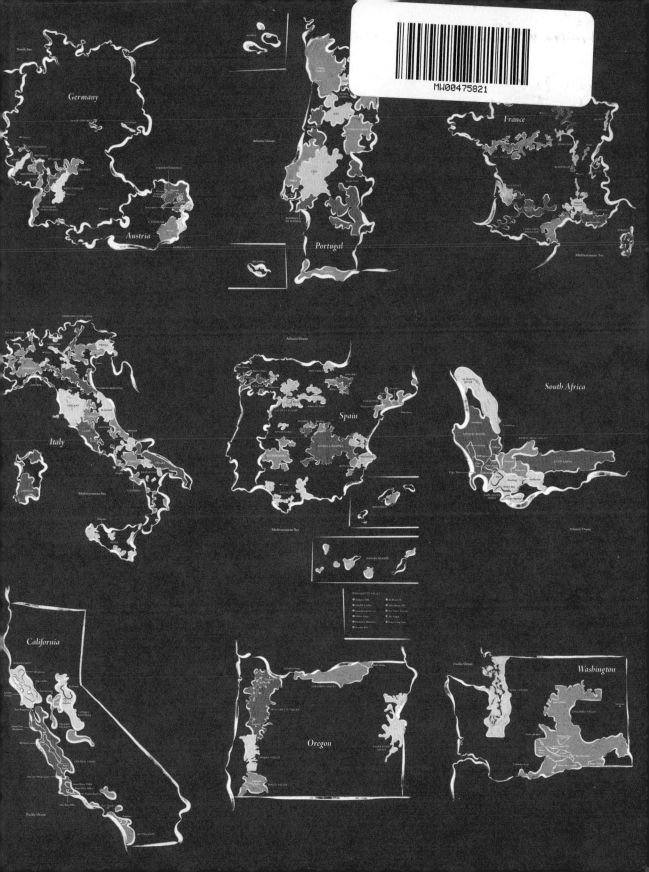

THE WORLD IN A WINEGLASS

The Insider's Guide to Artisanal, Sustainable,
Extraordinary Wines to Drink Now

RAY ISLE

SCRIBNER

New York London Toronto Sydney New Delhi

Scribner
An Imprint of Simon & Schuster, Inc.
1230 Avenue of the Americas
New York, NY 10020

First Scribner hardcover edition November 2023

SCRIBNER and design are registered trademarks of The Gale Group, Inc., used under license by Simon & Schuster, Inc., the publisher of this work.

For information about special discounts for bulk purchases, please contact Simon & Schuster Special Sales at 1-866-506-1949 or business@simonandschuster.com.

The Simon & Schuster Speakers Bureau can bring authors to your live event. For more information or to book an event, contact the Simon & Schuster Speakers Bureau at 1-866-248-3049 or visit our website at www.simonspeakers.com.

Interior design by Davina Mock Maniscalco

Manufactured in the United States of America

10 9 8 7 6 5 4 3 2 1

Library of Congress Cataloging-in-Publication Data has been applied for.

ISBN 978-1-9821-8278-6
ISBN 978-1-9821-8280-9 (ebook)

To anyone who has ever picked up a bottle of wine and thought,
"I wish I knew more about this . . ."

CONTENTS

1. There's a World in Your Wineglass 1
2. Sustainability, Organics, Biodynamics, Regenerative Agriculture,
   and More 12
      Sustainability 14
      Organic Viticulture and Winemaking 16
      Biodynamics 18
      Regenerative Agriculture 20
      About Natural Wine 22
      To Certify or Not to Certify 26
3. How to Drink Wine 29
4. Who Is in This Book and How It Is Organized 39

The Wineries

   Europe 45
     France 47
      Alsace 52
      Beaujolais 64
      Bordeaux 74
      Burgundy 86
      Champagne 121
      Jura and Savoie 136
      Languedoc-Roussillon 150

Loire Valley 159

Provence and Corsica 183

Rhône Valley 189

Italy 217

Northern Italy 221

Alto Adige–Trentino 222

Emilia-Romagna 229

Friuli–Venezia Giulia 232

Piedmont 242

Veneto 263

Central Italy 273

Abruzzo 274

Le Marche 280

Tuscany 284

Umbria and Lazio 318

Southern Italy 326

Basilicata, Calabria, and Puglia 327

Campania and Molise 330

Sicily and Sardinia 335

Spain 347

Galicia 351

Rioja and Navarra 361

Castilla y León 371

Catalunya and the Mediterranean Coast 381

The Islands 397

Portugal 403

Austria and Germany 419

Austria 421

Germany 434

Slovenia, Georgia, and Lebanon   453
    Slovenia   455
    Georgia   458
    Lebanon   464

The United States   471
  California   473
    The North Coast   478
    The Central Coast and Beyond   536
  Oregon   567
  Washington   605

The Southern Hemisphere   621
  Australia and New Zealand   623
    Australia   625
    New Zealand   635
  Argentina and Chile   643
    Argentina   645
    Chile   653
  South Africa   663

Acknowledgments   673
Appendix One: Finding and Buying the Wines in this Book   677
Appendix Two: Go-To Wine Importers   679
Appendix Three: A Selective Glossary   681
Photo Credits   689
Index   691

ONE

THERE'S A WORLD IN YOUR WINEGLASS

"The vine and the wine it produces are two great mysteries.
Alone in the vegetable kingdom, the vine makes the true savor of the earth
intelligible to man. With what fidelity it makes the translation!
It senses, then expresses, in its clusters of fruit the secrets of the soil."
—Colette, *Prisons et Paradis*, 1932

What is wine?

Say, if you like, that it's just fermented grape juice. Fair enough: you're right. But that's also like saying that a knife is just a sharp piece of metal. There's a world of difference between a machine-stamped blade with a polypropylene handle, and a carbon-steel chef's knife made by a master craftsman; so, too, with wine. At its best wine is an artisanal creation that edges toward, and possibly sometimes achieves, art. Wine is an alcoholic beverage—no question there—yet we drink it to amplify the pleasure of a meal and to heighten the joy of connecting with other people, rather than simply to achieve a buzz. Wine is fermented grape juice, but when made with grapes grown in carefully chosen locations, fermented and aged with intelligence, experience, and skill, it can also be something much greater than that.

At its heart wine is also an agricultural product. One sip of a great wine will tell you what kind of grapes went into it, where they were grown, even what the weather was like that year. The perfect temperatures in July in Napa Valley, or the rain in Piedmont in September, or the frost in April in the Loire Valley—all those can reveal themselves, for better or worse, in a single sip. Even more than they would if you were to eat the grape itself; wine's alchemical magic, the translation of the juice from the grapes by fermentation, somehow brings a mysteriously microscopic focus to all the broader influences of season, soil, and plant. Wine is grape juice transformed by yeast, guided by the human hand.

But the truth is that most of the wine in the world doesn't really summon that magic. While it does come from grapes that grew on vines, a vast percentage of the wine in the world is a mass-produced product that bears more resemblance to a can of Coke than it does to something handcrafted, distinctive, and honest. Its success is measured in the number of units moved off grocery store shelves, its market penetration, its profitability. It's differentiated into price segments: value, premium, ultra-premium, luxury—alarmingly like something you'd get at a gas station pump.

That's not to say that this kind of mass-produced wine doesn't taste good. It often does. But then, so do Taco Bell tacos. Why shouldn't they? Taco Bell tacos are designed by very smart people (or, if you prefer, "food innovation experts"). They satisfy any number of deep-seated flavor cues. They're savory and salty and meaty-cheesy, and they're seasoned with seven "authentic" spices and seasonings (what is an inauthentic spice? I wonder). They're delightfully crunchy. They remind me of my childhood: a sense of nostalgia. Of course, the Taco Bell innovation team is no stranger to nostalgia. Those sweet days of childhood, crunching tacos in the back seat of the family car . . . well. Nostalgia is great if you can wrap it in paper and sell it for $2.49.

I don't mean to beat up on Taco Bell tacos. If it's not clear, I actually like them. But, like bottles of industrial wine, Taco Bell tacos are sold by the millions, even by the billions. Where do they come from? Who creates them? They emerge from the hatch of the drive-through window, assembled by uniformed workers who, it's safe to guess, do not have a personal investment in the farms where that corn and beef came from. What's the source of that crunchy shell? What farmer raised those cows? Who wrote the recipe? Who's the guiding hand? Shareholders? Flavor scientists? A CEO?

Here's a kind of thought experiment. Picture a table with two bottles sitting in front of you. On the left, you have a bottle of Kim Crawford Marlborough Sauvignon Blanc. Take a sip. Odds are you'll think it tastes good (assuming you like New Zealand Sauvignon Blanc in the first place, which actually is a pretty big assumption, since some people just can't stand the stuff). Let's say you do like it. The wine's brisk and vivid, the flavor recalls a fresh grapefruit, it's appealingly tangy, it whets the appetite, and it costs a moderate $14 or so. It isn't odd or flawed.

And yes, Kim Crawford is a real person. I can vouch for that, since I've met him. And Marlborough is absolutely a place—it's a wine region on the north coast of New Zealand's South Island. (I can vouch for that, too. Been there. Plenty of vines.)

But at this point the actual Kim Crawford has absolutely nothing to do with Kim Crawford Wine. He and his wife, Erica, founded the brand in 1996. In 2003, they sold it to Vincor, a Canadian company, for $49 million (no need to feel bad for the Crawfords). In 2006, the international drinks conglomerate Constellation Brands bought Vincor for $1.3 billion. Today Kim Crawford Wines sells over 1.8 million cases each year in the United States alone. Back in 2019, Constellation announced a marketing campaign for Kim Crawford wines, centered on the tag phrase "Make It Amazing." The press release stated: "'Make It Amazing' celebrates the confidence Kim Crawford gives consumers by overdelivering on quality, taste, and value; and brings consumers' strong brand loyalty to life. . . . [It] is supported by a 360-degree integrated marketing plan including TV and digital advertising, social media content, dynamic displays at retail, strategic partnerships, consumer sampling, and experiential programming."

Hmm.

Now let's consider the second bottle on your table, a Greywacke Marlborough Sauvignon Blanc. Same grape; same region. The name refers to a type of hard sandstone, called greywacke, that's prevalent in the vineyards that owner Kevin Judd uses for this wine. Judd makes about forty thousand cases each year of his Sauvignon Blanc, which costs about $23 a bottle. He's a smart, somewhat taciturn, dryly funny guy, who was also the founding winemaker for many years at Cloudy Bay, the winery that effectively put New Zealand Sauvignon Blanc on the map in the early 1990s. (Like Kim Crawford, Cloudy Bay was eventually bought by a mega-corporation, in its case Moët Hennessy–Louis Vuitton, or LVMH; Judd left soon after.) Judd does not have a 360-degree integrated marketing plan for Greywacke. What he *does* have is a distinct, personal vision of what New Zealand Sauvignon Blanc and his wines particularly can be. He's involved in every decision regarding his wine—which vineyards grow the grapes for it, how they are farmed, when the grapes are picked, how the wine is made, how it is aged, when it is released, what the labels look like, what its price is.

It's worth pointing out that Greywacke Sauvignon Blanc does not come from a single small vineyard, and its production is not minuscule, except compared to something like Kim Crawford. You can find it in stores. It's not from an obscure, overlooked region in Europe that only a very few wine people (usually in Brooklyn) have heard of. It doesn't wear its artisanal nature on its sleeve. But it is what I'd call a real wine. The crucial difference is that the Greywacke bottle represents an individual winemaker's distinctive vision of how *that* specific grape variety grown on *that* specific type of land can express itself in liquid form. Both the Kim Crawford and the Greywacke are wines. No question. But, to me, the Greywacke provides some of that unusual mystery that wine can offer, that language that speaks of place and purpose; it expresses something more than just flavor. And the Crawford bottle, well. The label does everything in its power to convince you that the wine inside *is* distinctive and special—it "dazzles" with aromas, "bursts" with flavor, comes from "exceptional" vineyards, and "we proudly craft it." (I'm a bit unclear on who exactly "we" is—the people behind the 360-degree marketing plan?) But it's sort of like a Taco Bell taco. Tasty, for sure, but soulless. It makes me remember something that Eduard Tscheppe of the Austrian winery Gut Oggau said at a tasting I went to not long ago: "Most people just think of wine as a drink. And that makes sense, because it's mostly true. With a lot of wine there's only a distant memory of the soil and the climate in the bottle. It's really just an alcoholic beverage made by some company." Elena Pantaleoni, the brilliant, idiosyncratic owner of Italy's La Stoppa, phrases it a little more bluntly when she says, "There's a lot of elevator music when it comes to wine."

———————

Climate. Place. Seasons. The sun and the wind and the rain on vines. Agriculture: cultivating the soil, farming plants to provide crops. Grapes are an agricultural product. And an almost magical one—even with nothing but the wild yeasts found naturally on their skins, they can ferment into wine.

So forget for a moment about marketing, forget about bottles on shelves, even forget winemaking. Look at a bottle and start with a different question: How were the grapes grown?

Asking that question poses an odd quandary, because conventional farming—the use of systemic pesticides, industrial nitrogen-potassium fertilizers, herbicides like glyphosate, and so on—can result in perfectly good-tasting wines. Even extraordinarily delicious wines. And if the wine in your glass tastes good, then what more do you want from it? What does it matter what the grape grower's methods were?

I'd say this in response: consider food. We all make choices about what we eat. Some choices have to do with taste, some with nutrition, some with price and budget. But more and more, people are paying closer attention to where the food they eat comes from, how it was grown or raised, and whether the answers to those questions result in something that they feel comfortable putting into their bodies. An organic tomato, grown within a hundred miles of the market where you shop, purchased in season from the farmer who grew it, answers those questions very differently from a tomato that's harvested green on an industrial farm, artificially ripened with ethylene gas, and trucked across fourteen states to a miles-of-aisles supermarket in, well, wherever. Your hometown.

Those questions of origin—call it the who, where, and how of farming—can be political, ecological, or practical. The practical questions have always been with us. Should we slaughter the pig this week or next? Are the apples ripe enough yet to eat?

The ecological and political questions surrounding food are vast and complex—far beyond the scope of this book—and wine doesn't take part in all of them. But the changes in agriculture that occurred following World War II, as the Green Revolution took off and synthetic fertilizers, agrochemicals, pesticides, and mechanized farming became commonplace, do play into grape growing. Those developments gave farmers in vineyards a host of weapons to use against common vine issues such as mold, mildew, insects, and diseases. Inexpensive nitrogen fertilizers allowed them to increase yields dramatically and consistently. Chemical herbicides replaced days or even weeks of exhausting handwork. It seemed to many farmers, starting in the 1950s and 1960s, that science had ushered in a new age, one where nature, always capricious and sometimes overtly hostile, would now be subservient to man. Formerly devastating problems were now solvable. Plague of locusts? Try fenitrothion or chlorpirifos. Just make sure you stay out of the area afterward, unless you want your hormone system rewired. And be sure to mention that to your bee population as well.

Of course, it would be perverse not to recognize that in a global context, the large-scale, technological-agricultural developments of the post–World War II era have helped keep millions of people in developing countries from starvation. Famines, which in pre-industrial eras were typically caused by crop blights or weather conditions (drought, harsh winters, and so on), are still with us; but in the modern era they're more often (though not universally) the result of wars or political unrest. Science hasn't stopped war, but it's done wonders at controlling things like late potato blight, the cause of the

Great Irish Famine from 1845 to 1849. (Though even with modern fungicides, late blight still causes an estimated $2.75 billion in crop losses around the world each year. The current best-case solution? Genetically modified [GM] potatoes. Something to ponder.) But for all of industrial farming's successes, it's also a form of willed blindness not to recognize the environmental costs and underlying economic drivers tied to it.

Wine isn't a staple; no one will die if they run out of wine (hard to believe for some of us, but true). As a result, wine grapes don't have to be farmed as though they were wheat or rice or soybeans. Admittedly, if your ambition is to make 2 million cases of cheap-and-cheerful Chardonnay, then labor-intensive organic farming is probably not your wisest choice, financially (though I'd applaud you giving it a shot). Mass-production wines require mass-production grapes, and mass-production grapes generally require conventional, chemical-based farming. Which lands us back at that question of what people—what *you*—personally feel comfortable eating or drinking. As Mark Neal at Neal Vineyards in Napa Valley points out, it's strange (and frustrating, for organic growers like him) that wine often isn't held to the same standards as food. As he observes, "You go down the Whole Foods aisles, and people are throwing organic, organic, organic into the basket; then they get to the wine aisle and what the hell." It's a peculiar situation. If you prefer eating strawberries that weren't doused with difenoconazole—I sure as hell do—why not extend that preference to wine grapes?

But even outside questions of conventional versus organic (or similar) farming, growing grapes for wines that have personality and distinctiveness, and that express the character of the specific place they come from—wines of *terroir*, if you like—innately requires a different approach to farming. Philipp Wittmann, who makes sublime, stony Rieslings in Germany's Rheinhessen, describes it like this: "What we are doing is a kind of gardening, I'd say. It's very intense work in the vineyards. A lot of hours per acre, and a lot of handwork. It's the hope of producing perfect, ripe, healthy fruit in every season. You have to check every vineyard every single day: the leaf management, the soil, the fruit . . . and everything is different every year." That kind of labor-intensive, incredibly painstaking viticulture is the source point for almost all of the wines in this book. Unsurprisingly, it also goes hand in hand with shifts in recent years by conscientious winegrowers like Wittmann toward more Earth-friendly forms of farming.

One of the biggest changes in wine over the past couple of decades has been a boom in sustainable, organic, biodynamic, and similar practices in vineyards. Partly it comes from disillusionment, especially on the part of independent winegrowers, with the presumed benefits of conventional farming. Olivier Humbrecht of Zind-Humbrecht in Alsace describes it this way: "These chemicals allowed growers to multiply their production by three or four times. Less time in the vineyard, less hard work, three times the production, why say no? But then people started to see—ah, where are my butterflies? Where are my weeds? Where are my worms? Why do I have to start using more and more chemicals, and more and more powerful and harmful chemicals? And if you ask these questions, you start to see that the chemicals, by solving one problem, created other ones."

At the same time, there's also been an overall shift in public perception. Michele Manelli of Tuscany's Salcheto winery says, "If you want a funny story, the first years when people asked if I was organic, I'd say, 'No, my neighbor is, but I'm not!' Because the word 'organic' was a label of poor quality then, and quality winemakers didn't want to be in that constellation. Not anymore." (He adds, making a worthwhile point: "I still strongly believe that 'organic' doesn't have a taste. Nor does 'biodynamic.' They're practices. But they're very interesting practices, and I like the radical part, the refusal of the chemical shortcut.") The transformation of "organic" from a word implying poorly made, amateur, hippies-doing-their-thing wine to one implying an avoidance of chemicals that (a) might poison you and (b) might poison the planet is a fascinating change, one whose ripple effects are only widening.

What has recently pushed winegrowers even further along this path, or at least the kind of growers I'm writing about in these pages, is an increasing realization that trying to express a sense of place in a wine is essentially futile if you've managed to annihilate the *underground* life in your vineyard. Fred Loimer at Weingut Loimer in Austria comments, "Nature works with a combination of plants and animals to build soil life. When you walk on it, you're walking on life from millions of years. There's more life *in* the soil than there is above the soil." Climate, exposure, geology—they all play their parts in creating a sense of terroir. But more and more it's become clear that the microbial life of the soil holds just as important a role in why *this* wine from *this* place tastes distinctively different from *that* wine made from grapes grown just a stone's throw away. And one thing that chemical herbicides in particular are extremely effective at doing is not just killing weeds but snuffing out what lives underneath them as well. Steve Matthiasson, one of California's premier viticulturists, explains it this way:

"Using glyphosate [Roundup], for instance, isn't like pouring gasoline or boiling water into the soil. It's more that with herbicides in general, the problem is that not having plants growing in the soil means, first, that the soil is not getting fed with decaying organic matter when those plants die or the roots slough off, and, second, that the roots aren't tending and facilitating a healthy soil microbiome." In essence, by using systemic herbicides you will win the war on weeds, but in the process cause a famine and kill off your soil's billions of microbiological inhabitants by means of starvation.

————————————

Then there's winemaking.

A short course: Circa 6000 BC, people discovered that if you stuffed a bunch of grapes in a clay amphora, sealed it up, and waited a while, the result would be an intoxicating and (at least you hoped) palatable beverage. Progress after that was slow and incremental. In the 1300s and 1400s, the Cistercian monks of Burgundy were coming to the conclusion that individual small vineyards, though close to one another, could produce wines of differing character—this was the gradual invention of the concept of terroir. Glass bottles for wine? They don't appear until 1630. Or consider Champagne. From Christopher Merret's discovery in 1662 that adding a small amount of sugar to wine could induce a second fermentation (yes, an Englishman came up with that, not a French monk) to the invention in France of glass bottles strong enough to transport sparkling wine without often exploding took a hundred years or so.

Then the twentieth century marches in, and specifically the postwar period. At the same time viticulture was changing, a broad range of technological winemaking advancements—refrigeration for white wine production, cold stabilization, stainless steel tanks for fermentation, blanketing of wine with nitrogen or argon to prevent oxidation, sterile filtration, commercial single-strain yeasts—rapidly became commonplace in wineries. These changes certainly resulted in more *consistent* wine; there's a reason there are so few actively flawed wines in the market today, even at the bargain-basement level, compared to earlier eras. But larger, more uniform grape yields and more controlled winemaking don't necessarily translate to more *interesting* wine. So, while there are fewer foul-smelling, harsh, volatile, unpleasant wines being sold today, there are also far more homogenized, characterless, bland ones.

Progress—if that's the right word here—marches on, and a twenty-first-century winemaker's ability to modify or completely rewrite what nature gives in the vineyard is unparalleled. Processes such as reverse osmosis or "spinning cone" technology can imperceptibly reduce high alcohol levels. Industrial products such as Mega Purple, a 2,000-to-1 grape juice concentrate, help boost color and richness. A broad palette of designer yeasts can be utilized to highlight certain flavors and aromas (Scott Laboratories' NT112 has "good fructose utilization, enhances black currant aromas, and is recommended for wines destined for micro-oxygenation"). Need twenty thousand gallons of Cabernet to taste barrel-aged without buying several hundred expensive barrels? Try dangling a five-hundred-pound tea bag of oak chips in the juice, or even more efficiently, dump in a few gallons of liquid grape tannin. Merlot tasting slightly underripe? Try flash détente, where your grapes are superheated to 185°F, then pumped into a vacuum chamber—the water in the grape skins instantly turns to steam and blasts apart the microscopic vacuoles in the grape skins, intensifying color and tannins. Worried that the residual sugar in your "rich" red blend might re-ferment in the bottle? Zap the juice with Velcorin (dimethyldicarbonate), a sterilant/stabilizer that, while it breaks down into CO_2 and methanol in twenty-four hours, does require a hazmat suit and a respirator to work with. Less alarmingly but possibly more insidiously, commercial wines' flavor profiles are regularly manipulated to minimize vintage differences or to fit marketing strategies aimed at specific audiences, or both.

Still, if a winemaker chooses to farm organically, or chooses not to use liquid tannins or reverse-osmosis machines in their winery, that does not mean they are anti-science; often it's the opposite. Knowledge is awareness, and being wary of too much intervention or being concerned for the health of the environment doesn't automatically make you a Luddite. To pick one example among many, Elena Fucci, who farms organically in Italy's Basilicata region and makes stellar wines there, studied enology and agronomy at the University of Pisa before returning to found her eponymous winery. She says, "We work organically in the vineyard, but we also work in our vineyard with weather stations. It's not like we're watching the flowers to see if the petals look funny. The truth is that if you want to work organically or biodynamically, you need *more* knowledge of science, not less. It's too easy to say, 'I did nothing.' If you know the chemical processes, you know when to intervene intelligently. Then you can repeat quality, not have it be an accident every year."

Fucci is right. Doing nothing is not an option, because nature itself has absolutely no interest in making wine. Ripe grapes, left to themselves, will be eaten by bugs or animals, or fall to the ground and rot. Human intervention is required, both in the vineyard and in the winery. The real question is what kind and how much.

From its start, wine has been modified, adulterated, added to, subtracted from, and pretty much any other process that might make the vagaries of climate and season conform to the desires of man. Some artificial processes we don't mind at all—you'd have to look far and wide to find a wine lover who thinks refrigeration is evil. Others seem ill-advised to the point of lunacy: in the 1800s it was common to add plaster (gypsum or calcium sulfate) to wine to brighten its color and to moderate acidity, never mind that drinking those wines occasionally resulted in throat lesions. Colorant additives used at the same time included alum, elderberry husks, and coal tar derivatives. Even more alarmingly, lead acetate, which can cause organ failure and dementia, was sometimes added to wine as a sweetener. If you really want to make a wine dosed with weird additives, I'd actually much prefer you went for Mega Purple. It may be cheating, but at least you won't be giving your customers brain damage.

However, If you modify what nature has given you to a degree that nature isn't really represented anymore, if you even out the vagaries of the vintage and tweak the taste to fit a template or style, you may still be making wine, but to me what's left is a kind of denatured shadow of what wine can be. It may taste good, but it isn't interesting, or distinctive; it's an adult beverage product. Which is fine. Sometimes that's all you need. As a chef said to me once, "Sometimes rice is just rice. Not everything has to be special all the time." (But it would be a little nuts to write an entire book about non-special wines.)

What spurred writing *this* book is that I feel the actual experience of drinking real wine, wine made by individual vintners, ones who farm with respect for the planet and invest passion into their work, is simply different. Maybe it's worth drawing a line to food again. If you cook at home and decide to make eggplant parmesan, even though it's a complete pain in the neck to make homemade eggplant parm, the version that comes out of your oven will always taste different from what you buy in the frozen food aisle, among other reasons, *because you made it.* There is a different kind of pleasure to be found in eating something cooked with care at home than something assembled on an industrial food production line. Personal example: When I was a kid, my mother worked nights and my father would often make us hamburgers, operating under the delusional idea that if you mashed the burger against the hot pan until every micro-ounce of juice ran out of it, this was a good thing. Unfortunately, this technique is *not* a good thing: it's like putting a hamburger in the electric chair. But I loved those hamburgers, and even now, I remember them as being delicious. There's a reason the phrase "a home-cooked meal" has resonance, and it's not simply the familiarity of cliché. The point is that we make the decision to eat real food, as opposed to what the writer Michael Pollan has referred to as "edible foodlike substances," for a host of reasons. One is that knowing something was made by an actual person with an investment in their work, rather than a large corporation changes our experience of it. Of course, homemade eggplant parmesan and frozen TV dinners will both keep you alive. But eating something that has value to you provides a deeper form of satisfaction than eating something artificial or generic. And the same is true of wine.

This book isn't meant as an attack on mass-market wines, or the millions of people who enjoy drinking them. Life is complicated and stressful; if something gives you pleasure and doesn't cause anyone else harm, go for it. If you love Taco Bell tacos, go to town. Order four of them. Order a dozen.

And while it would be easy to demonize all corporate wine producers, and lionize all the little guys, the situation isn't entirely black-and-white. There are small-scale winegrowers who happily zap their vineyards with Roundup and dose their vines with chemical fertilizers, just as there are large-scale growers who farm organically and conscientiously (California's Bonterra comes to mind). Reputation and price are not infallible guides, either. Just as the $8 bottle of mass-market Aussie Shiraz you bought may have had its flavors custom-tailored to a consumer study, the $250, 98-point-score Napa Cabernet the next customer splurged on may have been reverse-osmosed down to a vaguely palatable 15.5 percent alcohol.

Instead, my hope here is to celebrate a specific realm of wines: ones whose grapes are grown with care and with concern for the environment; ones that express the character of the place they are from and the sensibility of the person who made them; ones that, if you let them, offer rewards beyond simple flavor. These are wines that can answer three simple questions: Where does it come from? Who made it? How did they grow their grapes and make their wine? If a wine can answer those questions, and the answers feel good to you, then it's time to find a corkscrew, get a glass, and drink it.

TWO

SUSTAINABILITY, ORGANICS, BIODYNAMICS, REGENERATIVE AGRICULTURE, AND MORE

"Agriculture must mediate between nature and the human community,
with ties and obligations in both directions."
—Wendell Berry, from "Renewing Husbandry"

I f you are not part of the solution, you are part of the problem. Yes, that might be a cliché, but when it comes to the environment, I can't help but feel that statement is true.

All farming, innately, is a give-and-take between man and nature. But balancing that give-and-take is complicated. Conventional, large-scale, mechanized agriculture largely ignores that two-way street. It takes more than it gives: with it we control nature to the utmost degree possible in order to produce as much volume—of corn, of strawberries, of pigs, of eggs—as possible. In some ways, it's hard to see a path out of this situation, given that 8 billion humans require a truly stupendous amount of food. Traditional (or, if you like, pre-industrial) farming methods weren't designed to feed a place like São Paolo, with its metropolitan population of almost 23 million people.

As mentioned, wine isn't a staple; a hundred million people won't starve if wine simply vanishes from the face of the earth. But as a result, there's more freedom to farm grape vines differently, without recourse to systemic chemicals and products, and conscientious growers and winemakers around the world are using that freedom to work in ways that team up with nature rather than tame it. (Vineyards supplying grapes for massive-production, industrial, beverage-product wines are far less likely to operate this way.)

Even so, green approaches in viticulture are subject to the same internecine conflicts that seem to plague all agricultural efforts in this realm. People who are vehement about organic viticulture think sustainability is little better than greenwashing. Biodynamics followers feel that organic viticulture, while it rejects systemic chemical inputs, doesn't concentrate enough on the ecological viability of the farm as a whole. People who work sustainably, unsurprisingly, get annoyed when someone with similar concerns about the planet tells them that sustainability is BS, and are more than happy to note that neither organic nor biodynamic viticulture addresses what happens outside the narrow realm of farming itself. (Winemaking practices are equally contentious: grow your grapes organically but use sulfur to keep your wine stable in the bottle, and hardline natural-wine lovers will look at you like you're Satan's right hand. So, too, with reactions to other additions or modifications.)

Also consider that nearly a third of wine's impact in regard to carbon footprint and climate change comes from the production and transportation of glass. If you send a wine to the other side of the world, you increase its carbon footprint three times. It's worth asking—not just for wine—what the real cost of consumer goods is when you take into account their effect on the environment. When you pick up one wine bottle and the glass weighs fourteen ounces, and you pick up another and it weighs two-and-a-half pounds (not an exaggeration), and both are being shipped from, say, Valparaiso, Chile, all the way to Chicago, what is the cost to the planet of the first bottle versus the second?

So, when it comes to wine, what is sustainability? What defines organic viticulture, or biodynamic, or regenerative? Unfortunately, different countries have different standards and different certifying organizations, and there is (as with every movement with noble goals, it seems) plenty of co-opting of terms by big producers and big business. Lately, there's been a spate of large-scale wine companies adding a "natural" wine to their portfolios. I'm going to go out on a limb and suggest that it seems somewhat unlikely that they really are in tune with Corrado Dottori of La Distesa's comment that "natural wine is not a 'brand'. It is a critical look ... at the economic-ecological catastrophe that is today's world."

Regardless of all the co-opting and all the internal debates, buying wines that you know came from vineyards that weren't zapped with systemic weed killers and pumped up with synthetic fertilizers is worth doing both for one's own body and, even if in a small way, for the world itself. Jason Haas at Tablas Creek Vineyard in Paso Robles, California, has it right when he says, "Agriculture has the potential to be part of the solution to these big picture problems, instead of being part of the problem." So do wine buyers.

Sustainability

Sustainable agriculture is defined by three main pillars: environmental protection (particularly in terms of conserving natural resources), social equity (workers' rights and fairness), and economic viability (you aren't sustainable if you go out of business). It's both a popular and broadly applicable term, less rigorous generally speaking than organic viticulture, and more easily bandied about in a kind of "well, of *course* we farm sustainably!" way. But followed diligently, it's an approach that makes a lot of sense.

The word itself comes from the Latin *sustinere*, "to hold," by way of the Old French *sostenir*, which means "hold up, bear; suffer, endure." In the fourteenth century, a time of plagues, it meant "endure without failing or yielding." Given the forest fires, heat spikes, violent hailstorms, and out-of-season, crop-destroying frosts that climate change seems to be giving us, that usage may well come back into play. But the modern use of sustainability more or less refers to avoiding the depletion of natural resources in order to maintain ecological balance. It's a good goal; it's also one that more and more vintners are aiming toward every day.

To look at some statistics, in October of 2012, 12.3 percent of the vineyard land in California was certified sustainable. According to the California Sustainable Winegrowing Alliance (CSWA), in 2021 that number had risen to 33 percent: 2,402 vineyards, comprising 204,857 acres of vines.

Do a close-up of Sonoma County, and the membership of the Sonoma County Winegrowers association is 99 percent sustainable. (You do wonder who the holdouts are.) Outside the U.S., the trends are similar. In New Zealand, 98 percent of the country's vineyards are certified sustainable. Consider Bordeaux, not exactly the fastest region around when it comes to change. In 2014, 34 percent of the total wineries in Bordeaux farmed either organically, sustainably, or were biodynamic certified; today that number is 65 percent, and the region is on course to have 100 percent of the region's wineries—six thousand, give or take—running some kind of certified sustainable program by 2030.

In vineyards, sustainable certification usually requires utilizing some form of integrated pest management, doing environmental risk assessments, maintaining biodiversity (at least to some degree), and other practices. Sustainable approaches to winery buildings include using recycled materials, relying on solar and other forms of energy generation, rainwater harvesting, natural lighting to reduce energy usage, using recycled paper for labels; that list goes on, too.

And then there are the social aspects of sustainability. Among many examples, wineries might provide daycare for vineyard workers' children or ESL courses for workers, or donate to local nonprofits. Carbon footprint is a consideration, too.

The hitch, as sustainability's critics point out, is that it's a fairly soft approach. Certification from the California Sustainable Wine Alliance, for example, doesn't actually ban synthetic herbicides, it just suggests they be used sparingly; the idea that you can be sustainable and still spray your weeds with glyphosate (Roundup) strikes many environmentally conscious people as hypocritical, to say the least, if not actually mendacious. The Napa Green sustainability organization puts glyphosate on its "restricted use" list, though if you avoid herbicides and neoniconitoids completely, you get a special "gold level" recognition. (In France, Emanuel Macron announced a plan to ban glyphosate completely by 2021, then backed down on it.)

Regardless, many of the requirements of sustainability as a practice are clearly valuable, and the fact that sustainability looks beyond the boundaries of farming to address climate and social issues is a plus. The question becomes, when it comes to the environment, is some action better than none at all? Personally, I feel it is, but—as they say—it's complicated.

Organic Viticulture and Winemaking

At its very basic level, organic viticulture specifies what you can and cannot use in your vineyard. What you cannot use is synthetic fertilizers and pesticides, as well as genetically modified seeds or crops. But contrary to what you might expect, organic grape growers *are* allowed to use chemicals, just none that are synthetic; and compounds that repel pests or act as fungicides are OK, as long as they are not systemic (i.e., absorbed by the plant and distributed through its sap and tissues). So, it's perfectly all right to use elemental sulfur in an organic vineyard to prevent powdery mildew, but it is definitely not all right to use Quadris Top (a combo platter of azoxystrobin and difenoconazole) for the same purpose.

The obvious benefit is that by farming organically, growers avoid using industrially produced fertilizers, pesticides, and herbicides, many of which have very questionable effects on the environment overall, possibly on your own or your workers' health, too, and distinctly negative effects on soil life. Conventional/industrial farming, at a baseline level, kills the soil; microbiological activity on conventionally farmed land is minimal; and there's a difference between living soil and dead dirt. But copper sulfate, commonly used in organic viticulture to control downy mildew, isn't environmentally ideal, either—it's a heavy metal that can damage soil life, and, as runoff, be deadly to fish, birds, and other creatures. The other problem with organic treatments is that they work on the surface of the plant (not being systemic). That's fine until it rains, after which you have to reapply them. That means that in a rainy season, organic vintners may need to spray up to four or five times, or even more. For this and many other reasons, in 2018, the EU dramatically tightened the limits on copper use in organic vineyards (a decision greeted with decidedly mixed feelings by organic vintners themselves).

Yet when you consider conventional versus organic viticulture, the choice is fairly clear for anyone who cares about the environment. And organic viticulture is a growing movement. In 2019, only 6.2 percent of the world's vineyards were certified organic, but that percentage is rising every year. In Italy, for example, organic vineyard acreage rose 57 percent between 2013 and 2018. Spain, which has more organic vineyard area than any other European country—247,000 acres as of 2020—has a growth rate even greater than Italy's. Organic viticulture is a rising tide, and a beneficial one (as opposed to what the melting of the polar ice caps might produce).

Then there's organic winemaking. Here the situation gets somewhat baffling. The USDA and EU certifications for organic *wine* (not organically grown grapes) differ primarily, and dramatically, in the level of sulfites allowed in the finished wine. USDA regulations allow 10 parts per million of added sulfites; EU regulations allow 100 parts per million for reds, and 150 parts per million for whites. So let's talk about sulfur briefly.

All wine contains sulfites, because sulfur compounds are a by-product of fermentation. The real point of contention is the presence of *added* sulfites. The upsides are straightforward: adding sulfites, specifically sulfur dioxide, to wine helps prevent oxidation, prevents random bacteria and microorganisms from growing in the wine, and prevents any residual yeasts from causing re-fermentation in the bottle (resulting in fizzy wine or the cork blowing out the top). Adding SO_2 early in the winemaking process can also affect the wine's taste and aroma, how it feels in the mouth, how it will age, and so on. The chemistry gets very complex very rapidly; refer back to your textbooks if you were a chemical engineering major during college, otherwise let's give it a miss.

There are also downsides to the addition of sulfites, though they do not cause "red wine headaches" or in fact headaches of any sort. If you have sulfite-sensitive asthma, sulfites will make you wheeze, cough, and have trouble breathing. But the incidence of nonasthmatic people with actual sulfite sensitivities is extremely low, and there are plenty of packaged or processed foods with higher sulfite levels than wine. If you've ever eaten precut frozen potatoes (e.g., French fries) or dried apricots, both of which typically have far more SO_2 than a bottle of wine, without ill effect, then it's a safe bet that your average bottle of Cabernet isn't going to do much to you either (except potentially get you drunk).

The impetus to make wine without sulfur additions descends primarily from the work of Jules Chauvet, the Beaujolais winemaker and wine scientist generally regarded as the "father of natural wine." His feeling was that the use of sulfur inhibited the true character of wine; it throttled native yeasts and stifled the expression of terroir. Chauvet befriended the Beaujolais vigneron Marcel Lapierre, who found his ideas alluring, and convinced several friends to follow them as well; they became the so-called "gang of four," and from them the natural wine movement more or less grew. The general feeling among natural and non-interventionist wine fans is that sulfur not only inhibits terroir expression but that it dulls down the flavors of wine overall, rendering it less full of life than it might be otherwise.

There's plenty of debate about this. Some natural winemakers are strictly anti-sulfur (the absolutist "zero-zero" movement). Others do not use added sulfur during the winemaking process, but do use small amounts at bottling, simply to keep wines both fresh and stable. Most winemakers in this book, regardless of whether they consider themselves "natural" or not, fall into a camp that basically feels that the less sulfur you can use, the better, but that it's also a valuable tool in small amounts (usually far less than what is allowed by law). Then there are conventional winemakers who don't really have a problem with sulfur use as long as it's within legal limits.

Because different countries have very different limits about how much added sulfur can be present in a wine before it is allowed to be labeled "organic," the whole situation for anyone simply trying to buy a bottle is very confusing. In the EU for a wine to be labeled organic, it must have less than 100ppm (parts per million) of sulfur dioxide for red wines, and less than 150ppm for white wines. For Chile, *any* wine made from organic grapes can be labeled organic wine; there is no sulfite limit. For Australia, it's 125ppm. On the other hand, the U.S. (the USDA, specifically) limits the amount to 10ppm added sulfur—essentially none. That's radically less than all other wine-producing countries, and effectively relegates using the USDA Organic seal to a very small group of producers who don't mind taking risks with the long-term stability of the wine they've made. Not being an anti-sulfur fanatic myself, I think the U.S. strictures are fairly absurd, and that we should follow the same standards as the EU. In the end, it's more important to ask how the grapes were farmed that went into the wine you are drinking. That's the crucial question. If organic farming matters to you, drink wines from grapes that were grown that way. It's less worthwhile worrying about whether the wine has the USDA Organic seal on it.

Biodynamics

When I think about biodynamics, I'm always drawn back to a quote from *The Magician's Nephew* by C. S. Lewis. In it, Digory, the main character, is transported by a magic ring to an odd wood—the Wood Between the Worlds. Lewis writes, "You could almost feel the trees growing. . . . This wood was very much alive. When he tried to describe it afterwards Digory always said, 'It was a rich place: as rich as plum-cake.'"

Strike out the word "wood" in the quote above and substitute "farm" or "vineyard" and you are basically talking biodynamics (though I doubt the devoutly Anglican C. S. Lewis would have approved much of biodynamics' founder, the Austrian theosophical philosopher, educational and agricultural theorist, spiritualist, ostensible clairvoyant, and all-around very odd human Rudolf Steiner).

But visit a biodynamic farm. Take a handful of the farmer's 500 prep in your hands. The biodynamic 500 prep is manure that's been buried in a cow horn during the fall and unearthed during the spring. Crumble it and smell it. It doesn't smell of dung; instead, it smells *rich*, just as the humming aliveness of the Wood Between the Worlds smelled to Digory in Lewis's book. Full of life.

The central point of biodynamics is to build life or vitality within the ecological whole of the farm—the soil, but also of course the vines, as well as the local flora and fauna—thus removing the need for outside inputs of any kind. Where biodynamics differs from other types of sustainable or organic farming is in its belief that farming can be attuned to the spiritual forces of the universe. You can thank its founder for that. (To take one example, Steiner felt that as you sleep, "the part of the astral body that permeates the solar plexus and the arms and legs is now the organ of perception, and with the aid of this organ man begins to feel the forces in his astral body that come from the Signs of the Zodiac." Absolutely, Rudolf.)

And yet. For all their questionable aspects, the "agricultural course" lectures that Steiner gave in 1924 in Koberwitz, Silesia (now Poland), started a movement that has become one of the principal approaches for farmers looking to work in harmony with nature. There are definitely some bizarre aspects to biodynamics, generally descending from Steiner's anthroposophical beliefs—that, for instance, "the cow has horns in order to reflect inwards the astral and etheric formative forces, which then penetrate right into the metabolic system so that increased activity in the digestive organism arises by reason of this radiation from horns and hoofs." It's almost needless to say that despite having plenty of ideas about agriculture, Steiner never worked on a farm a day in his life.

And *yet*. As Olivier Humbrecht of Zind-Humbrecht in Alsace says, "I'm very happy with something that you cannot explain scientifically, as long as there is a difference you can register. We can't explain, for instance, why using a certain preparation matters, but we can see the difference, and that is enough explanation for me." It should probably be noted that Humbrecht holds degrees in both enology and viticulture, and was the first winemaker to achieve the rigorous Master of Wine degree. He's an extremely rational guy (also an extremely smart guy). Yet he, and any number of brilliant vintners across Europe, the U.S., Australia, and elsewhere, all believe in the efficacy of biodynamics, and they feel that it is manifest both in the health of their vineyards and in the quality of their wines.

Personally, I'm of two minds about biodynamics. There's no question that the attention to detail it forces in farming a vineyard is beneficial; and its basic underlying principle, that a vineyard (or farm) should be considered an ecological whole, all of its aspects tied together either in health or ill health, seems like an inarguably good idea; so, too, its attention to biodiversity, the use of compost, and, concomitantly, its focus on soil health. I'm less convinced by but prepared to accept the idea that homeopathic levels of treatment (the various preps are typically diluted and sprayed over the vineyard in parts-per-million levels) could have beneficial even if not scientifically measurable effects. But I'm not convinced in the slightest that the constellations or planets affect plant health, or that manure buried in a cow horn attracts and absorbs etheric, life-giving forces from the earth. That latter aspect requires a Kierkegaardian leap of faith—as religion does—out of the rational into the irrational. That's why I feel that what's often termed "practicing biodynamics" or noncertified biodynamics, which is usually a form of taking the farming aspects of biodynamics and leaving behind the anthroposophical ones, seems like an entirely reasonable approach to the whole question. And yet, a life without some form of spirituality seems a fairly empty one, to me at least, and it's hard not to feel that there's more to the world than we, in our human hubris, can completely understand. As Damien Delecheneau of La Grange Tiphaine, another technically trained winemaker, says, "I come from a scientific background. But I understood at some point that there's something else above, or different. I call it supra, not super; this *moreness* in wine. You can't touch it. You can't measure it. That's what I found when I started working with biodynamics."

Regenerative Agriculture

Regenerative agriculture combines the principles of organic farming with the broader aspects of sustainability: it doesn't allow for synthetic inputs, and it also promotes practices that help with carbon sequestration, biodiversity, and soil health, among many other goals. And as Jason Hass of Tablas Creek, the first Regenerative Organic Certified vineyard in the United States, says, "A big piece of what differentiates regenerative agriculture is that you use natural processes to mimic what would happen in a wild ecosystem."

Organics and biodynamics are specifically focused on farming practices. Organic farming restricts what you can use to fight problems like downy mildew or insect pests, but only by substituting less ecologically problematic remedies (in theory; as mentioned, there is lots of debate about copper sulfate in this regard). In essence, it still treats the symptoms, rather than the root causes. Biodynamics focuses on the farm as an ecological whole. In that way it's much closer to regenerative farming—some skeptics feel that "regenerative" just means biodynamics without all the astrological woo-woo—but there are still significant differences.

Regenerative agriculture goes beyond the immediately local to require that farms minimize their use of limited resources like water and energy, and work specifically toward helping reverse climate change by improving soil health, increasing carbon sequestration, promoting biodiversity, and other strategies. Broadly speaking, the ambition of regenerative farming is to improve the land rather than damage it. Given that there are some 4 billion acres of farmland around the world (and nearly double that of pastureland), if proponents of regenerative agriculture could turn it into a mass, global movement, the earth would unquestionably benefit. Obviously, that's an uphill struggle.

Regardless: step by step, farm by farm. One of the key aspects of regenerative agriculture is its concentration on soil health, and in that context, farming without tillage. Tilling the soil, turning it over and breaking it up whether by use of a plow pulled by a horse or a Case Ecolo-Tiger 875 disk ripper, in theory increases the loss of soil carbon. In contrast, working with a continual cover crop and no tilling increases carbon sequestration and by extension the microbial life in the soil. Ivo Jermaz of Grgich Hills in California says, "Any green plant produces carbohydrates through photosynthesis—we all know that. But 50 percent of those carbs are used to feed microbes in a natural system. Every day that you have something green growing"—which in Jermaz's case means fifteen to twenty different species of cover crops at all times—"microbes are getting fed. They have to eat. If you have a cow or a dog, they have to eat; why not microbes?" Typically pasture-based animals are also added to the regenerative equation, for two reasons. They graze on the cover crops, which prevents the plants from going to seed and keeps their energy concentrated on growth, and also they produce manure, which they tread into the soil, both fertilizing it and adding additional microbial life.

(Some of regenerative farming dovetails very closely with the philosophies of the Japanese farmer, thinker, and writer Masanobu Fukuoka. Fukuoka proposed, and followed, a form of natural, noninterventionist, "do nothing" farming that requires no plowing or tilling, no chemical fertilizers or prepared compost, no weeding, and, overall, no wasteful effort. His theory was that human intervention into nature disrupts the natural balance, creating more problems than it solves. This approach is described in detail in his influential book *The One-Straw Revolution*.)

Regenerative agriculture, unlike organics or biodynamics, also requires attention to animal welfare and to farmworkers' conditions. Animals require the "five freedoms"—from discomfort, from fear and stress, from hunger, from pain and disease, and to express their normal behavior—and farmworkers must not just be paid a living wage, but their feedback has to be actively sought after and acted upon as well.

About Natural Wine

Well, what *is* "natural" wine?

Let's start with a legal definition, since the French, who do love a good bureaucratic regulation, made a stab at one in 2020. In March of that year, the Institut National de l'Origine et de la Qualité, otherwise known as the INAO, passed a ruling that for a wine to be certified "*Vin Méthode Nature*," grapes must be handpicked, not machine-harvested; they must be certified organic by one of several major certifying organizations; yeasts for fermentation must be naturally occurring in the winery or vineyard, not purchased; additions or adjuncts (citric acid, added tannins, Mega Purple, you name it) or intrusive/manipulative technical processes (spinning cone technology to reduce alcohol, for example) cannot be used; and sulfite content must be under 30mg/liter. Optionally, there's a second, more restrictive version of the certification, "*vin méthode nature sans sulfites ajoutés*," which requires absolutely no added sulfites.

Finally, problem solved! *Merci*, French governmental minions. That's natural wine. The hitch here is that the entire natural wine movement—and it is a movement—doesn't really *like* categorization. Or certification. Or government regulations. Or rules. Natural winemakers tend to have a very "You're going to tell me how to make my wine? Fuck off!" sensibility. It is essentially the punk rock of fermented grape juice.

So here's a short, more de facto definition of natural winemaking: nothing added, nothing removed.

Here's another: as little intervention as possible, zero intervention if achievable.

And here are some words: low-intervention, low-tech, lo-fi, untouched, un-fucked-with, raw, wild, savage, natty, alive.

That may help make things a bit clearer, but it's also worth taking a look at how "natural wine" got its start. Natural wine saw a slow, organic (appropriately) growth. To pick a good moment, though, let's land on 1978. That was when a young vintner in Beaujolais, Marcel Lapierre, dissatisfied with the wines of that era (lots of chemical treatments in the vineyards; lots of sulfur, chaptalization, and manufactured yeasts in the wineries) came under the sway of the *négociant*, winemaker and scientist Jules Chauvet. Chauvet's philosophy might be summed up in this quote from the book *Le Vin en Question*: "Wine, wine should be naked. I shall go even further; it is the wine without sulfur anhydride (SO_2), without sugar, without anything." That approach struck a chord.

Lapierre started talking to his friends, and soon the group—Lapierre, Jean Foillard, Jean-Paul Thévenet, and Guy Breton, dubbed by their U.S. importer Kermit Lynch "the gang of four"—began practicing what Chauvet preached. Over time awareness of their work and their wines spread, and started influencing like-minded winemakers throughout France. (Chauvet influenced vintners not in Beaujolais as well—Pierre Overnoy in Jura, for example—and also there were winemakers in other countries who landed on a similar noninterventionist philosophy without Chauvet's influence at all, such as Eduard Rebholz at Weingut Ökonomierat Rebholz in Germany's Pfalz region.)

By the mid 1990s, a few Parisian wine bars were focusing on these new "natural" wines. Other producers throughout Europe who were similarly dissatisfied with industrial farming and winemaking approaches were starting to be intrigued as well. (In Italy, particularly, there was a kind of cross-pollination from the work of Friuli's Josko Gravner, who had been inspired by the *qvevri* [amphora] wines of Georgia;

those, in essence, are the original natural wines, part of a tradition that stretches back more or less untouched for eight thousand years.)

Natural wines represent a truly minuscule fraction of the wine sold in the world—but over the years, the movement has unquestionably been influential. By 2000 or so, groundbreaking importers such as Jenny Lefcourt in the U.S. were focusing solely on natural wines; others, such as Kermit Lynch and Neal Rosenthal, had long had wineries in their portfolios that for all practical purposes were "natural" producers even if their primary focus was a somewhat broader umbrella of . . . well, let's call them real wines.

And that to me is the problem, and indeed part of the reason for this book. Because where's the line? Why, for instance, is Burgundy's Domaine de Villaine somehow *not* a "natural" wine producer while La Grange Tiphaine in the Loire is? Both farm biodynamically. Both use native yeasts, minimal sulfur, and don't manipulate their wines. In fact, Damien Delecheneau at Grange Tiphaine has more scientific training than Pierre de Benoist at Domaine de Villaine does. So why is one "natural" and the other not?

The truth is that philosophically there's very little difference between them. But, different importers. Different fans. Different *listeners*, you could say. Natural wine, as much as it is a philosophy and an approach to making wine, is also a social movement, a group identity. In a lot of ways, it's a club. And, as we all know from high school, what's the point of having a club unless there are people who can't get in?

Some aspects of the self-defining realm of natural wine do set it apart, principally a general (but not universal) willingness to accept some characteristics that most winemakers would see as flaws as, at worst, simply part of the character of the wine, and at best, virtues. These include brettanomyces ("Brett"), a yeast that produces volatile compounds that will make a wine smell (if you do not like Brett) of a sweaty horse, or a Band-Aid box, or a barnyard, or (if you do like it) appealingly funky. Volatile acidity is another. At low levels VA, as it's called, can either be mildly off-putting or actually appealing depending on your taste (at minimal levels, VA can sort of "lift" the flavors of a wine, or—perhaps a better way to say it—throw them into higher relief). At high levels, though, it smells of vinegar or nail polish remover or both. The flaw called "mouse," or *gout de souris*, is caused by compounds known as tetrahydropyridines, and will make a wine smell like a mouse cage and/or dirty socks;

that one's felt to be a negative by almost everyone (not exactly a surprise). Mouse occurs almost exclusively in natural wines, is only detectable after you taste the wine (it's activated by saliva, interestingly), and is pretty clearly tied to not using sulfur (SO_2) during fermentation. The bad news: natural winemakers largely abhor using sulfur during fermentation. The good news: not everyone can detect mouse. Some of us are anosmic to one, two, or all three of the primary compounds that cause it.

Is acceptance of these flaws a good thing? A bad thing? That depends on your definition of "flaw," of course. As the philosopher David Hume wrote in 1757, "Beauty is no quality in things themselves: It exists merely in the mind which contemplates them; and each mind perceives a different beauty." Of course, Hume argued as well for the presence of an objective standard as a kind of counterpoint to that. By general objective standards—i.e., the dominant idea of what wine should be—Brett is a flaw whether you intended to have it in your wine or not. But one of the natural wine movement's values has been to hold a mirror up to those general objective standards and say, "Wait a minute. Who says so? And who says they're right?"

For me, natural wine's birth as a corrective to chemical/industrial winemaking is inspiring, and its basic premise that less intervention is better than more makes a lot of sense. (Semantic quibbles that wine has always involved intervention—Farming! Crushing grapes! Refrigeration!—tend to elide the main point.) I find minor amounts of Brett or VA to be fine, *if they are in balance with the other characteristics of the wine* (but mouse is right out, sorry).

That said, I also find that too many natural wines allow acceptance of what are traditionally considered flaws to masquerade as expression of place. When Brett or VA or other intrusive notes blot out the character of the site or the nature of the fruit, I put the glass aside. A Brett-bomb doesn't smell of terroir; it smells of volatile phenol compounds. (And if you say to someone in that case that they "just don't understand the wine," then congrats: you're an old-school wine snob, just hiding under your cool-kid hat.)

In the end the best thing is to take the winemaker's sensibility and intentions into account. If those are entirely at odds with what you think wine should be, or if you simply find the result in the bottle unpleasant, don't drink the wine. Don't like punk rock? Don't listen to punk rock. On the other hand, just because you don't like Black Flag, or free jazz, or having your ears pummeled by Stravinsky's *Rite of Spring* does not mean you have no taste and only listen to yacht rock. The black-and-white anathemas issued by both sides—"all natural wine is crap" or "all conventional wine is crap"—are reductive and tiresome. (And I actively dislike, as is probably clear, the way that natural wine, despite its down-to-earth/of-the-people sheen, has actively co-opted some of the pretentiousness that always lurks around wine, and coupled it to indie-exclusionary-cool.)

The unfortunate rhetorical implication in the term "natural wine" is that all other wine is somehow unnatural, which creates a false division for wine buyers between a lot of terrific wine producers who are for all practical purposes making wine with the same respect for nature and dislike of overt manipulation. The actual border, which to me is far more significant, is the one between wine that's industrially or mass-produced, generic, and environmentally irresponsible and, well, real wine; that is, the kinds of wines and wineries covered in these pages.

To Certify or Not to Certify

Certification, basically a stamp of approval by an outside organization on your farming or winemaking practices, whether sustainable, organic, biodynamic, or regenerative, is a somewhat complicated issue. At first look, it seems simple: if you farm organically, for instance, certainly you should apply for organic certification, right? After all, that seal gives consumers a guarantee that what you *say* you are doing actually *is* what you're doing—and, in a world where words like "sustainable" and "organic" are more and more effective as selling points for food and wine, accountability matters.

At the same time, there are plenty of ecologically responsible growers who either do not want to be certified or who work outside the approved rule books. (And then there are growers who *are* certified, but for whatever reason decline to put it on their label.) Nigel Greening at New Zealand's Felton Road points out some of the problems: "We're now twenty-odd years into organics and most of our wine is not labeled organic. That's not because it isn't organic. It's just because of the sheer grief of the details of trying to deal with forty-five different markets around the world, each with their own organic rules and variations."

Certification is also complicated when it comes to biodynamics, because many growers use biodynamic practices in their vineyards, but have no interest in (or even antipathy toward) the more theosophical or quasi-spiritual aspects of the approach. Or they simply dislike the idea of paying a yearly fee to Demeter, one of the two biodynamic certifying organizations, which is based on a total percentage of the winery's sales (Demeter also raised eyebrows with U.S. grape growers by trademarking the word "biodynamic." If you are pro-Demeter, you'll agree with their argument that this prevents corporations and suchlike from hijacking the word and rendering it meaningless, the way the term "natural" essentially is when it comes to food. If you are anti-Demeter, you will probably instead see it as a fee-based money-grab. Both sides have a point).

In any case, each profile in this book clarifies whether a winery or estate is certified in whatever farming practices it follows. If an entry simply says "sustainable," "organic," or "biodynamic," then the owners have either chosen not to pursue certification or, in some cases, are in the process (organic certification usually takes about three years). If it says "certified organic" or "certified biodynamic," well, they are certified. Whether certification is a crucial consideration for buying someone's wine is up to you. But if it's any help, I didn't include anyone in this book who I thought was bullshitting me about their farming practices.

The following are the certifications most commonly found on wine labels (usually on the back on the bottle, though not always). There are a lot; this is by no means a comprehensive list. Also, some wineries will also state on the label, "made with organic grapes." This relates to the USDA's extremely low added-sulfite allowance for wines with the USDA organic symbol; in essence, "made with organic grapes" is the vintner pointing out that they grew their grapes organically, but that they think the USDA rules for winemaking itself are problematically restrictive (a fair call).

Sustainable
>   Certified California Sustainable Winegrowing (CCSW)
>   Certified Sustainable Wine of Chile
>   EntWine (Australia)
>   HVE (Haute Valeur Environmentale) (France)
>   Integrity and Sustainability Certified (South Africa)
>   LEED (for buildings; international)
>   LIVE (Low Input Viticulture & Enology)

Lodi Rules

Napa Green

New Zealand Sustainable Winegrowing

Salmon Safe (USA)

SIP (Sustainability in Practice) Certified (USA)

Sustainable Austria

Sustainable Wine Australia

Sustainable Wine South Africa

V.I.V.A. (Italy)

Organic

Agriculture Biologique / AB (France)

Argencert (Argentina)

Austria Bio Garantie / ABG (Austria)

BioGro (New Zealand)

CCOF (California Certified Organic Farmers)

Ecocert (France/EU)

Ecovin (Germany)

Euro Leaf (EU)

Letis (Argentina)

Nature et Progrès (France)

Oregon Tilth

Organic Farm New Zealand

USDA Organic

Biodynamic

Biodyvin (Europe)

Demeter

Respekt-BIODYVIN (Austria/Germany/Italy)

Regenerative

Regenerative Organic Certified (USA)

THREE

HOW TO DRINK WINE

"Wine is, after man, the most adept at telling stories. It is capable of broadcasting messages vast and ancient. It introduces itself with a complete set of identity papers. When I taste a wine, I taste everything that has ever happened in the land where it was raised. I meet the people who grew it and I feel the hands that touched it. I know it sounds like a bit of stretch to say that. But wine lives in and of itself."
—Luigi Veronelli, December 1984

know, I know: How hard is it? You pick up a glass, take a sip, and swallow. But look for a moment at any wine magazine in the world, and you're apt to read something along these lines: "Pale lemon-gold color. Exotic nose combines ripe pineapple, sultry mango, navel orange, peach skin, acacia honey, and smoky oak. The palate is concentrated and exotic, an electric fruit bomb with rich, tropical flavors of ripe pineapple, pear, apricot, and mango." The implication is that if you pick up a glass of that wine, then that's going to be your experience of it. And if that's not your experience, then . . . maybe you're doing something wrong?

But let's pause here. What makes an aroma "exotic"? And does the liquid in your glass actually taste like a mixture of pineapples, pears, apricots, and mangoes? And, even if it does, how does that help you? Will you derive more pleasure from it knowing that the wine smells—in theory—of pineapple, mango, orange, peach skin, acacia honey, and smoky oak? What if you don't smell those things? Are you some sort of nose-challenged loser? (Answer: No.)

Translating flavors and aromas into words is not easy. As the scholar Christopher Ricks once pointed out, literature is the only art where the criticism is in the same language as the art itself. Writing about taste or smell is like writing about music, or dance; you're using words to describe something nonverbal. But even so, it's pretty clear to me that wine writing of what could be called the American pseudoscientific taxonomy school—or the fruit-salad school—just doesn't do all that much for anyone who's actually drinking a glass of wine.

The real question, when it comes to describing a wine, is what matters? Does it *matter* that a wine tastes like raspberries rather than black cherries? Would you buy a wine based on whether it tasted like one or the other? Can you actually imagine how the wine will taste in your own mouth from a list like "mangoes, pineapples, pears, apricots, and oak"? The only place you'd normally find all those flavors together (sans the oak) is at a smoothie shop.

The words that writers use to describe wine fall roughly into three categories: factual, relational, and impressionistic. Saying a wine smells of new oak, if it was indeed aged in new oak barrels, is factual. The wine literally smells of new oak, because it has absorbed oak lactones, vanillin, and other compounds from the barrel. Stick your nose in a new oak barrel sometime, and you'll know exactly what that smell is. Saying a wine smells of raspberries, on the other hand, is relational—it smells "like" raspberries. There are no raspberries *in* the wine, but its aroma and flavor—to that taster at least—recall the aroma and flavor of raspberries. (Note that there is sometimes overlap between these two realms. When a wine smells "buttery," that's typically the compound diacetyl, a product of malolactic fermentation; the same compound is used to flavor movie-theater popcorn. There's no butter in the wine, but it really does smell like butter. Or at least like fake butter.) Then there are impressionistic descriptions: taut, fat, round, linear, graceful, electric, you name it.

Ideally some mix of all those types of words would conjure an impression of what that wine might *be* like, a kind of verbal echo that a reader could, however inexactly, use to summon a real sense of what they were about to taste. Unfortunately, a vast amount of the verbiage out there tends more toward a rugby pile-on of descriptor after descriptor, often modified by even more questionable adjectives: "crushed stone," "attractive plum," "succulent flowers," heading toward train wrecks like "the palate packs dried nori and wet kelp against wild black-plum and raw meat flavors." Uh . . . yum?

I've tried to shift the balance here to some degree. The most important information in these pages answers questions. It describes things that really do matter:

where the wine is from, how the vineyards were farmed, who made the wine. To me, "does it taste like blueberries?" or "how many months did it age in barrel?" is far less interesting than "what's the winemaker's story?" or "what's so special about this particular vineyard?" The descriptions of specific wines here truly are less important than the answers to those questions—though, I hope, helpful and evocative rather than useless. And yes, there are a few raspberries and wild cherries. Even "seashell minerality." (*Mea culpa!*) But only when I really, honest to God, felt that's what the wine reminded me of. So, in the realm of general advice, here's mine. Ignore the adjectives as much as possible. Just taste the wine.

Then there are point scores. For many years, people who care about wine have made a lot of their buying choices based on ratings or scores for wine, given by critics, typically on a 100-point scale. This system, which the wine critic Robert Parker effectively created in the early 1980s, changed how people bought wine. (It also made Parker and his *Wine Advocate* newsletter, along with rival publication the *Wine Spectator*, very influential.)

Admittedly, the 100-point system was a brilliant invention, because if there was ever a realm for decision paralysis, wine is it. Suppose you go into a store, and instead of the wall of Chardonnays you'd find at a BevMo or Total Wine, you're confronted with a wall of chicken soup. And, just as with the Chardonnays, there are not four or five brands of chicken soup, but dozens, even hundreds. Then you look closer, and you discover that the cans of chicken soup are priced anywhere from 50 cents to 50 dollars a can. *And*, most brands offer three or four variations, too—their basic soup, plus a "reserve" soup, plus who knows what else. Then, just to make it even *more* baffling, no ingredients are listed anywhere. Instead, all you find is paragraphs of alarmingly purple prose on every can's label, rambling on about how this particular soup was made by hand, or with care, or by soup people who've been making soup for ten generations in their castle in Italy, and how they "feel soup is really made at the farm," and how for *this* soup each chicken is fed organic feed and spring water, and then has its neck wrung lovingly by hand. Finally, there's some verbiage about how the soup tastes—but the words don't actually sound like the person is describing soup. No, instead there are "notes of citrus" or "hints of earth or minerals" or "laser-like acidity." In fact, the one flavor that's never mentioned on any of these cans of chicken soup is "chicken."

Is it any wonder that a system which rated wine on a simple scale became so popular?

But lately things have changed: the power of point scores for wines has started to diminish. Chalk it up to a savvier wine audience, the influence of social media, wine score grade inflation, you name it. There are a number of reasons, but among them is a greater interest in questions like how a wine was made or how the grapes for it were grown. A woman I was chatting with at a party not too long ago summed it up: "But what are these scores?" she asked. "I mean, who gives them out? Why would I pay attention to them?" She was in her early thirties and said she loved drinking wine. But what mattered to her was whether, in terms of origin and philosophy, a wine fit into a constellation of practices she cared about—far more than whether some critic had deemed it worthy of 93 points. To me her reaction made perfect sense. How do you assign a point score to the fact that someone's been farming their plot of land in Chianti for thirty years, knows every vine on the place, and grows their grapes according to biodynamic principles? Is that a 91? An 86? A 37.995?

Today, most sommeliers and restaurant wine buyers don't pay the slightest attention to scores. The opening of specialty wine shops throughout the country catering to organic, small-production, regional, and artisanal wines is also contributing to their decline. And when it comes to natural wine, a movement for which the philosophy and practices used to make the wine are the most important thing about the wine, traditional scoring systems don't make sense at all.

People like point scores because they're simple—they're meant to tell a customer how good the wine they're thinking about buying is going to taste. But can you taste organic-ness? What's the flavor of harvesting by hand on a forty-five-degree slope? Can a critic's palate discern whether a wine was made by an old Spaniard from grapes he grew on his own land rather than by a large corporation? How can a story have a taste?

Then there is context. Suppose you're on vacation in Italy. The scene is some backstreet trattoria in Rome (or Florence, or Siena, or Lecce—take your pick, they're all lovely). You're with someone you love, having a wonderful time. The food is amazing, and the red you randomly chose off the restaurant list is *exceptional*. You scribble down the name or snap a picture of it with your phone, and two months later, back home, you track down a bottle at your local liquor store. You take it home, open it for dinner by yourself, pour a glass, take that first sip, and what the hell? It doesn't taste anything like what you remember. That wine was great. This is just . . . *bleh*.

This is a pretty common experience.

But the wine is the same. Unless the bottle you just bought was somehow roasted in transit, which is unlikely these days, the liquid inside is exactly the same wine you drank in Italy. *You're* the one who's different.

Our experience of wine (and food, for that matter) is inescapably contextual. Who we're with, where we are, what sort of mood we're in, whether the sun is shining, whether a nitwit just backed into our car in the parking lot, whether we're in love, out of love, hungry, tired, graced with optimism or feeling like life is perfect crap, all of that plays into how a wine tastes to us.

This is, again, one reason why rating wines with numerical scores is so bizarre. Consider this scene: a wine critic sits at a table in a quiet room with a lineup of twenty Châteauneuf-du-Papes. The labels are hidden; the glasses, an ounce in each, are numbered one through twenty. The critic tastes each wine—smells it, swirls it, sips it, swishes it around in the mouth, spits it out. They make a few notes on a laptop, assign a score (92, 83, 100—as if a wine could be perfect!), and move on to the next one. Tomorrow, it's twenty more Châteauneufs. Or maybe twenty Sancerres, or twenty California Merlots.

No one on the planet actually *drinks* wine like this.

We drink wine in social situations, with other people. We drink it while we're falling in love with the person across the table from us, or in a bistro in a southern French town; we drink it while we're sorting out exactly what "fold in" means in the recipe we're cooking; we drink it when we're exhausted after a difficult day in the office, or on a porch looking over a lake at a house where we're spending a weekend.

All of those contextual details play into our perception of a wine. And unlike our blind-tasting critic friend, we also typically taste or drink wines knowing what winery made them, what country they came from, what year they were made, what the bottle cost, and much more. Additional context.

So suppose you feel that organic farming is a good way to treat the planet and that organic produce is something you strongly prefer to eat. Would it be so strange to think that your pleasure at opening a bottle of wine made with organic grapes might affect your enjoyment of what you're drinking?

The truth is that the story of a wine—knowledge of the people behind it and the place it came from, awareness of the honesty of how it was made and how that reflects your own beliefs—can deeply affect your experience of a wine. In fact, that's exactly *why* many wine critics taste blind. Knowing that the Châteauneuf-du-Pape they're about to give a rating to is from Domaine du Pegau, that it was made by the prodigiously talented Laurence Féraud, and that she is apparently genetically incapable of making anything other than stellar wines might predispose them to liking it and thus corrupt the theoretically objective score they're about to give it. Instead, they taste it *without* knowing any of that information.

Guess what: no one drinks wine *that* way, either. Seriously, why on earth would you want to?

I'm not arguing that quality is entirely relative. First, there's the initial question of whether a wine is well made or not. A table with three legs that falls over, for instance, is a bad table. A wine that tastes of burnt rubber or old vegetables, or that re-ferments in your closet and blows the cork out the top of the bottle, well, that's a bad wine.

But still, what about that question of quality?

People just getting into wine are sometimes told "a good wine is one you like."

It would be more accurate to say something along the lines of "It's totally reasonable for you to prefer wines that you like." Think about visual art. I may think my six-year-old daughter's stick drawing of a horse is the most beautiful thing ever made, but you'd think I was delusional if I said that it was a greater work than Botticelli's *Birth of Venus*, and you'd be right.

Similarly, let's say I love drinking mass-produced Australian Shiraz. Let's say I even prefer it to all other wines (the moon might also crash into the earth and wipe us all out tomorrow, but whatever). But anyone who knows anything about wine would think I was delusional if I told them that Yellow Tail Shiraz is a greater exploration of the potential of what wine can be than a bottle of, let's say, Domaine Chave Hermitage; and they'd be right.

Something that a lot of wine critics seem to have forgotten is that an aesthetic judgment is exactly that: a judgment. That critic dispensing 83- and 95-point ratings is biased both by their own palate as well as by their beliefs about what a certain kind of wine *should* taste like, just as art or theater or movie critics have their beliefs and biases. Robert Parker, the wine critic, whose ratings many accepted as purely objective, clearly long had a preference for richer, more powerful wines over lighter, more delicate ones.

Point scores make wine shopping easier, no question. But they're odd. Almost as odd as the idea of point scores for paintings. What does the *Mona Lisa* get, a 99? How about *The Card Players* by Cézanne? 95? 89? But wait, you say, they aren't comparable! One is a Renaissance masterpiece and one's a Post-Impressionist work from the late 1800s! So, OK then, within its competitive set (Post-Impressionism, Napa Valley Cabernet, whatever) Cézanne's *Card Players* gets a 99 and *Sunday Afternoon on the Island of La Grande Jatte* by Seurat gets a . . . 96?? Numerical scales imply scientific objectivity, a weird thing to apply to art, or even to wine. On top of that, there's simply no question that, even when tasting blind, each critic's own preferences, palate chemistry, quirks of smell, prejudices, mood, and so on inextricably affect their assessment of a wine. Even how *hungry* you are will. In the Nobel prize–winning psychologist Daniel Kahneman's book *Thinking Fast and Slow*, he cites an Israeli study that addressed this effect, in which eight parole judges' decisions were analyzed. Overall, only 35 percent of parole requests were approved. But when the researchers plotted the judges' decisions against what time of day they occurred, they found the approval rate shot up right after they ate, to about 65 percent. When they were hungry and impatient for lunch, or for their afternoon break, the rate dropped to about zero. Short version: pray to God if you ask for parole that you don't get a hungry judge.

Or pray to God that your Chardonnay, whose grapes you grew with such care and that you worked so painstakingly on in the winery, doesn't appear before a hungry wine critic. Because what is a wine critic but a judge, issuing verdicts about wine after wine? Which wines get parole, and which do not, and when did that stern character with his nose in the glass have his lunch? It's no wonder that the same wine might get an 86 from one publication, a 92 from another, and a 95 from a third. And yet each time, each critic insists their assessment is an objective one.

The only truly objective observation you can make about this is that, when it comes to assessing their own objectivity, wine critics are usually wrong.

Over the years, I've tasted tens of thousands of wines. I've definitely traveled tens of thousands of miles, to almost every country that makes wine, to write about them. I've tasted great wines and garbage wines and everything in between. And the one constant amid all that tasting, traveling, drinking, talking, and writing, though it took me a while to realize it, is that the wines I remember best all have one thing in common.

Surprisingly, it isn't how delicious they were.

The common thread between all those wines was that they offered something *more*. And that's what the wines in this book do. They offer something that expands beyond the direct chemical characteristics of flavor and aroma. That moreness might come from the winemaking or viticultural choices that went into making a wine. It might come from the history of the people who made it, or the fact that the wine expresses a vineyard site or a sensibility or both. It might be the way that specific wine seems distinct from every other wine you've ever tasted. It might be found in the way a wine tells a story.

The beverage product wines of the world can't do that. The Taco Bell tacos of wine offer all the moreness of . . . well, a Taco Bell taco. Real wines are more akin to when you stop at Edgar Rico's Nixta Taqueria, located in a former tattoo parlor on the east side of Austin, Texas, and order his duck carnitas tacos, with salsa cruda and radish and chopped onion on a homemade blue corn tortilla, made with Oaxacan blue corn that Rico nixtamalizes himself. That taco is one real taco, I can tell you. It will make a fast-food taco break down in shame at its own meager existence and weep like a small child. And the fact that maybe you can't get to Austin to eat Edgar Rico's tacos is beside the point, because there's undoubtedly a taqueria somewhere in your town—wherever your town happens to be—serving honest, real tacos made by a real person (as opposed to by a large corporation named, aptly and alarmingly in equal measures, Yum! Foods).

Another reason we remember our favorite wines so vividly is because the qualities that make them real are also wrapped into our *own* stories—where you were when you drank that bottle, who you were with, what moment it was in your life. The moreness that defines real wine amplifies the pleasure of drinking it, and it also acts as a fixative for memory. A wine that's just another commercial product may taste good, but that pleasant taste is its sole dimension; sort of the way a commercial jingle is not the same as Billie Holiday singing "Summertime." If those were my two choices, I know which one I'd want playing in the background if I were proposing marriage to someone. I'd also like a glass of real wine in my hand before I popped the question.

As a result, this book is not a typical wine guide. I think of it more as a collection of stories—lots and lots of stories—because personally I think it's far more useful to tell someone *why* a wine is fascinating, or exciting, or real, than it is to tell them something like "96 points: aromas of ripe blackberry and damson plums." If that's all you are told about a wine, what do you think about when you taste it? Not much, other than "yum" (assuming you like it) and "what the hell is a damson plum?" Skip the plums. Instead, find out how the grower farms their land, or what the winemaker's philosophy is, or how they moved to a tiny farm in the Ardèche after someone broke their heart in Paris. Seriously, you can decide for yourself if the damn thing tastes like plums.

Knowledge *is* pleasure when it comes to wine.

Add knowledge to memory and together they're a powerful force. Another example: A few years ago I dragged my best friend along on a five-country road trip for a story. Our final winery visit was to Nikolaihof, in Austria's Wachau region.

That afternoon we walked around in the estate's biodynamic vineyards with Nik Saahs, whose family owns the winery. At one point his dog, a long-haired dachshund, came bounding up. I asked what the dog's name was. "Oh, that's Lumpi. Here, Lumpi," Nik said, kneeling down to give the dog a scratch between the ears. He added, "Actually, he's the sixteenth Lumpi."

It turned out that the Saahses always have dachshunds, and those dachshunds are always named Lumpi. A long, amusing history of dogs, but not as long as the history of the estate itself. It was founded in AD 985, though the Romans made wine there as long as two thousand years ago; the ancient wooden press in its cellar was carved from a single elm tree. And if I buy a bottle of Nikolaihof today and drink it, the tingly freshness and purity of flavor of the wine is lifted by memories: the easy familiarity of long friendship, a comical series of identically named dogs, the vineyards slanting down to the slow-flowing Danube in the afternoon sun, a thousand-year history of making wine.

Put it this way: *our brains manufacture pleasure out of more than just the chemical makeup of the alcoholic liquid that's touching our tongues.*

But experiencing wine in that way doesn't require a trip across the ocean or an afternoon spent with a winemaker, though both can be great experiences. Another example: I've never met Diana Lenzi of Fattoria di Petroio in person (we've talked on the phone). Regardless, being aware that she worked as a chef in Rome but still somehow always knew she would return to her family's property to become a winemaker informs my experience of her Chianti Classico when I take a sip of it. Knowing that she was inspired by her mother and that her assistant winemaker is also a woman—and knowing how male-dominated the Italian wine world is— adds another layer. And every time I see a bottle of her wine, I remember that the part of Tuscany near Siena has a huge wild boar problem (they root up vines), and that Lenzi's suggested solution was that the town council start turning them into ragù, then market it to the world as "*Il Sugo di Siena.*" That makes me smile. Do I *need* to know that Petroio, like Nikolaihof, has existed since Roman times, or that her family has owned it since the 1920s and now farms the property entirely organically? No. Even without knowing that, the Petroio Chianti Classico would taste good; it's a delicious wine. But all those different pieces of the story change my experience of what I'm drinking. Lenzi's wines are real wines. They offer depth beyond flavor.

Does this mean that every single time you open a bottle of wine you need to learn its story and dwell on it before taking that first sip? Of course not. It's nice at times to stop thinking and simply be. If I'm at the end of a hike on a hot day and a friend offers me a cold Budweiser, I'm not going to turn it down. Drink what you like and be happy with what you drink. This book isn't here to make moral claims. But still, I think there's even greater pleasure to be found in opening yourself up to a different way of tasting, and to drinking a more rewarding kind of wine.

FOUR

WHO IS IN THIS BOOK AND HOW IT IS ORGANIZED

There are thousands and thousands of independent wine producers around the world who farm sustainably, organically, or biodynamically and who make great wines that express the places they come from. Writing about every single one of them would be a Sisyphean task (as would reading about them, because this book would weigh as much as a boulder). Here's how I've narrowed things down.

✦ **All of the wines in this book are from winemakers or owners I've talked to personally, or from wineries I've visited, or both.** The human element in wine is crucial. Terroir, the sense of place, is crucial, too; but terroir is always shown through the human lens of winemaking. Even the least-intervening winemakers decide what day to pick, decide whether to destem or not, decide when to bottle or not—the decision tree has a lot of branches. With winemaking the human hand is always present to some degree, even if your ambition is that it stay in your pocket. And if vineyards have terroir, then winemakers have stories. I've tried to tell the stories of the winemakers here in a way that I hope deepens the experience of tasting their wines.

+ **None of these wines have been tasted blind (and none of them have scores).** There's a general feeling in wine criticism that wines should be judged blind, without any knowledge of who made them, how much they cost, and so on, in order to ensure that ratings and recommendations are impartial.

That approach goes against exactly what I feel is most important, which is that knowing *who* made a wine, *how* the grapes were farmed and the wine was made, and *why* the vintner worked that way is vastly more valuable for wine drinkers than an assessment that ignores those aspects. Blind tasting denatures wine and sucks away much of what makes it so endlessly rewarding, and really, who gives a damn if a critic thinks a wine deserves 95 points and tastes of tobacco and morello cherries?

The argument for blind tasting is that it keeps critics from being biased and keeps consumers from being ripped off. My feeling is that actual knowledge is far more effective in that regard. Ratings are wines stripped of stories, and stories are what make wine (and much else in life) interesting. There are plenty of fake stories out there—that's most of marketing. But most of us these days have fairly refined bullshit detectors, and can separate the real from the fake fairly effectively.

+ **Why isn't Petrus in here? or Sassicaia? or Château Rayas? or . . . ?** Wine lovers will notice that a lot of very famous names are *not* included in this book. Many of them make wines from vines that are farmed both responsibly and brilliantly, and that without question express a personal vision and a sense of terroir. Domaine de la Romanée-Conti's La Tâche, for instance, is one of the greatest red Burgundies in the world, and would certainly fit all my criteria . . . but a bottle of it will set you back about $7,000. If a billionaire buys you a case of La Tâche as a Christmas present, by all means drink the stuff (or sell it and put a down payment on a house). DRC is an extreme case, but the sad truth is that many of the benchmark wines of the world have become so expensive that they're out of the reach of the average wine buyer, or even the wine buyer who's game to spend a fair amount of money. If you teamed up with nine friends to buy a bottle of Domaine Georges Roumier Chambolle-Musigny 1er Cru Les Amoureuses (a premier cru, not even a grand cru!) simply to have the opportunity to try it, you'd still be looking at more than $300 per person. That's nuts.

Even leaving aside price, most of those superstar producers have had hundreds, if not thousands, of pages written about them over the years. I'd rather call out a winemaker who's relatively unknown, or a domaine that hasn't yet hit everyone's awareness. The annals of "the world's greatest wines" are well thumbed. Put them aside for now. Part of the joy of wine is discovery.

✦ **Living on the land.** The distribution of the wineries here doesn't necessarily follow classic assumptions about which wine regions are most significant. In France, the Loire Valley is a hotbed of organic farming practices as well as natural wine producers. Bordeaux, on the other hand, produces far more wine overall but its most well-known châteaux tend to be owned by absentee multimillionaires (or multi-multimillionaires, or billionaires) or else large corporations such as LVMH or AXA Group. For this book at least, the Loire deserves more space.

Of course, absentee ownership—whether by corporations or individuals—doesn't mean that a winery won't produce very good wine; there are some extremely talented people working for corporate-owned wineries, and very rich investors certainly own some of the world's greatest vineyards. But with a few exceptions, I feel that being present on the land is a crucial component of being a great vigneron, the French term for someone who both cultivates the grapes and makes wine from them; on top of that, living on your own land provides a pretty formidable incentive toward farming it in a way that won't potentially poison you or your family or your workers, as many of the people I've interviewed here point out. (To every rule an exception, of course: Ridge Vineyards, for instance, which is owned by a [very hands-off] Japanese company, would be impossible to leave out; but those exceptions are few and far between.)

✦ **Most of the wines recommended in this book are under $100 a bottle.** It's a somewhat arbitrary cutoff, but also a realistic one: most of us don't wander around buying $500 bottles of first-growth Bordeaux or cult Napa Cabernet. On top of that, when it comes to famed regions like Napa Valley or the more famous villages of Burgundy, even prices for fairly modest wines have become alarmingly non-modest. A village wine from a large *négociant* in Burgundy may run you $75 or $80 these days; the average price of a bottle of Napa Valley Cabernet is around $75 as well. But Napa is just a tiny sliver of California, and Gevrey-Chambertin just one town in Burgundy. Young, ambitious winemakers (and old ambitious winemakers, for that matter) often can't afford to bootstrap their ventures in those regions. If you want that combo platter of value, talent, and passion, it often means heading to the fringes.

The truth is that *you can live an absolutely wonderful life of drinking wine without ever buying a bottle that's over $100.* There's a stupendous amount of very, very good wine in the world under that price, a lot of it from the kind of wine producers in these pages. Drink Agnés Paquet's Auxey-Duresses Les Hoz Rouge instead of Armand Rousseau Chambertin, and you'll have a great time, plus have cash left to send your kid to college. That said, all rules are made to be broken: there are certainly *some* wines in here more than $100. But by no means the majority.

For each wine, there's a simple key to the average bottle cost. Happy shopping. (Also see **Appendix One: Finding and Buying the Wines in This Book**, p. 677.)

$ from $5 to $20 a bottle
$$ from $21 to $50 a bottle
$$$ from $51 to $100 a bottle
$$$$ more than $100 a bottle

THE
WINERIES

Stéphane Tissot in his cellar, Jura, France

EUROPE

FRANCE

Domaine du Cellier aux Moines, Givry, Burgundy

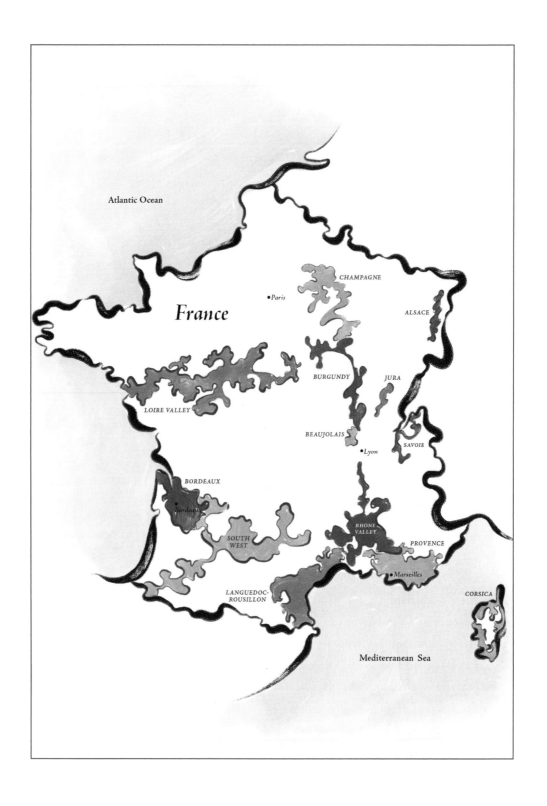

I f there is one country whose identity is inextricably linked to wine, it's France—certainly to most wine drinkers, and definitely to the French themselves. Though wine's origins don't lie here, France has done more to shape our understanding of wine than any other country. Some of the grapes we're most familiar with—Cabernet Sauvignon, Chardonnay, Pinot Noir, Merlot, Syrah, and many others—first rose to prominence in France. Many of the world's greatest wines are made here; and, perhaps more importantly, many of the world's most *distinctive* wines are made here, through a combination of brilliant winemaking and vineyards whose character is revealed in the wine that comes from them. The French, after all, created the concept of terroir. A French winemaker I once met described it with a musical metaphor: "The grape is the instrument, the winemaker is the player, the vineyard is the score." Who writes the score? "God, of course," he said cheerfully, "who else?" The nonreligious are free to offer up Mother Nature as an alternative.

I like his analogy because it doesn't diminish any of the sources of a bottle of good wine: the soil and climate, the vines, the grape variety, and the person who harvests and vinifies. All are important. In France you see that expressed in hundreds if not thousands of personalities and places, all as distinct from one another as Thierry Germain, of Les Roches Neuves in the Loire Valley's Saumur-Champigny region, is from Youmna Asseily, the warm, generous co-owner (with her husband,

Tony) of Château Biac in Bordeaux. Germain is apt to quote Goethe to you while walking in a vineyard; Asseily is likely to end up cooking you an entire Lebanese dinner the first day you meet her. Their wines are as different from each other as the people who make them.

In this book, the wine map of France looks slightly different than people might expect. Champagne is one of France's most famous wine regions. Dom Perignon is possibly the most famous wine made in Champagne, and is both delicious and also ages extraordinarily well in a cellar. But millions of bottles of Dom are made and sold each year. Whoever Dom's *chef du cave* is, no matter how talented he or she may be, they are beholden to the shareholders of LVMH, the vast luxury conglomerate that owns Dom Perignon (along with Krug, Veuve Clicquot, Ruinart, Mercier, and Moët Hennessy). In 2021 alone, LVMH sold more than 66 million bottles of Champagne. That's nearly one bottle for every man, woman, and child in France. Dom is an excellent wine, but so is Pierre Péters Les Chétillons, from a small, family-owned estate in Champagne. To some degree it's a question of where you'd like your money to go.

The wines of the Loire Valley are not nearly as well-known to the world, but right now, the Loire is one of the world's most exciting sources for what I'd call *real* wines—wines made from grapes grown in a conscientious, environmentally friendly manner, from a real place, by a real person. (Contra the U.S. Supreme Court, corporations are not actually people.) There are reasons for the Loire's profusion of exceptional, artisanal, independent wines. An acre of vineyard in Champagne will set you back about $600,000. An acre in Pouilly-Fumé, although it's the most expensive appellation of the Loire, will run you $65,000 or so. In Muscadet, where Claire and Fred Niger make sublime low-intervention wines at Domaine de L'Ecu, you might pay a mere $5,000—less than a hundredth of the price of that acre in Champagne. Is it any wonder that the Loire has been a magnet for young, ambitious, adventurous winemakers?

So, the vinous map of France here is skewed from the traditional one. The domaines and wineries I've profiled don't include many of the famous names wine lovers might expect to see. Bordeaux's reputation, for instance, has been built on the fame of its sixty-one classified-growth châteaux, with the pinnacle occupied by the five first growths—the Olympus of names like Latour, Mouton-Rothschild, and

Haut-Brion. The focus of this book is on wines that regular humans, with regular bank accounts, can afford. A $900 bottle of Château Latour, as good as it may be, doesn't qualify. And many of the storied properties of Bordeaux, like Latour, are now owned by multinational corporations or ultra-rich investors. Instead, why not look to names that are less renowned but no less deserving of respect: places like Château le Puy, whose vines haven't seen a drop of pesticide since its founding four hundred years ago; Château du Champ du Treilles, whose biodynamically farmed white Bordeaux is both delicious and also very affordable; and others.

There are more than twenty-seven thousand wineries in France. Vines blanket the country. France is only 1.4 times the size of California, but four times as many grape vines grow there. For every estate profiled in this book, there are ten or twenty or fifty more that I've never been to personally or whose wines I've never had, or whose wines are only sold locally (or, in some cases, are far too pricey). You could spend a lifetime trying to learn about every wine in France. Or you could, conceivably, taste a wine from each of these producers over the course of a year. It would be an ambitious project, but it definitely wouldn't be boring.

ALSACE

n terms of vineyard land, Alsace is tiny, a mere 38,000 acres of vines, a small fraction of what you find in Bordeaux (275,000 acres), never mind Languedoc (700,000). It's a slender strip of land, stretching for more than a hundred miles between the Vosges Mountains and the Rhine River on the eastern edge of France. Its winemaking history is long and chaotic. Many of the oldest winemaking families here settled in the region in the 1600s, fleeing the devastation of the Thirty Years' War, and in centuries following Alsace was ruled alternately by France and Germany, tossed back and forth as a kind of bargaining chip, or else, as in World War II, simply overrun. As the vintner Jean Trimbach says, "Historically, building anything in Alsace has been difficult, because it always gets destroyed." Alsace is a borderland, with all that entails.

Alsace is also remarkably green, not just in terms of its vines and forests but in how its small and typically family-owned estates are farmed. Over a third of Alsace vineyards are certified organic or are in conversion, and that percentage is only accelerating. Alsace has 12.8 percent (in 2022) of France's certified biodynamic vineyard acreage, representing 109 estates, a remarkable figure given that the region only has 5 percent of the country's total vineyard land.

Despite this, in recent years there's been an odd lull of interest in Alsace wines. What is there to say but that the winds of fashion blow strangely? The region makes some of the world's greatest dry Rieslings (a category that ought to be more popular than it is); excellent, affordable, sparkling crémants; complex, age-worthy whites from

Gewürztraminer, Pinot Gris and Pinot Blanc; delicately appealing Pinot Noirs (albeit not many—Pinot Noir represents about 11 percent of Alsace's vines, though that's increasing); and some of the world's greatest dessert wines. One hitch has been that Alsace's white wines can be dry, sweet, or anywhere in between, depending on the vintage and the producer's sensibility, but traditionally that information was never on the label. In the past, if you picked up an Alsace Pinot Gris, it might be anywhere from steely and tart to unctuously sweet, with no indication as to what you might be pouring into your glass once you pulled the cork. That changed in 2021, when the Alsace Wine Board mandated that wineries put a scale indicating the level of sweetness on every wine label. Smart move, too long in coming.

DOMAINE MARCEL DEISS • BERGHEIM

[certified organic / certified biodynamic]

Jean-Michel Deiss falls into the "wise old elf" school of French winemaking (as opposed to the "taciturn philosopher" school or the "passionate wild-haired youth" school). He's cheerful and twinkly, while at the same time inclined to saying things like "The concept of terroir is the concept of profundity."

Deiss has had plenty of intriguing things to say over the years. For instance: "Terroir is a concept that was invented because we wanted to go north with wines. In the south, in the sun, vines grow easily—the personality there is the grape. In the north, it's the personality of the place instead. And it's because of religion that we use this concept, because they wanted to create a great wine for religious wines in the north." Arguable, probably; interesting, definitely. Or: "You can be fooled by the label, the packaging, the aromas, but not by salivation." Context: he's talking about what he terms the "circular form of the winemaking"—essentially the correspondence between the nose and the mouth, and how a great wine will always keep you salivating. "Salivation is democratic," he notes. True enough.

Of course, being a wise old elf is valueless if what you make isn't good. That's not a problem here; the Deiss wines are stunning. The family has been in Alsace since the end of the Thirty Years' War. In 1947, Jean-Michel's father, Marcel, created the wine estate. Today the Deisses own roughly sixty-four acres of vineyards, all biodynamic and dedicated to "complantation" (mixing different grape varieties in a terroir, rather than planting a single variety). Modern Alsace focuses on mono-

---

> *"Every plant has the fantasy that it will grow all the way to the sun."*
> —Jean-Michel Deiss

---

varietal farming. Deiss, inspired by the mixed, pre–World War I vines at the family's Schoenenbourg grand cru vine-

yard, instead wanted to revive the region's historic, centuries-old ways of farming. In 1990, he planted the first modern vineyard in Alsace using this approach, giving his acreage in the Altenberg de Bergheim grand cru a willed chaos of thirteen traditional Alsace varieties (and breaking a number of local rules in the process). His epiphany moment, his son Mathieu says, was to focus "on the soil, not on the grape."

Today the wines are made by Mathieu, with Jean-Michel advising. Everything follows the basic philosophy he established: a rejection of technological domination of nature, and instead a return to a kind of farming and winemaking that argues for the primacy of place.

Domaine Marcel Deiss makes a few single-variety wines, the taut and compelling **Marcel Deiss Riesling ($$)** being one of them. But the real focus is on field blends, like the **Alsace Complantation ($$)**, a blend of Pinot Blanc, Riesling, Pinot Gris, Pinot Noir, Muscat à Petits Grains, Gewürztraminer, Sylvaner, Pinot Auxerrois, Pinot Beurot, Muscat Blanc, Rose d'Alsace, Traminer, and Chasselas Rose. "The idea was a wine that when you smell it and

taste it, you think, 'Alsace!'" Matheiu Deiss says. The **Engelgarten Cru d'Alsace ($$–$$$)** is one of several wines that Jean-Michel considers to be premier cru. (Alsace has no premier crus, so this is an ongoing battle.) It's a bolt of pure smoky citrus, "flinty and mineral," as Mathieu Deiss says. The **Grasberg Cru d'Alsace ($$$)**, from vines almost directly on limestone bedrock, is more fruit-forward and sweeter. The **Rotenberg Cru d'Alsace ($$$)** comes from their ripest site in Bergheim. Mathieu Deiss says, "We prefer here to have the complexity and depth and a bit of residual sugar than to make a dry wine without the depth." Of the various grand cru wines, **Schoenenbourg ($$$$)** comes from what's generally considered the greatest vineyard in Riquewihr; it's powerful and firm despite its sweetness. The **Altenberg de Bergheim ($$$$)** is sappy and luscious but with a spine of electric acidity, while **Mambourg ($$$$)** blends all five Pinot varieties (Gris, Noir, Meunier, Blanc, and Beurot) for a powerful, dry white loaded with warm spice notes.

DOMAINE TRIMBACH • RIBEAUVILLÉ

[organic]

Around 2009, Jean Trimbach says, the local nuns knocked on his door and asked if he would like to purchase their vineyard. "Which was kind of a shock, because we are Protestant, and the nuns and the Protestants, you know. But they were very happy to do the deal, and so were we."

Back when Trimbach's ancestors moved to Alsace, that never could have happened. That was in 1626, early in the Thirty Years' War, a conflict partly instigated by disgruntled Protestants in Prague tossing several Catholic lords out a window (miraculously, the defenestrated lords survived, either by the intercession of God or else by landing in a dung heap—the legend takes various forms). "Our family came from Switzerland, to work in the silver mines of Sainte-Marie-aux-Mines. But the southern parts of Alsace were already quite ruined because of the war, so some Protestants took their chance to move slightly north." The original Jean Trimbach found work as a cooper, making barrels, and that soon led to wine.

The Trimbachs farm 143 acres of grapes, mostly in the villages of Ribeauvillé, Bergheim, and Hunawihr. They also purchase grapes on long-term contracts from thirty-odd growers. All the vineyards, owned by the Trimbachs or not, are certified organic; the estate vineyards have been organic since 2008. "Even before that, we used no pesticides. We just didn't talk about it," Jean Trimbach says.

As for that real estate deal with the local nuns, it was for the convent's acreage in the grand cru Geisberg vineyard. "We're Protestant, but some people say our wines are more *Janseniste*—a bit stricter than just being Protestant," Trimbach says.

"They're made with finesse and elegance, intensity and energy, but are never super-broad. We have to wait for them. We like that precision, that tension, that finesse." Whether the Jansenists of the 1600s, who were notoriously not inclined toward fun, would have appreciated that, who knows.

Trimbach makes dozens of wines, in the dry, precise style that Frédéric Emile Trimbach established in the late 1800s. Look for the **Classic Riesling ($$)** (simply labeled "Riesling") for an introduction. The **Reserve Pinot Gris ($$)** suggests stone fruit and a hint of toasted nuts. The **Reserve Riesling Sélection de Viellies Vignes ($$)** is laser-sharp and lingering.

Though the Trimbachs are famed for their Rieslings, they make other varieties with equal facility; the floral, spicy **Gewürztraminer Cuvée des Seigneurs de Ribeaupierre ($$$)** for example, or the exotically rich **Pinot Gris Réserve Personelle ($$$)**. There are four grand cru Rieslings, all expressive of their individual sites. To pick one, the **Grand Cru Geisberg Riesling—Vignoble du Couvent de Ribeauville ($$$)** is steely and fresh, all talc-like mineral and lime/nectarine flavors.

The domaine's second most famous wine—one of the two "pillars of the house," as Jean Trimbach says—is its **Riesling Frédéric Emile ($$$)**. Jean Trimbach says, "It's a composition, like music, from two grand crus. Geisberg brings the power and richness, and Osterberg the tension and acidity." Then there's the **Riesling Clos Ste. Hune ($$$$)**, arguably Alsace's most famous wine. The walled Clos Ste. Hune vineyard is in the Rosacker grand cru; the wine it produces is pure and crystalline in character, but with deceptively rich layers of flavor.

DOMAINE WEINBACH • KIENTZHEIM

[certified organic / certified biodynamic]

If history had taken a different turn, Domaine Weinbach might still be a snail farm. Capuchin friars once owned the property, and in the 1600s they raised snails in an *escargotiere*, or snail park, inside the walled clos. The Faller family, who have owned Weinbach since 1898, still grow grapes on a nearby plot of vines historically known as Schnakator—the Snail's Gate. "But since 2021 we renamed it Caracol," Catherine Faller says. "It sounds nicer, I think." True, even if *caracol* is just Spanish for snail.

For many years, Weinbach was the first and only domaine in Alsace run solely by women. When Théo Faller died in 1979, his wife, Collette, took over (part of the long, brilliant history of French widows in wine). "She was absolutely certain she would continue. There was no question," Catherine Faller remembers. She and her sister Laurence soon joined their mother to help run the estate.

Catherine had not planned on this: "I was studying literature in Strasbourg when my father passed away. I was twenty-three. After he died my outlook changed. I realized that wine is more than wine. It's nature, it's history, it's people; it's never-ending. You keep learning every day from it."

Catherine took over the business side. Her sister Laurence was the winemaker, and it was largely through her impetus that the estate turned to organic and biodynamic farming. "But even before, we didn't use many chemical products," Catherine says. "It wasn't the heavy artillery, as we say in French. And the switch to biodynamics really allowed the terroir to express itself much better. But for us it's more a tool, a way of working, than a religion." Biodynamics also makes vineyards more resilient in the face of a changing climate, she feels. "Over thirty years, the starting date for harvest has moved one month earlier. When I was a little girl, harvest would start in mid-October, and my mother would prepare schnapps and hot water for the men at ten in the morning because it was so frigid. Now, we start in early September, and we give everyone cold water, because it's so hot."

Weinbach has seen its share of tragedies. Théo Faller died unexpectedly, and Laurence Faller even more so (she was only forty-seven), both from heart attacks. Shortly after Laurence's death in 2014, Collette Faller passed away, too, at eighty-five, indomitable to the end. "It was terribly sad," Catherine Faller says. She pauses for a moment. "But we have to go on. We always go on." Today she runs the domaine together with her two sons, Théo and Eddy, and still finds daily inspiration from the work she does. Looking back to when she was a student, she says, "Both literature and wine can carry you into another world. They take you somewhere. There are a lot of wines, of course, that don't take you anywhere, and a lot of books, too, I'm afraid—but the best, they open a door. And you come out the other side changed."

Weinbach farms ninety-four acres of vineyards outside the town of Kientzheim. Their basic varietal bottlings are among the best in Alsace, particularly the crisp **Domaine Weinbach Riesling** (\$\$), the softly citrusy, off-dry **Gewurztraminer** (\$\$), and the floral **Pinot Blanc** (\$\$). There are a number of special cuvée, terroir, and grand cru wines as well, such as the lightly off-dry **Gewurztraminer Cuvée Théo** (\$\$\$) (soon to be renamed **Cuvée Trait de Lou**) and the richer **Gewurztraminer Cuvée Laurence** (\$\$\$). The latter comes from the bottom of the Altenbourg vineyard; the **Altenbourg Gewurztraminer** (\$\$\$) comes from vines a bit higher up. "Our Gewürztraminers are voluptuous but not too exuberant," Catherine Faller says. "They don't smell like cheap perfume." (A direction Gewürztraminer all too often heads toward.) The supple **Riesling Cuvée Théo** (\$\$\$) comes from inside the domaine's walled clos vineyards, while the **Riesling Cuvée Collette** (\$\$\$) comes from old vines at the bottom of the Schlossberg Grand Cru. It's one of the estate's most beautiful wines, full of lime flavors and deep minerality. "It's a wine full of energy, like Collette, my mother," Faller says. The **Schlossberg Grand Cru Riesling** (\$\$\$) is the richest of the Weinbach dry Rieslings, providing incredible concentration and elegance. Recently, Weinbach has created a line of wines called MØ, made with zero sulfur. "This was my sons' idea," Faller says. "When they wanted to do it, I said,

OK guys, go ahead. But if the wines show *any* defect, they go to the distillery." Look for the lightly orange MVØ (\$\$), a blend of Pinot Gris and Gewürztraminer from the Vogelgarten vineyard.

DOMAINE ZIND-HUMBRECHT • TURCKHEIM

[certified organic / certified biodynamic]

Olivier Humbrecht is fascinating to talk to, because he's both deeply rational yet also so deeply appreciative of the aspects of the natural world that remain mysterious. He has a master's in enology and is one of the few winemakers who is also a Master of Wine, the notoriously difficult accreditation for professionals in the wine trade; yet he's firmly convinced of the value of biodynamic agriculture, even its more outré aspects. "I'm very happy to believe in things that you cannot explain scientifically, as long as there's a difference that you can *register* scientifically," he says. "If we do an experiment, and can compare the results, and there *is* a difference, then that's enough information for me. No one understands how life works. What made a few bits of protein turn into something that today is human? What made monkeys become monkeys, or men become men,

or horses become horses? Evolution, yes, but *why?* I don't know the answer, but I can see the difference between a horse and a man."

The Humbrechts have been making wine in Alsace since 1620. Olivier Humbrecht took over from his father in 1989, and today farms and makes wine from some one hundred acres of vineyards. From the start he wanted to work organically. His father farmed conventionally, though he eschewed chemicals as much as he could and used only organic fertilizers. "It wasn't what we'd call organic by today's standards," Olivier says. "But I'm not angry with the people of past generations. Working the old way, it took four people maybe three full weeks of hard physical work to plow one thirteen-acre vineyard. With conventional agriculture—modern agriculture—it takes maybe one guy, with one tractor, two days. And if the same guy does the herbicides, that'll take him maybe two hours.

"But then people started to see—ah, where are my butterflies? Where are my weeds? Where are my worms? Why do I have to start using more and more chemicals, and more and more powerful and harmful chemicals? If you ask these questions, you start to see that the chemicals, by solving one problem, created other ones. For a vine, it's like if you, as a human, were fed only intravenously instead of with fruits and vegetables and grains. An injection, a pill every day. So people started to say, maybe there *is* an alternative."

Zind-Humbrecht makes everything from basic varietal wines to ultra-limited *Sélection de Grains Nobles* (SGN) sweet wines. Among them, look for the basic **Zind-Humbrecht Riesling ($$)**, appealingly aromatic with a stony finish, and the rose-scented, spicy **Gewürztraminer ($$)**. The **Riesling Roche Calcaire ($$)** offers a bit more density and power than the basic Riesling, and the **Riesling Herrenweg ($$$)** even more length and expressiveness than that. The **Gewürztraminer Turckheim ($$$)** is made in a dry style but is still quite rich, with layers of golden fruit. **Gewürztraminer Rangen Clos St. Urbain ($$$)** is even more flamboyant, with classic lychee and rose notes, light sweetness, and tremendous concentration. Some people love Gewürz and some people find it cloying, but there's no question that Zind-Humbrecht's are among the best to be found. And the **Riesling Clos Windsbuhl ($$$)** comes from an ancient walled vineyard near Hunawihr that dates back to the fourteenth century. It combines elegance and power seamlessly, its flavors electrically energetic and long.

DOMAINE VALENTIN ZUSSLIN · ORSCHWIHR

[certified organic / certified biodynamic]

Marie Zusslin is the thirteenth generation of her family to grow grapes for wine in Alsace, but you wouldn't know that by talking to her—she wears that history very lightly. She and her brother Jean-Paul make their wines at their family's estate in the town of Orschwihr, following a tradition that began in 1691. But the current Zusslin sensibility really starts with their father, Jean-Marie, who converted the estate to biodynamic practices in 1997, making him a pioneer in a region that has since become a center of organic and biodynamic agriculture.

The siblings took over the estate from their father in 2000 and have continued his work. They collaborate with local farmers to produce compost for their vineyards, have added beehives and birdhouses around the estate, and farm much of the land using a horse rather than tractors. Since 2020, they've focused on agroforestry as well, planting trees amid the vines. Everything is handpicked. No chemicals or industrial products are used in the cellar, and sulfur is only used sparingly, at bottling, or not at all. (Since 2018, they've been making some of their wines with zero sulfur; because Jean-Paul's winemaking is so precise, they are uncommonly stable.)

The Zusslins are unusual in Alsace because a third of their production is sparkling Crémant d'Alsace. These are some of the region's finest sparkling wines. The **Valentin Zusslin Crémant Brut Zero Sans Soufre** (\$\$) is a green apple–scented, exceptionally fresh blend of Auxerrois and Chardonnay. Their **Crémant Rosé Brut Zero Sans Soufre** (\$\$), 100 percent Pinot Noir, suggests ripe strawberries with an earthy note on the finish. With the **Crémant Clos Liebenberg** (\$\$\$) "our idea is to show that crémant can be a terroir wine, not just a wine that reflects the winemaking process," Marie Zusslin says. It's Auxerrois with 10 percent Pinot Noir, light and crisp, with a firm, stony end.

Of the still wines, the **Riesling Grand Cru Clos Liebenberg Monopole** ($$$) has intense apple-orchard flavors with an oily texture (in a good way) and a stony finish. It's always fairly rich. "Liebenberg is an easy site to get ripe," Marie says, "and ripeness together with freshness is really the Clos Liebenberg style." The **Riesling Grand Cru Pfingstberg** ($$$) comes from the vines her grandfather planted in 1950. A powerful white, it has peach-honey notes, and "saltiness on the end—something that's happened with it only since my father started biodynamics," Marie says.

PRODUCERS PROFILED IN THIS CHAPTER

Marcel Deiss
Trimbach
Weinbach

Zind-Humbrecht
Valentin Zusslin

OTHER ALSACE PRODUCERS TO LOOK FOR

Jean-Baptiste Adam
Barmès-Buecher
Beck-Hartweg
Binner
Bott-Geyl
Albert Boxler
Dirler-Cadé
Pierre Frick

Josmeyer
Marc Kreydenweiss
Kuentz-Bas
Albert Mann
Eugène Meyer
Julien Meyer
Mittnacht Frères
Ostertag

BEAUJOLAIS

Le Beaujolais nouveau est arrivé!

The new Beaujolais is here! The line—doesn't everyone know it?—is the ubiquitous marketing slogan for Georges Duboeuf's Beaujolais Nouveau, once a phenomenon, now a weary, somewhat characterless fact of late-autumn life. But the *real* new Beaujolais is a very different thing, and it is definitely here, right now.

The renaissance in Beaujolais started in the early 1980s, with Jules Chauvet, the self-trained chemist, *négociant*, and winemaker often referred to as the father of the natural wine movement in France. Chauvet's feeling that wines should be "naked," unmodified by commercial yeast strains and by the addition of sulfur in the winery, and unmarred by the use of pesticides and herbicides in the vineyard, proved enormously influential. In Beaujolais, he directly mentored Marcel Lapierre, who in turn influenced his friends (among them Jean Foillard, Guy Breton, Jean-Paul Thévenet, and Joseph Chamonard), who in turn influenced . . . well. From Beaujolais to the world. Now the sons and daughters of that first generation of non-interventionist Beaujolais winemakers are producing their own impressive wines, too, as are many other young Beaujolais vignerons, such as Laura Lardy and Anne-Sophie Dubois.

In the early 2000s, wine lovers also began waking up to the realization that Beaujolais, natural or not, wasn't necessarily just a cheap and easy red wine from a kind of southerly, less prestigious appendage of Burgundy. Particularly that's true of the wines made in the ten crus of the region (from north to south, Saint-Amour,

Juliénas, Chénas, Moulin-à-Vent, Fleurie, Chiroubles, Morgon, Régnié, Brouilly, and Côte de Brouilly). There, Gamay, the grape of Beaujolais, transmits the character of where it's grown in much the same way that Pinot Noir does in Burgundy's Côte d'Or, albeit in its own distinctive way. The single disheartening aspect of this flowering of cru Beaujolais producers has been that the prices of the wines have risen. But even so, the best cru Beaujolais bottles still cost a fraction of the price of grand or even premier cru Burgundy.

Today Beaujolais is one of the most dynamic red wine regions in France. There's still plenty of anonymous, simple red streaming from its presses and vats—but when there's also such an abundance of ambitious, independent vignerons, both new and established, it's hard not to be excited for the region's future.

ANNE-SOPHIE DUBOIS · FLEURIE

[certified organic]

Anne-Sophie Dubois was born in Champagne (the seventh generation in a winemaking family), learned to make wine in Burgundy, and, continuing her southward path, landed in Fleurie. Her family purchased about twenty acres of vines there in 1992, and she took over the property in 2006, when she was only twenty-three. Her wines have impressed fans of both natural and conventional wines; she walks that subtle line where it's hard to decide which camp she might fall into.

Her vineyard forms what's essentially a natural amphitheater in Fleurie.

And her approach was influenced by a 2013 meeting with the enologist Jacques Néauport, who was more or less Jules Chauvet's right-hand man. Néauport pushed her toward less use of sulfur and less intervention in her winemaking overall, and her approach now is characteristic of the new wave of Beaujolais producers: handpicking, use of gravity flow rather than pumps, indigenous yeasts, zero additives, no fining, no filtration, and only a tiny amount of sulfur at bottling. She also ages her wines in old oak. Though Dubois has no use for oak flavors, wood is a natural substance, and she says that she prefers the slight transmission of oxygen that barrels allow: "The wine breathes through the barrel."

––––––––––

Dubois's affordable **Les Cocottes Fleurie ($$)**, released six months after the vintage, is juicy and bright, the epitome of *glou-glou*, a now-common French term for fun, quaffable, unpretentious wines. **L'Alchimiste Fleurie ($$)** is more serious, though perhaps that word somewhat contradicts the basic cheerful energy of Dubois's wines. L'Alchimiste comes from older vines, and typically has deeper, earthier black cherry flavors than Les Cocottes. Her top wine, **Les Labourons Fleurie ($$)** (formerly called Clepsydre, and renamed after she received organic certification in 2017), comes from the best and oldest vines in the *lieu dit* of the same name, and is vividly violet in hue and a touch more aromatic and complex than L'Alchimiste.

MEE GODARD • MORGON

[certified organic]

Mee Godard makes some of the most shimmeringly pure expressions of Gamay to be found in Beaujolais. Though born in Korea, she was adopted by a French couple as an infant. Her parents were not in the wine business, and she grew up in the suburbs of Lyon. Why wine? "It's in the crossroads of different passions I had since I was a child," she says. "I loved cooking, but I didn't want to be a chef—it seemed too hard! I love science, but when I was in biology at university, I really didn't know what to do with my degree. In truth, I probably wouldn't be doing what I am doing now, except for my eighteenth birthday dinner at Paul Bocuse. I had a wine there that completely changed my feelings about wine. I remember the experience vividly, though I can't remember the specific bottle."

Inspired, Godard moved to Oregon to get a degree in biochemistry, and followed that with an enology degree from Montpellier. She interned in Burgundy, but found her home in Beaujolais: "I had a *coup de foudre*, as we say." In 2012, a friend introduced her to an old grower in Morgon who was retiring and had no heirs. He wanted to sell, Godard wanted to buy, and today that vineyard is the basis of her wines.

Godard received organic certification in 2023. "I don't know if I will put it on the label, though. For me, it's more a question of health. My employees and I touch the vine leaves constantly; we're always in the vineyard. I don't want to poison the people who work for me. And also, because I consider it so crucial to the quality of the grapes, I want to keep my soil alive. I'm also focusing on agroforestry. I'd rather work in a direction that isn't just beneficial for the vines but for everybody."

Talk to Godard, and one minute you may be discussing the character of Moulin-à-Vent, and a few minutes later you may be talking about the French anthropologist Philippe Descola, and his theories on how the word "natural" has evolved in Western societies. It's always an exhilarating experience (and even better with a glass of wine nearby). But then, wine itself is a very complete field, as she says: "Sociology, history, economics, agriculture, enology, art—it's all there."

Godard works with vines in Morgon Côte du Py, Morgon Corcelette, Morgon Grand Cras, and Moulin-à-Vent Les Michelons. Her **Mee Godard Beaujolais-Villages ($$)** is velvety and bright at once, with lightly spicy notes on the finish. The four Morgons she makes all come from specific vineyard sites. The **Morgon Corcelette ($$)** tends, she says, to be fleshier and have more concentration. **Morgon Côte du Py ($$)** is "more complex, with more spice and more defined tannins." **Morgon Grand Cras ($$)** is usually more floral and silky. About her Moulin-à-Vent, she says, "It's hard to compare Morgon with Moulin-à-Vent, but for me it's more aerial, more delicate." The **Moulin-à-Vent Les Michelons ($$)** certainly proves that true.

DOMAINE LAPIERRE • MORGON

[certified organic / natural]

Domaine Lapierre was founded in 1909 by Michel Lapierre. Until the 1970s, the domaine was a reliably good but not particularly distinctive Beaujolais producer; that changed in the late 1970s, when Marcel Lapierre, Michel's grandson, met the pioneering French enologist Jules Chauvet. Chauvet guided him toward what is now thought of as natural winemaking— minimal or no sulfur; no enzymes, industrial yeasts, or other technical inputs; no chaptalization (adding sugar in underripe years).

Together with Jean Foillard, Jean-Paul Thévenet, and Guy Breton, Lapierre was one of several winemakers in Morgon influenced by Chauvet—the so-called "gang of four"—whose wines were brought to the U.S. by noted importer Kermit Lynch. They in turn were instrumental in bringing aware-ness of the natural wine approach to other winemakers throughout France. The stone gets tossed, and the waves ripple out.

What's sometimes overlooked, thanks to the halo of the natural wine legend, is how significant Lapierre also was in bringing attention to the quality of cru Beaujolais overall, particularly the wines of Morgon. His wines were reference points in the natural wine sphere, but even before that trend took off, they were known for being complex, brilliant reds, exemplars of the at-the-time lost potential of Beaujolais. Lapierre passed away in 2010, but son Mathieu and daughter Camille have carried on his work, making energetic, vibrant wines with minimal intervention and no new oak. They've also adopted some biodynamic practices in the forty acres of vineyards they own.

———

The **Marcel Lapierre Raisins Gaulois** (\$) is fresh and lively, made from higher-yielding vines in Morgon (above the AOC—Appellation d'Origine Contrôlée—limit, and so not labeled as Morgon). It's gulpable and fun, classic *glou-glou*. There's also the **Beaujolais "Le Beaujolais"** (\$\$), bright and easy-drinking as well, though with a little more depth. The **Morgon** (\$\$) is the winery's flagship wine, abundant with crunchy red berry and violet notes, and a landmark in the natural wine world. There's also the **Morgon Sans Soufre ($$)** bottling—zero sulfur—which appears on shelves momentarily each year before being snapped up by natural wine fans. Arguably it's a purer expression of the classic Morgon; either way, both of them are do-not-miss bottles. The top Lapierre wines are the **Morgon Roche du Py Cuvée Camille ($$$)**, which comes from a single two-and-a-half-acre plot of vines on the famed Côte du Py hill in Morgon, and the **Cuvée Marcel Lapierre ($$$)**, which comes from the family's oldest vines (one hundred plus years) both in Côte du Py and the *lieu dit* "Le Douby," near Fleurie. Generally speaking, Cuvée Camille is more lifted and red fruit–driven, while Cuvée Marcel Lapierre, which is only released in top vintages, is darker, spicier, and more earthy.

LAURA LARDY • FLEURIE

[organic / natural]

Laura Lardy is part of a longtime wine-growing family in the small town of Le Vivier, in the Beaujolais cru of Fleurie. "I'm the fourth generation; my vines are my father's vines. In the past it was all polyculture—animals, crops, everything. My father was the first to start selling bottles. That was in 1990, the year I was born; before it was just by the barrel."

Her father, Lucien, continues to make wine under his own name, and he and Laura both make their wines at his house. "Sometimes he's difficult in the cellar—'OK, if you do that, it's your problem!'—and sometimes he says, 'Ah, my daughter, she does that, she's very smart.' But we play off each other, and I learn from him. Without my father, I wouldn't have any of what I have now."

When she graduated from school, Lardy told her parents she wanted to work in wine, but in the early 2000s Beaujolais was going through a difficult time economically. Instead, she became a hairdresser. "I was happy, because I was a little wild as a kid, and it taught me to speak to people more easily, to communicate." But after a couple of years, wine lured her back in. She laughs now, remembering that when she'd see her former salon clients in the street, they'd say, "Oh—you cut *vines* now, not hair."

Lardy rents her vineyard land from her father. "My work, more and more, is better practices in the vines. When I work with a new site, I shift it to organic, but it does take a long time. I do all the manual work myself in the vineyards." And in the winery: she's a one-woman operation. She works in a classic, semi-carbonic style, solely with native yeasts, neutral oak, and minimal sulfur (only at bottling). "When I started, I said, 'Ah, if one day I make wine, I won't use any sulfur!' You know, zero sulfur—it's been a thing to say a long time in Paris, 'OK, I'm cool, I drink zero-zero wines.' But then you make your wine, and you think, do I want this to oxidize? This wine that I put so much work into? And if you use just a tiny amount of sulfur, even if the bottle travels overseas, there's no oxidation, ever."

Lardy's juicy **Laura Lardy Beaujolais-Villages Blanc ($$)** is an unpretentious, appealing white. Her **Beaujolais-Villages Gourde à Gamay ($$)** is, as she rightly says, "a lot of fun." A post-fermentation blend of red and rosé, it's light-bodied and ideal with a slight chill. She farms vines in four of Beaujolais's crus: Fleurie, Morgon, Moulin-à-Vent, and Chénas. Her **Fleurie Les Côtes ($$)**, from fifty-year-old vines, has the floral delicacy of that cru. The **Moulin-à-Vent ($$)** is impressively supple and silky. **Morgon Côte du Py ($$)** comes from that cru's most famous site, a hill of decomposed schist that gives more power and depth to Gamay's essential fruitiness. Lastly, her **Chénas La Fayarde ($$)** is delicate and graceful, possibly the most lifted of her wines, though not the richest. "Chénas is so small, people forget it," she says. Hers offers a good reason why they shouldn't.

CHÂTEAU THIVIN • CÔTE DE BROUILLY

[certified organic]

"The covered yard rang with the sound of voices, wheels, heavily-shod footsteps, as the estate's forty grape-pickers were going down for their meal, accompanied by their robust, winey odor. I would really have liked to follow them." That's the novelist Colette, writing about the 1947 grape harvest at Château Thivin. Have things changed? Not much.

Thivin is the oldest estate on Mount Brouilly. First built in the 1300s—the date 1383 is still carved over the door to one of the cellars—it was bought by the Geoffray family in 1877, at auction during the height of the phylloxera plague, when that microscopic root louse destroyed over 40 percent of France's vines. A wise purchase: phylloxera was defeated and the property thrived, surviving two world wars, helping create the Côte de Brouilly appellation during the Great Depression, offering its hospitality to Colette among many others, and making some of the best wines of Beaujolais decade after decade. It's now managed by Claude-Edouard Geoffray, the great-grandnephew of the founder.

The grapes are still picked by hand, and undoubtedly, after picking grapes for hours on a steep hill in the hot Beaujolais summer, the pickers still have a robust, winey odor. No insecticides are used, herbs and flowers fill the vineyard rows, and sheep graze among the vines during spring until bud-burst. Natural compost fertilizes the ground. The Geoffrays own twelve different plots of vines, principally in Côte de Brouilly, totaling about forty-four acres.

Winemaking here is straightforward: a mix of whole-bunch or de-stemmed grapes, use of gravity rather than pumps as much as possible, not much new oak. Harvest, winemaking, the place, the vines, the wine—not that much has changed when you come down to the soul of Château Thivin. Even today, forty to fifty pickers come for harvest, stay at the winery, work and eat together. More are volunteers from around the world and other wineries than in Colette's day, but another scene from her memoir *The Blue Lantern* evokes the moment: "Voices hazy with early morning fatigue arose from the heights of a neighboring vineyard and then declined, descending ever lower as the sun rose higher. I could picture the slow work of picking, the baskets filled, the increasingly parched throats of any who thought to slake their thirst by biting into a bunch."

Château Thivin's red wines are concentrated but silky, with blue-red fruit and fine-grained tannins, influenced by the volcanic soil of the Côte de Brouilly hill. The **Château Thivin Côte de Brouilly ($$)** comes from south-facing parcels averaging fifty years old. The **Côte de Brouilly Cuvée Zaccharie ($$$)**, named after the founder of the estate, is a blend from two parcels of their oldest vines. The family also makes the **Brouilly Reverdon ($$)**, a lighter, more delicate red from vines in the broader Brouilly appellation, and a small amount of two floral, lightly citrusy whites, the **Beaujolais-Villages Blanc Cuvée Marguerite ($$)** and **Beaujolais Blanc Clos de Rochebonne ($$)**.

PRODUCERS PROFILED IN THIS CHAPTER

Anne-Sophie Dubois   Laura Lardy
Mee Godard   Château Thivin
Domaine Lapierre

OTHER BEAUJOLAIS PRODUCERS TO LOOK FOR

Guy Breton   Domaine de la Grand Cour
Domaine Chapel   Sandrine Henriot
Pierre-Marie Chermette   Jean Claude Lapalu
Damien Coquelet   Johan Lardy
Georges Descombes   Yvon Metras
Louis-Claude Desvignes   Clos de la Roilette
Domaine Diochon   Julien Sunier
Jean-Louis Dutraive   Domaine des Terres Dorées
Alex Foillard   Jean Paul et Charly Thévenet
Jean Foillard

BORDEAUX

Bordeaux may be the single most famous wine region in the world. Yet not everyone realizes that there are essentially two Bordeauxs. One is populated by the sixty-one classified growths of the Médoc, the premier grand cru *classés* of Saint-Émilion, and the superstar châteaux of Pomerol. This is the Bordeaux of glamour and of money, of Petrus and Château Mouton Rothschild, of wines collected and cellared, sold at auction, and even counterfeited or faked—sometimes quite brilliantly, if nefariously—because of their absurd value.

Then there's the other Bordeaux. Though it overlies the first one geographically, in terms of wealth and reputation this second Bordeaux might as well be an entirely different country. This is the Bordeaux of small châteaux (note that any wine-producing estate in Bordeaux is termed a château, whether there's an actual château on the property or not), of independent vignerons, and of grape growers eking out a living from fifteen or twenty acres of family land. There are more than 6,300 grape growers in Bordeaux, but only a microscopic fraction make $500 bottle wines, and while an acre of classified-growth land in Pauillac might sell for $900,000, an acre of vines in Entre-deux-Mers goes for $30,000.

For this reason, while Bordeaux makes some of the world's most sought-after, expensive wines, it's also one of the world's best sources for affordable, excellent reds. Currently, it's very easy to track down a very good bottle of Bordeaux for $35 or $40. The average price of a bottle of Napa Valley Cabernet, just to give a comparison, is now above $70 (again, cost of land plays a giant role). That said, most truly low-end Bordeaux, the $10 and under realm, comes from grapes farmed conventionally and with an eye toward production rather than quality. Only a small percentage of the 500 million or so bottles that Bordeaux produces each year cost more than $15, with most of the bottles priced below that ending up in French supermarkets, UK chain groceries, and so on.

And yet. More and more producers here are leaning away from chemical-heavy viticulture, whether through France's HVE sustainability certification (*Haute Valeur Environmentale*) or through organic viticulture. (There are also a few biodynamic producers scattered through the region, but they are a negligible percentage of the total.)

Today, many of the world-famous Bordeaux properties are owned by foreign investors, major corporations, billionaires, multibillionaires, multi-multibillionaires, and so on. But there are still beautiful family-owned properties throughout this vast region, with wines being made by individual vignerons driven by empathy for the environment and a personal vision for their wines. It can take some hunting, but they can be found.

CHÂTEAU BIAC • CADILLAC CÔTES DE BORDEAUX

[certified sustainable]

Château Biac isn't a château with fairy-tale towers. Instead, it's a small manor house, built in 1755 by the Baron of Langoiran, its peach-colored walls, terra-cotta shingles, and white shutters surrounded by thirty-seven acres of vineyards. Nor are the owners French. Tony and Youmna Asseily, and their winemaker son Gabriel, who live here, are Lebanese. They purchased Biac in 2006 on the advice of Patrick Léon, for twenty years the technical director at the first-growth Château Mouton Rothschild. Léon became the Asseilys' winemaking consultant until his death in 2018, and has been succeeded in the role by his son Bertrand.

The Asseilys farm in accordance

with France's HVE sustainability certification, avoiding systemic herbicides and pesticides, as well as chemical fertilizers. As Gabriel Asseily says, "I found a baby deer on the property the day my sister's son Luca was born. It lives in the woods nearby; Luca will come play here in the vines. Why would I spray rubbish all over our vineyards?"

The south-facing amphitheater of Biac provides perfect drainage for the vines and an optimal exposure; the slope and the river below work together to provide an ideal balance of humidity and ventilation. Not that Tony Asseily knew any of this when they bought the property. All he'd been looking for was a summer home: "I didn't want to chew my fingernails up to my elbows out of worry about frost, hail, and the weather in general. I had absolutely no intention of making wine." But vines are even better than mythological sirens at luring people to an un-looked-for fate, and today the Asseilys make about thirty-five hundred cases of wine each year.

Château Biac ($$$) is Cabernet Sauvignon and Merlot (in varying percentages depending on vintage) with small amounts of Petit Verdot and Cabernet Franc, and is silky despite its underlying power. **Felix de Biac ($$)**, dominated by Merlot, trades in some of the power for earlier drinkability. There's also **Felicie de Biac ($$)**, an alluring white that's predominantly Sauvignon Blanc with a touch of Semillon, and **Secret de Château Biac ($$)**, a dessert wine, can challenge many more esteemed Sauternes despite its humbler Cadillac Côtes de Bordeaux appellation.

CHÂTEAU BOURGNEUF • POMEROL

[certified sustainable]

Château Bourgneuf is a rarity these days: an estate in Pomerol whose wines are affordable. But the Vayron family has always sold their wines at a reasonable price. "When you open a bottle of wine, you don't want to feel pressure because it costs a fortune," Marie Vayron says.

The Vayrons bought Bourgneuf in 1840, and today the winery is run by eighth-generation Frédérique Vayron, Marie's sister, who took over the winemaking in 2009.

Bourgneuf's seventeen acres of vineyards are farmed sustainably in line with France's HVE certification program. Frédérique has also started replanting trees and bushes on the property, working with a local association formed to bring back native plant species to Bordeaux. "We're not organic, but that may be a matter of generations," Marie Vayron says. "My father is wary of it, and my sister would never switch without his approval. It would be disrespectful, and would break that link of trust they have between them."

Bourgneuf's vineyards are 90 percent Merlot and 10 percent Cabernet Franc, though Frédérique Vayron is slowly increasing the percentage of Cabernet Franc in the vineyard as a hedge against climate change. But in slow fashion: "Pomerol is a very small kingdom, and Merlot is its coin," her sister, Marie, says. There are two wines. The first, **Saison de Bourgneuf** ($$), is open and generous on release, with modest tannins and a touch of new oak. **Château Bourgneuf** ($$$) is a very classically styled Pomerol, with velvety tannins and rich, dark fruit; an elegant wine that over time in a cellar takes on black truffle notes. "After ten years or so," Marie Vayron says. "To me, that's the terroir identification of older Pomerol, that black truffle component."

CHÂTEAU DU CHAMP DES TREILLES • SAINTE-FOY CÔTES DE BORDEAUX

[certified organic / biodynamic]

"Purity and delicacy are what we're aiming for," Corinne Comme says about her white wine, which she makes, together with two similarly pure reds, with her husband, Jean-Michel Comme, at this small estate in the eastern reaches of Bordeaux's Entre-deux-Mers.

Corinne is a renowned biodynamic consultant in Bordeaux and beyond, and Jean-Michel was famously the estate director at the fifth-growth Château Pontet-Canet for more than thirty years (he instituted biodynamics there at a time when the concept was all but unheard of in Bordeaux). Champ des Treilles is their home estate. Its roots lie in the vineyard land that Jean-Michel's grandparents farmed after moving to France from Italy in the 1920s.

The Commes were among the first in this part of Bordeaux to farm organ- ically, then with biodynamics, and they still work as they always have: biodynamics, plus other practices tied to the idea of listening to nature rather than trying to modify it: no green harvesting, no leaf removal, no tractors, using infusions and teas from local herbs and plants to protect against vine diseases, and working with the phases of the moon. Jean-Michel has noted that the technical training he got as a student taught him to trust only modern science, but that his grandparents always felt that science didn't have every answer. Today he feels that their approach, "physically strenuous but logical and respectful of life," is the better choice.

The Commes farm twenty-four acres of vines just outside the town of Margueron, many of them more than sixty years of age. Their **Domaine du Champ des Treilles Vin Passion Blanc** ($) is one of Bordeaux's great steals, a smoky, melony white that dances across the palate. They also make two reds, the **Petit Champ Rouge** ($), crunchy and bright, aged in old oak vats, and the **Grand Vin Rouge** ($$), richer and darker, mostly Merlot, and aged in French oak barrels.

CHÂTEAU LE PUY • FRANCS CÔTES DE BORDEAUX

[certified organic / certified biodynamic]

Chemicals have never touched the soil at Château le Puy. That's "never" as in for sixteen generations, possibly even longer.

Le Puy is unlike any other Bordeaux estate. The Amoreau family, which owns it, has been making wine since 1610 on the stony outskirts of Bordeaux's Right Bank. It's a long way from the manicured, wealthy estates of Pauillac and Margaux, and if you ask Pascal Amoreau about the grand châteaux of the Médoc, he'll shrug and say with a twinkle in his eye, "The Médoc? What is that? I don't think I know what you mean."

For many generations the family farmed without chemical fertilizers or pesticides because they simply didn't exist at the time, but when the massive shift toward those products occurred, following World War II, they still refused. "With my grandfather, it was about saving money," Pascal Amoreau says. "When the salespeople came to him after the war, he said, 'I've been farming my vines for forty years without chemicals, and they're doing very well. Why should I pay for this stuff?'"

But the next generation, Pascal's father, Jean Pierre, understood the ecological

---

"The people who used to mock us now come to the estate and ask how we do things."
—Pascal Amoreau

---

aspects. "My father knew that chemical agriculture made no sense. If it's bad for your body, he felt, how can it be good for the grapes? Yet we were considered the crazy people of the village."

Le Puy technically lies within Francs Côtes de Bordeaux, though the Amoreaus choose not to be part of the appellation. The family owns three estates: Le Puy, which covers 173 acres; Saint Roc, smaller at 75 acres; and a recent acquisition, Closerie du Pelam, from a friend of Pascal Amoreau's who wanted to retire. "It's all organic and biodynamic," Amoreau says. "We don't know how to do anything else!" Only part of their land is devoted to vines. The rest is ponds, forests, and fields, aimed at creating biodiversity.

Winemaking here falls into the broad realm of "natural" winemaking without taking on that label: no fining, no filtering, minimal or no sulfur (if the wine is considered stable enough, or, for their Barthélemy cuvée, in every vintage), little or no new oak, spontaneous fermentation through native yeast. "It's not a production method for us, it's a way of life," Amoreau says. "But we don't put it on the back label, because we don't sell organic wine, and we don't sell biodynamic wine. We sell Château le Puy."

He adds, "When you share a bottle of Le Puy, you don't just share a bottle of wine, you share an outlook, a way of doing viticulture. There's a quote from Jean-Paul Sartre, I think, that 'emotion is a sudden dive of our consciousness towards the magic.' I think we need to dive toward the magic in wine."

Compared to most red Bordeaux, Le Puy's wines are lighter and more delicate, and they shimmer with energy and freshness. "People call us the Burgundy of Bordeaux," Pascal Amoreau says, "but that's not our phrase. I say that we make identity wine, and the identity is Château le Puy."

The **Château le Puy Rose-Marie** (\$\$) is a full-bodied rosé made from Merlot. "With the rosé we tried three times," Pascal Amoreau says. "First with Cabernet Sauvignon. Pah. Awful. Then half Cabernet and half Merlot. Awful. Third try, 100 percent Merlot? It's amazing. But my father was skeptical even so. He was in the cellar and said, 'Why are we doing this rosé? What's the point?' and I said, 'So me and my friends can drink it!'" **Duc des Nauves** (\$\$) comes from a site lying a little lower than the main estate. It's aged in cement and bottled after one year, and is more fruit-forward than the rest of Le Puy's wines. **Emilien** (\$\$\$), the flagship wine, is 85 percent Merlot, the remainder divided between Cabernet Sauvignon, Cabernet Franc, Malbec, and Carménère. It is extraordinarily age-worthy: vintages from the 1920s still show beautifully. **Barthélemy** (\$\$\$) comes from the Le Roc estate, and is 85 percent Merlot with 15 percent Cabernet Sauvignon. Black cherries, forest leaves, a subtle gamey wildness—it's darkly compelling, and a fine argument against the idea that wines made without sulfur cannot age.

CHÂTEAU SMITH HAUT LAFITTE • PESSAC-LÉOGNAN

[certified organic / biodynamic]

Smith Haut Lafitte, under owners Florence and Daniel Cathiard, is the rare top-level Bordeaux château that is fully committed to organic and biodynamic viticulture. The history of the estate dates back to the 1300s, when it was founded by a French nobleman named Verrier du Bosq; he probably couldn't have anticipated that in the 1700s a Scottish sailor would acquire the place and append his name to it. Regardless, the renaissance of the property started in 1990 when the Cathiards purchased it.

They quickly stopped using chemical products, moving over time to fully organic viticulture—all 193 acres of vines were certified organic in 2019, and the estate has also been biodynamic since 2021. The Cathiards prefer to call their approach "bio-precision," as they stick to the less spiritual aspects of biodynamics and also extensively utilize phytotherapy (tisanes of herbal products such as horsetail, nettles, and oak bark to help fight fungal diseases and gray rot, applied across the vineyard). Additionally, their carbon reduction efforts resulted in Florence being invited to speak at COP21 in 2015 (the annual U.N. Conference of the Parties regarding climate change).

Florence notes that her father actually intended to name her "Nature," but luckily her mother thought that was an absurd choice of a name. Even so, the connection seems to have been made; as she says, "The planet is damaged to a point where it can no longer heal on its own. It's time to take care of it as much as we can."

The **Château Smith Haut Lafitte Blanc ($$$$)** is one of Bordeaux's greatest white wines, and priced as such; it's a kaleidoscope of flavors, nevertheless always retaining incredible precision. **Le Petit Blanc ($$)**, from younger vines, is a shade less complex but still very impressive. The **Les Hauts de Smith Blanc ($$)**, a counterpart to Le Petit, shifts character slightly as it is 100 percent Sauvignon Blanc (no Semillon) but shows no lack of creamy, alluring citrus flavors.

The grand vin **Château Smith Haut Lafitte ($$$$)** is Pessac at its finest, roughly two-thirds Cabernet and a third or so Merlot, with small amounts of Petit Verdot and Cabernet Franc, rich with tobacco-edged black fruit and silky but powerful tannins. **Le Petit Smith ($$)** may have less power, but it offers an earlier-drinking elegance that's hard to resist. Similarly, **Les Hauts de Smith ($$)** consistently overdelivers at what—for this level of Bordeaux—is a remarkably modest price.

CHÂTEAU LES TROIS CROIX • FRONSAC

[sustainable]

Les Trois Croix, owner Bertrand Léon says, is a very old estate. "One part was created in 1712; that's written on the top of the door of the cellar. And the appellation itself is very old—in the sixth century Fronsac was the favorite wine of Charlemagne." Given that pedigree, it seems a shame that Fronsac is now considered far less prestigious than the Médoc and its grand estates.

Betrand's father, Patrick, who bought Les Trois Croix in 1995, knew both the grand and the humble parts of Bordeaux very well. He was born near Fronsac, but he became one of France's most renowned winemakers and was for two decades the head of Château Mouton Rothschild. (He passed away in 2018.)

"My father knew how good Fronsac could be," Bertrand recalls. "But it lives in the shadows of Saint-Émilion and Pomerol. It's an outsider appellation—the quality is very, very good, but the price is not that high."

Les Trois Croix has close to fifty acres of vines, 80 percent Merlot and the rest Cabernet Franc. The former owner loved herbicides and used them with abandon. "When you do that on 100 percent of the surface, the roots stay 100 percent on the surface," Bertrand says. He and his father stopped the herbicides, reworked the soil, and slowly brought the land back to life. Bertrand farms now according to what he calls "antiquated biological protection," about 80 to 90 percent organic but with the freedom to use "products made by innovation but with a good mindset," in years when mildew pressure is too high. "When you're organic, you use copper, but if you use too much copper, it's very bad for the soil. It's difficult for people to understand. When people see 'organic,' they tend to think, 'It's safe! Organic, good! Not organic, *pfff*!' It's not that simple."

Château Les Trois Croix ($$) has plummy Merlot fruit that resolves into a stony, tannic finish; not sharp, but firm. "Our tannins are very ripe, but we also get freshness," Bertrand Léon says. "We're right on top of a hill, so it's about a foot of clay, then after that limestone, limestone, limestone, and that gives freshness."

DOMAINE DE L'A • CASTILLON CÔTES DE BORDEAUX

[certified organic / biodynamic]

Stéphane Derenoncourt is one of Bordeaux's leading winemaking consultants, whose clients range from star châteaux like Pavie Macquin and Smith Haut Lafitte to a host of smaller, less well-known properties. But for his home estate he chose the outlying region of Castillon Côtes de Bordeaux. He says, "The best sites in Castillon, those on the limestone plateau and slopes, are as good as those in Saint-Émilion, and certainly far better than the myriad Saint-Émilion vineyards found on the sandy valley floor of the appellation."

Domaine de l'A is a joint project between Stéphane and his wife, Christine (also a consultant; they work together). The property was farmed organically for twenty years before they bought it, and they have continued that approach—it was one of the reasons they were first attracted to the site. (They were certified as of 2020, but do not put it on their label.) He and Christine are also longtime practitioners of biodynamics. Much of what they've learned through using organics and biodynamics at l'A has also informed their consulting; along with Jean-Michel and Corinne Comme, they've been influential figures in leading other Bordeaux growers in this direction.

Today the Derenoncourts farm roughly twenty-seven acres of vines, mostly Merlot (70 percent) and Cabernet Franc (29 percent) plus a tiny amount of Chardonnay. Leaving aside the Chardonnay—under a thousand bottles are made each year—there is one wine: **Domaine de l'A ($$–$$$)**. Polished, with supple tannins, it offers layers of blue and red fruit, often a faint, toasty espresso note, and impressively pure flavor.

PRODUCERS PROFILED IN THIS CHAPTER

Château Biac

Château Bourgneuf

Château du Champ de Treilles

Château Le Puy

Château Smith Haut Lafitte

Château Les Trois Croix

Domaine de l'A

OTHER BORDEAUX PRODUCERS TO LOOK FOR

Vignoble Paul Barre

Château Chantegrives

Château Chasse-Spleen

Domaine de Chevalier

Château Coutet

Château Falfas

Château La Fleur Garderose

Château Fonroque

Château Grand Puy Lacoste

Château La Grave (Fronsac)

Château des Gravieres

Château Guiraud

Château Haut-Marbuzet

Clos du Jageuyron

Château Jean Faure

Château Malartic-Lagravieres

Château Mazeyres

Château Pontet-Canet

Roc des Cambes

Château Tour des Termes

Château de Vieille Tour

BURGUNDY

The ribald *How I Liberated Burgundy* by the BBC war correspondent Wynford Vaughan-Thomas recalls a moment in World War II when the Germans were in retreat, but the French commanders were hesitant to press the advantage. The reason? The location of the German forces between Chalon and Dijon: "It would mean war, mechanized war, among the Grand Crus!" an officer told the author, aghast. The generals would be pilloried for it. France would never forgive them. At the last moment, though, "a young sous-lieutenant turned up and said, 'Great news, *mon colonel*, we have found the weak point in the German defenses. Every one is on a vineyard of inferior quality!'" With this information, the French happily attacked.

Terroir is everything in Burgundy, and if you're going to drive a tank over some vines, for god's sake do it over some Bourgogne rouge and not over a grand cru. This idea, that a wine can express the character of a particular site—its soil, its weather, its exposure to the sun, its actual identity—originated in Burgundy in the 1300s and 1400s with the Cistercian monks of the Abbé de Cîteaux. The monks weren't conversant with microbiology, geological strata, or any of the scientifically analyzable aspects that might contribute to terroir, but they could determine that a wine from *this* particular section of *this* particular slope had a different character from one grown on another plot of land, perhaps one where the soil drained slightly differently and the orientation to the sun shifted somewhat east. This was the origin idea of the cru, as well as of the concept of terroir itself. Over the centuries it has spread throughout the world of wine.

In Burgundy it reigns supreme. Here's just one example. Regarding his wine from the Chaignots Premier Cru, in the northern part of Nuits-Saint-Georges, Grégory Gouges of Domaine Henri Gouges says, "That area, the part next to Vosne-Romanée, makes wines that are a little more elegant, more fine, compared to the southern part. The south part is more sweet, more powerful. Les Pruliers, for instance." No one in Burgundy would blink an eye at this, and in fact Nuits-Saint-Georges contains forty-one different premier crus, each with its own distinctive character. Les Pruliers is no more than five hundred meters or so from Les Saints-Georges; suggest to a Burgundian that their wines might be interchangeable, and they'd look at you as if you'd said a duck is really the same as an eagle.

The difference of course is in the details, some large (a duck will not swoop from the sky to carry off your Pekingese in its talons) and some—many, with Burgundy—quite small. But the differences are there. And that singular level of nuanced expression is what makes this wine region unlike any other.

It also makes Burgundy very complex. People spend years learning the details of the 1,247 *climats* (delineated vineyard sites, essentially, of historical significance) of the Côte d'Or, which stretches from Dijon in the north to Santenay in the south. Add in the many, many more climats of Chablis, northwest of Dijon, and the Côte Chalonnaise and the Mâconnais to the south, and you have a monumental task ahead of you. For the generalist wine lover, that's akin to climbing Everest when all you really wanted to do was take a nice hike.

What's crucial to know is that the wines of Burgundy are essentially ranked by a historical sense of the quality of the vineyard they come from. So the largest and least prestigious designation is simply Bourgogne, a broad regional designation (rouge or blanc); after that, village wines (Chablis, Gevrey-Chambertin, or Nuits-Saint-Georges, for example); premier crus (Nuits-Saint-Georges Les Pruliers, Gevrey-Chambertin Clos Saint Jacques); and grand crus (Musigny, Corton-Charlemagne, Bonnes Mares). In total, Burgundy makes about 3 percent of France's wines. Pinot Noir and Chardonnay are the heart and soul of Burgundy. But there's also a small amount of Aligoté grown here, a white grape largely dismissed in the past that has now seen a flurry of interest, and even tinier amounts of Sauvignon Blanc and Sauvignon Gris planted in the equally tiny appellation of Saint-Bris.

The top wines of Burgundy are among the most coveted in the world, and today have reached stratospheric price levels. That's the simple reason that many of the great names of Burgundy, despite their devotion to expressing terroir and their inclination toward nonchemical viticulture, aren't in this book. Domaines like Dujac, Leflaive, Georges Roumier, Coche-Dury, Romanée-Conti, and so on would all fit these pages philosophically, but when a domaine's basic Bourgogne Blanc sells for $150, its audience is really limited to the multimillionaires of the world. So best advice for drinking these wines? Befriend a multimillionaire. (Or become one yourself, what the hell.)

The *good* news is that much of the excitement in Burgundy can now be found in what were long considered less prestigious places, villages like Montagny, Fixin, and Bouzeron; broader, long-dismissed appellations like the Hautes-Côtes de Beaune; or once-denigrated grapes like Aligoté. In these realms, younger, independent producers are making wines that far exceed old expectations—and that are priced at a level you don't have to mortgage your house to afford.

DOMAINE BERTHAUT-GERBET • FIXIN

[sustainable]

Amélie Berthaut is part of the younger generation of Burgundian winemakers who are shaking things up in a place that does not particularly love being shaken. Mostly this group of talents is based in under-recognized villages and appellations—the Hauts Côtes and the Côte Chalonnaise, towns like Montagny, Mercurey, Savigny-les-Beaune, Aloxe Corton, and Fixin, where Berthaut's family has been making wine for seven generations.

"Fixin is very small, about 250 acres total. Gevrey is five times that. Gevrey is the big name; Fixin is hidden in its shadow." Fixin (pronounced *fissin*) is adjacent to Gevrey and, historically, has been known for similarly muscular wines, but without Gevrey's reputation for elegance. "Rustic tannins, huge wines," Berthaut says. "My father made wines like that. But that's the winemaking they were doing at the time. He also used to machine harvest; everyone did. People still use this word, 'rustic,' about Fixin," she says, a little wearily. "We're trying to change that. It will take time, but it's a good challenge."

Berthaut took over in 2013, when she was twenty-three. But first she needed to fall in love with the prospect of making wine: "I wanted to do anything *but* wine. My parents worked so hard, all the time, and I didn't want that. They loved what they did, but as a child I never saw them, unless I wanted to work with them. When I was in school, I used to do my homework on the barrel heads with chalk."

Berthaut decided to become an agricultural engineer, but a required internship necessary for her degree changed her course. It needed to be at a farm, but "given my family history, I wasn't going to learn about cows," she says. A vineyard also counted as a farm, and she ended up at Domaine de la

Tour du Bon in Bandol. "Agnès Henry, the owner, was wonderful. She ran the estate brilliantly, but wasn't nearly as stressed as my parents."

Domaine Berthaut-Gerbet owns forty-two acres of vineyard both in Fixin and in Vosne-Romanée. "We're not certified organic, and we'd rather not be," Berthaut says. "We'd rather be free. But we haven't used any herbicides for a very long time, and we only use copper or sulfur."

The family's Vosne-Romanée acreage comes from her mother's side; Berthaut-Gerbet is a recent amalgamation of Domaine Denis Berthaut in Fixin and Domaine François Gerbet in Vosne-Romanée. Berthaut's mother, Marie-Andrée, ran the latter with her sister for forty years. Berthaut, for her part, seems content to make her wines in Fixin. "I could never work in Vosne. My father is really proud, but he's really nice. My mother . . . well. When you run your own domaine for four decades, it can be difficult to pass it on." Perhaps that formidable character runs in the Gerbet family: François, Marie-Andrée's father, first turned up in Vosne-Romanée in 1943 to help liberate Burgundy from the Nazis, arriving in a tank nicknamed "The Slayer."

Amélie Berthaut makes a few grand cru wines, but like all Burgundy grand crus these days, they're stunningly expensive. Her Fixins are another story: brilliant Burgundies that don't cost a fortune. Even more affordable is the juicy, dark-fruited **Domaine Berthaut-Gerbet Hauts Côtes de Nuits ($$)**, from a vineyard on her mother's side. "The Hauts Côtes aren't famous appellations, but they're good vineyards for the future," Berthaut says. "They're higher and cooler." There's also a fine **Bourgogne Rouge Les Prielles ($$)** and a similarly impressive **Côtes de Nuits Villages ($$)** from forty-eight-year-old vines in Brochon.

The **Berthaut-Gerbet Fixin Rouge ($$$)** is all crunchy red fruit, fresh and bright; a far cry from "rustic." The **Fixin Les Crais 1er Cru ($$$)** is red- and blue-fruited with floral notes. Berthaut says, regarding the **Fixin En Combe Roy ($$$)**, "It's a very small parcel, with old vines planted in the 1950s." Think tingly, dark, juicy raspberries with a little rhubarb added in.

Berthaut's top Fixin premier crus come from the adjoining Les Arvelets and Les Hervelets vineyards. Hervelets is a newer effort: "I find Arvelets has more elegance," she says, "but maybe that will change. We've only been making Hervelets since 2017." Her **Fixin Les Hervelets 1er Cru ($$$$)** has whole-cluster herbal notes and a dancer-like musculature, fine and taut. About the **Fixin Les Arvelets 1er Cru ($$$$)** she says, "This is a great vineyard. It's only Fixin, not a famous appellation. But it's better than many famous vineyards." The wine's deep blueberry and cherry notes, potpourri spice, and sustained, complex flavors support that claim.

DOMAINE SIMON BIZE & FILS •
SAVIGNY-LÈS-BEAUNE

[certified organic / biodynamic]

"The world is never perfect," Chisa Bize says. This is an understatement in Burgundy, where variable weather (ever more, thanks to climate shifts) and the foibles of the Pinot Noir grape would drive winemakers to despair if not for the transparent brilliance the wines can achieve. (Chardonnay is more forgiving, but making wine in Burgundy is rarely easy no matter the variety.)

Domaine Simon Bize was founded in 1880 in Savigny-lès-Beaune. Today it is one of Savigny's most recognized domaines, but the road hasn't been smooth. The worst blow came in 2013, when Patrick Bize passed away suddenly, leaving his wife, Chisa, and sister Marielle in charge of the property. He had been running the domaine for two decades at the time of his death, and was the architect of Bize's reputation today. He had also, largely through Chisa's influence, shifted it toward organic and biodynamic viticulture.

Today the property remains a source for stellar Savigny-lès-Beaunes. It has been a complicated shift. Patrick was a much-loved member of a local family, but Chisa was born and raised in Tokyo, and Burgundy retains its small-town wariness of outsiders from other parts of France, much less Japan. Yet even the most local of locals has to admit that under her direction, the Simon Bize wines have stayed consistently remarkable.

Of the domaine's fifty-four acres of vines, twenty are farmed biodynamically. The rest could be considered "organic-plus"; Chisa Bize has reduced her reliance on copper and sulfur with homeopathic, plant-based compounds, and has taken other measures such as adding thirteen hundred pounds of basalt dust to the vineyards to make a better environment for microorganisms. "Basalt has energy," she says simply. Life in the soil is key for her: "The previous generation felt the soil should be very clean—nothing green, nothing but vines. That's not nature. The younger generation here understands that that has to change. Microorganisms can't live in soil like that." In the winery, she's also experimented with zero-added-sulfur cuvées and even an "orange" Bourgogne Blanc—a shock to the elders of Burgundy, possibly, but change often is.

Domaine Simon Bize makes two main Bourgogne Blancs, the **Domaine Simon Bize Bourgogne Blanc Les Champlains ($$)** and the **Bourgogne Blanc Les Perrières ($$)**. The former is a bit more generous thanks to the inclusion of 5 percent Pinot Beurot (Pinot Gris), the latter stonier and more direct. The **Bourgogne Blanc Akatcha ($$)** is 100 percent Pinot Beurot, fermented for a week on the grape skins, resulting in a copper-hued wine with vivid flavors and fine tannins. The **Savigny-lès-Beaune Blanc ($$)**, a blend from three vineyards, is supple and citrusy; the **Savigny-lès-Beaune 1er Cru Aux Vergelesses ($$$–$$$$)** is racy and mouthwatering, with more complexity than it might initially seem.

For reds, the **Bourgogne Rouge Les Perrières ($$)** has more presence than most Bourgogne Rouges, with streamlined tannins and juicy cherry fruit. The village **Savigny-lès-Beaune ($$$)** is a step up in complexity and depth. Then there are six premier cru Savigny-lès-Beaunes, all excellent. Arguably the most famous one, the **Savigny-lès-Beaune Les Serpentières ($$$–$$$$),** comes from the first vineyard that Chisa Bize started farming biodynamically. "It's the beginning of that story," she says. The wine is lovely, with lifted floral notes and vivid red fruit that can mislead you about its underlying strength.

DOMAINE DE CASSIOPÉE • MARANGES

[certified organic]

Every time the church bell in Sampigny-les-Maranges tolls the hour, Ratapoil starts singing. Ratapoil is Talloulah Dubourg and Hugo Mathurin's black Labrador, and don't think for a moment that I mean howling—Ratapoil's response to the bell, even down in the Domaine de Cassiopée cellar, is a kind of operatic ululation, lovely, albeit in a rather eerie way.

Dubourg and Mathurin (and Ratapoil) founded Cassiopée in 2020. The couple met in enology school, and have worked at a small roster of well-regarded names—she at Clos de Tart and Benjamin Leroux, he at Domaine Roulot and Frederic Mugnier. They purchased the estate in 2019 from its previous owner, a Dane who'd made a go of making wine there. "He wanted to make natural wine, but he used a ton of new oak, and he didn't know how to farm, so a neighbor farmed everything for him, 100 percent chemically." When the Dane called it quits, Dubourg says, she and Mathurin were in the right place at the right time: "He hadn't listed it online—if he had, everyone in Burgundy would have been here in two days. And he was happy, he said, to sell to young winemakers who wanted to have a family here."

They converted the land, a little more than twelve acres, to organics and received certification in 2023. The couple are in their twenties, and Dubourg says, "Our generation, we realize that organics is the first step we have to do to work better—for our children and eventually for their children. But it's not a final step: we want to work the soil less, too, to plow with less depth. To work differently than before. But we also have to understand why older generations chose to work the way they did. They didn't *intend* to kill the soil." Mathurin also adds that arguments that organic viticulture is too expensive are absurd. "Look, if two young people in Maranges can be organic and still make money, don't tell me you can't do that in Puligny or Meursault."

As to the domaine's name, Dubourg says, "We didn't want to give our names to the estate, and we work a lot with the moon and with biodynamics. So it felt right. Plus, it may be the name of the daughter we hope to have one day."

The Cassiopée wines are minimal intervention without being rigidly natural. Regarding sulfur, for instance, Mathurin says, "The goal isn't to make no-sulfur wines simply to make no-sulfur wines, but to use as little as absolutely possible, or none if it's not needed." Overall, they're fresh, vivid, elegant expression of Hautes Côtes de Beaune and Maranges. There are two Aligotés, the **Domaine de Cassiopée Mitancherie ($$)** and **En Gerlieus**

($$). The former is like drinking electric lemongrass; the latter is deeper and more textural, and comes from much older vines. Their **Maranges Les Plantes Blanc ($$)** is minerally and racy. "For us, it's the most classical white wine we make," Dubourg says.

Of the reds, the **Hautes Côtes de Beaune Le Paizets ($$)**, from sixty-plus-year-old vines, is earthy and spicy. Those spice notes are shared by the **Maranges Bas du Clos ($$$)**, from ninety-plus-year-old vines just behind the couple's house (the cellar is below the house), along with cassis-scented fruit; the **Maranges Les Plantes Rouge ($$$)** comes from even older vines (110 years) and has lovely dark cherry fruit and mocha notes, zesty acidity, and a terrific mouthfeel. Cassiopée makes a few other wines as well; all are very small production, but all well worth seeking out.

DOMAINE DU CELLIER AUX MOINES • GIVRY

[certified organic / certified biodynamic]

Givry, in the Côte Chalonnaise, is too often overlooked. The last time it boasted true fame was when its wines were (it's said) the favorites of King Henri IV. That was around 1600. Philippe Pascal, the owner of Domaine du Cellier aux Moines, says, "There are great terroirs in the Côte Chalonnaise, comparable to what you find in the Côtes de Beaune and Côte de Nuits. But here, after phylloxera and World War I, we also had the emergence of the steel industry, thirty miles away. All these big factories demanded a lot of manpower, plus at the time the wine business was very difficult. Men left the vineyards for the mills, so vineyards here didn't develop at the same pace. Since the 1970s we've been catching up."

The history of Cellier aux Moines stretches back almost nine hundred years. "The 'cellar of the monks,'" Pascal says with a shrug. "Maybe it's a terrible name, but we're hardly going to change it now. It was founded by the same Cistercian monks who planted Clos Vougeot, the sister vineyard of the Abbé de Cîteaux."

He and his wife, Anne, switched to organics in 2015; they began working with biodynamics at the same time. "I knew even before we began that it was the right direction. It's helped us make wines that are more precise. Biodynamics somehow gives the terroir the ability to speak louder, to transmit more energy in the bottle.

"But is it because of biodynamics, or because bio forces you to become a better farmer?" he asks. "That's hard to say. I do know that you no longer have chemistry as a safety net. And in the end that the grape has more energy, and the *wine* has more energy." Pascal pauses, thoughtfully. "What is energy, to quantify it? I don't know. But it's that undefinable expression the wine gives you when you taste it."

Clos du Cellier aux Moines makes several whites. The **Clos du Cellier aux Moines Aligoté Sous les Roches ($$)**, from vines planted in 1945, suggests green apples and lemon zest, with a kind of dusty spice note. The **Mercurey Les Margotons ($$)** is creamy, full of orchard fruit flavors. The **Montagny Les Combes 1er Cru ($$$)** is my favorite of Pascal's whites (even more than his savory **Chassagne-Montrachet Les Chaumées 1er Cru [$$$$]**, a more prestigious site). The Les Combes wine is gorgeously aromatic, with a kind of lime blossom fragrance, its flavors long and lasting. "It has that exotic twist on the nose, which is tied to the vineyard having five percent Muscadelle in it," Pascal says.

The primary red wine is the **Clos du Cellier aux Moines 1er Cru Givry ($$$)**, a fragrant, luscious red Burgundy with toasted spice notes from a percentage of whole-cluster fermentation; it threads the richness Givry can offer through a needle's eye of fine focus. The layered, more powerful **Clos Pascal Monopole Givry ($$$)** comes from a minuscule plot of prephylloxera vines on the steep hill behind their house. "When phylloxera killed the vines in the 1800s, the owner just let it go to bushes. So that vineyard was not included in the Givry appellation, because abandoned vineyards were not included. We had to lobby to get it back in. It's a great terroir, very stony, planted with no trellising—the vines just go up to the sky."

CHANDON DE BRIAILLES • SAVIGNY-LÈS-BEAUNE

[certified organic / certified biodynamic]

One of the most acclaimed domaines in Savigny-lès-Beaune, Chandon de Brialles has for many years also been one of the most forward-looking in terms of ecological practices—or possibly backward-looking, since part of François de Nicolay's approach since 2013 has been primarily to use horses in his thirty-four and a half acres of vineyards. "We introduced horses because we saw how good they were for the soil. We started in Corton with one horse, then one for our acreage in Ile-des-Pergelesses . . . then another horse . . . then another horse." He laughs. "We stopped at four."

The domaine was founded in 1834, though its tiny subterranean cellar dates back to the 1100s. François de Nicolay is the seventh generation of his family here; he took over in 2001 from his mother, who had been farm-ing organically since 1988. "She understood that the herbicides and systemic chemicals weren't good for either the vines or the environment as a whole," François says.

De Nicolay was the proprietor of a wine shop in Paris when his mother called him to ask "the key question," as he puts it: whether he would return home to run the domaine. "It took me ten minutes to think about it. I had also become interested in biodynamic wines, and I told her I had ideas about how to make our farming even better. She said, 'That's your problem now, not mine!'"

Fair enough. De Nicolay started biodynamics in 2005 and was certified in 2011. "But I'm not a spiritualist. I use biodynamics as a practical method. My task is to make good wines and to pro-tect the environment at the same time."

Chandon de Briailles's wines are pure and expressive, transparent expres-sions of their terroirs. The **Chandon de Briaille Savigny-lès-Beaune Ile-des-Vergelesses 1er Cru blanc ($$$)** is a fine example: citrus and orchard fruit flavors playing against each other, with that effortless elegance that good Savignys often have. The **Corton Blanc ($$$$)** comes from vines mostly in

Corton Bressandes, but it can't be labeled as such (as it is white). "My parents planted Corton Blanc in the 1960s," de Nicolay says. "It's in a red area, so when we finally replant, we'll shift to red. The nursery originally sent the wrong plants!" It's deep with pear, apricot, and red apple flavors and often a wildflower honey accent.

For reds, the **Savigny-lès-Beaune Les Lavières 1er Cru ($$$)** suggests red and black currants and violets, ending on a mineral-saline note. François de Nicolay says, "There's only a few inches of soil in Lavières before you hit mother rock—that limestone gives the seaside character to the wine." His **Savigny-lès-Beaune aux Fourneaux 1er Cru ($$$)** comes

from vines planted in 1956, with a little more clay, and is a bit rounder and richer. The **Pernand-Vergelesses Ile des Vergelesses 1er Cru ($$$–$$$$)** offers black cherry flavors and soft tannins, with floral accents. "It's a fantastic terroir," de Nicolay says of this cru. "Quite far from the town of Pernand, so you get that warmth that you don't get in the valley." The **Aloxe-Corton Les Valozières 1er Cru ($$$)** comes from two-thirds acre of vines directly below Corton Bressandes, and is dense and powerful, one to age. Of the grand crus, the **Corton Bressandes Grand Cru ($$$$)** stands out for its seductive blueberry–red cherry flavors and remarkable combination of power and elegance.

CHANTERÊVES • SAVIGNY-LÈS-BEAUNE

[sustainable / organic]

Chanterêves, a partnership between husband-and-wife winemakers Guillaume Bott and Tomoko Kuriyama, has quickly made a name for itself in the new wave of *négociant-vinificateurs* that have come into being in Burgundy.

Kuriyama was born in Japan, into

a food- and wine-loving family. Her maternal grandmother taught cooking, her father collected wine, and so it isn't a complete surprise that she ended up doing a degree in enology and viticulture (at Germany's Geisenheim University). Her course for Burgundy was set during a stint as a harvest intern at Domaine Simon Bize, where she met Guillaume Bott. That was in 2005. They fell in love, married, and started Chanterêves in 2010. (Bott himself grew up in Dijon, where his father had a plumbing and air-conditioning company. "My younger brother runs it now," he says. "When you're a winemaker, it's *very* good to have a brother who works in plumbing.")

Kuriyama and Bott work with a handful of growers throughout Burgundy, and they're among those pushing for recognition for Burgundy's less acclaimed appellations: Hauts Côtes de Beaune, Chorey-lès-Beaune, Nuits-Saint-Georges Villages, Auxey Duresses, and others. Their domaine vineyards are organic, with some biodynamic practices; the purchased fruit isn't necessarily organic, though they look for farmers whose approach is in sync with their own.

The Chanterêves wines ferment in wooden tanks with no temperature control, using all native yeasts. "We avoid intervention," Kuriyama says. Sulfur use is minimal, though they do use some at bottling. The focus is clarity, energy, and precision.

Are these natural wines? "We make wines we want to drink," Kuriyama says. "We don't want to produce 'natural' wine, no, even though most of what we drink is natural these days. I don't know—if you aren't 'natural,' then you are unnatural?"

Kuriyama and Bott's passion for what they do is infectious. They are serious winemakers and growers, but there rarely seems to be a moment when they aren't smiling. What is the point if not passion and delight? "An Australian winemaker who was visiting once asked what we were paying for our Chassagne Montrachet premier cru grapes," Kuriyama recalls. "I told him, and he said, 'I don't see how you can possibly make any money!' But we're not in this to make money. You'd have to be completely insane if that was why you did what we do."

Chanterêves makes five different Aligotés, and all of them are excellent. To take two examples, look for the **Chanterêves Aligoté Les Monts de Fussey ($$)** or the **Bas des Ees ($$)**, both from the vineyard land they purchased in 2020.

Also look for their **Auxey-**

Duresses Les Hautés ($$$), a golden-lemony white that embraces the palate, and their poised, fragrant **Savigny-lès-Beaune Dessus de Montchevenoy** ($$$), from vineyard land they own above the 1er cru Aux Gettes. "It's very isolated," Kuriyama says. "We have to fence it because badgers come and eat the grapes." Standouts among the many Chanterêves reds include the lively, almost prickly **Bourgogne Hauts Côtes de Beaune Paris l'Hopital** ($$$), off granite soils just west of Maranges; the **Chorey-lès-Beaune Champs Longue** ($$$), from a tiny parcel of forty-five-year-old vines, full of crunchy berry flavors; the **Nuits-Saint-Georges Villages Les Tuyaux** ($$$), darkly spicy and powerful, made with 100 percent whole-cluster fermentation since 2014; and the lovely **Savigny-lès-Beaune Dessus de Montchevenoy Rouge** ($$$), with its lifted stem-spice fragrance and fine blue and red fruit. Buy it, and be happy that the badgers didn't eat all the grapes first.

DOMAINE CHEVROT • MARANGES

[certified organic]

Brothers Pablo and Vincent Chevrot are deeply tied to Maranges, the small town that's the southernmost commune of the Côte de Beaune. They were born and raised here, and their grandparents lived across the road from the small winery where they work, and sold wine in bulk to the big *négociants*. "My father was at school when my grandfather died in 1967, and had to come home to run the winery. He decided to sell our wine in bottles instead—he was one of the first people in Maranges to do that," Vincent Chevrot recalls.

There's none of the stiffness you sometimes find in Burgundy's more famous villages here in Maranges. Vincent, in his mid-thirties, in sunglasses, a black T-shirt, and shorts, definitely shows no pretension. Nor does the winery, which often has a Ping-Pong table set up on the crush pad. "Very important for team building!" he says.

But there is tradition. The family home, surrounded by electric-blue Chardon Marie flowers in the summer months, was built in 1798. The old part of the cellar dates from the same era, and the reputation of Maranges as a source for powerful, rustic Burgundies probably dates back that long as well. "Some terroirs *are* big here. They make strong wines, and if you do too much extraction, they get that way much too fast. The old people liked hard wine," Vincent says, punching his fist into the palm of his other hand, the way you might sock a baseball into a glove. "But not so much anymore. We've changed."

The family's forty-seven acres of vineyards are certified organic. "My father was taught at school that chemicals were good," Vincent says. "They did give him time—for birthdays, for spending time with us, for business. So maybe they weren't one

---

> *"I prefer a wine that has personality over one that's one hundred percent enologically perfect."*
> —Vincent Chevrot

---

hundred percent bad. But my brother and I felt we had to change. The main thing is that we're in the vines—us and also our employees—so all of us are exposed to any chemicals we might use. Beyond that, there's the broader environment to consider. But you have to certify, I feel. In Burgundy, if you ask, ninety percent of people will say they're organic. But I can tell you, there's a lot of faking going on."

The Chevrots stopped using sulfur several years ago except for minimal amounts at bottling. That led to reducing their use of new oak, too. "Wines without sulfites, if you put too much new oak on them, it isn't good. It just shows more." In essence, these are wines made with very minimal intervention, without really being in the natural wine camp. "I prefer a wine that has personality over one that's one hundred percent enologically perfect," Vincent says. "But I don't want one hundred percent crazy, either."

And regarding his brother's name, Pablo? Not a very French moniker. Vincent laughs. "Well, my grandfather was Paul, and we have Spanish origins from my mother . . . and my brother was conceived in South America. So! He's Pablo. And Vincent, well. Everyone in Burgundy is called Vincent."

The Chevrots' lemon-zesty, supple **Domaine Chevrot Bourgogne Aligoté Cuvée des Quatre Terroirs ($$)** is an excellent example of the variety. For whites, there's also a floral, delicate **Hauts Côtes de Beaune Blanc ($$)** and a firm, rather dignified **Maranges Blanc ($$)**. The bright, lively **Domaine Chevrot Bourgogne Pinot Noir ($$)** is excellent for the price; the two vineyards it comes from are both classified as Maranges Villages, but the wine is labeled as Bourgogne Rouge to keep its price down. But the Chevrots' **Maranges Sur le Chène ($$)** is the true steal. As Vincent says, "If you don't know Burgundy, this is a great wine to start with." With its floral, black-currant nose and mouth-coating flavors, it takes the innate power of Maranges and gives it remarkable finesse and detail. The **Santenay 1er Cru Clos Rousseau ($$$)** is a step up in elegance. Vincent says, "Maranges has more on the attack, more power. Santenay has less power but more balance, and the flavors are a bit longer."

DOMAINE EDMOND CORNU • LADOIX

[sustainable]

If you stand outside the cellar doors at Edmond Cornu in the late afternoon on a November day, looking through the village of Ladoix-Serrigny, up at the slopes of the Côte de Beaune, you'll understand one reason why the heart of Burgundy is called the Côte d'Or. To the left and right a rich seam of golden leaves covers the hillside, fading toward Beaune in one direction, Nuits-Saint-Georges in the other.

Domaine Edmond Cornu was established in 1875. Pierre Cornu says, "When my great-grandfather died, the property was divided between five or six kids. Each had maybe a third of a hectare. Is that a domaine or not a domaine?" A Gallic shrug. Pierre is in his fifties. His father, Edmond, who still helps out, is in his seventies. In the 1920s, Pierre says, his grandfather bought their first plow and started working the vineyard with a horse. Then, in 1961, his father sold the horse to buy the family's first tractor. "That's when he started bottling our wines, because he actually had enough time then."

It's hard to believe now that Burgundy was once poor, and that people here simply scraped by as best they could, for decades and decades and decades. Things are clearly different now, but the connection to an unostentatious farm life permeates the air at places like Cornu. The Cornus own roughly forty acres of vineyards in the northern part of the Côte de Beaune, plus a small plot of vines in Corgoloin in the Côte de Nuits. Pierre says, "Things change. My father's generation would use chemicals to remove all the weeds. Now we plant

weeds! When we first started using cover crops, my father would check the vines and say, 'What kind of work is *that?*' But later he started to say, 'OK. It looks pretty nice.'"

Ladoix has never been as well-known as some of the neighboring towns are, and Pierre says that "for years the wines were just labeled Côtes de Beaune Villages, because no one knew Ladoix." That's changed, but the Cornu wines are still very fairly priced, possibly a trailing aftereffect of their village's lack of recognition. These aren't wines that are sold back and forth between collectors, never to be opened. Instead, they're expressive, honest Burgundies, capturing Pierre's sense of what it means to be a vigneron: "Our job is like a pianist's—but the instrument we play isn't a Steinway, it's Pinot Noir. And we don't play Beethoven or Chopin, we play Ladoix or Aloxe Corton."

The **Edmond Cornu Aligoté ($$)** is less sharp and lean than many Aligotés. Coming from sixty-year-old vines, it has a green apple and talc character that's extremely appealing. The **Chorey-lès-Beaune Les Bons Ores ($$)** has all the direct, dark-berry appeal of Chorey but also a fair amount of grace.

"The gravel in this vineyard makes a fairly elegant wine," Pierre Cornu says. The **Ladoix Vieilles Vignes ($$)**, from vines planted in 1926 and 1960, captures that red berry/dark fruit balancing act that seems characteristic of Ladoix, the northernmost village in the Côte de Beaune; its wines live in a kind of transitional place between the Côte de Beaune and the Côte de Nuits. The **Ladoix Premier Cru Le Bois Roussot** (\$\$\$) comes from a vineyard high up the slope overlooking Ladoix. It has the alluring scent and flavor of black cherries, and a rich juiciness that grows tangy and then ends on firm mineral notes. The **Ladoix Les Carrières** (\$\$\$) is more lifted and high-toned, the flavors all red currants and red berries. And the **Ladoix Premier Cru La Corvée** (\$\$\$), powerful and profound, can age effortlessly for years. Cornu also makes a reasonable amount of **Aloxe Corton Vieilles Vignes** (\$\$\$), elegant and red-fruited, more tart than the Ladoix VV, with a faint licorice note. Finally, there's a tiny amount of **Corton Les Bressandes Grand Cru** (\$\$\$\$), complex and vivid, its black and red fruit graced with sweet spice notes, but only about four hundred bottles come to the U.S. each vintage.

DOMAINE HENRI GOUGES • NUITS-SAINT-GEORGES

[organic]

Of the famous villages of the Côte de Nuits, Nuits-Saint-Georges has always been the odd one out. Unlike Vosne-Romanée or Morey-Saint-Denis, it has no grand cru vineyards. Yet it can produce profound wines, especially from the premier cru Les Saint Georges vineyard (which many people feel is a grand cru except in name). And if there is one producer to know in Nuits-Saint-Georges, it's Domaine Henri Gouges.

The domaine was founded in 1919. "There were a lot of Gouges before us in wine, but as grape growers," Grégory Gouges says. Henri Gouges, his great-grandfather, was one of the first growers to bottle and sell his own wines (rather than selling them to a *négociant*), and was instrumental in creating the Nuits-Saint-Georges appellation in 1936. (Note that "nuits" refers to the walnuts grown in the area since Roman times, not to the night; *nux* is Latin for nut.) He was also, by all reports, an excellent cook. Françoise Gouges, his granddaughter, recalls him keeping live pike in the bathtub, to be cooked later in the day.

In the 1940s and 1950s, Henri

Gouges made powerful, somewhat unforgiving wines, and for many years that was one of the signatures of the domaine: intense tannins, muscular strength, red Burgundies that took a long time in the cellar to develop. Grégory says, "Our wines today aren't softer than the older wines, but maybe a little more accessible."

Work in the vineyard has been without any pesticides, herbicides, or chemical fertilizers since 1985. "We have no label, no certification, but we've been organic for a long time," Grégory says. "My father started it, and after three or four years, he discovered the soil was alive again. As the years went by, we discovered more and more life in the vineyard, too—*le faune, le flor,* flowers and vegetables, and everything to do with animals big and small. But we don't put anything on our labels, because it's not something we do in order to market our wines or increase our sales. It's just a philosophy we follow for ourselves."

Even if they are more accessible, and even as the viticulture has shifted away from the conventional practices of the 1960s and 1970s, the Gouges wines have remained unerringly true to their long-established character. Drinking them can feel like a trip back to the Burgundy of an earlier era. "It's important not to do a revolution, but an evolution," Grégory says. "And it's very important for us, now, to recognize what the past generations here made, with less technology and with less money perhaps. We may have better techniques today, but we have to use that knowledge in a good way, to respect the terroir, to respect Pinot Noir, and to respect the generation before us."

―――――――

The domaine makes two white wines, a supple **Bourgogne Pinot Blanc ($$)**, with orchard fruit and toasted bread flavors, and a small amount of alluring, complex **Nuits-Saint-Georges La Perrière Premier Cru Blanc ($$$$)** that's also made with Pinot Blanc. (Or, as this particular variety is known, "Pinot Gouges." Grégory Gouges says,

"In 1932, in the middle of Les Saint Georges, Henri found one shoot of white grapes on a vine; the rest was Pinot Noir. He grafted this over and after twenty-five years was able to plant a small parcel, La Perrière, with it. In 1990, my uncle Christian did a DNA analysis and the result was that it was a white Pinot Noir. Some people call it Pinot Gouges, some say Pinot Mutánt—mutated Pinot.")

But reds are the heart of the domaine's identity, starting with its appealing **Côte de Nuits Villages ($$)**. As good as that wine is, the personality of the Gouges wines is more fully evident in the firm, substantial, village **Nuits-Saint-Georges ($$$)**. The Gouges premier crus have become substantially pricier in recent years (along with the rest of Burgundy), but they're brilliant wines regardless. The **Nuits-Saint-Georges Clos de Porrets Premier Cru ($$$$)** has a kind of upright military character in most vintages, stern and somewhat unforgiving, but impressively potent and complex. "Today a lot of people want easier wine," Grégory says. "Porrets keeps a little of the old austerity." The **Nuits-Saint-Georges Chaignots Premier Cru ($$$$)** comes from the northern part of the appellation: "That area, the part next to Vosne-Romanée, makes wines that are a little more elegant, compared to the southern part," Grégory says. "The wines of the south part are sweeter, more powerful—Les Pruliers, for instance." Henri Gouges acquired about seventeen acres of Les Pruliers in 1920, from which the **Nuits-Saint-Georges Les Pruliers Premier Cru ($$$$)** comes. Finally, there's the **Nuits-Saint-Georges Les Saint Georges ($$$$)**, a profoundly age-worthy, complex, intense red Burgundy. "It's the best of Nuits-Saint-Georges," Grégory says. "In it you have all that classic structure, but when you taste the wine, you also find more elements than in any of the others; it's so complex and full." It's also far outside the basic price parameters of this book, but any profile of Domaine Henri Gouges would be incomplete without mentioning it.

THIBAULT LIGER-BELAIR • NUITS-SAINT-GEORGES / MOULIN-À-VENT

[certified organic]

Thibault Liger-Belair has been farming organically since his first vintage, and follows some biodynamic practices, but he is not particularly interested in having someone else certify that part of his approach: "I believe in science, I believe in soil, and I believe in God. I don't need to believe in biodynamics." Also, like many conscientious farmers currently working in Burgundy, Liger-Belair feels that the conventional farming practices of the past forty-five or fifty years resulted in a host of problems. "We were considering the soil as though it were a big factory," he says. "Add what the vine needs. Add fertilizers. And this, add that. But what's much more important is what the *soil* needs. That's been my work—understanding what the soil needs."

He goes on: "I follow the principles of Hildegard of Bingen. A saint from the fifteenth century in Germany. I started to look at her teachings, about all the plants that can be good for humans. We make teas from those plants for the vines: chamomile, dandelion, willow tree. It may sound strange, but the name of the willow in French is *saule*, because of the salicylic acid—it's in the bark and the leaves. I don't know exactly everything that happens in the soil, but step by step, we begin to understand. The only problem is that we only do one vintage per year!" Speak all that as fast as you can, with energy practically popping off your fingertips, and you have an idea of the man.

Liger-Belair's family has been in wine since 1720. "We were wine merchants, but my father never worked in the wine business. My grandfather told him not to do it. That was in the 1970s, in the middle of the oil crisis." French wine was in disastrous economic shape at that time; his grandfather's advice made sense. Nevertheless, Liger-Belair, a teenager at the time, would still dutifully go every weekend to Nuits-Saint-Georges to see his grandparents. "I started spending time with a friend of my father's there, a neighbor, who made wine. He worked constantly. I asked him one time, 'Why don't you stop? Take the weekend off, take a rest.' And he told me, 'I prefer to be with my wine, with my vineyard, than to be on a sofa in front of my TV.' I was fourteen, and that really got into my head, so when I was sixteen, I told my father this was what I wanted to do."

Liger-Belair is part of the growing cadre of Burgundy producers who also own land and make wine in Beaujolais. "When I finished my studies in 1996, I rented an old house in the vineyards in Moulin-à-Vent. I saw how beautiful it was every morning when I opened the window, and I decided that land that beautiful couldn't possibly produce bad wines."

The **Thibault Liger-Belair Moulin-à-Vent Vieilles Vignes ($$)** is a touch flamboyant, in the best way, very pretty, with a creamy texture and black and red berry flavors. His **Bourgogne Les Deux Terroirs ($$)** is an oddball of a wine, and a brilliant bargain. "The idea was to make a 'super-*passetoutgrain*,' combining the terroirs of Beaujolais and Burgundy. It's Gamay—two-thirds cru Beaujolais and one-third from Burgundy." The wine is lovely, floral and berry-bright, resolving into earthy-peppery notes. The **Bourgogne Les Grands Chaillots ($$)** is fragrant and full of cherry liqueur flavors, round and mouth-filling. "It's much more difficult to make a good Bourgogne rouge than a good grand cru," Liger-Belair says. "But I focus on it, because it's the calling card for our domaine." His **Nuits-Saint-Georges La Charmotte ($$$)** "is always soft and elegant at the beginning, then you feel the freshness and intensity." The **Chambolle Musigny Vieilles Vignes ($$$)** has all the silkiness that village has at its best, and saturated flavors that are somehow also delicate and lifted. And the **Nuits-Saint-Georges Les Saint Georges 1er Cru ($$$$)**, despite being quite pricey, is a stellar red Burgundy, full of the power and darkness of Nuits, exotically spicy, complex, deeply flavorful, and lasting.

DOMAINE BRUNO LORENZON • MERCUREY

[organic]

When people rattle off a list of the great villages of Burgundy, Mercurey is never named. It has the disadvantage of being in the Côte Chalonnaise, south of the more famed Côte d'Or; there are no grand crus here. Bruno Lorenzon, a lean former rugby player who makes some of Mercurey's best wines, and who is also rarely inclined to mince words, says, "Socially speaking, it's more classy, more important, to open a Chambolle-Musigny than a Mercurey, even if the Chambolle is crap."

Lorenzon farms twenty-seven acres of vineyard split between Mercurey and nearby Montagny. This is family land. The Lorezons have been growing grapes here for a hundred years, since Bruno's great-grandfather arrived. He works organically, as his father did. "He stopped using chemicals in the vineyards forty-five years ago," he says, "before the fancy wave of organics. But three years ago, I gave up the certification. You shouldn't hide behind a label; there are too many people hiding behind 'organic' marketing. You can be organic, and still be shit. You can be biodynamic, and still be shit."

In the cellar, Lorenzon doesn't acidify, nor does he ever chaptalize in poor vintages. "You take the vintage as it is. I try to make in the winery what I'm given in the vineyard." No sulfur is used until a minimal amount at bot-tling. But he also doesn't believe in natural fermentation—or at least the sort of natural fermentation that simply works with yeasts found ambiently. Instead, he selects yeasts from his vineyard, propagates one strain, and keeps that to use each year. In essence, he says, "You take away everything you don't need. You don't add any makeup to the wine. But for that to work, you need great vineyards."

His wines, both white and red, are an argument for the idea that Mercurey, despite its secondary status, does have terroirs equal to those of Burgundy's more famous names. But Lorenzon himself isn't pretentious about it. "A wine, a premier cru, should be able to live for twenty years. But if it's a beautiful day, and you're with a friend, you should be able to open it and enjoy it in the moment, right now."

———

Highlights among Lorenzon's whites include the **Domaine Bruno Lorenzon**

"People ask, 'Let's see, it's forty percent new oak, what about your pH?' Shut up, and sit down. Just taste it. Just be inspired."
—Bruno Lorenzon

Mercurey 1er Cru Champs Martin Blanc ($$$), a precise white with light mango notes and a creamy texture, and the **Mercurey 1er Cru Pièce 15 Blanc ($$$)**, part of a series of *"pièce"* wines, inspired by his grandfather. "He was very close to me, and he said, 'In each block there is some amount of great terroir—you have to find the best vein, like a vein in your body.'" It's somehow rich but light all at once.

That's a quality Lorenzon wants in his reds, too: "Pinot for me should be lifted. A floating island. But it has strength. It's like a rugby player—you can be only a hundred and fifty pounds, and still be a great rugby player." His **Mercurey 1er Cru Champs Martin Rouge ($$$)** expresses that with its vivid, bright red fruit, floral aromas, and fine tannins. The **Mercurey 1er Cru Pièce 13 Rouge ($$$)** is firm and structured, with whole-cluster savory notes. "It's got a lot of grip," Lorenzon says. Finally, the **Mercurey 1er Cru Carline Clos des Champs Martin ($$$$)**, named for his sister, comes from a single block of sixty-five-year-old vines just over an acre in size. It's round, red-fruited, darkly spicy, "and usually richer," Lorenzon says. "There's a little more clay here. It has a touch of the Rhône Valley in a way."

DOMAINE CHRISTIAN MOREAU • CHABLIS

[certified organic]

Moreau is one of the historic names in Chablis. The family's presence here dates to 1814, when Jean Joseph Moreau, a *tonnelier* (cooper) from Montbard, founded the *négociant* house of J. Moreau et Fils in Chablis. This remained a family company until 1974, when the Moreaus sold half of the firm to the giant Canadian liquor company Hiram Walker; in 1985, the remaining half also went to Walker, which then sold the company to the French *négociant* company Boisset. But Christian Moreau long regretted losing the family name, and in 2002, when the Moreaus regained the rights to their own vineyards and to make and market the wines from them, he founded Christian Moreau Père et Fils.

It's a rare happy outcome to the family-sells-to-giant-corporation story. Moreau owns about thirty acres of vineyards, skewing toward grand cru sites—Les Clos, Clos des Hospices (a part of Les Clos), Valmur, Vaudésir, and Blanchot. Grapes are harvested by hand from densely planted, low-yielding vineyards that have been certified organic since 2013. Fermentation is solely with natural yeasts, in steel for the village wines, and in 30 to 45 percent oak for premier and grand crus (about 10 percent of that new). Fabrice Moreau, Christian's son, currently makes the wine.

Moreau's basic village **Chablis ($$)** is a perennial value, with exactly the crisp fruit and mineral finish you'd hope for. The domaine's **Vaillons Premier Cru ($$$)**, from seven different parcels, with vines averaging over fifty years old, adds roundness and depth. Of the grand crus, Christian Moreau says, "the **Vaudesir Grand Cru ($$$$)** is the most delicate, with a lot of finesse. **Valmur Grand Cru ($$$$)** is a bigger wine, and needs a bit more time to express everything. The **Les Clos Grand Cru ($$$$)** is a mix of both, not as light as Vaudesir, not as big as Valmur, and a long aftertaste." It's a show-stopper, with lemony intensity and a chalky, stony finish. Finally, there's the domaine's **Les Clos Grand Cru Clos des Hospices ($$$$)**, a tiny half-acre site within the Les Clos Grand Cru. Silky and poised, it's probably the finest expression of the character of the domaine and a stellar grand cru Chablis.

DOMAINE MOREAU-NAUDET • CHABLIS

[organic]

Starting in 1991, Stepháne Moreau worked to bring his family property in Chablis from relative anonymity to the forefront of the region, crafting gorgeously terroir-expressive, mineral-driven wines that over the years accumulated a devoted following. His models were two friends: Vincent Dauvissat, one of the region's iconic names, and Didier Dagueneau, the wild-haired, daredevil genius of Pouilly-Fumé.

Moreau's family had been in Chablis for generations, and the domaine was founded by Stepháne's great-grandfather. But when Stepháne took over, he instituted needed changes. He reduced yields, switched to manual harvesting and organic farming, started using spontaneous fermentation with natural yeasts, reduced the level of sulfur use, and, perhaps most unconventionally for what's been the arc of style in Chablis, harvested later, creating a style that was both ripe and full-bodied yet laser-focused—a difficult tightrope to walk.

His partner through all this was his wife and co-vigneron, Virginie Naudet. They met in Irancey, a chance encounter one evening when Stéphane came into the restaurant her parents owned. "I didn't know Chablis that well," she says, "but we met, we drank some glasses together, and eventually we were married." There: a Hollywood romance in nineteen words. Even then, she says, he knew what he hoped to do with his family's property someday. "It was very important to respect nature for him," Virginie says. "When he took over, he worked more and more that way, with the weather, doing organic and *biodynamie*. But he was working alone, so it was very hard."

Moreau-Naudet's distinctive label, a white hand holding a white grape between thumb and forefinger against a low stone wall, represents that balance between labor and nature. Originally the estate had a traditional label, but Virginie never liked it. "I said, 'Can we change this boring label?' So, one day, Didier Dagueneau came to Chablis, and after many glasses of wine, he and Stéphane drew this hand. I looked at it the next morning—it was terrible! So I called a professional artist to redraw it."

The story takes a hard turn: Stéphane Moreau died unexpectedly in 2016, at only forty-seven. But Virginie kept on. "For me, it was impossible that Moreau-Naudet would be finished," she says. "Stepháne worked very hard for a very long time, and he passed away very suddenly. It was impossible for me, in my head, in my heart, to even contemplate selling."

Today the Moreau-Naudet wines are as good as they ever have been. Most recently, Virginie has been working with agroforestry as well. "We had nature in Burgundy. Then people removed it. And now we're going back to what we had before. Thirty or forty years ago, wine producers were ripping out all the trees to plant more vineyards. Now we're reversing that trend."

She has pressed forward against other people's expectations, but not her own. "I continued, and my daughters will continue after me. It was very difficult for the first two years after Stéphane was gone. But with time, I learned and learned; I must do this, I must do that; time after time, year after year. I started alone, but I did it." She flexes her arm in a gesture of strength, a woman who can arm-wrestle tragedy and win.

Moreau-Naudet makes a range of stellar Chablis from sixty-two acres of vineyard. The **Domaine Moreau-Naudet Petit Chablis ($$)**, fresh and focused, comes from a small plot of younger vines and is aged nine months in stainless steel before bottling. The village **Chablis ($$)** is easily one of the best village Chablis to be had, drinking more like a premier cru (at a distinctly not-premier-cru price). The **Chablis Vieilles Vignes Les Pargues ($$$)** comes from a two-and-a-half-acre *lieu dit* of fifty-plus-year-old vines between the Vaillons and Montmains premier crus. Chalky, lemon-zesty, complex: impossible to resist. There are four premier cru wines (Montmains, Vaillons, Fôrets, and Montée de Tonerre) and one grand cru (Valmur). All are superb Chablis, minerally and intense, brimming with energy; personally, I'm partial to the filigreed power of the **Fôrets Premier Cru ($$$$)**, but it's impossible to go wrong with any of them.

DOMAINE AGNÈS PAQUET • HAUTES CÔTES DE BEAUNE

[sustainable / certified organic]

Agnès Paquet was born in Meloisey in the Hautes Côtes de Beaune, "a *very* big city," she dryly notes. "Three hundred people!" Her parents were not in the wine business, but in the 1950s her grandfather bought a vineyard in Auxey-Duresses, which he rented out to local vintners. When he passed away, her parents decided to sell it. "But I told them I would make the wine myself," Paquet says. "They thought I was young and crazy. But they were supportive. They just said, look, this will be very difficult, what you are trying to do, for at least ten years. And they were right—though it was actually eleven."

Paquet's first vintage was in 2011. She still lives in Meloisey, making wine in what was once her great-grandfather's house. She's also part of that wave of new talents who've brought unexpected acclaim to places like Auxey and the Hautes Côtes de Beaune, along with Domaine de Cassiopée, Chanterêves, and others. "When I started, I would always say 'the Hautes Côtes de Beaune in Burgundy,' because no one knew where the Hautes Côtes were," she says. "But when I started, no one knew Auxey, either. They didn't even know how to pronounce it. 'Do you say Aussy, or Oxy?' 'Well! The most important thing is to talk about it in the first place!'" she says. (It's pronounced "Aussy.")

Paquet stopped using herbicides in her vineyards in 2004, went fully organic in 2008, and received certification in 2022. "But being organic doesn't necessarily mean you're sustainable," she points out. "We try to be both. So, we minimize the use of tractors in the vineyard to use less carbon, for instance. We're actually trying to minimize *all* mechanical interventions. But it's not easy. I'd love to have all my vineyards worked by horses, but it's just too expensive."

In the winery, Paquet uses only indigenous yeasts, and minimal sulfur. "I just want the terroirs I work with to talk by themselves," she says. "I don't want to 'make' wine, just create the most purity possible with the least intervention."

The **Agnès Paquet Aligoté Le Clou et la Plume ($$)** comes from young vines in Meloisey and vines in Meursault. Softer and rounder than some Aligotés, it suggests green apples and lemon hard candies (without the sweetness). Her **Auxey-Duresses Les Hoz Blanc ($$)** is from the original estate vineyard her grandfather bought. It's fresh, stony, and elegant, with a Chablis-like minerality. Her **Cuvée Patience No. 12 Auxey-Duresses ($$)** is also from the estate vineyard, but solely from ninety-plus-year-old Chardonnay vines; it's held a little longer before release, giving it a faint honey-hay note and more texture and depth. For her **Bourgogne Pinot Noir Les Croquamots**

($$) she uses only foot-treading. "I like it! It's very gentle on the grapes," she says. Juicy dark cherry flavors are the hallmark here. Her **Hauts Côtes de Beaune Rouge ($$)** tends to be spicy and aromatic, and comes from vines in Meloisey. And her **Auxey-Duresses Les Hoz Rouge ($$)** comes from both twenty-year-old and sixty-year-old vines. The fruit is vinified and aged separately, then blended before bottling. Full of floral notes and blue and red fruit, it fills the mouth with flavor, then ends on creamy tannins. Finally, don't overlook her **Aligoté Pet Nat Ali Bois Bois et les 40 Buveurs ($$)**. The name means "Ali Drink Drink and the Forty Drinkers," and the wine itself is as fun as the play on words: lots of fresh green-apple/tangerine fruit, foamy bubbles, and a very faint touch of sweetness. "We always have some in the fridge for when we come back from a bike ride," she says.

SYLVAIN PATAILLE • MARSANNAY

[certified organic / biodynamic]

Sylvain Pataille is a striking figure in Burgundy today, not just for his shaggy beard and mane of curly hair, but because he is both a consulting enologist for a number of top domaines while at the same time making, under his own name, some of Burgundy's most idiosyncratic, expressive, distinctive wines.

Pataille didn't grow up in a winemaking family, but he did grow up in Marsannay, and as he says, "All my clients as an enologist were my friends when I was growing up. And since my parents weren't winegrowers, I started with the vines that growers didn't want anymore—particularly Aligoté."

The renaissance of Aligoté owes a lot to Pataille's passion for it, and his persistence in convincing people that, rather than being a second-rate white grape, Aligoté was capable of producing wines of true complexity and expressiveness. It wasn't easy. "When we started with Aligoté, it was three euros a bottle," he recalls. "The glass and the cork were half of that. It was impossible. No one wanted to *try* them. Not buy them—they wouldn't even try them. If you were an Aligoté grower, you tried to *lose* as little money as possible, not make money."

That's changing, albeit slowly. But one ironic benefit of the lack of love for Aligoté was that vines were never replanted, and old vineyards are still in the ground. That has resulted in, for Pataille, some remarkable finds, and over time he's built up his domaine from the single hectare (2.47 acres) he started with in 1999 to more than thirty-seven acres today (not solely Aligoté; he makes remarkable Marsannay Blanc and Rouge as well). He has been certified organic since 2008 and has worked biodynamically since 2014, but is not certified. "The controllers—the system—is too dogmatic," he says. "I like the method but not the dogma."

He refers to the way he works as the new old Burgundy. "We're producing the wines our grandfathers would have. With low sulfur, with natural yeast, basket pressing—we own six of them—and with fifty-year-old vines because they were never replanted. Back in the 1990s and 2000s, all the critics wanted Pinot Noir to be black, to be oaky; it made some of us lose our identity. In the lab where I was working then, it was a method; make the wines in the Bordeaux and Rhône style. You have to live in your time, this is true. But an honest wine shows the soil of where it's from, the climate, the vintage. Identity is very, very, very important. I don't want my wines to taste like they come from anywhere but here."

Pataille uses only native yeasts and minimal sulfur in his winemaking. "We have to be scientists, but scientists who work traditionally," he says. "I trained as an enologist, with many, many books, but I can't imagine today making wines except with almost no sulfur." To start with, he makes a handful of Aligotés; here are some standouts. The basic **Sylvain Pataille Bourgogne Aligoté ($$)** is a classic, with flavors of fresh quince and vivid acidity. The **Bourgogne Aligoté Les Auvonnes au Pépé ($$)** is more golden apple, rounder, and more smoky. **Bourgogne Aligoté Le Charme aux Prêtres ($$$)** is from, he says, "for me the best cru for Marsannay whites." The soil is marl and limestone, and gives this cool minerality, with strength." Pataille's **Marsannay Blanc ($$$)** has a dancerly elegance, and is flinty and citrusy. His **Marsannay Le Chapitre ($$$)** vibrates with life, all lemon zest, green apple, and stony notes.

Pataille makes one of the world's great rosés, as far as I'm concerned: his **Fleur de Pinot Marsannay Rosé ($$$)**. It's lovely and complex, a Marsannay rosé with the grace of a premier cru red; for it he uses "my best old vines and my best grapes." His **Marsannay La Montagne Rouge ($$$)** suggests roses and dark cherries, with a lot of mouthwatering juiciness. His **Marsannay Clos du Roy ($$$)** is a balance to that: more powerful, with more blue fruit notes and a luscious density. There are several others.

DOMAINE DE VILLAINE • BOUZERON

[certified organic / biodynamic]

Pierre de Benoist co-owns and manages this distinctive domaine located in the often-overlooked Côte Chalonnaise village of Bouzeron. The other owner is his uncle, Aubert de Villaine, the former (as of 2019) director of Domaine de la Romanée-Conti, a name that is never, ever overlooked. But since DRC's most affordable wine runs about $3,000 a bottle—no exaggeration—that domaine is not in this book.

Domaine de Villaine, on the other hand, is. And though Aubert de Villaine is still involved, it's very much de Benoist's show. A bearded, compact man, he's energetic and passionate when he speaks, and deeply devoted to biodynamic viticulture (though he feels the requirements for certification are too formulaic). "For me it's not a culture but a method," he says. "It applies information to the vineyard, a link between the ground—the underground, the under*world*—and the vegetable, the human, and the sky."

Occasionally de Benoit drifts into a philosophical-mystical zone that can be a bit hard to follow, as when he points out that the new part of the cellar respects "the number of God, 1.64444 . . . another magical number, of course. What I wanted to do was build this cellar respecting that number, and also to do it without plans, like the ancient Egyptians with the pyramids. We used water from Bouzeron for the concrete;

I also used some of the lees from our wine in the concrete, to inform the cellar of its purpose. It was a way of asking, how can we apply biodynamics *outside* the vineyard, even to the cellar's construction?"

The lesser status of Bouzeron and the Côte Chalonnaise as a whole, irks him. "I'm sure we have the same level of terroir as the Côte d'Or," he says. "Different terroir, but the same level. After all, we created the first wine trade here, well before the Côte d'Or. But then I come from the Côte Chalonnaise, so of course I would say that." He's quite possibly not wrong: the monks at Cluny planted vines in Bouzeron in the twelfth century, so winemaking here stretches back at least as far as it does in the Côte d'Or. "In the Côte d'Or, they have grand crus." He shrugs. "In Côte Chalonnaise, we simply have great Burgundy."

It's impossible to talk about Bouzeron without talking about Aligoté, Burgundy's other white grape, long maligned and now unexpectedly fashionable again. De Villaine, who purchased the estate in 1971, was an early defender of the variety, and instrumental in helping create the official Bourgogne Aligoté de Bouzeron appellation in 1979 (now just Bouzeron). "When you taste a Bouzeron Aligoté," de Benoist says, "that saltiness it has is expressing the memory of the dead sea that existed in Burgundy two hundred million years ago."

Everything here is vinified in wood rather than stainless steel, most in large, old *foudre* (casks). There are no enzymes, additives, manufactured yeast, and what little sulfur is used at bottling is "volcanic sulfur, a gift from the ground," de Benoist says. Of the many whites, the **Domaine de Villaine Bouzeron ($$)** comes from seventeen small parcels of Aligoté vines averaging sixty-five years old. "It's full of vegetable memory," de Benoist says. (And, orange and ripe apple flavors, with mouthwatering acidity.) The **Rully 1er Cru Margotés ($$$)**, from his coldest cru, has lovely texture and spice, while the **Rully 1er Cru Cloux ($$$)**, from a slightly warmer terroir, is savory, its flavors long and sustained. The **Rully 1er Cru Rabourcé ($$$)** is creamier and richer, showing more orchard fruit character.

Of the reds, the **Bourgogne Côte Chalonnaise La Digoine ($$–$$$)** is aromatic, full of floral berry and stem-spice notes. It's irresistibly juicy and very appealing. The **Rully 1er Cru Cloux Rouge ($$$–$$$$)** has a concentration and depth not usually associated with Rully. The polished **Santenay 1er Cru Passetemps ($$$$)** comes from a vineyard the domaine purchased in 2011. "My ancestor, who created DRC, was a *négociant* from Santenay. I wanted in a small way to open the wine of my ancestor," de Benoist says. In recent years the prices of the Domaine de Villaine wines have risen because of their tangential proximity to the aura of DRC, but they're still well worth seeking out.

DOMAINE ELENI ET EDOUARD VOCORET • CHABLIS

[certified organic]

Eleni and Edouard Vocoret are part of the new generation in Chablis, making profoundly expressive wines from their small domaine effectively on their own. The two met in New Zealand while working harvest and are in every way a team—in the vineyard, in the winery, in life. Except for driving the tractor. "I'm not interested," Eleni Vocoret says. "I don't really enjoy it, and he loves it, so why bother?"

Edouard Vocoret's family has been in Chablis a long time, and his family's holdings amount to 125 acres of vines or so. But he learned winemaking with the organic Mâconnais vigneron Daniel Barraud, whose whole philosophy, Eleni Vocoret says, "was about knowing the vineyard and being able to control the whole process yourself."

As a result, in 2013 the Vocorets—both of whom are winemakers—took over about 12.5 acres of Edouard's family's vineyards, mostly village Chablis plus a tiny amount of premier cru land. "The family was still spraying, so the first thing we did was stop using all herbicides," Eleni says. "Then we changed everything about the farming, step by step." They started working the soil mechanically rather than chemically, changed the pruning method for the vines, minimized the use of tractors, and started harvesting everything by hand. Since 2018, they've been certified organic, and are now using some biodynamic preparations, "to try them out," Eleni says. "We'll see. If we do biodynamics, we'll do it the way we feel and think is good, not the way someone tells us to do it."

They're a tiny operation. Until 2021, it was only the two of them. Since then, they've hired one more person. "It was getting a little bit much," Eleni says. (They also have two small children.) "But we still try to be everywhere all at the same time. It's a cliché, that wine is made in the vineyard, but seriously, it is."

The Vocorets make four wines, but they'll soon be making several more, as they recently took over an additional twelve acres of land from Edouard's family, including vines in the Valmur grand cru and premier cru land in Fôrets, Montée de Tonnerre, and others. "From four, we're going to twelve cuvées," Eleni Vocoret says. "A lot!"

Instead of combining all their village Chablis into one wine, the Vocorets bottle three separate parcel-specific village Chablis. The **Eleni et Edouard Vocoret Chablis Les Pargues** ($$) comes from vines in the next valley over from the premier cru of Montmains, and is classically Chablis in its steeliness and minerality. "It's very straight, almost austere," Eleni says. **Chablis Boucheran** ($$), from two acres of vines between the Vaillons and Montmains premier crus, is more open, "very aromatic and easy to drink," and the **Chablis Bas de Chapelot** ($$), she says, "is the most opulent; it could almost be a premier cru because it has so much structure and volume." It comes from a larger parcel, about eight acres, just below Montée de Tonnerre. Lastly—at least until the wines from their new vineyards are released—the Vocorets make a small amount of **Chablis 1er Cru Les Butteaux** ($$$), from sixty-year-old vines. It's elegant and full of chalky, seashell minerality.

PRODUCERS PROFILED IN THIS CHAPTER

Berthaut-Gerbet
Simon Bize & Fils
Domaine de Cassiopée
Domaine du Cellier aux Moines
Chandon de Briailles
Chantêreves
Domaine Chevrot
Edmond Cornu
Henri Gouges

Thibault Liger-Belair
Bruno Lorenzon
Christian Moreau
Moreau-Naudet
Agnès Paquet
Sylvain Pataille
Domaine de Villaine
Eleni et Edouard Vocoret

OTHER BURGUNDY PRODUCERS TO LOOK FOR

Daniel et Julien Barraud
Château de Beru
Albert Bichot
Domaine de Bongran
Boyer-Martenot
Bret Brothers /
  La Soufrandiere
Philippe Colin
Dominique Cornin
Domaine des Croix
Domaine Dandelion
Joseph Drouhin
Vincent Dureil-Janthial
Jêrome Galeyrand
Génot-Boulanger

A. F. Gros
Guffens-Heynan/Verget
Benjamin Leroux
Claire Naudin
Philippe Pacalet
Petit-Roy
Patrick Piuze
Domaine de Roally
Domaine des Rouges Queues
Olivier Savary
Taupenot-Merme
Camille Thiriet
Domaine Valette
Vins Saisons

CHAMPAGNE

What is there to say about Champagne that the Champenoise haven't already said? The region is home to the greatest sparkling wines on earth, and also the greatest marketers of sparkling wine on earth; Champagne's ability to promote itself has been second to none for generations. That's caused some ironic problems. The name is so universally embedded in people's minds that it's become a general term for any wine with bubbles, much like Kleenex (when's the last time you asked for a "facial tissue"?). As a result, the CIVC (Comité Interprofessionel du vin de Champagne) goes to great, sometimes absurd, lengths to try and stamp out what they see as unapproved use of the Champagne name, as when they threatened in 2013 to sue Apple for proposing to call one of its iPhone colors "Champagne." They also took the Australian wine writer Jayne Powell to court for referring to herself as "Champagne Jayne," apparently for deigning to write about, in addition to Champagne, sparkling wines that weren't Champagne. Powell won; bravo to her.

It would be easy to write the Comité off as overly litigious, if it weren't for the fact that if you *don't* actively try to regulate the trade use of names of products that are inextricably tied to their places of origin—Champagne, Prosciutto di Parma, Roquefort, even Jersey Royal potatoes—then corporations all over the world will happily hijack those words, profiting on their reputation, and soon you will find "Napa Valley Cabernet Sauvignon" that is made in China from grapes grown in Shandong. (Not to single out China; large U.S. wineries did this for years. In fact,

Korbel still makes "California Champagne" thanks to a loophole in the trade rules that grandfather in its label.) The reason Europe has traditionally been far more inclined to regulate names like these is because so many European foods and wines are named for, and defined by, the places they come from.

But of course, real Champagne only comes from the Champagne region in northern France. The residents there certainly do make a lot of it—300 million bottles a year or so, from eighty-four thousand acres of vines, farmed by sixteen thousand different growers. It's worth noting that the vast proportion of those grapes are sold to a handful of giant houses (Moët, Vueve Clicquot, Mumm, Laurent-Perrier, etc.), which are in turn owned by an even smaller handful of giant commercial entities. Which isn't to say that those wines aren't sometimes exceptionally good: Krug makes wonderful Champagnes. But Krug is owned by a mammoth luxury-goods conglomerate (LVMH) worth some $329 billion, which makes me, at least, consider those oh-so-delicate bubbles in a slightly different way.

The great change in Champagne in the recent past has been an alternative to all that: the rise of what's called grower Champagne, or, by irreverent sommeliers and wine geeks, "farmer fizz." Starting in the 2000s, more and more bottles began to appear in wine stores and on restaurant menus from individual estates that grow their own grapes and make and bottle their own wines rather than selling all of their fruit to the large houses (the French term is *récoltant-manipulant* as opposed to *négociant-manipulant*; if the code on the back of a Champagne bottle says RM, then it's from a grower). It's worth noting that many of these grower Champagne producers started much earlier than that—Champagne Pierre Péters started in 1921, for instance—but the explosion of attention is much more recent.

What grower Champagne gives, aside from the in-itself interest of a wine from a specific site or terroir, is some kind of transparency as to how the grapes might have been grown, and, in most cases, winemaking that is more artisanal than industrial. As always, though, *small* doesn't necessarily mean *good*: there are uninteresting grower Champagnes as well, and certainly ones made from conventionally farmed grapes using every technological winemaking trick in the book. Once again, knowing who made it, how they made it, and why they made it the way they did is a wine lover's best weapon.

Champagne was also for many years one of the most chemically farmed regions in

France. Herbicides, systemic pesticides, and chemical fertilizers were standard; even ground-up urban garbage, known as *boues de ville*, was used as fertilizer here from the 1970s to 1990s. (Thankfully, the latter is no longer legal.) And though conventional farming is still the dominant mode, there's progress toward a more responsible overall approach. In recent years, the CIVC adopted a two-ounce lighter bottle as a standard, which doesn't seem like much but actually lowers Champagne's carbon footprint by about eight thousand metric tons; the stated goal is to reduce carbon emissions by 75 percent by 2050. The CIVC also stated in 2018 that they would pursue a ban on herbicides in the region . . . but then they reversed and in 2022 said, "the ban on herbicides will not be included in the Champagne AOC specification." Instead, it is now a "strong goal." Hmm.

Despite all this, there are dozens and dozens of small producers in Champagne, as well as some larger ones, who do farm conscientiously, and who use winemaking processes that aren't reliant on an endless arsenal of industrial enological products. There are exquisite wines to be found here, and plenty of them. And Champagne is a fascinating beast. Because its wines are typically blends of grapes (Chardonnay, Pinot Noir, and Pinot Meunier most prominently, though there are actually seven that are allowed; the others—Pinot Gris, Pinot Blanc, Petit Meslier, and Arbane—constitute under 1 percent of what's grown), and often blends of years, Champagne is most often by its nature a wine of process as much as it is a wine of place. The human hand plays a big role here. How that hand wields its power makes all the difference.

BILLECART-SALMON • CÔTE DES BLANCS

[certified sustainable]

Billecart-Salmon is one of the few remaining family-owned major Champagne houses, owned and operated by the Billecart-Salmon family for more than two hundred years. The Billecarts, who have lived near Mareuil-sur-Aÿ since the 1500s, long owned vineyards in the area. In 1818, Nicolas

François Billecart married Elisabeth Salmon, whose family owned vineyards in the Côte de Blancs village of Chouilly. In short order the couple decided, together with Elisabeth's enologist brother Louis, that a Champagne business might not be a bad idea. Mathieu Roland-Billecart, the house's seventh-generation president, concurs. "We're happiness merchants," he says.

Family, he says, is key. "It brings beautiful things, though sometimes headaches. It's a bit like Christmas dinner with your family all the time. But on the big things, we always agree, and when times get tough, we agree even more. Quality, focus, caring for our people—we always agree on those. But if you change the color of the curtains? Then things get exciting."

But family ownership in itself isn't enough. The family has to be present, too. Roland-Billecart says: "Think of a restaurant. When the chef or owner walks the floor every day, things are better. I'm based at the estate, I live and breathe the estate, and I'm involved in everything from winemaking to grape growing to marketing to sales." So are other family members; there is no board of directors at Billecart, and twice a week the tasting team—five family members, the cellar master, and the vineyard director—meets to assess the wines, taste every single base wine, and agree on every blend. The family has records of every single meeting going back for decades.

Billecart-Salmon owns 247 acres of vineyards, which will be certified organic by 2025 (currently they're certified HVE3, the highest level of the French *Haute Valeur Environmentale* sustainability certification). The house rents another 247 acres, farming those sustainably. Though large compared to grower Champagne producers, Billecart is small in the realm of historic Champagne houses; substantially less than a tenth the size of Moët, for instance.

The non-vintage **Blanc de Blancs Brut ($$$)** is a perfect example of the Billecart style: electric and almost thrumming with energy, minerally and precise. The house is probably most famous for its non-vintage **Rosé Brut ($$$)**, which was first made in the 1840s (the current style comes from the 1970s). It's salmon-hued, creamy, and complex, with red berry and citrus fruit, made with about 7 to 8 percent red Pinot Noir from old vines around Mareuil-sur-Aÿ. The non-vintage **Sous Bois ($$$$)**, unlike most of the Billecart wines, receives a short aging in old oak barrels "to add some roundness," Mathieu Roland-Billecart says. It ages longer than most non-vintage cuvées, about ten years. "By then it's gained what we want the wood to give, not oakiness, but richness, generosity. It loves a twenty-four-month-aged Comté cheese." (I can attest that this is true.) The **Brut Nature ($$$$)**, unlike most brut natures, receives long aging on its lees, to give it more roundness; it's a lovely Champagne, with aromas of brioche, apricots, and tangerine peel, taut but not austere. "Anyone can make brut nature," Roland-Billecart says, "you just zero out the sugar. But to make one that has balance, that's harder." The house's prestige cuvées are expensive, but not brutally so (except for Clos Sainte Hilaire). The **Cuvée Elisabeth Salmon Brut ($$$$)**, to choose one, is one of Champagne's best rosés, made from 55 percent Pinot Noir and 45 percent Chardonnay, with 9 percent red wine. The wine ages on its lees for ten years before release, and is irresistibly complex and aromatic, with flavors that last and last.

DEHOURS ET FILS • VALLÉE DE LA MARNE

[certified sustainable / organic]

Champagne Dehours is, in the end, a happy story. Ludovic Dehours started the estate in 1930, between the wars, and Robert Dehours built it into a respected small grower. But he passed away unexpectedly at fifty, and the family had to go into a joint venture with a financial company to keep afloat. Robert's son Jêrome Dehours, lean, bearded, and thoughtful, recalls that he was still in school at the time: "And when I began to work, they'd taken over the business, they were making all the decisions about how to farm, and I quickly decided that I didn't remotely have the same vision. In 1996, I broke the shackles and made a new start. My family owned a small amount of vineyard land, but I had no clients, no material, no winery, nothing. It wasn't easy!"

The first year, he made five thousand bottles, practically nothing in Champagne terms. Today he farms a little more than thirty-five acres across forty different small plots in the Vallée de la Marne, and makes about one hundred thousand bottles a year—still tiny, in a region where Möet & Chandon makes something on the order of 28 million, but a success story nonetheless.

Dehours works organically; he was also one of the first estates in Champagne to qualify for France's HVE certification. "The idea is work with our conscience first. No chemical products—nothing like herbicides, pesticides, none of that. If we can, we use only copper and sulfur, and we use only natural products for fertilizer as well. But we also try to use only local producers and products. Our philosophy in the cellar is the same, too:

a minimum of interference, a very low level of sulfites, traditional presses, and no enzymes or anything like that at all.

"But still, for me, the crucial thing is the expression of the terroir and the vintage. The problem of environmental pollution is very important, of course. But the life in the soil is, too, because it's critical to the expression of terroir."

Like several other cutting-edge grower Champagne producers, Dehours works with perpetual reserves, created over years (a blend of vintages is kept in a large tank or vat, and a portion drawn off each year, then replaced with an amount of the new vintage). In his Grand Réserve, for instance, the perpetual reserve (which is stored in a large wooden vat) is composed of every vintage from 1998 on. "It's a big question of balance, though," he says. "We're always on a tightrope, trying to balance. Trying not to fall."

The **Dehours et Fils Grande Réserve Brut ($$)** is the estate's flagship cuvée, made 83 percent from the wine of the vintage (predominantly Pinot Meunier, with 25 percent Chardonnay and 8 percent Pinot Noir), with the remainder from the perpetual reserve Jêrome

has created for it. It's also a total steal. The **Brut Nature ($$$)** comes from the same cuvée but with zero dosage, steely and intense. The **Les Vignes de la Vallée ($$$)** ups the percentage of reserve wine to 33 percent and adds substantially more lees aging, giving it a rich, savory depth. The rose-gold **Oeil de Perdrix Rosé Extra Brut ($$$)** is herbal, citrusy, and precise. There are a number of single-vineyard wines, two of which stand out because Dehours decided to create them entirely from perpetual-reserve wine starting in 2013.

The **Brisefer Extra Brut ($$$)** leans toward scintillating green apple and citrus notes, while **La Croix Joly ($$$$)**, from 100 percent old-vine Pinot Meunier from a small plot in Troissy, has a luscious texture that's impossible to resist, even as it remains pinpoint precise.

LARMANDIER-BERNIER • CÔTES DE BLANCS

[certified organic / certified biodynamic]

Pierre and Sophie Larmandier were very early adopters in Champagne of both organic and biodynamic viticulture. Pierre took over his family's small Champagne house in 1988, and realized by the early 1990s that if he was going to have any life left in the soil of their vineyards, he would have to stop using chemicals. As he and Sophie's son Arthur says, "His approach was unusual, because he started doing organics and biodynamics at the same time. He felt that wines he'd tasted that were biodynamic were more pure and expressive, and he wanted that for his wines, too."

Pierre's overall situation was unusual, too. His father had passed away when he was eighteen; when he returned to take over in 1988, his grand-

mother had been running the estate, "at a time when a woman running a Champagne estate was unheard of," Arthur Larmandier notes. "But the result was that he was free to do what he wanted— single-vineyard wines, organic viticulture. My great-uncle actually came to him and said, 'You're going to ruin the estate! You're destroying what your father did!' So many local people spit on him, essentially—they thought he was bringing vine diseases to the entire village, not just the estate. So for ten years he killed himself, working, plowing, while everyone else was just spraying herbicides all the time, even in winter."

Today Pierre Larmandier's efforts have been vindicated. Larmandier-Bernier makes brilliant Blanc de Blanc

Champagnes from its forty-five acres of grand and premier cru vineyards (and one rosé), and has done so while farming biodynamically for more than twenty years. Needless to say, Pierre Larmandier neither destroyed what he'd inherited nor brought ruin to his neighbors' vines. Instead he proved to be a forerunner of what has become an ever-increasing group of Champenoise vignerons working in environmentally responsible ways.

Larmandier-Bernier's two anchor wines are the non-vintage **Larmandier-Bernier Longitude Blanc de Blancs Extra Brut ($$$)** and the **Latitude Blanc de Blancs Extra Brut ($$$)**. Longitude comes from sites with chalk that lies close to the surface, making for a more linear, taut cuvée. "It's a north-south line running from Vertus to Oger to Avize to Cremant," Arthur Larmandier says. It typically is made two-thirds from the current vintage, with one-third being reserve wine from a perpetual cuvée. With Latitude, "the idea was to do something quite rich. So it's the sites with deeper chalk," Arthur says, "where we get grapes with a rounder flavor profile." The blend is similar: two-thirds current vintage, one-third perpetual cuvée. (It's worth noting that "rich" for Larmandier-Bernier is still fairly steely compared to many producers' wines.) The family's **Rosé de Saignée Premier Cru ($$$)** suggests strawberries and red currants, with savory, spicy notes on the end. There are also three single-vineyard vintage wines. The **Terre de Vertus Premier Cru Brut Nature ($$$)** comes from a single plot of vines outside the town of Vertus. It's always made with zero dosage, Arthur says; "at the end you get some tension, some saltiness, which is why we keep it brut nature." **Les Chemins d'Avize ($$$)** has a lovely aroma of sweet citrus blossoms and white peaches, and comes from sixty-five-year-old vines. "It's our smallest production wine." Finally the **Vielle Vigne du Levant ($$$$)** comes from a small east-facing parcel in Cramant known as "Borron de Levant" (the name means sunrise). "The clay in the soil here gives it richer, more buttery notes," Arthur says, and it indeed has a kind of golden aroma and flavor—think nuts, ripe citrus, buttered brioche.

MOUSSÉ FILS • VALLÉE DE LA MARNE

[organic]

Cédric Moussé is one of an ever-growing group of younger talents in Champagne who are reviving the reputation of Pinot Meunier, long considered the country cousin to the more urbane Pinot Noir and Chardonnay that dominate most traditional Champagne blends. "Meunier was a black sheep until twenty years ago," Moussé says. "But that wasn't completely wrong. It's the Champagne variety that can't handle large yields. When nitrate fertilizers arrived, production in Champagne went crazy. It jumped like 30 to 40 percent." That boom in production was great for profits, but not for quality. "Meunier doesn't like to be pushed, so during that period, the wines that came from it just weren't very good. But when we shifted to organic viticulture, we decreased our production 25 percent—and the wines were just . . . *wow*."

The Moussé family has been farming in the Vallée de la Marne, in the town of Cuisles, for five generations. They began making wine under their own name in 1923, during the grim years following World War I. "It was a complicated time for France," Cédric says; an understatement to say the least. "The big brands had no money to buy grapes, so my great-grandfather Eugène had to start making his own

---

> *"We have a revolution going on today in Champagne, a beautiful, pure revolution."*
> —Cédric Moussé

---

wine. But our town was small and poor, and he had no customers. Through that entire period, he and my grandfather would load up a horse and cart with wooden boxes full of twenty-five bottles of wine, and take them to the train station five miles from our house, and send them to Paris. That's how they survived."

During World War II, both Cédric's great-grandfather and his grandfather Edmond were in the French Resistance, and when American or English pilots were shot down and would parachute into the area, "my family would rescue them, and take care of their injuries. The Vallée de la Marne is very hilly—a lot of places to hide. But it was extremely dangerous. My grandfather and his brother were both caught and sent to prison camp. Eugène, my great-grandfather, died at Ravensbrück after eight months. My grandfather Edmond survived at a different camp for eleven months, was finally released, and walked back to France from Germany."

In the 1970s, Cédric's father, Jean-Marc, was one of those who found the new, chemical-driven approach to farming appealing. But Edmond Moussé had never used chemicals, and still had horses for plowing. The two didn't agree, but "my father won the argument and started using chemicals to kill the weeds," Cédric says. "Eight years later, my grandfather organized a tasting of the past fifteen vintages—the vintages before my father started spraying all this shit on the vines, and the vintages after. There was no comparison. After that tasting my father stopped completely; he let the grass grow back in the vineyard. He could taste the decline in the wines, could smell how tired the Meunier was. My grandfather was completely right."

Today the vineyards are organic. Cédric is moving them toward biodynamics, and bringing in more compost and more animals—chickens and sheep, "and I use horses for one plot that's near my house. The animals are all great for the ecosystem as a whole." In the winery, he works without any enological products and only uses tiny amounts of sulfur. "Most sulfur in wine is from the distillation of petroleum products; I developed a machine to burn natural sulfur. It's very pure, and very efficient. With one drop you can protect a large quantity of wine."

He adds, "We have a revolution going on today in Champagne. A beautiful, pure revolution. There are twenty or thirty new growers every year moving over to organics. The problem is that you need seven years to change the vineyard over, and then three or five to change the wine. Everything takes time in Champagne. But this is the direction that everyone is taking."

Cuisles, almost alone in the Vallée de la Marne, lies on a specific type of green clay soil. "It's the same green clay you use in cosmetics, for a mask, and it's ideal for Meunier. I want to make the purest possible expression of that." Moussé's twenty-four acres of vineyards are planted almost exclusively to

Pinot Meunier, with a small percentage of Pinot Noir (12 percent) and an even smaller amount of Chardonnay (3 percent). Moussé's signature and most easily found wine is the nonvintage **L'Or de Eugene Brut ($$)**, a supple melange of orchard fruit flavors and chalky minerality, 80 percent Pinot Meunier and 20 percent Pinot Noir, that's half from the current vintage and half from a perpetual cuvée that he started in 2003. The vintage **Terre d'Illite Brut ($$$)** is named for that green clay in Cuisles; it's 95 percent Meunier with a touch of Pinot Noir, silky but with bright citrus notes. The top wine is the **Special Club Brut ($$$$)**, entirely Meunier from the Les Fortes Terres vineyard, powerful and complex, even opulent in style.

PIERRE PÉTERS • CÔTE DES BLANCS

[organic]

If you want to drink great Champagne from Mesnil-sur-Oger, you can open a bottle of Salon ($1,000) or Krug Clos des Mesnil ($1,500, give or take), or you can leave those bottles to the Elon Musks of the world and delve into the wines of Champagne Pierre Péters.

Rodolphe Péters's family has lived in Mesnil-sur-Oger since the 1850s, first as grape growers and then, starting with Rodolphe's great-grandfather in the late 1800s, making their own wines. Early on, most of what they made wasn't sparkling. "Even the big houses made quite a bit of still wine then," Péters says. "My great-grandfather didn't make sparkling wine until right before World War I. He made the first vintage under his own name, Camille Péters, in 1921." In that era, there were only five or six independent growers in all of Champagne.

Camille Péters passed away during World War II, when his son, Pierre, was only eighteen. Pierre had five younger sisters and a mother to support; Rodolphe says, "He was in charge of the family. So he made the decision to use his own name, and the first vintage of Pierre Péters was 1944."

The Pierre Péters wines are crystalline, taut, mineral-driven Champagnes, made entirely from Chardonnay. Also, the reserve wines used to amplify the depth and complexity of the new vintage are drawn from a perpetual cuvée, similar to a solera in sherry, a method that Rodolphe Péters first proposed to his father in 1997, years before he started actually working at the winery. "I graduated with an enology degree in 1992, but I didn't take over the winery until 2011. I worked for fifteen years at other wineries. That's our mode: one person running the estate, generation after generation. My father would tell me, 'OK, you can come for harvest, you can come for tastings, you can participate in the blending, but you can't actually work here yet.' And I would say, 'Dad, this is crazy. In fifteen years, I am still going to be an apprentice! It's like trying to become a sushi chef.'"

The family farms forty-seven acres, primarily in Mesnil-sur-Oger, but also in Oger, Cramant, and Avize. "I'm not certified, but I've been working organically for eight years now," Rodolphe says. "We also plant using our own genetic material, a massale selection from our own vines. You know, you need a transmitter between the terroir and the wine—that's the vine. And the quality of the vine material decides the purity of that transmission."

He adds, "Pierre Péters is a bigger ship these days. My wife and I try to protect our kids from the pressure of that. 'Do you work with your father? Will you take over the winery when he is gone?' Those questions. People will always ask them, and the answer can be difficult. For me, making wine, running our family's company, that was always my dream. And I've lived it like a dream, a passion. But it *has* to be a passion. It's far too much to do just out of obligation."

Champagne Pierre Péters makes about thirteen thousand cases of wine per year; a reasonable size for a grower, albeit minuscule compared to the large houses. The **Pierre Péters Cuvée de Réserve Brut ($$$)** comes from vineyards in all four of the grand cru towns where Rodolphe grows vines, and is one of the best non-vintage brut Champagnes to be found. The **Réserve Oubliée Brut ($$$$)** has a greater percentage of reserve wines and spends more time on lees, marrying the essential raciness of the Péters style to more developed notes of toasted nuts and honeycomb. **L'Esprit Brut ($$$)**

is the vintage cuvée, fragrant and elegant. **Rosé for Albane Brut ($$$)** was first produced in 2007; before that the domaine only ever made 100 percent Chardonnay Champagnes. Rodolphe Péters named the wine for his daughter, and uses *saignée* Pinot Meunier to create a rosé that's citrusy and floral. The most famous Pierre Péters wine is undoubtedly the **Cuvée Spéciale**

Les Chétillons Brut ($$$$), an extraordinarily complex blanc de blancs that comes from three separate small parcels of old vines in Mesnil-sur-Oger, which Camille Péters had the foresight to purchase back in 1930. Typically released seven years after the vintage, it's one of the great wines of Champagne: beautifully layered, balancing richness and mineral precision effortlessly.

LOUIS ROEDERER • REIMS

[certified sustainable / organic]

Louis Roederer is inarguably one of the great Champagne houses, yet in many ways is one of the most unusual as well. It remains family owned, when most of the major houses are owned by luxury goods conglomerates; two-thirds of the grapes used for its wines come from estate vineyards, vastly more than the usual percentage (the rest are from vineyards farmed under long-term contracts); and all of those estate vineyards benefit from sustainable, organic, and biodynamic practices.

Pinot Noir has long been Roederer's backbone. The first vineyard land

that Louis Roederer bought, in 1845, was in Verzeney. "He was in love with the Pinot Noir from Verzeney," says longtime chef du cave Jean-Baptiste Lécaillon. Pinot accounts for fully two-thirds of Roederer's 605 acres of vines; it also makes up about sixty percent of the blend for Cristal, the house's famed prestige cuvée. (Side note regarding Cristal: It was created for Tsar Alexander II of Russia in 1876, and its bottle has a flat bottom because the tsar, ever wary of assassination, specifically wanted to make sure no one could hide a bomb under it. Ironic second side note: Alexander was in fact killed by a bomb, but it was thrown under his carriage on a street in St. Petersburg.)

Roederer began converting its estate vineyards to organics in the 1990s, Lécaillon says. "In Champagne, in the 1960s and 1970s, with herbicides and pesticides, we destroyed a lot of biodiversity; we destroyed the magic of the soil—the fungi, the bacteria, the weeds, the insects, all the things that work together to create terroir. So we needed to regenerate our soils." The house uses no herbicides or synthetic pesticides, utilizes compost made on-site with biodynamic preparations, and implements herbal tisanes to reduce reliance on copper (approved in organics) by twenty to thirty percent. Half the estate is certified organic; the other half is certified sustainable at the highest level of France's HVE program (and is effectively organic). Lécaillon says, "The more organic you are, the more full of life you are in your soil, and the more difficult it is for a disease or problematic insect to settle there. But my real goal is to make great wines. I can be very proud to have super-organic grapes, but if they don't produce good wine, it's a waste of time."

Roederer makes a broad range of Champagnes. The numbered **Louis Roederer Collection Brut ($$$)**, a multi-vintage blend that's typically sixty or so percent current vintage plus thirty percent wines from a perpetual reserve, is one of the best basic brut cuvées in Champagne. It fulfills Lécaillon's statement that "with all our wines we play on this sweet-sour, acidity-creaminess opposition. It's life-giving." The **Vintage Brut ($$$)** and **Vintage Brut Rosé ($$$)** have a similar stylistic bent, albeit being more expressive of the character of each year; there's also a floral, citrusy **Blanc de Blancs Vintage Brut ($$$$)**. A small amount of **Brut Nature Blanc ($$$$)** comes from 25 acres of biodynamic vines on the property, and is minerally and precise; there's also a similarly electric **Brut Nature Rosé ($$$$)**. And then **Cristal Brut ($$$$)** and **Cristal Brut Rosé ($$$$)**, both pricey (the latter remarkably so), but both thrillingly refined and complex, and both able to age for decades in a cellar.

PRODUCERS PROFILED IN THIS CHAPTER

Billecart-Salmon

Dehours et Fils

Larmandier-Bernier

Moussé Fils

Pierre Péters

Louis Roederer

OTHER CHAMPAGNE PRODUCERS TO LOOK FOR

Agrapart

Françoise Bedel

Bereche & Fils

Bollinger

Cedric Bouchard

Emmanuel Brochet

Chartogne-Taillet

Ulysse Collin

Marie Courtin

Dhondt-Grellet

Pascal Doquet

Doyard

Drappier

Duval-Leroy

Egly-Ouriet

Fleury

Olivier and Marie Horiot

Hugues Godmé

Benoît Lahaye

Laherte Frères

Georges Laval

David Léclapart

Leclerc-Briant

A. Margaine

Jerome Prevost

Louis Roederer

Savart

Jacques Selosse

Vilmart & Cie

Vouette & Sorbée

JURA AND SAVOIE

As you drive along the Route de Trousseau, which is named for a grape that originated in Jura, it's worth knowing that there is also a Route de Poulsard—another grape—in the next town over. And, if you glance over at the right moment, you will see a cement bus shelter where someone has spray-painted "SAVAGNIN POWER!" next to a raised fist, celebrating yet another grape. Wine is at the heart of life here.

Jura is not a forgotten corner of France, but it's close: of the roughly 89 million people who visit the country each year, only a negligible fraction find their way here. As a result, in a world where almost nowhere feels untouched anymore, this tiny slice of eastern France truly does. Tucked between Burgundy and Switzerland, it's a patchwork of vineyards, rolling hills, and farmland. On its eastern border, the land gradually rises into waterfall-strewn outcrops and crags, bucolic and dramatic all at once.

And its wines are fascinating. They're expressions of a tradition that's persisted for centuries, untainted by the lures of industrial production and international style. Yet for decades, almost no Jura wines were bought by anyone outside the region (particularly strange when you consider that Beaune, the heart of Burgundy, is only an hour away). Chardonnay and Pinot Noir, the two great grapes of Burgundy, are also both used to make world-class wines in Jura. Plus, the wines made from Jura's native grapes—the ones that get faux-political graffiti and streets named after them—can be remarkable. That's partly due to the approach traditionally used for making white wine here, in which the vintner allows a thin film of yeast to grow over the surface of the wine in the barrel as it ages. *Sous voile* wines, as they're called (literally, "under a veil"), have a savory, saline, oxidative character that is utterly distinctive.

The Savoie, south of Jura and east of the Rhône, and also bordered by Switzerland, is even less known to most American wine drinkers. It has roughly the same small vine acreage as Jura (about five thousand acres), a similar climate (continental, but influenced by the Alps), yet different grape varieties: Jacquere, Altesse, and Chasselas for whites, Mondeuse and Persan, primarily, for reds. Never heard of them? You aren't alone. But the wines can be compelling: brisk, minerally whites, full of acidic zip, and light-bodied, savory reds, all of which can be found at very modest prices and are definitely worth seeking out.

MICHEL GAHIER · ARBOIS

[natural]

Michel Gahier is a rock star of the natural wine world, but he is one of the most unprepossessing rock stars you might ever encounter.

Knock on the old wooden door that opens onto the main road of Montigny-lès-Arsures, and Gahier may open it. He's lean and professorial, with curly gray hair receding from his high forehead and round, black-rimmed glasses; his gaze is direct and forceful, though his manner is quiet. Inside, the small, stone-walled tasting room has an old table and some wooden

chairs, and empty bottles lined up atop a small cabinet. On one wall there's a colorful poster, an old advertisement for absinthe, with an elderly roué in a pointy hat and ruffled collar reaching for a pretty, red-haired, absinthe-drinking girl in a nineteenth-century dress. "*Absinthe Parisienne. Bois, donc tu verras après*"—"Drink, so you'll see later" indeed.

Gahier has been making wine for more than thirty-five years. His parents also made wine, and grew grains, and raised cattle for meat and milk.

"They would grow what they ate," he says. But when Gahier himself was getting started, he says, his primary problem was that he hadn't figured out yet what *not* to do. A winemaker neighbor, from his father's generation, lived next door and would watch him work. One time when Gahier was vinifying some red wine, the neighbor waved him over. "What you're doing is an absolute mess," he told the young vintner. The older man's recipe was simple: don't touch the wines. Gahier says now, "When you're young, you do a lot to make the most beautiful wines, and as you get older you learn to do nothing."

He adds: "There's no approach. What I do is simple. Most of the work is in the vines. We make the wine, we put it in *foudre*, and when it's ready we bottle." He stopped using sulfur more than twenty years ago, partly pushed that way by a notable local chef, who yelled at him at one point, "Don't put that shit in your wines the way the rest of them do!" Gahier smiles at the memory. "He was huge—four hundred pounds—and when he yelled you could really hear him. He was like a bear. *'Don't use chemicals, it's just crap!'* He would express *very clearly* when he did not like something."

Though Gahier has seen Jura wines rise from utterly forgotten to having an actual following once again, it's been a long road. "I only kept going because I was young then, and I was very lucky to meet a few people who would taste and think, 'Hmm—what's going to happen to these wines in twenty to thirty years?' They knew they would last; *I* knew they would last. I make real wines that can age, not Mickey Mouse wines that die after four years."

Gahier farms about twenty acres of vineyards around Montigny-lès-Arsures, using no chemical fertilizers or pesticides of any kind, working by hand. "I don't follow any sort of label. It's not organic, it's not biodynamic. I follow the moon, and I do it my own way. I just want to make good wines like the older generation did." He knows his vineyards intimately, knows the rocks that populate the soil. Taste with him, and he'll use the wall of the

> *"With wine, you have to choose: Are you a farmer, or a businessman? Because once you start talking about business, there's no point in talking about terroir."*
> —Michel Gahier

tasting room as show-and-tell. "The benefit of having a home built by poor people is that you have all the rocks from around the area," he says. "The bits and pieces. Only the rich people get the nice, even stones."

———

Gahier's **Chardonnay Les Follasses ($$)**, like all his wines, is made in Jura's classic oxidative style, aging *sous voile* under a veil of yeast, its green apple and quince notes edged with hazelnut and honey. "You can drink it in its youth, but it also ages well, Chardonnay grown on white marl," he says. The **Chardonnay Les Crets ($$)** comes from a hilltop vineyard full of red clay. "The clay retains water, which helps the wine's acidity," he says, and the wine is indeed electrically bright on the palate, with spiced apple and a touch of caramel. The **Chardonnay La Faquette ($$–$$$)** is savory, with light yeasty notes and a distinctive saltiness. It ages for one year in large *foudre*, then a further three years in smaller barrels *sous voile*. "If you want to make wines like this, you can't use chemistry," Gahier says.

Thirty-year-old Trousseau vines are the source for his red **Le Clousot Trousseau ($$)**, a lightly funky, strawberry-earthy red, juicy and wildly drinkable. The **La Vigne de Louis Trousseau ($$)** offers similar strawberry character with tingly lemony acidity. From older vines, it's a wine meant to age, Gahier says. Finally, there's the **La Grands Vergers Trousseau ($$–$$$)**, from sixty- to seventy-year-old vines on a gentle slope with superb sun exposure. Gahier considers this to be his greatest red. It's savory and complex, definitely has a little reductive funkiness when young, and is full of wild red berry flavors and licorice accents.

VIGNERONS LES MATHENY • ARBOIS

[organic / natural]

It's unclear when you meet him whether Emeric Foléat ever actually sits down. He's extraordinarily animated, constantly talking with his hands, with an infectious, impish smile and, seemingly, an opinion about everything on earth. But for all that he is a modest winegrower: "You have to be humble at all times," he says. "If someone tells you that you're making amazing wines, you have to remember that it is still just wine."

Foléat's stone-walled cellar, in an old farmhouse off a side street in his tiny hometown, is the size of the average American garage. Old barrels and a few small tanks fill the space; an upturned barrel serves as a table. He farms without synthetic chemicals, essentially working organically, but is disinclined to fit himself into any particular camp: "We all want to save the world, but we all have iPhones in our pockets. People want labels. They should want authenticity instead."

Foléat's winemaking is similarly uncategorizable. He vinifies each of his parcels separately, allowing them to develop at their own pace in old, neutral *tonneaux* (large, nine-hundred-liter barrels), sometimes leaving parcels aside to age on their own and be bottled separately, allowing some to develop a *voile* of yeast, some not; it's almost impossible to generalize about his approach. He's also not dogmatic; he uses minimal amounts of sulfur, but also feels the natural wine world's concerns about it are overstated. "My grandfather, when he was in the Resistance during the war, hiding in the woods from the Germans, sometimes had to go six days without food. He didn't ask if there was sulfur on the vegetables he ate; if he could find anything to eat, he ate it. We create our own problems." The goal instead, he says, should be to create the cleanest wine possible with the fruit you are given each year to work with. He also points out that problems like how much sulfur to use are fairly insignificant ones, comparatively, and tells another story. One day when he was a teenager, he was chopping wood, helping out his grandfather. After a few hours he said, just as a general complaint, "Man, I'm dying of hunger." His grandfather promptly grabbed a stick, whacked him with it, and yelled, "You have no idea what it's like to feel hunger!" Point taken.

The **Vignerons les Matheny Arbois Chardonnay ($$)** is typically deep gold in hue, earthy and honey-tinged, a savory, focused, full-bodied white. The red **Poulsard ($$)** is darker and more robust than many Jura versions, intense with meaty strawberry flavors and substantial tannins. The winery's **Trousseau ($$)** is similarly dialed up, with darkly sweet fruit and earthy tannins; it's almost fierce on release. "Come back in fifteen years, then drink it," Foléat quips. His **Vin Jaune ($$$)** is less yeasty than some, suggesting dried straw on the nose; it's fine and complex, with nut-skin and earth notes.

DOMAINE DE MONTBOURGEAU · L'ETOILE

[organic]

Picture a classic French country house, with climbing vines on its cream-colored walls turning scarlet in the late November grayness. It lies down a long drive from an old gate; the first thing you see through the trees is the slate shingles of the roof. The proprietor here is Nicole Deriaux. In her late fifties, she's direct and friendly, though it's hard to miss the force of will behind the modest demeanor.

Montbourgeau lies just outside the village of L'Etoile in the southwestern part of Jura, which gets its name, almost certainly, from the abundance of tiny starfish fossils in the soil here—when I was there, Deriaux brought out a box of them she'd collected over the years and tipped them out onto the wooden table in her tasting room. They looked like prizes a child might find in a box of cereal, though they were 180 million years old or so.

The vines here, Chardonnay and

Savagnin, roll down the hillsides onto the flats near the cellar. "There's no label saying so, but we work organically," Deriaux says. "We do have one plot we can't farm with a tractor, so we're thinking of using horses—if we do, we might ask for the certification. It takes working seven days a week. I couldn't do that before, but now that my sons Cesar and Batiste are here full-time, we can."

The old cellar under the house is full of wooden *foudre*, traditional large wooden casks. "It's important that wine sees wood rather than steel," she says. "I can't say why, but it's important. The wines just taste a bit more pure." She

and César, who is now the full-time winemaker, did a blind trial in 2020 to confirm this feeling: wood won. Her other son, Batiste, concentrates on the viticulture. Their presence has allowed Deriaux to relax a bit more. "We live and work in the same place, so work-life balance is always an issue. If you have dinner, do you talk about work? At breakfast? My father and I could never keep work and life separate. But for years my sister and I had an old dream of having a swimming pool—ever since we were children. And now we have one! It definitely helps with getting away from work. Even if you can still see the cellar from it."

The Montbourgeau wines are made in the classic *sous voile* style of Jura, giving them a deeply savory tang that's unmistakable. They are aged in barrel, never racked, never topped off. It's a deeply old-school, traditional approach," Deriaux says. "Why was it created? Who knows! Because people in Jura were lazy? They used to forget the wines for months. Or maybe it was simply to make something different from Burgundy."

The **Domaine de Montbourgeau**

Chardonnay l'Etoile ($$) is light gold, crisp and clean, with a faint, delicate yeastiness and orchard fruit flavors. **L'Etoile En Banode ($$)** comes from a single parcel of Chardonnay and Savagnin planted by Jean Gros in 1970. "My father loved Chardonnay," Deriaux says. "He was like the wines he liked. Big, round, joyful; he was a very joyful man." It's less driven by *voile* yeastiness, very finely nuanced, with citrus and green apple and lots of salinity on the end. The winery's

Savagnin ($$) is pungent and earthy, a high-acid white that's very lemony, lifted and tart. The **Cuvée Spéciale ($$)** is Montbourgeau's top Chardonnay. "It's a simple vinification: the juice goes into wood, there's alcoholic fermentation in barrel, malolactic in the spring, then aging on lees. That's all. Four years later, you have your wine." With its deep *voile* character, lemon peel and fresh-turned earth notes, and electric zestiness on the palate, it's one of those wake-up bottles that makes you think "wow!" and "this is fascinating." Montbourgeau also makes a classic **Vin Jaune ($$$)**, made entirely from late-harvested Savagnin, aged for at least seven years before release. It's earthy and complex, smelling at times of smoke, dried pears, and/or cheese rind, endlessly complex.

DOMAINE RATTE • ARBOIS

[certified organic / certified biodynamic]

Domaine Ratte occupies a small winery space in an industrial block on the outskirts of Arbois, flanked by a car repair garage and a building supply store. It's unpretentious and direct, just like Françoise Ratte, who with her husband, Michel-Henry, makes a range of ambitious reds and whites from roughly twenty-two acres of vines, half of which are more than seventy years old. The couple farms biodynamically. Françoise's reasons for this are environmental but also personal: "My father died from chemicals," she says.

"He sprayed in the vineyards with no mask, no suit. But *everyone* did. You have to understand, for his generation, for my father and his friends, the chemicals were magic. No rot, no disease, no weeds. But they were not good for him."

As a result, no chemicals have touched the Ratte vines since Françoise and Michel-Henri took over, and they never will. They also stick to low-intervention winemaking, borrowing from old traditions—for example, they destem their grapes in the vineyards, using wooden racks designed for that purpose, a method that probably last had popularity before World War I. "We try for a very minimum of manipulation," Françoise says. "We don't use

> "For his generation, for my father and his friends, the chemicals were magic. No rot, no disease, no weeds. But they were not good for him."
> —Françoise Ratte

much new wood, because our wines have energy without it. And just enough sulfur at bottling—one or two grams—that we're able to sleep at night."

These are natural wines, but they are not "natural" wines: precise, energetic, cleanly made, vivid, but not funky or outré. They're also, despite the basically old-school nature of the operation here, modern in style, in that the Rattes do not work in the *sous voile* oxidative tradition. Instead they make what are termed *ouillé* wines, without long-term oxygen contact . . . which is to say more or less the way wines are made everywhere *but* Jura. It's a kind of reverse contrarian approach, but for Françoise the main point is that the Ratte wines are made the way that she and Michel-Henri like them.

The basic **Domaine Ratte Chardonnay ($$)** is full-bodied, with great limey acidity; in contrast, the **La Regole Chardonnay ($$)**, from chalkier soil, has a savory character, deeply mineral and lemon-zesty. The **Grand Curoulet Melon d'Arbois ($$)** comes from a small parcel of land marked by an abundance of fossilized oysters in the ground; whether that directly affects its bright apple-quince flavors and minerally, saline finish can be debated, but there's no debate that it's a lovely white wine. The **Arbois Savagnin**

Naturé Ouilé ($$)—*Naturé* is the old name for Savagnin, Françoise says—has a pineapple-upside-down-cake scent and a pleasing zap of acidity, with lots of tingly mineral notes on the finish. And the **Arbois Trousseau Les Corvées ($$)** comes from an old variant known as Trousseau a la Dame. "Very tiny berries, very thick skin," Françoise says, "so you have more color and body than classic Trousseau." Pure, clear ruby in hue, all raspberry liqueur and smoky earth, lifted by vivid acidity, it's a thrilling Jura red.

DOMAINE DE LA RENARDIÈRE • ARBOIS

[certified organic / biodynamic]

A stop to see Jean-Michel Petit in the tiny town of Pupillin is a joy, not just because his wines are delightful, but because Petit has a wicked sense of humor and a disinclination to edit himself in the slightest. After an hour, you will know what he thinks about a lot of things, and you'll probably have been laughing half the time as well. He farms according to biodynamic principles, but has zero interest in getting certified: "Demeter [the biodynamics organization] charges 450 euros a year, so I said, 'Bullshit!' Doing biodynamics doesn't cost anything. Cow shit? We have plenty of cow shit in Jura. Plus, I can't get certified because about 20 percent of my vineyards are biodynamic, they're organic and experimental. Certification? *Pfff.* I need to pay some people to come judge the decisions I make?"

Official certification or not, though, he's convinced of the value of this way of working. "My friend, a soil scientist, said, 'Jean-Michel, please, not you—biodynamics is crap!' But two years ago, he tested our soils. He came back shamefaced, because the lab had run the tests twice, and the organic matter was far greater in the biodynamic soil both times. 'I'm a scientist,' he told me, 'and I can't believe this but . . .'"

Petit established Renardière in 1990, and today farms eighteen and a half acres of vineyard, all of which is certified organic (Demeter's certification can go to hell, but apparently organic certification is OK; who needs consistency?).

Much of the vineyard land that Petit farms is old vines, and it took several years, he says, to understand the nuances of the different sites. "I thought when I started, because I got my vines from old farmers, they'd explain the terroir to me. But it was like, 'Oh, Chardonnay from here, Chardonnay from there, we just blend them.' I had to learn the harmony between the grape vine, the soil, and the terroir myself."

Petit's wines come to the U.S. in very tiny quantities, but if you see a bottle, nab it. The **Domaine de la Renardière Arbois Chardonnay ($$)** is fresh and bright, with lemony acidity and a hint of creaminess. The **Cuvée Jurassique Chardonnay ($$)**, from twenty-year-old vines on limestone soils, has more mouth presence—it's a bit oilier, in a good way—with green apple and citrus flavors. The **Les Vianderies Old Vine Chardonnay ($$$)** is usually riper and a bit more flamboyant, the apple flavors shading from green to red. Petit's **Ploussard ($$)** is a pure pleasure, pale transparent ruby-hued,

with spicy strawberry flavors and hints of anise. The **Trousseau a la Dame ($$)** is earthier and softer. Finally, there's an impressive **Vin Jaune ($$$)**, all pungent *sous voile* notes and savory flavors, plus a distinct orange peel character. "You know how you take orange peels and put them on the radiator, and it makes the whole room smell good?" Petit says. "That's what I'm looking for when I smell barrels of Vin Jaune."

DOMAINE ANDRÉ ET MIREILLE TISSOT • ARBOIS

[certified organic / certified biodynamic]

If you say that you'd like to come by and taste with Stéphane Tissot, and that you're leaving a generous two hours for the appointment, people who know him will laugh and say, "You'll be there for four, at least." On my visit in 2019, Tissot talked animatedly as we wound through barrels, *foudre*, tanks, and amphorae in the crazy quilt of rooms and passages that is his cellar. He'd happily amalgamated several different groups for tasting—a journalist or two, a young French chef and his team from Paris, a couple of Chinese wine collectors. The

entire group wound up at a long table with a couple of bottles on it . . . which turned into five bottles . . . which turned into ten . . . more and more arrived. In the end there was a line of thirty bottles, stretching the length of the table. Tissot poured, talked, sat on the edge of the table, stood, gestured, tasted, drank. His wines' energy is only matched by the energy of their maker. Four (yes) hours passed swiftly. It was one of those long, joyous tastings where, when you finally leave, you find that you walked in at full daylight and now it is night.

Stéphane Tissot's father, Andre, and mother, Mireille, founded the domaine in 1962. Stéphane started working there in 1989, took over the viticulture in 1995, and later took on the winemaking as well. Today he and his wife, Bénédicte, farm 125 acres of vineyard, scattered from Château Chalon to the north of Jura (but mostly in Montigny). He's received substantial acclaim for his wines, but unlike those of similar Jura stars Overnoy and Ganevat, prices largely remain under $100. There are a dizzying number of cuvées, all precise, vivid expressions of local terroir.

A moment that changed Tissot came in 1991, when he went to Australia to work a harvest as an intern. There, he realized that the winery where he was working was using exactly the same manufactured yeast that his family was using back in Jura. "The same bag, the same company, the same strain. I thought, 'Something is wrong here,'" he says. That moment pushed him toward the use of native yeasts and spontaneous fermentation, and in 1995 toward organic (and later biodynamic) viticulture. As he has written, "The industrialization of wine is the end of all these identities, these nuances, these characteristics that are part of the magic of a bottle."

Stéphane Tissot's wines are excellent across the board. In general, Tissot uses new oak sparingly and minimal sulfur only at bottling (zero sulfur for reds), and makes a surprisingly high percentage of sparkling crémant (about 25 to 40 percent of his total production). Unlike many Jura vignerons, he also makes a substantial amount of wine overall, so Tissot bottles are findable, at least with a modest amount of searching.

His **Crémant de Jura Indigène** (\$\$) is a lively, effervescent blend of Chardonnay, Pinot Noir, Trousseau, and Poulsard, full of honeysuckle and citrus flavors. The **Arbois Chardonnay Patchwork** (\$\$) is a blend from many of his vineyards, full-bodied but zesty, with citrus and stony notes.

His single-vineyard Chardonnays are a fascinating study in terroir, because they're typically all made exactly the same way, with the same percentage of new oak (12 percent); in effect, they offer a master class in soil character. The **Côtes du Jura Chardonnay Sursis** (\$\$\$) comes from vines in Château Chalon planted on *lias*, a clay soil dating from between the Triassic and Jurassic eras. Lots of reductive flinty notes here; lots of citrus; a savory finish. His **Arbois Chardonnay Les Bruyères ($$$)** is from a vineyard defined by *trias*, an older clay soil. Tissot says, "With *trias*, you don't have the citrus character of *lias*; it's more a smoky, rustic personality." Bruyères tends to be more powerful, more earthy, and, yes, smoky in nature. The **Arbois Chardonnay Clos de la Tour de Curon ($$$$)**, his top wine, comes from limestone soils and is entirely different: more delicate, with white peach and floral notes. (Its seeming lightness is deceptive: it ages beautifully.)

For reds, the **Arbois Rouge Cuvée D.D. ($$)** is 40 percent Pinot Noir, 40 percent Poulsard, and 20 percent Trousseau, a lightly feral, tingly wine with vivid wild berry fruit. The **Singulier Trousseau ($$)** is less funky and more delicate, with raspberry pastille notes and lovely transparency. Tissot also makes two amphora wines, the juicy, ebullient **Poulsard en Amphore ($$)** and the silky **Trousseau en Amphore ($$)**, whose flavor hints at cured meat but is primarily luscious strawberry-raspberry fruit: "Amphoras bring a sweetness to the wines," he says. There's also the polished, complex **Arbois Pinot Noir En Barberon ($$)**, made with whole-cluster fermentation from grapes grown on clay—"The clay soils strengthen the wine's spice," Tissot says.

PRODUCERS PROFILED IN THIS CHAPTER

Michel Gahier

Vignerons les Matheny

Domaine de Montbourgeau

Domaine Ratte

Domaine de la Renardière

Domaine André et Mireille
Tissot

OTHER JURA AND SAVOIE PRODUCERS TO LOOK FOR

JURA

Domaine Berthet-Bondet

Domaine de la Borde

Croix & Courbet

Domaine Désiré

Joseph Dorbon

Domaine Labet

L'Octavin

Domaine Overnoy-Cricquand

Domaine Pignier

Domaine de la Touraize

Domaine de la Tournelle

SAVOIE

Domaine des Ardoisieres

Patrick Bottex

Domaine les Hauts Lieux

Domaine Labbé

Domaine Louis Magnin

Vignes de Paradis

André & Michel Quenard

Renardat-Fâche

LANGUEDOC-ROUSSILLON

The Languedoc makes more wine than any other region in France. It's vast, stretching from just above the town of Perpignan in the west to around Nîmes in the east, hugging the Mediterranean shore all the way. For many, many years it was known for oceans of light red *vin de table*, the staple drink of every French household, bistro, and bar. In 1980, one out of two adults in France drank at least one glass of wine a day—these days consumption is far lower—and much of that came from Languedoc, millions upon millions of glasses.

The French coined the phrase *"plus ça change, plus c'est la même chose"* ("the more things change, the more they stay the same")—but no. Things *have* changed for Languedoc. While it still produces a vast amount of wine, something that seven hundred thousand acres of vineyards will allow you to do, Languedoc now has more organic vineyard land than any other French region, some seventy thousand acres, nearly a third of the total for the entire country. Yields have been reduced from the once spectacularly high levels of the 1970s and 1980s across much of the region; winemaking has improved; and the sheer affordability of land compared to more prestigious regions has drawn any number of independent vintners here, especially to hillside sites along the northern borders of the region. Languedoc's subregions gradually achieved their own identities, with places like Faugères, La Livinière, and Pic St. Loup becoming official sub-appellations (and producing, often, excellent wine). Climate change is an issue—the region has always been warm, and in the past thirty years harvest dates have advanced three weeks earlier, with temperatures in the region sometimes reaching 115 degrees or higher—but even so, the lack of humidity makes Languedoc ideal for organic grape growing.

Without question, there's still plenty of inexpensive, relatively anonymous wine made here. It's no longer so much carafes of *vin de table* as it is internationally marketed, branded wines such as Fat Bastard and Red Bicyclette, perfectly quaffable but not very interesting; so is Diet Coke. Then there are interesting characters like Gérard Bertrand, who, while he does make a huge amount of affordable Languedoc reds, whites, and rosés from purchased fruit, also owns more certified biodynamic vineyards than anyone else in France. And then there are estates along the model of the groundbreaking Mas de Daumas Gassac, which Aimé Guibert founded in the mid-1970s intending to prove that Languedoc could be the source of world-class wines, not just everyday plonk. He more than succeeded, and has been followed by dozens (if not more) equally ambitious vignerons.

Languedoc and Roussillon are often mentioned in the same breath (literally as a hyphenate, Languedoc-Roussillon) but are in truth quite different. First, there's the matter of scale: Languedoc dwarfs Roussillon's production, making nine times as much wine. The terrain is also different: Roussillon is tucked up against the Spanish border, a realm of sloping river valleys surrounded by mountains, the snowcapped Pyrenees rising to the west, and the Corbières Massif and Albera Massif flanking them. There's also less concentration solely on vineyards in Roussillon than in Languedoc, with peach and nectarine orchards here and there, and plenty of Spanish influence as well (many of the residents speak Catalan); its robust red wines go as well with the local *Boeuf a la Catalane* as they do with cassoulet.

GÉRARD BERTRAND • LANGUEDOC

[certified organic / certified biodynamic (depending on estate)]

Gérard Bertrand farms more biodynamic vines than any other producer in France, and possibly more than any other in the world—more than 2,400 acres. Given the painstaking handwork involved in biodynamic farming, that's a truly remarkable feat (and he's still increasing that acreage).

Bertrand, a charismatic, six-foot-four former professional rugby player, grew up in Languedoc, near Narbonne; his father and grandfather both made wine. He came to biodynamics because of health issues. "I had a liver issue when I was twenty-two, which for a winemaker is a problem—and for a Frenchman is a disaster!" he says. "It was until I consulted with a homeopathic doctor that I felt healed. I saw the change that it made in my life, and it inspired me to be open and curious about what plant treatments could

do for the health of my vines and the soil. I experimented first at our family home in Cigalus; the results were remarkable." That was twenty years ago; since then he's never wavered on his course.

The crucial consideration, for Bertrand as for other biodynamic growers, is soil life. "Biodynamic farming goes much further than organic farming," Bertrand says. "We view the soil as a living organism to be treated with respect and use biodiversity as a barometer for how well we get this right. Biodynamics is also an approach that recognizes our place within the ecosystem, adding a spiritual dimension to the relationship between the land and those of us on my team working on it. Ultimately, I feel, this brings an awareness to how we relate to our environment and our impact on everything around us."

Bertrand makes an enormous amount of wine, not all of it biodynamic (his most inexpensive wines use quite a bit of purchased/*négociant* fruit). But a

surprising amount is. While his widely available, citrusy **Change Sauvignon Blanc ($)** is not certified biodynamic, the fruit for it is certified organic. Of the biodynamic whites, the **Domaine l'Aigle Chardonnay ($$)** is fresh and bright, with peachy notes. The **Château l'Hospitalet Grand Vin Blanc ($$)** blends Vermentino, Roussanne, Viognier, and Bourboulenc and is full of ripe orchard fruit flavors, accented by white pepper. **Cigalus Blanc ($$–$$$)** from his home estate, is an unusual (and surprisingly successful) blend of Chardonnay, Sauvignon Blanc, and Viognier, a kind of southern French mashtape of Bordeaux, Burgundy, and Rhône influences.

Of the reds, the certified organic **Naturae Cabernet Sauvignon ($)** is a reliable bargain. For the biodynamic wines, look for the red-fruited **Domaine de l'Aigle Pinot Noir ($$)**; the richly spicy **Château l'Hospitalet Grand Vin Rouge ($$)**, a blend of Syrah, Grenache, and Mourvèdre; and the polished, black-fruited **Cigalus Rouge ($$–$$$)**, among others.

CHÂTEAU MARIS • MINERVOIS LA LIVINIÈRE

[certified organic / certified biodynamic / regenerative]

On a basic level, the origin story of Château Maris is a familiar one: wine lover decides to make wine. As always, the details give it shape. In 1988, British Robert Eden was working for the late wine broker and Burgundy guru Becky Wasserman. He first discovered the wines of the Languedoc when he was seeking out good-value Chardonnays for customers, and focused in on the wines of La Livinière. "I had a tasting group—we were young, so we were *extremely* serious," he says with a laugh. "La Livinière kept producing wines in the style that I liked, and then on one trip down there I had the misfortune of meeting a real estate broker . . ." What can you do?

Languedoc is a far less expensive place to buy land than regions like Burgundy. Château Maris was in the village of La Livinière; there was no pretty house, no beautiful view, "and there weren't many buyers for an ugly property with no vines nearby and a rundown cellar," Eden recalls. But in

1997, together with his financial partner Kevin Parker, he bought the property.

That first year he made wine that tasted awful. Fine: it was a terrible year in Languedoc. But the next year, 1998, was a great vintage, and the grapes Eden harvested *still* tasted awful. A friend asked him if he'd tested his soil. "I remember thinking, 'I'm in France, what are you talking about? It's the best soil in the world!' But we tested our soil and discovered it was deader than the road outside. Zero organic matter, very heavy traces of chemicals—pesticides, herbicides, synthetic fertilizers, even some that had been banned ten years earlier. It was in a disastrous state. But the beautiful thing is that you can regenerate life into soil. You can bring it back."

The initial answer was manure. *Lots* of manure. "Probably more than sixteen hundred tons of it," Eden says. "We were farming close to two hundred acres then, and putting ten tons of compost on it per year, and every ten tons of compost needs twenty tons of manure. That's a lot of shit. And it steams! It doesn't sit there quietly in a corner. We take up residence in La Livinière and it's 'Hey, here's what the Englishman is bringing to the village, a giant pile of shit.' It didn't exactly make me popular."

But it did bring the soil back to life. It was also the start of Eden's dive into biodynamic viticulture. "When I started, my understanding of the plant-soil relationship was pretty poor. I just didn't connect the health of the soil to the health of the plant and to the taste of what it produces," he says now. "Nature is naturally resilient. A vine doesn't need us to survive. But we can definitely fuck it up."

As with other people who've headed down the same path, biodynamics became a part of Eden's life. "It's a philosophy that actually grabs you in the end. You appreciate the plant—vegetable life—as a very sensitive being. It becomes spiritual because every spirit is important. And look, when you farm using an abundance of chemicals, it's not healthy—not for the people who are consuming what you grow, and not for the people working in the field, either! One of the most important reasons I went organic, and then biodynamic, was to stop my workers from inhaling all these poisons. We need to preserve each other as well as the natural world."

Recently, Eden built a new winery for Maris. It's entirely made from hemp (specifically hemp bricks, made with lime and a molasses-based fixer). "Our earlier winery was this very successful concrete building, filled with stainless steel, energy-consuming lights, and so on. But I realized that it had nothing whatsoever to do with what we were doing in the vineyards. They were two different religions! The gods weren't even similar. What we have now is a plant-based, recyclable building. You could knock it down and toss the bricks into the vineyard and the soil would love it." Because the hemp works as insulation, Château Maris requires no air-conditioning; a grass roof provides insulation; the veranda is covered with solar cells, which provide all needed energy; rainwater is collected, and dirty water from wine production is recycled. There's really no other winery like it. Eden is justifiably proud, but recognizes that it's only one person's effort. "Humans are messing things up, and at a rapid rate. But I try to do what I can in my space. I often use this quote from Jane Goodall: 'Every single person every single day can make a difference.' I try to make a positive difference in the environment for future generations. And if that inspires others, great."

Château Maris makes a wide range of wines from 111 acres of estate vineyard, plus a number of other wines from purchased fruit (these have organic but not biodynamic certification). The *négociant* wines, labeled simply Maris, can be remarkable deals: the red-fruited, medium-bodied **Maris Rouge Blend** (\$), a combo of Merlot and Syrah, is hard to beat at the price; so, too, the lime-zesty **Maris Vermentino** (\$) and the juicy Syrah-Grenache blend **Le Zulu** (\$–\$\$). There are several others.

Of the estate wines, **La Touge** (\$\$) is a complete steal: a smoky, black-fruited, black-peppery blend of 70 percent Syrah and 30 percent Grenache, with supple tannins, that's typically findable for just over \$20. **Les Planels** (\$\$) comes from thirty-five-plus-year-old, terraced Syrah vines and balances herbal garigue notes against ripe black currant and blackberry fruit. The estate's top wine, the plush **Les Amandiers** (\$\$\$), comes from a 2.5-acre plot of old-vine Syrah and is full of enveloping blue fruit and spice notes (and a good smack of new oak—allow it a few years in the cellar or some time in a decanter to mellow). Robert Eden says, "With Syrah in La Livinière you get a lot of the power of the heat of the south, but you get this freshness from the Montagne Noire behind us. That's the typical characteristic of the variety here."

MAS DE DAUMAS GASSAC • LANGUEDOC

[organic]

Mas de Daumas Gassac started making world-class wines in the Languedoc when no one, anywhere, thought that the region was good for anything other than generic French table wine. That attitude has changed, largely thanks to the singular vision of Aimé Guibert. He was still overseeing his family's glove business in Millau when, one weekend in 1970, he and his wife, Véronique, were driving through the Hérault countryside. A bar owner tipped them off to an old *mas* (farmhouse) for sale in the Gassac river valley. When they stopped by, it was a classic *coup de foudre*, at least in a real estate context.

Grapes had grown on the property since the time of Charlemagne, but the vines had long been abandoned. So the Guiberts weren't sure what to plant—melons, asparagus, possibly other vegetables? Samuel Guibert, who now runs Daumas Gassac with his siblings, recalls that "they were good friends with the dean of the enology school of the University of Bordeaux, so they asked him, 'Should we plant carrots or potatoes?'

He came down, walked the property, and told them, 'I have found in this valley something I've never seen anywhere else in Languedoc. It's a terroir that will allow you to create a truly great wine.' Which is why you can now taste a twenty-year-old wine from us instead of twenty-year-old asparagus."

The Guiberts followed the dean's advice and planted vineyards, but even though the greatest enologist of the time, Emile Peynaud, signed on in 1978 to make their first vintage, the reputation of the region was so dire that wine merchants simply refused to sell the Guiberts' wine. That lasted until 1982, when the French magazine *Gault & Millau* described Damas Gassac as "the Château Lafite of the Languedoc." International acclaim soon followed, and the Guiberts—and the dean—were vindicated.

The Daumas Gassac vineyards cover just under one hundred acres, scattered in small plots amid the local scrub and forest; Aimé Guibert was very keen from the start not to destroy the diversity of the native plant and animal life. The domaine is organic, and always has been (not certified, though, as Aimé disliked bureaucrats of any kind). "We inherited a land free from chemicals at Daumas Gassac, and we've kept it that way," Samuel Guibert says.

Mas de Daumas Gassac's fame is founded on its eponymous red, the **Mas de Daumas Gassac Rouge ($$$)**. Like the vineyard itself, it's primarily Cabernet Sauvignon (75 percent) with a whole host of other varieties. Focused and cedary, more red-fruited than black, it can be austere when young, but is able to age effortlessly for decades, picking up notes of warm spice, dried herb, and tea leaf. There's also the **Mas de Daumas Gassac Blanc ($$$)**, a similarly complex blend of roughly equal parts Viognier, Chardonnay, and Petit Manseng, slightly less Chenin Blanc, and then a dollop of fourteen or so other rare varieties. Citrus-melony with bright acid when young, it, too, ages gorgeously, developing rounder pear-melon notes and taking on a nutty, waxy character. There's also a bright rosé sparkling wine, the **Mas de Daumas Gassac Rosé Frizant ($$)**. The **Mas de Daumas Gassac Cuvée Emile Peynaud ($$$$)** is the estate's top wine, made only five times in the last forty years. It comes from a small plot of particularly stony, poor soil, and is 100 percent Cabernet Sauvignon, powerful but refined, saturated with flavor.

There are also a number of more affordable wines from Moulin de Gassac, a project that Aimé Guibert started in the 1990s to keep local farmers' vines in the ground by purchasing their fruit at a fair rate. All three of the main Moulin de Gassac wines are excellent bargains: the **Moulin de Gassac Guilhem Blanc ($)**, a floral, light-bodied white that blends Grenache Blanc, Sauvignon Blanc, and Terret; the red-currant-and-citrus **Guilhem Rosé ($)**; and the lively, medium-bodied **Guilhem Rouge ($)**, a typical Languedoc blend of Syrah, Grenache, and Carignan, full of spicy berry flavors.

PRODUCERS PROFILED IN THIS CHAPTER

Gérard Bertrand   Mas de Daumas Gassac
Château Maris

OTHER LANGUEDOC-ROUSSILLON PRODUCERS TO LOOK FOR

Amistat   Mas Amiel
Domaine d'Aupilhac   Mas Cal Demoura
Léon Barral   Mas Jullien
Clos de Fées   Matassa
Domaine Gauby   Maxime Magnon
Grange des Pères   Château d'Oupia
Le Clos du Gravillas   Domaine Rimbert
Domaine de Majas

LOIRE VALLEY

The Loire is the longest river in France, and while charming foot paths run here and there along its banks, it would be ambitious to walk its length. In terms of wine-growing areas alone, the Loire travels some 450 miles from the Côte Roannaise in the east to the Bay of Biscay. In its valley are nearly 7,000 wine estates in 87 different appellations, cultivating almost 173,000 acres of vines.

The Loire Valley is the largest source of white wine in France, home both to famous appellations (Sancerre, Vouvray, Muscadet) and little-known ones (Cour-Cheverny, Jasnières, Fiefs Vendéens, and many more). Three grapes produce most of that wine: Melon de Bourgogne, which dominates the Muscadet vineyards around Nantes; Chenin Blanc, the grape of Savennières, Vouvray, Montlouis, and other middle Loire regions; and Sauvignon Blanc, in the upper Loire, where the vignerons of Sancerre, Pouilly-Fumé, and other appellations make their bright, citrusy wines. There are reds as well, mostly from Cabernet Franc, but also Côt (Malbec) and Gamay, among other varieties. The Loire's weather and soils are varied, as well they might be—the place is huge. The damp, ocean-influenced climate of Muscadet is very different from the continental climate of Touraine; the limestone and quartz of Sancerre bears little resemblance to the slate and schist of western Anjou.

That vast variety is also echoed by the range of sensibilities here. The Loire makes a tremendous amount of inexpensive sparkling wine—it's the second-largest sparkling wine producer in France after Champagne. Most of that disappears into

French supermarkets. Similarly, as it's almost impossible to find a wine list anywhere that doesn't offer Sancerre these days, there are plenty of generic versions of that popular wine floating around as well. And yet the region is also filled with small-scale, interesting, ambitious vignerons; some are historic names, some are more recent, and a surprising number are devoted to making noninterventionist, natural wine. Many of the latter are recent arrivals. As the Loire restaurateur and organic farmer Rémi Fournier told me, "A lot of people here who make natural wine, they're not sons of local vignerons. What they needed was a place they could afford; many of them came from outside the Loire. They were attracted by the Chenin, of course, but they were also attracted by how little land cost. They could *afford* to fail. And the top wines of the region were organic for a long time: Nicolas Joly, Clos Rougeard, Guy Bossard at Domaine de l'Ecu in Muscadet. The first wave came in the 1990s, then there was a second wave, and a third, and a fourth—now, what, the fifth?" He laughed, and poured me some more wine.

That a bootstrapping, no-money and no-rules, try-anything sensibility of natural wine is firmly ensconced here is almost ironic, at least when you look around at the Loire's plethora of spectacular châteaux, those fairy-tale country homes for past French nobility that are now tourist attractions. But there they are, castles and organic vineyards alike. In the course of a morning, you could stop by winemaker Damien Delechenau's modest family property, La Grange Tiphaine, walk his vineyards, taste his brilliant natural wines, then spend a few hours wandering the vast stone hallways of the Château de Chambord, a little under an hour away. A fine study in contrasts, just like the Loire.

BERNARD BAUDRY • CHINON

[certified organic]

Chinon is the homeland of Cabernet Franc (at least since the 1100s, when it was first planted here by monks) and the source for some of the greatest wines made from that grape: savory, herbal, energetic reds. And many of Chinon's best Cabernet Francs are made at Domaine Bernard Baudry.

Bernard Baudry was the last of five children, and he was twelve years younger than his oldest brother. Running the family wine business was not an option. Still, he studied viticulture and enology in Burgundy in the early 1960s, and, influenced by the groundbreaking Chinon winemaker Charles Joguet, decided not only that he wanted to make wine, but that he wanted to make wines that would express their terroir, that would speak of where they were grown. He set off on his own.

Baudry didn't have money to buy a vineyard, so he leased land, slowly building a reputation for wines that offered more depth and complexity than what was being made in Chinon at the time. Eventually he was able to buy vineyards, and today, he and his son Mathieu farm seventy-four acres of vines, about two-thirds of which they own (the rest is under long-term contract).

Everything is organic. "In the 1970s, in the eighties, the nineties, most of the wineries here were producing very high yields in the vineyards, using chemicals, fertilizers," Mathieu Baudry says. "My dad was cautious—not so much ecologically driven as that he believed that if you wanted to show how the soil affects

the wine, you can't use herbicides, you can't use MKP [mono-potassium phosphate fertilizer]. He preferred to plow the land, and force the roots of the vines to go deep. But he knew this by experimenting, by tasting and tasting—you don't find the smokiness in the wines of Grézeaux, for instance, until the roots grow far down."

He adds, "The chemicals, you know, they're so *easy*. You have your yard at your house, you spray it with Roundup, voilà, it's clean! No weeds! I'm not crazy organic—you won't see green billboards when you drive up to our place—but it just makes sense. To make wine that expresses the soil, that soil has to be as alive as possible."

Mathieu's arrival in 2001 also brought a move toward less interventionist winemaking, and, crucially, less extraction. "For me, Cabernet Franc always has a nice herbal character, but back in the 1980s, even the 1990s, it was too much. We'll open an '86 and my father will taste it and say, 'Wha!! What did I do? So much extraction.'" So, from 2001 onward, no pumps; no *pigeage* (punching down the surface layer of fermenting wine), instead only gentle pump-overs; no fining or filtering. "I like to say, winemaking is very simple," Mathieu says. "It's full of details, but the details are mostly about removing things you're doing, rather than adding them. Humans, you know, we like to *do* things. A lot of people

> *"A lot of people think you have to do this, do that, add this, add that. But the grape, she just needs you to be there."*
> —Mathieu Baudry

think you have to do this, do that, add this, add that. But the grape, she just needs you to be there." He only uses indigenous yeasts, again a decision in service of terroir: "I can't imagine using yeast I bought from the winery supply shop and then telling you about the smokiness that the gravel soil imparts. It would be absurd." He pauses, thoughtfully. "Making wine is not so difficult if you don't think of yourself as the boss. 'You, grape! You will do this kind of wine, for this kind of consumer!'" Then he laughs.

The Baudrys make five different red Chinons, along with two whites and a rosé. Though they could qualify as natural wine given Mathieu Baudry's noninterventionist approach, he's wary of that label. "I think of what I do as a common-sense approach. Plus, I don't like belonging to groups. I prefer to be free, and I don't like the rigidity the natural wine group sometimes has— the 'what I do is right, and my neighbor is wrong.'"

The **Bernard Baudry Chinon Rouge Les Granges ($$)**, from the estate's youngest vines, is fruity and direct; a good introduction. The **Chinon Rouge Cuvée Domaine ($$)** comes from slightly older vines and has a bit more structure. The three top reds, each from a single small vineyard, are the domaine's defining wines (and to this day not overwhelmingly pricey, a rarity). The **Chinon Rouge Les Grézeaux ($$)** comes off the old terraces near the river. Mathieu Baudry says, "It has a distinctive smokiness, but it's always a bit shy." From southeast facing, clay-limestone slopes replanted by Bernard in 1995 after being abandoned during World War II, the **Chinon Rouge Clos Guillot ($$)** is precise and linear, with red fruit and, often, a blood orange note. "It doesn't go left, it doesn't go right, it's just very straight," Mathieu says. Finally, the **Chinon Rouge Croix Boisée ($$$)**, Mathieu says, "would be a grand cru, if we had a classification like that." More full-bodied, it comes from vines on clay and white limestone, its vivid red fruit bolstered by chalky tannins and a saline note.

JACKY BLOT / DOMAINE DE LA TAILLE AUX LOUPS • MONTLOUIS-SUR-LOIRE

[certified organic]

Jacky Blot, who passed away in the spring of 2023 at age seventy-five, for many years made some of the finest Chenin Blancs in both Montlouis and Vouvray. But Blot wasn't from a winemaking family, or from money. His father was an agricultural laborer, and while Blot said that as a child they always had "real products, simple but real, with real flavor—butter from the churn, chickens from the farm," that direct connection to the land faded over time.

Yet something crucial lingered. Blot's brother became a pastry chef in Paris, and one day an acquaintance of his brought over a bottle of 1959 Burgundy when Blot was visiting. "I tasted it and a light bulb went off," he later said. Blot was in his twenties, a parachutist in the French military. (An unlikely path into winemaking, but so many are.) Work took him to Tours, where he eventually became a wine broker. That led to his purchase of a few acres of land in Mountlouis-sur-Loire in 1988.

Blot's hope, or plan, was to recapture Montlouis's once-vaunted reputation: "If we have a great terroir, and we plant the right vines on this terroir, and we make wine the same way that people who produce great wines make them, then we should be able to make great wine." Meanwhile, as his work as a broker took him around France to different wine regions, he tasted and talked with winemakers. "I think of it like a painter who visits several schools and, in the end, creates his own style of painting," Blot said.

His farming was adamantly organic since his start in 1988. At the time, most Montlouis fruit was farmed conventionally, and sold either to the local co-op or to large producers in

Vouvray. Chenin Blanc in general was picked underripe and then chaptalized to bring the alcohol up to a legal level. "They were all made with sugar," he recalled recently. "But that was the past. And today there are an enormous number of organic growers in Montlouis. We're no longer alone."

Domaine de la Taille aux Loups, as well as its sister property in Bourgueil, Domaine de la Butte, carries on under Jacky's son Jean-Philippe. Most of the vineyards are in Montlouis, though they also have two vineyards in Vouvray, and the Bourgueil estate is one large swath of old vines on a single, south-facing hillside.

The sparkling **La Taille aux Loups Brut Tradition ($$)** is made in the classic method (second fermentation in the bottle) and is vividly fresh and zesty; the more unusual **Triple Zéro ($$)** is made with the old-school *pétillant naturel* method (a single fermentation in the bottle) and receives zero chaptalization, zero *liqueur de tirage*, and zero dosage (hence triple zero). Soft, fine bubbles, a savory creaminess, lots of lemon and green apple fruit— it's a truly delightful sparkling wine.

There are a number of dry Chenin Blancs in the portfolio, from both Montlouis and Vouvray. The most affordable is **Remus ($$)**, which is also the only one that comes from a number of different sites. **Clos de Mosny ($$)** comes from a walled vineyard in Montlouis that Blot purchased in 2011; it's full of orchard fruit and citrus flavors, and is intensely aromatic. **Les Hauts de Husseau ($$)** comes from seventy-plus-year-old vines in one of the highest sites in Montlouis. Mouthwateringly tart, it has fine citrus flavors and a finish that seems etched into stone. **Clos de Venise ($$)** would be labeled Vouvray but for the labeling turf war between that appellation and Montlouis (see the profile of François Chidaine, on page 165, for more on that); for now, it's simply Vin de France. But it's a beautiful Chenin: silky and stony at once. **Bretonniere ($$)**, the domaine's formerly-known-as-Vouvray wine, is equally impressive, more chalky than flinty, with the same round-but-bright lusciousness that the Venise has.

There are also several reds from Blot's Domaine de la Butte in Bourgueil, all Cabernet Franc, all lifted and vibrant, very much in the style of the whites. The **La Pied de la Butte ($$)** is the lightest and most affordable. **Le Haut de la Butte ($$)** comes from vines at the top of the hill and is savory and layered. The best of this trio is **Mi-Pente ($$)**, from the center of the vineyard. It's herbal and forest-spicy, with abundant black- and red-currant fruit.

DOMAINE FRANÇOIS CHIDAINE • MONTLOUIS-SUR-LOIRE

[certified organic / certified biodynamic / regenerative]

Montlouis-sur-Loire, or Montlouis as it's often just called, is the tiny scrapper of French Chenin Blanc. Its roughly eleven hundred acres of vines, located on a low-lying, sandy, pebbly plateau between the Cher and Loire rivers, are a fifth of what you'll find in its more famous neighbor to the north, Vouvray. But Montlouis's reputation in recent years far exceeds its size, thanks to a small group of vignerons that includes François Chidaine.

Chidaine has been organic since 1992 and biodynamic since 1999; more and more, he's also focused on regenerative practices. "We're a biodynamic estate, and at the same time we've developed a kind of soil-preservation farming approach. It's a response to climate change. If you use ground cover, you can store carbon. We use cereals, legumes, and so on. We pasture animals to re-create microbial activity in the soil. And we are adding

> *"We need to rethink the landscape. We need to counter the effect of three or four centuries of farming that have been destroying microbial diversity in the soil."*
> —François Chidaine

hedges back," he says. "With climate change, we've also lacked water for a long time. With this approach I can store water. The year 1997 was a landmark for climate change." That year was good vintage in the Loire, but one that marked the beginning of a string of devastating April and May frosts; in the past decade, frost has been a consistent rather than occasional threat, in some cases destroying 80 to 90 percent of the Loire harvest, as in 2021. "We can still try to change the way we work," Chidaine says. "We can still rethink it. We have to start working for the future."

There are quite a few Chidaine wines (including a recent joint venture in Spain), but here are some standouts. His **Montlouis Méthode Traditionnelle Brut ($$)** is a terrific sparkling value. It's 100 percent Chenin Blanc from vines that are twenty to fifty years old, floral, citrusy, and rich with flavor. From Montlouis, **Clos de Breuil ($$)** comes from a single-vineyard parcel of thirty-five- to eighty-year-old vines on one of the highest points in the appellation. It's made in a dry style, with Montlouis's characteristic interplay of mouthwatering acidity, crisp green apple flavor, and stony minerality. His **Les Bournais ($$–$$$)** comes from a small site on a cliff above the Loire River. Intensely aromatic, Les Bournais also can age beautifully, heading into rich, textural lemon curd, quince, and citrus peel flavors after a decade or so.

Chidaine also makes excellent Vouvrays, though they are currently not labeled as such. In 2009, Vouvray passed a regulation that starting in 2014, any wine labeled "Vouvray" had to be vinified within the appellation's borders, no matter whether the grapes were grown there or not. It was a blow—seemingly directly aimed—to vintners like Chidaine with vineyards in both regions, but whose wineries are located in Montlouis (literally about two miles from Vouvray). Regardless, Chidaine's **Argiles Vin de France ($$)** comes from fifteen- to fifty-year-old vines in Vouvray, taking its name from the clay-filled soils of the appellation. Rich but dry, it suggests beeswax, chalk, and the bright crunch of a Granny Smith apple. His **Baudoin Vin de France ($$–$$$)** comes from a little less than seven acres of vines in one of Vouvray's most storied vineyards. It's an intense Chenin Blanc yet it glides across the palate in an irresistibly effortless way.

DOMAINE DELAPORTE · SANCERRE

[certified organic]

Matthieu Delaporte's family started making wine in Sancerre in the seventeenth century, and was one of the first domaines in the region. "Chavignol is where everything started," he says. "At that time, of course, families were making wine, raising animals, making cheese. There was a cheese cave in every cellar in the village. But these days there aren't any goats at the wineries." No goats, but extremely good Sancerre; that seems a fair trade-off.

The Delaportes own eighty acres of estate vineyards, three-quarters Sauvignon Blanc, the rest Pinot Noir. Matthieu, who took over in 2010 at age twenty-two, has shifted the estate toward organics, eliminating use of herbicides, pesticides, and synthetic fertilizers and returning to hand-harvesting. He's also reduced sulfur use substantially, partly for personal reasons: "I had a huge asthma attack working in the winery. A winemaker who's allergic to sulfites is . . . a problem."

Even with the changes he's made, the past is still inescapable here. Not long ago, Matthieu found some wines that his great-grandfather had bottled just after the Second World War. "They were probably bottling wine before that, too, but mostly they were making it in barrels and sending the barrels off by train. These were under my grandparents' house, in perfect condition. A hundred bottles of 1947 Sancerre. They taste amazing! But they also make me think of my great-grandfather, making wine year after year through both world wars."

Domaine Delaporte's Sancerres are what you wish Sancerre would taste like, but it rarely does. The flagship **Domaine Delaporte Chavignol Sancerre** (\$\$) is an irresistibly juicy white, full of ruby-red grapefruit flavors and hints of freshly mown grass. The **Sancerre Silex** (\$\$), from fifty-plus-year-old vines on flint (silex) soils, is floral and smoky, more delicate in character. The top wine is the **Sancerre Les Monts Damnes** (\$\$\$), about which Matthieu Delaporte says, "Monts Damnes is kind of a grand cru of Sancerre, even though there are no grand crus here, technically. The vineyard is between a 40 to 50 percent slope. It was called Monts Damnes—the damned mountain—because 'you have to be absolutely damned to work that kind of hill.' It was insane to farm on that kind of slope a hundred years ago. It's still a challenge." Delaporte's Les Monts Damnes has that vineyard's signature depth and complexity of flavor, with an herbal, waxy character that's hard to describe but deeply alluring. The domaine also makes a savory, expressive **Sancerre Rouge** (**$$**) and a very appealing **Sancerre Rosé** (**$$**), both from Pinot Noir.

DOMAINE DE L'ECU • MUSCADET SÈVRE-ET-MAINE

[certified organic / certified biodynamic / natural]

The Domaine de l'Ecu story starts with Guy Bossard, who returned from France's then mandatory military service in 1972 intent on making wine in his hometown of La Landreau, as his father, grandfather, and ancestors had before. Controversially among local growers, he removed all use of chemicals on the property and received organic certification in 1975 (biodynamic in 1988). He was also among the first to focus on the complex terroirs of the region, and, rather than release his wines as soon as possible, age them *sur lie* for months, adding texture, complexity, and depth. If there's been a reevaluation of the potential of Muscadet, a lot of the credit for that goes to Guy Bossard.

By 2010, he was ready to retire, but none of his children were interested in following him. Enter Frédérick (Fred) Niger, a local lawyer and wine lover who was passionate about organic and biodynamic wine, and also sick of his current career. As his wife, Claire, recalls, "One day he got up and said, 'OK, that's enough.'" Niger sold his business to cover the tuition for an enology degree, and around the same time met Bossard, who lived nearby. They connected, Bossard sold Niger the estate, and the two of them worked together until 2014, when Bossard finally did retire.

Niger has followed much the same path as his mentor, though his wines are clearly his own, and there have been changes, mostly toward an even more noninterventionist approach. He and Claire work together, farming L'Ecu's forty-two acres of vineyards and making wine in the domaine's small cellar. Organic and biodynamic farming is not easy here. There's mold and mildew pressure from the region's notoriously damp, cool weather; as one droll local saying observes, "it's fun to live in Brittany if your best friend is a frog."

Most of the L'Ecu wines are fermented in more than one hundred amphorae of varying sizes, from 1,450 liters down to a handful of small 160-liter urns. Niger also likes to play monastic songs to the wines as they age, though Claire says, "During harvest, it might be Eminem instead." Everything is hand-work; as Fred has written, "We have renounced all technological artifice in our cellar to break with the movement of wine standardization, and to preserve the link uniting each of our cuvées to a terroir and a vintage."

Domaine de l'Ecu makes over a dozen different cuvées. There are three primary ones. The **Domaine de l'Ecu Classic ($–$$)** comes from the estate's younger vines and is meant to be drunk in its salty, citrusy youth. Then there are the two wines that really define L'Ecu: **Granite ($$)** and **Orthogneiss ($$)**. Both have been labeled as Muscadet Sèvre-et-Maine in the past, but in 2020 the Nigers were told that their wines were "atypical for the appellation," so now they are simply labeled Vin de France. The former, from granite soil, tends to be rounder, albeit in a bright, vibrant way, with more stone-fruit flavors; the latter is more citrus-driven, with plenty of oyster shell and saline notes.

There's a large roster of smaller cuvées. To pick a few favorites, **Virtus ($$)**, formerly called RedNoz, is a semi-carbonic, zero-sulfur Cabernet Sauvignon that's fruity and energetic and full of life. **Taurus ($$)**, a white from a tiny parcel of forty-five- to fifty-year-old Melon de Bourgogne grapes, aged for twenty-four months on lees, is fuller-bodied and more powerful than the Granite and Orthogneiss wines. **Mephisto ($$)**, a Cabernet Franc that spends two years in amphorae, is full of the crisp raspberry-cherry and spicy-savory tobacco-leaf characteristics that make good Loire Cabernet Franc such a pleasure.

VINCENT GAUDRY • SANCERRE

[certified organic / certified biodynamic]

The best way to describe Vincent Gaudry may be to borrow something that Pascaline Lepeltier, a master sommelier and a walking encyclopedia of France's Loire Valley, said to me about him: "He's not tattooed, he's not a wild man, and he's shy, so he's never been the sommelier catnip. But he's absolutely brilliant."

He's also, when he wants to be, very funny and charming. During a visit a few years ago, he was building a new bottle storage building with giant slabs of limestone—truly huge, five to six tons apiece. "It's like Egypt and the pyramids," he said, because they were lifting the stones with a hand-cranked winch. I expressed my surprise at this method—which seemed more than a little labor-intensive—and he said, "But with one bottle of Sancerre, yes! You have the power. That's why we're out of wine."

More probably Gaudry was out of wine because he does not make very much, and because more and more people (even those sommeliers to whom he was not formerly catnip) have caught on to how good his wines are.

Gaudry worked initially with his father, but in 1993 they were still using chemicals in the vineyard, and after one instance of spraying he became extremely ill. As a result, in 1995 he told his father, "Either we change everything or I go work somewhere else." They shifted to organics, then quite quickly moved to biodynamics. Why the latter? "I wanted more answers," he says.

Are these traditional Sancerres? Do they defy expectation? Break the mold? It depends on when your mold was made. Sancerre was legally established as a wine region in 1936, but at the time the business was largely *négociants* from Paris buying barrels to sell in Parisian bistros. It's only in the 1980s and 1990s that modern

Sancerre, that happy go-to white on wine lists everywhere, really came into being. Gaudry isn't modern. He farms with horses, doesn't filter his wine, uses only a tiny amount of sulfur when he bottles. "These wines are like the wines of the 1960s. Made and aged in barrel. And if everything goes well, at least a year and a half aging," he says. "The most difficult thing, making wine, is to know *not* to do anything. A lot of things you do as a winemaker are to reassure yourself. They have nothing to do with the wine. To let yourself go—that's the most difficult thing."

If you taste with Gaudry in his cellar, the room may be tiny and freezing and lit only by a single candle, but the mood will be warm and thoughtful. The **Vincent Gaudry Melodie de Vieilles Vignes Sancerre ($$)**, from fifty- to ninety-year-old vines, is all smoke and lemon/grapefruit peel. His **Scorpio Sancerre ($$)**, designated on the label by the astrological sign, has crystalline aromas of gumdrop, melon, and citrus, with a stony finish and beautifully sustained flavors. **Pour Vous Sancerre ($$$)** has an earthy, wet character (admittedly an odd adjective to use for a liquid, but still, smell the wine). It's savory and dense. **À Mi-Chemin Sancerre ($$$)** is mouth-filling and salty, with ruby-red grapefruit flavors. And Gaudry's **Sancerre Rouge Vincengetorix ($$)**, made from Pinot Noir, is a total pleasure: spicy, gamy, with toasted herb notes and savoriness throughout.

THIERRY GERMAIN / DOMAINE DES ROCHES NEUVES • SAUMUR-CHAMPIGNY

[certified organic / certified biodynamic / natural]

Take a walk in Thierry Germain's Mémoires vineyard in Saumur-Champigny on a late fall day. Even under a blustery wind, the centenarian Cabernet Franc vines here seem to grasp at the sun, something you can later taste in the coiled intensity of the wine Germain makes from them. Germain has some of that intensity himself. He thinks deeply, and cares passionately about his vineyards. He also farms biodynamically and extends those principles to the organization of his estate as well: "For me the crucial part of biodynamics is the social part. In 1990, I helped a vineyard worker buy his own property—it was a scandal here. I got a lot of shit for it. But part of biodynamics is helping the world move forward. Every morning I have breakfast with my team; I've been doing that for thirty years. There's no 'general manager' and so on—everybody is able to give input and advice."

Germain largely adheres to natural winemaking principles. "Added sulfur is what keeps conventional wines alive," he says. "Minerality and acidity are what keep real wines alive." His wines express the honeycombed limestone terroir of Saumur; they're taut and vivid, brilliant expressions of what this under-regarded Loire appellation has to offer. Germain himself is a fascinating conversationalist. At one point he might explain that Rudolf Steiner's 1924 lectures, the urtexts of biodynamics, are about agriculture overall, not just viticulture, and that they were inspired by *The Metamorphosis of Plants* by Goethe. "Something with Goethe is that he really makes things concrete. I want people who come to this estate to understand that biodynamics is concrete." He also works with an eighty-year-old German medium to feel the energies of his vineyards, he says, and work on changing bad energy to good; admittedly an undertaking most people would not feel was concrete in the slightest. No matter. The medium visits from Zurich twice a year. "It's a very important moment for me each time."

———

Germain makes more than fifteen different wines. Every single one is worth seeking out. To call out a few: the white **Domaine des Roches Neuves Saumur Blanc l'Insolite ($$–$$$)**, made from the fruit of ninety-year-old Chenin Blanc vines, is silky and rich, but at the same time lifted by electric acidity. The **Saumur Blanc l'Echelier ($$$)**, from slightly younger vines (seventy years) in a three-hundred-year-old walled *clos*, is perhaps a touch more savory; both are thrilling white wines.

The **Domaine des Roches Neuves Saumur-Champigny Rouge Domaine** ($$), Germain's most affordable Cabernet Franc, is a bright, floral, medium-weight red, its red berry flavors underlined by a light bell pepper note. His **Terres Chaudes Saumur-Champigny** ($$–$$$) is "for me the most varietally Cabernet Franc of my wines, in terms of aromatics and texture." My take: it tastes like a forest filled with blueberries. Germain's **Saumur-Champigny Rouge Mémoires** ($$$) comes from a one-hundred-plus-year-old plot of Cabernet Franc vines. Following the holistic biodynamic principle that a vineyard is just part of a larger ecological whole, Germain gives credit to the trees that surround Les Memoires for the distinctive character of this wine. "Trees help to bring light. If there is no light aboveground, there's no light belowground, and light brings life." How Les Memoires's violet-scented flavors can be dark and powerful yet at the same time ethereal is a mystery, but it's a mystery that's fascinating to drink.

LA GRANGE TIPHAINE • MONTLOUIS-SUR-LOIRE

[certified organic / certified biodynamic / natural]

Winemakers Damien and Coralie Delecheneau are among the natural wine movement's second-generation stars. They combine technical knowledge—he with a degree in enology from the University of Bordeaux, she with one from the University of Reims—with a thoughtful, noninterventionist approach. As regards the use of sulfur as a preservative, controversial within the natural wine world, Damien says, "There's a lot of religious thinking about wines without sulfites. But I don't think winemakers necessarily need to make all their wines without any sulfites—I don't make wines to throw them away because they've gone bad."

That scientific mindset plays against an understanding that there's more to the world than science: "I come from a scientific background. But I understood at some point that there's something else above, or different. I call it supra, not super; this *moreness* in wine. You can't touch it. You can't measure it. That's what I found when I started working with biodynamics."

The Delecheneaus' thirty-seven acres of vineyards, at their home in Montlouis-sur-Loire and also in Touraine and Touraine-Ambroise, have been organic since 2007 and biodynamic since 2014. Some, particularly in Montlouis, are ancient—for instance, Côt (Malbec) planted in the 1880s, around the time Damien's great-grandfather Alfonse Delecheneau founded the domaine.

The operation is small, just the Delecheneaus plus three employees. There's nothing fancy here. If you talk to Damien, he's likely to be tinkering with a tractor or tromping the vineyards in work boots, his dog Lou sometimes by his side and sometimes dashing off amid the vine rows in pursuit of possible rabbits. In the winery, old concrete vats fight for space with hoses and other winemaking accoutrement, and a downstairs space is packed with barrels three-high on racks. "If you're here in the Loire, you have to accept that you have to make great wine at really great values," Damien says. "It's not a wealthy region. You can't hire troops of people to do your work. And you can't overprice your wine, because the region won't sustain that. But it's an amazing moment here right now, because you're seeing history being written. The world is just at the beginning of discovering the quality of what the Loire has to offer."

Among the Delecheneaus' white wines, the **Domaine La Grange Tiphaine Clef de Sol Montlouis sur Loire Blanc ($$)**, from eighty-year-old Chenin Blanc vines, is a standout, floral and lightly honey-scented, full-bodied but vibrant with tangy kumquat flavors. Its counterpart among the reds, the **Clef de Sol Touraine Red ($$)**, a 65/35 Cabernet Franc/Malbec blend, bright violet in hue and full of ebullient red fruit, is lovely, too, and refreshing with a slight chill. The *pet-nat* **Nouveau-Nez ($$)**, sparkling Chenin Blanc bottled just before it finishes fermenting, is faintly cloudy, appealingly citrusy, and purely fun to drink.

There are many others, and they are all exciting wines, but the Delecheneaus' **Côt Vieilles Vignes ($$$)**, from 115- to 120-year-old Malbec vines, aged half in neutral oak and half in concrete eggs, bears calling out for its intensity and focus, all blueberries, earth, violets, and that indescribable "supra-ness" Delecheneau describes.

DOMAINE HUET • VOUVRAY

[certified organic / certified biodynamic]

Domaine Huet is arguably the most acclaimed producer in Vouvray. Founded in 1928 by Victor Huët, it was run for fifty-five years by his son Gaston Huët, a legend in French winemaking. Gaston Huët passed away in 2002, and since 2003, the property has been owned by Hungarian winemaker Istvan Szepsy and New York financier Anthony Hwang; daughter Sarah Hwang runs the winery and lives there. She's well aware of Huet's stellar reputation: "Is there an expectation? Of course! But we could embrace it or fight against it, and we've chosen to embrace it. Ultimately, we're a few pages in a huge book. Our job is to make sure that the story is still being written, and written properly."

It is, unquestionably, a remarkable story. Victor Huët fought in World War I, and returned from the front with his nerves shattered and his lungs damaged by mustard gas. Before the war, he had owned a bistro in a small town west of Lyon; after the war, he abandoned it for the countryside, looking for a peaceful place to live and make wine. He found that in Vouvray. Gaston, who took over from his father in 1937, had his life upended by war as well. He fought for the French, was captured by the Germans in Calais, and spent five years in a prisoner-of-war camp in Silesia before being freed in 1945—whereupon he walked back to France, arriving almost skeletally thin but with a burning determination to restart his life. Despite the postwar disrepair of the Huet vineyards and lack of supplies (bottles, pruning equipment, the horses taken by the German army) he managed to make wine that year, one of the greatest vintages of the twentieth century in France.

Huët was joined by his son-in-law Noël Pinguet in the 1970s, and in the late 1980s they shifted the domaine to biodynamics. They were among the first in France to head in this direction, receiving certification in 1993. Benjamin Joliveau, the current winemaker, says, "Noël didn't have any prejudices. He was very scientifically driven—he studied math at university—and he couldn't really *believe* in biodynamics because he couldn't explain it. But after five to ten years, he saw the effects in the vines, and then, even if he couldn't explain it, he had to admit it worked."

Domaine Huet's three vineyards (Le Haut Lieu, Le Mont, and Clos du Bourg) total seventy-four acres. They are close together—take the winding little road out of town, stone walls on either side hemming you in, and you can soon reach any of them—but they are quite different. "Clos du Bourg makes wines that are more aerial and complex," Joliveau says. "It's clay on limestone that gives it its structure." The vineyard faces south, and at the bottom drops right off; the top of the church spire in Vouvray peeps into view. "Le Haut Lieu has more productive soil, which gives it more fruit. And the flint at Le Mont makes the wine more strict.

It's a very short wine when young, but that changes over time." Everything is hand-harvested at Huet, unusual in a region that, as Joliveau notes, is 90 percent machine-harvested. "But seventy percent of that is sparkling, and half of that goes to supermarkets all over France. It's low-cost, big-production wine. I won't say anything about the quality," he says with a smile.

The cellar at Huet is a warren of old, small cellars under the streets of Vouvray, excavated in centuries past to provide stone for castles and châteaux, and all connected over time. "It's very humid," Joliveau says. "Great for wines, or for mushrooms." Though these underground chambers are filled with wooden vats and barrels, very few of those are new; some date back to the 1960s or '70s. "We aren't looking for the taste of wood," Joliveau says. "We also don't make every style of Vouvray every year"—meaning sparkling, dry, semi-dry, and sweet—"that's not our decision. That's nature's decision. She's unpredictable, and we just adapt to what she gives us."

Though in some sense Huet only makes three wines (plus a sparkling Vouvray), because all of their production is vineyard-designated, the nature of Vouvray means that each of those wines has three different versions:

sec (dry), *demi-sec* (lightly sweet), and *moelleux* (sweet). There are also the *premiere trie* wines, a top selection from the *moelleux* barrels, and Cuvée Constance, a rare, ultra-limited sweet wine using fruit from some or all of the three vineyards. The map may be a bit confusing, but the destination is unquestionably a beautiful one.

The sparkling **Domaine Huet Vouvray Petillant ($$)** is full of salty, yeasty orchard fruit notes, "and really nice bitterness," Joliveau says. "Bitterness for a long time had such a negative connotation, but it's quite important for Chenin Blanc." The **Le Haut-Lieu Vouvray Sec ($$)** suggests straw and lemon peel, with fine, bright acid. "It's easy drinking, a good first step," Joliveau says. **Le Mont Vouvray Sec ($$$)** is stony, with a kind of crystalline, penetrating character.

The **Clos de Bourg Vouvray Sec ($$$)** may be even more mineral, with more power and depth, yet it's also more generous in its youth.

The lightly sweet demi-sec wines like the **Le Haut-Lieu Demi-Sec ($$$)** shift the dry cuvées's flavors more toward a supple, red-apple richness, the sweetness offset by the wine's light bitterness. "A demi-sec has to be better than just good," Joliveau says. "Because if it's not good, it's awful. Just sugar and alcohol." The **Le Haut-Lieu Moelleux ($$$)** furthers that sweetness, with the wine taking on an unctuous character, with candied apple and lime flavors. *Moelleux* wines technically are required to be thirty grams per liter of residual sugar, but Huet's are typically at least forty-five grams. The sweet wines from Huet also age spectacularly well.

NICOLAS JOLY / LA COULÉE DE SERRANT • SAVENNIÈRES

[certified organic / certified biodynamic]

No one has been more influential in spreading the word of biodynamics throughout the wine community than Nicolas Joly. A thinker, an evangelist, an iconoclastic winemaker (though he rejects that term), a magnetic speaker, and a figure of some controversy, he's a direct link from the writings and philosophies of Rudolf Steiner to any number of European and New World vignerons, through his own work, through his books, and through the biodynamics-focused group he founded, Return to Terroir, which now numbers 175 members from 13 different countries (membership requires organic certification for at least three years, plus biodynamic certification for at least two).

After receiving an MBA from Columbia, Joly worked in finance for three years, for J.P. Morgan. That life didn't suit him (no surprise, given his later trajectory) and he returned to take over his parents' estate, La Coulée de Serrant, in the Loire Valley, in 1977. The property was ancient: Cistercian monks planted the first vines there in the 1100s, and it has produced wine ever since—2023 is Coulée de Serrant's 893rd consecutive vintage. It's also one of only three single-estate appellations in France (the other two are Romanée-

> "Forget about your knowledge. Take the wine. Swallow. Feel the music."
> —Nicolas Joly

Conti in Burgundy and Château Grillet in the Rhône).

Asked why he left finance to help run a family wine estate, Joly says, "My first answer would be fate. Why did I start with biodynamics? Same answer, I have no idea. But I was deeply linked to nature, to fishing, hunting, from my father. I had that feeling for understanding wind, soil, harmony with plants; I didn't know it consciously, but it was inside me."

Joly has spoken at length about biodynamics. But two things he's said recently seem apropos: "Biodynamics slowly takes you to an understanding of the invisible world, and how elementary forces linked to the soil, linked to the water, linked to the leaves, linked to the flowering process, or linked to the fruitification—how all of them are different, how all of them are acting." Similarly: "When you understand that a plant, a vine, has the capacity to capture what you call energy, whether it is the moon, stars, sun, planets, whatever—and that this lands on an earthly level, that's where biodynamics is working if it is well done."

Joly loves to talk, at length, and tends to head into the transcendent. He's eminently quotable, but for every comment like "the greatest result that biodynamics will have is that farming will return to being an art," which is aphoristically brilliant, you get something more gnomic like "if you have to interfere in your cellar, it means you have lost something from what Kepler was calling music of the spheres—I'm not saying the wine will be bad; you are losing that secret connection to the deepness of the appellation, and you learn this from one year to another."

Over the years I've interviewed Joly several times. There are any number of pithy, penetrating remarks from those conversations, but here are a few:

"Chemical fertilizers are salts. If you want to know what a fertilizer does, eat a tablespoon full of salt."

...and...

"If you add yeast, then you are obliged to *feed* that stupid yeast. So, you add an enzyme. And then you have to add something so that the enzyme

will live, and at the end what do you have? It is not wine."

...and...

"All of this is playing music. What we discuss, talking about wine, is music. A wine that touches you is pure music. And all this intangible organization, this secret world you move in with biodynamics, is music. And when you grow your vines to capture music, instead of trying to capture a market, then people will follow you."

Joly is a brilliant musician, but even the best musicians get weary. He was born in 1945, and is now in his late seventies. Most of the work of the estate is currently handled (brilliantly) by his daughter, Virginie, though he is always, indefatigably present. And the wines are as good or better than they have ever been.

The Jolys farm 39.5 acres of vines on three vineyard sites in Savennières, all Chenin Blanc. From their vineyards they produce three wines, following a noninterventionist approach—very little new oak, only spontaneous fermentation with native yeasts, no fining, no filtering, and only a minimal amount of sulfur at bottling.

The aromatic **Savennières Les**

Vieux Clos ($$$) comes from 13.5 acres of twenty-five- to thirty-year-old vines designated AOC Savennières. Formerly known Les Clos Sacrés in the U.S., it's the most open and inviting of the Joly wines. The **Savennières Clos de la Bergerie** ($$$) is designated AOC Savennières Roche aux Moines, and comes from the eastern-facing side of that site. It's richer and deeper, with golden orchard-fruit flavors, apricot and pear, sometimes shading into pineapple. **Clos de la Coulée de Serrant ($$$$)** is Joly's most famous wine, probably the most famous wine in the Loire Valley, and, at its best, one of the greatest dry white wines of France. It comes from a historic 17.2-acre monopole of forty-five- to fifty-year-old vines at the eastern edge of the Savennières appellation, overlooking the Loire River. As with its proprietor, what is there to say that hasn't been said? It's full-bodied and rich but framed by bright acid and exquisite minerality, seductively aromatic, its flavors suggesting stone fruits and citrus peel. With time it ages into a kind of stony, layered, honeysuckle lusciousness.

DOMAINE AUX MOINES • SAVENNIÈRES

[certified organic / biodynamic]

At Domaine aux Moines the first residents who are likely to greet you are Nelson and Nestor, two large, black dogs. Their approach is to growl ferociously at any visitor for about thirty seconds, then flop over in the driveway and start to scratch themselves, having proved to their satisfaction that they are, indeed, extremely dangerous. The next resident to greet you will be Tessa Laroche, Domaine aux Moine's winemaker.

The Laroches founded Domaine aux Moines in 1981. At the time, Loire wine was in the doldrums, and estates like this one were worth a fraction of what they are today. It's hard to imagine now, as you stand in front of the château itself and look down and across the great Roche aux Moines vineyard, that at one point this place might have been considered a bad investment. But it was. As Tessa Laroche says, "My parents bought this entire domaine for the price of a good apartment in Paris."

That domaine comprises fifty-four acres of land, almost thirty of those planted with vines. "The monks planted vines here because they thought it might be good for grapes," Tessa says. "They were right!" La Roche aux Moines is a small appellation unto itself within Savennières, and its rules require that all vineyards in it be farmed organically. That suits the Laroches just fine (their vines were certified organic in 2011; they also use biodynamic practices, but are not certified). Yields are low, harvest is done by hand, and all fermentations use indigenous yeasts.

Chunks of broken stone appear in the vineyard here and there; the La Roche aux Moines appellation is mostly schist (with some sand and veins of volcanic rock). This gives the wines a flintiness and focus that Savennières doesn't always show. Picking one up on a cold, sunny February day, Tessa says, "You can actually pick up a ten-pound chunk of schist here and split it apart into layers." She proceeds, with very little effort, to do just that, peeling the rock apart into slabs. "It's a very distinctive soil." Indeed.

Domaine aux Moines makes two wines, both elegant, focused expressions of Chenin Blanc (once in a great while they do a sweet wine as well). The **Domaine aux Moines Le Berceau des Fées ($$)** takes its name from a row of trees on the property (known rather poetically as "the cradle of the fairies") and comes from younger vines. The straightforwardly named **Domaine aux Moines Savennières—Roche aux Moines ($$$)**, the flagship bottling, comes from forty-five-plus-year-old vines. It's intense and powerful, but somehow delicate as well, a beautiful and distinctive Savennières. It can age effortlessly for years.

PRODUCERS PROFILED IN THIS CHAPTER

Bernard Baudry

Jacky Blot / Domaine de la Taille
  aux Loups

François Chidaine

Domaine Delaporte

Domaine de l'Ecu

Vincent Gaudry

Thierry Germain / Domaine
  des Roches Neuves

La Grange Tiphaine

Domaine Huet

Nicolas Joly / La Coulée
  de Serrant

Domaine aux Moines

OTHER LOIRE VALLEY PRODUCERS TO LOOK FOR

Catherine & Pierre Breton

Château de Brézé

Domaine Vincent Careme

Chéreau Carré

Domaine de la Chevalerie

Domaine du Closel

Mathieu Cosme

François Cotat

Pascal Cotat

Claude and Etienne Courtois

Didier Dageneau

Domaine Guiberteau

Domaine des Huards

Richard Leroy

Luneau-Papin

Alphonse Mellot

Eric Morgat

Agnes et Rene Mossé

Clos Naudin / Foreaux

Domaine de la Noblaie

Domaine de la Pépière

Domaine les Pierres Ecrites

François et Julien Pinon

Jo Pithon

Theirry Puzelat

Olga Raffault

Claude Riffault

Frantz Saumon

Brendan Stater-West

Clos du Tue-Boeuf

Domaine Vacheron

PROVENCE AND CORSICA

R ight now, in terms of wine, Provence is known for one thing: rosé. And lots of it. Which is fine—the revivification of dry rosé, which shambled back into the world circa 2010 like some kind of cheerful pink Frankenstein monster, is on the whole a good thing. But too much success can be difficult: while there are quite a few wonderful Provençal rosés around, there's also now an ocean of mass-produced, semi-flavorless, pink alco-water, probably best drunk as French beachgoers do, *à la piscine*—in a big glass with a heaping handful of ice cubes (*piscine* literally means swimming pool).

But there are excellent rosés to be found in Provence, as complex as any white or red; the wines of Clos Cibonne are good examples. And there are the brooding, dense reds of Bandol, where the Mourvèdre grape reaches its greatest heights, as well as lighter-spirited, more easy-drinking (yet still impressive) wines from Aix-en-Provence and Les Baux de Provence, as well as the little-known but lovely whites of Cassis. Oh, and lavender, and sunflowers, and buttery olive oil, and the Mediterranean sun, and the beaches. And, of course, all that rosé, which is more than 90 percent of all the wine made here and is so enjoyable, if you happen to be sitting on a terrace by the sea. Well. Maybe Provence's problem is that it's just so damn pretty.

Then there's Corsica. It's closer to Provence than it is to any other French wine region, but at the same time it might as well be another country entirely. Corsica's culture and personality are very much, even fiercely, its own. So, too, Corsican wines. The place is mountainous, wild, and isolated, with vineyards pocketed here and there and often reached by roads that could daunt even those with zero fear of heights. The primary grapes are the red Niellucciu (Sangiovese) and Sciacarellu, and the white Vermentinu and Biancu Gentile, plus a heap of other even less known local varieties. The vineyard area in total is small, under ten thousand acres total, and estates tend to be small as well. The wines range broadly in style, but the best are some of the hidden gems of French wine.

CLOS CIBONNE • CÔTES DE PROVENCE

[certified organic]

Drive along the coastal roads near Le Pradet in the Côtes de Provence appellation and you will see old signs: "Tibouren: This way." This is the route to Clos Cibonne.

Tibouren is a grape native to this place, but very few people cultivate it. As Claude Desforges says, "It accounts for only two percent of the grapes grown in our appellation. And we have eighty percent of those Tibouren vines ourselves. Partly it's geographical. Tibouren grows best along the coast; you have to have ventilation. The skin is very fine, and it rots easily—you have to have the wind off the sea."

Clos Cibonne overlooks the harbor of Toulon on the Mediterranean coast; it has plenty of wind off the sea.

But the other reason so little Tibouren is grown is that it's basically a pain in the neck. It's fragile, low-yielding, easily subject to grape maladies, and after the phylloxera epidemic that swept France in the late 1800s, local farmers stopped growing it, almost universally.

But a few plants survived, and when Andre Roux took over Cibonne from his father in 1930—the Rouxs had owned the property since 1793—he started planting Tibouren again. "You had to be courageous to grow it!" Desforges says (Andre Roux was his wife's grandfather). "Andre Roux was courageous, and also a little . . . well. He was an intense person."

Roux dedicated his life to wine made from Tibouren. The grape is red, but what it excels at is rosé; not pale pink, innocuous wine-water, but rosés that are complex, aromatic, and layered with flavor. "The DNA of Cibonne was based on this grape," Desforges says. "It was never in doubt. The unevenness of the bunches"—one of the things that most farmers dislike about Tibouren—"gives you more and less ripe grapes at the same time, so you get a backbone of acidity you wouldn't otherwise have."

Rosé at Cibonne is aged in large hundred-year-old oak casks (when they need repair, the family calls the same local cooperage that made them in 1903). Over time the surface of the wine in the barrel is covered by a veil of yeast, known here as *fleurette*, a similar approach to that of both the *sous voile* wines of Jura and fino sherries in Spain. "The fleurette creates this unique profile that adds to the whole picture of the wine, and also to the wine's longevity. We also use only indigenous yeasts, which makes a big difference," Desforges says. "We don't make a commercial, simple, citrusy rosé. We make old-fashioned wines that show off their terroir. These other rosés are a fashion, and we have never followed fashion."

Clos Cibonne farms all fifty-nine acres of its vineyard land organically. Fifteen of those acres are a fairly recent addition. "We were quite lucky to expand," Desforges says. "What I love about the new vineyard land is that we've maintained all the olive trees between the rows in the vineyard— grapes, olives, grapes, olives. It's a really beautiful spot. I love to go there in the evenings and watch the sun set. You can see the mountains in the distance."

The winery makes five rosés and one red. **Cibonne Tentations ($)**, the only one not entirely from estate fruit, doesn't receive the barrel-aging that the other cuvées do and is bright and direct, a good summer sipper. **Clos Cibonne Tradition Rosé ($$)** is the wine that has driven the winery's fame (in an "if you know, you know" way). Ninety percent Tibouren with a touch of Grenache, it ages under fleurette for a year in century-old *foudre*. Scintillating orange in hue, it's substantial, its spicy orange and berry notes underlain by an earthy, savory quality. There is really no other rosé like it. **Cuvée Spéciale des Vignettes ($$)** is a limited selection made from the oldest vines on the property, and is 100 percent Tibouren. Made in the same way as the Tradition, it's more darkly peach-orange in hue, a touch more complex. **Cuvée Caroline ($$)**, another small cuvée, adds small percentages of Grenache and Syrah. **Cuvée Marius ($$)**, named for Andre Roux's grandfather, is the winery's top rosé and a kind of nod to historical winemaking practices. The grapes are harvested late, at higher alcohol levels, and aged two years in barrel. It's the color of onion skin, tastes of dried fruits, and is substantial and complex; yet still a rosé.

The **Cuvée Speciale ($$)** is the property's only red, a wine full of tobacco, red fruit, herbal *garrigue* (scrubland) notes, and heaps of white pepper. "That's the typicity of Tibouren, that white pepper," Desforges says. If you ever need a bottle to prove to someone that wine can indeed smell distinctly of pepper, this is the one.

MAS DE GOURGONNIER • LES BAUX DE PROVENCE

[certified organic]

The Cartier family has been devoted to organic viticulture since 1975, and were one of the first certified organic wine estates in Languedoc, if not in all France. The family grew fruit, vegetables, and grains outside of the village of Les Baux starting in the 1700s, supplying the local abbey with produce; they planted their first vines in the 1950s, and today their charming, squat bottle of Les Baux de Provence Rouge is one of the most widely available certified organic French wines to be found—both very affordable and very good.

The estate is run by Luc Cartier together with his son Lucienne and daughter Eve. They farm 111 acres of vines, along with about 50 acres of olive trees (the Mas de Gourgonnier olive oil, also organic, is excellent). Around the vineyards the Provençal landscape stretches out, covered with pine trees and the wild, aromatic *garrigue* of the region, full of the scents of lavender, juniper, thyme, and rosemary that people often find in the red wines of Provence. All the winemaking is done with indigenous yeasts, in stainless steel or large, old oak barrels, and, for their *sans soufre* cuvée, zero sulfur.

———

The **Mas de Gourgonnier Alpilles Blanc ($)** is a lively blend of Grenache Blanc, Vermentino (or Rolle, as it's known in southern France), and Roussanne. The winery's **Les Baux de Provence Rosé ($)** is classic and light-bodied in the Provençal rosé style, only unusual in its inclusion of Cabernet Sauvignon together with Grenache and Mourvèdre. The **Les Baux de Provence Rouge ($)** has for many years been a staple for anyone interested in a full-bodied, lively, southern French red, whether they knew it was organic or not. It's incredibly reliable and also a total pleasure to drink. More recently, inspired by time that Eve Cartier spent in California working with small producers there, there's also the **Les Baux des Provence Rouge Sans Soufre ($)**, made with zero sulfur addition. It's a little more rustic and vivacious than the main cuvée, a bit the wilder younger brother (or sister).

PRODUCERS PROFILED IN THIS CHAPTER

Clos Cibonne   Mas de Gourgonnier

OTHER PROVENCE AND CORSICA PRODUCERS TO LOOK FOR

Provence

Château La Coste   Château Pradeaux
Domaine de Fontsainte   Château Simone
Domaine du Gros Noré   Domaine Tempier
Clos Sainte Magdelaine   Domaine de Terrebrune
Domaine Henri Milan   Domaine de Trévallon
Château de Pibarnon

Corsica

Comte Abbatucci   Clos Canarelli
Antoine Arena   Yves Leccia

RHÔNE VALLEY

We take it for granted these days that the Rhône Valley produces some of France's greatest wines. The red wines of Hermitage and Côte Rôtie are arguably the world's definitive Syrahs; tiny Condrieu makes luscious, sought-after whites; Châteauneuf-du-Pape is a byword for powerful Grenache-based blends that channel the Mediterranean sun into velvety layers of flavor. And there's much more to the Rhône, unquestionably one of France's greatest wine regions.

But in the decades after World War II, that wasn't the case. The steep slopes and terraced vineyards of the northern Rhône were often simply abandoned—the farming was extremely hard, near-impossible to mechanize, and the wines sold for a price that couldn't justify the effort involved in making them. This was true even into the early 1990s. As the vigneron François Villard recalls, "When I bought my first land in Condrieu, the woman who sold it to me was so relieved that she kept saying, 'Thank you! Thank you!'" That's hard to imagine now, when an acre of Condrieu would cost you a fortune (if you could find someone who was willing to part with one), and vineyard land on the terraces of Hermitage and Côte Rôtie would be more like multiple fortunes.

The southern Rhône was better off in that era, simply by being easier to farm, but even so, most of its wines were sold in bulk and bottled by local co-operatives, and were neither prestigious nor particularly exciting. There were exceptions, like Château Beaucastel in Châteauneuf-du-Pape, but they were few and far between.

No more. Today top Châteauneufs, Côte Rôties, and Hermitages sell for hundreds of dollars, and the superstar wines of Cornas and Gigondas aren't far behind.

The Rhône Valley is big—the Côtes du Rhône appellation alone covers some 140,000 acres (it's the largest appellation in the region, responsible for nearly half of all Rhône wines). The Rhône produces some of France's most full-bodied, generous reds. Grenache is the southern Rhône's mainstay, with its gift for channeling the region's warmth and glorious sun into opulent, silky-smooth wines, though it's typically blended to greater or lesser degree with other varieties, primarily Mourvèdre, Syrah, Carignan, and Cinsault. White wine only accounts for a small percentage of what's made here (whites only account for 10 percent of Rhône wine overall), but in the right hands and in the right places, southern Rhône whites can be compelling.

The much smaller northern Rhône—its six crus produce a tiny but influential 6 percent of all Rhône wine—is all about Syrah. The cooler weather and steep hillside vineyards of Hermitage, Côte Rôtie, and Cornas, which often seem carved directly into the stone, produce powerful, savory, long-lived reds unlike any others in the world. Crozes-Hermitage and St.-Joseph may not reach the same heights, but the best producers there are superb. There are also white wines here: Condrieus, made from the Viognier grape, are singularly alluring, both stony and voluptuous at once. Hermitage also produces world-class white wines, and Saint-Péray, if not at quite the same level, very good ones.

Organic viticulture is burgeoning here, as everywhere in France. Currently organic vineyards account for 13 percent of the region's area, and the number of certified organic producers climbs every year—today there are more than twenty-two hundred. If there's one issue that presses on Rhône grape growers, though, in terms of the environment, it's climate change. The Rhône, particularly in the south, has always been a warm region. Now temperatures are rising to over 115 degrees Fahrenheit on some summer days. Harvests for many vintners are a month or more earlier than they were thirty years ago.

Laurence Feraud, at Châteauneuf-du-Pape's acclaimed Domaine Pegau, has also noted a distinct increase in the number of vines that simply die each summer. "It's so hot, and there's no water. It's like apoplexy. We try to do our best, but it's difficult because our average loss now is a minimum of three thousand plants per year. What can you do?"

Good question. And one being asked around the world.

CHÂTEAU DE BEAUCASTEL • CHÂTEAUNEUF-DU-PAPE

[organic / biodynamic]

Château de Beaucastel is one of the great estates of Châteauneuf-du-Pape. Vines have grown here for more than two thousand years, since the days when the Roman empire ruled the region. The property's fortunes rose and fell over the centuries, but since the Perrin family purchased it in 1909, it's been impeccably run for more than a hundred years. It lies in a cool, northern sector of the appellation. Marc Perrin says, "We get more mistral here. Strong north wind, which has a huge impact on temperature—it's a much cooler climate than the parts of Châteauneuf that don't get the mistral." That's one reason the Mourvèdre variety, a key part of Beaucastel's wines, does so well here. "It's at the northern limit of ripeness," Perrin says, "but like anything in life, if it is extremely hard to do, sometimes the results are better."

The Perrins are organic and biodynamic, but don't trumpet that fact. "My grandfather Jacques made the decision to farm organically after World War II. It was very unusual at the time. He did yoga, too—everyone thought he was crazy."

> *"We've been organic since 1950, and working biodynamically since 1974. But we never claim it on the bottle. It's like something my uncle used to say: 'Some people go to church just to be seen at church, and others go simply because they believe.'"*
> —Marc Perrin

Châteauneuf-du-Pape is often misunderstood, Perrin feels. "People usually think it's a big wine, rustic, but it isn't. It's much more balanced, elegant, not heavy, not rustic whatsoever. One of the big problems in wine is people's preconceptions." It could be argued that one of the big problems in the entire *world* is people's preconceptions. It could also be argued that a lot of Châteauneuf-du-Pape these days actually is, unfortunately, heavy. Beaucastel doesn't fall into that realm. As Perrin says, "The key is always balance. Châteauneuf has the potential to age thirty, forty, fifty years, and you don't want to compromise that. Even in the richest vintages, I feel Beaucastel is always incredibly balanced."

The Perrins' **Coudoulet de Beaucastel Côtes du Rhône ($$)** is one of those happenstances of law as much as nature. The vineyard lies literally ten feet outside the border of the Châteauneuf-du-Pape appellation, directly across a small road from Beaucastel's main vineyard. Is the wine the same as Beaucastel? Not quite. But it is rich and potent, full of ripe red fruit and pepper, and at a third the price, that's very hard to argue with. There's also a **Coudoulet de Beaucastel Côtes du Rhône Blanc ($$)**, a blend of Bourbolenc, Marsanne, Viognier, and Roussanne that plays its citrus and stone-fruit flavors off each other nicely. The **Château de Beaucastel Châteauneuf-du-Pape Blanc ($$$$)** is somehow lusciously rich but bright, pulling alluring orchard fruit and melon flavors from a blend of Roussanne, Grenache Blanc, Clairette, and Bourbolenc. The **Château de Beaucastel Châteauneuf-du-Pape ($$$$)** is simply one of the great wines of the Rhône. It deftly balances rich red and black fruit flavors, spice notes and firm tannins, and with age becomes even more complex, taking on truffle, sandalwood, and herbal garigue notes, the wild rosemary-lavender-thyme scene of the Rhône hills.

JULIEN CECILLON • ST.-JOSEPH

[certified organic]

Though Julien Cecillon's family has been making wine for ten generations, and his uncle was the famed northern Rhône winemaker Jean-Louis Grippat, Cecillon saw no future for himself in wine. "I was just starting business school, and my uncle was going to sell the estate; his daughters wanted to quit the business, and I didn't have the cash to buy it. So that link with the past was broken."

Cecillon ended up in banking but

hated it, and came home to look for a job in the wine industry. With no experience, that didn't prove easy, but eventually Yves Cuilleron took a chance on him. "Yves said, OK, you work for me, I pay you, I'll give you a place to stay, we'll make good wine. It was a magical year. I owe him a lot."

Other jobs followed, among them a stint in California, where he met his wife, business partner, and fellow winemaker Nancy Kerschen, and by 2011 the couple knew they wanted to start a winery. Though part of his family's land had been sold, Cecillon still had seven and a half acres of vineyard. From it, he and Nancy produced two thousand bottles of St.-Joseph in 2012. To make ends meet, he taught in the local business-viticulture school, and worked in a program aimed at reducing the use of chemicals in vineyards in the area. "I learned a lot about that issue, and about the health of farmers as a result. I did three classes a week for five years—vineyard owners, fruit growers, olive growers. Every class had

twenty-five farmers, and each time I'd ask everyone to say something about themselves. And every single day I had someone say, 'Yeah, I have something to say. My son died last year, my wife has issues, my father died from cancer.' They never said, 'Oh, it was definitely the chemicals'; it was almost a secret. They felt a lot of shame about it."

Cecillon still thinks a lot about the stories he heard from farmers when he was teaching. "When I speak with the old farmers in my village, they give me the vision they had in the 1970s: If you were organic back then, you were a loser. You were the dumbest of the dumb. Because you were refusing modernity. A few people had the strength to fight that, but they were considered to be the worst farmers in town." That's changed. "Today, in the Rhône, everyone mostly understands the huge challenge we have in front of us in terms of the earth. It's terrifying, but it's also exciting. You're not just making wine to drink now; you feel like an actor in something bigger than you are."

The **Famille Cecillon Saint-Péray Gemini Blanc ($$$)** is a blend of 70 percent Marsanne and 30 percent Roussanne, rich and full-bodied, with a honeyed edge. Cecillon also makes a small amount of his **Viognier Invictus Vin de France ($$)**, equally lush in character, all apricots and cream.

Cecillon is part of a small but growing group of young Rhône winemakers making Gamay from Ardèche, in this case the **Gamay La Savane Vin de France ($$)**. "I fell in love with this vineyard," he says. "When we saw it first, it was neglected—the grass was higher than the vines, and it was full of foxes and rabbits." The **Saint-Joseph Babylone ($$$)** comes from the old-vine parcels that Cecillon and Kerschen used to start their business, some of them more than a century old. It's smoky and savory and polished; the name is an homage to their bilingual life together. **Crozes-Hermitage Les Marguerites ($$$)** comes from a single parcel on the back side of the Hermitage hill that the Cecillons took over in 2020. "It's a magical terroir," Cecillon says. He also makes a brooding, powerful **Cornas Saint Pierre ($$$)**, meaty and dark and deserving of time in a cellar.

CHÊNE BLEU • VAUCLUSE

[certified sustainable / certified organic]

"Most people, when they think of buying an old vineyard, it's Peter Mayle, a vineyard in Provence, a beautiful place to escape to," Xavier Rolet says. "I started from a different place. I wanted an environment that was complex, an environment that hadn't been polluted. We don't talk about it much, but conventional viticulture is one of the most chemically intensive forms of agriculture. I was looking for a place that had been abandoned for a long time."

What Rolet found was an estate sixteen hundred feet up in the hills, in an overlooked part of the Rhône Valley, which had been abandoned for about fifty years. "It had all the raw material, and the geology was incredibly complex. And there were native oak forests all around, which were a little bit of a barrier against pollution. The only problem was that it needed about fifteen years of rebuilding and restructuring." (Today he and his wife, Nicole Rolet, jointly run the property.)

Chêne Bleu's viticulture is organic with some biodynamic methods. Native grasses and native flowers grow between the vine rows, and biodiversity abounds (birds, insects, sheep). Wastewater from the winery is sent to a half-acre bamboo forest, where microorganisms in the soil degrade the biological matter in the water; bees are kept throughout the property to aid in pollination; wildlife corridors are maintained; compost is made from garden and vineyard residues; the list goes on.

"I've had an interest in conservation for a long time," Xavier Rolet says. "It became obvious to me that agriculture in general, and viticulture in particular, could have a huge impact in resolving the issue of climate change. Focusing on carbon and methane emissions is helpful, but they're minor compared to agriculture overall, which, post–World War II, is almost exclusively composed of intensive chemical farming. We've lost hundreds of millions of acres around the world to bad agriculture. Chêne Bleu was an opportunity for me, in a practical way, to do something about that. On a modest scale, maybe, but something."

The **Chêne Bleu Viognier IGP Vaucluse ($$)** pulls freshness from the altitude of the vineyard, and warm, rich fruit from the property's southern-Rhône latitude. **Le Rosé ($$)** blends Grenache, Syrah, Mourvèdre, and Rolle (Vermentino) for a red-fruited rosé with more body and character than the typical Provençal style; a second rosé, the **Pont de Arts Vieilles Vignes Réserve Spéciale ($$$)**, comes from old vines. It puts rosé on a level with top white wines: complex, nuanced, floral, with lasting flavor and depth. **Aliot ($$$)** is the property's top white, primarily Roussanne with Grenache Blanc, Clairette, and Rolle, its rich, orchard fruit flavors balanced by bright acidity.

The two reds are **Abelard ($$$)**, 85 percent old-vine Grenache with 15 percent Syrah, supple and full-bodied with ripe red fruit flavors and cedary spice notes, and **Héloïse ($$$)**, which flips the varietal makeup (Syrah 70 percent/Grenache 26 percent/Roussanne 4 percent). It's intense and peppery, with a little more edge.

CHÂTEAU DE SAINT COSME • GIGONDAS

[certified organic / biodynamic]

Château de Saint Cosme is the oldest winery in the southern Rhône. A Roman legionnaire first made wine here in the second century AD; vats carved into the limestone under the château remain from that era. Middle Age documents reference vinegrowing here, and the property has been in owner Louis Barruol's family since 1490. But for the vast portion of its modern history, the wine from Saint Cosme's vineyards was sold in bulk to *négociants* in Burgundy and Châteauneuf-du-Pape. "Nobody knew us," Barruol says. "My father was primarily a farmer."

Château Saint Cosme (pronounced like "comb") lies just north of the picturesque village of Gigondas, up against the crags of the Dentelles de Montmirail. Barruol took over the estate in 1992, when he was only twenty-three. His first goal was to restore Saint Cosme from its ruined state. He has an aesthetic streak—he'll compare wine to Rodin's sculptures, noting how that artist was able to generate emotion while remaining true to his raw materials—but also a steely will (this is someone who regularly played rugby up until he was forty-eight). By the late 1990s, he had brought Saint Cosme to the top ranks of southern Rhône producers, where it remains. In 2019, he also purchased Château de Rouanne in nearby Vinsobres, another great terroir whose reputation had declined (for years it was the primary source for Barruol's *négociant* Côtes du Rhône). He shrugs. "I get bored easily, so I need new projects."

Château Saint Cosme has thirty-seven acres of vines, a third of them planted before World War I. The property has never been farmed with chemicals, and these days Barruol works biodynamically, but is not certified: "I don't choose to get certified and I never will. The certification for biodynamics for France has been built by people from Burgundy, Champagne, and the Loire, where the climate is totally different from here. Using silica is a requirement for certification—that's nonsense. Use silica on vines in the southern Rhône in June, and you'll see how your wines are after that." (Silica—ground-up quartz, basically—enhances photosynthesis and ripeness, in theory, two things that aren't remotely lacking in the sunny southern Rhône.) Barruol says, "I like biodynamics in terms of what it brings to agriculture. But my spirituality is mine, and I don't need a guide for that. I also don't like the group effect of bio; biodynamics adherents are often not very open-minded. They tend to think they own the truth."

At Château de Rouanne he farms 153 acres of vines, again biodynamically.

The estate, which lies a few miles from Saint Cosme, in Vinsobres, was the property of a local noble family from the twelfth century to the nineteenth century. After that, it changed hands three times before Barruol bought it. "We're going slowly at Rouanne," he says. "When you take over a place, you don't make a huge amount of wine quickly. Never forget, a cook cooks every day, and as winemakers we only cook once per year."

Barruol's *négociant* wines are labeled simply Saint Cosme, while the domaine wines are labeled Château de Saint Cosme. Quality is high for both, though the *négociant* grapes are not necessarily certified organic or biodynamic. For the non-domaine wines, the red **Saint Cosme Côtes du Rhône ($$)**, much of the grapes for which still come from the biodynamic vines at Château de Rouanne, is a stellar buy, as are the bargain-priced **Little James Basket Press Blanc** and **Rouge ($)**. The **Saint Cosme Crozes-Hermitage ($$)** is also a standout: smoky, dark, and savory.

The **Château de Saint Cosme Gigondas ($$$)** is a benchmark for the appellation. Seventy percent Grenache with smaller portions of Mour-

vèdre, Syrah, and Cinsault, it's a mélange of red and black fruit with complex herbal notes and supple, fine-grained tannins. Barruol makes several single-site Gigondas bottlings. For a splurge, look for the gorgeously aromatic **Gigondas Le Poste ($$$$)** with its peppery red/blue fruit and violet floral notes.

The Château de Rouanne reds are dark and powerful, but retain elegance because of the coolness of the site. But first, surprisingly, is a fresh, bright sparkling wine, the **Rouanne Brut Nature ($$)**. Barruol says, "I got the idea after one year of working there—it was so cold in the winter, all the time; and it seemed my Mourvèdre tasted ripe at twelve percent alcohol, so . . ." The **Château de Rouanne Vin-**

sobres (\$\$) bursts with plum, berry, and white pepper notes; it's an excellent value, too. There are also three single-site bottlings. To pick a favorite, the **Rouanne et les Crottes Vinsobres (\$\$\$)** comes from the middle of the slope in the vineyards; it suggests the wild herbs of the region, against a layered backdrop of blue and red fruit and smoke. "The name can be traced back to the fourteenth century on the old map of the property we have," Barruol says. "It's the essence of what we make at Rouanne."

YVES CUILLERON • CONDRIEU

[certified sustainable / organic]

In 1986, Yves Cuilleron had no plans to become a winemaker: his primary goal was to become a mechanic. But after graduating school, he learned that his uncle wanted to retire and planned to sell their family's northern Rhône vineyards, a patrimony that stretched back several generations—but that were at the time, more or less a money-losing proposition. Yves felt differently. "So, I said, maybe I can keep them?"

"I was the right generation," he says. "At the time, there was a lot of free land, and none of it was very expensive. So my thought was to rapidly expand what we owned, because I was sure the reputation would come back. It had to. In the nineteenth century, the vineyards of the northern Rhône had the same reputation as the best Bordeaux, the best Burgundy."

Cuilleron now farms 173 acres, in six different crus (Condrieu, Côte Rôtie, Saint-Joseph, Saint-Péray, Crozes-Hermitage, and Cornas), as well as in the broader Colline Rhodanniennes IGP. His approach is certified sustainable and practicing organic (he started conversion to certified organic in 2022), but also very much his own. "My vinification is my vinification; it's my philosophy, my idea. Same in the vineyard. But it started with my uncle—during the eighties, he was one of the first to let grass start to grow in his vineyards again. He never used herbicides, never used pesticides, and I followed him. I saw that the important thing was balance. If you begin to use chemical products, you need more and more each year. And if you keep that balance, you need less and less."

Cuilleron produces a number of exceptional bargains from the relatively recently created Collines Rhodaniennes appellation. His **Yves Cuilleron Viognier Les Vignes d'à Côté ($–$$)** summons a lot of the aromatic splendor of Condrieu for a fraction of the price. Similarly, the **Syrah Les Vignes d'à Côté ($–$$)** has that signature northern Rhône black-pepper-plus smoked-meat savoriness without the price tag of Cornas or Côte Rôtie.

Cuilleron also makes plenty of different wines from the northern Rhône's famed crus. Among the whites, the **Condrieu La Petite Côte ($$$)** comes from south-facing terraces in Chavanay, and offers textbook floral-peachy intensity and a creamy, luscious texture; the **Condrieu Les Chaillets ($$$)**, from old vines in Chavanay, is firmer and stonier, still full-bodied and seductive but a bit more regal in bearing.

Cuilleron's **Saint-Joseph Rouge Les Pierres Seches ($$)** is savory, full of blue-black fruit and pepper, not massive but certainly muscular. The name, literally "the dry stones," refers to the handmade stone walls used to hold up the steep terraces in northern Rhône vineyards. His smoky **Côte Rôtie Bassenon ($$$–$$$$)** comes from a tiny vineyard in the southernmost part of the appellation. Those are just a few—Cuilleron makes more than forty wines, and all are well worth trying.

DOMAINE ALAIN GRAILLOT • CROZES-HERMITAGE

[organic]

Alain Graillot, who passed away in 2022, probably did more than any other vintner to raise the Crozes-Hermitage appellation from overlooked obscurity to international recognition.

Before Graillot arrived in Crozes-Hermitage, he'd never made a wine in his life. He studied chemical engineering, and in the 1980s was working for a pharmaceutical corporation in Paris. "Basically, he had a midlife crisis," his son Maxime Graillot says. Alain was turning forty, hated the work he was doing, and loved wine. "He had friends in Burgundy," Maxime recalls, "but he always said, 'I didn't feel like settling in a place with three months of fog and then endless winter.'" The Rhône Valley beckoned. He moved there in 1985.

Graillot had a vision of the wines he wanted to make, influenced by his Burgundian friends: fresh, precise reds, moderate in alcohol, made with whole-cluster fermentation. It was a style that had fallen out of favor in the Rhône, but he was firm about it. "My father was a big man of soft powers," Maxime says. "He had strong beliefs and he knew how to get to his point."

Alain Graillot himself didn't work in a strictly organic way, "but the pharmaceutical company he'd worked for in Paris also sold agricultural products, so he had an understanding of what to avoid," Maxime says. "And when I came back in 2004, I moved everything to organic. But I did that for me, my kids, and my neighbors, not for anyone else. I'm not certified. I don't need other people to believe me,

and I don't need to prove to myself what I'm doing."

Maxime is outspoken, expressing opinions that are sometimes blunt, and often very funny. Currently he and his brother Antoine are implementing agroforestry practices on the property, planting trees both in the vineyards and around them: "First, it's good to have trees! But we also live right in the middle of Crozes-Hermitage, and people used to share the land here with peach trees, cherry trees, apricots—and even if it was industrial agriculture, at least it was diverse. It's a very short-term vision to have monocultures." He's also noted distinct climatic changes in the twenty-five years he's been making wine. "In France traditionally you look for maximum ripeness, because you're in northern Europe. With climate change you can't work that way anymore. But there are still a lot of people who do, and then you have to add acid, and reduce alcohol, and blah blah blah. It's absurd."

He adds, "We *cannot* keep living the way we've been living for the past twenty years. I'm not saying we have to go back to the stone age; I'm not saying we have to stop international trade. But we don't pay the right cost for things—there should be trade that's based on the cost to the planet. A T-shirt from

China might cost 99 percent less to produce, but it might cost 99 percent more when you take into account the cost to the planet of getting it to France. If wine needs to reflect that, I'm OK with it. Even if I sell less wine. My brother and I, our ambition is not to rule the world with Alain Graillot Crozes-Hermitage."

The one Graillot white is the **Crozes-Hermitage Blanc ($$)**, made with 80 percent Marsanne and 20 percent Roussanne. It's rich with orchard fruit flavors, but bright and zippy as well.

The reds are entirely Syrah, made with no new oak and 100 percent whole-cluster fermentation. (Two signs that Alain Graillot put up long ago still hang in the winery: "No Destemmers!" and "No Dogs!" "My father hated dogs," Maxime says, with a shrug. "Normally, all the winemakers have a dog. Not my father. That's why I have a cat and two chickens.") The **Alain Graillot Crozes-Hermitage ($$–$$$)** is a benchmark of the northern Rhône, floral, savory, taut, and vivid, a superb cool-climate Syrah with an herbal edge from the whole-cluster winemaking. "When you do things whole cluster, you always get a green character," Maxime says. "But if there's strong, powerful fruit, you'll balance that, and the herbal notes will be noble." That's even more clear in the **Crozes-Hermitage La Guiraude ($$$)**, a selection of the best barrels from the first wine (usually about one out of ten). Lastly, there's a small amount of **Saint-Joseph Rouge ($$)**, from two small parcels, made exactly the same way as the Crozes; it's typically a little lighter and more red-fruited, but still complex and lasting. (The Graillots also have an ongoing project in Morocco together with the local Thalvin winery. The **Syrocco Syrah du Morocco [$–$$]**, made from organically farmed fruit, is an affordable pleasure, more fruit-forward than the Graillot Rhône wines but equally enjoyable.)

E. GUIGAL · CÔTE RÔTIE

[organic (estate vineyards)]

"It finishes extremely well, but it starts badly."

That's Philippe Guigal, talking about the origins of E. Guigal, his family's company. The Guigal name is practically synonymous with Rhône Valley wine; the family's widely available Côtes du Rhône red manages the remarkable trick of being produced in very substantial quantities while still being extremely good; its famed La-La's, the trio of single-vineyard Côte Rôties comprised of La Turque, La Moulin, and La Landonne, are benchmarks not just for that appellation but for the Rhône Valley as a whole. In fact, in the third decade of the twenty-first century, it's hard to think of the Rhône Valley at all without thinking of the name of Guigal.

Contrast that with Etienne Guigal's start.

Etienne Guigal was born in the eastern Loire Valley in 1909. His father died when he was six months old, leaving the family with almost nothing. Bad enough, then worse. According to Philippe Guigal, "When my grandfather was eight, his mother told him,

'I love you, but I don't have enough money to raise three kids, and you're the smartest. You'll have to leave and be on your own.'"

We think of wine as being tied to luxury and romance, but there's nothing romantic and certainly nothing luxurious about being thrown out of your home at age eight, to find your way in the world. Etienne found work looking after cows and goats in the Haut Loire.

"This was very, very hard," Philippe continues. "The Haut Loire is much colder than the Rhône, and my grandfather sometimes talked about how he remembered walking in the snow without shoes." After five years of this, Etienne headed to the city of Saint-Étienne to try to find work in a factory that made guns. He looked older and stronger than his age, and the foreman agreed to hire him, but, Philippe Guigal says, "then the guy asked, 'How old are you?' My grandfather said, 'I'm twelve,' and the guy said, 'What? I can't hire you!' My grandfather started to cry. 'I have no work—I have no choice,' he said." The foreman took pity on him and agreed to hire him, but told him, "If you see someone with a tie and a jacket in the factory, you have to hide."

It's hard today to imagine the poverty and difficulty of life in France following World War I. In 1924, Guigal moved farther east to join his brother in Côte Rôtie, where the older boy was working as a migrant laborer, picking apricots. Pickers were needed because so many men of working age had died in the war. This is where the story turns. "He wasn't very interested in apricots," Philippe Guigal says, "but he saw the crazy hillsides we have here. 'What's going on there?' he asked. His brother told him, 'It's grapevines, but the work's too hard and they aren't worth anything. They're going to disappear.' And my grandfather said, 'Hm . . . I don't think so.' Then he saw a vineyard on one of the slopes, and asked some of the local people about it. They told him it was the best vineyard in the region. He said, 'I'm going to buy it one day.' He had absolutely nothing! Not one cent! But that was La Mouline. And then he met a maid who was working at Château d'Ampuis, and fell in love. He told her, 'One day I'll buy this house, too.'"

Etienne Guigal kept that promise, but it took some time. He founded his eponymous firm in 1946, after working his way up the ladder at the renowned Rhône producer Vidal Fleury. By 1965, he was successful enough to buy La Mouline, the vineyard he'd seen on the hill, and he almost lived long enough to buy Château de Ampuis, too. (His son Marcel fulfilled that part of the dream, purchasing Château d'Ampuis in 1995. E. Guigal is now headquartered there.)

Today, the Guigals own roughly 185 acres of vines in the northern Rhône and 190 acres in the south, and purchase fruit from growers with whom they have long-term contracts. They make wines in almost every significant Rhône appellation (the estate-owned vineyards cover all of Guigal's northern Rhône production, except for Crozes-Hermitage; the southern Rhône wines are primarily from contract vineyards). And as Philippe Guigal says, "We're a one hundred percent family-owned business, and for us that's extremely important. Twenty-five years ago, I could have named twenty-five family-owned wineries of significant size in the Rhône Valley. Not now."

They farm their own vineyards

without synthesized chemicals or fertilizers, and have for many years. Philippe Guigal says, "In the 1960s, my father, Marcel, subscribed to a publication called the *Organic Paisan*. He was always convinced of the importance of working this way, but he never claimed it overtly. If you remember France in 1968, the hippie culture—some people at the time might have thought my dad was in this movement, 'nature is beautiful,' but that wasn't really him. It's probably more linked to the fact that Côte Rôtie is only twenty-five minutes south of Lyon, and Lyon was always the center of the French chemical industry. Having that example close by was probably more of an influence."

Most of Guigal's inexpensive wines are *négociant* bottlings, so the family does not handle the farming for those wines. It's accurate to say, though, that much of the *négociant* fruit is sustainable, and some of it is organic. (Though definitely not all.) All of the domaine vineyards, on the other hand, including those of Château Nalys, the Guigal's recently acquired Châteauneuf-du-Pape property, are farmed organically.

Among the domaine wines to look for is the impressive **E. Guigal Crozes-Hermitage Blanc** (\$\$). Crozes-Hermitage Blanc can be a hit-and-miss proposition, but Guigal's melony, chalky bottling, predominantly from their estate vineyards, overperforms for its price. The family's **Cuvée Lieu-Dit Saint-Joseph Blanc** (\$\$\$) is a step up from that in terms of complexity and depth. From the southern Rhône, the

Domaine de Nalys Saintes Pierres de Nalys Blanc (\$\$\$) is succulent and rich, though not too much so; the grand vin **Château de Nalys Blanc** (\$\$\$–\$\$\$\$) is primarily Roussanne, giving it more floral and stony notes.

Among the reds, the **Saint-Joseph Lieu-Dit Rouge** (\$\$\$) is powerful but supple, with plenty of black Syrah fruit and spice notes. The single-vineyard **Saint-Joseph Vignes de l'Hospice** (\$\$\$\$) comes from a single steep plot of older Syrah on granite soil; it's very fine and pure, and thrillingly aromatic. For a sense of why Guigal is so respected as a Côte Rôtie producer, the spicy, savory, profound **Château d'Ampuis Côte Rôtie** (\$\$\$\$) provides a good idea. It's worth the splurge for a special occasion. (The famed La-La Côte Rôties—La Turque, La Mouline, and La Landonne—are now so expensive—$400-plus a bottle—that they're outside the scope of this book.) The **Domaine de Nalys Saintes Pierres de Nalys Châteauneuf-du-Pape Rouge ($$$)** is a full-throttle, luscious, southern Rhône red that nevertheless maintains impeccable balance. The grand vin **Château de Nalys ($$$$)** red is primarily Grenache, along with a good whack of Syrah, plus smaller percentages of Mourvèdre, Counoise, and Vacarèse. It is more structured and powerful than the Saintes Pierres; still approachable when young, but it definitely will benefit from several years aging.

Leaving aside the wines from vineyards they own, the Guigals have a remarkable gift for sourcing extremely good fruit and/or finished wine for their *négociant* bottlings. The basic **Côtes du Rhône Blanc ($)** and **Côtes du Rhône Rouge ($)**, the latter speaking to the family's northern Rhône home with its high percentage of Syrah, are both stellar deals. The same can be said of the **Guigal Crozes-Hermitage Rouge ($$)** and **Gigondas ($$)**. And the **Côte Rôtie Brune et Blonde ($$$)** is a classic. Made from both estate and purchased fruit, it's a rare instance of an excellent Côte Rôtie that's actually relatively widely available.

DOMAINE DE LA JANASSE • CHÂTEAUNEUF-DU-PAPE

[organic]

On the advice of her parents, Isabelle Sabon planned to become a teacher. "That's what my mother always told me. Be a teacher. You'll have more time. Which made sense, because when I was young, my father and mother were *always* working." Her father founded Domaine de la Janasse in 1972. In that era most Châteauneuf-du-Pape was still sold in bulk and bottled by cooperatives. Building recognition for an estate wasn't easy. Sabon's parents grew tomatoes and other crops to make ends meet, and her mother had a second job at the local bank. "It was important for my parents that my brother and I did not feel obligated to work in wine. So I learned chemistry, and planned to teach it. . . ." She laughs. "But in the end, I became an enologist."

Because for all the work, there *is* something in wine. Today Isabelle and her brother, Christophe, farm 222 acres of vineyards in Châteauneuf, Côtes du Rhône, and the Principauté d'Orange (an IGP region between Châteauneuf and Côtes du Rhône AOCs). "For us it's enough," she says. "But my father always wants to buy new vineyards, even though he's retired. Recently he wanted to buy some land in Cairanne, and we were like, 'stop!'"

The Janasse property is in conversion to certified organic, but Sabon notes that nothing will really have to change for the certification. "When my father started, he farmed conventionally, because the people who sold you the products were the people who told you how to farm. But for twenty years we haven't used any chemical products at all."

Though running the domaine may not be as grueling now as it was for Sabon's parents, it's still hard work. Yet it's also tremendously fulfilling: "Each year is a new challenge when you make wine. Last year, frost; this year, hail. But those two months of harvest are one of life's great pleasures. And yes, there are difficult years. But my father always told me, nature gives to you, so you have to learn that she can also take."

Janasse's Côtes du Rhônes and IGP wines are some of the finest values in the Rhône. All come from estate fruit. "We never buy grapes, and we never buy wine," Sabon says. The **Domaine de la Janasse Viognier Principauté d'Orange ($)** and the **Rosé Méditerranée ($)** are two to look for, as are Janasse's Côtes du Rhônes, all of which are very good. The crisp **Côtes du Rhône Blanc ($$)** comes from a twelve-acre vineyard just outside Châteauneuf's borders. The basic **Côtes du Rhône Rouge ($$)** is at the usual high standard for this property, but for a few dollars more, go for the deeper, more substantive **Côtes du Rhône Réserve ($$)**, which could easily be mistaken blind for a Châteauneuf-du-Pape, or the spicy, herbal 100 percent Grenache **Côtes du Rhône Les Garrigues ($$)**, which comes from a small plot of one-hundred-plus-year-old vines. (There's also an excellent Côtes du Rhône from a property they purchased in the town of Plan de Dieu in

2014, the **Clos Saint Antonin Côtes du Rhône [$$]**—seek it out.)

About Grenache, Sabon says, "Grenache can make a wine that's powerful but also elegant; with tannins when it's young, but silky tannins; and with the complexity of a blended wine, without the blend. And only Grenache can do this—pure Syrah or pure Mourvèdre won't have the elegance or the freshness it does." The **Domaine de la Janasse Châteauneuf-du-Pape Chaupin ($$$)**, which is 100 percent Grenache, deepens all those characteristics. Janasse also makes its **Châteauneuf-du-Pape Tradition ($$$)** from a number of vineyards they own; it's 65 percent Grenache with Syrah, Mouvèdre, and Cinsault, and is darker and more muscular, albeit in that velvety Châteauneuf way. At the top of the range is the **Châteauneuf-du-Pape Vieilles Vignes ($$$$)**, a blend from the oldest vines on the property. It's more powerful and structured than Chaupin; more imposing, to be sure, and a gorgeous Rhône red . . . but to my mind not necessarily better.

DOMAINE LA MONARDIÈRE • VACQUEYRAS

[certified organic]

Domaine La Monardière, helmed by the young Damien Vache, is one of the bright lights in Vacqueyras, an appellation that is itself one of the brighter lights in the southern Rhône as a whole (particularly for those in search of compelling wines at a not-painful price). Vache's family has grown grapes for years: "The estate and the majority of the vines were in my family forever," he says. "But it's really since my parents took over in 1987 that we began to make and sell our own wine."

When Vache began working with his father, Christian, in 2007, they also started the certification process for organic viticulture, though the older man had been de facto farming that way, without herbicides or systemic pesticides, since 2000. "I think what made my father switch was some of the winegrowers around him, people he knew and liked, who worked that way—Denis Alary in Cairanne, for instance." Damien notes that he benefited from his father's disinclination toward chemicals, since he played in the vines constantly as a small child. Helping out with work started early, too: "I first drove a tractor when I was eleven or twelve. It was great fun! I loved it."

The Vaches farm fifty-four acres of vineyard. Damien, his wife, and their three young sons live in the middle of the vines, and his parents are there, too, he says. "It's a very family situation. I'm not sure which is more work, though, the vineyard or my boys. But I really love both."

Compared to neighboring Gigondas, Vache says, the wines of Vacqueyras have softer, more elegant tannins, and are more approachable when they're young. He also feels Vacqueyras is undervalued for its whites, so 20 percent of his vines are white varieties, unusual for the region. The **Domaine La Monardière Galejade Blanc ($$)**, a complex, full-bodied blend of Roussanne, Grenache Blanc, and Clairette, shows why that's a smart decision.

Vache's **Côtes du Rhone Les Calades ($–$$)** is a fresh, vivid red; it comes entirely from the estate's vines in Vacqueyras, but because it contains more than 10 percent "accessory" grapes (Counoise, Cinsault, and Cari-

gnan), Vache is required to label it as Côtes du Rhône. The **Vacqueyras Les 2 Monardes ($$)** blends 70 percent Grenache and 30 percent Syrah. It's a generous, dark-fruited red with pepper and wild herb notes. The **Vacqueyras Vieilles Vignes ($$)** is from vines averaging sixty plus years old, and is two-thirds to three-quarters Grenache, depending on the vintage, with the rest split between Syrah and Mourvèdre. Earthy and dark, with plush tannins and firm acidity, it amps up the character of Les 2 Monardes, adding a touch of gaminess from the Mourvèdre. All of the Monardière wines are absurdly underpriced for what they offer.

DOMAINE DU PEGAU • CHÂTEAUNEUF-DU-PAPE

[sustainable / organic]

Sometimes life as a winemaker starts early. "When I was quite small, my grandmother asked me all the time to climb up and dip my fingers into the tops of the large casks. I was agile, so I could get up there easily, and tell her if they were full or not," Laurence Féraud says. But her path wasn't a direct one. Not long after that, Féraud went to live in Avignon with relatives on her mother's side. But the vineyards remained in her memory, and now and then she would visit, reconnecting with a different life. "It's funny. When I was a teenager, I wanted to be a shepherd, of all things. I loved the idea of reading a book under the trees and watching the sheep."

Her grandparents made wine and sold it to the local co-op in bulk. But by the time Laurence had finished a degree in enology and then in business, she had other ideas. She returned home and convinced her father to start his own winery. "I was ready to come back," she said. "I had a good job in Paris, and I wasn't going to make any money in Châteauneuf, but between all the money I was spending

in Paris and the money I wouldn't be earning in Châteauneuf, either way I was going to be poor!"

Things have changed. Domaine du Pegau now makes some of Châteauneuf-du-Pape's most respected wines, and the estate's organic vines cover 178 acres in Châteauneuf-du-Pape and several other southern Rhône appellations. "It's probably more than twenty years now that we've been working organically, but we're not certified," Féraud says. Regardless, what she's concerned about today are the climate changes happening in the southern Rhône. She's seen more and more vines simply die during the summer, she says, thanks to temperatures that regularly reach 115 degrees Fahrenheit or higher (irrigation is not allowed in Châteauneuf-du-Pape). And with the heat, the grapes are smaller, too. "If they're the size of black currants, we can press and press, but there's no juice," she says.

Pegau remains a family winery, as it was when Laurence Féraud was growing up. Her son Maxim now works with her, and her father, who is eighty-four, still weighs in. "Three generations, it's not always easy to work together," she says with a shrug. "But it's important."

Féraud's Châteauneuf-du-Pape wines are labeled as Domaine de Pegau (the word is an ancient Roman term for a wine pitcher), and the rest of her Rhône wines as Château Pegau. She also bottles a very good, very affordable, *négociant* Côtes du Rhône under the Sélection Laurence Féraud label. The winemaking is traditional: whole-cluster fermentation in old oak, and nothing more than that; not all that different from the years when Féraud was climbing up on top of barrels to dip her fingers in the wine.

The **Château Pegau Côtes du Rhône Blanc Cuvée Lône ($–$$)** is a crisp white full of orchard fruit flavors. **Pink Pegau ($)** is a salmon-hued, palate-whetting rosé. The **Château Pegau Côtes du Rhône Cuvée Maclura ($–$$)** and **Côtes du Rhône Villages Cuvée Setier ($$)** both have a peppery, black olive, and black fruit intensity, the Setier with a bit more tannic structure. Féraud's **Domaine Pegau Châteauneuf-du-Pape Blanc Cuvée Réservée ($$$)**,

mostly biodynamic Clairette with percentages of Grenache Blanc, Roussanne, and Bourboulenc, impeccably balances richness against freshness. Her **Châteauneuf-du-Pape Cuvée Réservée ($$$)** is one of the benchmark wines of Châteauneuf, earthy and powerful, full of old-school savoriness. Pegau's Châteauneuf vineyards are divided between the three main soil types: stony soil, "which gives you the upfront power and the jamminess, the fat," Féraud says. "The sandy soil gives length, the notes on the back end, and the deep taste of fruit from mineral soil. Then clay, which gives something very deep in the mid-palate, those licorice and black currant characters." Lastly, there's the ultra-limited **Châteauneuf-du-Pape Cuvée da Capo ($$$$)**, only made in top vintages from three separate vineyards in the La Crau section of Châteauneuf. It's a brilliant wine, but in recent years its price has climbed into the stratosphere.

DOMAINE GEORGES VERNAY • CONDRIEU

[certified organic / biodynamic]

"Viognier should have disappeared," Christine Vernay says. "But my father was absolutely convinced that he had to save it." This was in 1953. After two world wars, the northern Rhône was depleted, its vines too hard to farm and its wines largely forgotten. There were only a few acres of Viognier left in the world, two and a half of which were in a block of vines planted by Georges Vernay's grandfather in 1937. "He felt that Condrieu was a special terroir, this place where Viognier has a distinctive taste, unlike anywhere else—you can plant lettuce, potatoes, peaches, apricots anywhere. But here, only Viognier. It can't be reproduced."

Vernay restored acres of dauntingly steep terraces, the *chaillées* of the northern Rhône, and replanted them with Viognier vines. Today, the variety is planted throughout the world, and Condrieu is renowned for its wines; much of that is due to Georges Vernay. Not for nothing was he known as "the Pope of Condrieu."

Since 1996, Vernay's daughter Christine has helmed the estate. When she took over, it was unprecedented for a woman to run a domaine here, but she brushes off the distinction. "Of course it was difficult, but it would have been the same if I were a man—because the challenge was to be as good as my father!"

The domaine has effectively been organic from the start. "You know, for a lot of winemakers, it was amazing to have these chemical products—you could work a hectare of vines easily yourself," she says. "But for our family that way of working was always a bit weird. I've always been convinced, from the beginning, that to stop erosion and to promote the life in the soil, we had to work this way. Though I do remember my mother always complained about my father having to fight the grass between the rows with a hoe."

Georges Vernay passed away in 2017, at age ninety-two. In 2020, Christine's daughter Emma Amsellem joined her, and since her arrival, the Vernays have been shifting to biodynamics. "It's not like you can come in and announce, 'All right! Bio! Let's go!'" Emma Amsellem says. "But we'll be certified by the end of 2023, I hope. It's that idea of 'when you go slowly, you go well, and you go far.'"

Domaine Georges Vernay makes stellar Condrieu, and also a broad range of wines from Côte Rôte, St.-Joseph, and the recent Collines Rhodaniennes IGP. "Collines is near the Condrieu appellation, not in it, but the quality is quite high because it's so close," Christine Vernay says. The domaine's wines from the Collines Rhodaniennes are spectacular values. The **Domaine Georges Vernay Pied de Samson Viognier ($$)** is Condrieu in all but name, and the **Fleur de Mai Syrah ($$)** and **Saint-Agathe Syrah ($$)** are similarly suggestive of Côte Rôtie.

The **Les Terrasses de L'Empire Condrieu ($$$)** comes from a patchwork of old-vine parcels in Condrieu. The impressive **Les Chaillées de Enfer Condrieu ($$$)** gets its name from what old farmers called the vineyard: "the terraces of hell." Emma Amsellem

says, "It faces right into the sun, and there are a lot of stones, so the stones burned the skin of the people who worked there." The **Côteau de Vernon Condrieu ($$$$)**, from fifty-to-eighty-year-old vines, is the domaine's top Condrieu, and quite possibly the greatest wine in the appellation. Rich, complex, impeccably balanced, it's one to save up for.

The **Domaine Georges Vernay Blonde du Seigneur Côte Rôtie ($$$)** is fresh and floral, an elegant Syrah from three parcels of vines on granite soil. "A lot of white pepper and violets," Christine Vernay says. Her **Maison Rouge Côte Rôtie ($$$$)** is the domaine's top red wine and comes from very old vines. "It has the same elegance, but also density," Christine says, along with darker fruit and plenty of intensity.

FRANÇOIS VILLARD • CONDRIEU

[certified organic (estate) / organic (négociant)]

François Villard comes from humble origins. His father grew corn in the

farmland between Viennes and Grenoble, and Villard himself started out as a cook at a hospital in Viennes. "That's when I became interested in wine," he recalls with a laugh, "probably because I was not very excited by the food! I took a sommelier course, and decided somehow to become a winemaker. I bought my first land in 1988, planted my first vines in 1989, and made my first wine in 1991. Four hundred bottles! I started from nothing."

Villard is now one of the most recognized winemakers in the Rhône, making between four hundred thousand and five hundred thousand bottles a year. He owns 106 acres of vineyards, and works with another 90 or so, in every region in the northern Rhône except Hermitage. His timing was fortunate. When he started in the early 1990s, the northern Rhône was in a decades-long slump. "When I bought my first land, the woman who sold it to me was so relieved I bought it, saying, 'Thank you! Thank you!' That was in Condrieu. It cost almost nothing." Today, the price of that first acre of land would be vastly higher, if you could even find an acre for sale.

As of 2022 all of his vineyards are certified organic, though Villard first stopped using herbicides in 1998, and cut back on all other systemic agricultural chemicals beginning in 2005. Still, he notes, the kind of conventional farming he was doing before 1998 was part of what helped the northern Rhône get back on its feet, by making farming here less grueling and more productive at a time when prices for the region's wines were stunningly low (that, too, has changed).

Villard is in his sixties, but shows little sign of slowing down. Recently he's started buying land in La Côte St. Andre, northwest of Grenoble. "Ten years ago, I thought, maybe I'll have to reduce my level of activity. But finally, no. I just choose more carefully. I'm like an old soccer player. I choose my match."

Taken together, Villard's three Condrieus, the **François Villard Condrieu De Poncins ($$$)**, **Condrieu Le Grand Vallon ($$$)**, and **Condrieu Les Terrasses du Palate ($$$)**, are a master class in the terroir of this tiny but remarkable wine region. He also makes the excellent, affordable **Viognier Contours de Deponcins ($$)** from vineyards that aren't quite within the Condrieu boundaries and a pretty, fresh **Saint-Péray Blanc ($$)**, mostly

Marsanne, from an appellation even smaller than Condrieu, and several other whites.

Villard's reds are less oaky and oomphy than they once were, with a more lifted, streamlined character in recent vintages. A few to look for are the affordably priced **Syrah L'Appel des Sereines** ($); a peppery, lively wine labeled simply as *vin de France*; the savory, cassis-and-black-olive-scented **St-Joseph Poivre et Sol** ($$); the powerful but balanced **Cornas Jouvet** ($$$); and the violet-scented, polished **Côte Rôtie Le Gallet Blanc** ($$$), which comes from schistous vineyards in Ampuis and St. Cyr. His **Seul en Scène** ($$$) is also superb, a generous, black-fruited Syrah that's a testimony to the potential of the up-and-coming Collines Rhodanniènes region.

PRODUCERS PROFILED IN THIS CHAPTER

Château de Beaucastel
Julien Cecillon
Chêne Bleu
Château de Saint Cosme
Yves Cuilleron
Alain Graillot

E. Guigal
Domaine de la Janasse
Domaine la Monardière
Domaine du Pegau
Georges Vernay
François Villard

OTHER RHÔNE VALLEY PRODUCERS TO LOOK FOR

Domaine Alary
Domaine des Amphores
Pierre André
Domaine l'Anglore
Domaine Aphillanthes
Franck Balthazar
Domaine de Beaurenard
Le Clos de Caillou
Michel Chapoutier
Domaine Charvin
Clusel-Roch
Domaine Combier
Domaine Faury
Pierre Gaillard
Yves Gangloff
Domaine Gour de Mautens

Domaine Gramenon
Domaine Lionnet
Maxime Magnon
Domaine de Marcoux
Domaine Monnier-Perréol
Domaine Montirius
Domaine de la Mordorée
Domaine la Remejeanne
Domaine Romaneaux-Destezet/
  Hervé Souhaut
Rene Rostaing
Saint Jean du Barroux
Domaine Santa Duc
Jean Michel Stephan
Eric Texier

ITALY

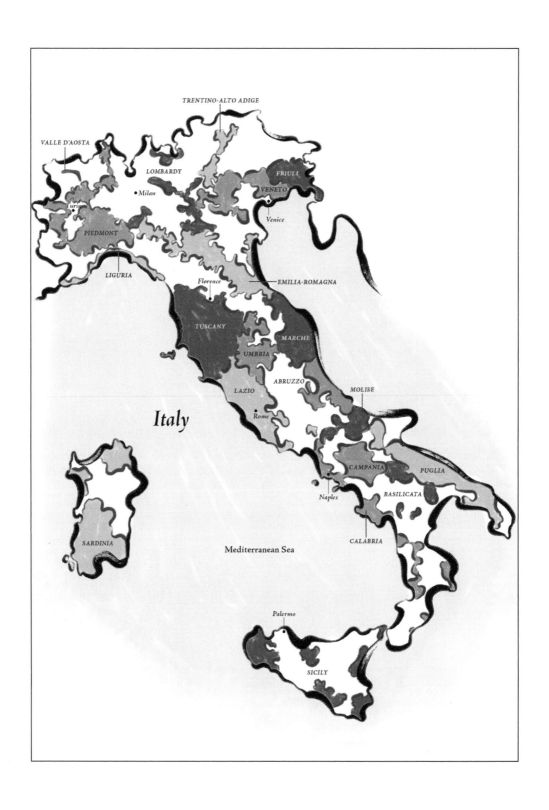

taly's vast number of native grape varieties, estimated at more than two thousand, is unequaled by any other wine-producing country, though only around four hundred or so are in commercial production.

Only four hundred! Add to that the not-quite-as-staggering but still daunting number of official wine denominations (also more than four hundred), which range from the deeply familiar, such as Chianti Classico, to the utterly obscure—Cacc'e Mmitte di Lucera, anyone?—and you have a recipe for melting the brain of most casual wine drinkers. Thank god so many of the wines are so good.

Italy makes more wine than any other country, roughly 19 percent of what's produced in the world, and has been making wine for thousands of years. The oldest recorded evidence goes back to the Copper Age, around 4000 BC; traces of salt of tartaric, naturally occurring during winemaking, have been found in urns at an archaeological site in southern Sicily.

Move on, past the Etruscans and Phoenicians, past the Roman Empire, past the Renaissance (there are still Italian producers who got their start in that era), to the beginnings of what we now think of as Italian wine in the late 1800s. That is when Barolo gets its start (at least what we now know as Barolo; it was sweet, rather than dry, until the mid-1800s); when Baron Ricasoli in Tuscany first wrote down a distinct "recipe" for Chianti (70 percent Sangiovese, 30 percent Canaiolo, and white varieties such as Malvasia and Trebbiano; it has since changed); when the first Brunello di Montalcino was bottled; and more. That burst of ambition was interrupted by the devastation of two world wars, with a global depression sandwiched between them.

The fire was rekindled in the 1960s, the beginning of the modern era in Italian wine. The vast majority of Italian wine had always been an everyday staple, a jug to put on the table at lunch or dinner, made locally by families for their own consumption, or with grapes from peasant farmers laboring under the traditional structures of Italian agriculture—*mezzadria* (a form of sharecropping, basically) and in the south the effectively feudal *latifondo* system, in which, as winemaker Elena Fucci in Basilicata says, "farmers were basically slaves to the noble landowners." Both agriculture and winemaking typically were not aimed toward quality so much as quantity. In the 1960s and 1970s, that began to change, with small estates (often owned by farming families who used to sell their grapes to large producers or local cooperatives) arising with a focus on making high-quality wine. Somewhat in parallel with that but slightly later, conscientious grape growers began questioning the assumed benefits of conventional, chemical-based agriculture, and an interest in sustainable, organic, and biodynamic approaches started to occur. In a kind of ecological snowball-rolling-downhill way, that movement picked up speed and dimension over the years, to the point where 19 percent of the vineyards in Italy are now farmed organically, nearly three times the global average.

It's been true for centuries that there is effectively no place in Italy where vines are not cultivated. But what's true today is that there is also effectively no place in Italy where you can't find wines that vividly express the identity of where they come from, that are made from grapes grown with respect for the soil and the environment, and that are of truly exceptional quality. And the initial postwar wave of talents who pushed these changes forward starting in the 1960s is now being strengthened by an ambitious younger generation who are building on their work, as with the groundbreaking Elisabetta Foradori's sons Emilio and Theo and daughter Myrtha at her eponymous Trentino winery; or who are starting their own inspiring projects, like Angela Fronti at Istine in Chianti Classico, whose single-vineyard wines are some of the leaders in Chianti's very competitive race for brilliance.

NORTHERN ITALY

Northern Italy's wine regions stretch from the foothills of the Alps, bordering on France, Switzerland, and Austria, down to the fertile plains south of the Po River. No surprise, then, that the wines span a vast variety of styles and characters, from the cool-climate, Alps-influenced whites (and Pinot Noirs) of Alto Adige to the fruity red bubbles of Lambrusco, taking in everything from more than 70 million cases of everyday Pinot Grigio and Prosecco each year to world-class reds from Barolo and Barbaresco along the way.

ALTO ADIGE–TRENTINO

There's no question: the Alto Adige (also known as Südtirol) is one of the most stunningly beautiful wine regions in Italy, if not the world. A narrow valley bordered by mountains on either side, it's also one of Italy's smallest wine regions; its modest thirteen thousand acres of grapes represent about 1 percent of Italy's production. Much of the wine here is made by local cooperatives, though often at a very high level; most of the best wines, and certainly most that come from organic or biodynamically farmed vineyards, come from independent producers. Cool-climate whites comprise about two-thirds of the region's wines, with Pinot Grigio, Pinot Bianco, Traminer, and Sauvignon being the mainstays, followed by less-known varieties like Kerner, Müller-Thurgau, and Sylvaner. The third of Alto Adige wine that's red is primarily Schiava (Vernatsch), Pinot Noir, and Lagrein.

Trentino is the southern half of the Alto Adige–Trentino region. It's not quite as narrow, not quite as steep, and not quite as small—about twenty-five thousand acres of vineyards—but still a mountainous region. If Trentino doesn't have quite the cachet of Alto Adige, that's probably because much of the Pinot Grigio grown here (the most widely planted variety in the region, with Chardonnay coming second) is destined for large production, relatively uninteresting wines designated with the broad Delle Venezie appellation. Even so, there are a number of exceptional producers to be found here, if you look.

FORADORI • TRENTINO

[certified organic / certified biodynamic]

Does Elisabetta Foradori make natural wines? Inasmuch as she still makes wine—she has handed the reins at Foradori over to her children for the most part, and lately has been concentrating on making cheese—the answer is, well, yes and no. But while not dogmatically natural, her adherence to biodynamics and her noninterventionist winemaking approach put her close to that camp.

Elisabetta Foradori was born in the town of Mezzolombardo, in a house in the middle of vineyards that her father farmed and made wine from. At the time, he mostly sold his wine in glass demijohns, as was typical in the area, to bars and trattorias.

But her father died unexpectedly, and very young—he was only thirty-eight. Elisabetta was twelve at the time. Something was kindled in the daughter's heart; by the time she was nineteen, in 1984, she had graduated with a degree in enology. She returned home to run the family winery, and her passion, she soon found, was to try and rehabilitate the reputation of the grape Teroldego. But their land was in grim

shape, after years of agricultural chemicals and mechanized farming—the vines could produce the simple trattoria reds her father had made, but not wine at the level she wanted to make. But that was true for many if not most European vineyards in the decades following World War II. Reliance on chemicals, vines bred to produce as much quantity as possible, and machine harvesting were the order of the day. As Foradori and many others have observed, most of the world's agriculture involves applying an industrial protocol to nature, an approach in turn driven by generating profits for those industries: the makers of chemical fertilizers, pesticides, genetically modified seeds. Foradori's approach is in opposition to that: grapes, she feels, should carry the soul of the earth, not the soul of a chemical company.

Foradori started growing vines from seed rather than relying on nursery clones, planting massale selections from old-vine material, and trying to build biodiversity in the vineyard. By the mid-1990s, her Granato red was generally felt to be one of Italy's top wines. Yet she still wasn't satisfied, and in 2000 began working biodynamically, in essence to try and recover a connection to nature she felt she had lost. She moved her approach in the cellar away from the type of controlled winemaking she'd been taught in school, toward a less interventionist sensibility.

In person, Foradori is an intriguing combination of intensity and liveliness; she can seem quite serious one moment, relaxed and smiling the next. She's been tremendously influential for a lot of young Italian vintners, and for younger women winemakers around the world—a bit like the Patti Smith of wine in that way. There's no question she's made an indelible mark on the world of Italian wine, and even now, with her children Emilio, Theo, and Myrtha overseeing the day-to-day business of the winery, she's still deeply present. The family is a close one, working together, and working in harmony with nature in their vineyards in the foothills of the Dolomites.

All of the Foradori wines come from their seventy-four acres of vines. Among the standouts are the **Foradori Lezèr** (\$\$), which is a pale, transparent ruby, midpoint between a red and a rosé, and is made mostly from Teroldego with a handful of other local varieties. The **Foradori Teroldego** (\$\$) is one of the best examples of this spicy Trentino grape, with red fruit, lively acidity, and an herbal-foresty aroma. **Granato** (\$\$\$) is a benchmark northern Italian red, made with fruit from very old, pergola-trained vines. There are also several single-vineyard Teroldegos, all extremely good; for instance, the stony, spicy **Teroldego Sgarzon** (\$\$\$), from a cooler site in the valley of the same name.

Foradori also makes compelling whites from little-known (in the U.S. at least) local varieties, like the **Fontanasanta Nosiola** (\$\$), from a grape that had faded away to less than a few hundred acres of vines at the turn of the millennium. Foradori farms about four acres of what's left, and after harvest ferments and ages the wine for eight months in clay amphorae. The result is a straw-colored white that deftly balances savory and fruity notes.

GARLIDER • ALTO ADIGE

[certified organic]

Garlider is about as far north in Italy as you can go before you hit Austria, with its vineyards perched on the hills of the Alto Adige's sunny, rocky Isarco Valley, outside the town of Velturno. Here Christian Kerschbaumer and his wife, Veronika, are making shimmering Alpine white wines, aged in neutral oak to keep their stony clarity intact.

The Kerschbaumers farm about ten acres of vines, with the forested slopes rising even higher behind them and the valley spread out gloriously below. They use no chemical or systemic inputs whatsoever, and also try to keep the use of organic treatments like copper sulfate to a minimum. All harvesting is by hand. The land itself has been farmed for generations: the Garlider family worked it from 1489 to the early 1900s, when Christian's grandfather purchased the farm. Until the early 2000s, the family sold the grapes to the local co-op, a typical practice for the Alto Adige (most wineries here are still co-operatives), but then Christian took over, intent on making his own wines.

The winemaking is straightforward, though unadorned might be an even better word. Spontaneous fermentation with native yeast, white wines fermented and aged in stainless steel, and the one red (a Pinot Noir) aged in neutral oak. As pure as the air here, essentially.

The zippy **Garlider Müller-Thurgau ($$)** is a refined expression of this often-nondescript variety. That's true even more of the stony, vivid **Pinot Grigio ($$)**, which is apt to make even Pinot Grigio–haters reassess their feelings about that often-abused grape. The **Grüner Veltliner ($$)** has amplitude but not weight, its grapefruit and grapefruit zest flavors punctuated by white pepper notes. Finally, the **Blauburgunder ($$)**, aka Pinot Nero, aka Pinot Noir, is the only one from the entire Isarco Valley. It's brisk and fresh, a cool-climate, mountain Pinot with light, graceful tannins and a savory-spicy finish.

J. HOFSTÄTTER • ALTO ADIGE

[sustainable]

It's hard to imagine J. Hofstätter without the irrepressible, irreverent Martin Foradori Hofstätter at its helm, but in fact three generations before him have run this expansive Alto Adige estate. The winery was founded in 1907 by Josef Hofstätter, a locksmith who also owned a small restaurant in Tramin, and has gradually grown through the years (partly through marriage in 1959, which brought in the Foradori family's vineyards). Today J. Hofstätter farms some 136 acres on both sides of the Adige Valley, as well as at their Maso Michei estate in Trentino (and another 12 acres in Germany's Mosel region).

As Foradori says, "The way we farm means doing the minimum necessary to keep our vineyards healthy—no herbicides, manure composts, subsoiling, copper and sulfur rather than systemic treatments, using solar panels for our energy needs, strategizing about equipment to minimize fuel production . . ." It's a long list.

Martin's father, Paolo, was instrumental in bringing Pinot Noir (or Pinot Nero, as it's locally known) to attention in the Alto Adige, and also the first to formalize single-vineyard wines here—his 1987 Vigna St. Urbano Pinot Noir paved that path, with the result that "vigna" is now the approved terminology for single-vineyard bottlings here. "And all those names, the specific vineyards, are not fantasy names," Foradori says. "They're historical names from three hundred years ago or more."

The **J. Hofstätter Pinot Grigio** (\$–\$\$) is a standout in a world of fairly insipid versions, peachy and crisp, and the winery's elegant **Chardonnay** (\$\$) is an equally impressive value. On the less expensive side, look also for the crisp, fragrant **Maso Michei Müller-Thurgau** (\$\$) from Hofstätter's new, high-altitude property in Trentino. The single-vineyard white wines from Hofstätter are all exceptional, particularly the **Vigna Kolbenhof Gewürztraminer** (\$\$\$), a dry, precise, beautifully focused expression of this sometimes overblown variety. "It's not the *Miami Vice* style of Gewürztraminer," Foradori says. "No padded shoulders!"

For reds, the estate's three Pinot Noirs offer increasing degrees of complexity and depth, from the appealing and affordable **Mezcan Pinot Nero ($–$$)**, to the more savory **Riserva Mazon Pinot Nero ($$)**, to the profound **Barthenau Vigna St. Urbano Pinot Nero ($$$)**, and the complex, age-worthy **Vigna Roccolo Pinot Nero ($$$$)**, from vines planted in 1942. "My father was seven in 1942, and participated in planting this parcel," Foradori says. "There's a lot of history here."

MANINCOR • ALTO ADIGE

[certified biodynamic]

On a spring day, Count Michael Goëss-Enzenberg is as dapper as his biodynamic vineyards are unruly: goldenrod-colored pants, maroon pocket square, a houndstooth jacket. Around him the vines grow amid flowers, grasses, chickens, sheep, birds, bees. ("This is a paradise for bees," he says.) He and his wife took over here from his uncle in 1991; his family has owned the property since 1662, when a relative married the granddaughter of the founder, the grandly named Hieronymus Manincor.

Around the beginning of the 2000s, Goëss-Enzenberg came to the realization that the soil in his vineyards was dying, and in 2005 converted to biodynamics. "After one year we noticed an enormous difference—just the change in the smell of the soil from that year to the next was enormous. Nature changes rapidly when you are good to nature." Manincor was one of the founding estates of the respekt-BIODYN organization, and by 2009 was certified biodynamic.

Today there are 119 acres of vines here, along with almost 150 acres of apples. The winery is underground, insulated by the vineyard soil above; geothermic energy helps regulate temperatures, and a biomass plant that uses apple and vine cuttings and wood chips from the surrounding forest provides additional energy. The interdependence of everything on the estate, its ties to nature in all its aspects, makes it seem an oasis of sorts—and a very Tyrolean one, with Lake Kaltern blue and shimmering in one direction, and the crags of the Alps rising to the sky in the other.

For whites, seek out the dry **Moscato Giallo** ($$), abundantly floral and fruity, and the aromatic **Réserve della Contessa** ($$), a full-bodied blend of Chardonnay, Pinot Bianco, and Sauvignon. The red **Schiava Kalterersee der Keil** ($$) carries lots of flavor despite its transparent ruby hue; served lightly chilled, it's excellent with charcuterie (like speck, the lightly smoky local version of prosciutto). For more power, look for the **Réserve della Conte** ($$), a blackberry-peppery blend of Lagrein, Merlot, and Cabernet Sauvignon. For Pinots, there's the **Pinot Noir Mason** ($$), spicy, savory, and abundant with red cherry fruit. Goëss-Enzenberg says, "What I'm looking for with Pinot Noir is the fragility of the fruit, the delicacy." There's also the higher-end **Mason di Mason** ($$$), which comes from the oldest vines in the highest-altitude parcels of the vineyard. It's a step more complex, both aromatically and on the palate, but unfortunately it comes and goes from the U.S. market somewhat unpredictably.

EMILIA-ROMAGNA

Ask most Italians what Italy's greatest food region is, and you'll often get Emilia-Romagna as the answer—it's the home of balsamic vinegar, Parmigiano Reggiano cheese, prosciutto di Parma, ragù Bolognese, tortellini . . . the list goes on. Add in its extraordinary wealth of great restaurants, both humble and exalted, and one understands why it's named as the greatest.

For wine, though, Emilia-Romagna has mostly been known for mass-produced, industrial Lambruscos (Riunite is the classic example, which at one point sold more than a million cases *per month* in the U.S. alone) or relatively generic white Trebbiano. Even so, there's been a groundswell of artisanal Lambrusco producers dedicated to making wines far more expressive and complex than what people have come to expect from the region; sommeliers and wine directors have caught on to this trend, even if most wine buyers have yet to. And, pocketed away here and there, there are also ambitious, rule-breaking producers like La Stoppa. There, Elena Pantaleoni is one of the most insightful producers of natural wine to be found anywhere. An hour in her company can make you forget that something like Riunite even exists.

LA STOPPA • COLLI PIACENTINI

[certified organic / natural]

Elena Pantaleoni is a brilliantly articulate advocate for natural winemaking, or at least for what could be considered its origin point as a philosophy rather than as a set of specific rules. "I'm not a fan of ideological winemaking," she says. "If I need to use sulfur, I use sulfur. People arrive and say, 'Ah, you are a "natural wine" producer.' But wine has been made this way for six thousand years."

La Stoppa sits on a hillside in the tiny Colli Piacentini wine region. From its fifteenth-century tower, far below to the north you can see the city of Piacenza. Beyond it, on the other side of the Po River, lies Lombardy; beyond that, the Alps. "It's a very border place. We're closer to Genoa in Liguria than we are to Bologna," Pantaleoni says.

The estate was founded in the late 1800s by a wealthy lawyer from Genoa. Pantaleoni's father, Raffaele, bought it in 1973. When her father passed away, in 1991, Pantaleoni took over. She was twenty-six, owned a book and music store in Piacenza, and had no experience making wine. But she felt she owed an obligation to her family to

keep La Stoppa going. "Wine for me is a medium to talk about a choice I made," she says. "To make my home in the country, to make wine, to live this way."

She made changes, switching to organics, replanting international varieties on the property with native ones, shifting toward a less interventionist approach to winemaking. None of this was whimsical. "Before asking *how* to do things, it's important to ask *why* to do things," she says. "All my decisions are made with respect—to the place, to the people here, to my customers."

La Stoppa's eighty acres of vineyards are certified organic, but Pantaleoni doesn't put that on her labels. Organic viticulture, she feels, should be a starting point, not the end goal. "For me, being a natural producer means understanding where you are, then understanding what grapes are suited to the place, understanding how to farm them, and then making the wines."

She adds, "With wine it becomes very difficult for the consumer to understand what's industrial and artisanal. For example, there isn't a guide for cheese anywhere that would put artisanal mozzarella on the same page as industrial mozzarella, which is basically plastic. But wine ratings do that. Besides, if you are passionate about wine or music, eventually you get bored of the more commercial versions—there's a lot of elevator music when it comes to wine."

Pantaleone's wines are made in stainless steel or concrete, each tank fermenting on its own, with no temperature control and no sulfites. In the wood vessels particularly, fermentation often continues in the springtime; this can result in a certain amount of volatile acidity. Technically a flaw, it doesn't really bother Pantaleone: "First, it adds to drinkability. Second, what is a defect? My wines, for some people, may have defects. But VA, Brett, reduction, those 'flaws' are what make my wines what they are after all these years. And there's always fashion in what's a defect and what's not: look at jeans with holes. For my mom, this is a defect. But someone young might pay two hundred dollars for them. The real defect is doing something dishonest, doing something you don't believe in. There's a big lack of honesty everywhere. Contributing to that is the real flaw."

The La Stoppa wines are often aged for several years, and released when Pantaleoni deems them ready. Her **Trebbiolo Rosso ($$)** is about two-thirds Barbera and one-third Bonarda, a little tingly, with vibrant but earthy dark fruit notes. "Talking about natural wine, it's good to have some wines that are easier to drink, that can attract the public without fear," she says. **Macchiona ($$)** blends equal parts Bonarda and Barbera for a supple red with earthy black cherry notes, spicy tannins, and often a little leathery funk from Brett. **Ageno ($$)** is a no-sulfur, skin-contact blend of Malvasia, Trebbiano, and Ortrugo. Ruddy orange, it has firm tannins, tangy acidity, and a flavor that recalls mocha and orange peel. The sweet, multi-vintage, micro-production **Buca delle Canne ($$$)** comes from a tiny parcel of one-hundred-plus-year-old Semillon vines. Think ginger, candied orange peel, honey, all of it sweet and bright, the aromas lifted on an unapologetic hum of volatile acidity. Flawed? If you're a technocrat, possibly. If you're an artist, not so much.

FRIULI–VENEZIA GIULIA

riuli, in the northeast corner of Italy between the Veneto, Slovenia, and Austria, was kicked back and forth like a soccer ball in earlier eras of conquest. The Roman empire ruled it, followed by the German nobility in the Middle Ages, the Venetian Republic in the 1400s, the Austro-Hungarian empire in the 1800s . . . it's a long list. Today it is part of Italy, but at the same time very much its own place, the spirit and character of the local culture having persisted through centuries of rule by others. "Stubborn and a little crazy" is how one local winemaker described the Friulian personality to me. Regardless of whether that's true, the region does seem to produce a surprising number of iconoclastic winemakers who refuse to follow anyone's direction but their own.

As a result, in conjunction with its cool climate and (in Colli Orientale, Collio, and Carso) its steep, hillside vineyards, Friuli is quite possibly the source of Italy's greatest white wines. And it is definitely the origin point for both the use of amphorae in winemaking in Italy (and eventually other countries) as well as for skin-contact "orange" wines, largely thanks to the pioneering work of vintners such as Josko Gravner.

The main native grape varieties here, for whites, are Friulano (formerly Tocai Friulano), Ribolla Gialla, Verduzzo, and Picolit (the last in minuscule amounts). There's also plenty of Sauvignon, Pinot Grigio, and Chardonnay. For red varieties, a true expression of Friuli can be found with Refosco, Schiopettino, and Pignolo, but the region also produces very good Merlot, along with some Cabernet Sauvignon and Cabernet Franc.

There are four main subregions. The flat, gravelly Friuli Grave is the largest, and responsible for more than half of Friuli's production. Unfortunately, much of that is Pinot Grigio destined for simple Delle Venezie bottlings and Glera headed into cheap Prosecco. More exciting are the hilly regions on the eastern border, filled with terraces of vines and wild cherry blossoms in the spring. These are Colli Orientali del Friuli, east of Udine; the cooler Collio, south from Colli Orientale and bordering on Slovenia; and Carso, in the hills near Trieste.

BORGO DEL TIGLIO · COLLIO

[organic]

Sometimes being fired by your own mother can turn out to be a very good thing. In 1981, Nicola Manferrari was twenty-three and working at his mother's pharmacy in Cormòns. When his father died unexpectedly that July, his mother told Nicola that he would have to deal with the grape harvest at their small family vineyard himself. He did, and once the grapes were in, he decided to take a few days off with his girlfriend. He informed his mother of this plan from a payphone by the side of the road. She in turn demanded that he return and work at the pharmacy instead. He refused, so she fired him.

But Manferrari's mother often fired him. It was her response whenever he did something that irritated her, which happened a lot. She'd usually rehire him a few days later. This time, though, he chose to stay fired. Being a pharmacist was his mother's plan for his future, not his. It wasn't a *bad* idea: running a pharmacy close to the then Yugoslavian border meant owning a very successful business, since in addition to local customers, people from the Communist side would frequently sneak over to buy medicines unavailable to them. But for Manferrari it was the *wrong* idea. He had no interest in being a pharmacist; he'd found he loved working the harvest, and working for his mother (obviously) wasn't an ideal situation.

From that moment Manferrari devoted himself to wine, and to Tocai (now called Friulano). A surprising choice. Friulano is a difficult grape to grow and to vinify, his son Mattia Manferrari says. "It has very thin skin, so it's very vulnerable to rot and mold. And it tends to produce a lot, which is good if you're a farmer selling to the co-op, but not good if you're aiming for quality. And my father wanted to make elegant, world-class wines." At that time, the variety was usually made into bulk wine, or sold in glass jugs to local restaurants. "It was sort of regarded as a farmer's wine that needed to be forgotten," Mattia says. "It belonged to Collio's past, not its future."

Nicola Manferrari felt differently. He believed great wine could made from Tocai. Soon, better winemaking and better viticulture combined with the old vines he'd inherited proved him right. His wines received acclaim, particularly from the influential writer, critic, publisher, and activist Luigi Veronelli. He still makes them today, now assisted in the vineyards and cellar by Mattia, who's been helping out at the winery since he was in elementary school.

The Manferraris farm twenty acres of vines in three different vineyards: their original property in Brazzano; a second, cooler parcel near the village of Ruttars; and a third, Ca' delle Vallade, in a cold valley that channels the constant wind. Wind is a part of life here, particularly the bora, a biting wind from the northeast that blows in the winter. "During February or March, if you're pruning and the bora blows, you have to stop. You'll freeze," Mattia says. "And in Trieste, when it blows, you have to hold on to something or you'll get knocked over."

The Manferraris follow their own approach. "We firmly believe that there is no single recipe you can apply to every vineyard around the world," Mattia says. "We'll never get certified organic, because we work our own way. For instance, if you're going to be organic in Friuli, you have to spray a lot of copper. To me that's a problem. It's a powerful fungicide, but it stays in the soil. We want our vineyards to be around for a long, long time. If we spray copper over and over, what does that do to the biome of the soil? Our soil is the most important thing we have. It's our treasure. So my father and I will do anything to preserve its life."

The **Borgo del Tiglio Collio Bianco** ($$) is a complex, beautiful expression of the Collio region's overall terroir. It's round and supple, with floral and orchard fruit notes. A savory, tartly citrusy **Sauvignon** ($$$) comes from the winery's vineyard near Ruttars; there's also a 100 percent **Friulano** ($$$) that, unsurprisingly given Nicola Manferrari's devotion to the variety (which he still prefers to call Tocai), is one of the best to be found in Friuli. Then there are two single-vineyard whites, "the soul of our winery," as Mattia refers to them. **Ronca della Chiesa** ($$$–$$$$), he says, "symbolizes our origins, the old vineyards that my father inherited. The vines are seventy years old now; we want them to live much longer." It's layered with orchard fruits, spice, and almond notes, a luscious white that somehow also retains intense verve and focus. The other white is the equally brilliant **Studio Bianco** ($$$$), a combination of Friulano, Sauvignon, and Riesling that's full of lingering nectarine and white peach fruit with flinty minerality and a seductively silky texture.

For reds, there's the relatively affordable (for this winery) **Collio Rosso** ($$), a firm, taut 100 percent Merlot, and the profound, complex **Rossa della Centa** ($$$$). It's also Merlot, but from a small section of vines near the family's house. "When we get it right, and when the vintage allows it, it's a unique wine—it has to have the right personality," Mattia says.

LIVIO FELLUGA • FRIULI

[sustainable]

Livio Felluga, who passed away in 2016 at 102 years of age, had a life that encompassed the history of modern winemaking. He was born in 1914, one of eight children, in Istria, which at that time was a part of the Austro-Hungarian empire. The family had vineyards plus a small trattoria on the Isola d'Istria, and Livio learned early on about viticulture from his grandfather. After the First World War, the family moved to Grado, a tiny island just off the coast near Trieste. "It was the Hamptons of the Austro-Hungarian empire," Livio's granddaughter Laura Felluga says, "and it stayed that way after it became part of Italy." Livio was ten. The family started selling their Istrian wines there, and, she says, "that's where my grandfather learned that wine would define his identity."

Then, World War II. Felluga left home, fought in northern Africa, and was taken prisoner by the Allies. Re-

---

"Elegance doesn't mean weakness."
—Livio Felluga

---

located to Scotland, he spent three years picking potatoes; his family assumed he was dead. Only after the end of the war did his mother receive a packet of letters that he'd written over the intervening years.

Felluga finally returned home in the late 1940s. But he had no access to his family's former vineyards; Istria was now a part of Yugoslavia, under Communist rule. Yet he knew he wanted to grow grapes, and

that he wanted to own the land that he grew the grapes on, so he bought some small, abandoned vineyards near the Friulian town of Rosazzo. As Laura Felluga says, "My grandfather was born in Austria-Hungary, but he spoke a Venetian dialect, and when he got to Friuli he was like a foreigner in his own land."

Laura Felluga sees that patchwork of influences as a strength. "One thing we like to say is that in a world where every message is being simplified, we want to go the opposite route. Our region has always been a borderland; it has so many layers of tradition. You walk through our vineyards—in 1915, this was Austria, in 1930, this was Italy—and the borders shift through the centuries. Every group that invaded us left some new tradition. And new grape varieties: Sauvignon was brought in by the Hapsburgs, Pinot Grigio and Merlot by the French. This richness and diversity is the biggest asset we have."

The *azienda agricola* Livio Felluga is now owned by Livio's four children, and the next generation is involved as well. "What we do is all about my grandfather's vision, and keeping to that," Laura Felluga says. "And we are always respectful to nature, but we've never wanted to put achieving a certification before following the actual philosophy. And, since we've never stopped since my grandfather first began buying land, many of our plots have been organic from the start. We constantly work towards having the smallest impact possible."

Livio Felluga (until his passing, the winery and the man were effectively one and the same) makes primarily white wines. The family's **Livio Felluga Pinot Grigio ($$)** is a heartening reminder of the potential of this often uninteresting variety, full of orchard fruit flavors lifted by a light tartness, with a sleek, mouth-coating texture. The **Friulano ($$)**, from the region's signature grape, is focused, precise, and stony. **Illivio ($$)** "was created by my father as a birthday gift to my grandfather when he turned ninety," Laura Felluga says. "The intention was to represent his personality—fiery but elegant." It's a vivid, vanilla-scented, melony blend of Chardonnay, Pinot Blanc, and a touch of Picolit. **Terre Alte ($$$)** is one of the great wines of Friuli. A blend of Friulano, Sauvignon, and Pinot Grigio, round and complex and generally irresistible, able to age for a decade or more, it comes from ancient vines in a vineyard close to the Abbey of Rosazzo. "When you're at the abbey," Laura says, "you can really appreciate our landscape. Facing south, you see the sea sparkling; you're framed on either side by the Dolomites; and in front of you is this sea of vineyards." **Abazzia di Rosazzo ($$$)** is the other side of the Terre Alte coin. Effectively the same blend, made in the same way, it expresses itself differently: more mineral and linear, lightly herbaceous, ending on a firmly stony note. "The two vineyards are different ages, though both are very old," Laura Felluga says. "Some of the oldest vines, we don't even know when they were planted." Abazzia de Rosazzo, too, ages very well, though as Laura says slightly ruefully, "We always speak about how well our wines age . . . but then we always end up drinking them."

GRAVNER • CARSO

[biodynamic / natural]

Josko Gravner is the only winemaker I know of who keeps a simple wooden chair on a platform in his cellar so he can sit there and think about his wine. Is he making it the right way? Should he have a different approach? Is it truly the wine he wants to make?

Gravner is idiosyncratic and brilliant. A tremendously influential figure—whether he wanted to be or not—he's the most significant modern inspiration for fermenting and aging wine in amphorae, and for making skin-maceration (or "orange") white wines. Locally, his choices were usually seen as capricious or bizarre (admittedly, not an unusual problem for visionaries), but as he says, "There are two ways to make wine. One is to look at the customer and make something to please them. The other is to look inside yourself and make wine you want to

---

"As a child, I fell in love with the earth."
—Josko Gravner

---

make, that fulfills you. I expect ninety percent of the population not to like my wines. That doesn't bother me."

Gravner's family has lived near the small town of Oslavia, near the Slovenian border, for more than three hundred years. He started out making wine in his father's cellar, and selling it in bulk (standard for the time). In the 1980s, he began making wine with modern techniques, using stainless steel tanks for fermentation. His work received acclaim, but he felt dissatisfied. His wines were from the Collio, but he felt they tasted like they could have been from South Africa or Napa Valley or Chile. "In the 1980s," he says, "I realized stainless steel was a mistake and brought wood back to the cellar. But that was another mistake, because I used French *barriques*, not *botti*," the large oak ovals traditional in the region. He switched out the small barrels for *botti*, and also, in the mid-1990s, started experimenting with fermenting his white wines on their skins. When he tasted the results, he was convinced. By 1997, all of Gravner's wines were fermented on their skins, with no temperature control and no manufactured yeasts. "I only have two words," he says, "*vivo* or *morte*. Alive or dead. And if you add industrial yeast, your wine is automatically dead."

The crucial turning point in his winemaking came the same year, 1997, when a friend brought him a 250-liter *qvevri*, or amphora. Gravner buried it in the earth, full of grapes, and found that the fermentation it brought was much slower, much longer, and extracted from the grape skins the quality he was looking for. "It was an emotional experience," he recalls. "My heart beat faster. The amphora really taught me how to find the source of how to make wine. So, I decided to change my practices entirely."

Today, a decision to use amphorae for winemaking is simple; search "winemaking amphorae for sale" and buy one. In 1997, it was unprecedented. The sole source for the amphorae he needed was the country of Georgia, largely because Georgia was the sole place where this ancient style of winemaking still existed. And, in the late nineties and early 2000s, Georgia was dangerous, a snarl of political unrest and criminal gangs. To buy his *qvevri*, Gravner had to travel with armed guards, in an armored car, carrying cash. "It was very unsafe, and also the poverty was incredible. It was like going back a hundred years."

Gravner's rigorous questioning of his own choices isn't limited to winemaking. In 2012, he uprooted every white variety he was growing except for Ribolla, the native grape of his region. Some of the land went to other purposes; his Godenza vineyard, where Pinot Grigio vines grew, is now home to four Tibetan goats and a horse. In Pusca, where he had planted Chardonnay and Sauvignon (despite the Slovene meaning of that name—it translates as "barren, infertile land of little value"), he ripped out the vines and planted a forest. He says, "Whenever I make a mistake, it teaches me something. Errors are your best school, if you are capable of admitting you made a mistake." He's also dug rainwater ponds in his largest vineyards, and planted trees on the vineyard terraces to provide homes for animals and birds. It's a way of bringing back the whole of nature to the vineyard, an attempt to reestablish a balance that intensive, monoculture farming takes away. "To make wine for me is not to look forward but to look back. That's where you find what you're looking for. And simplicity in everything."

Gravner releases his wines when he feels they're ready, which may be ten years or more after the vintage. He makes one red these days, from the local Pignolo variety, **Gravner Breg Rosso ($$$)**, which is made in amphorae, then aged in oak *botti* for five years, and then aged a further five years before release. It's toasty-herbal, flinty, all wild berries and plush, gripping tannins. **Gravner Ribolla ($$$)**, his defining wine, is made in amphorae and also aged for years before release. Golden-cidery in color, with surprising tannic grip, it is far more savory than fruit-driven, deep and complex. It makes you think of nut skins, citrus peel, dry spices. "As a child," Gravner says, "I fell in love with the earth." One taste, and that's easy to tell.

VENICA & VENICA • COLLIO

[organic]

The history of Giampaolo Venica's family, like many in Friuli, defies national borders. His great-grandfather farmed in the Collio region as a citizen of the Austro-Hungarian empire. After World War I, when Friuli became Italian, so did the Venicas. They bought the farm they now own in 1930, and kept it through World War II. "Wine was just part of the daily cycle," Giampolo says. "We had grape vines, cherry trees, apples, plums, and all of it was sold in the local market at the time. Then, in the 1960s, my father and uncle started to make wine for our own consumption, and to sell at the trattoria we owned then."

The Venicas farm just under a hundred acres of vines, spread out over the Collio hills on more than twenty different sites. "The big guys buy the big pieces of land, so you take whatever's left," Giampaolo says, "a lot of small parcels surrounded by forest, or on steep hillsides."

The Venicas have never used herbicides, and Giampaolo has also pushed his family toward organic viticulture (though currently he's taking a break from overseeing the vineyards: "Family stuff can be a lot. The same decision you make in two seconds yourself takes a month, a lot of conversations—

you say this, I say that, and so on").

If he hadn't stayed in wine, he adds, he probably would have been a chef. "I remember my grandmother cooking in the kitchen. I have wonderful memories of that. Every time I drink a wine from Friuli, ours or someone else's, it makes me think of all the smells from that restaurant." Partly for that reason, his solo project—a kind of adjunct to Venica & Venica—is called Dalia Maris. Dalia was his grandmother's name. "It's also a flower," he says, "and so it gives a sense of the land. And Stella Maris, in Italian, is the north star. A sailor navigating on a ship, he looks for the north star—and this project, for me, is a journey. And because it's outside my family, it also gives me a sense of freedom."

The **Venica & Venica Pinot Grigio Jesera ($$)** is light gold-copper in hue due to a day or so of maceration on the skins, floral on the nose, with ripe pear and nectarine flavors. The winery's **Sauvignon Ronco del Cerò ($$)** comes from the hillside vineyard land that Daniele Venica purchased in 1930. It's classic Friulian Sauvignon, full of citrus zest and grapefruit flavors, bolstered by lively acidity. The **Friulano Ronco delle Cimè ($$)** is made with grapes sourced from four different vineyards and has the density and mineral depth of this variety when it's grown well.

Giampaolo Venica's Dalia Maris wines are exceptional, but made in extremely small quantities. "It's three thousand bottles total," he says. "I'm doing everything myself; I just put my phone on airplane mode and work in total silence." His ambition is to make Friulian wines from native white varieties that lean more toward the richness and mineral depth characteristic of Rhône whites rather than the high-acid, low-pH style that's currently in fashion here. If you taste the **Dalia Maris B Bianco ($$$)**, the top wine from this new project, you'll likely agree that his goal isn't just possible, he's attained it. A blend of roughly 80 percent Friulano and 20 percent Ribolla Gialla, it's luscious and mouth-coating, intensely flavorful; whatever minerality might be defined as, this has it. The **Piccolo Bianco ($$)** comes from fruit that didn't quite make the cut for the top wine. Even so, it's still remarkable: full-bodied, seductive, savory, and a total pleasure to drink.

PIEDMONT

Piedmont and Tuscany vie for being the Italian wine region that inspires the most passion, much as Burgundy and Bordeaux do in France. There are other similarities, too: Nebbiolo, the great red grape of Piedmont, has, like Pinot Noir, an uncanny ability to translate small nuances of terroir into specific character in a wine. Also, like Pinot Noir, it's a capricious, thin-skinned, difficult variety, good at making winemakers throw up their hands in dismay at its unpredictability when they aren't dancing for joy at its sublime expressiveness.

Not that the wines of Piedmont (or Piemonte, if you are Italian) are limited to Nebbiolo. The region itself is large—it stretches from the foothills of the Alps, north of Turin, south to the less formidable Appenines, which block it from the Mediterranean. East-west, it runs from the Ticino River in the east to the Alpine French border in the west. The heartland of Piedmont, though, in terms of wine, is the hilly region around the towns of Asti and Alba. And the heart of *that* is the Langhe, the source of two of Italy's greatest red wines, Barbaresco and Barolo.

As winemaker Luca Currado, who was born here, likes to say, "In Tuscany, they have 'under the Tuscan sun.' In Piemonte, we have 'under the Piemontese fog.'" He's entirely right. Anyone who has driven through the hills of Piedmont on an autumn night will recognize that alarming feeling of being able to see no more than a foot or so in front of your car as you navigate the narrow, winding roads—a situation that does not seem to stop local drivers from blowing by you at sixty miles an hour, apparently entirely unconcerned with visibility, or even survival.

Barolo, in the hills southwest of Alba, is tiny: about seven miles long and five miles wide, a tiny realm of spectacularly valuable vineyard land. That wasn't always the case. As Giuseppe Vajra of G.D. Vajra notes, "You have to remember, up through the 1980s, the wealthy land was the flatland. The hillsides, the vineyards, those were poor." The same is true of Barbaresco, even smaller and located east of Alba. Both are home to some of the greatest vineyard land in the world, and for many years you could buy it for a song. No longer: an acre of vineyard in a top Barolo cru now runs over $1 million.

The greatest Barolos and Barbarescos have risen in price accordingly, but even so, there are many, many producers here making terrific wine under $100 a bottle. And if you look to the humbler red grapes of the region—Barbera and Dolcetto, and the more obscure Pelaverga—and to Piedmont's white varieties—such as Cortese (the grape of Gavi), Arneis, Timorasso, and Nascetta—wonderful and affordable wines abound. Roero, northeast of Alba, is particularly a growing source for excellent whites.

But back to Nebbiolo, the grape of Barolo and Barbaresco. It's named for that Piedmontese fog—*nebbia* is Italian for fog—and seems to thrive nowhere else as it does here (plenty of people have tried to grow it in other places; the results are typically grim). Nebbiolo can be magical. Nor does a wine made from it have to be a $250 rarity to attain that state. Wines made from Nebbiolo present a mysterious study in contrasts: graceful but powerful, perfumed but grounded in the earth, fiercely tannic but delicate, too. As winemaker Chiara Boschis says, the magic lies in how Nebbiolo "stays on your tongue, how it's ethereal. And who doesn't want the ethereal?"

BORGOGNO • BAROLO

[certified organic]

Borgogno is the oldest continuously operating winery in Barolo, and if you venture down into the winery's cellar, you will believe it—there are ranks and ranks of old vintages stretching into the darkness, in a place where wine has been made since 1761. True, most of those bottles only date back to after World War I, but it's still awe-inspiring. The credit goes to Cesare Borgogno, who in 1920 began cellaring half of every vintage he made—an unheard-of practice at the time, and one which Borgogno continues to this day.

Since 2008, Borgogno has been owned by the Farinetti family, but in many ways, very little has changed. Winemaking is done as in the past: long, spontaneous fermentation in concrete with native yeasts, long aging in Slavonian oak barrels, no enzymes or other additives. As Graziella Defilè, proprietor along with her husband, Oscar Farinetti, says, "We work respecting what was done in the past, innovating today—but with continuity with what has been done by those who went before us. When we bought Borgogno, we swore to safeguard its

traditions. It's also important, I feel, to emphasize that everything came from the hands of a farmer here, Bartolomeo Borgogno, more than two hundred and fifty years ago. He was a peasant with a passion for the land who founded a winery at a time when only the aristocracy was the protagonist in this world."

One innovation the Farinettis have instituted is, in fact, a return to tradition in terms of the farming. They started converting Borgogno's vineyards to organic viticulture in 2015; in many ways more akin to how Cesare or even Bartolomeo Borgogno would have farmed than the chemical approaches of the postwar years. Lately, Graziella adds, "we've pushed further—in one portion of the vineyard we've switched to enzymatic treatments such as orange peel and seaweed; they help the plants go into a kind of self-defense mode against diseases. More nature, less chemistry. We have to protect this land and take care of it. Wine begins with agriculture—in his book *Vino al Vino*, Mario Soldati wrote, 'Wine is the poetry of the earth.' And so it is."

Borgogno makes a dizzying range of wines. So, a few standouts. The **Borgogno Derthona** (**$$**) is 100 percent Timorasso, a formerly obscure Piedmontese white variety that's now seeing a minor renaissance; it's bright and orchard-fruity, with a distinctive honey note. The ruby-hued **Barbera d'Alba Superiore** (**$$**) is red-fruited and fragrantly spicy. The basic **Langhe Nebbiolo** (**$$**) hews to a softer style for Nebbiolo, with classic dark cherry flavors. There's also the **Langhe Nebbiolo No Name** (**$$$**), so called because of an annoying run-in the Farinettis had with the Barolo authorities (who certify wines to approve their use of the Barolo name). With one vintage, the Farinettis ended up with two lots of their classic Barolo, made in exactly the same way from the same grapes; they submitted them both, and one was approved but the other wasn't. Graziella Defilè says dryly, "For us, this was absurd." They resubmitted the wines, and the second identical wine was downgraded again. "We couldn't call it Barolo, but for us it was Barolo. So we gave it a label of protest, 'No Name.'" Of course the wine proved to be a huge success.

The **Borgogno Barolo Classico** (**$$$**) is, indeed, in a classic style: slightly austere on release, elegant, with fine, taut tannins and elegant red fruit. The **Barolo Riserva** (**$$$$**) is similar in character but more structured and built for long aging; a good thing, given the thousands and thousands of bottles of back vintages resting in Borgogno's cellar.

CHIARA BOSCHIS—E. PIRA • BAROLO

[certified organic]

Chiara Boschis crackles with energy. Whether she's talking about her wines, or her project to bring life back to a tiny mountain town in Castelmagno, or about being a woman in the very male-dominated world of Piedmont winemaking, she's fiercely animated and also fiercely funny.

Boschis first hit visibility as a member of the "Barolo Boys" group in the early nineties—she was, needless to say, the only woman in the group. The group, all friends and all winemakers, did a lot of experimentation: in the vineyard, in the cellar. (Notoriously, Elio Altare, another member, chainsawed his family's old wooden tanks into pieces and replaced them with French oak *barriques*. He was then disinherited, though later his sisters gave the estate back to him.) The winemakers in the group were rebelling against the poor vineyard practices, high yields, and often defective or oxidative winemaking that marked a lot of Barolo at that time, and that rebellion got the Barolo Boys plenty of attention.

What's probably more revolutionary in Boschis's case—outside of the fact that she's a stupendously talented winemaker—is that she fought her way to the top ranks of Barolo producers at a time when women were in many ways barred from that course. She says, "My father always said to me, 'Why do you like to be in the first line? In the first line, you get the bullet in the head!' But I say that if you are in the first line, you get there first."

She adds, "In my generation there were *no* women in the cellar. It was heavy, heavy work. That's why I bought machines so early, to move things. Because the attitude, it was 'Eh, if you want to be like a man, OK, work like a man. Move that *barrique*.' At that time, when they saw a woman who wanted to act like a man, people were not very approving. For years I was working like crazy, seven days a week, every night. The boys of Barolo"—meaning the boys of the *town* of Barolo, not the Barolo Boys—"would be in front of the winery in the bar, watching me work late at night, cleaning tanks, and they'd be saying, 'Hey, hey, you are never going to be married.' 'Well!' I'd say, 'Certainly not to you!'"

Boschis farms twenty-seven acres of vines in Barolo, Serralunga, and Monforte d'Alba. "It's a holistic approach. We use worm-digested compost, from a place called 'Worm Up.' It costs two thousand euros per hectare, so that's twenty thousand euros of worm shit every year! But it's the *best* shit. I also have a lot of hotels for birds, hotels for insects, a lot of work with plants for birds and insects to eat. We don't do atomic war with a cannon of chemicals. We use bows and arrows."

Boschis was also instrumental in creating the first organic district in a major Barolo cru, Cannubi Bio, and has convinced twenty-four of the twenty-six growers in the cru to participate. "I told them, 'Leave less money to your nieces, and leave them a better place.' Everybody says the quality is in the vineyard. Of course. You need the best exposure, the right soil, the ideal drainage. But the small percentage that the human being does, that has a huge impact on the vineyard—for good *or* for bad."

Chiara Boschis's wines have power and richness, but since the 1990s have pulled back on oak quite a bit; they were once entirely aged in new oak barrels, but that's now down to about 30 percent. Her **Chiara Boschis— E. Pira Dolcetto ($$)** is all black- and red-raspberry fruit, dark and spicy and chewy. Her **Barbera d'Alba ($$)**, dark ruby in color, suggests blueberries and dusty spice, with zingy acidity. She makes three Barolos. The **Barolo Cannubi ($$$$)** is the wine that first brought her fame, and lives up to its reputation with lush dark cherry fruit, sleek but substantial tannins, and hints of licorice. "It's super-smooth—a silk glove," she says. Her **Barolo Mosconi ($$$–$$$$)** is more chewy and aggressively tannic, with an iron note overlying its dark berry fruit. Finally, the **Via Nova Barolo ($$$)** is a blend from all three of the villages where she has vineyards, spicy, crisply tannic, bright, tremendously alive. "We're lucky. Having vineyards in three different villages allows us to show the perfect classic Barolo. Mosconi, in Monforte d'Alba, is strong; Serralunga, more vivid and punching; Barolo, where Cannubi is, more elegant and perfumed."

G. B. BURLOTTO • VERDUNO

[organic]

A modest door in a stone wall in the little town of Verduno, an oval brass plaque the size of your hand that says "*Ditta Comm. G. B. Burlotto—*

Produzione Vini Classici—Verduno Piedmonte." Walk through, and you've stepped back in time. The old fermentation cellar: brick floors, glass-and-iron doors, old oak fermentation vats. It looks onto a modest courtyard with a spreading cypress tree, the arched windows of the family's home and the winery's offices framed in red. The house and cellar were built in the late 1700s, and Burlotto winemaker Fabio Alessandria says, "We like to keep it the way it was then."

Until recently Verduno was one of the lesser-known villages of the Barolo region; now its star is ascendent. Giovan Battista Burlotto, who founded Burlotto, was Fabio's great-great-grandfather. "From the beginning we've been living and working here," Fabio says. "I think today we are the oldest family in the Barolo area working with the same brand, in the same place, with the same vineyard. There's always been a direct continuity."

Today the family owns forty-two acres, mostly in Verduno. Winemaking is staunchly traditional—foot-treading, long maceration on the skins, aging in old-school large oak *botti*—and the wines are stellar. Burlotto has also been a longtime proponent of the nearly forgotten, now newly popular Pelaverga grape. "In the middle of the 1900s, my grandfather was the *last* of the pure Pelaverga producers," Fabio says. "In 1964, he made less than a thousand bottles. The grape probably would have died off, but eventually my parents decided to work with the other producers in Verduno to find the best plant material and the right vines." Extinction averted.

The **G. B. Burlotto Pelaverga ($$)** is transparent ruby, with toasty cherry and black pepper flavors, intensely pure and fresh. There's also a strawberry-scented, lightly herbal **Dolcetto d'Alba ($$)** and an impressive **Barbera d'Alba ($$)**, full of blueberry fruit and hard not to love. Burlotto's **Freisa ($$)** is firmly tannic, with potent flavors and a light mushroom-earth note. "I call Freisa the country cousin of Nebbiolo," Fabio says. His **Langhe Nebbiolo ($$$)** expresses Nebbiolo's lighter side, with sweet currant flavors and gentle tannins. Finally, there are five Barolos. The **Burlotto Barolo ($$$)** has lightly resinous floral notes, red berry flavors, and a hint of violets.

It's a standout Barolo *normale*. **Aclivi ($$$$)** comes from the family's best Verduno parcels, "made with the old philosophy of the blend." With more power than the *normale*, it deserves a few years of age before opening. The cru Barolos are expensive, but it's worth noting that the **Burlotto Monvigliero Barolo ($$$$)** is extraordinary, from a vineyard "known for its aroma and elegance," Fabio says. Its aroma suggests cherries, mint, orange peel, and dark chocolate; its flavors are equally complex.

CERETTO • ALBA

[certified biodynamic]

Ricardo Ceretto, one of eleven children, escaped poverty to found his eponymous wine company in Alba the 1930s. He grew to be one of the town's most successful wine merchants, but he didn't own any vineyards. Nor did he want to. His sons Bruno and Marcello had different ideas, though. Inspired by the wines of Burgundy, they wanted to own land, grow Nebbiolo, and make Barolo and Barbaresco, rather than buying wines made by farmers and selling them under the Ceretto name.

According to Federico Ceretto, Bruno's son, Ricardo Ceretto stood with his sons on the balcony of their building in Alba and said, "You want me to buy seven acres of Bussia"—one of the Barolo crus—"when I could buy twenty acres of Dolcetto? Nebbiolo, I wait three years to get paid, Dolcetto I sell tomorrow? No. This is crazy." He pointed out at the town. "See all this? That's my market. Every cantina, every store, every hotel, every house. You want to do Nebbiolo, leave and do it yourself."

Bruno and Marcello did. Their mother helped them buy that vineyard land in Bussia, and for a year father and sons split their business (and didn't speak). Then the mother interceded and said to the father and his sons, "*Basta*. Stop being idiots. Get together again."

Since then, Ceretto, first under Bruno and Marcello and now under the next generation, cousins Lisa, Roberta,

Alessandro, and Federico, has become one of the most significant wineries in both Barolo and Barbaresco. It's a family business; Federico says, "My father and uncle are really one entity, Bruno-Marcello. Since 1969, they've had one bank account for the both of them." And though the day-to-day operations have been passed down, neither of the brothers, who are both in their eighties, plans to retire anytime soon. Federico recalls an acquaintance asking his father why he didn't take a break, play some golf, relax a little. Bruno's response, at age eighty-four, was "You love golf? Go to Sicily and play golf. We have a winery to run."

The family owns three hundred acres of vines, largely in cru sites—Bricco Asili, Bricco Rocche, Cannubi, others—all biodynamic. After following a more international, oak-influenced style in the 1990s and early 2000s, the wines (under Alessandro Ceretto's hand) have pulled back from that flashiness, with the percentage of new oak dropping to about 10 percent, the use of *botti* reinstated, and overall a shift to more elegance and subtlety now present.

Though the winery is more known for reds, the **Ceretto Blange Arneis Langhe ($$)** is a great example of this white variety, all pear–green apple flavors with a light tingle from a tiny amount of carbon dioxide retained after fermentation; it brightens the wine without actually making it effervescent. Ceretto's classic **Barbaresco ($$$)** offers spicy, dark berry flavors and often a light minty note. The **Barolo ($$$)** is equally classic: savory, dark cherry flavors, plus plenty of round but firm tannins.

There are several single-cru bottlings from the winery. The **Barbaresco Asili ($$$$)**, with its exotic twist of spice, creamy density, and sweet tannins, is one of the best. "Asili is the paradise of Nebbiolo in Barbaresco," Federico says. "These vines were the first ones Marcello planted, back in the 1960s." The **Barbaresco Bernadot ($$$$)** suggests cherries and smoke, and on release is usually a little more austere than Asili. Ceretto's **Barolo Brunate ($$$$)** shows all the lush charm of this cru, full of darkly fragrant cherry liqueur notes, hints of lemon peel, and fine, very firm tannins. **Barolo Prapó ($$$$)** tends to suggest black currant rather than cherry, and is polished and chewy. The family's top wine, the **Barolo Bricco Rocche** ($$$$), is lingering and complex, fragrant, perfectly poised; the flavors descend at the finish into gripping, stony tannins. About the latter two, Federico Ceretto says, "Bricco Rocche is the flagship, the iconic wine, but the pure austere concentration of Serralunga that you get in Prapó is bigger." Ceretto's top wines are quite expensive, but for those with a fat wallet, they're worth the investment.

PIO CESARE • ALBA

[sustainable]

Among the uncountable losses of the Covid-19 pandemic was the premature death of Pio Boffa, the larger-than-life force behind Piedmont's Pio Cesare winery. Boffa was a driven, talented, charismatic figure, a daunting person to have to replace. But his daughter Federica Boffa, who took over the winery at age twenty-four following his passing, seems more than up to the challenge.

"It's a lot of pressure, and a lot of responsibility," she admits. "You can never be prepared to lose your father, and for me, the most important person in my life. My father was the face of the winery; he was a big show. Sometimes it could be difficult working with him, of course. He always expected the best."

Pio Cesare, which Federica now manages together with assistance from her cousin Cesare Benvenuto, was founded in 1881 in Alba. Continuity is key here: family ownership and also winemaking continuity. From 1881 until now there have only been four winemakers. "Being loyal to the family style through all these years has always been crucial to us," Federica says. "Same family, same building, same facilities, producing almost the same style of wine—despite climate change, despite new clones, despite changes in taste. We've never followed any trends or fashions. Our labels have never changed in over one hundred and forty years." The winery itself was built on the ruins of the ancient Roman walls of Alba, and founder Pio Cesare had one of the first passports issued by Italy. "I live on top of the winery, which is sometimes good and sometimes not so good," Federica says. "You never stop. But our hands, our hearts, our feet, our brains are our business."

Pio Cesare sustainably farms 170 acres of vineyards in Barolo, Barbaresco, and Colli Tortonesi, using no chemical treatments on the vines. Though the family style has been consistent, it's also shifted somewhat in recent years, lowering the wines' formerly somewhat formidable levels of extraction and also reducing the use of new oak.

Wines to look for include the elegant, flinty **Pio Cesare Piodilei Chardonnay ($$$)**, about which Federica says, "We took out three acres of Nebbiolo in Barbaresco to plant Chardonnay—you can imagine my grandfather's reaction." The **Langhe Nebbiolo ($$)**, which uses grapes from family holdings in Barolo, Barbaresco, and Diano d'Alba, is energetic and fragrant, easily drinkable on release. Pio Cesare's two flagship Nebbiolos are great examples of two of those appellations. The **Barbaresco ($$$)** is more red-fruited—cherry and currant—with firm tannins and light tarry notes, whereas the **Barolo ($$$)** is darker, more powerful, and more intense. "The heart of the Barolo is always Serralunga," she says. "There's a faithfulness to our idea of Barolo there—very masculine, very powerful." Also don't miss the winery's single-vineyard **Barbera d'Alba Fides Vigna Mosconi ($$$$)**, a brilliant Barbera with a depth, complexity, and balance this variety doesn't always express. "*Fides* means faith, or trust. My father called it that because we bought land in Serralunga and could have made much more money planting Nebbiolo on it. But he had this trust in Barbera to make a great wine there."

ELVIO COGNO • NOVELLO

[certified sustainable / organic]

Elvio Cogno, who passed away in 2016, was one of the architects of the rebirth of Barolo in the 1960s. A former chef, he abandoned cooking to make wine, partnering with Giuseppe Marcarini at the Marcarini estate in La Morra. His 1964 Marcarini Brunate was one of the first single-cru Barolos, and is one of the historical benchmarks in the region. Eventually that partnership dissolved, and in 1990 Cogno returned to his hometown of Novello to start again, purchasing an eighteenth-century farmhouse, Cascina Nuova, in Barolo's Ravera cru. His son-in-law Valter Fissore, who worked with Cogno for twenty-five years before the older man's passing in 2016, says, "Moving to Novello wasn't an easy step. He bought this winery when he was sixty years old. Can you imagine, starting from nothing at that age? That took incredible willpower."

Today Fissore and his wife, Cogno's daughter Nadia, run the winery, in the restored *cascina* (farmhouse), the old granaries now serving as the wine cellar. It's a beautiful place, a standout in a region jammed with beautiful places.

From the top of the hill in Ravera it's possible to see, on a clear day, the Alps in one direction and the Ligurian Sea in the other. The focus remains as Elvio Cogno intended: extraordinarily expressive single-cru Barolos from thirty-seven acres of vineyards around the winery. The farming has been effectively organic for more than fifteen years now, without any industrial fungicides, herbicides, or pesticides. As Fissore notes, he and Nadia and their children live directly in the center of their vineyards; he'd just as soon all of them stay healthy.

The Cogno wines are made in a low-intervention manner, though Fissore is not in the "natural wine" camp in the slightest (he, like many other producers in this book, provides one reason why that boundary line is somewhat absurd: working naturally is a spectrum, not a country whose borders are controlled by checkpoints and guard towers). Simply put, the wines are made with the grapes from their vineyards and with yeast strains local to Novello; no chemicals, no adjuncts, no enzymes, no commercial yeasts.

"Commercial yeasts give you boring wines," Fissore says. "'Oh, it tastes like banana!' Why would I want my wine to taste like a banana?"

Elvio Cogno was also instrumental in the rebirth of Nascetta, a once-forgotten white variety that now produces some of the Langhe's best white wines. Fissore recalls, "In 1991, my father-in-law and I tasted a 1986 bottle of Nascetta from a winery that had disappeared—it was like a great Sauternes, but dry. And I thought, 'Wow, why aren't we making this? Why are people growing Chardonnay instead?' It's Piedmontese, it has a long history—if you want Chardonnay, go to Burgundy!" Cogno himself had been feeling exactly the same way, so in 1994, the two men made a thousand bottles of Nascetta. Today Fissore makes about twelve times that much (though still not what you'd call an abundance).

"My father-in-law was a visionary," Fissore says. "I followed his knowledge and his vision. Nascetta was a wine that had completely disappeared, and now there are forty producers making it. Do we make money on it? No. But that's not the point. The point is passion."

The **Elvio Cogno Anas-Cëtta ($$)** is 100 percent Nascetta, fermented in a combination of wood and stainless steel. Straw-colored, lemony, and fragrant when young, it turns a twelve-karat golden hue as it ages, taking on more exotic fruit notes (mango, for example), becoming rounder and more smoky. Fissore makes two Barberas, the more affordable **Bricco dei Merli Barbera d'Alba ($$)**, with tart plum and herbal notes, and the remarkable **Pre-Phylloxera Barbera d'Alba ($$$)**. The latter comes from a tiny, 120-year-old plot of vines that Fissore refers to as "a museum. I dedicated this wine to my father-in-law, because when he was at Marcarini, he used to make a Dolcetto called Bosca di Beri on sandy soil in La Morra. This is from there." It's exquisitely complex, with robust blackberry fruit, aromatic herbal notes, white pepper, and a kind of savory meatiness; it's also more tannic and muscular than most Barberas. The **Montegrilli Langhe Nebbiolo ($$)** is made with 40 percent carbonic maceration and no wood. Full of vivacious red berry fruit, "it's a bit nearer to the character of Pinot Noir," Fissore says.

The four Elvio Cogno Barolos are among the best in the entire region. The **Elvio Cogno Barolo Cascina Nuova ($$$)**, from younger vines, is meant to be easier drinking, a Barolo to enjoy now, rather than to put away for twenty years. **Barolo Ravera ($$$)** is the estate's signature wine. "It's our pride," Fissore says. "Thirty years ago, no one made Ravera as a cru. Now, many do." Think dark cherries, deep spice notes, a hint of graphite. The **Barolo Bricco Pernice ($$$)** echoes the graphite note in Cascina Nuova, but is more brooding and powerful; a wine to age. Finally, there's the **Barolo Vigna Elena Riserva ($$$$)**, named for Valter and Nadia's daughter, which comes from a single two-acre, hillside vineyard planted to the Nebbiolo Rosé subvariety (there's also Nebbiolo Lampia and Nebbiolo Michet). "Compared to Lampia, Rosé has more finesse—more Burgundy character, more rose petals. A bit less power," Fissore says. But power isn't what the Cogno wines are about. What Fissore strives for is elegance and complexity. "Wines you can enjoy with food, where you always want a little more," he says. "Not some super-boomba wine where you can't drink another glass."

DIEGO CONTERNO • MONFORTE D'ALBA

[certified organic]

Are you considered an upstart if your winery was founded eighteen years ago? In Barolo you are, of course. But Diego Conterno's experience in the region predates his own brand; for more than twenty years he worked with his cousins at Conterno Fantino, until the partnership crumbled. He sold his share in that winery, launched Diego Conterno in 2005, and today works alongside his son Stefano in the southern part of Barolo.

Stefano, red-haired and energetic, says, "When my father sold his part of Conterno Fantino in the early 2000s, he changed everything: the brand, the wines, but not the Ginestra property. He decided to restart not with new land but with a new philosophy. Only indigenous grapes, cement fermentation rather than stainless steel, *botti* rather than *barriques*." Their eighteen and a half acres of vines have been certified organic since 2013.

These expressive, elegant Langhe wines don't skimp on power but don't rely on it for effect, either. The sole white wine, the **Diego Conterno Nascetta ($$)**, has that variety's classic green apple–lime aromatic notes. It's medium-bodied and entirely refreshing. The winery's **Dolcetto d'Alba ($$)** is all blueberry and raspberry fruit, a bit chunky and intense (the nature of Dolcetto, I find). Stefano says, "Dolcetto is very difficult fruit and very difficult wine. The skins are very soft. A simple wine, but difficult to work." The **Barbera d'Alba Ferrione ($$)**, named for the area in Monforte that lies outside of Barolo's official boundaries, is all blackberry and lemon zest acidity, with modest tannins; the **Langhe Nebbiolo Baluma ($$)** is a pleasure, with crunchy red fruit, gripping tannins, and a faint note of cured meat.

The **Diego Conterno Barolo ($$$)**, dark ruby in hue, is chewy and relatively dense with firm, sweet tannins. It comes from three vineyards within Monforte d'Alba: San Giovanni, Bricco San Pietro, and Ginestra. There are also two wines from the Conterno's five acres of prized vines in Ginestra, **Barolo Ginestra ($$$$)** and **Barolo del Comune di Monforte d'Alba ($$$$)**. The former comes from the oldest vines, planted in 1942, and is held a year longer before release. The Comune wine is more red-fruited, less powerful, but still impressive; the Ginestra, full of savory currant flavors, a light toasted character, and chewy, dense tannins. Age it.

ODDERO · LA MORRA

[certified organic]

Mariacristina Oddero's family first started growing grapes at the start of the nineteenth century, and in 1878 bottled their first wine with the Oddero name on it. "It was a group of samples that my great-great-grandfather Giacomo sent to a store in Milan," she says. "There were a few other producers doing bottles in the 1870s, Borgogno for sure, Pio Cesare maybe. But not many." Oddero was among the first.

The tasting room at Oddero is filled with family photos that reflect that history, and from them it's clear that Mariacristina, who is petite and elegant, distinctly resembles her mother and grandmother before her: a line of strong-willed women who wielded much more influence in the winery's history than people might have realized at the time.

"The women in the past in this area were very strong, but very humble," she says. "Though my grandmother also used to say that men can't pour wine for people and talk at the same time. She was a pharmacist all her life, one of the first pharmacists in Alba. It was a beautiful pharmacy, she worked very hard, and it was *very* successful.

Her money bought the vineyards. My grandfather *selected* the vineyards, but the money came from her." There's a glint of pride in Mariacristina's eye. "In Piedmont, women have always been behind a lot of family decisions, just not publicly."

When she joined the winery in the late 1990s, after earning a viticulture and enology degree, she and her uncle Luigi soon began to butt heads (her father Giacomo and Luigi had run the winery since the 1950s). Not entirely surprisingly, she won that battle—the line from *A Midsummer Night's Dream* "though she be but little, she is fierce" comes to mind. Luigi departed. She won another battle when she started organic viticulture in 2008. "My father, when he first came and saw the cover crops in the vineyard, called me *la regina del gramone*, the queen of the weeds." She laughs. "But three years later we received certification. I'd love it if someday in the future all the vineyards in Barolo became organic."

Oddero makes wine from eighty-six acres of vineyards, with cru holdings in Rocche, Vigne Rionda, Bussia, Villero, and Brunate. Everything is certified organic. The winery makes two Barberas, the **Oddero Barbera d'Alba Superiore ($$)**, lightly herbal with focused berry flavors, and **Nizza ($$)**, made from purchased fruit in Barbera d'Asti. Nizza has broader flavors, with higher acid and a bit more bite. "I love both, but Alba is closer for me, because we have vineyards there," Oddero says. "Asti, for me, the nose is a bit wild, not the ethereal nose of Alba." The winery's **Langhe Nebbiolo ($$)** is all dark cherry and tobacco, with drying Nebbiolo tannins. The **Barolo ($$$)**, blended from vineyards in La Morra and Castiglione di Falletto, has a firm austerity, dark cherry and raspberry flavors, and gripping tannins. "My father is ninety-five now, and for him this *is* Barolo. The old school of Barolo," Mariacristina says. "He's an old man; he likes the classics." Oddero also makes a number of cru Barolos, all excellent. Two to compare are the **Barolo Brunate ($$$$)**, which balances dense, coating tannins against its baking spice and red cherry flavors, and the **Rocche di Castiglione ($$$$)**, more floral, with creamy raspberry flavors and a fine, precisely delineated structure.

GIOVANNI ROSSO • SERRALUNGA D'ALBA

[organic]

In person, Davide Rosso often seems like an Italian winemaker grafted into real life from Fellini's *La Dolce Vita*, with his gravelly voice, cigarette dangling between his fingers, and elegant flop of jet-black hair. He has that *sprezzatura* manner as well—especially when standing at the tasting counter in his winery, where as often as not he'll be drinking a gin and tonic rather than a glass of wine. The diffidence masks an extremely talented winemaker, though, who's producing some of the Langhe's best Barolos.

The Rossos have farmed vineyards around Serralunga d'Alba since the 1890s, though they've been in the region longer than that. Asked how long, Davide lifts his hands and says, "I don't know—long, long, long, long time." The real stride forward came from his father, Giovanni, whose ambition in terms of restructuring and restoring their vineyards, with an eye to making excellent wine, was vital; when Davide took over in 2001 at age twenty-seven, he followed his father's path. "We are traditional," he says, about both farming and winemaking, which means working organically in the vines, long, slow fermentation in cement tanks, and aging the wines in traditional old oak *botti* in the cellar.

He also started a project on Mount Etna in 2016, buying a fifty-year-old vineyard twenty-two hundred feet up on the side of the volcano. Not exactly close to the Langhe, but when asked why, he says, "Because I love it! It's a place where, when you are there, you have energy. There's no scientific explanation. But that energy, with it you can make a great wine."

First, the Etna wines. The **Giovanni Rosso Etna Rosso ($$)**, mostly Nerello Mascalese with a touch of Nerello Cappuccio, is ruby-hued, smoky, and bright with cranberry-inflected red fruit. Davide's **Etna Bianco ($$)** is, he says, "a mix of stuff—Cataratto, Grecanico, Ansonica, etcetera, etcetera." (The "etcetera etcetera" gets a cigarette wave.) Lemony and textural, it ends on a salty mineral note.

In the Langhe, highlights include one of the best **Langhe Nebbiolo ($$)** deals around, an easy-drinking Nebbiolo with floral accents that's hard to resist. The **Giovanni Rosso Barolo ($$)** comes from vineyards in Serralunga, Barolo, and Castiglione Falletto; think violets and red cherries, with the underlying tensile strength that Serralunga in particular tends to impart. Of the cru wines, the **Barolo Ceretta ($$$)**, has a spicy aroma and sweetly plummy fruit, ending on softly gripping tannins. "Ceretta is the little stranger in Serralunga," Davide Rosso says. "Typically Serralunga is calcareous soil, or in the northern part more sandy clay. Ceretta is on the border of the two, a mix of both. It's sweeter, rounder, more feminine, not typical of Serralunga." The **2018 Barolo Serra ($$$)** is, on the other hand, he says, "a typical expression of Serralunga: more tannic, more balsamic, more vertical. There's only three hundred meters [a thousand feet] between it and Ceretta, but they're completely different."

Then there are two wines from the famed Vigna Rionda vineyard. The **Giovanni Rosso Ester Canale Rosso ($$$$)** is labeled as Langhe Nebbiolo but is far more complex and alluring than most actual Barolos. It's a beautiful wine. What to say about the **Ester Canale Barolo ($$$$)**? It's a stupendous wine, but at an equally stupendous price, roughly $400 a bottle.

G. D. VAJRA • BAROLO

[certified organic]

"After World War II, my grandfather and grandmother were young and broke and in love," Giuseppe Vajra says. "My grandfather had been among those who stood up to Mussolini, so, because he'd been part of the resistance, he was able to get a job in the Italian defense department. But that meant moving from the Langhe to the city, to Torino. So that's where my dad grew up. But he'd always had this crazy dream of being a farmer, like being an astronaut, or a race car driver. Then, in 1968, he got caught on the streets during the youth protests. My grandfather sent him back to the family farm, to keep him out of trouble. And that's when the seed exploded."

The Vajra estate is located in Vergne, the highest village in the com-

---

"You don't need art or poetry or a glass of wine in order to stay alive. But what's the point of life without those things?"
—Aldo Vajra

---

mune of Barolo. The family has farmed there, growing grapes and other crops, since the 1880s—the name at the time,

and up until the 1960s, was the more traditionally Piemontese Vaira. Aldo Vajra was fifteen when he was sent back to the farm to stay out of trouble; by 1971, when he was eighteen, he was studying viticulture and had converted the estate (which at the time was selling grapes to other producers, not making wine) to organic farming. The Vajras were among the first, if not the first, in Piedmont to head in this direction. "My father was fortunate to have a professor who was early in the movement to do chemical-free farming," Giuseppe Vajra says. "But they had to meet after hours in the professor's office to discuss the topic, because all of the university's agricultural research was funded by chemical companies at the time."

Aldo Vajra became a viticulture instructor, and, as Giuseppe says, "luckily found the only crazy woman who could put up with him, my mother. She came from a farming family, so she understood him. Together they created Vajra."

It wasn't an easy task. At the time, in Piedmont, the only lands with real value were the flatlands. The hillsides and vineyards were for the poor.

And when Aldo Vajra finally decided to make wine rather than just grow grapes, it was 1972, a spectacularly bad vintage in Barolo. Essentially, the weather forced his hand: "I had grapes, but in 1972 no one wanted them," he recalls. "So, I had to transform my grapes into wine. I also have to thank my uncle. About the 1972 vintage, he told me, 'Listen, Aldo, if you manage to sell this wine, we have to go out for a nice dinner. But sell it fast, because it's going to be dead by summer.'" Not what one would call an auspicious start. Despite that, the young farmer persevered, and nature rewarded him in 1975 with what he recalls as his first "magical vintage—I can still taste that wine. All the flavors in the world, like a candy."

Today Vajra farms close to one hundred acres of vines. This is a family effort: Aldo and Milena still oversee everything, but their children Giuseppe, Francesca, and Isidoro are part of the equation. It's a gravitational pull, it seems. Giuseppe says, "At fifteen, I wanted to be a heart surgeon—I even passed my medical exams. And I was wary of working in a winery. I asked, 'Dad, what is the social purpose of what you do?' He said, 'Giuseppe, if you want to save lives, go be a doctor. We don't save lives. You don't need art or poetry or a glass of wine in order to stay alive. But what's the point of life without those things?' That's the night I decided to devote myself to making wine."

The **G. D. Vajra Langhe Riesling Pétracine** (\$\$) is crisp, zesty, and dry, all golden apple, lime peel, and chalk. (When Aldo Vajra bought the vineyard—after the deal was signed—the former owner said, "Oh, by the way, don't plant Nebbiolo in that corner over there." Awkward, since Vajra had bought the place specifically to plant Nebbiolo. But he'd had a crush on Riesling since the 1970s, he says, and planted two blocks of Rheingau clones. The results speak for themselves.)

The **Claré J.C. Langhe Nebbiolo** (\$\$) is part of a new line of wines from Vajra that lean more toward natural winemaking (or toward the past). It's very light, a pale ruby color, with fresh strawberry notes and a light tingle on the palate. **Coste & Fossati Dolcetto d'Alba** (\$\$) is violet-hued and full of dense purple-berry juiciness. The **Barbera d'Alba** (\$\$), with its lovely dark berry fruit, leans to the second of what Giuseppe calls "the two poles of Barbera—one crisp and raw, the other rich and lush." The **Barbera d'Alba Superiore ($$)** is chewier, and usually needs some time after release. "It's a bit of slamming the big encyclopedia on the table," Giuseppe says. Peppery and plummy, the **Kyè Freisa Langhe ($$$)** pulls a lot of elegance out of this sometimes rustic old variety. Vajra's **Langhe Nebbiolo ($$)** is typically floral, with bright bing cherry fruit. The **Barolo Albe ($$$)**, Vajra's most affordable Barolo bottling, comes from several high-elevation vineyards and often has a faint mocha edge to its red currant and red cherry flavors. Vajra's three cru Barolos are all exceptional, and remain mystifyingly well priced for Barolos at this level. **Barolo Costa di Rosa ($$$$)** is smoky and floral, with silky but powerful tannins and sweet cherry fruit. Vajra's **Barolo Ravera ($$$$)** is darker and more brooding, sweetly dense with juicy, compelling raspberry fruit. "Iron oxide is the distortion pedal in this wine," Giuseppe Vajra says, referring to Ravera's distinctive soil. Finally, the **Barolo Bricco della Viola ($$$$)** is a picture of elegance from the highest vineyard in the commune of Barolo, the "Hill of Violets." Vajra's vines there date back to 1949. The wine is layered and subtle, its fragrant beauty concealing a fair amount of power.

VENETO

Ah, Veneto. In the way that Venice, one of the most beautiful cities on earth, is now overrun with hordes of tourists descending on it from the vast cruise ships that park in its lagoon, so too the Veneto wine region, capable of producing sublime, expressive wines, is unfortunately overrun with millions upon millions of bottles of mass-produced, characterless Proseccos and Pinot Grigios. There are brilliant versions to be had of those wines, but you definitely have to work to find them.

Is it the Veneto's fault it's so fertile? It produces more wine than any other Italian region, the vast majority of it white, with endless acres of grapes planted on the Piave and Adige river plains, and inland from the shores of Lake Garda. But throughout the region there are also areas where complex, ambitious wine can be made: the hills of Valpolicella (home to Amarone) and Soave, and some estates in Prosecco; also, Franciacorta is the source for Italy's best high-level sparkling wines. One quick tip is, in the more productive regions like Soave and Valpolicella, to look for "classico" on the label, which designates that the wine is from the original demarcated boundaries of the region, as opposed to the thousands of acres added later on to satisfy supermarket demand. Another tip, as always, is simply to look for great winemaking. There are plenty of banal Soaves to be found, but those of Dario Pieropan (and his father, Leonildo, before him), to give one example, are gorgeous, complex wines.

ALLEGRINI · VALPOLICELLA

[sustainable / certified organic (La Grola vineyard)]

In the 1950s and 1960s, Giovanni Allegrini spearheaded a quality revolution in Valpolicella. His daughter Marilisa recalls, "In that era in Valpolicella, the hillside vineyards were abandoned. When my father bought La Grola and Palazzo delle Torre, the two vineyards that are the heart of our estate, no one wanted them. And everybody thought he was crazy." (He also nearly bankrupted the family buying them.)

"Everybody thought he was crazy" might be the tagline for any number of brilliant wineries, but of course Giovanni Allegrini wasn't crazy. He was right. And smart, because he bought excellent hillside vineyard land, mostly near the town of Fumane, for a very good price. He also brought a renewed rigor to both viticulture and winemaking in Valpolicella, and was one the first vintners here to make ambitious single-vineyard wines.

Today Allegrini is a very large family company, with properties in Brunello di Montalcino and Bolgheri as well as in Valpolicella, but its roots remain in the hills of Fumane. Marilisa, elegant, erudite, and possessed of incredible willpower and drive, is CEO, overseeing the business side and acting as the face of the company (her brother Franco oversaw the winemaking until his death in 2022). She has been a force in Italian wine for forty years.

Allegrini farms all of its nearly three hundred acres of vineyards in Valpolicella sustainably, and the seventy-five-acre La Grola vineyard, which contains La Poja, is certified organic. Additional work includes efforts toward biodiversity and carbon footprint reduction. (Also, the family's Tuscan properties are both certified organic.) And though the company unquestionably makes a lot of wine, it remains completely defined by the family's ownership.

The basic **Allegrini Valpolicella ($)** is a remarkably good wine for a modest price, full of ripe plummy fruit and light tannins. **Palazzo delle Torre ($$)** comes from the vineyard of the same name (where the stunningly beautiful, Renaissance-era Villa delle Torre stands). For it, a small amount of *appassimento* wine (Amarone, basically) is blended in with the finished Vapolicella, adding depth and richness. **La Grola ($$)** comes from Allegrini's organic hillside cru of the same name. It's 90 percent Corvina with 10 percent Oseleta, full of ripe, dark berry and plum fruit and soft, palate-coating tannins. **La Poja ($$$–$$$$)**, Allegrini's top non-*appassimento* wine, is 100 percent Corvina from a single parcel at the top of the La Grola vineyard. It embodies Giovanni Allegrini's belief that Valpolicella, and the Corvina grape, could produce a world-class, terroir-expressive red wine.

About Allegrini's **Amarone della Valpolicella Classico ($$$)**, one of the benchmarks of the appellation, Marilisa Allegrini says, "The traditional style of amarone has that port-like aroma, high alcohol, and residual sugar. We changed our methods to make a wine that still has that distinctive, dried-grape aroma, but with no sugar and no oxidative character. My brother didn't like to say that it was 'modern,' just that it was an innovative style." Allegrini's Amarone is far more food-friendly and elegant than many; a higher percentage of Corvina (45 percent or more) adds to its freshness. The **Amarone della Valpolicella Classico Riserva Fieramonte ($$$$)** comes from a vineyard the family has owned for generations but that had to be ripped out in 1985 thanks to vine diseases. Franco Allegrini replanted it in the early 2000s to create this powerful, ink-dark, black-fruited, formidable wine.

BERLUCCHI • FRANCIACORTA

[organic (estate vineyards) / sustainable (purchased fruit)]

Without Franco Ziliani, there would *be* no Franciacorta, though according to his daughter Cristina, "What my father always said was that he didn't create Franciacorta, he discovered it." In the 1950s, when he was in his twenties, Berlucchi tasted Champagne for the first time. "Wine in Italy at the time wasn't a cultural thing," Cristina says. "I remember the carpenters working on my father's house one time were drinking wine while they were working. It was to feel stronger, more powerful; like an energy drink. And most of the wine of Italy back then just wasn't very good. In those years a steak was *much* more expensive than a bottle of wine."

Nevertheless, her father became a winemaker, then met a nobleman named Guido Berlucchi, who was making a small amount of white wine at his estate. With that memory of Champagne in his mind, Ziliani suggested they make something similar. "Berlucchi thought he was a little bit crazy, but my dad was determined." And in 1961, the first bottles of sparkling wine ever labeled Franciacorta appeared.

Ziliani's success was rapid. "Even though people thought it was weird, making sparkling wine from Franciacorta, they really liked it," Cristina Ziliani says. Eventually her father bought out Berlucchi, and while the company has grown exponentially, it remains family owned.

Berlucchi is not small. The Zilianis own 320 acres of vineyards, all farmed organically, and control another 980, which they require to be farmed sustainably at the very least. "We push them toward organic, but it's difficult with the climate changes—we have much more rain than we once did," Cristina says. "Still, we have a sustainable protocol that every farmer we work with has to follow; no herbicides or pesticides at all, even if the vineyard isn't fully organic. And we pick all the grapes ourselves, so we always know what's happening."

The sparkling **Berlucchi '61 Extra Brut Franciacorta** ($$) is citrusy, crisp, and vividly fresh, made from 85 percent Chardonnay and 15 percent Pinot Nero and aged for twenty-four months on lees. The **'61 Satèn** ($$), which is 100 percent Chardonnay, is soft and creamy, with peach and citrus flavors. The zero-dosage **'61 Nature** ($$$) is bone-dry and steely, with laser-like focus. At a slightly higher price, the **Cuvée Imperiale Brut** ($$) adds complexity and layers of flavor. For a splurge, look for the **Palazzo Lana Extrême** ($$$), which spends seven years on the lees and an additional six months aging before it's released. Copper-gold in color, it's luscious and complex, with rich toasted bread, citrus zest, and orchard fruit notes.

CA' DEI ZAGO · PROSECCO

[biodynamic / natural]

Prosecco made in the *col fondo* style is the original, old-school Prosecco. The second fermentation occurs in the bottle, but the wine is not disgorged—meaning that the lees remain in the bottle (the term translates literally as "with the bottom"). *Col fondos* are cloudy-hazy, tangy, and have softer bubbles and less sweetness than the modern style. They're typically bottled under crown caps rather than cork, and are sadly a vanishing species.

Ca' dei Zago has been making *col fondo* Prosecco since the 1920s, and Christian Zago, its young, fifth-generation winemaker, has no interest in stopping. Zago farms according to biodynamic principles, too, a rarity in a region mostly known for industrial, mass-production sparkling wines.

Ca' dei Zago lies in the hills just south of Valdobiaddene—you can see the town from the vines—and has from its inception never been farmed with chemical fertilizers or other treatments, only cow manure and compost. There are sixteen acres of steep, terraced vineyards, primarily Glera, but with a smattering of old local varieties like Verdiso, Perera, and Bianchetta. Zago points out that because there's no possibility of adjusting sugar or acidity with *col fondo* wines, no freedom to add anything that did not *come* from the vines, the method requires that your farming be exceptionally good. (In essence, *col fondo* wines translate the vineyard to the bottle much more directly than either traditional or Charmat method wines do.) "When you drink *col fondo*, you drink wine, nothing else," he says.

The **Ca' dei Zago Valdobbiadene Frizzante Col Fondo ($$)** comes from vines averaging about fifty years old, planted by Christian Zago's grandfather. It's a softly fizzy, almost creamy sparkling wine, with shimmering citrus notes, nice mineral depth, and a savory, leesy quality. Give it a light shake to distribute the lees at the bottom of the bottle, or drink it as the locals do, pouring off the clear wine to serve first, then finishing with a glass of bubbles that's practically opaque with cloudy sediment.

PIEROPAN • SOAVE

[certified organic]

1978, Soave. In the U.S., people were buying more Soave than any other Italian wine—"There are almost as many people in love with Soave Bolla as there are people in love" ran one TV tagline—and the vast majority of it was insipid, overcropped, flavorless dreck. Yet not *all* of it. In 1971, Leonildo Pieropan had been the first in the region to adopt the French concept of a cru wine, one from a single high-quality vineyard. Then, in 1978, he released the first vintage of La Rocca, and it remains to this day one of the benchmarks of the region. Andrea Pieropan says, "If you think that only just recently, in 2019, did the Soave *consorzio* actually break down the region into official geographical zones—the first step towards arriving at single-vineyard wines—this gives you an idea how much of a pioneer my father was." Leonildo fermented La Rocca in large barrels and *tonneaux*,

rather than traditional cement tanks, and released it two years after the harvest. "At that time, trying to sell a white wine from Soave two years after the harvest? That was like trying to fly to the moon," Andrea says. "It took him ten years to sell the first bottle. Critics would say, 'This wine is not Soave.' And my father would say, 'No, the *rest* of the wines aren't Soave. This one is.'"

Even now, much of Soave is industrially produced, "and anytime you use a grape for massive production, you can't make great wine," Andrea says. La Rocca was also one of the first white wines, he adds, that showed Italy that it was possible "to play in the premier league with indigenous Italian varieties. The idea my father had was to make a great Italian white wine that was authentic to the place where it came from."

The first Leonildo Pieropan founded

Pieropan in the 1880s; he was a surgeon, but abandoned that career after his first operation because he hated the sight of blood. It was with the later Leonildo, who passed away in 2018, that the family vineyards grew from a few acres to over 150; more than forty years ago the Pieropans also shifted to organic viticulture. The second Leonildo also instituted green harvesting, the practice of cutting some of the crop early to increase the quality of the remaining bunches. "In the 1970s, Soave was about quantity, not quality," Andrea says. "People would come into our vineyards and look at the grapes lying on the ground and say my father was completely crazy." A familiar refrain.

———

The **Pieropan Soave Classico ($–$$)** is a spot-on example of what Soave can be when it's produced with care: the aroma suggests blossoms and green apples, with a note of almonds, and it's racy and crisp. The single-vineyard **Calvarino Soave Classico ($$)** is made with fruit from thirty- to sixty-year-old Garganega and Trebbiano vines. "In Soave, Trebbiano gives more pear aromas and more tart malic acid," Andrea Pieropan says. "Garganega gives more white flowers—cherry blossoms—and more body and structure." **La Rocca Soave Classico ($$)** comes from a hillside vineyard with more clay soils, located just below a medieval castle. Entirely Garganega, it's made from grapes that are picked late, toward the end of October or in the first week of November. Light gold, with deep aromas and flavors of stone fruits, nuts, and sometimes honeysuckle, it's a rich wine, but buoyed by bright acidity. The late harvest date was initially a problem, Andrea Pieropan recalls: "People used to come during the night and steal our grapes. Everyone else finished picking about two weeks before we harvest La Rocca, so they probably thought, 'What does it matter? He clearly doesn't want them.' After two or three years of this, though, my father was pretty angry, so he built a wall with a gate to keep everyone out."

PRODUCERS PROFILED IN THIS CHAPTER

Alto Adige—Trentino

Foradori

Garlider

J. Hofstätter

Manincor

Emilia-Romagna

La Stoppa

Friuli–Venezia Giulia

Borgo del Tiglio

Livio Felluga

Gravner

Venica & Venica

Piedmont

Borgogno

Chiara Boschis—E. Pira

G. B. Burlotto

Ceretto

Pio Cesare

Elvio Cogno

Diego Conterno

Oddero

Giovanni Rosso

G. D. Vajra

Veneto

Allegrini

Berlucchi

Ca' dei Zago

Pieropan

OTHER NORTHERN ITALY PRODUCERS TO LOOK FOR

Emilia-Romagna

Lini
Paltrinieri
Moro Rinaldini

Vigneto Saetti
Terrevive

Friuli

Gradis'sciutta
Edi Kante
Lis Neris
Miani
Radikon
Ronchi di Cialla

Ronco del Gnemiz
Scarbolo
Skerlj
Vignai da Duline
Vodopivec
Zidarich

Liguria

Laura Aschero

Punta Crena

Piedmont—Alto Piedmont—Lombardy

Anna Maria Abbona
Fratelli Alessandria
Antoniolo
ArPePe
Brovia
Piero Busso
Castello di Verduno
Capellano
Cavallotto
Damilano

Ferrando
Fabio Gea
Ioppa
Malvirà
Bartolo Mascarello
Walter Massa
Poderi Colla
Ada Nada
Francesco Rinaldi
Rivetto

Rovellotti

Luciano Sandrone

Trediberri

Mauro Veglio

Trentino—Alto Adige

Abazzia di Novacella

Kofererhof

Pacherhof

Pojer & Sandri

Tieffenbrunner

Val d'Aosta

Grosjean

Lo Triolet

Veneto

Bisol

Borgoluce

Bussola

Cantina Filippo Filippi

Corte Sant'Alda

Gini

Inama

Masi

Angiolino Maule / La Biancara

Musella

Tenta Santa Maria

CENTRAL ITALY

The center of Italy is blessed with warm days and cool nights during the summers, temperate winters, and fertile land planted with acre after acre of grape vines (or olive trees), the terrain growing dramatically craggy and mountainous as you head over the Appenines in the east and drop down to the Adriatic Coast. This is the homeland of Sangiovese, Italy's most planted red grape, whose name derives from the Latin *sanguis jovis*, the blood of Jupiter. But there are plenty of other significant red varieties as well, and some of Italy's most well-known (though not always the best) white wines are made here, too: Frascati in Lazio, outside Rome, and Orvieto in Umbria.

The anchor of central Italian wine is Italy's most famous wine region, Tuscany. Home to Chianti, Brunello di Montalcino, and a host of other famous subregions, Tuscany, with its medieval hilltop towns, warm terra-cotta tones, olive groves, and, yes, vineyards, is many people's platonic ideal of the Italian countryside. More than that, though, Tuscany produces some of Italy's greatest wines, and is also, after Sicily, home to a greater percentage of organically farmed vineyard land than anywhere else in the country.

The task for wine lovers is to sift through the super-abundance of bottles from central Italy that fill store shelves and find the producers who aren't willing to coast on the region's basic gift for making easy-drinking, unexceptional reds and whites. There are plenty of these winemakers, many more than those portrayed here.

ABRUZZO

The narrow region of Abruzzo lies sandwiched between the Appenines and the Adriatic Sea. More than 65 percent of the land here is mountainous, and a good chunk of what's not is coastline, so vineyards perch where they can between these two boundaries. As with many Italian regions, Abruzzese winemaking was dominated by large co-ops from the end of World War II on through the seventies, eighties, and nineties. Even today, nearly 80 percent of Abruzzo's grapes go to co-op wines. But that's not all that surprising, in a place where there are more than 6,000 grape growers but only 250 or so wineries.

The Montepulciano d'Abruzzo grape is the backbone of production, making everything from light, simple, fruity reds to—when it is grown and vinified well—spicy, more complex wines that still retain the variety's innate fresh red berry vivacity. It's also made into Cerasuolo d'Abruzzo, the local rosé, which is deeper in color and usually far more interesting than the vast amount of pale-pink rosés that flood stores every summer. Whites primarily come from Trebbiano, but the Pecorino variety has also been a focus in recent years, particularly for the region's newer, more ambitious winemakers.

Abruzzo, more than most other Italian wine regions, still feels wild. There aren't many people, and much of its landscape isn't developed. Cristiana Tiberio, one of the region's most talented winemakers, says, "Most of our region is mountains. It's all rock and stone and forests. Abruzzo is a place where, in May, you can ski in the mountains, then jump in your car, drive for twenty-five minutes, and swim in the Adriatic. And there's a lot of biodiversity—wolves, deer, wildcats, bear. I love to walk in the mountains, but every time I start, I think, 'OK, please, I just don't want to meet a bear.'"

The history of Abruzzese wines is long. The Etruscans made wine here, then the Romans, and the story goes that Hannibal gave his army wine from Abruzzo to restore their strength after their legendary crossing over the Alps. It seems unlikely that he also gave the wine of Abruzzo to his famed elephants, but who knows? There's no question that a drunken elephant would be a formidable foe.

EMIDIO PEPE • ABRUZZO

[organic / biodynamic]

For almost sixty years now, Emidio Pepe has been championing the potential of Trebbiano di Abruzzo and Montepulciano di Abruzzo. His early desire to prove that these two local varieties were capable of creating long-lived, world-class wines has been satisfied—these days, no one doubts that his wines are exactly that. But, even at ninety, he has hardly retired. While most of the work is now done by his two daughters (and two granddaughters), as any of them will say, "nothing has really changed." The vision remains the one he started with.

That vision is summed up by Pepe himself when he says, "Our whole wine-making process is based on respecting the wine as if it were a human being."

The Pepe family has been farming grapes in Abruzzo since the late 1800s, but until Emidio took over in 1964, their crop was always sold to the local co-op or to *négociants*. Pepe abandoned that, determined to make his own wine. He started with the family's three and a half acres of pergola-trained vines—the classic vineyard practice in Abruzzo, where the vine trunks are trained high on wooden poles, and the canopy of leaves truly is a canopy, spreading out on wires above head height. Through the years, he's kept to this traditional approach, though the family now farms a little more than thirty-seven acres of vines.

His vineyards are in the north of Abruzzo, ten minutes from the Adriatic Sea and forty minutes from Gran Sasso, the highest peak of the Appenines. The vines are descendants from a small, ancient plot that Pepe particularly liked back in 1964; these ancestral clones play into the distinctive signature of his wines. The farming is biodynamic, but the basic tenets of biodynamics were already present in how Pepe had worked from the start: no chemical products in

---

"Our whole winemaking process is based on respecting the wine as if it were a human being."
—Emidio Pepe

---

the vineyard, paying attention to the phases of the moon—"my grandfather worked this way"—and above all a focus on creating living soil. Living soil equals living wine. So: biodynamic preparations, cover crops, and a rotation system for the land surrounding the vineyards to increase diversity in soil microorganisms, indigenous yeasts, and crops as well. (The family also makes olive oil, pasta, and flour from a heritage wheat strain, and dried chickpeas and chickpea flour.)

The winemaking follows a similar path. Grapes are destemmed by hand by being rolled over a net, and crushed by foot in wooden tubs. "It's all very traditional." Fermentation happens in glass-lined concrete tanks. "No filters, no sulfites, no racking [moving wine from one barrel to another either to remove sediment or expose it to oxygen]. If you rack," Pepe says, "the first time it's like a well-dressed man taking off his jacket. The next time, he loses his shirt. Then his pants, and after that? He has nothing left."

Emidio Pepe makes four wines (five, if you count a younger-vine Montepulciano that's sold only in Italy). There's a small amount of lightly herbal **Emidio Pepe Pecorino Colli Apruntini** ($$$), coming from one and a quarter acres of vines; it's bright and brisk, with orchard fruit flavors. His flagship white is his **Trebbiano d'Abruzzo** ($$$), golden-hued, full-bodied, and immensely flavorful (think citrus peel, ginger, and apples, often with a savory, cheese-rind note). Since the Trebbiano does malolactic fermentation in bottle (extremely unusual), it sometimes has a very faint effervescence when opened. Pepe's **Cerasuolo d'Abruzzo** (**$$$**), the classic, deeply colored rosé of Abruzzo, is all earth and cherries. Absurdly small amounts come to the U.S., so if you see it, buy it. Pepe's greatest wine is his **Montepulciano d'Abruzzo Selezione Vecchie Vigne** (**$$$$**). It's released after a minimum of five years aging (it's also decanted to remove sediment and rebottled, if more than seven years old). This is a profound red: smoky, earthy, full-bodied, richly flavorful with dark berry and bacon notes, powerful but also elegant. "That elegance comes from all the elements of the wine," Pepe says. "They are all integrated, no one overpowers the others."

TIBERIO · ABRUZZO

[certified organic]

"Ever since I was a teenager, I've had a great passion for wine," Cristiana Tiberio says. "As a wine lover, yes, but as a curious wine lover—I wanted to understand, to know."

Cristiana is the co-proprietor and winemaker, with her viticulturist brother Antonio, of their family's eponymous winery, which their father, Riccardo, founded at the turn of the millennium. Before then, he'd been working as the export manager for a large commercial winery, but in 1999 he came across a singular, sixty-year-old vineyard of Trebbiano Abruzzese vines; it changed his and his family's life.

"A lot of different kinds of Trebbiano grow in Abruzzo," Cristiana says, "so when you see a wine labeled Trebbiano from here, it's usually a blend, mostly using Trebbiano Toscana. Trebbiano Abruzzese is rare. I remember my father told us, when he said what he was thinking of doing, 'We won't just be buying a vineyard, we're buying an old, historic heritage. Not just for us, but for the future of the wine culture of Abruzzo.'" She laughs. "So, we all said, yes! Please! Buy the vineyard!"

Riccardo Tiberio had come from a family of farmers, so in essence the family went back to that tradition.

Cristiana and Antonio pulled the weeds, pruned the overgrown vines, learned the terroir and the variety. "We spent five years reviving it before we had our first fruit," Cristiana says. "Really, that was probably the most significant period in my winemaking life. Making wine in the end is really about developing a sensibility that's tied to your place. Wine isn't just this narrow process of turning sugar into alcohol. It's a complex, infinite world made up of soil, wind, sun, vines, and also the person. The winemaker is a part of the terroir, too."

Tiberio is located near the medieval town of Cugnoli in the Abruzzese hills, a thousand feet up and twenty-three miles from the Adriatic Sea. The climate is cool, with breezes flowing from both the Appenine Mountains and the ocean. Wildlife is abundant. Wolves, bear, deer; rock and stone and forests; and it is, as Cristiana says, "very crystalline light, very clean. It's a very pure area, and that leads to very pure flavors in the fruit."

The Tiberios farm seventy-four acres of organic vines: Trebbiano Abruzzese, Pecorino, and Montepulciano d'Abruzzo. There are also eight acres of forest on the property, and eight acres of alfalfa, which attracts beneficial insects. "And we don't use any plastic," Cristiana says. "We only use willow or raffia to tie things down, so when it falls to the soil it's not a problem. We only use hot water to clean the winery, no chemicals. Native yeasts for fermentation. Even lighter glass for our bottles—wine doesn't need a heavy bottle!"

The Tiberio wines are exceptionally pure and focused. "We use stainless steel, which was a very unpopular decision at the beginning, because in the classical wine world, important wines are aged in oak, or maybe concrete," she says. "But for our wines, anything other than stainless steel overwhelms the flavor. They lose that precision, that engagement with the terroir. Which is what I *don't* want. I don't want to make 'great' wines. I want to make wines with a precise identity."

Riccardo retired in 2008, handing control of the winery to Cristiana and Antonio. "Mostly he takes care of the vegetable garden now," she says. "He's seventy-five, and he worked so hard for his entire life that I'm happy if he can just *enjoy* the vineyard, instead of being stressed by the work it needs."

But even with the work it requires, the vineyard is where she goes herself to find solitude and peace. "The winery is too chaotic. For some decisions, I need the silence." She pauses thoughtfully. "Wine is—in some ways it's sad to say—the great love of my life. I'm happy to wake up at four a.m. to work all day long, even when it's very tough; I'm happy on those summer days when it's so hot you can't even breathe, or those days in the winter that are bitterly cold. And, in the spring, you have the canopy of leaves, and always a light cool breeze, and through the branches of the vines you can see the mountains. It's very beautiful. And it's home."

Tiberio's superb **Trebbiano d'Abruzzo ($–$$)** is as crisp and clean as mountain air, grapefruit and jasmine scented, a thrill to drink and also a stupendous bargain. The very limited **Fonte Canale ($$$)** comes from particularly ancient vines—ninety plus years—and is even more laser-focused, with floral and citrus notes and a stony finish. The winery's **Pecorino ($$)**, Cristiana Tiberio says, "shows the original character of Pecorino—sage, rosemary, kiwi—and a lot of texture." The **Cerasuolo d'Abruzzo ($$)** is a juicy, irresistible example of the classic Abruzzese style of rosé: much deeper in color and fuller in flavor than pale pink Provençal versions. "Cerasuolo can't be a soft, round wine—it needs to keep the crunchiness, the vibrancy, the electricity that it gets from mountain fruit," Cristiana says.

Tiberio's **Montepulciano d'Abruzzo ($–$$)** red is much brighter and livelier than most; drinking it is like biting into wild berries on a sunny day. "Stainless steel respects the terroir; the wine keeps that vivid red fruit," she says, "and a little clove and cinnamon." **Archivio ($$)** comes from a single small portion of the winery's historic Montepulciano d'Abruzzo vineyard. It's an intense wine, full of smoky red fruit and spice flavors. The **Colle Vota Montepulciano d'Abruzzo ($$$)**, on the other hand, is lighter and more transparent, but the pale hue belies its intensity of flavor. It's a stellar red, weightless but with flavors that last. If only there were more of it!

LE MARCHE

Bordered by Emilia-Romagna above and Abruzzo below, Le Marche, on the Adriatic Coast, is primarily known as a white wine region. That's thanks to its most famous wine, Verdicchio di Castelli di Jesi (and the slightly less well-known Verdicchio di Matelica), planted throughout the low-lying limestone hills in the province of Ancona. Almost always a crisp, pleasant wine, in the right hands it can gain a stony intensity and layers of flavor that are thrilling when its young and that age beautifully over time.

For reds, there are the Rosso Conero and Rosso Piceno appellations, both producing wine with varying percentages of the Montepulciano grape. Rosso Coneros, which are a minimum of 85 percent Montepulciano, tend to be robust, powerful wines, a blend of red and black fruit flavors bolstered with substantial tannins. Many of them amply qualify for the adjective "rustic," but the best can be nuanced and polished. Rosso Piceno moderates Montepulciano's rough strength with more or less equal amounts of Sangiovese (the rules allow 35 to 85 percent Montepulciano and 15 to 50 percent Sangiovese; up to 15 percent of other local red varieties is also permitted).

Le Marche's wines tend to get overshadowed by those of more famous regions, but the best are distinctive expressions of the terroir of this lovely coastal region. Plus, it's a lovely place to visit, and not nearly as crowded as more famous destinations. Long gone are the days when the marchese worked as tax collectors for the popes, which gave rise to the saying *meglio un morto a casa che un marchigiano al uscio*, or "better a corpse in the house than someone from Le Marche at the door!"

BUCCI • CASTELLI DI JESI

[certified organic]

For a long time, Verdicchio dei Castelli di Jesi was more famous for the bottle it came in—tall, slender, green, with a curved shape drawn from ancient amphorae—than the wine's actual quality. The bottle came out of a competition held in 1954, which was won by a Milanese architect; the wine itself, back in those days, came from over-cropped, conventionally farmed grapes treated indifferently in wineries. Ampelio Bucci was determined to change all that.

His family had farmed in Castelli di Jesi since the 1700s, but Bucci worked in the fashion world. When he returned to Le Marche, he focused his efforts on creating Verdicchios of true quality. Together with consulting winemaker Giorgio Grai, he did just that, using only estate fruit cultivated to provide lower yields and greater intensity; he bottled his first wine in 1983.

The Bucci estate is a true farm, nearly nine hundred acres of wheat, corn, beets, sunflowers, olive trees, and grape vines. The grapes occupy less than a tenth of that land, so the winery's total production is not that large. The vineyards have been farmed organically since 1999 (certified since 2002), though Bucci doesn't promote it. He has said that he doesn't want people to think his choice to be organic is simply a marketing idea.

The vines are primarily Verdicchio, with a few acres of Sangiovese and Montepulciano, all between the Adriatic Coast and the Appenine Mountain range. There are four wines; two whites and two reds, enough to satisfy Ampelio Bucci's vision, which was to express the varieties and landscape of his region.

The **Bucci Verdicchio Classico dei Castelli di Jesi ($$)** is exactly what you would hope for: elegantly poised, with no oak influence (Bucci uses large, old oak casks, but no new oak), floral and citrusy with a distinctly mineral finish. The **Villa Bucci Riserva Verdicchio Classico ($$$)** is one of Italy's great white wines, polished and complex in its youth and able to age far longer than one might guess; think decades, not just years. There are also two reds. The **Bucci Rosso Piceno Superiore Pongelli ($$)** moderates the muscular tannins of Montepulciano with brighter, less brooding Sangiovese (it's a fifty-fifty blend), while the **Villa Bucci Rosso Piceno Riserva ($$$)** layers on a bit more intensity and depth of flavor, playing Montepulciano's black, plummy fruit against the red, cherry-inflected flavors of Sangiovese.

LA DISTESA • CUPRAMONTANA

[organic / natural]

La Distesa's Corrado Dottori is, among many other qualities, one of the best *thinkers* about natural wine. As he writes on his blog, "Natural wine is not a '*type of wine*.' It is a counter-culture movement. Natural wine is not a '*method*.' It is an ethical and aesthetic attitude. Natural wine is not a '*brand*.' It is a critical look (one of many possible) at the economic-ecological catastrophe that is today's world."

Dottori's observation gets to the heart of the divide between natural wine and the vast majority of the wines in this book, which are made in a manner respectful to nature, without winemaking interventions, and are expressive of where they come from, but which aren't social statements. His point is that "natural wine" extends beyond wine—it's as much (or more) about social, ecological, and political issues as it is about how the wine is actually made, even if the practical result is wines that are made with as little intervention as possible.

La Distesa has been organic from the start. Dottori also uses some biodynamic practices, but he isn't inclined toward Steiner's mysticism. Today there are twenty-one acres of vines at La Distesa, cover crops such as favas, vetch, peas, and wild alfalfa growing between them, along with several acres of barley, wheat, and legumes, and several more of olive trees. Dottori also isn't particularly interested in making single-variety wines, preferring old-school blends of different local grapes, and his winemaking is classically natural—minimal intervention, no fining or filtering, native yeasts, no sulfur. That is, if such a thing as "classically natural" exists.

All of the La Distesa wines are made in small amounts. Of them, the **La Distesa Terre Silvate ($$)** is probably the easiest to find (hit your local natural wine bar). A blend of Verdicchio and Trebbiano from three different vineyards, it's pale gold and savory; a small portion of the wine also stays on its skins for several days during fermentation, giving some nice texture overall. For **Meticcio ($$)**, white and red grapes are harvested together and co-fermented, resulting in a transparently pale red (or dark rosé, take your pick) that's full of lively red berry character. **Nur ($$)** is what Dottori refers to as an "ancestral" wine, made from Trebbiano, Malvasia, Verdiccio, and Pecorino, that receives a couple of weeks of skin exposure and zero sulfur. Cloudy gold, a bit funky, a bit tannic, a bit herbal, a bit wild. **Nocenzio ($$)** is a red blend of Sangiovese and Montepulciano, made in open-top wooden tanks with a fair amount of whole-cluster fermentation. It's juicy, lively, light-bodied, herbal, and, per the winery, "to be consumed in large gulps."

TUSCANY

What to say about Tuscany that hasn't already been said? Italy's most famous wine region is lodged in the imaginations of people around the world as the incarnation of what Italian countryside is supposed to look like. Hills covered in vines and olive trees, groves of cypress trees, picturesque medieval hilltop towns, quaint piazzas where you can sip an espresso under the Tuscan sun with several thousand other vacationers . . . well. It's not exactly undiscovered.

Tuscany's primary grape is Sangiovese, the heart of Chianti, Brunello di Montalcino, and Vino Nobile di Montalcino, among other wines. Nearly two-thirds of the vines here are this variety, which is ideally suited to the region's temperate climate and its soils, particularly *galestro*, a kind of rocky marl, and *alberese*, a more compact clay/limestone soil, both common to the center of Tuscany (there are other types as well—Tuscany is big, about 8,900 square miles, and its geology is a jigsaw puzzle). Bordeaux varieties can also do well, particularly on the coast: Cabernet Sauvignon, Merlot, Cabernet Franc. Tuscan whites definitely trail behind the reds, but the local varieties Vernaccia and Vermentino can both make some excellent wines.

Chianti is Italy's most famous wine. Not always its best, and in fact for many years a lot of Chianti was pretty awful, but over time the straw-covered fiasco filled with diluted, insipid red, best consumed quickly so you could get on to jamming a candle in the top of the bottle, has receded into memory. There's still plenty of anonymous, large-production Chianti around, but the quality revolution that started in the 1990s (better plant material, less overcropping, better winemaking) changed Chianti dramatically. For many years, also, 10 to 30 percent of white grapes were required to be included in Chianti, an absurdity in terms of quality but a boon for local farmers with acres of uninteresting Trebbiano. It took until 2006 for local lawmakers to eliminate white varieties from the approved blend. The heart of Chianti, and the source of most of its best wines, is Chianti Classico, between Florence and Siena.

Today, there's a second quality renaissance going on in Chianti, with a focus on terroir-driven, 100 percent Sangiovese wines, an interest in some of the more forgotten local grapes such as Mammolo and Pugnitello, and a pullback from the use of new oak as well as from the inclusion of Bordeaux varieties (fine if you want to make a super-Tuscan, but why, if what you want to make is Chianti?). As Diana Lenzi at Fattoria di Petroio observes, "I have to phrase this in a way that won't get me hanged by my neighbors, but I do feel that Chianti Classico did everything in its power to butcher its reputation back in the seventies and eighties. You never knew what you were going to get in the glass—the wine could be modern or classic, round or tannic, diluted or powerful, you name it. Our identity was gone. Now the best estates have gone back to what the land wants them to do. It's an incredible return to our origins and a very exciting time for Chianti."

Brunello di Montalcino is Chianti's smaller, fancier, southern neighbor: while its wines are also made from Sangiovese, they have more prestige and command higher prices. Are they better? On average, possibly, but brilliant Sangiovese is brilliant Sangiovese wherever it is grown: the best wines are comparable regardless of appellation. That said, Montalcino is a warmer region, and wines here tend to be darker, richer, and more powerful. They're made from the Sangiovese Grosso subvariety, which tends to be somewhat more tannic. Brunello is also a relatively recent arrival in the world of wine—the first Brunello di Montalcino was bottled in 1888 by Ferruccio Biondi-Santi. (Biondi-Santi remained family-owned until 2017, when it was bought by a French investment group.)

Vino Nobile di Montepulciano is the third iconic Tuscan wine produced from Sangiovese, but somehow the least appreciated. The same form of Sangiovese is used here as in Montalcino, though in this case it's called Prugnolo Gentile. Salcheto's Michele Manelli says, "We're more continental than Montalcino or Chianti Classico. More difference day and night. And more clay than Montalcino; and more oxidized sands in the soil, which help with vibrancy and acidity. Our Sangiovese has the ca-pacity to move more in the direction of elegance than power. Not everyone here is going that direction, but it's an opportunity for Vino Nobile."

Then there are the so-called "Super Tuscans," essentially a movement that started in the 1970s to make high-end, complex wines that combined the local Sangiovese with Bordeaux varieties (or left the Sangiovese out completely). The most thrilling examples of these tend to come from Bolgheri, in the broader Maremma region on the Tuscan coast. These can be extraordinary wines, but are often the province of people whose wallets bulge with cash; the Ornellaias and Sassicaias of the world don't come cheap, to say the least (and aren't in this book, as a result).

There are plenty of other Tuscan wines, too, from the white Vernaccia di San Gimignano to the vibrant, Sangiovese-driven wines of Morellino di Scansano to up-and-coming places like Montecucco. And in Tuscany as a whole, there's an ever-growing movement toward sustainable and organic viticulture. Today Tuscany is second after Sicily, with 15 percent of its vineyard land being farmed organically. Yet it is also home to growing concerns among winemakers about the effects of climate change. The past decade has seen a number of uncharacteristically hot summers, with temperatures in July and August sometimes climbing to 104 degrees or higher. It's not a problem to be solved on a local scale, but it's possible to moderate the effects. Piero Lanza at Fattoria Poggerino notes, "With the extremes of climate we're experiencing, organic viticulture is even more important now. The vines are stronger, the roots are deeper, and they are able to withstand the climatic changes better."

STEFANO AMERIGHI • CORTONA

[certified biodynamic / natural / regenerative]

Most people don't think of Syrah when it comes to Tuscan wine, but Stefano Amerighi doesn't think like most people. In his late forties, with a mane of ink-black hair, beard, and chunky black glasses, he looks more like the coolest professor you ever had than he does a winemaker, and while you couldn't say he has an academic vision of wine, exactly, he *is* remarkably erudite. And his winery crew—early twenties, tattooed, casual—do sometimes seem more like students or acolytes rather than workers.

Amerighi makes his wine in Cortona, "the only Italian appellation that's based on Syrah," he says. He grew up on his family's farm. "I started in 2000 with biodynamics, so we've never had any chemicals here. It was all pasture before. My grandfather died of cancer, like so many farmers in this area. When I started, I said, 'I don't ever want to use any chemicals in this vineyard.' And I haven't."

He picked the particular hill his vineyards are on, he says, because in 1997 he was in Rome, at a wine tasting, and he had a glass of the 1995 Ten-

imenti d'Alessandro Bosco Syrah. "For me it was a kind of vision. I came back home to my father and said, 'I've tasted a great wine! A great *Syrah*! Where is Manzano?' And he looked at me and said, 'It's two kilometers from here.'"

That wine woke him up to the taste of Syrah. He planted his vineyard in 2000 and opened his winery in 2001. When he began, he was influenced by his experience working with Sangiovese with Piero Lanza at Poggerino ("no whole cluster, long maceration"), but he's gradually shifted that toward using whole bunches during fermentation, and no oak. "Syrah in this part of the world doesn't need wood," he says. "At all. It changes the taste completely. And I don't like wines that remind me of barrels!"

He works more in the natural wine realm than the conventional one, albeit with his own twist. "For me the natural approach is not only to not add sulfites, to not filter, to not change the balance of the wine, but also to have a social vision with the people who work for you." This comes out of biodynamics: "The idea is to develop an agricultural organism that's very complex. First, we did our vineyard, then we brought in the cows, then the chickens; we planted fruit trees; now we're growing heirloom grains for beer. But there's a social part to the anthroposophic vision. You want your workers to be employed all year long, and if you have animals on the farm, you can do that, because there's always work to do. The people are part of the vision as well." He shrugs. "All the local guys used to say to my father, 'He's a crazy boy, a *bischero*'—literally a tuning fork, but Tuscan dialect for a fool—'he'll destroy the family property and his own property, too!' But that was twenty-two years ago. At the time it was *very* rare to find a natural wine. Now they come and ask me about how I work."

Amerighi farms roughly twenty-seven acres of vines, but he makes only thirty-five hundred cases of wine each year. A good portion of his production always gets sold off for distillation. "You can only make natural wine if you're willing to do that," he says. Because he works without sulfur and with whole-bunch fermentation, "the environment is just wonderful for bacteria, so you have to be very careful." It's essentially a form of vinous edge-walking, and sometimes a barrel goes over that edge. At that point, it gets sold off and isn't bottled. Amerighi also recently planted a terraced vineyard up in the mountains just outside the Cortona appellation, where the climate is cooler, as a hedge against global warming.

The **Stefano Amerighi Syrah ($$)** is a bright, tart red with flavors of blackberries, cured meat, and olive tapenade—deeply savory, in other words. There's also a lively, cherry-scented **Rosato ($$)** that's more substantial but no less refreshing than typical rosés. His top wine, **Syrah Apice ($$–$$$)**, comes from parcels at the top of the hill, and stays sixteen to eighteen months in ceramic vessels, then two years in bottle.

It's leafy and smoky (particularly in cool vintages), and "the color of the arancia sanguignate, the blood orange," Amerighi says. Finally, there's a minuscule amount of one-hundred-plus-year-old, ungrafted Pecorino from Le Marche, aged for several years before release, called Noè Vino Bianco ($$). It's fascinating, but it's nigh-on impossible to find, partly because it's been several years since a new vintage appeared.

AVIGNONESI · MONTEPULCIANO

[certified organic / certified biodynamic]

"My husband, Max, would say I ended up here by mistake," Virginie Saverys says. "I bought a ruin in Tuscany in 2007, and it was a mistake to even buy a pair of shoes in 2007." That ruin, purchased just before a worldwide recession, was Avignonesi. Though it had been a wine estate for many, many years, the previous owners had let it run down. "Suddenly, from being a wine lover, I was a winery owner. And then of course I made a lot of mistakes, which have cost me a lot of money."

Today, though, Saverys can take pleasure in what she has accomplished here: four hundred acres of organic and biodynamic vines; a commitment to biodiversity, with beehives, sheep, and vegetable gardens on the property; and vineyard workers who are paid fairly, on actual contracts (much of the vineyard work in Italy is done by immigrant labor through external farming companies; exploitation is not uncommon). "In addition to wanting to make excellent wines, I want to feel good about myself when I look in the mirror in the morning," Saverys says. "Initially when I came here, people were saying, 'Ah, this woman, she's just rich, she's going to be a Marie Antoinette, and graze her little sheep and wear bows in her hair.' They were very surprised to find me here at the winery, working, and with respect and fairness and in an ethical way with our staff."

From the start, Saverys knew she wanted to farm biodynamically. Organics removes chemical and systemic products from the vineyard, she says, but doesn't add life. "Biodynamics is more like going to a homeopathic doctor and working proactively. You're creating a better immune system. Your soil becomes healthier, which you don't get with organics alone; there are more bacteria, nematodes, mycorrhizae, and so on. When I took over Avignonesi, I thought, 'This is it. This is exactly what fits.'"

Avignonesi's flagship wine is the **Avignonesi Vino Nobile di Montepulciano ($$)**, a red that shows the darker, denser side of Sangiovese while retaining freshness and focus. The winery's **Poggetto di Sopra Vino Nobile di Montepulciano ($$$)** comes from a single, thirty-two-acre vineyard. "To me, Poggetto is probably the most elegant single vineyard we have," Saverys says. "It's a gentle wine." **Desiderio ($$$)** was one of the earlier Tuscan Merlots to appear. Under the previous ownership it was often very oaky; even the critic Robert Parker—"a guy I thought owned shares in every cooperage in the world," Saverys says with a laugh—told her that he hoped she would use less oak on the wine than the former proprietor. Today it's a beautifully balanced red; light herbal and leather notes accent the succulent red fruit. Avignonesi's **Vin Santo ($$$$)** and **Vin Santo Occhio di Pernice ($$$$)** are expensive (extremely so, in the case of the latter), but they're two of Tuscany's greatest Vin Santos, complex and layered, with flavors that last and last. "The sad thing is that people these days no longer drink sweet wines," Saverys notes. "They're beautiful, but they're hard to sell."

COL D'ORCIA • MONTALCINO

[certified organic / biodynamic]

The largest organically farmed estate in Tuscany, with more than nine hundred acres of vines, Col D'Orcia also produces honey, pasta from ancient grain varieties, even tobacco for cigars. Five years after receiving organic certification in 2013, owner Count Francesco Marone Cinzano moved on to biodynamic farming, and in 2021, he started a substantial project aimed at reducing the winery's carbon footprint. "I feel a duty towards protecting this environment," he says. With his swept-back gray hair, trimmed gray beard, green jacket, and scarf—at least the last time I saw him—he looks the image of an Italian nobleman, twenty-first-century style.

"It's hard to imagine now, given the success of Brunello di Montalcino, but when my father purchased Col D'Orcia, Montalcino was one of the poorest municipalities in Italy. It was very isolated. People survived on what the land could produce. So that's the concept we try to apply now: we have our sheep and goats, our poultry, beehives; just last week I released a few pheasants to nest in the vineyards. It gives you so much joy to walk through those vineyards and come across a nest full of eggs. Small pleasures!"

Cinzano's main concern currently is climate change, and how it's affecting the wines of Montalcino. Over the past twenty years, he says, they've seen picking dates for Sangiovese come earlier and earlier. "In 2012 we even started in the last days of August, which was unheard of in the past. These days, the main issue we face is dehydration. We have heat waves, day and night for two or three weeks, which leads to overripeness in the grapes. That's something we absolutely want to avoid; it destroys the elegance and finesse of the wine."

Despite rising temperatures in Montalcino, Col D'Orcia's wines remain elegant, classically styled reds that are saturated with flavor but not weighty. The **Col D'Orcia Rosso di Montalcino ($–$$)** is bright, forwardly fruity, and has lightly grippy tannins. The estate's **Brunello di Montalcino ($$$)** is a good notch more complex, full of silky wild berry fruit, dried-tobacco nuances, and plush tannins. "What is the magic formula for Brunello di Montalcino?" Cinzano asks. "The terroir here. Our soils are from different geological eras, but they all have a high percentage of limestone, which is key to the character of Brunello."

The **Poggio al Vento Brunello di Montalcino ($$$)** comes from a ridge of sandy soil high up in the estate, and is both more refined and more intense. **Olmaia ($$$)** is 100 percent Cabernet Sauvignon, with minty oak notes and ripe black currant fruit. Col D'Orcia is also one of the few wineries to still make a sweet, honey-floral **Moscadello di Montalcino ($$)**. "It's a wine that dates back to the Middle Ages," Cinzano notes. "Most of the wines made for religious services in Tuscany were made from Trebbiano, except in Montalcino, where Moscadello was used." A curiosity, but a delicious one.

PODERE LE BONCIE • CHIANTI CLASSICO

[organic / biodynamic]

Giovanna Morganti is a philosopher. That might be said about a number of winemakers, but in her case, following her agronomy studies, she took time off to get a degree in philosophy. "From an academic perspective, I had been *vino, vino, vino*, so I took a break."

That break turned out to be necessary, because "if you're good at making wine, there has to be a philosophical element; also spiritual, but not in a confrontational way. You're at the mercy of nature. If you get a hailstorm that destroys everything in five minutes, all you can do is pray." Though, she admits, "What you actually end up doing instead is cursing."

Le Boncie is in southeastern Chianti Classico, next to what was once

> *"The use of chemical inputs makes everything taste the same. It makes wine homogenous, without personality."*
> —Giovanna Morganti

the tiny hamlet of San Felice. Morganti built her winery herself, next to her house. Below it, following the undulations of the terrain, are the vines that she farms. Stand in the center of the vineyard on a sunny day, and you'll see the towers of Siena in the distance; behind you, you might hear one of Le Boncie's roosters crowing out his impressiveness.

The land was once her father's. He planted vines on it in 1968, and after he passed away in the mid-nineties it became hers. By that time, she'd worked as an agronomist at a couple of local wineries, "but I was always thinking of creating my own wine." After her philosophy studies, in the mid-1980s, she went to work for Castello di Volpaia, which was where her love of wine really kicked back in. "And that's where I really started to believe I could do this myself," she says. "Volpaia was the start of the *grand amore* for me. It also cut the umbilical cord with my family."

Morganti uses biodynamic practices but isn't interested in following the official requirements the certifying organizations for biodynamics set down. Like so many others, she was first introduced to biodynamics by

Nicolas Joly of Clos de Coulée de Serrant. "It was a newborn concept in viticulture at the time, so I really learned as I went."

She adds, "Biodynamics is a complex stream of inputs. It's not a protocol. It bothers me that people tend to think of it that way. But regardless, we use some organic methods and some biodynamic. We're a bit too anarchic here to follow a specific structure." She also doesn't mention either word on her wine labels. "Too often it's a game, just to get the certification and put it on the label. It doesn't involve following the true spirit of the idea. With Le Boncie, we're small enough that we can work on trust."

Podere le Boncie Cinque ($$) is the baby of the three wines that Giovanna makes, a direct, bright, lively red that's basically a bright glass of summertime. It's the younger brother of her top wine, Le Trame. **Chiesamonte ($$)** comes from the vineyards owned by a nearby church, which she leases and farms. It's a darker, less firmly acidic red, all dark cherry and blueberry, juicy and sustained. The flagship of the line is **Le Trame ($$$)**, a pure expression of the Le Boncie site. Aromatically it suggests wild raspberries, red cherries, dried herbs, and a hint of earth; on the palate it's powerful though still medium-bodied. The name means "the intrigues," and as Giovanna says, "Le Trame is more complex, more mysterious. It's tricky. It changes in the glass." As a side note, none of the Le Boncie wines are labeled as Chianti Classico. Morganti left the appellation in 2011, objecting to regulatory changes by the *consorzio* that she felt were driven by large, commercial producers.

FONTODI • CHIANTI CLASSICO

[certified organic]

Fontodi is one of the few contemporary wineries, possibly the only winery west of the country of Georgia, with the capacity to make its own amphorae. But that's one of the benefits of your family having been in the terra-cotta business since 1650. If you go to Florence, and look up at the roof of the Duomo, the tiles you see there were made by the Manetti family. Despite the acclaim that Fontodi has received for its Chiantis, the roots of the family, eight generations deep, lie in clay, brought to the surface and fired in furnaces in Greve.

But in the 1960s, Dino Manetti was passionate about wine, his son Giovanni recalls. "His dream was to buy a vineyard and make wine, specifically in Panzano. He'd always been a big fan of the wines from here, and this property at one time had a brilliant past." But after two world wars, the Fontodi property had been ruined and abandoned. "When my father bought it, it was completely destroyed. He called it a *bella dormentada*—a sleeping beauty—and every day after working at the terra-cotta company, he would take the car, drive here, and work on

restoring the cellar and replanting the vineyards."

At first, this was a hobby. Then, in 1979, Dino Manetti moved his entire family there. "I was sixteen, so it was a shock to say the least," Giovanni recalls. "I had to drive a Vespa to Florence to go to school. In the winter, I froze every day."

The winery is located outside Panzano, midpoint between Florence and Siena, in the valley known as the Conca d'Oro, the valley of gold. It received the name because the bowl of the valley faces directly south, making it an ideal microclimate for Sangiovese (or, others say, because it used to be planted with wheat, which looked golden). The family's 240 acres of vines have been farmed organically since 1990. At the time, Dino Manetti himself was skeptical about organic viticulture. But he told his son, "I trust you. Just don't disappoint me."

Giovanni Manetti laughs, and mimes staggering under the weight of an enormous burden: "It was like having a big stone dropped on your back. Boom! OK, Father. Yes! Do not disappoint!'" Setting aside the burden, he says, "I knew I had to do it. Up until then, I was using chemical products to spray, but I didn't like the smell. I knew something was wrong. It was a little scary to make the switch, but the older workers at that time, the ones who used to work in the vineyards before the Second World War, were very helpful. They told me, 'Giovanni, no problem, we can do it. This is how we used to work. We know it is possible.'"

Manetti also incorporates bio-dynamic techniques into his farming (not that he's against science, he says; the vineyard also has sensors to track humidity and rainfall, helping forecast fungal attacks). All of these practices, he feels, increase the quality of the Fontodi wines. "What you want is to make wines of strong personality that can't be made anywhere else in the world. Otherwise, you lose. You've lost the game. If you want to transfer terroir into the bottles, you have to be organic or biodynamic. Otherwise, it just doesn't work."

Manetti's approach in the cellar is essentially the same as in the vineyard: as little intervention as possible, meaning spontaneous fermentation, no enzymes, very little sulfur, and bottling only on the descending moon. He controls everything. "I don't buy grapes. I can only make wine from grapes I grow myself. If I can't do that, then I'll go back to Florence and make terra-cotta again."

About the **Fontodi Chianti Classico ($$)**, Manetti says, "I age my Chianti Classico for two years, because at one year it's not ready, believe me. It has muscles. It needs that time." It's a terrific Chianti Classico, year in and year out, polished and precise. The **Dino Chianti Classico ($$)** is made in amphorae. "My great-great-grandfather used to make amphorae for wine, but our company stopped production in 1930," Manetti says. "Now that they've became fashionable again, we've restarted. Amphorae provide something very pure in wine—just flowers, fruit, minerals, that's it." (Unfortunately, there are only about a thousand bottles per year of this strawberry-scented red.) Fontodi makes two single-vineyard Chiantis, both benchmarks for the region. **Vigna del Sorbo Chianti Classico Gran Selezione ($$$)** is firm and powerful when young, with a hint of new oak; over time that melds with the wine's dark cherry and licorice notes. Lastly, there's **Flaccianello della Pieve ($$$$)**, one of the wines that started the "Super Tuscan" movement. Though always slightly closed when it's released, it is stunning after several years of age. Made from 100 percent Sangiovese, it comes from three small high-elevation vineyards on the property where the rocky soil gives small clusters of small grapes. "So, more concentration," Manetti says. "More color, more perfume, more intensity, more everything." Yet balanced and beautiful. It is a great wine.

ISTINE • CHIANTI CLASSICO

[certified organic]

The Fontis are farmers. For decades, their main business was servicing vineyards that belonged to other wineries. "In Tuscany, there are noble families who own a castle, hundreds and hundreds of acres of land. That's not my family," Angela Fonti says. But it was a successful business, and Fonti grew up both with wine and amid wine (her uncle owns the Caparzo winery in Chianti Classico). She studied winemaking, and began a career as an enologist.

But in 2011, something changed. "I was thirty. I was working at a winery in Cortona, making Syrah. But my blood is Sangiovese. And, specifically, Sangiovese from Radda. It wasn't a clear decision, starting our own winery. But I knew if I didn't do it then, I never would."

She also laid down a condition: "I told my family, if we don't go organic, I won't come back and do this. To me, that wasn't so much a choice as a duty. And now, when I taste the wines from our three vineyards, the differences between them are far more evident than they were in 2013, when we started the conversion."

Fonti has received justifiable acclaim in recent years for her three single-vineyard Chianti Classicos, but don't ignore her entry-level **Chianti Classico**

($$). Aged in traditional large barrels, it's leafy and crisp, bright with berry fruit. Of the three single-vineyard wines, the **Chianti Classico Cavorchione ($$$)**, the lowest altitude of the three, is a finely drawn red, with tight, straw-like tannins. The **Chianti Classico Casanova dell'Aia ($$$)** tends to come off more herbal, and to Fonti "is the most Radda in style—good acid-ity, never too concentrated, elegant and spicy." Finally, the namesake **Chianti Classico Istine ($$$)** is spicier and darker-fruited, sometimes with a light peppermint note. Fonti's top wine, **Le Vigne ($$$)**, is a mix of the three vineyards. It's deeply saturated in flavor, summoning suggestions of black cherry and espresso, held in by fine, linear tannins.

LAMOLE DI LAMOLE • LAMOLE

[certified organic]

The town of Lamole, the saying goes, "is the antechamber of paradise." That's a comment on its altitude—it's one of the highest areas in Chianti Classico, as close to the heavens as you get in this hilly, vineyard-covered region. Lamole is also the smallest of the new Chianti Classico UGAs (*Unitá Geografiche Aggiuntive*), terroir-specific subzones established in 2021. "It's two hundred and fifty acres total, and of that we have about forty percent," says Andrea Daldin, longtime winemaker and general manager of Lamole di Lamole. "Our big project over the last fifteen years was converting from conventional agriculture to organic, and ultimately as sustainable as possible as

> *"Climate change. All we can do is carry out research in the vineyard and try to accommodate it. You can't fight the sky."*
> —Andrea Daldin

well—thinking of that in the sense that sustainability's DNA is social, economic, *and* environmental responsibility.

The estate's vineyards lie at about 2,200 feet to 2,300 feet altitude. In the past that altitude plus the immediate microclimate made grape growing often an exercise in frustration (hence local growers throwing up their hands in dismay and leaving for better prospects). Daldin says, "Until 2010, in ten vintages we'd have seven rainy, cold ones and three hot ones. Now that seems to be the reverse. We've had to change our cultivation and vinification because of that—for instance, planting more Sangiovese Grosso [the biotype of Sangiovese found in Montalcino, to the south], which has bigger berries; in hot vintages they maintain balance more easily than regular Sangiovese."

Daldin farms using the winery's own organic compost, and with precision spraying for organic copper and sulfur treatments to reduce the amounts needed. "We also use natural defenses—algae, aloe vera, propoli—to fortify the leaves and grape skins against mold and fungi. And a distillation of tree barks and local plants from the nearby woods, which keeps out the wild boar and also helps with water stress." Daldin also shifted to native yeasts for fermentation a few years back. "We gain more spiciness, more gripping acidity, but beautiful balance as well. They're just more complex wines than they were before."

The **Lamole di Lamole Maggiolo Chianti Classico ($–$$)** stays silky despite some firm Sangiovese tannins, with classic herbaceous Chianti Classico notes mingling with red berry fruit. **Lareale Chianti Classico Riserva ($$)** comes primarily from a specific site on the hill near the winery, and adds some savory depth to that basic character. "*Lareale* is traditional Tuscan slang for a little district or place," Daldin says. The winery's impressive **Vigneto di Campolungo Chianti Classico Gran Selezione ($$$)** is typically richer and darker, more muscular, with mouth-coating tannins and black cherry fruit. "This is from our oldest vineyard," Daldin says. "Steep and terraced, and very high up."

LE MACCHIOLE • BOLGHERI

[certified organic]

Le Macchiole is one of the stars of Bolgheri, a very star-filled sky when it comes to wine estates. But it could easily have ceased to exist, if Cinzia Merli were not as strong-willed and passionate as she is. She and her husband, Eugenio Campolmi, had taken her family's small vineyard, which at the time was making table wine for her family's equally unassuming *tavola calda*—a cafeteria-style, steam-table restaurant—and through the 1990s had transformed it into one of Italy's most acclaimed wineries. It was an amazing success story. Then, in 2002, Eugenio passed away from lung cancer. He was forty.

Merli was thirty-five, with two small children, loans they had taken to expand the business, and a local wine community that in a standardly chauvinistic way assumed she would soon give up and sell the property. Bad assumption.

Today Merli runs Le Macchiole together with her two sons, and it would be easy to argue that it is even more acclaimed than it was when Eugenio died; also that the wines are even better. But it wasn't easy. Merli recalls,

"My first harvest alone was the worst weather in fifteen to twenty years. Immediately I thought, OK, this is a sign. And that wasn't even enough, because the next year was the 2003 vintage." The summer of 2003 was the hottest recorded in Italy in three centuries, and caused an estimated twenty thousand or more deaths, together with massive crop damage across the country. "I thought, OK, maybe this is not my work, my destiny," Merli says. "But my brother convinced me to wait one more year. And I was lucky, because 2004 was a great vintage."

Merli converted to organic farming soon after her husband's death: "I went organic *because* Eugenio got sick. I didn't want to expose anyone else at the winery to those risks."

Le Macchiole, like most Bolgheri producers, concentrates more on French varieties than on Sangiovese. Merli jokes about it: "I'm a wine producer in a new area, focusing on international varieties . . . and I don't even like international varieties!" Even so, her most famous wine, Paleo Rosso, is 100 percent Cabernet Franc. "We discovered that in this variety we had all the charm and complexity we wanted. Clean, fresh, with great emotion. It's a variety that—I'm really convinced—is perfect for the area," she says.

Merli makes that comment while sitting at a table at La Pineta, an old fisherman's shack a few feet from the sea, which cooks some of the best fish in Italy. It's late spring and the windows are open; the blue curtains in the dining room, in their white window frames, flutter in the wind off the water. On the table is a grilled sea bream, *orata*, caught that morning within sight of the restaurant. Her Paleo Rosso, contrary to expectation, goes perfectly with it. Why? "Because the wine is not heavy—not *pesante*," she says. The word means physical weight but also intensity of feeling, emotional weight; as in too much to carry, not in pounds but in effort. Merli herself has carried a lot, and yet, as with her wines, she contains a surprising lightness, a kind of cheerful resilience that's impossible not to feel lifted by when you're in her presence.

Le Macchiole's excellent, lively **Bolgheri Rosso ($$)** is a blend of Merlot, Syrah, Cabernet Franc, and Cabernet Sauvignon. Despite Bolgheri's propensity for rich, powerful reds, Merli looks for energy and lift, she says; even more in recent vintages. Her **Paleo Rosso ($$$$)** exemplifies this, vivid and complex, its dark fruit edged with savory herb and mocha notes. The white **Paleo Bianco ($$$)** is a nuanced, fragrant blend of Chardonnay and Sauvignon Blanc. **Scrio ($$$$)**, spicy and intense, is one of the few Syrahs in Italy that can rival top Rhône versions. Then there's **Messorio ($$$$)**, one of Bolgheri's top reds, which puts it in a class with the Sassicaias and Ornellaias of the world. It's an alluring Merlot, dense and powerful, with fine, plush tannins, layers of dark fruit, and lots of richness, though it remains elegant somehow as well. (It is also very expensive, but writing about Le Macchiole without mentioning it makes no sense at all.)

CASTELLO DI MONSANTO · CHIANTI CLASSICO

[organic]

In 1962, Fabrizio Bianchi of Castello di Monsanto realized that he could produce something special from one particular site at the top of the hill on his property. He called the wine Il Poggio, and it was the first single-vineyard Chianti Classico. Laura Bianchi, his daughter, who now runs Monsanto with him and makes the wines, says, "My grandmother on my father's side was from Piedmont, so he came in with a kind of Piemontese sensibility. Tuscany at the time was straw-covered flasks, big-production, inexpensive wines." In that era, the idea of a single-vineyard Chianti Classico was beyond novel; more like baffling, at least to wine buyers. "Il Poggio was more expensive than the usual wines from Chianti," she recalls. "For the first five years, he had a very hard time selling any of it."

The history of the town of Monsanto stretches back to AD 998. Castello di Monsanto's vineyards surround the town—not hard, as the population is only two hundred—and then a girdle of cypress forest surrounds the vineyards. "It's a patrimony of micro-organic elements," Laura Bianchi says about the forest, "and it also protects us from frost." Nor is anyone likely to change that: cut down a cypress tree in Tuscany, and you can expect a five-thousand-euro fine.

Castello di Monsanto makes a number of wines from the estate in addition to Il Poggio. Laura Bianchi says, "What's important is that the style of the wine doesn't change. We believe in what my father started sixty years ago, and we try always to improve the quality, but not change the style. Our philosophy is to protect tradition. The old methods and the old culture." That sensibility is aided by the fact that all the rest of the Monsanto vineyards are planted with a massale selection from Il Poggio. "We call it the mother," Bianchi says. Everything here is hand-picked, across fifty-two separate parcels of vines (there are 178 acres of vineyard total), and the property is farmed with organic methods but not certified.

Among the many Monsanto wines, the **Castello di Monsanto Chianti Classico Riserva ($$)** remains one of the best values around in traditionally styled Chianti, full of fragrant red and blue fruit, with bright, juicy acidity. If you are looking for a benchmark to rate other Chianti Classico against, it's an inarguable choice. The **Sangioveto Grosso ($$$)** comes from a vineyard about three hundred meters (a thousand feet) from Il Poggio. Fragrant, lightly minty, with red currant and berry flavors, it has warm, toasted spice notes and a firm structure. (Sangioveto is the historic name for Sangiovese in Chianti Classico.) **Nemo Cabernet Sauvignon ($$$)**, from vines planted in 1976, is a very Tuscan interpretation of Cabernet, with taut, crunchy tannins, dark fruit, and light vanilla notes from oak. And the **Il Poggio Chianti Classico Riserva Gran Selezione ($$$)** is one of the great wines of Chianti Classico, and quite happily, for wine lovers at least, not yet priced as such. It's powerful and somewhat unyielding when young, but can age for decades. Dusty and slightly resinous aromatically, with layers of red cherry fruit, forest herbs, and a little toast, it ends on firm, drying tannins. It was the first single-vineyard Chianti Classico ever made, and remains one of the best.

MONTESECONDO • CHIANTI CLASSICO

[certified organic / biodynamic / natural]

Silvio Messana, founder of Montesecondo, is a slender, thoughtful man, quick to smile, with a flop of gray hair across his forehead and oval, wire-rimmed glasses. He's a musician as well as a winemaker—he spent his college years at the Berklee College of Music in Boston, and later produced film scores in New York City.

It wasn't until 2000 that Messana moved back for good from New York and began to make his own wine, on land his father had purchased outside the town of Cerbaia in 1963. "I had no idea! I just bought four tanks and started." Even today he seems amused by this decision.

For the first two years he farmed

conventionally. "I just did what my neighbors did. But I didn't like the wines. Then I went to a talk Nicolas Joly from Coulée de Serrant was giving about biodynamics and thought, *that* sounds interesting." The next day he came home, threw out all the chemicals he'd been using in the vineyards, and started the shift to biodynamic farming.

Messana farms forty-four acres of vines, and also buys grapes from an additional six organic acres for a new label he launched in 2019. His winery is a former tractor shed, with some small tanks, two rows of clay amphorae, a few barrels, and not much else. It suits his approach, which is low-intervention and unpretentious. "I like working with the essentials," he says. "In the end, you don't need much to make wine." Native yeasts drive all the fermentations; a minimal amount of sulfur is used, only at bottling. Messana's wines have a purity of ex-

pression that's compelling; the natural wine markers—sometimes an oxidative character to the whites, fermentation in amphorae for some wines, a hint of volatile acidity now and then—seem to serve the expression of place and fruit, rather than mask it.

Messana himself has said he is ambivalent about the term "natural wine," though not the winemaking approach itself, and, he suggested to me recently, maybe the natural wine movement has run its course anyway: "It's like when free jazz arrived. It broke things up. But then the free jazz movement was over, and it went to people using part of that language within the broader tradition of jazz."

He adds, "Music is music. But often when you listen to new music, you don't understand it at first, because your brain isn't used to it. Natural wine opened a door for conventional winemakers to think about taste differently."

The **Silvio Messana Garnaccia ($$)** is a golden-hued Vernaccia (the name of the wine is an old local term for the grape) that receives ten days maceration on skins before spending eight months in a concrete tank. Think red

apples and spice. (The Silvio Messana wines are his new line, made with fruit from vineyards he doesn't own himself.) Messana created his **Montesecondo Rosso Toscana ($$)** as a lively, lighter, un-oaked approach to Chianti

Classico. The DOCG (Denominazione di Origine Controllata e Garantita) authorities refused to certify it as Chianti Classico, citing its lighter color, so he renamed it simply Rosso Toscana. Either way, it's a delight. His **Montesecondo T'in Sangiovese ($$$)** is juicily ebullient with its rhubarb–strawberry–red cherry character; it's a transparent, totally delicious expression of Sangiovese. And his **Montesecondo Chianti Classico ($$)** is impressive: dark-fruited, herbal, and complex. "It's in a bit of oak," Messana says. "You know, more conventional, so they don't give me a hard time again."

FATTORIA DI PETROIO • CHIANTI CLASSICO

[organic]

Diana Lenzi of Fattoria di Petroio didn't plan to be a winemaker. She studied to be a chef, and eventually worked in the Michelin-starred restaurant Acquolina in Rome. But Fattoria di Petroio, which her father had founded in the 1980s, was part of her life and part of her family. She says now, "I always knew I would end up back here one day."

Cooking and winemaking are not all that different, when you think about it, especially if you consider a winery not that much more than a great big kitchen. Lenzi still cooks frequently, both for visitors to Petroio and when she heads back to Rome to do guest stints in her chef friends' kitchens, which she does often. But she has no regrets about leaving the restaurant life. "I was very happy, but my father couldn't keep taking care of Petroio," she says.

Petroio is located in the tiny town of Quercegrossa, midway between Siena and Castellina. The property is 247 acres of forests, olive groves, and vineyards (37 acres). It's been organic from 2015, and Lenzis have been diligent about providing a refuge for local fauna: deer, fox, porcupines, wild hare, even the ever-problematic wild boars that now overrun Tuscany. Those, Lenzi would just as soon see fewer of. "The *cinghiale*, the wild boar, have invaded us. They completely rip things up; we've lost a fifth of our crop to them more than once." Then her chef side adds, "On the other hand, they taste great. So, my proposal is that the town of Siena create a wild-boar ragù. We can call it 'Il Sugo di Siena,' put it in beautiful jars, and market it around the world. It's certainly a better idea than the one some genius came up with not long ago: bringing in wolves to get rid of the boars. Now we have wolves *and* boars."

More seriously she adds: "I cook and I produce wine in exactly the same way. I start with the ingredient, which has to be the absolute best I can find. If I do a tomato sauce from my own garden, with nothing else but olive oil and basil that I've grown, I'll knock people out of their chairs. Because they'll taste the earth, they'll taste the taste of a real tomato, they'll taste everything. If I use a so-so industrial tomato instead, I can do the most intricate, complicated, tomato-gelatin dish ever, and they'll forget it before they're even done eating. Wine is exactly the same. I have beautiful, healthy grapes here— those are my ingredients. A wine that's made from industrially farmed grapes, it might be perfect but it will also just be flat, pleasant, uniform. When you taste it, you may think it's OK, but you'll never think it's spectacular."

The **Fattoria di Petroio Chianti Classico** ($) is classic in style, full of cherry and spice notes. Lenzi's **Chianti Classico Riserva** ($$) is 100 percent Sangiovese, aged twelve months in large French *tonneaux*, then an additional month in *barrique*. It's darker and more structured, with an oaky edge (though not an overbearing one). The **Poggio ai Grilli Chianti Classico Gran Selezione** ($$$) is complex and velvety, its innate approachability masking its capacity for long-term aging.

FATTORIA POGGERINO • CHIANTI CLASSICO

[certified organic]

In the 1980s, Piero Lanza says, the general feeling about Radda, his part of Chianti Classico, was "*Sfigato! Que sfigato!*" Which more or less translates as "How unlucky we are! How fucking unlucky!" The grapes wouldn't ripen, the acidity was incredibly high, the color was very light. No one wanted the wines. "But now we're OK, and the places that are much closer to Siena are too hot; it's much harder to do balanced wines. Now everyone is looking for Radda, for wines that show the land they come from, rather than big, dark wines with lots of oak, where after one glass you say, '*Basta!*' 'Enough!'"

Poggerino is a small part of what was once a large estate owned by Lanza's grandfather. When he died in 1972, the vast majority of the land went to Lanza's uncle (first-born male; the usual story), who then sold it to a corporate wine group. What is now Poggerino went to Lanza's mother. She planted the first twelve acres of vines in 1973, thinking she would make wine. It didn't go that well. Lanza says, "In the 1970s, wine here was the price of water, and the quality was awful." But

she kept at it, working together with Lanza's father, and the first vintage of Poggerino was in 1980. "My father was a banker, and like a lot of people who want to get into wine, he liked the sunshine and the butterflies, but not the work so much," Lanza says with a laugh. "After a few years on a tractor, he said, 'I'm tired of this.' The truth is that the two things you absolutely need to make wine are discipline and patience."

Lanza finished an enology degree, and in 1988 he moved to Poggerino to take over from his father. (He and his sister Benedetta run the estate; she oversees the *agriturismo*.) "I had no idea about how to actually make wine," Lanza says. "Learning from a book is one thing, the real practice is another." But he worked and learned, and now it's been more than fifteen years since he's been doing everything on the estate himself: "agronomist, enologist, business manager . . . I like to say that Poggerino has a human scale: one human."

Lanza has been organic for nearly twenty years, though he didn't bother with certification until 2019. "At school in the 1980s, we learned to use chemicals to control everything. Herbicides, systemic products, chemical fertilizers. But over the years I became more sensitive to the land." He says this while standing in the Poggerino vineyard, which lies in a south-facing bowl with forest on all sides. No matter what time of year it is, there's always a light breeze rustling through the vines. "We're quite high up," Lanza says. "We have the combination of altitude and forest—hot days, but the forests help keep things cool at night. We have to fence everything, though, because we have thousands of wild boar and deer in the area."

And pumpkins. The guy who looks after the winery's vegetable garden grows them. *Big* pumpkins. "We had the world's largest pumpkin in 2021," Lanza says. "It weighed twenty-seven hundred pounds. My goal in the vineyards is balance, and a twenty-seven-hundred-pound pumpkin is pretty much the opposite of that. But he loves growing them, and I want him to be happy, so how can I say no?"

With one exception, the Poggerino wines are 100 percent Sangiovese, and are beautifully pure expressions of the variety. The most affordable, **Poggerino Il Labirinto ($)** is a juicy, simple pleasure, and a serious bargain. The estate's **Chianti Classico ($)**, all high-toned fruit with light herbal notes, is transparent ruby in hue and tart in a palate-freshening way. **Chianti Classico Riserva Bugialla ($$)** spends eighteen months aging in *botti* and a year in bottle before release; it's firm and tart, with smoky red fruit and lasting flavors. The **Chianti Classico Nuovo ($$)** ages in a cement egg rather than *botti*, which makes it a little softer and rounder, and brings out the earthy notes in the wine (unfortunately, there's not much of it around). Lanza also makes **Primamateria ($$)**, a robust fifty-fifty blend of Merlot and Sangiovese, and an appealing **Brut Rosato Frizzante ($$)**, 100 percent Sangiovese aged in the bottle on lees for almost four years; it's crisp, lively, and full of berry flavors. All of the Poggerino wines seriously overperform for what they cost.

QUERCIABELLA · CHIANTI CLASSICO

[certified organic / biodynamic]

Querciabella owner Sebastiano Castiglione was one of the first Tuscan vintners to adopt biodynamic farming methods, in 1998. In addition, his devotion to ethical production of his wines has resulted in Querciabella's becoming entirely plant-based in 2010 (classical biodynamics utilizes animal products such as cow horns filled with manure for its preparations). The result is truly vegan wine that sacrifices nothing to quality.

Querciabella was founded by Castiglione's father, whose inclinations were much more traditional. In 1988, Castiglione recalls, they hired a new winemaker. "He and I had a brief conversation, and we both agreed the wines should be organic; we converted right then and there, and never looked back. But I didn't tell my father—I knew he'd never agree. So, ten years later, I made the suggestion that we become organic. He said, 'It's impossible! We can't do it!' And I said, 'Well, we've actually been doing it for ten years now.'"

When Castligione moved to biodynamics in 1998, he started with the approved biodynamic preparations. "But I've been an animal rights activist since I was fifteen. I don't want animals exploited or used in any way, so quite soon I wanted to shift from that. We were already growing cover crops, so I said, why don't we grow plants we can use for green manure? And we don't use horns or bladders or anything stupid like that. We did experiment with a ceramic horn, but I decided against it."

What Castiglione did do was go back and read Rudolf Steiner's works again. "The most important thing he said was that you have to adapt your techniques to your ecosystem. But what's now the requirement for certification— the dogmatic principles espoused by the German and Austrian followers— contradicts the original idea of Steiner's work, which is that you adapt *dynamically* to your environment."

Talking with Castligione is exciting. The only hitch is that he's a very private man, so chances to meet are relatively few; but he's both extremely smart and extremely outspoken. He's emphatic that biodynamics is better than organics, for instance. "If you count the microorganisms in the soil, biodynamic viticulture is thousands and thousands of times better than organic. And even if you grow grapes organically, there are still innumerable substances allowed during vinification that are horrible. There is so much chemical crap in wines that people normally drink. It's horrible. If you looked at a list, you'd be scared. You *should* be scared." On the other hand, he's even less fond of conventional agriculture: "Conventional wine producers often say there's no science showing that biodynamics works. Fine. You can have that. But there's plenty of science that shows that pesticides, herbicides, and chemicals will give you cancer, kill you, whatever. So, let's start from there."

Querciabella is surrounded by forest land, and Castiglione's fondness for animals has meant being creative when it comes to managing the predations of deer and wild boar. "If you don't put up fences, you don't have grapes. It's that simple. But we use a grid for our fences that smaller animals can get through—we don't want to disrupt their paths. Just the deer and the boar are kept out. We also had a tiger once that couldn't get through. It was the middle of the night, and I heard it roaring. It had escaped from one of those idiotic personal zoos. I remember waking up and thinking, 'Well, *this* is not normal!'"

The affordable **Querciabella Mongrana** (\$–\$\$) blends Sangiovese with Cabernet Sauvignon and Merlot; it's aged in stainless steel and cement, and is medium-bodied and lively. There's a white version as well, the **Mongrana Bianco** (\$–\$\$), a blend of Vermentino and Viognier that's full of stone-fruit flavors. **Querciabella's Chianti Classico** (\$\$) is one of the best basic Chianti Classicos you can find, full of mouth-filling wild berry flavor. The even better **Chianti Classico Riserva** (\$\$\$) ages for a little more than a year

in 20 percent new French oak, and in the bottle for at least another year. It adds layers of complexity and structure. **Batàr** (\$\$\$\$) was one of the first "Super-Tuscan" whites, and is still one of the best. Half Chardonnay and half Pinot Blanc, with *bâttonage* (stirring) in barrel (20 percent new) on lees for nine months, it's richly apple-peachy, with a creamy texture and citrus peel accents. Its red counterpart is **Camartina** (\$\$\$\$), a formidably dark-fruited blend of Cabernet Sauvignon and Sangiovese.

ROCCA DI MONTEGROSSI • CHIANTI CLASSICO

[certified organic]

Marco Ricasoli-Firidolfi's estate in Chianti, Rocca di Montegrossi, dates back to the seventh century, when the fortress for which it was named was built by the founder of the Ricasoli-Firidolfi family. As happens to fortresses, the building was destroyed and rebuilt several times over the next fourteen centuries. The family also acquired the much grander Castello di Brolio in 1141—they were in the habit of acquiring castles, at one point owning more than a dozen of them—and this was where the "Iron Baron," Bettino Ricasoli, first codified in 1872 the blend of varieties for Chianti. Over time, the family split into several branches. (One still owns Castello di Brolio.) On the Ricasoli-Firidolfi side, Marco's brother owns the nearby Castello di Cacchiano, and Marco himself owns Rocca di Montegrossi. If you are confused, welcome to the history of Italian nobility.

For all that weighty heritage, Marco Ricasoli is a surprisingly low-key, easygoing fellow, thoughtful about viticulture and winemaking, passionate about the environment, and surprisingly sanguine about the complexities

of property and family. Though his father grew up in Castello di Brolio, the property and the Ricasoli name and title went to Marco's uncle. "My father was the second son," Marco says, "so Ricasoli would never be his."

Today Rocca di Montegrossi comprises about fifty acres of vines in Monti in Chianti, about four miles from Gaiole. Forty acres of olive trees also grow on the property (the oil is excellent), along with a couple of hundred acres of untouched forest. The vineyards and olive groves have been organic since 2006. The vineyards lie at the top of a bowl encircled by hills; a line of ancient cypresses marks the upper boundary. "In September and October, the bottom of this valley is a sea of fog," Ricasoli says, "but up where we are, it's sun and blue skies."

There are also solar panels on the estate, producing enough energy from the sun that the winery needs almost no electricity from the grid. "From the beginning I've been very involved in the natural argument," Marco says. "I farm organically. All the rain we get goes into reservoirs. Solar panels heat all our hot water. We're one of the greenest wineries in Italy. But it's very important for *all* of us to be protective of nature. It's one of the biggest fights with my kids—don't waste water, don't waste electricity. Turn off the lights!"

Rocca di Montegrossi's **Chianti Classico ($$)** is finely focused, with Sangiovese's bright red-cherry character fully on display. The **Chianti Classico Riserva San Marcellino Gran Selezione ($$$)** is named for the small church at the center of the vineyard; the vines were planted the year of Marco's birth, by his father. Darkly spicy, with dried aromatic herb notes, it's sleek and expressive, and made only in top vintages. **Geremia ($$$)** is primarily Merlot with a small amount of Cabernet Sauvignon. Named after the long-ago founder of the Ricasoli family, it's violet-edged, smoky, and dark-fruited, with a savory meat note and firm tannins. Finally, the winery's sweet **Vin Santo ($$$)** is made from Trebbiano grapes dried for three months on vertical nets—Marco's invention. "It's like a curtain of grapes, so you don't have to use dirty wood racks with twenty years of mold on them." The wine is then aged for eight years in small barrels, or *caratelli*, of mulberry, oak, and cherrywood. It's layered and seductively sweet and complex, a true *vino di meditazione.*

SALCHETO • VINO NOBILE DE MONTEPULCIANO

[certified sustainable / certified organic]

Salcheto's owner, Michele Manelli, grew up near Brescia in northern Italy. "It's a very industrial area, and as I got older, I really felt this deterioration of our lifestyle, this feeling of an abuse of something important." Manelli remembers swimming as a boy in the Mella River— all the children did, he says, up until it became so polluted that they were told to keep away from it entirely. "So it's very personal. I don't want to dwell too much on the sadness of that, but the values I brought to the winery came out of that experience."

Manelli bought Salcheto in 1997, when land in Vino Nobile wasn't nearly as expensive as it's become today. "It was my first wine project and my first serious life project," he says. "When I was a kid, I dreamed of being a farmer, a businessman, and a politician. Now I've been able to put together all three. I farm, but I also run a winery and sell wine, and in the last decade I've been very engaged in trying to push wine as a whole toward higher sustainability levels. I'm doing what I dreamed of doing."

Manelli farms his 148 acres of vineyards organically, but strongly feels that sustainability is even more important: "I like the radical part of organic farming, the refusal of the chemical shortcut. But I believe even more in sustainability. Organic is just the process, kind of closed in its tower—a golden tower, but still a tower. Organics alone doesn't consider a lot of the ecological and social challenges we're facing, such as climate change, carbon use, fair working conditions, and so on. There are so many environmental aspects that organics—and biodynamics, I should add—don't address, that our world of seven billion people, all living together, needs to address. This is not a criticism; I'm just saying that we need

to push in the right direction in *many* ways."

Salcheto only uses oak from responsibly managed forests, uses lighter-weight bottles to lower carbon footprint, purifies and reuses all its wastewater, is energy independent (using things like reflective light tubes to bring light from outside to illuminate the lower levels of the cellar), produces its own composts and biodynamic preps. (Manelli uses some biodynamic techniques, but says he'll never get certified: "I have a problem with this whole supposed astrological connection between the air, stars, and so on.") It was also the first winery to have certified the carbon footprint of a bottle of wine, and also the first in Italy to adopt a welfare plan for its vineyard workers.

"Even in the Italian wine industry you have abuse of labor, even modern slavery—not a lot of the latter, but it's out there," Manelli says. "So these are real challenges, especially when you consider that nearly one worker out of two in farming in Italy is a migrant."

Manelli also helped found and is the president of Equalitas, an Italian organization dedicated to promoting and certifying sustainability for wineries. His passion is evident when you speak to him, and despite the scale of the world's enviromental and social problems, he also is a remarkably positive, cheerful presence. "I feel the environmental problems are like a gigantic mountain that we—Salcheto—have very, very slightly had an effect on. As one winery we're just a grain of sand in a vast sea of sand. We make four hundred thousand bottles a year, but Europe produces twenty-six *billion* bottles each year. Still, in terms of the carbon savings Salcheto has been able to make over the last decade using lighter bottles, our estimate is that it's about three million kilos. That's equal to planting five thousand trees!

"But to offset the climate challenges we're all facing we need *millions and millions* of those trees. The point is that everyone has to do something to make a difference. We can't all sit around waiting for some solution to come from above. Everyone has to take at least a small responsibility, or we'll never make it as a species."

Manelli also hopes, with his wines, to give Vino Nobile di Montepulciano more of the reputation that it actually deserves (it tends to be overshadowed by both Brunello di Montalcino and by Chianti Classico). "Our Sangiovese runs more in the direction of elegance than power," he says. "I think Vino Nobile has a great identity, we're just a little late in writing it down." His **Salcheto Vino Nobile di Montepulciano ($$)** is indeed elegant, while still having plenty of the robust dark fruit typical of Prugnolo Gentile (Sangiovese) from this area. The **Vino Nobile di Montalcino Riserva ($$$)** is along similar lines but more fragrant and complex. **Salco ($$$)** comes from the oldest vines on the property, and spends two years in wood and then four years in the cellar before release.

Manelli also recently released a line of no-sulfur, no-intervention wines called Obvius; effectively natural wines, but without the "natural wine" imprimatur. "I asked myself, if I made wines with total nonintervention, what would be the result? What tastes will we get from this. Oxidation? VA? Brett? I was with everyone else in calling these faults, but this project changed my vision of wine. I still want to do my modern wines, that are made using sulfur. But now I consider Brett, and oxidation, and volatile acidity not so much absolute faults as possible characteristics. They're part of the basket of tastes." The **Obvius Rosso ($$)** is a good example, juicy and dark and faintly feral. A good one for some wild-boar ragù.

FATTORIA SELVAPIANA • CHIANTI RÙFINA

[certified organic]

It sounds like a fairy tale: The old nobleman, childless, realizes that the children of the man who looks after his vineyards love the land as much as he does, and so he leaves them his entire estate. But that's truly the story at Selvapiana. Francesco Giuntini Antinori's family had owned Selvapiana since the early 1800s. But as Federico Giuntini recounts, "Francesco, my adoptive father, never got married. And Franco, my actual father, was the estate manager. So, at a certain point, Francesco decided that my sister and I were the ones who should inherit his property. He first told us this in 1987. I'd just finished high school, and one day he said, 'Stay at Selvapiana this weekend, I need to talk to you.' I wasn't actually very happy about that—I was young, and I wanted to go out in the city and have fun. But we went on a walk through the woods, and he told me what he intended to do.

"We all thought he was joking! We assumed he would leave the estate to his cousins. But my father passed away in 1990, and a few years later Francesco came to the winery office on a Monday morning and said, 'Now we go to the *tribunale* and make this official.'" Giuntini still seems a little amazed himself. "It's *una fabula*. But I do like to think that what my sister and I have accomplished makes him feel that he didn't make a mistake."

Today Selvapiana is unquestionably the most respected producer in Chianti Rùfina, and one of the most respected in Chianti as a whole. It's been a long journey, though. "From the 1950s straight through to the 1980s were tough times in our region," Giuntini says. "People grew grapes, but they were all sold to the *negociants* for the fiasco—the straw flask. The cheap wine." Selvapiana itself was in poor shape: the vineyards weren't well cared for and the winery was old and dilapidated. "We had to bring it all back to life," Giuntini says. "But we did. My son, when he tastes the wines from when I first started, is always surprised. He says, 'You didn't know anything, you didn't have any experience, and the winery was in terrible shape—but the wines are still good!'"

Even before Giuntini started, his father, Franco, and his soon-to-be-adoptive-father, Federico, had made some notable wines. Selvapiana was one of the first Chianti estates to make a Riserva from 100 percent Sangiovese and also one of the first to release a single-vineyard wine, Bucerchiale, whose first vintage was 1979. After Giuntini started, he made changes—restoring the winery,

buying barrels (there were none left), and, in 1992, converting the vineyards to organic farming.

Today Giuntini farms 145 acres of vineyard. He oversees the estate, and his son Francesco (named after Giuntini's adoptive father: "I owe everything to him") makes the wine.

And Francesco Giuntini Antinori, who set this fairy tale in motion, still weighs in from time to time. "But he's mostly retired," Giuntini says. "He's ninety now." He pauses thoughtfully. "It's funny. When I left high school, I knew I wanted to make wine, and my best friend was planning to do charity work. I told him, 'When we meet again in our sixties, I will have saved Selvapiana and you will have eliminated hunger in the world!' I don't think he's quite managed that, unfortunately. But Selvapiana is doing well."

The basic **Selvapiana Chianti Rùfina** (\$) is one of the great values in Tuscan wine, round and juicy yet with firm tannins. The **Villa Petrognano Pomino Rosso** (\$\$), from the tiny Pomino DOC, is more rustic and powerful, with fuzz-tone tannins and dark berry fruit. There are also two single-vineyard

wines from the winery's Rùfina vineyards, the earthy, red-cherry-rich **Vigneto Bucerchiale Riserva** (\$\$) and the darker **Vigneto Erchi** (\$\$\$), with its sanguinary and graphite nuances. "Erchi is a little more round and supple in the mouth, and Bucerchiale is a more Pinot-style Sangiovese," Giuntini says. There's also one white wine, the brisk, lively **Pomino Bianco Villa di Petrognano ($$)**, as well as a standout **Vin Santo del Chianti Rùfina ($$$)**, its candied citrus, dried fig, and caramel flavors lifted by racy acidity.

TENUTA DI VALGIANO · COLLINE LUCCHESE

[certified organic / certified biodynamic]

The Valgiano estate lies in the hills above Lucca, between the Appenines and the Tyrrhenian Sea, its vineyards surrounded by a girdle of untouched forest land. As on many biodynamic estates, the farming here isn't limited to grapes. Owners Moreno Petrini and Laura di Collobiano also produce small amounts of honey, eggs, and olives, and raise pigs, chickens, and rabbits. All this is achieved without chemical interventions, even including the traditional copper/sulfur treatments for mildew that are allowed in organic viticulture—instead Petrini and Collobiano spray fresh cow's milk on the vines during humid conditions.

The Colline Lucchese appellation is one of Tuscany's least well-known and, in many ways, least changing; in 1968, there were 988 acres of vines here, and in 2022, there were 1,037. "It's a very tiny appellation," Moreno Petrini says. "Outsiders rarely invest here. It's almost frozen in a way. But then, Lucca was always its own insular republic. We were never under the rule of Florence; never under Tuscan domination. We're very proud of that."

Moreno grew up in the outskirts of Lucca and, as a boy, could see from his house the hillside estate he now owns. "We used to play here as kids—I could go blind and still know exactly where I am, anywhere on this property." When he bought it, the estate was in disrepair. The former owner's sole interest in life was hunting, and he raised horses and hunting dogs on the property for that purpose. "There were all these cages

> *"If I could explain our wine, I'd become a writer. I prefer that the wine explain itself."*
> —Moreno Petrini

in the courtyard full of dogs," Moreno says. "It was like a gulag for dogs. But I loved this place because of the horses." (He was, and is, an accomplished rider.) "When the guy decided to sell, I knew I wanted to buy it."

Moreno is quick to note that he and Collobiano—whom he'd been living with at the time on a nearby, even more rundown estate—didn't have a clue what they were doing when they took over Valgiano. They began by farming conventionally, the same way their neighbors did, planning to make a day-to-day quaffing wine, nothing more. But they realized that the estate offered more than that. At the same time, they started to question their viticultural approach, too. "I was buying products at the farm supply store, all of them with skulls and bones on the labels. I wanted to work differently, but I didn't know how. Then I found this book by Nicolas Joly, *Wine from Sky to Earth*."

Joly's book was the proverbial flashbulb going off for Moreno and Collobiano. "There's a process with biodyamics . . . we don't know exactly what's going on, but I promise you that it works," Moreno says. Together with longtime winemaker Saverio Petrilli they make their wine using native yeasts, with open-top fermentation, foot-crushing the grapes. "For my generation, the fight has been against industrial winemaking," he says. Nothing at Valgiano is modified, nothing adjusted; the vintage is the vintage. Referring back to the cold, wet 2014 vintage, Moreno says, "This story that some winemakers tell about how dark and ripe their wine is? In 2014? Please. Don't tell me Jesus died of a heart attack. We both know that's not what happened."

The **Palistorti di Valgiano Bianco** (**$$**), a blend of Trebbiano, Vermentino, and Malvasia, is lightly grapefruity-peachy and medium-bodied. **Palistorte** (**$$**), which means "crooked posts," gets its name from what locals used to call the vineyard, because there were so many stones in it. The second red from the estate, it's full of direct cherry-plum flavors, and subtle herbal notes. The flagship wine, **Tenuta di Valgiano** (**$$$**), a blend of Sangiovese, Syrah, and Merlot, has an architectural elegance that almost conceals its intensity and power, but not quite.

UMBRIA AND LAZIO

Lazio has two big problems with its reputation as a wine region. The first is that historically much of the wine here has been just OK: pleasantly quaffable whites (and some reds) destined for the thousands of trattorias, *ristorantes*, and osterias of Rome. The second is Rome itself. The Eternal City might as well be called the Eternally Famous City, because its radiance tends to obscure everything else around it.

Even so, there are good wines to be found in Lazio, particularly from the local red Cesanese variety, and usually in the hands of younger vintners who aren't satisfied with the Lazio's overall reputation. Damiano Ciolli is one fine example.

Umbria, on the other hand, *should* be better known. But it, in turn, lies in the very large shadow cast by its northern neighbor, Tuscany. Its climate may be similar, but its wines are distinct to the place: Orvieto, an often banal white that, in the right places, made by the right winemaker, can be brilliant; and powerful, tannic, intense reds made from the Sagrantino variety. Giampiero Bea's Pagliaro Sagrantino di Montefalco, for example, is one of the great wines of Italy.

PAOLO BEA • MONTEFALCO (UMBRIA)

[organic / biodynamic / regenerative]

A walk through the Paolo Bea vineyards was one of the early inspirations for this book. I wish I could say that it was the beauty of the landscape, or the autumn sun descending toward the horizon, but the defining moment was when Giampiero Bea showed me some of the leaves on the vines at the edge of his property. They looked like they'd been torched: discolored, shriveled, burnt. Bea farms organically, but, across a small culvert, his neighbor tended to spray heavily with weed-killing herbicides. "It drifts over," Giampiero said. "This is what happens. But he's not willing to change."

One person farming conscientiously is never enough. Giampiero let go of the leaf and shrugged. There wasn't anything he could do, other than keep making his family's extraordinary wines.

Giampiero's father, Paolo Bea, now in his eighties, founded the winery in 1973. But the Bea family has lived in the hills of Umbria near the walled town of Montefalco since the 1500s. Today, Giampiero and his brother Giuseppe do the work. There are twenty-seven acres of vines here, five acres of olives, as well as fruit trees, vegetable gardens,

and animals. There's no technology in the vineyards except for a couple of humidity measuring stations; organic treatments like propolis and nettle teas are used for vine problems. Regenerative strategies are used, such as growing artichokes to improve the soil's iron content. (The artichokes get eaten when they appear in May, and then the stalks and leaves are plowed back into the soil in September.) Paolo Bea stopped using chemical treatments and fertilizers back in 1969, and his sons continue with his vision. You get the sense, visiting, that the human element here is just one minor part of the whole, participatory but transient. That's clear even in the design of the cellar, where a wall of solid rock has been left exposed, the water that seeps across its surface serving to keep the cellar just humid enough (Giampiero was an architect before joining the family business). The humility the Beas feel about the human role in the process is clear, too, when Giampiero says, "My wine is an expression of terroir. I like to assist in the process, not dominate it."

The **Santa Chiara Umbria Bianco** ($$$), made from Grechetto, Malvasia, and other varieties, spends two weeks on its skins; orange-gold hued, it suggests fresh melon and herbs. Giampiero uses Trebbiano Spoletino for the **Arboreus Umbria Bianco** ($$$) from vines that were trained decades ago to grow up maple or elm trees with the grapes hanging ten or fifteen feet above the ground. Dark gold in color, Arboreus gets three weeks or more of skin contact; the result is pineapple-y, waxy, lemony, peppery; complex and utterly distinctive. **Rosso di Veo** ($$$) comes from the Beas' younger Sagrantino vines. It's full of strawberry-cherry fruit, bright and zippy, with a meaty note hiding underneath. The **San Valentino Montefalco Rosso** ($$$) comes from the vineyard of the same name, from vines that are fifty plus years old. Primarily Sangiovese, its lifted flavors suggest red cherries with fresh herbs and often a light coffee note. From the Pipparello Vineyard, Giampiero makes the **Pipparello Montefalco Rosso Riserva** ($$$) from Sangiovese together with Montepulciano and Sagrantino; it's silkier than San Valentino, spicy and strawberry-cherry inflected. The most profound wine from Bea is the **Pagliaro Sagrantino di Montefalco** ($$$$), from a single vineyard at thirteen hundred feet elevation. This is Sagrantino in all its wild intensity, full of deep, dark fruit with hints of espresso and dried herbs, powerful and tannic, almost feral.

PAOLO E NOEMIA D'AMICO • LAZIO

[certified organic]

Paolo and Noemia d'Amico's Villa Tirrena estate, which is both home and winery, lies hidden away at the end of one of those winding Italian country roads along which one drives, thinking, "I must have missed it—did I miss it? There can't possibly be a winery here." Yet there is, and from the expansive garden behind the home, the land drops away to an extraordinary view over Umbria's Calanchi Valley and the medieval hilltop town of Civita di Bagnoregio (the winery lies right on the border between Lazio, Umbria, and Tuscany). The steep valley itself was mined by the Romans for basalt; the d'Amicos' eighty-plus acres of vineyards float above it, a kind of Italian Shangri-La of vines. That feeling of magical unreality is intensified by the d'Amicos' mazelike sculpture garden, which features works by artists as disparate (and well-known) as Anish Kapoor, Banksy, and Igor Mitoraj (and while a great art collection doesn't necessarily imply great wine, it certainly makes visiting the property a fascinating experience). The d'Amicos farm organically, and overarchingly see wine and art as related forms of expression. This can get a little mystical—the couple plays classical music in their vaulted cellars to the barrels of aging wine—but the relationship doesn't feel so much forced as natural.

Winemaker Guillaume Gelly makes a number of compelling wines here. The citrusy **Noe Orvieto ($–$$)** is more minerally than many Orvietos thanks to the volcanic tufa soil at the estate; the **Calanchi Chardonnay ($$)** is similarly crisp and focused, and is made with no new oak and no malolactic fermentation. **Notturo dei Calanchi ($$)** is the only Pinot Noir from Umbria that I've ever run across, but its bright cherry fruit and lively character suggest that the region might have a hidden talent for the variety. **Tirrena ($$)** is a robust, plummy blend of Merlot and Syrah. Lastly, **Atalante ($$)** shows that Umbria has a facility for Cabernet Franc just as Tuscany does. Subtly herbal, with polished dark fruit, it's an impressive Umbrian red.

DAMIANO CIOLLI • OLEVANO ROMANO (LAZIO)

[organic / biodynamic]

"I was born to the sound of my grandfather hammering rims on casks, so I was never going to do anything else with my life than make wine," says Damiano Ciolli, whose wines are some of the most singular expressions of Cesanese, the often-overlooked local grape of Lazio.

Ciolli's father and grandfather were farmers, growing grapes and selling them to other producers, making only a small amount of their own wine. When he took over in 2001, he was determined to change that. "I was around my grandfather and my father when I was young, and I didn't like that they worked like beasts to produce as much fruit as possible. I decided I was going to make better wine and less of it. Wine that people would respect."

With his partner-in-life, Letizia Rocchi, who has a PhD in grapevine physiology and winemaking, Ciolli started working organically, and also lowered yields to increase quality. Bucking tradition can be difficult: "My father came from a culture of not wasting anything," Ciolli says. During his second year, when Ciolli was green harvesting—cutting off bunches of grapes before they're ripe, to intensify flavors in the remaining clusters—he recalls that "my father had to leave because he felt sick to his stomach. Then he came back with the tractor to pick up all the grapes on the ground. He hid them, so that other farmers wouldn't think we were *pazzo matto*." (Lunatics, essentially.)

The **Damiano Ciolli Botte Ventedue ($$)** blends the local varieties Trebbian Verde and Ottonese for a fresh, peachy white. **Silene ($$)** is Cesanese d'Affile that's fermented in stainless steel and aged for a year in cement tanks. It's bright and fresh, full of crunchy cherry fruit. **Cirsium** ($$) is full-bodied and firmly tannic, with dark fruit and a kind of foresty herb note—it tastes, more or less, the way you'd think it would, if you were standing in these wildflower-filled vineyards, surrounded by dark trees and then, above, the bright, open Mediterranean sky.

SERGIO MOTTURA • ORVIETO (UMBRIA)

[certified organic]

Sergio Mottura is a farmer, but he's just as likely to meet you in his home in the small town of Civitella d'Agliano in a blue blazer and beige linen pants. Yet there's nothing pretentious about him. Rather there's a kind of calmness in his manner, similar to the calm eloquence of his wines.

Mottura owns eighty-nine acres of vineyards, which have been in his family since the 1930s. He's devoted to the grapes indigenous to his region. "When I started at twenty-one," he says, "my uncle had one tank of Grechetto in the cellar. I tasted this; it was a wonderful wine. Why mix it with anything else? And why use international varieties? In Italy, we have more than three thousand varieties of our own—why use Syrah? Or Sauvignon? Or Viognier?"

Mottura's winery is powered entirely by solar energy, and he has farmed his vineyards organically since the 1960s. He says, "I asked myself back then, why would I use chemicals? My children play among these vines." The porcupine depicted on his wines' labels ties to that decision. When Mottura stopped using conventional fertilizers and herbicides, he found that the local porcupines returned to his vineyards. "Now, there are a *lot*," he notes, sounding a little ambivalent about the prolixity of these porcupines.

The **Sergio Mottura Orvieto ($)** is 60 percent Grechetto and 40 percent Procanico. It's an excellent expression of Orvieto, a wine that too often seems uninspired. His **Poggio della Costa ($$)** is a profound white for a nominal price, given its quality. Made from Grechetto from a single, steep, seventeen-acre vineyard, fermented and aged in stainless steel, it suggests pears and apples and a light flinty smokiness. It ages impressively well, too. **Latour a Civitella ($$)** draws fruit from five of Mottura's best vineyard parcels, and is aged in French oak barrels. Golden-hued and lightly nutty, it's a richer expression of Grechetto than Poggio della Costa, but no less complex.

PRODUCERS PROFILED IN THIS CHAPTER

Abruzzo

Emidio Pepe

Tiberio

Le Marche

Bucci

La Distesa

Tuscany

Stefano Amerighi

Montesecondo

Avignonesi

Fattoria di Petroio

Col d'Orcia

Fattoria Poggerino

Podere le Boncie

Querciabella

Fontodi

Rocca di Montegrossi

Istine

Salcheto

Lamole di Lamole

Fattoria Selvapiana

Le Macchiole

Tenuta di Valgiano

Castello di Monsanto

Umbria and Lazio

Paolo Bea

Damiano Ciolli

Paolo e Noemia d'Amico

Sergio Mottura

OTHER CENTRAL ITALY PRODUCERS TO LOOK FOR

Abruzzo

Antica Tenuta Pietramore

Le Marche

Andrea Felici

La Staffa

Tuscany

Castello di Ama
Fattoria dei Barbi
Il Borro
Boscarelli
Tenuta di Capezzanna
Castell'in Villa
Colombaia
Felsina
Ficomontanino
Bibi Graetz
Grattamacco
Montenidoli

Monteraponti
Montevertine
Pacina
Marchesi Pancrazi
Podere le Ripi
Michele Satta
Sesti
Talenti
Tolaini
Uccelleria
Castello di Volpaia

Umbria and Lazio

Arnaldo Caprai
Fongoli

Tabarrini

SOUTHERN ITALY

The wine regions of southern Italy stretch from about ninety miles south of Rome down to the very tip of the Italian boot, including the islands of Sicily and Sardinia. Here Sangiovese gives way to varieties like Aglianico, Negroamaro, Nero d'Avola, and others. All produce robust wines, especially in the hot weather of southern Italy's summer months; to find elegance, vintners usually seek out altitude, planting high in places like the slopes of Monte Vulture in Basilicata or the slopes of Mount Etna in Sicily.

Southern Italy also *feels* different from northern or even central Italy. Arabic and Spanish influences are much more prevalent in the history of southern Italy; historically, its economy was much more agrarian than the north's, a divide that only increased after the Industrial Revolution; and it was poorer. The south sees the north as boring and work-obsessed; the north sees the south as loud and backward. These are clichés, of course, but that doesn't stop people from subscribing to them—just ask someone from Milan their opinion of Naples.

Regardless, southern Italy's wine regions are some of its most exciting. There are few Italian reds as shimmeringly mineral as those from Mount Etna right now; few Italian whites as compelling as great Fianos and Falanghinas from Campania. Sicily has the largest percentage of Italy's organic vineyards by a good measure (27 percent), helped by its hot, dry weather and lack of mold and disease pressure as a result; coming second behind it is Puglia, neck and neck with Tuscany.

BASILICATA, CALABRIA, AND PUGLIA

Basilicata, Calabria, and Puglia comprise the instep, toe, and heel of the Italian boot, respectively. Puglia makes more wine by far than the other two; it's effectively an ocean of grape vines and olive trees. Fertile soils and hot weather lead to abundant crops, and that's what Puglia has. For years its wines were a secret weapon for bulking up the fruit and richness of those from colder northern Italian regions. That practice has largely died away, but even so, most of the grapes here go for simple, everyday drinking wine destined for supermarket shelves around Europe. Yet scattered throughout the region are ambitious producers; they just take some hunting to find.

Calabria, the toe of the boot, is still deeply rural, a source for plums, citrus, wheat, olives, and, of course, grapes; also, the fiery red Calabrian pepperoncino. For centuries the region was also extremely poor. Its land is mostly mountains surrounded by coastline (summer tourism drives some of the economy here). Wines here are primarily red, mostly from the local Gaglioppo grape.

Basilicata shares with Campania a devotion to the powerful Aglianico variety, mostly grown on the foothills and slopes of the extinct Mount Vulture volcano. It's a tiny place, the instep of the boot, and in some ways more vertical than horizontal. Fully 93 percent of its land is either mountains or rugged hills.

ELENA FUCCI • BASILICATA

[certified organic]

Aglianico is not an easy grape. In the wrong hands, it can be brutally tannic and acidic, a grape that makes ill-tempered wines that would rather punch you in the head than delight your palate.

Then there are Elena Fucci's wines, which take Aglianico's innate power and transform it into elegance. Fucci is based in Basilicata, the instep of the Italian boot, in the town of Barilla. "I was born upstairs from the cellar, in my family home," she says. "I was going to study genetic engineering, but when I found out my parents were going to sell our vineyard and the house I grew up in, I changed my mind that day."

Her parents were both teachers. Her grandfather farmed grapes, but sold them to the local co-op. "He wanted my father to study, not farm. So, my father did. He's a teacher; so is my mother. But at eighteen, I started working in the vineyard with my grandfather, learning from him."

Fucci made her first wine in 2000: one grape variety, one vineyard, one wine. Twenty-five hundred bottles total. In 2004, the year she received her winemaking degree, she made seven thousand bottles. Today she makes about thirty thousand. Still small, but a substantial improvement from that first vintage.

Her ancestors, she notes, weren't nobility. They were farmers. They didn't have thousands of acres of land; there was no long tradition of winemaking to draw on. In her great-grandfather's time, she says, farmers, *contadinos*, "were basically slaves to the noble landowners. This is why the south of Italy was so much less developed than the north," she says. "But my great-grandfather was able to buy land he was farming because the owner wasn't from here—he was Tuscan, from Florence. He had a son, but the boy died horseback riding at an early age, so he had no heirs. And he thought about things differently than the landowners here."

The vineyard land that Fucci's great-grandfather bought spreads out in an amphitheater on the slopes of Mount Vulture, the highest vineyard on the mountain. It's cold in the winter here, and cold in the spring; the last snows come in March. Fucci farms about nineteen acres, all Aglianico. "I work organically in the vineyard, but I believe in science; I also have weather stations placed throughout. It's not like I'm watching the flowers to see if the petals look funny. Why? Because if you have the parameters, the data from the weather, you'll know if there's disease pressure. Or if I know the climate is going to be a problem in terms of one insect, then I can address the issue in the right way. To me, if you want to work organically or biodynamically, you need *more* knowledge of science, not less."

Fucci possesses a rare combination of artistic passion for her wines and a classically scientific rigor of thought. She also has an undying interest in experimentation. "Right now we're doing experiments in amphorae. Everyone says, 'Oh, the Greeks and Romans did that!'" Her gaze is piercing from under her dark bangs, but she's also quick to smile: "Well, of *course* they did, they had nothing else! For me, what's actually interesting is how the polymerization of the polyphenols is changed by Italian terra-cotta, which is quite porous. But that isn't romantic. It's chemistry!"

The **Elena Fucci Aglianico del Vulture Titolo ($$$)** is Fucci's primary wine, and is one of the best Aglianicos in Basilicata, elegant yet powerful, with an aroma that suggests floral iron, if such a thing exists. Her **Titolo by Amphora ($$$)** is aged in unlined clay amphorae for eighteen months and is rounder on the palate, its tannins a little more relaxed, but it's no less complex and often has a slight smokiness.

There's also a juicy rosato, the **Titolo Pink Edition ($$)**, which swoops into the market each year around June and disappears just as rapidly. A few years ago, she also released the first vintage of wines made from an old plot of vines owned by friends of her grandfather, the **Elena Fucci Sceg Aglianico del Vulture ($$)**. It's a bit more rustic and muscular. (*Sceg* is a local dialect word for pomegranate.)

CAMPANIA AND MOLISE

O happy land! That's Campania, whose name derives from the Latin *campania felix*, the happy countryside. And it is happy, in wine terms, its broad swaths of vineyards lying inland from Naples and the Amalfi coast, growing local varieties under the buttery southern Italian sun. This is a volcanic region—ask the former residents of Pompeii—and that soil character shows through in the wines, often giving the whites a flinty, smoky edge, and the reds a core of minerality inside the ripe fruit that the region's warm weather provides.

The principal red grape here is Aglianico, which can produce anything from teeth-shattering tannic reds without much fruit to moderate their structure, to intense, characterful, long-aging reds that are as good as anything the north of Italy has to offer. As always, the right vineyard, farmed with skill, and a talented winemaker willing to respect what the terroir expresses are the keys to putting the latter in a bottle rather than the former.

Winemaking history here stretches back millennia. The white Falanghina grape is thought to have been used for Rome's storied Falernum (or Falernian) wine, aged in amphorae for years until it was oxidized and brown, and priced according to its rarity: "You can drink here for one *as*—if you give two, you will drink better—if you give four, you will drink Falernian," read an inscription found preserved in a wine bar at the site of ancient Pompeii. (The bronze *as* was a coin; two of them could buy you a loaf of bread.) The ancient Greek historian Strabo wrote of Campania that it was "the most blest of all plains. And, indeed, it is from here that the Romans obtain their best wine, namely, the Falernian, the Statanian, and the Calenian . . ." Though Campania's reputation has ebbed and risen again and again over the centuries, there is no question that indeed it is a blessed region for wine.

Tiny Molise, on the Adriatic coast, may be Italy's most overlooked wine region; it's also the second smallest after Val d'Aosta, with a little more than 13,000 acres of vines (for comparison, Puglia, to the south, has about 217,000 acres). Montepulciano is the primary grape here, making lively reds similar in style to those of Abruzzo to the north.

MASTROBERARDINO • CAMPANIA

[sustainable]

Mastroberardino and particularly Antonio Mastroberardino have been at the forefront of restoring the ancient grape varieties of Campania, carrying on a family tradition that stretches back to the 1700s.

World War II nearly put an end to that history, though. A good part of the Mastroberardino cellar was built as a bomb shelter in the summer of 1943. Antonio Mastroberardino, fifteen at the time, spent days there with his family while the Allies shelled the area around Naples, then went straight to harvest. By the end of the war, the family estate was more or less in ruins. Undaunted, and despite his youth, he decided to rebuild the winery and re-

plant the vineyards, choosing to concentrate only on the native grapes of Campania: Aglianico, but also Fiano de Avellino, Greco di Tufo, Coda di Volpe, and Piedirosso, all of which were either minimally planted or even in danger of extinction at the time. For many years, Mastroberardino was the only vintner bottling estate wines from Campania's heritage varieties (most Campanian wine then was sold on the bulk market, and local varieties were ripped out in favor of more familiar grapes such as Sangiovese and Trebbiano). He was also instrumental in reviving the reputation of Aglianico, and the most famous wine made from it, Taurasi. "We love Aglianico for its personality, but it's a tough variety," his son Piero Mastroberardino admits. "But its history here goes back to Roman times, to Pompeii. It's a difficult variety, but it proves that you have to truly engage your brain and your heart when you make wine, unless you want to end up with vinegar."

Antonio Mastroberardino passed away in 2014, and today the estate is run by Piero, the tenth generation of the family to make wine here. ("I learned to ride a bicycle and played soccer in our cellar," he says.) Mastroberardino owns more than 490 acres of vines, spread across almost all of Campania. Farming is sustainable, with a focus on biodiversity, responsible water management, reduction of CO_2 emissions, and social policies—working with suppliers who follow similar environmentally friendly protocols, training employees on environmental issues. Piero Mastroberardino says, "Viticulture is part of a natural balance, but it's also social."

Mastroberardino makes a plethora of wines, ranging from the very affordable to the quite expensive. For a baseline, look at Campania's native white grape varieties, like the **Mastroberardino Fiano di Avellino ($$)**, delicate and floral, or the richer, stonier **Falanghina di Sannio ($$)**. In a similar vein for red, the **Irpinia Aglianico ($$)** is an excellent introduction to this variety's intensity of flavor, without the formidable tannins it sometimes shows. The **Radici Taurasi ($$)** and **Radici Taurasi Riserva ($$$)** are benchmarks in Campanian wine, and in large measure helped the Taurasi appellation achieve DOCG status in 1993. Full-bodied, powerful, full of black plum and spice notes, and firmly tannic, both are drinkable in their youth—the Riserva possibly only for the brave—and both age impressively in a cellar.

QUINTODECIMO · CAMPANIA

[certified organic]

Luigi Moio is heir to several generations of winemaking knowledge, and he's also an academic who teaches enology at the University of Naples. In his wines one feels both the history of Campania—its vineyards, its mountains, its traditions—together with a kind of pure intellectual precision.

Moio was born in Mondragone, north of Naples, where his father, Michele, helped revive the ancient Roman Falerno del Massico appellation. Until 2001, Moio primarily worked as a consultant for other wineries in the region, but then he and his wife, Laura, established Quintodecimo in the forested hills of Irpinia, inside the Taurasi DOCG. The Moios farm sixty-two acres of vineyards, avoiding all chemical herbicides, fertilizers, and pesticides, and utilizing practices such as green manure and revegetation. Only native yeasts are used for fermentation.

The **Quintodecimo Exultet Fiano di Avellino ($$$)** is a prime example of the Moios' gift for balancing incisive focus with generosity of flavor: it coats the palate, yet its tree-fruit flavors are precise, carried forward on crystalline acidity. Among the whites, there's also the **Giallo d'Arles Greco di Tufo ($$$)**, the name a reference to the golden hue of Greco grapes at harvest time (and to Van Gogh), and the **Via del Campo Falanghina ($$$)**, from a single vineyard in Mirabella Eclano, which suggests ripe orchard fruits and fresh herbs; like the others, it also ages effortlessly in a cellar.

All three reds are made from Aglianico. **Terra d'Eclano ($$)**, the most affordable, pulls grapes from all five of the Moios' vineyards to produce a broad portrait of the estate; it's ink-dark, as Aglianico typically is, with plum-berry flavors and gripping tannins. **Vigna Quintodecimo Taurasi Riserva ($$$$)** comes from some of the first vines Moio planted at his estate. It channels the power and intensity of Aglianico into surprising elegance, its layers of dark flavor tightly bound up when young, but opening up over time. The **Vigna Grand Cerzito ($$$$)** comes from a small parcel of Aglianico planted in 2004 on volcanic soil, rather than clay-limestone, as Vigna Quintodecimo is. It's not as dark and brooding as Vigna Quintodecimo, either; side by side, the two are both world-class reds and also a fascinating comparison.

SICILY AND SARDINIA

Who would think that making wine from vineyards on Mount Etna, especially when all those vineyards had ever been known for was anonymous bulk wine, would result in some of the most exciting and sought-after Italian wines? Add to that the fact that Etna is an active volcano, with significant eruptions most recently in 2018 and 2021, and it becomes even more unexpected. But that's the case. Etna's wines are now some of the most profound, terroir-expressive wines in Italy.

The rest of Sicily shouldn't be ignored. Though there's still a vast amount of inexpensive, ripe, dark red and bargain-basement white made here, there are also exciting artisanal wines being made throughout the island, from projects like Feudo Montoni in the remote center to the low-intervention, organic wines of COS on the island's southeast coast.

Sicily's climate is essentially classic Mediterranean-island gorgeous, warm and dry, though it can be extremely hot in the summer (leading to super-ripe, jammy flavors if growers aren't careful) and surprisingly crisp, even cold, in higher-altitude vineyards in the center of the island. Due to the climate, there's very little pressure here from vine problems like powdery mildew or rot, which makes Sicily an ideal place for organic farming practices; as a result, it has more organic vineyard land than any other region, fully 27 percent of the country's total. The most widely planted red grape is Nero d'Avola. The less well-known Frappato makes light, crisp reds that are finding more favor as tastes shift, and on the side of Etna, Nerello Mascalese has risen from total obscurity to a source for some of the most elegant, terroir-transparent reds around. For whites, the native varieties Cataratto, Grillo, Inzolia, and Carricante (on Etna) are the names to remember. There's also plenty of vineyard acreage planted to international, easier-to-sell varieties.

Sardinia is slightly smaller than Sicily and, once you get away from the glamorous, park-my-yacht-here Costa Smeralda, wilder and more rugged. It only has a fourth of the vineyard land Sicily does, most of its scant arable land being devoted to grains like wheat and spelt, and citrus fruit. Vines are mostly planted to the red varieties Cannonau (Grenache) and Carignano (Carignan) and the white Vermentino. The reds tend to be fleshy, low in acid, with ripe, dark fruit flavors and herbal-spice aromas; the best Vermentinos tend to come from the northern Gallura region, and are crisp and green-apple-citrusy: classic ocean-influenced white wines.

FRANK CORNELISSEN • SICILY

[organic / natural]

Belgian-born Frank Cornelissen established his estate in 2001 on Mount Etna, several years before the explosion of new wineries that now dot the volcano's slopes. His start was microscopic, not to mention unlikely: a single acre of vines three thousand feet up on the side of an active volcano, in a region that at the time was not only not fashionable but essentially entirely ignored (it has since become the coolest place in Italian wine, so to speak, somewhat ironically for a volcano). If southern Italian wines were seen as rustic and clunky in the 1980s and 1990s, the wines of Etna were sloshing around the bottom of that pretty grim bucket.

Cornelissen saw in Etna what others didn't: austere volcanic soil, altitude—cooler temperatures and greater luminosity—and a native grape variety, Nerello Mascalese, with the potential to produce lighter-bodied, terroir-expressive red wines.

He decided to work with as little intervention as possible. That meant no spraying, not just of conventional herbicides, fungicides, and pesticides, but also of organic treatments (i.e., copper and sulfur, though he did relent on that in 2013 and 2015 to avoid his vines dying). He uses no fertilizers and makes all his own compost on-site, and now farms about fifty-four acres of vines, along with five acres of olive trees. He uses some biodynamic techniques, but not according to the approved biodynamic calendar, since he feels his vineyards live on their own schedule. "All possible interventions on the land we cultivate, including any treatments, whether chemical, organic, or biodynamic . . . are all a mere reflection of the inability of man to accept nature as she is and will be."

Cornelissen extended the same philosophy to his winery at a time when noninterventionist winemaking wasn't even really a term: no industrial yeasts, no additives, no oak, and minimal sulfur (zero, until recently). He quickly became a star in the natural wine world, and has remained one ever since.

The early Cornelissen wines were often unpredictable. Today they still have some of the unedited funkiness of natural wine, but that's balanced against expressiveness and distinctive character (and much more consistency). **Susucaru ($$)** looks like a dark rosé but is a red wine, and is mostly Nerello Mascalese from several different vineyards. It's simple, tart, and inviting, all smoky strawberries and wild herbs. **Munjabel Rosso ($$–$$$)** is Nerello Mascalese from fifty-plus-year-old vines that gets skin contact for about fifty days. It's richer and earthier, with herb and black cherry flavors and a kind of energetic liveliness. There are several single-vineyard (or, on Etna, *contrada*) wines. The **Munjabel CR**, or **Campo Re ($$$)**, is a good example, from a small plot of seventy-plus-year-old vines. Then there's **Magma ($$$$)**, Cornelissen's top wine. It's also a single-vineyard bottling, earthy, complex, and dark-fruited, from vines planted around 1910 at close to three thousand feet. It's been a sought-after rarity in the natural wine world for many years now, and the price has risen accordingly.

COS · SICILY

[certified organic / biodynamic / natural]

Take three idle college friends, home for the summer, give them some Nero d'Avola grapes and an abandoned cellar to work in, and forty or so years down the line you may end up with one of the most influential wineries in Sicily.

COS was founded by Giambattista Cilia, Giusti Occhipinti, and Cirino Strano, two of them architecture students and one, Strano, a medical student. They were home for the holidays with time on their hands, and Cilia's uncle suggested they make some wine. They did, then continued to make it through their college years, shifting their studies in part toward winemaking. By the time they graduated, they had founded a winery. This was in Ragusa, on the southeastern tip of Sicily. At the time, it was a nearly dead place for wine, and COS was instrumental in reviving the DOCG-status wine Cerasuolo di Vittorio (there are now more than forty producers).

COS's greater significance in Sicily, though, was its early adoption of biodynamic viticulture, which the trio started in 2000. Giusto Occhipinti, who emerged as the group's guiding force, has likened vineyards to a winemaker's life savings: a repository of something valuable, that needs to be protected. No chemicals or synthetic treatments have ever been used on COS vines. COS was also among the first Italian wineries outside Friuli to bring back the tradition of winemaking in clay amphorae, and the first in Sicily to work in what has essentially become the template for natural wine: no fining, no filtration, no sulfur (except for a minimal amount at bottling). Nothing but grapes and native yeasts and time.

Only Cilia and Occhipinti are still involved in the business today, and the wines are made in a new winery they designed and built in 2007. All wines ferment in resin-lined concrete vats, then are aged either in old Slavonian casks or in the 150 clay amphorae the partners own. Either way, these are exciting wines to taste, lifted and vibrant, and deeply expressive of the terroir they come from.

The **COS Cerasuolo di Vittoria ($$)** helped revive the vanished reputation of this light-bodied southern Sicilian blend. It's a combination of Nero d'Avola and Frappato that offers silky, black cherry–raspberry, herb, and spice flavors. The winery's **Frappato ($$)** has a similar liveliness, though it's more purely on the red-fruit spectrum. The Pithos wines are so called for their aging in amphorae (*Pithos* is the ancient Greek word for amphora). The **Pithos Bianco ($$)** is 100 percent Grecanico, yellow-orange in color, with orchard fruit and honey notes. **Pithos Rosso ($$)** has the same blend as the winery's Cerasuolo di Vittoria, but is aged seven months in amphorae; it's earthy and juicy, with tingly acidity. There's also the white **Zibibbo in Pithos ($$)**; Zibibbo is the Sicilian name for Muscat of Alexandria. It's a boisterous mix of melon, citrus, and apple flavors, with a lot of skin-contact texture. Slightly kooky, and entirely engaging.

TENUTE DETTORI • SARDINIA

[certified organic / certified biodynamic / natural]

Sardinia's Alessandro Dettori makes what many people would consider to be natural wine. Even the label on his bottle makes it clear: "No product with synthetic chemicals, except sulfur, is used in the vineyards and in winemaking. We do not add yeasts, enzymes, or any other adjuvant in the vinification and maturation of our wines. They are not filtered, clarified or barriqued. . . . There may be some natural sediment and CO_2. Each bottle can be different."

But making "natural" wine wasn't his goal when Dettori got started. He really just wanted to make the kind of wines his grandfather had, wines he himself had helped make when he started assisting the old man as a boy. Nothing fancy: his grandfather's wines were sold locally, to friends, customers from town, and simple trattorias. It was everyday wine, for everyday people, honest and unpretentious, made with grapes, the native yeasts growing on the grape skins, and nothing else.

Time passes. Dettori went off to

university, spent some time as a drummer in a rock band, and eventually moved to Brazil. But when his grandfather passed away in August of 1998, Dettori put down the drumsticks and returned home to finish the harvest.

Today he farms sixty-four acres of vineyard, and also grows grains, vegetables, fruit, and olives. The vines look small and scruffy—they're trained in the traditional Sardinian bush-vine manner called *sa sardisca*, and are set far apart, cover crops and grasses growing between them. This part of northwest Sardinia is a windy, remote place. Hawks wheel overhead and wild boar trot through in the scrubland around the vines. The vines are the ancient native varieties of the region: Retagliadu Nieddu (Cannonau), Monica di Sorso, Pascale, Vermentino, and Moscato di Sennori. The farming, too, is from a former time. Taste and instinct are the only guides. Fermentation is in the same small concrete tanks Dettori's grandfather used. No filtration is done, and no other substances are added at all.

As the back label on bottles of Dettori's wines says, "We are modest-sized artisans of the earth. You will understand, then, when we say that we do not follow the dictates of the market, but produce wines that we like, wines belonging to our culture. They are what they have to be and not what you want them to be."

———

Dettori's vineyard, Badde Nigolosu, is divided into several plots, each of which is bottled on its own. The golden-hued **Tenute Dettori Bianco Romangia** (\$\$) is 100 percent Vermentino di Sennori and rich with red apple and honeysuckle notes. The winery makes three different single-vineyard Cannonaus. The **Tuderi Rosso Romangia** (\$\$) comes from vines around forty years old, and is juicy but bright, its red fruit flavors accented with garrigue-like herbal notes. **Tenores Rosso Romangia** (\$\$), from eighty-year-old vines, is more transparent (though still a rich wine), with black pepper and raspberry flavors and firm tannins. The top wine, **Dettori Rosso Romangia** (\$\$\$), comes from vines that Alessandro Dettori's great-grandfather planted in 1863. It's powerful, dark, and meaty, sometimes with a touch of sweetness— Amarone-like, in a way, without the need for drying the grapes first.

FEUDO MONTONI • SICILY

[certified organic]

Feudo Montoni is hidden away in the center of Sicily, high up in the mountains, no other wine estates around, just a few farmers growing wheat. "We're in the center of old Sicily," owner Fabio Sireci says. "This part isn't the Sicily for tourists. It's the Sicily for explorers. Everything here is stopped in time."

Here, Sireci and his partner, Melissa Muller, farm 370 acres of land, 109 of which are grapes. "It's important that the vineyard is surrounded by other crops," he says. "Chickpeas, lentils, wheat, all of it organic—it's like a ring that defends the vines from nonorganic neighbors." No chemicals are used, nor have they ever been. The only fertilizers are nitrogen-fixing cover crops, such as rye grass.

Sireci and Muller also grow tomatoes, raise chickens, have beehives, and let a neighboring shepherd graze his sheep on their property. "Our life goal is being self-sustainable," Sireci says. "We don't believe in being part of the industrial agricultural world."

Talking to Sireci is sometimes more like talking to a professor than a winemaker: "We have to extend this concept of history when it comes to wine. In wine, one year of a human life is like twenty years for a winery. Where we are, the history of the winery starts in the twelfth century; the building we make our wine in was built in 1469." Sireci's grandfather bought the estate in the late 1800s. At the time it was mostly wheat fields. Wheat was profitable, and wine, Sireci says, was largely a secondary pursuit. "But my grandfather was passionate about it. He wanted to know where the vines came from, what the grapes were. And because we're so isolated, we have some of the purest biotypes of these grapes that exist." Every new vine at Feudo Montoni is grafted from other vines on the property, a practice going back to the 1800s.

Sireci adds, "For me, the concept of organics is in the word, at least in Italian: *biologico*, which comes from *bios* in Greek, which means life. Yes, it's a tool, it's not putting anything chemical into your vineyard, but what's more important is the sense of contribution to the *bios*, to life. It has to give something to the community as well. Of course, it's important not to kill someone with chemicals when you give them a glass of wine! But where we are, the center of Sicily, is *not* a rich region. It's impoverished. Organics requires much more handwork than conventional agriculture; you need a community to take part in it. And that means I can give twenty employees a good life, a good job, and they won't have to emigrate. Working the way we do, I won't solve the problems of the world, I know. But at least I won't make them worse."

Feudo Montoni's vineyards are located high up, and the result is acidity and freshness, even in Nero d'Avola. "Twenty years ago, people would tell me about our wine, 'This is not Nero d'Avola.' But all they knew were the wines of the coast and south," Sireci says.

About the **Feudo Montoni Della Timpa Grillo ($$)** Melissa Muller says, "There's a typical Sicilian cake that comes from Arabian times here, *cassata*, that's full of candied fruit and color—for me, that's Grillo." The winery's flinty **Vigna del Masso Catarratto ($$)** is "very straight, very cutting, yet very subtle," Sireci says.

There are two Nero d'Avolas, the more affordable being **Lagnusa Nero d'Avola ($$)**. Blackberries, tea leaves, crisp acidity—it's a very bright version of a grape that's often brooding and blunt. **Vrucara ($$$)** comes from a little more than five acres of pre-phylloxera vines that were on the property when Sireci's grandfather bought the land in the 1800s. "We estimate they're over one hundred forty years old," Sireci says. Intensely flavorful, the wine has savory notes of leather and dried herbs plus plenty of velvety dark berry fruit, yet it's not weighty at all. It's one of Sicily's most compelling reds.

GIROLAMO RUSSO • SICILY

[organic]

Giuseppe Russo remembers what the wines of Etna used to be like. His father, who sold charcoal for a living, had a dream of owning a vineyard. Eventually his health made him change his career, and in 1991, at age forty, he invested in a few acres of vineyard on the slopes of Etna.

At the time, Russo says, "there were people who knew how to farm a vineyard well—if there's a tradition here, that's the tradition. But people just made wine for themselves and their family, or maybe to sell to a local bar. The feeling about Etna wine was that it came out in the spring after harvest, and if you didn't drink it by fall, it went off."

Russo's father worked the same way, selling grapes and making a small amount of wine only when he had some fruit left over. "But he died quite suddenly in 2003," Russo says, "while he was in the vineyard. It was a huge shock for me. I was ending work on my thesis at school, and I had to decide what to do—sell off the land, or continue with it, and make his work *my* work."

For a time, he did both, farming, making wine, and teaching literature and music in the local high school. But with each successive harvest, he felt himself grow more connected to making wine and to the land he'd inherited from his father. "I won't say I decided, because I couldn't decide, but the events of my life brought me to wine. And I named my wine Girolamo Russo because of his name, because my father was my fate."

Russo organically farms twenty acres of vineyard on the northern slopes of Etna, planted almost entirely to Nerello Mascalese. It isn't easy: "Etna is very difficult. If you don't respect the volcano, there's no second chance." At first, he says, he looked for ripeness, concentration, and power in his wines, "but while I was looking for that, I found elegance."

In the winery, he uses spontaneous fermentation with native yeasts, very little if any sulfur, no new oak. And his life as a literature teacher and a pianist informs his winemaking as well. "If I'd been an agronomist or an enologist, I couldn't have made the wines I make. Making wine is a matter of analysis, but you also have to understand some nuance, no?" he says. "With winemaking, just in the way that an artist or a composer puts together a piece, you have to start at the beginning, which is the fruit. Then you have to allow yourself to be taken away by *that* specific fruit in *that* specific moment. Each harvest, you have to do this. You have to compose something different. Just like the beauty in music, this is the beauty in winemaking."

The **Girolamo Russo Etna Rosato ($$)** comes from younger Nerello Mascalese vines. Pale pink and zippily fresh, it's hard to resist. The citrusy, herbal **Nerina Etna Bianco ($$)**, named for Giuseppe's mother, is a blend of Carricante, Catarratto, Inzolia, Grecanico, Minnella, and Coda di Volpe. The **'a Rina Etna Rosso ($$)** is not an entry-level wine, Russo says, though it is his most affordable red. Instead, he feels that by blending fruit from three *contradas* (a named vineyard, basically, which may have several owners), he is able to make a sum greater than the parts, a composite picture of Etna terroir. With its red cherry fruit and a light herbal edge, medium-bodied and vibrant with acidity, it's a classic Etna red. His **Feudo Etna Rosso ($$$)** comes from a single *contrada* in Randazzo and is full of cherry-peppery notes, supported by fine-grained tannins. The **San Lorenzo Etna Rosso ($$$)**, by contrast, comes from eighty-plus-year-old vines in a different Randazzo *contrada* and tends to be a bit more delicate, floral and transparent.

PRODUCERS PROFILED IN THIS CHAPTER

Basilicata, Calabria, and Puglia

Elena Fucci

Campania and Molise

Mastroberardino   Quintodecimo

Sicily and Sardinia

Frank Cornelissen   Feudo Montoni
COS   Girolamo Russo
Tenute Dettori

OTHER SOUTHERN ITALY PRODUCERS TO LOOK FOR

Basilicata

Gianfranco Fino   I Pastine
Cantine Madonna delle Grazie   Valentina Passalacqua
Musto Carmelitano

Calabria

'aVita   Giuseppe Calabresi

Campania

Lonardo   Mila Vuolo
Guido Marsella

Sicily

Marco de Bartoli
Benanti
Bosco Falconeria
Calabretta
Il Censo
Criante
Salvo Foti
Graci
Murgo

Arianna Occhipinti
Pala
Passopisciaro
Fattorie Romeo del Castello
Tasca d'Almerita
Tenuta delle Terre Nere
Valle dell'Acate
Aldo Viola

Sardinia

Argiolas
Pala
Santadi

SPAIN

Comando G's Rumbo al Norte Vineyard, Gredos

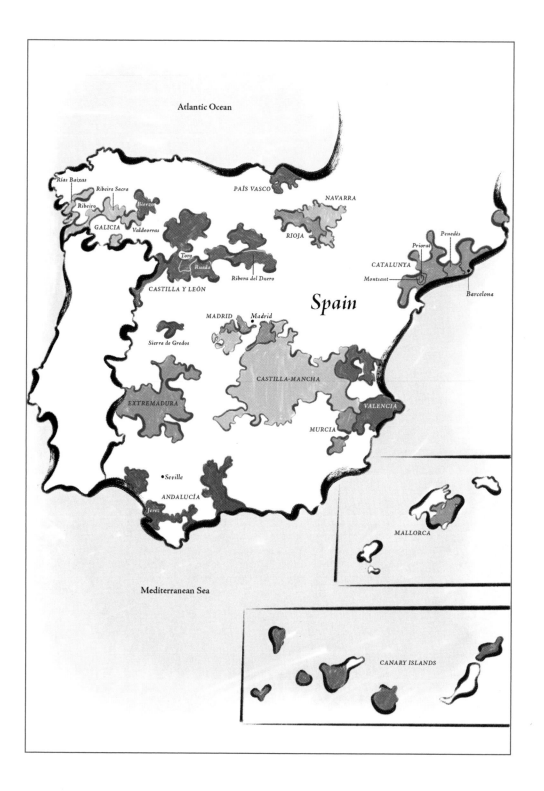

S pain tends, for U.S. wine drinkers, to run last in mind out of the three largest European wine-producing countries. That's not very forgiving, but mass public opinion rarely is. Spanish wine doesn't benefit from our national romance with Italian food and culture, and it doesn't have that vague halo of prestige (deserved or not) that French wine has. (Don't discount the halo: one psychological study poured participants two glasses of exactly the same wine, informing them that one was from California and one from New Jersey, and asked them to rate their relative quality. You can guess the results.)

It's an entirely unfair situation. Spain's wines are fully as adventurous, vibrant, and distinctive as anything found in France and Italy. Younger-generation winemakers are pushing into natural or low-intervention realms, the ongoing project of rediscovering overlooked regions remains robust, and the great wines of Spain are truly some of the great wines of the world. All of that is even more impressive given Spain's late start in the modern wine era. As France and Italy dug themselves out from the destruction of World War II, Spain remained stifled under the dictatorship of Generalissimo Francisco Franco until 1975.

There's no question, especially in classic regions like Rioja, that much of Spain's wine production still lies in the hands of large companies (or regional co-ops) buying fruit from hundreds of small growers. There's also no question that in the late 1990s and early 2000s Spain, like many other places, spent a good measure of its energy producing massive, over-oaked, hyper-extracted reds, particularly at the higher end of the market. But there's ambition everywhere here today, not to mention a vast natural resource of old-vine vineyards that often have survived—perhaps ironically—because of decades of neglect. That may be a bleak way to ensure low-yielding ancient vines aren't ripped out, but it's an effective one, without which some up-and-coming regions like Gredos, in the mountains west of Madrid, would never have achieved their recent fame. Ferment (yes) is everywhere: whether that's winemakers working with indigenous grape varieties in the Canary Islands, ambitious small producers popping up in the corporate cracks in Rioja, or growers focusing on organic or biodynamic practices around the country, it's present, and impossible to ignore.

GALICIA

Galicia doesn't look like "Spain" at all. It looks like Ireland. There are pine forests and rocky coasts, and a kind of Atlantic moodiness that seems very much at odds with passionate Spanish activities like bullfighting and flamenco. Rías Baixas, the most recognized wine region of Galicia, is damp when there isn't rain, and when there is rain, it's just plain wet. Albariño vines thrive here in this drizzly corner of a country mostly known for its arid plains and Mediterranean heat. What's funny about that is that, while Rías Baixas is misty and cool and all gray-green-Atlantic, Albariño itself is pretty much the spot-on embodiment of Galileo's famous saying that "wine is sunlight, held together by water." You could argue that no other grape variety pulls that off so well.

Albariño's success has been a boon for Galicia, which historically has been a poor province. (One reason grape vines were trained so high here in the past was so that people could grow vegetables and raise chickens underneath them from September until June.) Many Albariños are light, simple, and affordable, made by large producers or co-ops, and are released as soon as possible after harvest. But the best Albariños are subtle, layered, minerally whites. And adventurous winemakers in Galicia have also delved into the potential of other local varieties like Godello (particularly in Ribeira and Valdeorras) and the red grape Mencía in Ribeira Sacra, where vineyards cling to the walls of the steep canyons carved by the rivers Miño and Sil, and in stony Monterrei.

DOMINIO DO BIBEI • RIBEIRA SACRA

[certified biodynamic]

A reference point in Ribeira Sacra, Dominio do Bibei was founded in 2001 by proprietor Javier Dominguez. Its seventy-nine acres of vines, which range from fifteen to more than one hundred years old, are planted to the varieties of this rugged part of Galicia, and grow in dauntingly steep, terraced vineyards perched above the Río Bibei, a tributary of the Sil.

In essence, Dominguez says, he has worked to recover the past in this dry region. That means red wines that avoid concentration and lean toward delicacy that, when young, give a sense of what bigger, more extracted wines become once time in the bottle has allowed them to age and become more transparent. "What I remember, from thirty or forty years ago, are these wines, that feeling," he says. "The cut of these wines is Atlantic, without any touch of the Mediterranean."

All the winemaking here is either in concrete or in old, neutral wood. Oak influence is not something Dominguez is after: "Why work so hard and so carefully on a wine, if all you smell in the end is a French forest?" Overall, his winemaking is non-interventionist without heading into the occasional funk of the natural winemaking world. "You have to respect nature, but sometimes you have to use science," he says. Then he tells a story about a biodynamic farming acquaintance who was also deeply invested in homeopathic medicine: "He had an aneurysm, and the doctor said, 'you need an operation,' but he refused. Four days later, *pfft!*" At the same time, Dominguez isn't afraid of the risks inherent in a low-intervention approach: "You have to go deep into your defects, because that way you find your personality. And I prefer to drink a wine with personality over one that is perfect."

Dominio do Bibei's **Lapola ($$)** adds Albariño and a tiny amount of Doña Blanca to Godello for a white that's precise and lightly herbal, wrapping up on a mineral note. **Lalama ($$)** is primarily Mencía, and is floral and red-fruited with a savory edge. **Lacima ($$$)** increases the percentage of old-vine Brancellao in the blend, adding a rocky austerity. The property's top wine, **Dominio do Bibei ($$$)**, 80 percent Brancellao and 20 percent Mouratón, favors ethereality over power, with flowing aromatics and superfine tannins.

DO FERREIRO • RÍAS BAIXAS

[organic]

Drive up to Do Ferreiro, on a drizzly day under a gunmetal sky. The gray Atlantic crashes to your right. By the roadside Albariño vines are trained on granite posts to head height or higher—bunches of grapes, dewed with rain, hang down. The high trellising allows for ventilation and prevents rot, a problem here. But it's exactly this damp, ocean-cooled climate, Gerardo Méndez will tell you, that allows this region to produce the wines it does.

The word *ferreiro* means ironworker in Gallego. Méndez's grandfather worked with iron for a living, though he used to make wine for his friends, and would always offer a glass whenever anyone came over. Today the family is just as hospitable, and Albariño vines—some more than two centuries old—grow outside their house, but their wines are sold throughout the world.

"Albariño is a different kind of white, because it's like a red," Gerardo Méndez says. "You can have it with seafood, but then go on to meat. It's salty, strong-flavored from the sea; Albariño tastes of salinity. With Albariño, when you eat, the wine disappears; when you drink, the food disappears." This last is a bit Yoda-like, but you get the gist.

The **Do Ferreiro Albariño ($$)** is a classic example of Albariño's appeal: salty, zesty, crisp, as suggestive of the Atlantic and the rocks it crashes against as you could wish for. **Do Ferreiro Cepas Vellas ($$$)**, made from a single small vineyard planted in 1785, is complex, layered, age-worthy, electric on the palate, with flavors that last and last. **Do Ferreiro Rebisaca ($$)** is more forwardly fruity, but still retains that Rías Baixas chalky-saline mineral character.

FORJAS DE SALNÉS • RÍAS BAIXAS

[organic]

Forjas de Salnés is one of the most acclaimed among the new wave of Galician producers. Founded by Rodrigo "Rodri" Méndez, its first vintages appeared in 2005; the name is an homage to the Forjas de Salnés ironworks, which Mendez's grandfather, who started life as a blacksmith, built into a major local business.

Méndez, whose uncle Gerardo owns the nearby Do Ferreiro winery, makes stellar Albariños. But perhaps even more significant are Méndez's red wines. During the 1970s and 1980s, as Albariño slowly gained popularity, farmers in Galicia began uprooting the red varieties native to the region—they are often hard to grow and always hard to sell, but Albariño was the opposite. Méndez's grandfather Francisco took a different course. In 1980, instead of ripping out grapes like Caíño, Espadiero, and Loureiro Tinto, he grafted and replanted them. Rodri Méndez, who started helping out in the vineyards as a boy and had learned from him, brought his grandfather's respect for Galician history with him when he founded Forjas.

Méndez farms about thirty acres of vines, most of them venerable, and some, as at his Finca Genoveva vineyard, truly ancient—more than 160 years old. Everything is farmed without chemical interventions other than copper and sulfur and harvested manually. Méndez's friend Raul Perez consults on the winemaking, which is broadly noninterventionist: not much temperature control, native yeasts, and no added enzymes or anything of that ilk.

The largest production wine from Forjas is undoubtedly the **Forjas de Salnés Leirana Albariño ($$)**. Laser-focused, with a kind of glassy minerality, it's a great deal given its modest price. The smaller-production **Leirana Finca Genoveva Albariño ($$$)** comes from a single plot of vines planted in 1862, and is aged on its lees for a year in neutral oak. It's electric with citrus and saline notes, complex and long. The **Cos Pes Albariño ($$$)** uses winemaking techniques from Galicia's past: indigenous fermentation with whole clusters and skins, aging in neutral wood barrels, no fining at all. The result is a very textural, savory expression of Albariño.

For the reds, the entry-level **Goliardo Tinto ($$)**, a blend of Caíño, Espadeiro, Loureiro, and Souson, is light-bodied and savory, full of fresh Atlantic influence. Méndez's **Goliardo Loureiro ($$)** comes from Loureiro vines planted in 1972, it's both black- and green-peppery, with dried herb notes. The tiny-production **Finca Genoveva Tinto ($$)**, from Caíño vines planted in 1862, is Méndez's most profound red. Aromatic and herbal, with dusty earth notes and a bolt of brilliant red fruit that lasts, it's a beautiful expression of Galicia's coast through a red wine lens.

ADEGAS GUÍMARO • RIBEIRA SACRA

[organic]

At one point on a visit to Guímaro, I asked Pedro Rodriguez about the purpose of the large hook that was hanging above the big wooden doors that led into the winery. "Oh, that's for the *matanza*," he said. "When we slaughter the pig. You hang him on the hook so the blood can drain out."

Guímaro is a winery, but more than that it's also a traditional Galician family farm, with chickens, rabbits, pigs, and a substantial patch of vegetables. The Rodriguez family has lived in the area around the tiny town of Brosmos for generations; Pedro's grandparents met in the vineyards. (Guímaro's best wine was once a blend of two vineyards, one inherited from his grandmother's family and one from his grandfather's, but she didn't like that very much, Pedro reports: "She said hers by itself should be the best.")

For many years the Rodriguezes made small quantities of wine only for themselves and to sell in glass *garrafones* to local bars, but in the early 1990s they built their own winery and began bottling their own wines. They called the wine Guímaro after Pedro's grandfather's nickname—the word means "rebel" in Gallego.

Today Rodriguez farms twenty-two acres of his own land, along with forty leased from small growers in the area. Over time he has reduced yields and eliminated the use of chemicals in the vineyards, switching to organic viticulture. He has also started planting heirloom grape varieties, such as Caíño, Merenzao, Souson, and others, in high-elevation sites in the area. Farming here is backbreaking: on the steepest slopes, Rodriguez has to haul the baskets of ripe grapes up on metal tracks using a hand-powered winch.

The **Guímaro Blanco** ($$) is crisp and lively; the **Cepas Viejas** ($$), from older Godello vines, is more textural. The unoaked **Mencía Tinto** ($) is one of the great steals in Spanish wine: fragrant and fresh, a bolt of pure red Mencía fruit. **Camiño Real** ($$) is primarily old-vine Mencía, along with other local varieties. It's fragrant and peppery, filled with vibrant red-fruit flavors. The floral, spicy **Finca Capeliños** ($$$) is perhaps the best of Rodriguez's three single-vineyard reds, and comes from just over an acre of ancient Mencía vines.

PAZO SEÑORANS • RÍAS BAIXAS

[certified organic]

Pazo Señorans could serve as a model for the classic eighteenth-century manor houses of Rías Baixas, with its sunlit courtyards, manicured garden, and commanding view of the region. And its Selección de Añada Albariño could similarly serve as a model for the heights that variety can reach here.

The grapes for Selección de Añada are grown on a small, old-vine parcel directly behind the winery, on shallow soils over what is effectively a solid layer of granite. The wine stays in stainless steel tanks on its lees for an extended period—eighteen months or more—and is stirred regularly. "When we started making Selección Añada in 1995, people thought it was odd," says technical director Ana Quintela Suárez. "White wines were all supposed to be young!" She adds, "What I wanted to recall was the ancient Albariño style, from a time when the wine was kept in big wooden tanks— rounder and richer, perhaps not with such fresh fruit but with much more elegance."

When owner Marisol Bueno and her husband, Javier Marque, bought the property in 1979, the Rías Baixas D.O. (*denominación de origin*) didn't exist. They were instrumental in its creation, and Bueno was the first president of the D.O. (she also ran the winery, furthering a rich tradition of women making wine in Galicia). Today the winery is in the hands of her daughter, Vicky Mareque Bueno, continuing that legacy.

Aromas roll out of a glass of **Pazo Señorans Selección de Añada Albariño ($$$)**—apples and pears, hazelnuts, a cool herbal quality. Underneath everything is a velvety, savory sense of leesiness. There's a polished, stony reserve to this wine, even as it fills your mouth with flavor.

The more affordable, straw-colored, basic **Albariño ($$)** is also impressive; less layered, but bright with tart citrus and stone fruit flavors. Suárez says, "The influence of the sea, six miles away, is very important." She's right: it's as if you can taste the proximity of the Atlantic in the rocky, salty finish.

ZARATE · RÍAS BAIXAS

[organic]

Visit Zarate and you'll find granite posts used to support Eulogio Pomares's Albariño vines. Granite is the story in the Val do Salnés, and about his El Balado Albariño, I once wrote that it tastes of what granite would taste like if granite were made into wine.

Pomares's estate lies close to the sea, on a strip of granite and sand that ends a couple of miles to the east in the stony hills. Outside the sixteenth-century house is a tiny parcel of old, ungrafted vines. "No one quite knows how old they are," Pomares says. "More than a hundred and fifty years, though."

Zarate was founded by Vincente Zarate, who came to Rías Baixas from Rioja in the 1760s, built a house in Cambados, married a local girl, and started a winery. Eulogio is the seventh generation to live on this land. He started making wine himself in 2000, but says, "I was always making wine. When I was four or five, I remember being in big barrels, crushing grapes with my feet." For the first couple of years, he made one wine, then in 2003

he created a second from the tiny El Palomar vineyard (the name means "pigeon house"), which was planted in 1850. Soon he started working with another tiny old vineyard, Balado, where the gnarled, gnome-height vines are encircled by an ancient stone wall.

The Zarate farm encompasses sixty-two acres, but only seventeen of those are planted. Pomares farms no-till organic, with permanent natural cover crop and no use of pesticides or herbicides. He uses shells from the coast in lieu of fertilizers to provide the calcium and magnesium that vines require, and local seaweed goes into his compost. "The only problem," he says, "is the mildew," a standard issue in humid, seaside regions. His top wine, El Palomar, is made in a single 2,300-liter old oak barrel, rather than in the stainless steel tanks typical of Albariño production today. "Rías Baixas is a young region in some ways," he says. "Winemakers now don't realize what the old men were doing before— Albariño is famous because of the wines they made this way."

Eulogio's basic **Zarate Albariño ($$)**, fermented with wild yeast and aged on its lees, is precise and stony. There are three single-parcel whites. **Balado ($$$)**, from vines planted in 1950, tastes more or less like it was carved out of rock rather than vinified. Pomares says, "For me, Zarate is not about fruit; these are mineral wines." **Tras da Viña ($$$)** offers fierce acidity, yet despite that is the most approachable of these three on release. The ancient vines of **El Palomar ($$$)** give it tremendous complexity, and also ageability: eight years after the vintage it's golden-hued, singing with honeysuckle, lemon curd, spice, and savory lees characteristics. Pomares's sole red that arrives in the U.S. is **Fontecón ($$)**, a peppery, herbal blend of Espadeiro and Caiño.

PRODUCERS PROFILED IN THIS CHAPTER

Dominio do Bibei

Do Ferreiro

Forjas de Salnés

Adegas Guímaro

Pazo Señorans

Zarate

OTHER GALICIA PRODUCERS TO LOOK FOR

Adegas Algueira

Daterra Viticultores

Godeval

Gomariz

Nanclares y Prieto

La Perdida

Eladio Pineiro

Quinta da Muradella

Valdesil

RIOJA AND NAVARRA

More than 160,000 acres of vineyards make up Rioja, Spain's most famous wine region, all strung along the meandering course of Spain's longest river, the Ebro, as it cuts its way between the Sierra de Cantabria in the north and the Sierra de la Demanda in the south. This is a region of small family farms, many just an acre or two, and the vast majority of the grapes from those vines still go to local co-ops or large-scale producers. To put it another way, there are more than 14,000 grape growers in Rioja, and only 571 wineries. (Navarra, to the northeast, is even more extreme, with some 27,000 acres of vineyard and only 87 wineries.)

Even so, some of Spain's greatest wines are made here. And more and more producers, large and small alike, are focusing on wines that express the terroir of this place—in a way, what's happening in Rioja is not dissimilar from the rise of grower Champagne, though with less visibility. There's also been an increased interest in organic and sustainable vineyard practices, though the vast majority of vineyards here are still farmed conventionally.

Tempranillo, arguably Spain's greatest red grape, reaches its apogee here, whether in the resolutely old-school wines of López de Heredia, estate-grown expressions by producers such as Remelluri, or in the hands of small-scale grower-vignerons. There's also a new-wave movement of young Rioja producers, who are focusing on site and ecologically friendly farming techniques. Their wines are a distinct departure both from traditional Rioja as well as from the oaky, super-rich *alta expresión* wines of the 2000s.

361

ÁLVARO PALACIOS • RIOJA, PRIORAT, AND BIERZO

[organic]

Álvaro Palacios owns wineries in three regions spread across the north of Spain. When he's not in Rioja, his home, he's in the Priorat, where he helped build a forgotten region into a world-class source of Grenache-based reds; when he's not in the Priorat, he's in Bierzo, making wine from precipitous, ancient vineyards strung in a jewel-like chain across the steep hills. "During harvest, I drive twelve hundred miles every week," he says. "It's crazy. But what else can you do?"

Palacios was born in 1964 and grew up at his family's Rioja winery, Herencia Remondo (now Palacios Remondo), the seventh of nine children. He began working in the winery shop at age ten, refilling six-liter carafes with cheap Rioja for the truck drivers passing through town. By his twentieth birthday, he was helping with the winery's exports, heading off to England, France, and the United States. But he wasn't content. At that time, trends in Rioja were toward as much production as possible, as much mechanization as possible, and wines that were essentially industrial products. "My father had

turned me into the perfect machine," Palacios says. "I had every skill I needed to run the winery, and what did I do? I told him, 'Dad, I'm moving to Priorat to make my own wine.' I can't imagine how I'd feel if a child of mine said that to me."

That was in 1989. The person who had first realized the Priorat's potential was René Barbier (later the founder of Clos Mogador), who happened to work in the export department at Herencia Remondo. "My father and René, those two guys were my heroes," Palacios says. "But they were completely different. My father was very correct, very traditional. René was a total hippie. We'd tour around Europe together doing sales trips in his old motor home."

Barbier's enthiusiasm for the Priorat drew in several other young winemakers as well, and the wines that they made in the Priorat brought them worldwide acclaim. "We knew this was going to be a great region," Palacios recalls. "Garnacha is one of the few grapes that can transform heat and aridity into something vibrant, complex, and refreshing. No one wanted it in the old times because the yields were so low."

Ten years later Palacios's nephew Ricardo told him about another impoverished region with long-ignored, old-vine vineyards, on the other side of Spain: Bierzo. Ask Palacios about it, and he'll make a kind of what-can-you-do gesture. "I always go to places that are beautiful and that have slopes, hillsides, and mules and horses for farming. It's the egoist in me, too. There's nobody there, so you get to be first."

Descendientes de J. Palacios focuses on the Mencía grape, producing complex reds with the tensile strength of Bordeaux and the aromatic nuance of Burgundy from stubby, hundred-year-old vines near the small town of Corullón. "Bierzo is a mystic, religious place," Palacios says. It's also even steeper than the Priorat—his Corullón vineyard is a one-wrong-step-and-you're-gone place, stuck so far up in the hills that even the locals told him he'd never get ripe fruit off of it. "It's extreme viticulture," he admits.

In 2000, Palacios's father died, and he immediately returned to Alfaro, in Rioja, to help run (and, eventually, take charge of) the family winery. He has no regrets: "You always remember the town where you first ate bread. That's home. Priorat is where I made myself, but Rioja is where I was born."

He cut production at Palacios Remondo from 2 million bottles a year to eight hundred thousand, and started concentrating on estate fruit. He also followed his passion for Garnacha. Tempranillo is king in Rioja; it's like Cabernet Sauvignon in Napa Valley. Garnacha is usually used as a blending grape, to moderate Tempranillo's tannins and add some juiciness. Yet Palacios soon began grafting all of the winery's Tempranillo vines over to Garnacha. He firmly believes that the climate and land of Rioja Orientale (formerly Rioja Baja) aren't really suited to Tempranillo.

"Some people say about a wine like La Montesa—our flagship wine, which is 90 percent Garnacha—that it's not Rioja. But it's from Rioja! When I first started replanting, I talked to some of the old farmers in Alfaro. They'd say to me, 'Alvarito, what are you doing up there? It looks like you're planting green beans.' But then they tasted La Montesa and said, 'Ah—that's what Rioja here used to be like.' My life has been about finding these flavors."

Palacios makes a substantial range of wines from Bierzo, the Priorat, and Rioja. Some, like his legendary L'Ermita, are stupendously expensive (as in $1,000-a-bottle expensive). But most range between $30 and $120 or so, and they're excitingly expressive no matter which property they're from.

In Priorat, the **Álvaro Palacios Finca Dofi** ($$$$) is his flagship wine, made from the first vineyard he worked with there (then known as Clos Dofi), from biodynamic fruit. It's Garnacha with a small percentage of Carignan and a tiny percentage of white grapes, complex and rich with flavor. His **Vi de Vila Gratallops** ($$$) is the equivalent of a village wine in Burgundy, made with grapes from six different organic, old-vine plots near the town of Gratallops. The **Les Terraces V.V. Priorat** ($$$), a sixty-forty blend of old-vine Grenache and Carignan, comes primarily from Palacios's estate vineyards, plus a small amount of purchased old-vine fruit.

From Bierzo, the fragrant **Descendientes de J. Palacios Villa de Corullon** ($$$), from biodynamic or organic old-vine vineyards around the village, is, like the Gratallops, what Palacios would consider a "village" wine. There are also two single-vineyard wines priced similarly to Finca Dofi, **Las Lamas** ($$$) and **Moncerbal** ($$$). Both are superb. (La Faraona, the top of the range, is priced stratospherically. Stick to the others, unless you win the lottery.)

In Rioja, the **Palacios Remondo La Montesa** ($) is an absurd steal. It's a brilliant, lively glass full of cherry and raspberry flavors, a total pleasure to drink. **La Propiedad** ($$), from old-vine estate fruit, is deeper and more complex. **Plácet Valtemolloso** ($$$), the sole white that Palacios makes, is 100 percent Viura. It's a succulent, pale golden wine that ages better than one might guess. Finally, Palacios makes three inexpensive (but very good) wines from purchased grapes, one from each property: **Petalos de Bierzo** ($), **Camins del Priorat** ($$), and **La Vendimia** ($) in Rioja. They are all excellent introductions to his style and sensibility.

GRANJA NUESTRA SEÑORA DE REMELLURI • RIOJA

[certified organic]

Remelluri is one of the great estates of Rioja. Wine has been made here since the 1300s, when the Hieronymite monks who lived in the Nuestra Señora de Toloño monastery, high atop a nearby mountain, founded a farm on the site. The modern era of Remelluri starts in 1967 with Jaime Rodríguez Salís, a writer and archaeologist, and his wife, Amaia, a writer and artist. Their first wine was released in 1971, though as their son Telmo Rodriguez, who has run the estate since 2009 with his sister Amaia Rodriguez Hernandorena, says, "Yes, 1971, a terrible year! Which came just after the legendary Rioja vintage of 1970. But in 1970, my father sold all his grapes to the co-op in Bastida. Oh well!"

Telmo oversees the winemaking (along with running an abundance of his own projects throughout Spain); Amaia, who lives there, oversees the viticulture. The property, which lies in the foothills of the Sierra de Toloño mountains, is one of the most beautiful in Rioja. From the uppermost vineyard you can see the Ebro Valley laid out before you; look the other way, and the ruins of the old monastery are visible atop the crags. Seeing them immediately makes you wonder how the hell any monks got up there in the first place, much less built an entire monastery.

Organic farming has been the rule since the 1970s, with the entire production certified organic since 2014. In addition to grapevines, almond, peach, fig, and olive trees grow, beehives hum, and native plant growth throughout the property is encouraged. Essentially, Amaia works in line with the basic principle of biodynamics—that the estate is a unified ecological whole—and utilizes some biodynamic practices, but isn't trying to be "biodynamic" per se.

Remelluri's 275 acres of vines are divided into more than 100 individual parcels. All are vinified separately with indigenous yeasts and minimal intervention. The **Lindes de Remelluri** (\$\$) wines are a pair of impressive and relatively affordable reds made with non-estate fruit from farmers in two villages (Labastida and San Vicente) the family has long worked with. The flagship **Remelluri Rioja Reserva ($$)** is a layered, complex, entirely absorbing expression of the entire estate, both powerful and elegant. The **Rioja Gran Reserva ($$$)** comes from the oldest vines on the property. It's often brooding and backward on release, but tremendously complex with age. And the **Rioja Blanco ($$$$)**, though pricey, is unlike any other Spanish white. For it, Telmo Rodriguez decided he wanted to erase the question of grape variety by co-planting nine different grape varieties in eleven different sites around the estate (to this day, he's cagey about the specifics). It manages to be both fresh and luscious at once, a dizzying swirl of flavor ending on distinct mineral notes.

R. LÓPEZ DE HEREDIA • RIOJA

[organic]

"We have letters from my great-grandfather to his sons," María José López de Heredia says. "Thousands of letters. Giving them advice, telling them what he knew, questioning them, testing them. And in every single letter he wrote about the pride he had in Viña Tondonia. There are a million clues in each one about how this vineyard, for him, exemplified quality. Every single letter is a lesson, an explanation of this gorgeous philosophy about doing things well."

Her great-grandfather Rafael López de Heredia y Landeta founded Bodegas López de Heredia in 1877. It is a singular place, with a singular philosophy; in many ways, when you taste the wines or when you visit the old cellars, their ancient walls covered in black mold, you feel that time has stopped. But as María José says, "It's not that we are determined not to change, but that we choose to get to know our history, to respect it, and to change it to the minimum possible.

"I have known so many people in wineries, they employ a new winemaker and suddenly that person says, well! We can *improve* these wines! But for me, saying that you have improved something means that it was not good enough before. It's a matter of respect: for me, for the work my father did, the work my grandfather did, that my great-grandfather did, that our ancestors did." At the same time, she notes, it's impossible to re-create the past. You can't work with oxen, the way vineyard workers did here in the 1920s; you wouldn't try plowing your vineyard with a plow from the 1800s. "That's being romantic and, allow me to say, a bit stupid." María José is nothing if not direct.

She, her sister Mercedes, and their brother Rafael are the current caretakers of the family's bodega and its vineyards. The past is unquestionably present here: fermentation still happens in large, old, wooden vats, many dating back to the 1800s; aging occurs in the maze-like underground cellar, in American oak barrels coopered at the winery; mold covers the walls and cobwebs drip from the ceilings. In the vineyards, the farming is organic, with some biodynamic practices, but, María José says, "we're not officially biodynamic, because biodynamics seems to me a religion. I agree 100 percent with the philosophy, though."

Only native yeasts are used, the wines are not filtered, and if the reds are fined, egg whites are used. "People ask us, do you have wines for vegans?"

She sighs. "Yes, we have wines that are not fined. But we won't make a marketing issue out of something that we have been doing forever. And we don't adapt our wines to the market's demands."

In the past decade or so, López de Heredia's wines have been more successful than ever before. They are released, as they always have been, when the family feels they are ready to drink, typically years after the vintage. They are a picture of a Rioja that once was, yet that is somehow still current. The past echoes forward into the present. "We made wine throughout the Spanish Civil War," María José says. "Very bad wine, I assume, because the vines were basically abandoned—there was no money to pay the workers—but, somehow, we made wine. But today, look at Ukraine: How are we living in the twenty-first century with this going

"We've disappointed a lot of people: Why don't we do something more modern? But we've never wanted to do something different, because we like and respect so much what we did in the past."
—María José López de Heredia

on? And somehow our importer there is still selling wine. I thought, the other day, how can anyone in the middle of such a war still sell wine? But in the middle of the Civil War here, we were living, and still selling wine; people were killing each other, but at the same time people were living, and falling in love, and having children. They kept on going."

Which is what López de Heredia does: it keeps on going. And, as María José says, "Years of experience, if you are not a fool, do mean something."

López de Heredia makes wine from three vineyards, Tondonia (about 247 acres), Bosconia (37 acres), and Cubillas (59 acres). Tondonia is the most famous, and sits above the right bank of the Ebro at sixteen hundred feet altitude, looking across to the town of Haro and the winery. Bosconia is about a mile away; Cubillas, two miles. The **Viña Cubillo Crianza ($$)** is the bodega's most affordable red. It's firmly but not aggressively tannic, with lovely red cherry and leather notes. Moving up, the **Viña Bosconia Reserva ($$)** spends five years in barrel and four in bottle before release, its deeper aroma and flavors suggesting black cherries and baking spices. The **Viña Tondonia Reserva ($$$)** is the flagship, from the vineyard that Rafael López de Heredia y Landeta first planted in 1877. Complex and layered, it seems to dance between youth and age; a kind of elegant tension that's hard to put into words, but is definitely a pleasure to drink. **Gran Reservas ($$$$)** of both Bosconia and Tondonia are released only in great years, and after lengthy aging— ten years in barrel, and at least nine in bottle. They are both sublime wines, Bosconia a bit richer, Tondonia more classically austere.

Then there are the whites. Even the most youthful, the **Viña Gravonia Crianza Blanco ($$)** spends four years in barrel and five years in bottle before release, giving it notes of toasted nuts and citrus flowers. The **Viña Tondonia Reserva Blanco ($$$$)** is aged even longer, six years in barrel and six in bottle, resulting in a tremendously complex aged white. It's more or less impossible to describe, but a melange of stone fruit, caramel, honeysuckle, and toasted nuts gives an idea. Finally, there's the winery's unicorn-like **Viña Tondonia Gran Reserva Rosé ($$$$)**—unicorn-like in that these days it's rare enough that people justifiably wonder if it actually exists. Suffice to say, it's a stellar rosé, and after four years in barrel and five in bottle, nothing like the pale-pink, mass-market bottles that tend to fuel that market.

PRODUCERS PROFILED IN THIS CHAPTER

Álvaro Palacios

Granja Nuestra Señora
 de Remelluri

R. López de Heredia

OTHER RIOJA AND NAVARRA PRODUCERS TO LOOK FOR

Finca Allende

Anza

Bodegas Aroa

Viñedos Hontza

Bodegas Muga

Marques de Murrieta

La Rioja Alta

Olivier Riviere

Sierra de Toloño

Viña Zorzal

CASTILLA Y LEÓN

The Duero River, which becomes the Douro in Portugal, meanders west through the northern plateau of Spain before dropping in altitude and traversing gorges and canyons as it heads toward the border between the two countries. The middle stretch of the river is bounded by vineyards, principally those of Ribera del Duero and Toro, where the red Tempranillo grape (known locally as Tinto Fino or Tinto de Toro) is dominant, and Rueda, where the white Verdejo grape grows, and it more or less bisects the large region of Castilla y León.

Ribera del Duero is an arid place—it's one of the highest altitude wine regions in Europe—with bitterly cold winters and blazing summers. In 1985, there were only nine wineries here; today there are many more. Like most Spanish red wine regions, it went through a late-1990s to early-2000s period of making massive, super-extracted wines, but thankfully that has calmed down. There's now a focus on finding more balance, on wines that bolster the region's red fruit juiciness with bright, firm acidity.

Rueda is all about Verdejo, a grape whose citrus flavors recall those of Sauvignon Blanc without that variety's signature grassy-bell-pepper character. Plenty of non-descript Verdejo is grown for co-op production, and is pleasant but forgettable. But a few producers here are more ambitious, working organically and with an eye on terroir.

The history of Toro's wines stretches back centuries. They were the drink of choice at the University of Salamanca, founded in the 1200s; they accompanied

Christopher Columbus on his voyages to the New World. As late as 1719, Jean de Vayrac wrote in his *Etat présent de l'Espagne où l'on voit Géographie Historique du Pays*, in an account of a visit to Spain, "Toro is home to the most luscious wines and the most beautiful women." That assessment might not fly today, but as it comes from an eighteenth-century Frenchman, you have to make some allowances.

Bierzo, which though it owes a lot to Galicia in both climate and the style of its wines, politically resides in Castilla y León; the mountains surrounding it separate it from Asturias to the north and Galicia to the west. In a sense, it's a transitional place, making wines that are neither as powerful as those of Ribera del Duero or Toro, but not as cool-climate Atlantic as those of Rías Baixas, for instance. The aromatic, graceful Mencía grape drives most of Bierzo's reds, and whites are largely made from Godello, but there are smatterings of other varieties planted as well.

Lastly there's Sierra de Gredos or, as it is most often simply called, Gredos. Gredos is one of Spain's most exciting wine regions right now, and all of that excitement is centered around Garnacha (Grenache) and the transparent, minerally, delicately complex wines it makes from the region's mountainous vineyards.

Officially, Gredos is not a legal appellation, partly because it exists in three separate adjoining provinces (Toledo, Avila, and Madrid) and thus is under three different political jurisdictions. But geographically it's a whole. Daniel Landi, co-winemaker for Comando G and a Gredos native, says, "Politicians love borders. But those don't apply here. To put it simply, Gredos is the mountains. The grapes don't care what political province they're in." Consequently, labels may say Vinos de Madrid, D.O. Mentrida, Sierra de Gredos, or any of a variety of other designations. It's a little confusing, but the fact that politicians love borders often results in confusion (or worse).

Vineyards here are usually at two thousand to four thousand feet, planted both in the foothills of the Sierra de Gredos and in narrow, rock-choked mountain valleys. This is hard land, all granite and sand, bitterly cold in the winter and hot in the summer. But, as in the Priorat twenty years ago, the extremes of the climate and soil in Gredos are now being translated into some of Spain's most compelling wines.

DOMINIO DE ÁGUILA • RIBERA DEL DUERO

[certified organic]

It takes a certain amount of chutzpah, or talent, or determination, or some magical combination of all three to travel to Burgundy as a winemaking student and somehow convince Domaine de la Romanée-Conti to take you on as an intern, but that's exactly what Águila founder, Jorge Monzón, did. After coming home to Ribera del Duero, Monzón took the terroir-focused sensibility he'd acquired at DRC and brought it to bear on the vineyards near his home town of La Aguilera.

He and his wife, Isabel Rodero, founded Dominio de Águila in 2010. They focus on old-vine parcels largely abandoned or ignored by larger producers; the sort of vineyards that in different parts of Spain in different eras have fueled the ascension of regions like Priorat and Gredos. Yesterday's leavings are today's treasures, when it comes to the nuance and complexity of old-vine cuvées.

Today Monzón and Rodero organically farm seventy-five acres of extremely old vines and an additional twelve acres of younger vines (they sell grapes to local wineries in addition to making their own wine). They follow organic practices, and also borrow some biodynamic/holistic approaches like using herbal extracts from valerian and mielenrama to help vine health.

Dominio de Águila's **Pícaro del Águila Clarete ($$)** is an exploration of a classic Spanish style of light red wine (not exactly rosé, but not exactly not, either). Red and white grapes—Tempranillo, Bobal, Garnacha, and Blanca del País—are foot-trodden, macerated on the skins for a day or two, then fermented and aged in neutral oak barrels. The **Pícaro del Águila Tinto ($$)** is a similar co-fermented blend of red and white grapes that spends longer on the skins, extracting an intense ruby color. The red **Reserva ($$$)** is 95 percent Tempranillo with a host of other varieties, from their oldest vines. It's floral and fragrant, full of deep wild-berry flavors. Finally, there's a remarkably minerally, salty, honeyed **Albillo Viñas Viejas Blanco ($$$$)**.

Albillo more or less means "the white grapes that grow here." Given that the vines are more than a hundred years old, that makes perfect sense.

BERNABELEVA • GREDOS

[biodynamic]

Bernabeleva's story starts in the early 1920s, when Dr. Vicente Álvarez-Villamil purchased a small estate high in the foothills at the eastern edge of the Gredos Mountains. He named it Bernabeleva, or the Path of the Bear, after the Celtic carvings of bears on boulders around the property, and he planted Grenache vines with the hope of making distinctive wine from them. But Spain's Civil War in the late 1930s put an end to that dream.

His family held on to the land, though, and in 2006 two of his great-grandchildren, Juan-Diez Buines and Santiago Matallana Buines, started rehabilitating the now-eighty-year-old vines. Today the family owns about eighty-six acres in Dr. Álvarez-Villamil's original Cantocuerdas Vineyard: the almost one-hundred-year-old Garnacha and Albillo vines he planted, plus younger plots of Macabeo, Garnacha Blanca, Malvar, and Moscatel de Grano Menudo. Vines are often farmed with mules, working according to the phases of the moon, and each parcel is vinified separately, using native yeasts and very little new oak.

The Bernabeleva wines are superb across the board: elegant, weightless, aromatic. As an introduction look for the **Camino de Navaherreros ($)**, which uses Grenache from all of the estate's vineyards. It's a stellar deal. The **Navaherreros Tinto ($$)** is a blend from the estate's older parcels, with more intensity though not more weight. **Navaherreros Blanco ($$)**, the only white currently imported to the U.S., is primarily Albillo with a little Macabeo. Of the single-parcel wines, which are made in quite small amounts, the elegant but powerful **Arroyo de Tortolas ($$)** comes from a steep, tiny plot of sixty-five-plus-year-old Grenache planted at about twenty-four hundred feet; **Viña Bonita ($$$)**, from a plot of Grenache planted in 1929, is more shimmering and ethereal. Taste the two side by side if you can.

PAGO DE CARRAOVEJAS / OSSIAN VIDES Y VINOS • RIBERA DEL DUERO / RUEDA

[sustainable / certified organic]

Pago de Carraovejas was the inspiration of Seville-based restaurateur José María Ruiz, who was looking for the perfect wine to serve with the classic dish of his region, roast suckling pig (*cochinillo*). That quest led him to Ribera del Duero, where instead of simply buying some wine, he founded a winery on twenty-two acres of vineyards outside Peñafiel.

That was in 1987. Today the estate is run by his son, Pedro Ruiz, who has developed several other wineries as well, among them his Ossian project in Rueda. Carraovejas is large, nearly 350 acres, but is farmed organically in its entirety.

Ossian, which Pedro Ruiz purchased in 2016, lies an hour southwest. Most Rueda Verdejo is pleasant-to-anonymous, industrial-production wine. Ossian is the opposite. Its heart is twenty-two acres of one-hundred- to two-hundred-year-old, pre-phylloxera Verdejo vines, situated at the highest altitude in Rueda and farmed organically since the winery started in 2005. It's the oldest certified organic vineyard in Rueda, not to mention one of the oldest vineyards, period, anywhere.

Pago de Carraovejas's principal wine is the **Pago de Carraovejas Ribera del Duero ($$$)**. It's a picture of the entire estate, dark-fruited and velvety, with light vanilla-coconut aromas from a mix of French and American oak barrels.

The floral, vivid **Ossian Quintaluna ($$)** is a remarkable deal, given a good percentage of old-vine fruit goes into it. **Ossian Viñas Viejas ($$)** comes entirely from the estate's ancient Verdejo vines. It's bright and piercing, then in the mouth it's surprisingly rich and layered, somehow creamy despite the crisp acidity. Finally, there's **Capitel ($$$$)**, from a single small plot of pre-phylloxera vines, more than 150 years old. It's very fine and complex, akin to the Viñas Viejas but with even more depth.

COMANDO G • GREDOS

[certified organic / certified biodynamic]

Snow-covered mountains rising up into the sky. Soil that looks utterly unforgiving. Stubby, gnarled, ancient Grenache vines eking out survival among the stones. "The weather is extreme—mountain weather," Comando G's cofounder Daniel Landi says. The region is poor. At the entrance to one farm, a set of old mattress springs is being used as a gate, secured with wire. "They reuse everything. Because there is no money. None." This is Gredos. "We came from disaster," Landi says, "but there was great potential."

Madrid is only an hour away, but here in the mountains west of the city it's a different world. When Landi and his friend and fellow winemaker Fernando García started in the early 2000s, Gredos was almost abandoned. What wine there was, he recalls, came from a local co-op producing modest amounts largely sold in bulk, or from his family's own small estate, which had essentially been abandoned. "I grew up hearing our lands were bad lands," Landi says. "When I was young, I felt like everyone thought this. The price of grapes was so low you couldn't possibly live on it. And when we started, everyone in the town felt the same way. 'You're here, doing agriculture? You are at the bottom of the bottom. You'll never make great wine here.'"

But Landi and García had a passion—Grenache—and because Landi had grown up here, he knew Gredos harbored ancient Grenache vines. (Like a lot of old vines in Spain, they had never been pulled out, simply because the value of the land itself had dropped so much that replanting made no sense.) Everyone young had moved to the city. Landi and García, perversely, moved back.

They started Comando G in 2009. Both had full-time jobs, but every Tuesday they'd head out after work, driving to different villages, looking for vines: high-altitude, north-facing, ancient vineyards. Older farmers thought they were crazy, and told them to stop being stupid and to buy vineyards nearer to the villages.

"We spent ten years being explorers in a free land," Landi says. Thanks to the success of their wines, there's much more competition for vineyards these days. But even with that, "Gredos is one of the only places left in Europe with grand cru vineyards that are still cheap."

The two have worked organically and biodynamically since the start. In terms of winemaking, Landi says, "We're looking for freshness. Minerality is the most important thing. Fruity wines are not what we're after. Fruit is important, sure, but the mineral is crucial. When the stones talk, you listen."

As for the name, officially Comando G comes from Gredos, granite, and Grenache. But the actual origin lies with a character from a cartoon series both Landi and García watched when they were growing up. "Comando G was on a team of five guys trying to save the universe," Landi says. "So, we were two guys trying to save the universe from Cabernet. It was Comando Garnacha."

The Comando G wines have become more and more sought after in recent years, but the introductory-level **La Bruja de Rozas** ($$) is still fairly available. Medium-to-light-bodied, with wild herb and berry aromas and flavors, it's a profound bargain. The **Rozas 1er Cru** ($$$) comes from fifty-to-sixty-year-old vines grown at three thousand feet in the Valle de Tiétar; it's similar to La Bruja, with more structure and complexity.

The grand cru wines from Landi and García have become alarmingly expensive, but they're too sublime to leave out. **Las Umbrías** ($$$$) is the lightest and most delicate, pale ruby in color, with a gossamer weightlessness and pure strawberry notes. "It's a red wine with the soul of a white wine," García says, "because it's about texture, not tannins and extraction." **Tumba del Rey Moro** ($$$$), which translates rather exotically as "Tomb of the King of the Moors," is less herbal, leaning more toward spiced red fruit; it comes from a 1.7-acre vineyard in the Alto Alberche sub-region. **El Reventón ($$$$)** is darker and fuller, chewier, with North African spice notes (cinnamon, allspice, pepper). "This is on slate, not granite," Landi says. "It's our Priorat. It's *not* Priorat, but it's our version of it." Their most acclaimed wine, **Rumbo al Norte ($$$$)**, comes from a sandy three-quarter-acre vineyard filled with huge boulders. "There are more stones than vines," García says. This is not remotely an exaggeration: the place looks like the surface of the moon. Tense and withholding when young, after a few years the wine opens up to supple, saturated flavors, somehow staying transparently ethereal as well. Production is minuscule, unfortunately.

BODEGAS Y VIÑEDOS RAÚL PÉREZ • BIERZO

[organic]

Raúl Pérez makes his home in the rugged, northwestern Spanish region of Bierzo, but his influence extends across all of Spain. He got his start in 1994 as the winemaker at his family's property, Castro Ventosa, when he was twenty-two. A little more than a decade later,

> **"It's not whether a wine is better or worse, it's whether a wine has personality."**
> —Raúl Pérez

he created his own winery; in short order he also became the consulting winemaker for some of Spain's best wineries.

Pérez was born in the town of Valtuille de Abajo in Bierzo. It's a place where most people labor in the vineyards; where for a midmorning snack, workers head to a café for a bowl of tripe in olive oil and a coffee with a shot of *orujo*, the local grape brandy, then head back to the vines. Pérez's family has farmed here for more than two hundred years.

That rootedness is deceptive, though. Pérez makes wines throughout Spain, in Asturias and Cantabria;

in Ribeira Sacra, where he helps out his friend Pedro Rodriguez at Guímaro; in Monterrei; in Rías Baixas; and he also has projects in various Portuguese regions, along with some in Bordeaux and Argentina. Ask him when he sleeps, and he says, quite cheerfully, "Almost never."

Pérez's own wines appear under the Bodegas y Viñedos Raúl Pérez label. Farming for his own vineyards is organic, though not certified. Generally speaking, Pérez is not one to follow anyone else's rules, but his general philosophy is that everything he does should be in tune with the environment, both viticulturally and also in the winery, where he fine-tunes his approach to each specific site.

The earthy, peppery **Viñedos Raúl Pérez Ultreia Saint Jacques ($)** is one of the great bargains of the wine world. A blend of Mencía with tiny amounts of Bastardo (Trousseau) and Garnacha Tintorera (Alicante Bouschet), it is, he says, "the best overall representation of Bierzo wine." **Ultreia Godello ($$)** is the white counterpart to Saint Jacques, lean and minerally, and usually very low in alcohol. Perez's La Vizcaina project concentrates on hillside areas around his hometown. The **La Vizcaina La Poulosa ($$)** shows dusty, crunchy blue fruit with a tea-leafy end. The **La Vizcaina El Rapolao ($$$)** comes from a tiny parcel of forty-five-year-old vines and has more of a dark cherry and licorice character. Both are Mencía with small percentages of Bastardo and Garnacha Tintorera. **El Pecado ($$$)**, Pérez's most acclaimed red, is made at the Guimaró winery in Ribeira Sacra from half a hectare of one-hundred-plus-year-old vines (mostly Mencía). There are simply too many other wines from Pérez to cover all of them, but it's worth noting his **Sketch Albariño ($$$$)**, which gained notoriety for being aged underwater off the Galician coast (he actually only ages thirty bottles per year underwater, not all of it, Pérez says). Regardless, the sixty-plus-year-old vines themselves are "right in front of the sea—you could jump in." The wine mingles tropical and citrus fruit, smoky and full-bodied but lifted by powerful acidity. Pérez says he started making it because he was having problems with stress. "My doctor said, 'Go to the sea! Don't work! But I saw the grapes, and . . .'" That's Raúl Pérez in a nutshell. His doctor, he adds, was really pissed off at him about this.

PRODUCERS PROFILED IN THIS CHAPTER

Dominio de Águila

Bernabeleva

Pago de Carraovejas / Ossian
  Vides Y Vinos

Comando G

Bodegas y Viñedos Raúl
  Pérez

OTHER CASTILLA Y LEON PRODUCERS TO LOOK FOR

4 Monos

Alvar de Dios

Rubén Díaz

Gulp/Hablo

Penalba Herraiz

M. Isart

Orly Lumbreras

Bodega Marañones

Viña Mein

Mengoba

MicroBio Wines

Hacienda Monasterio

Daniel Ramos

Finca Torremilanos

Finca Villacreces

CATALUNYA AND THE MEDITERRANEAN COAST

The long Mediterranean coast of Spain and its inland wine regions represent a wildly varied realm of styles, grape varieties, and historical approaches. The proximity of the sea and the climate it brings inform much of what is produced here, from Empordà on the Spanish border down to Murcia in the south.

Unfortunately, though there are distinctive independent winemakers throughout, the bulk of the wines produced in the two southernmost regions, Valencia and Murcia, are more or less exactly that—bulk wines, inexpensive and relatively pleasant, but unexciting. There's potential here, but it remains somewhat obscured.

Catalunya is a different story. Its independent political spirit seems to shade over into its wines as well. While the vast majority of affordable, sparkling Cava made in Penedès is resoundingly generic, the region is also chock-full of creative, noncorporate, even brilliant talents, making complex sparkling wines along with ambitious reds and whites from Garnacha, Monastrell, Xarel·lo, and a bevy of other local grapes. Plantings of ancient vines, particularly Garnacha, in the inland regions of Terra Alta, Costers del Segre, and Conca de Barberà also produce bottles worth seeking out. And then there's the Priorat, one of Spanish wine's greatest success stories, and Montsant, which encircles it.

Regarding the Priorat, rarely has a wine region shot so rapidly from utter invisibility to world renown. Before 1989, what reputation the Priorat had was as little more than a supplier of dark, hefty blending wines to producers in other regions, and even that business was fading. Vineyards were abandoned. It was impossible for winemakers even to earn a subsistence living on their meager fruit. The idea of making fine wine here was, seemingly, absurd. The transcendent origins of this beautiful, austere, rocky region—the monastery at Scala Dei was founded in the thirteenth century after monks saw a vision of a golden ladder rising into Heaven—were long since forgotten.

So, enter a second vision, thanks to a group of young, renegade winemakers led by René Barbier, at the time the export manager for Rioja's Palacios Remondo winery, but whose family had roots in the area going back to the 1800s. Barbier saw potential: old-vine Cariñena and Grenache, their roots diving deep for nutrients and water into the rocky, slate-chunked hillsides; useless for large-production commercial wines, possibly perfect for great, site-expressive reds.

Barbier convinced a group of winemaker friends to join him, and attention came quickly. By the late 1990s, Priorat reds were among the most sought after in Spanish wine. That buzz subsided in the late 2000s, but the region still makes wines that justify the acclaim: big yet balanced, full of dark cherry and blackberry fruit, their richness counterpointed by underlying minerality. When Priorat wines are well made, that abundant fruit stays fresh, and though they are close to or beyond 15 percent alcohol in most cases, you probably won't notice (unless you drink an entire bottle). The best producers have pulled back both on new oak and ripeness without losing the heart of what makes these wines special.

In a way, visually, the Priorat recalls the hinterlands of New Mexico or Arizona: scrub, dust, tough little trees. There were more than twelve thousand acres of grape vines planted here before phylloxera struck in the late 1800s. By 1989, there were a little less than two thousand. Today, there are about five thousand acres. And despite the success (and price) of the wines, this is not a polished wine region. The towns still sometimes seem almost empty. During the day, you can listen to the church bell in the town square of Gratallops, population 175, marking the hours. At night, you'll hear nothing but wind, or silence.

GRAMONA • PENEDÈS

[certified biodynamic (estate fruit); certified organic (contract fruit)]

Though officially founded in 1921, Gramona dates back to 1881, when Pau Battle founded Celler Battle. The thought was to sell sparkling wine to France, whose vineyards at that time were being ravaged by phylloxera. Xavier Gramona says, "My grandfather realized that the Xarel·lo grape was the only one that could travel to France without oxidation. So he decided that if he built a cellar, he could become wealthy."

Gramona sources grapes from about 750 acres of organic vineyard. The family's own 178 acres are biodynamic. Sustainability efforts beyond organics and biodynamics are also key to their approach: using geothermal energy; recycling all water used at the estate; raising horses, cows, and sheep in the middle of their vineyard holdings to provide manure for compost and ingredients for biodynamic preps (they plow about a third of their own land by horse); using lighter bottles to reduce their wines' carbon footprint. All without sacrificing quality on the altar of production and, Xavier says with a smile, without accepting the primacy of some other sparkling wine regions. "The paradigm of Champagne being the only great sparkling wine has to change. You can make great sparkling wine anywhere in the world if you have the right terroir and the right grape varieties."

Though Gramona primarily makes sparkling wines, it also produces very good still wines. **Gramona Gessamí** ($), an aromatic white blend of Sauvignon Blanc, Muscat, and Gewürztraminer is a steal at about $20. **Mart Rosat** ($$) is a salmon-hued wine made from the rare Xarel·lo Vermell variety (a pink-skinned variant); it's tart and strawberry-scented.

For bubbles, **La Cuvee Brut** ($$), made from the classic local blend of Xarel·lo, Macabeu, and Parellada grapes, is aged thirty plus months on the lees and is creamy and complex, plus a great value. **Imperial Brut** ($$) is made from grapes sourced from the thirteen members of Aliances per la Terra, a Penedès grower organization dedicated to promoting organic and biodynamic farming, plus some estate fruit. It has a similarly creamy texture to La Cuvee, but with more aromatic complexity and a bit more autolytic character—think fresh-baked bread. **III Lustros ($$$)**, aged a minimum of seven years before release and entirely from the family's biodynamic Font de Jui vineyard, is a world-class sparkling wine, with complex aromas and remarkable depth. **Celler Battle ($$$$)** takes grapes only from the oldest vines at Font de Jui, and is aged even longer before release (one hundred months, minimum). It's wonderful stuff, though at twice the price of III Lustros I'm not entirely convinced it delivers twice the actual pleasure. A minor quibble, I suppose.

MAS MARTINET / VENUS LA UNIVERSAL • PRIORAT AND MONSANT

[organic / regenerative]

Sara Pérez was nine in 1981, when her parents, Josep Lluís Pérez and Montse Ovejero, moved their family to Spain's Priorat. They were biologists and teachers, and while at the time the Priorat was desolate and impoverished, "they saw the imminent richness of the region," Pérez recalls. It was a strange moment. There was no school of viticulture and enology in all of Spain at the time, and certainly not in the Priorat. "You could study to be a secretary if you were a girl, or a mechanic if you were a boy, so everyone was leaving the area." So, somewhat idealistically, her parents founded just such a school. It didn't take long before they founded a winery, too, influenced (along with Álvaro Palacios) by the arrival of Priorat visionary and Clos Mogador founder René Barbier. They christened it Mas Martinet. In 1989, her parents' first vintage, Pérez, was seventeen. By 1996, the Priorat had become world famous, and, at twenty-four, back from receiving a degree in biology, she was making the Mas Martinet wines.

Not that it was easy being a woman winemaker in Spain. Pérez says that she didn't notice the roadblocks at the time as much as she does in retrospect: "I think I was telling myself a nice story, not permitting myself to see the difficulties. At home my parents never said to me, 'You can't do this because you're a woman.'" She laughs. "What they did say to me was 'You *have* to do this, because you're the oldest!' My two brothers were little. They were just sitting around being cute." Working at Martinet wasn't a problem, but Pérez also started making the wine at Cims de Porrera, housed in the town of Porrera's old co-op. "All the growers selling us fruit there were between sixty and eighty years old, and all of them were men. It's a tiny village. And I was young, and I have always been very direct. So, at the co-op, I was yelling, I was using bad language—when you have to fight a lot to get things done, you have to make space." She gestures at elbowing an imaginary person out of the way. "One day an old man said to me, 'With that mouth, you'll never get married.' I was like, 'Oh. My. God. If I *don't* speak like this, you won't ever listen to me!'"

Pérez has lost none of her will and energy, but it's balanced by passion for what she does, and a kind of rambunctious positivity; it's hard, talking to her, not to get caught up in her delight in things. "I'm really quick," she says, snapping her fingers. "When I have a vision, I go ahead, and I go fast. Ahead, ahead, ahead."

That's how Venus la Universal was born. By the late 1990s, Priorat reds were pushing the envelope in terms of richness, extraction, sheer power (and alcohol). They garnered tremendous acclaim, but they could be exhausting to drink.

She wanted to make a wine more defined by elegance and tension, and found her answer in Montsant, which essentially encircles the Priorat. "It was like coming from the heat and darkness into the light and freshness, with a lot of flowers and the breeze from the sea. I said, 'Hey, I need to make wine here!' But *Montsant? Really?*" She says the name the way a New Yorker might react to the idea that great vineyards could be found in New Jersey. "But I discovered how amazing Carignan could be here, and so in 1999 I started trying to create something new." The soil in the Priorat is *llicorella*, a kind of broken schist, almost pure rock—"soil" is actually a generous word for it. It's a harsh place, and one that seems to concentrate light and heat into powerful, dark, intense wines. Montsant, with its decomposed granite soils and less arid climate, was gentler. For a year Pérez had no name for her new wine, until she went on a trip to Rome with some friends. "I was in the Uffizi Gallery, and I saw Botticelli's *Birth of Venus*, and I was just blown away," she says. "I had been searching for this strange beauty in my wines, and this was exactly it."

Today Pérez makes wine at both Mas Martinet and at Venus la Universal, where she lives (the latter since 2005 has been a joint project with her husband, René Barbier, Jr., who makes Clos Mogador). Both properties are farmed more than organically, in a sense; Pérez has a master's degree in agri-ecology, a discipline that combines different visions: organic, biodynamic, permaculture, and more. "It's a holistic approach; you respect everything. In a vineyard, not everything is vines. It's one living organism that should be more or less autonomous. And when you come in and harvest the grapes, you're removing a lot of energy from the system, so you need to restore that. It's an exchange between the farm and the farmer, in a way." She uses biodynamic preparations, but isn't

certified ("I have some problems with anthroposophic philosophy"); sheep help manage the ground cover; no pesticides or fertilizers are used; the local community is involved ("the sheep belong to a girl here in Falset who's studying to be a shepherd"); and the buildings on the property are fashioned from simple materials—hay, clay, wood ("so if in thirty years someone decided to remove them, there won't be anything bad left behind").

That sensibility plays into what could almost be Pérez's motto; words she wrote about a decision she came to with her husband some years ago: "*Hace ya unos años que con René decidimos pasar por este mundo intentando dejar una huella emocional, no material.*" ("We decided to move through the world together leaving an emotional footprint, not a material one.") "To find plentifulness inside yourself—that's the richness we're looking for," she says. "Not more objects. If I have a new car, or a new sofa, I don't care. Because in the end none of that actually matters."

Of the Mas Martinet wines, **Martinet Bru ($$)** comes from three different vineyards, and has sweet, dense, purple fruit lifted by bright acidity, with mineral notes that suggest rocks warming in the sun. "For me this wine is a door into understanding Priorat," Pérez says. **Clos Martinet ($$$)** is more fragrant and complex, with dark fruit, licorice, and floral notes.

The Venus la Universal wines are lighter-bodied and more taut than Mas Martinet's. Partly that's a stylistic choice; partly it's the difference between the Priorat and Montsant. **Dido Blanc ($$)** blends local varieties—Grenache Blanc, Macabeu, and Xarel·lo—and gets a small amount of skin maceration before pressing, giving it a textural character along with its stone fruit flavors. **Dido ($$)** is 100 percent Grenache, bright ruby in hue, with lively, crunchy berry fruit; it's partly fermented in clay amphorae. **Venus ($$$)**, Pérez's first wine from Montsant, blends old-vine Carignan with small amounts of Grenache and Syrah. Violets and mulled spices, tart and crunchy, full of energy—it's a wonderful red that's deceptively long-lived as well. Pérez also makes a couple of wines that fall into the "natural" spectrum: zero sulfur, minimal intervention. Among them is the **Venus de Cartoixà ($$$)**, which is Xarel·lo from a single sixty-year-old parcel. It's apple-tangy, earthy, and salty on the finish. "I remember my first sensation of touching the leaves in this vineyard," Pérez says. "They felt like rice paper. Very sensual—it transported me to Japan for some reason." Whether the wine will do that as well, who knows. Try it and perhaps you'll see.

CLOS MOGADOR • PRIORAT

[biodynamic]

René Barbier was export manager for Bodegas Palacios Remondo when he had an idea, or perhaps more a vision, of making wine in the Priorat. Barbier's family had roots in the area as deep as those of the tough old Carignan and Grenache vines hidden away on the re-

> *"I want harmony, but I like the small mistakes. There's no perfection in wine."*
> —René Barbier Meyer

gion's steep, rocky slopes. His grandfather had founded the well-known René

Barbier winery in Penedès (it's now a mass-market brand owned by Freixenet); his family owned land near Gratallops. The potential was inarguable. The poor soils and brutal climate were terrible if what you wanted was huge harvests of commercial grapes, but for ambitious, low-yielding viticulture that could produce truly expressive wines, they were ideal.

Barbier is a genial, soft-spoken man when you meet him, albeit with an occasional mischievous glint in his tone, but the relaxed manner is deceptive—he's the one who convinced the other four in the original Priorat group of winemakers to move there, at a time when the place was more or less a desolate vinous wasteland. In 1999, he started tasting wines made with the old-vine Carignan found in the area. This led to a new, Carignan-focused project, Clos Manyetes, and also to removing most of the Cabernet from Mogador and replacing it with Carignan. "There's a multi-*cépage* tradition here," he told me. "Two hundred years back, there were thirty-odd varieties growing in the Priorat. So it's very nat-ural to adapt the winemaking to the vineyard."

That remark was in 2002. Today the elder Barbier has stepped back, and his son René Barbier Meyer is in charge of winemaking at Clos Mogador. That work has changed, too. The first vintage using indigenous yeasts was 2006. "My idea was to make the wine as natural as possible," Barbier Meyer says. He's also substantially reduced the use of sulfur since the early days, and moved from new oak *barriques* to making the wine almost exclusively in *foudre* (ten times as big as *barriques*, they give far less oak influence). "Today the wine's pH is lower, too," he says. "The wines are brighter. The year 2017, for instance, was very hot and dry, but still the wines are fresh. That's because of the viticultural changes we've made, for sure."

Barbier Meyer adds, "I want harmony, but I like the small mistakes. There's no perfection in wine. Some people say, ah, it's a little rustic. But I *like* that rusticity. Even so, in the Priorat you have to be careful, because it's easy to go too far."

Nelin ($$$), the winery's white wine, is a blend of Grenache Blanc, Marsanne, and Roussanne with "a lot of local grapes." (One of those, a variety called Cana Vellas, Barbier Meyer says, is known locally as "Old Lady Strangler.") Aromatically Nelin suggests dry straw from a little skin contact, stone fruits, a tiny oxidative note; on the palate, it's savory, salty, complex. **Clos Mogador ($$$)** itself is 55 percent Grenache ("such an amiable, delightful grape," Barbier Sr.

says), 25 percent Carignan, 10 percent Syrah, and 10 percent Cabernet Sauvignon. It still has the deep, dark cherry fruit of Priorat Grenache, with pepper, baking spice, and violet aromatics. But it is fresh, bright, and lifted, with fine, chewy tannins and the Priorat's schist-driven minerality on the end.

RAVENTÓS I BLANC / CAN SUMOI • PENEDÈS

[certified organic / certified biodynamic]

Occasionally, your donkey wanders off. It's one of those things—some days it rains, some days are windy, some days the donkey ends up at the Café de la Plaça in the middle of town. Perhaps in small Catalan towns like Sant Sadurní d'Anoia, donkeys sometimes feel a late-afternoon desire for good coffee; who can say? Regardless, when the donkey wanders off, you go get it.

It was when Manuel Raventós, who co-owns Raventós i Blanc with his son Pepe, went to retrieve the donkey that he got what he refers to as a "dark look" from one of the old men at the bar. The men are at the Café de la Plaça every day. It's where they go to

drink coffee and talk about the world. But on this day in 2012, Manuel felt that the dark look seemed to be saying, "You are betraying Cava and betraying Sant Sadurní!"

The reason for that look was Manuel and his son Pepe's decision in 2012 to quit the Cava denomination of origin and to stop labeling any of their wines as Cava. Instead, their intent was to create a new appellation, Conca del Riu Anoia, and also to prove that Penedès could make world-class sparkling wines on par with Champagne. The Conca del Riu Anoia appellation would have much more stringent rules than Cava. Among them were that grapes would have to be grown organically or biodynamically (almost all Cava vineyards are conventionally farmed), the wines aged at least eighteen months (Cava requires nine), and every wine would need to be vintage dated (much Cava is non-vintage). "They're the strictest wine regulations in the world, including Champagne," Pepe Raventós said to me once, with pride.

This secessionist move also stirred controversy locally because the Raventós name is deeply, inextricably tied with Cava. In 1872, a member of the family created Spain's first sparkling wine. Codorníu, which the family cofounded (in 1551) and which relatives of Manuel and Pepe's still own, is one of the largest producers of affordable sparkling wine in the world. And Josep María Raventós i Blanc, Manuel's father, was instrumental in the creation of the Cava denomination in 1972.

Pepe says, "Look, Cava is a great value Spanish sparkling wine. But our dream is to help nature produce the best possible expression of mineral-driven sparkling wine. And the Cava name doesn't help anymore with that."

He and his father have the vineyards to make that happen. The land surrounding the Raventós i Blanc win-ery has been in the Raventós family since the 1490s (or possibly before; the Black Plague wiped out most of Catalonia immediately prior to that, so records are thin). Pepe Raventós is the twenty-first generation to farm it. Leather-bound ledgers in the winery contain handwritten records of the family's wine business, back to the mid-1800s. Leafing through them is time travel, the entire history of Cava in neat black numbers, starting when it was known in Catalan as Xampáyn; years of good harvests and bad; boom sales during wartime (Pepe's great-grandfather realized early on that whenever the Germans started a war, one of the first things they did was overrun Champagne); visits from Spain's king.

Pepe Raventós's most recent project is Can Sumoi, a joint venture with his childhood friend Francesc Escala. In 2016, the two discovered a dilapidated estate two thousand feet up in the Sierra de l'Home mountains and set about rehabilitating it. The focus here is natural wines, from seventy-five acres of old-vine Montonega, Xarel·lo, and Sumoll. If you visit, it feels like a step back in time. The place is isolated, the vines are ancient, and the farmhouses on the property, largely untouched, date back to the end of the seventeenth century. The wines echo that pre-industrial sense. The farming is biodynamic (as it is at Raventós i Blanc), the winemaking uses little or no sulfur, indigenous yeasts, no additives or filtration, and is as low-intervention as humanly possible.

"What I'm trying to do, it's not the highway," Pepe Raventós says, about both Raventós i Blanc and Can Sumoi. "It's the little road. It's steep, and it takes time. And this place, where we are, has so much potential. I am convinced of that. We're going to make wines so good they will make you cry."

Unlike most Cava, all Raventós i Blanc sparkling wines are vintage dated. The **Raventós i Blanc Blanc de Blancs** (**$$**), from organically farmed, thirty-year-old vines, is pale gold in hue, delicate, and aromatic; it has the apple-citrus notes typical of Cava, but with a finesse that recalls Champagne. **De Nit** (**$$**), a rosé, is streamlined and elegant, with a floral-citrus aroma and a light yeasty note. **De La Finca** (**$$**) comes from the best sections of the estate vineyards. Aged for thirty-two months before release, it has aromas and flavors of nuts and toast in addition to citrus fruit, but more importantly, it's distinctive: clearly a wine that expresses the place it comes from. **Textures de Pedra** (**$$$**) comes from the highest-altitude vines on the estate and is beautifully fragrant, with peach and toast aromas and flavors. Finally,

there's the extremely small production **Raventós i Blanc Manuel Raventós** (**$$$**), which is aged for seven years in the bottle. It satisfies the question of whether the Raventós wines have the capacity to age like top Champagne: they do.

The **Can Sumoi Ancestral Montonega** (**$$**) is a *pètillant naturel* (or *pèt-nat*) made from a local clone of Parellada. It's floral, lightly fizzy, and refreshing. **La Rosa** (**$$**) blends Sumoll, Montonega, and Xarel·lo for a pale orange-pink wine that's citrusy, chalky, silky, and lasting. **Perfum** (**$$**) is an unusual white blend of Malvasia, Macabeu, Moscatel, and Montonega that's aptly named; it's floral and fragrant, a pleasure to drink. And the **Xarel·lo** (**$$**), from two different plots on the estate, offers electric acidity laced with green apple and herb notes.

RECAREDO · PENEDÈS

[certified biodynamic]

Ton Mata, the third generation at Recaredo, manages this distinctive sparkling wine producer: distinctive because the wines are solely made with estate fruit, from vineyards that are biodynamically farmed with tremendous respect for the land they come from. Thoughtful and eloquent, Mata has for many years now pushed toward a more responsibly farmed, terroir-expressive model for Spanish sparkling wine, the vast majority of which is sold by three enormous companies—Freixenet, Codorníu, and García Carrión. (Each makes millions and millions of cases of Cava every year.)

"I feel Xarel·lo is one of the great white grapes of the world," Mata says. "And we have wonderful vineyards here. But they're not cultivated well and in the end these grapes go to a kind of wine that's generic. That's the opportunity we're missing!"

Recaredo was founded by Ton Mata's grandfather Josep Mata Capellades in 1924. "He was a football player for Español, the national team, and had a part-time job disgorging Cava," Ton Mata says. Capellades built his cellar directly under his house in Sant Sadurní.

"The second generation, my father and his brother, started buying vineyards, and the third generation made our wines all estate," Ton Mata says. In 1999, Recaredo became organic, and in 2006, it shifted to biodynamic, becoming in 2010 the first estate in Penedès to achieve certification. "Organic agriculture kills with natural products, but biodynamics brings life," Mata says.

Walking through Recaredo's 124 acres of vineyards near Sant Sadurní, the mountain of Montserrat rising in the distance, you can see that life, with cover crops growing beneath the stubby, gnarled vines. Fallow vineyards are planted with legumes (sainfoin for livestock to graze on and a local chickpea variety, *cigronet de l'Anoia*; both help restore soil fertility).

"We want the best for the next generation," Ton Mata says, "but I love tradition as well. Sant Sadurní is still a village. If I go to the Café de la Plaça for a coffee, the old, old generation is there every day, talking about the village, the politics, the everything—every day after lunch they're all there to take a coffee. It's still a wonderful place."

Unlike most Cava, all of Recaredo's wines are vintage dated, and all are zero dosage ("brut nature"). The **Recaredo Terrers Brut Nature ($$)**, aged for four years on lees, has orchard fruit flavors lifted on citrusy acidity, and an elegance and minerality that commercial, mass-produced Cava simply can't compete with. (Note: since 2019, Recaredo's wines are no longer labeled Cava but Corpinnat, the name registered by a group of Penedès wineries dedicated to wines made from 100 percent organic vineyards, harvested by hand, made on the winery premises, and containing at least 90 percent indigenous grapes.) The flavorful, brilliant ruby **Intens Rosat Brut Nature ($$)** is made from Monastrell and Garnacha. **Serral del Vel Brut Nature ($$$)**, which launched with the 2008 vintage, is a single-vineyard bottling from a high limestone plateau that ages for eight years on the lees. The **Reserva Particular Grand Brut ($$$$)** was first released by Josep Mata Capellades, Recaredo's founder, in 1962. It was the first long-aged Cava ever, and is made in tiny amounts from the estate's oldest vineyards (planted in 1950 and 1955). Finally, **Turó d'en Mota ($$$$)**, Recaredo's top wine, is 100 percent Xarel·lo from a single vineyard planted in 1940. Made in minuscule quantities, it is a spectacular sparkling wine: thrillingly precise yet also fanning out on the palate with breadth and density, with flavors that last and last.

FAMILIA TORRES · PENEDÈS

[sustainable]

In 2007, Miguel A. Torres saw the former U.S. vice president Al Gore's documentary *An Inconvenient Truth* and decided that as a winery "we had to accelerate. Of course, ecology was always a part of our philosophy. We live from the earth and we are also a family-owned company, so this combination always led us, and still does, to care for our land and resources. Not just for this generation, but also for future generations."

Revelations like this happen frequently; acting upon them, not so much. But soon after Miguel A. Torres's realization, Familia Torres launched its climate protection program, Torres & Earth, and it has since invested more than 15 million euros in renewable energy, biomass, energy efficiency, reforestation, and more. "Between 2008 and 2019 we also reduced our carbon dioxide emissions by 30 percent per bottle," Miguel says, "and our plan is now to reach 55 percent per bottle by 2030, becoming 'climate positive' by 2050."

That's a lot of bottles: Torres sells more than 12 million each year. It's the largest wine producer in Spain, and also has outposts in California (Marimar Estate) and Chile (Miguel Torres Chile). That does raise the question of what they are doing in this book, which is devoted to wineries of place, working at non-industrial scale. Short answer: do that much for the environment, you deserve recognition. Plus, while the more affordable Torres wines are made in enormous quantities, the family's smaller projects produce some of Spain's most compelling wines.

"Practically every vine grower in the world was already noticing climate change three to four decades ago, as vines are very sensitive to temperature shifts," Miguel A. Torres says. "We need to drastically decarbonize our world economy to contain the increase in global temperatures, and this requires the participation of all: governments, countries, sectors, individuals. We have to work together." To that end, in 2019 Torres, together with Jackson Family Estates in California, also created IWCA, International Wineries for Climate Action, a collaborative group focused on reducing carbon emissions across the wine industry. The current membership includes the Symington Family in Portugal, Cullen Wines in Australia, Herencia Altés in Spain, and others. More are being added yearly.

IWCA is only one of Torres's initiatives. Additional projects the family has undertaken include reforestation in Chilean Patagonia, where the family has planted trees across nearly fifteen thousand acres to recover the region's original forest landscape and to capture CO_2; implementing carbon capture and reuse strategies at the company's wineries (CO_2 is a natural byproduct of winemaking, but is typically dispersed into the atmosphere rather than reused); and utilizing solar panels, geothermal wells, and biomass boilers to reduce nonrenewable energy consumption. "A lot of wineries base their decisions about whether to invest or not in carbon-reduction programs on purely economic criteria," Miguel A. Torres says. "My experience is that if you take that as a starting point, it won't happen. You have to think and act with a long-term perspective. It's crucial that we act together to put a stop to this madness that will make our earth almost uninhabitable at the end of this century."

Torres makes a multitude of wines from vineyards across Spain. A few to look for include the **Familia Torres Gran Coronas Cabernet Sauvignon Reserve ($–$$)**, a perpetual value; the jasmine-scented white **Viña Esmerelda ($)**; **Purgatori ($$)**, ripe and red-fruited, made with Cariñena, Garnacha, and Syrah from the family's 494-acre organic estate of the same name in Costers del Segre; and the darker, more powerful **Pago del Cielo Celeste Reserva ($$)** from Ribera del Duero.

The family has also been on a multi-decade quest to revive native Catalan grape varieties, many of which dwindled toward nonexistence after phylloxera devastated Spanish vineyards in the late 1800s. **Familia Torres Forcada Blanco ($$)**, for example, is a crisp, focused white from a nearly extinct Penedès variety, while the top-of-the-line, single-vineyard **Grans Muralles ($$$$)** is partly made from Querol, a red variety that was unearthed after the family ran advertisements in village newspapers about their hunt for forgotten vines and varieties. It's a fascinating project.

PRODUCERS PROFILED IN THIS CHAPTER

Gramona

Mas Martinet / Venus
  la Universal

Clos Mogador

Raventós i Blanc / Can Sumoi

Recaredo

Familia Torres

OTHER CATALUNYA AND MEDITERRANEAN COAST PRODUCERS TO LOOK FOR

Albet i Noya

Avinyó

Parès Baltá

Ca N'Estruc

Cans Rafols dels Caus

DIT Celler

Escoda Sanahuja

Espelt (and Anna Espelt)

Herència Altés

Mustiguillo

Familia Nin-Ortiz

Partida Creus

THE ISLANDS

A dmittedly, it's a little odd to group Spain's wine-producing islands into one category, since the Canary Islands lie in the Atlantic off the coast of northwest Africa, and Mallorca is in the Balearic Islands, an archipelago in the Mediterranean. But the vineyards in both places are defined by their proximity to the sea.

Mallorcan wines were practically forgotten for many years, at least internationally, hidden behind the island's fame as a vacation destination. But once you escape into the interior, leaving the beaches and nightclubs of Palma behind, there are wineries here, a few of them very good indeed. The island's local varieties, including Callet, Manto Negro, Pansal Blanc, Giró Blanc, and Gargollassa, are found nowhere else. There's a fair amount of Cabernet Sauvignon and Chardonnay planted as well, but for a true sense of the Mallorcan wine, stick to the indigenous grapes. Mallorca may have a minimal presence within the broader world of Spanish wine, but it's an intriguing one.

The Canaries, on the other hand, have enjoyed surprising popularity in hipper restaurants and wine shops in recent years. Partly that's because their character fits the way tastes have changed—there's a vogue now for crisp, lighter-bodied reds and minerally, taut whites. Additionally, wines from volcanic regions have seen a similar pop in interest (and the Canaries are nothing if not volcanic; witness the spectacular 2021 Cumbre Vieja eruption on La Palma). Perhaps it's also the deeply Instagramable lunar landscapes of vineyards here—scrubby, low vines growing in stone-rimmed pits in the jet-black volcanic sand on Lanzarote and Tenerife, protected against the constant Atlantic wind. And it's definitely due to the work of ambitious, restless winemakers on the islands.

Even if wines from the Canaries still take some searching to find, there are more of them than ever in the market. The best, from local varieties such as Listán Negro, Malvasía Volcánica, and Negramoll, are thrilling.

ÀNIMA NEGRA • MALLORCA

[biodynamic]

Mallorca may be best known for beaches, but if you visit Ànima Negra, in the southeast part of the island, it's hard to imagine there's a beach within a thousand miles. The ground under your feet is hard and dry, with low trees and even lower vines. The winery itself is a massive stone structure, part of a country estate outside the tiny town of Felanitx that dates back to the thirteenth century. Before wine, it was devoted to dairy farming.

Pere Obrador and Miquel Àngel Cerdá, both of whom grew up in Felanitx, founded Ànima Negra in 1994. "When we started here, this place was full of cows," Pere Obrador recalls. "It took a *long* time to have a winery that didn't smell like cow."

The two partners farm 150 tiny parcels of local grape varieties—Callet, Mantonegro, Fogoneu, Premsal Blanc, and Giró Ros—all within six miles of the winery. Most of the vines are fifty to eighty-five years old. No fertilizers, chemical insecticides, or herbicides are used, and Obrador and Cerdá also follow biodynamic practices. Fruit trees grow here, too: apricots, peaches, plums, cherries. Fermentation is solely with indigenous yeasts (the partners have propagated a kind of "bank" of yeasts from their oldest vineyard at the winery). In essence, the philosophy is "humility in the presence of the land," as Obrador and Cerdá put it, something that's reflected in the character of their wines.

Ànima Negra's one white wine is called **Quibia ($$)**, a word which more or less translates as a "worry-free state of mind." It's made with Callet, Premsal, and Giró Ros, but for the Callet (a red grape) the juice is drained off the skins before it has time to take on any pigment. Pale straw in hue, it has a lot of texture but is low in alcohol (around 11.5 percent), with peachy notes and a distinctly saline finish. **ÀN/2 ($$)** is their introductory red, a blend of old-vine Callet, Mantonegro, Fogoneu, and Syrah fermented in stainless steel and concrete. It's savory and fresh, with vivid spice notes. **ÀN ($$$)**, the flagship red, is made almost entirely from Callet, which can recall a cross between Cabernet Franc and Syrah. It's a concentrated wine, with smoke and leather notes floating above the dark berry fruit.

VIÑÁTIGO • CANARY ISLANDS

[organic]

Juan Jesús Méndez of Viñátigo has been at the heart of a burst of ambitious winemaking in the Canaries. He took over his family's winery in the early 1990s, at first concentrating on the same varieties they'd always made, Listán Blanco and Listán Negro. But eventually he shifted toward recuperating ancient, largely forgotten local grape varieties and, essentially, mapping them onto terroirs specifically suited to them on the island of Tenerife. (He also works with old-vine plantings throughout the island.) All of Viñátigo's farming is done organically, with some biodynamic practices; indigenous yeasts are used for fermentation, and sulfur is kept to a minimum.

Because phylloxera never reached the Canaries, vines here are not grafted onto American rootstocks, as in the vast majority of European vineyards. That, plus the austere volcanic landscape and soil, gives Canary Islands wines a distinctiveness that Méndez has been brilliant at expressing. When you add to that Méndez's work with grapes like Gual, Marmajuelo, Vijariego Blanco, Tintillo, Baboso Negro, and others—just a few of the more than eighty native varieties he has helped catalogue—you land on wines that are truly unlike any others.

The **Viñátigo Listán Blanco ($$)** is salty and brisk, suggestive of the Atlantic coast. Of the more esoteric white varieties, the winery's **Marmajuelo ($$)** is flamboyant and tropical, while the **Gual ($$)** is smoky and luscious, yet with bright acid and a minerally finish. There's also Méndez's **Ancestrale Blanco ($$$)**, a 100 percent Gual made as if it were a red wine, with three weeks' skin contact (an orange wine, essentially, though the Gual grape is so light-colored that it barely tints the wine). Herbal and complex at first, it broadens on the palate, taking on layers of flavor.

His **Listán Negro ($$)** comes from a plot of one-hundred-plus-year-old ungrafted vines and is peppery and black-fruited, yet light-bodied at the same time. He also makes a varietal **Negramoll ($$)**, gently tannic with red fruit flavors; **Ancestrale Tinto ($$$)**, a fifty-fifty blend of Tintilla and Baboso, is dark, powerful, and intense; and **Ensamblaje Tinto ($$$)**, a blend of Baboso, Vijariego Negro, and Tintilla that's complex and full of currant-raspberry flavors and warm spice notes.

PRODUCERS PROFILED IN THIS CHAPTER

Ànima Negra (Mallorca)   Viñátigo (Canary Islands)

OTHER CANARY ISLANDS AND MALLORCA PRODUCERS TO LOOK FOR

4 Kilos (Mallorca)   El Grifo (Canary Islands)
Los Bermejos (Canary Islands)   Tajinaste (Canary Islands)
Envínate (Canary Islands)
Frontón de Oro (Canary
   Islands)

PORTUGAL

The Douro Valley

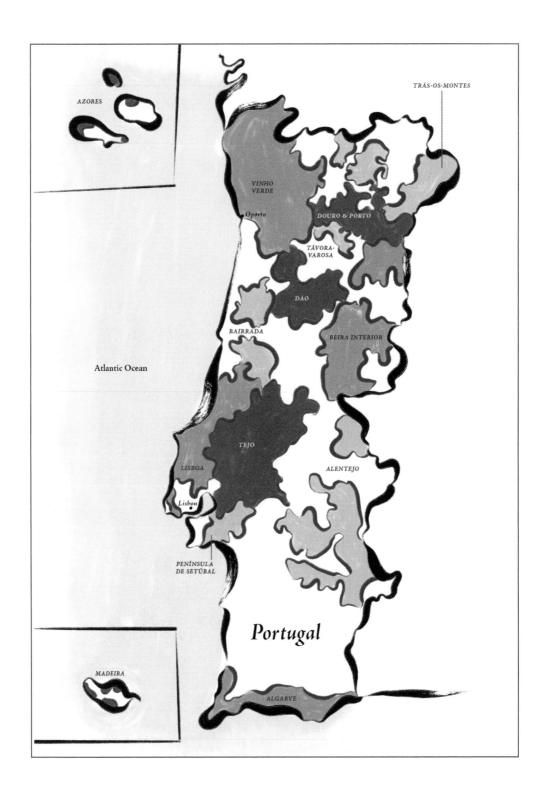

AZORES

TRÁS-OS-MONTES

VINHO
VERDE

Oporto

DOURO & PORTO

TÁVORA-
VAROSA

DÃO

BAIRRADA

BEIRA INTERIOR

Atlantic Ocean

TEJO

LISBOA

ALENTEJO

Lisbon

PENÍNSULA
DE SETÚBAL

Portugal

MADEIRA

ALGARVE

Why Portugal's wines don't get more attention in the U.S. is a long-reigning mystery among both American wine pros and the Portuguese themselves. What's not to like? Salty, citrus-zesty whites; reds that range from delicately transparent to earthy, powerful, intense, and, with Port, one of the world's great sweet wines—and all typically underpriced for what they offer. Perhaps it's in the Atlantic nature of Portugal to be somewhat less self-promotional than its warmer, more Mediterranean neighbor Spain. Walk into a *taberna* in Jerez, and you get flamenco, all stomping of boot heels and percussive guitar and swirling red dresses; hit a *tasca* in Lisbon late at night and it's fado, Portugal's haunting, mournful style of singing, with cheery lyrics like those in Amália Rodriguez's "Água e Mel," "But if I tasted the new wine . . . My god why am I still so alone?"

Regardless of what the gray Atlantic does to one's worldview, it definitely helps define coastal Portuguese regions like Vinho Verde, Colares, and Bairrada, not to mention Madeira and the recently revivified wines of the Azores. Head inland, and temperatures rise precipitously during the summer; not for nothing the old saying that Portugal's Douro Valley, home to some of the country's most exciting table wines as well as Port, offers "nine months of winter and three months of hell." (As regards Portuguese relations with Spain, an old Douro farmer once gave me another local saying: "The only thing that comes from Spain is bad winds and bad marriages." Ouch.)

Portugal mostly relies on its distinctive, native grape varieties for its wines. Some are shared under different names with that bad-marriage neighbor next door: Alvarinho (Albariño in Spain), Jaen (Mencía), and Tinta Roriz or Aragonese (Tempranillo in Spain), for example. Others are purely Portuguese: Touriga Franca, Castelão, Baga, Touriga Nacional, Arinto, Tinta Barroca, Alfrocheiro Preto . . . the list stretches on and on. There are literally hundreds, including the evocatively—or alarmingly—named Esgana Cão, which translates as "Dog Strangler," apparently a commentary on its rather impressive level of acidity. Pour some with a plate of Italian strozzapreti pasta ("priest strangler") and you've got quite an evening ahead of you.

The country is currently the tenth largest producer of wine in the world (though the Portuguese drink more wine per capita than almost anywhere else—bravo, Portugal). Only a small percentage of its vineyards are certified organic, about 2 percent, but the number grows each year. There are more than a hundred thousand vineyards in Portugal, but the vast percentage of them are tiny and their fruit goes to regional co-ops and large producers; when you are farming for as much crop as you can get, the incentive to work anything other than conventionally is minimal.

Regardless, Portugal's bevy of independent wineries and estates are often farming more responsibly and making truly exciting wine in the process, from Alentejo in the south to Vinho Verde in the north, and everywhere in between. There's a burgeoning number of young winemakers working in a spectrum that ranges from crisper, chillable, less extracted reds to full-on, zero-intervention, natural winemaking (occasionally referred to as the "new Portugal"). And the early wave of groundbreakers, the most prominent of whom is inarguably Dirk Niepoort, keep innovating. It's an exciting wine realm here, and for many wine drinkers, one that's just waiting to be discovered.

ANTÓNIO MAÇANITA • AZORES AND ALENTEJO

[organic]

There was once a time when the Azores—a nine-island Atlantic archipelago some one thousand miles west of Portugal, now known mostly as a vacation spot—were a vital part of the European wine world. "Up until 1852," António Maçanita says, "you had nearly fifteen thousand acres of vines on these islands, producing over two and a half million gallons of wine every year. Then it all ended."

Two disasters happened in short succession: in 1854, an epidemic of powdery mildew destroyed crops; then in 1857, the root louse phylloxera arrived, and killed the islands' vines (as happened throughout Europe). By 1859, wine production on the islands had dropped to a negligible six thousand gallons per year. Half the population emigrated. The existence of the Azores as a wine region was over.

But open a bottle of Maçanita's Azores Wine Company Arinto dos Açores. The wine smells of grapefruit peel and volcanic stones; it tastes stony, too, with notes of fresh citrus and sea spray. Maçanita, who also makes wine in Portugal's Alentejo region, has va-

cationed in the Azores since he was six. In 2000, he tried planting his first vineyard there, but it was destroyed by a storm. "The ocean pounds on the rocks, and that atomizes the salt in the water, and then the winds from the storm basically salt your vineyard. And then it's dead. *That's* why people here build stone walls around their vineyards."

He tried again, and now amid this jagged terrain—the islands are essentially outcroppings of black volcanic basalt—Maçanita farms more than three hundred acres of vineyards. That's a far cry from the Azores' mid-1800s heyday, but it is by far the largest new vineyard development there in centuries. His success has also raised the image of the islands' wines, and local farmers who were once being paid a bleak seventy euro-cents per kilo of grapes now can sell their fruit for upward of four euros per kilo.

A rise in interest in cool-climate and also volcanic wines has helped boost the region's reputation. "Our vineyards are on the same latitude as New York," Maçanita says. "We don't have to hunt for cool weather. We're looking for sun." But when the sun comes, the wines are remarkable. "Everyone wants to bite into terroir," he says. "They want to taste it. And you can do that in the Azores."

Maçanita also makes excellent wines in Alentejo. Fitapreta, his estate there, lies outside the ancient Roman city of Evora. It's one of several ambitious projects in this sun-drenched, southern Portuguese region responsible for shifting its image from a steady supplier of ripe but largely uninspiring reds to a source for excellent wines made from indigenous varieties.

The lime-scented, saline **Azores Wine Company Verdelho o Original** (\$\$) comes from vineyards dug into the volcanic stones of the tiny island of Pico. (Verdelho found on the islands is not the same as the variety found on Portugal's mainland; it's genetically slightly different.) **Arinto dos Azores** (\$\$), pale gold in hue, smells of grapefruit, mint, and sea spray; with its snappy acidity and stony finish, it's a killer accompaniment for oysters on the half shell. For reds, there's the appealingly crisp, savory **Tinto Vulcânico** (\$\$), a brain-spinning, co-fermented field blend of Aragones, Agronòmica, Castelão, Malvarsico, Merlot, Touriga Naçional, Saborinho, and Syrah; and the **Isabella a Proibida** (\$\$), a neon-purple wine made from the obscure Isabella variety, a hybrid of European Vitis Vifinera and American Vitis Labrusca grapes.

At Fitapreta, Maçanita works sustainably in his vineyards and with as little intervention as possible in the winery. The **Signature Series Branco de Talha** (\$\$) is fermented in a single thousand-liter amphora from the local white varieties Roupeiro and Antão Vaz, then transferred into stainless steel. It's honey-tinged, with good minerality and sweet fruit. The **Fitapreta Tinto** (\$\$) utilizes traditional Alentejo varieties for a soft-textured, rich red that speaks of the region's inviting warmth. **Fitapreta a Touriga vai Nua** (\$\$), or "the Touriga Goes Naked," plays on the Portuguese saying *o rei vai nua*, "the king goes naked." It's made from Touriga Nacional, often regarded as the king of Portuguese grapes—hence the wordplay—with no oak and partial carbonic maceration, turning what's often a powerful, even brooding variety into a light, chillable, easily quaffable red.

NIEPOORT VINHOS • DOURO VALLEY

[organic]

The first wine that Dirk Niepoort ever made, back in 1990, was an old-vine blend of local Portuguese varieties, from a vineyard called Quinta do Carril in Portugal's Douro Valley. He called it Robustus. The name was apt: the wine was, as he recalls, "a monster." It was massive and powerfully tannic, almost overbearing in its intensity—but still, he felt, quite good. At the time, almost no one else in the Douro was making table wines. Port ruled the region, as it had since the 1700s. The Niepoort family business, which Dirk's father, Rolf, directed, *was* Port.

Niepoort made four barrels of Robustus, then he headed off to Australia to work the harvest. When he returned to Portugal several months later, he stopped by the family cellars in Oporto to taste how his wine was progressing. But the wine wasn't there. "My father," he recalls, "had given away three of the four barrels I made to the workers. He said it was shit."

The Niepoort family has been in the Port business since 1842, when they moved to Portugal from Holland. Dirk Niepoort is the fifth generation to work for the family company, and since 1997, he's been in charge of it. Prior to his involvement, Niepoort Vinhos was purely a Port trading company. They purchased finished wines from growers in the Douro and blended, aged, and bottled them in Oporto, selling the results under the Niepoort name (standard practice at the time). Neither his father nor his grandfather, he says, ever spent a single night up in the Douro; they lived and worked in Oporto. "We were a good house, but we were a secret."

Dirk Niepoort is curious, ambitious, talented, and also extremely stubborn. Despite his father's disgust at Robustus, he kept going. Today he organically farms more than two hundred acres of vines in the Douro and makes a large range of Douro wines. Add to that a number from other Portuguese wine regions—Dão, Minho, Vinho Verde, Bairrada—as well as the family's substantial Port business. Then there are collaborations with other winemakers, some in Portugal and some not. Referred to as the "Niepoort Projectos," these collaborations usually head into the unexpected. What about making a white wine from Jerez, aged under a veil of yeast like a Fino Sherry, but not fortified? Why not make a bi-regional Dão-Douro blend?

What's distinct about Niepoort is his approach to wine as a whole, and his ability to communicate that sensibility. From the beginning, he has seen wine—whether in the Douro or in the world at large—in terms of what might be possible, rather than what has already succeeded. This doesn't mean his technical approach to winemaking is radically experimental; if anything, it's the opposite. "I mix old-fashioned thinking and traditions with modern possibilities. We do very simple wine. We don't use industrial yeast, no chemicals except for sulfur; it's noninterventionist winemaking. The first duty of a good winemaker is *not* to interfere."

In a way, Niepoort tends to see what might be rather than what is. A group of old, high-altitude Douro vineyards filled with obscure white varieties like Rabigato and Côdega do Larinho—grapes that, for decades, had been destined for anonymous bottles of white Port? Perhaps instead those vineyards could be a source for an extraordinarily complex, minerally white: the Niepoort Redoma Branco. A dry red from ancient Douro

vineyards—made by foot-treading in old stone *lagares* (large, shallow stone tanks), the way vintage Port is traditionally made—could include the stems, a technique borrowed from Burgundy. That's Charme, a gorgeously aromatic wine that manages to channel the innate power of Douro reds into Burgundian finesse. As a Portuguese sommelier once told me, Charme "is a wine that really has the sensibility of a great Pinot Noir, but using Portuguese grapes. No one had thought to do that before. It was like dropping a bomb on people's ideas here."

Several years back, Niepoort told me, "Probably the person who had the biggest influence on me was José, our Port blender when I was younger. His life was Niepoort. He never missed a working day in his entire life until he went into the hospital—he passed away in 2009 at age ninety-six. It puts everything in perspective." This was at a dinner at his property in Bairrada, bottles everywhere, a flame-hued sunset guttering into night. But fathers are inescapable influences, too. Later that night he said, "One day I had a birthday party and I opened and decanted a magnum of my 1991 Redoma. Later I looked around and wondered, where was the wine? And my father had drunk most of it. I thought, well, it can't be *that* bad." He shrugged. "I make what I want. Then I try to explain it to people. That's what I do."

There are dozens of Niepoort wines; so, a few signal efforts. The **Twisted Tinto ($)** is a bright, juicy blend of classic Douro varieties such as Touriga Nacional and Touriga Franca; it's inexpensive and delicious. The **Docil Branco Loureiro ($$)**, from Vinho Verde, concentrates on one of the signature varieties of that region. It's floral and vividly citrusy. **Redoma Branco ($$)** is his flagship white, complex and aromatic. Made from a forty-year-old vineyard planted with Rabigato, Côdega do Larinho, Arinto, Gouveio, Boal, and Viosinho grapes, it could also easily win an award for "best collection of really obscure white grapes." **Nat Cool Bairrada ($)** is an irreverently labeled, light-bodied red made with no sulfur, from the Baga grape, in a style somewhat similar to Beaujolais. (There are several Nat Cool wines from different regions, all a bargain and all a pleasure to drink.) **Redoma Tinto ($$)** is the wine that proved Dirk Niepoort right about the potential for dry wines in the Douro. Young, the wine is full of intensity, its wild strawberry and dark plum flavors bolstered by powerful tannins; it also ages beautifully. **Charme ($$$)** comes from seventy- to one-hundred-year-old vines near Pinhao, in the Douro Valley, the grapes foot-trodden in granite *lagares*. Currants, red cherries, the wildflower and wild herb aromas of the Douro—extremely expressive, it's also finely balanced and effectively translates Burgundian elegance into Douro character, as its name suggests (Charme: Charmes-Chambertin). The Niepoort **Vintage Port ($$$)** and **Colheita Port ($$$)** are, since the table wines have received so much acclaim, reminders that Niepoort started with Port. The single-vintage, tawny Colheitas are full of caramel, dried citrus, and toasted nut flavors. It's an unusual style that Niepoort specializes in, and the winery regularly releases older (and quite beautiful) vintages into the market.

FILIPA PATO & WILLIAM WOUTERS • BAIRRADA

[biodynamic]

Filipa Pato, the daughter of Bairrada's groundbreaking Luis Pato, and her Belgian sommelier husband, William Wouters, are emblematic representatives of the "new Portugal"—young winemakers working in environmentally responsible ways, making minimal intervention wines that are pure expressions of native Portuguese grapes and their terroirs. Or, as she puts it, "authentic wines without makeup."

Pato and Wouters are based in Bairrada, on the coast north of Lisbon, a region long known for austere, intensely tannic wines made from the local Baga grape. Pato grew up at her father's winery, and later worked harvests in Bordeaux, Mendoza, and the Margaret River region in Western Australia before returning to launch her own wines in 2001. Her focus is the indigenous grapes of her region: Baga, Bical, Arinto, Cercial, Maria Gomes. She works primarily with old vines on Bairrada's poor limestone soils, and has farmed according to biodynamic principles since the start (one of very few producers in Portugal to do so). Wouters joined her in 2003, and handles the business side of the company, though they are very much a team in all aspects.

Filipa Pato's wines are marked by their vivid energy and lift, a far cry from the old-school, rustic, weighty reds and relatively anonymous whites that Portugal used to be known for. The **Filipa Pato & William Wouters Bairrada Branco Dinamica ($$)** is a bright, stony blend of 80 percent Bical and 20 percent Arinto. **Nossa Calcario ($$)** steps up the complexity, adding some richness and orchard fruit notes to that baseline drive and minerality. It's 100 percent Bical from vines in Ois do Bairro, Pato's hometown. The sparkling **Beiras Brut Rosé 3B ($$)** is 80 percent Baga and 20 percent Bical from various Bairrada vineyards (Baga, Bical, Bairrada = 3B), full of vivid raspberry fruit and salty minerality. Her **Bairrada Tinto Missão ($$$)** is the winery's top wine, a layered, dark, evocative red from a single vineyard

of 130-year-old, pre-phylloxera Baga vines.

LUIS SEABRA VINHOS • DOURO

[organic]

Luis Seabra is one of the brightest stars of the "new Portugal" group of winemakers, coupling terroir-focused winemaking with his own minimal intervention style, and making some of the most exciting table wines currently to be found in the Douro.

His family's roots lie in the Douro, but Seabra was born on his father's coffee farm in Angola. He returned to Portugal in the 1970s, and studied viticulture in college. Initially he taught; then worked in soil research; then made wine for a large co-operative before joining up with Dirk Niepoort in the early 2000s. He was an instrumental part of Niepoort's wildly influential table-wine program (the Douro region at the time was still almost exclusively known for Port, with the almost sole exception of the iconic Portuguese red Barca Velha).

Seabra works across three regions, Douro, Dão, and Vinho Verde, farming a total of seventeen and a half acres of vines. Most of the vineyards are ancient and remote, often on steep slopes at high altitude; some Seabra owns, and some he contracts from local farmers. He avoids all chemical treatments unless there's a risk of losing the entire vineyard to disease. His wines are intensely expressive, light on their feet, and speak directly of the stony, schist soils and ancient vines they spring from.

Taken togther, the white **Luis Seabra Vinhos Xisto Ilimitado Branco ($$)** and its red sibling **Xisto Ilimitado** ($$) offer one of the best introductions possible to the cutting edge of Portuguese wine, and for a modest price, too.

The white is a field blend of Rabigato, Codega, Gouveiu, and Viosinho from older, high-elevation vines in the Douro's Cima Corgo subregion (basically, the middle stretch of the Douro). It's stony and crisp, all citrus and crunchy green apple fruit. The red is a jigsaw puzzle of local grapes—Touriga Franca, Tinta Amarela, Tinta Roriz, Rufete, Tinta Barroca, Malvasia Preta, and (heading into the realm of real obscurity) Deonzelinho Tinto—that's darkly fruity and peppery. **Xisto Ilimitado Indie ($$$)** is a single-vineyard red, more layered and more aromatic, with a distinct note of dried tobacco.

Seabra also makes one white from old vines in Vinho Verde, his **Granito Cru Alvarinho ($$$)**; and a stony white from old-vine Encruzado, Bical, and Sercial in the Dão, his **Grand Cru Dão Branco ($$$)**, inspired, he says, by his memories of tasting old Dão whites from the 1960s.

SOALHEIRO • VINHO VERDE

[certified organic / biodynamic]

There's a French term, *garagiste*, generally used for small-scale winemakers who work out of a tiny facility rather than, say, a grand château. In João António Cerdeira's case, he truly started as a *garagiste*. In 1982, he removed the family car (a red Ford Escort) from his garage and replaced it with the equipment he needed to make wine. The result of that decision became Soalheiro, both one of Vinho Verde's best producers and also one of the few to farm organically.

The story, and the name, actually starts a few years earlier, in 1974, when the country emerged from more than fifty years of authoritarian rule. That was also the year that Cerdeira planted Alvarinho grapes on a small site known locally as *soalheiro*, "sunny," a reference to its daylong exposure to the sun; possibly less politically significant overall, but mildly revolutionary in his hometown. Most vineyards at that time in the Monção e Melgaço region were field blends of different varieties, planted on high pergolas at the borders of land farmed for more lucrative crops like corn. Cerdeira planted only Alvarinho. Initially he sold his grapes. Then, after the family car got relegated to the street, he started to make wine.

Since then, Soalheiro has grown to thirty-five acres of vines over a number of different vineyards, all in Monção e Melgaço, on the south banks of the Minho River, which forms Portugal's northern border with Spain. Today the estate is run by Cerdeira's winemaker son António Luís; his daughter Maria João, who trained as a veterinarian, oversees the vineyards and was the force behind the family's shift to organic viticulture in the mid-2000s. In 2021, the family decided as well to convert to biodynamics. They also work with an association of small, local growers that they helped form, to help shift over to sustainable practices.

The **Soalheiro Alvarinho Classico (\$)** is a spot-on expression of this variety, fresh and lively, balancing tropical (pineapple) and citrus (grapefruit) flavors. **Allo (\$\$)** is a blend of 70 percent Loureiro and 30 percent Alvarinho, and is lighter-bodied and more floral. **Granit (\$\$)** comes from vineyards planted solely on granite soils, less fertile than others in the region; they give the wine a taut stoniness that's quite striking. The **Primeiras Vinhas Alvarinho (\$\$)** is the top wine and comes from the original vines that João António Cerdeira planted in 1974; it gets fermented partly in old oak casks on its lees, adding a savory depth that the Classico doesn't have.

WINE & SOUL • DOURO VALLEY

[sustainable / organic]

The first time I ever tasted with Sandra Tavares da Silva, co-owner with her husband, Jorge Serôdio Borges, of Wine & Soul, we were joined by a young sommelier from South Africa, his wife, and their small child. At one point, driving down from the quinta to visit a vineyard, they vanished. We turned back and found them standing next to their rental car. There was a six-inch gash in one of the tires. "Driving on schist," Tavares da Silva said thoughtfully, "is like driving on knives."

That's the Douro. But that inhospitable schist is why vine roots dive as much as thirty feet below the earth's surface, seeking water as the vine tries to survive. The wines that result can be stunning, but the work involved in making them can be backbreaking. And that's if you have an actual winery. Wine & Soul occupies a small, old warehouse in the steep Vale de Mendiz. "It was totally ruined when we bought it in 2004. No roof, nothing, just stones," Tavares da Silva says. She and Serôdio Borges rebuilt the place by hand. You're already farming in broken rock, so why not add a little more difficulty to the project?

The couple, both winemakers—Tavares da Silva, when she moved to the Douro in 1999, was the first woman winemaker in the region—were working for other companies when they founded Wine & Soul. They were in their twenties, essentially starting from scratch. "We didn't have anything," she says. "And we wanted a company name that would say something about us, about our way of being in business, and our wines. Most people understand our philosophy—what we like is to make wines that express the land, the soul of the land."

Port has been the signature wine of the Douro for centuries. But Wine & Soul's focus is on table wines, made in small amounts from old vineyards often planted to dozens of varieties (more than forty recognized grape varieties grow in the Douro). "These old vineyards would be lost in the Port business," Tavares da Silva says. "That's why from the beginning we wanted to make wine from them."

The couple farms organically and sustainably, and extends that philosophy toward trying to improve the Douro's social environment as well. They are members of the Bagos D'Ouro charitable institution, which helps provide education and social help for children and teenagers in need in the region; though the Douro Valley is rightly acclaimed for its wines, poverty here among local farming families is a constant. It's about helping the land, but helping the people who work the land as well.

The **Wine & Soul Quinta da Manoella Vinhas Velhas ($$$)** comes from the property of the same name in the Vale de Mendiz, planted by Jorge's great-grandfather more than a hundred years ago. The wine, a blend of thirty or so local varieties, is foot-trodden in old granite *lagares*, then aged for twenty months in neutral French oak. "There's a lot of Tinta Francisca in the blend," Tavares da Silva says, "an unusual variety that gives red fruit flavors and lots of juicy acidity." The couple also makes two more wines from the estate, **Manoella Branco ($$)**, a field-blend white that offers a kind of citrus-filtered-through-stones zestiness, and **Manoella Tinto ($$)**, a juicy, layered red suggesting wild berries and spice. **Guru ($$)**, a white from a fifty-year-old vineyard planted with indigenous varieties, has toasty notes riding above its stony orange-lemon character. **Pintas ($$$)**, the wine that launched Wine & Soul, comes from a five-acre vineyard of eighty-plus-year-old vines in the Pinhão Valley, planted with more than forty indigenous varieties. It's foot-trodden in *lagares*, aged in French oak for twenty months, and is a stellar Douro red, full of explosive blackberry and raspberry flavors, all lifted by floral aromas and supported by fine-grained, powerful tannins. The more affordable **Pintas Character ($$)** comes from vineyards adjacent to Pintas itself (*pintas*, by the way, means "spots"; the vineyard was named after the couple's dog). It's similar in character if slightly less powerful and complex. Wine & Soul also makes a small amount of very good **Vintage Port ($$$)**.

PRODUCERS PROFILED IN THIS CHAPTER

António Maçanita   Luis Seabra Vinhos
Niepoort Vinhos   Soalheiro
Filipa Pato & William Wouters   Wine & Soul

OTHER PORTUGAL PRODUCERS TO LOOK FOR

Blandy's   Poeira
João Pato Duckman   Quinta da Pellada /
Taylor Fladgate   Quinta de Saes
Viúva Gomes   Quinta do Vale Meão
Anselmo Mendes   Quinta do Mouro
Luis Pato   Symington Family

AUSTRIA AND GERMANY

Weingut Loimer, Kamptal, Austria

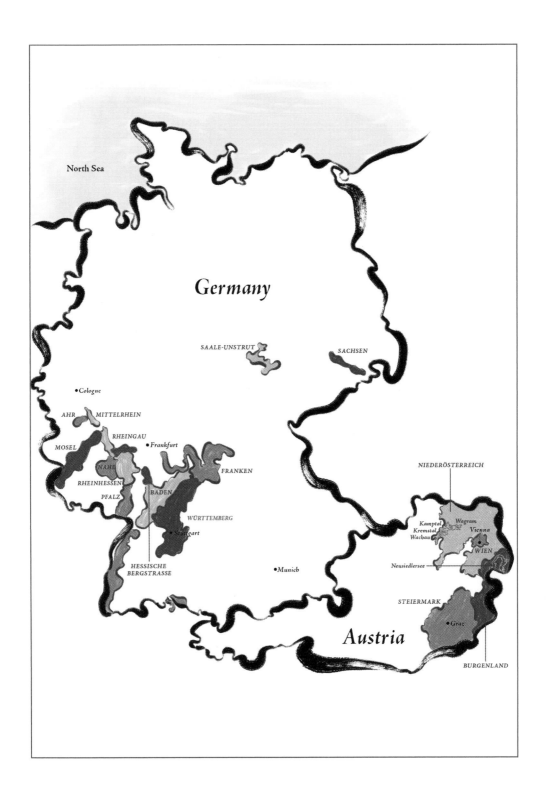

AUSTRIA

Austria's winemakers are among the world's leaders in ecologically aware viticulture and winemaking. Over the two decades from 2000 to 2023, the country's percentage of organically certified vineyards rose from 1.7 percent to 22 percent, a robust 22,465 acres, and more still are farmed organically but not certified. Of those organic vineyards, 15 percent are certified biodynamic either by Demeter or respekt-BIODYN. (The respekt group was founded in 2007 by a number of like-minded vintners including Fred Loimer, Bernhard Ott, and Fritz Wieninger.) Also, a further 18.3 percent of Austria's vines are certified sustainable under the government "Sustainable Austria" program.

Most of those vines grow in the eastern part of the country; if you prefer to head west, strap on some skis and go to Innsbruck, the site of the 1976 winter Olympics. The largest and most prominent region is Niederösterreich, north and east of Vienna. It contains the famed subregions of Kamptal, Kremstal, and Wachau, the former's vineyards split by the river Kamp, a tributary of the Danube, and the vineyards of the latter two lying along the Danube itself. Wachau's vineyards, particularly, rise steeply and beautifully in terraces along either side of the Danube; it's a stunningly beautiful region, which along with its two neighbors makes some of the world's greatest white wines.

Burgenland, in the east along the Hungarian border, makes both red and white wines, and has also been a nexus for Austria's natural wine scene. Steiermark, or Styria, in the southeast, is a source for sublime Sauvignon Blancs. It's also worth noting the small region of Wien, in and around Vienna (in the late Middle Ages, vines were grown within the city's walls, in what's now the old town center of the city). Wien has seen a boom of interest in recent years for its Gemischter Satz wines, traditional field blends of different grapes, fermented together. Under the rules of the category, no one grape variety can constitute *more* than 50 percent of the blend, an inverse of typical European grape region regulations. Gemischter Satz wines were and are the drink of choice in Vienna's old-school *heurigers*, or wine taverns. There's not much that's better than sitting outdoors at a *heuriger* on a sunny Austrian summer day, under the vine arbors, sipping Gemischter Satz and snacking on spicy Liptauer cheese with fresh-baked bread.

GUT OGGAU • BURGENLAND

[certified biodynamic / natural]

Stefanie Tscheppe-Eselböck and her husband, Eduard, are stars in the natural wine world, and their Gut Oggau wines, with their distinctive pen-and-ink portraits of faces on the labels, are sought after by natural wine bars around the world. But the Tscheppes haven't let that go to their heads. They are still firmly rooted to their land in eastern Austria, and to the abandoned farm that they bought in 2007 and turned into Gut Oggau.

Nothing was there when they moved in. "The vineyards were thirty to sixty years old," Eduard says, "and they'd been abandoned for at least a decade. But in the 1950s it had been one of the best estates in our area."

During their first harvest, they realized that they wanted to be as low intervention as possible. "No makeup," as Eduard says. To see the potential for the vineyards, they were adamant about adding nothing, and taking nothing away. "Natural wine wasn't even really a term then," he says. "It was a little naive—we just jumped right in."

Stefanie adds, "It was a crazy thing to do. Our first child had just been born. We had a huge bank loan. Nobody liked the wines. Nobody liked the labels. We basically thought, *oh shit!* But we also thought maybe there will be someone, somewhere who will like what we're doing."

The Gut Oggau wines are all vineyard blends of parcels that the Tscheppes feel have similar characters; they're pre-defined by the vineyards, as Eduard says. They farm more than twenty different parcels, and are certified biodynamic. "Organics is good, but with organics you hit a wall," Eduard says. "Especially with how out of balance the earth is now. You have to figure out how to climb that wall to reach real balance in your vineyard, and biodynamics is that ladder." They make their own compost, and also have started using horses, though that's been somewhat of a be-careful-what-you-wish-for experience.

"It was a big dream of ours for a long time," Stefanie says, "but in our town we have more horses than humans. We needed to find a stable where the horse could stay. We did, but after two years, the owner said, 'You have to move, you're stressing me out! You're always here, your kids are here, it's too much chaos.' So we bought small stable. But then our trainer said, 'One horse? You can't have one horse in a stable. A horse needs a companion!' So we bought another horse. Then he said, 'Yes, but when you are out working, one of the horses will *still* be alone.' Shit! So we bought a third horse. They're not very well trained, but that means they're just like our family."

––––––––––

The Gut Oggau wines all have names, and portraits on the labels that go with those names. "When we started, we felt the wines tasted so individual," Stefanie says. "They all had character—they were living personalities in the barrel. So we illustrated faces that felt in tune with the character of each wine." Some representative examples include the tart, grapefruity **Gut Oggau Theodora ($$)**, a pale, rose-gold blend of Grüner Veltliner and Welschriesling, fermented briefly on skins in old

barrels, aged in those barrels for nine months, then bottled (as all their wines are) unfiltered, unfined, and with zero sulfur addition. **Atanasius ($$)** is a juicy, light-bodied red blend of Zweigelt and Blaufränkisch. **Edmund ($$$)** is copper-yellow in hue, hazy, and full of tannic apple-skin and golden apple flavors that spends a full two weeks on skins. The electric-purple **Josephine ($$$)** is a dark-berried blend of Blaufränkisch and Roesler that suggests walking through an autumn forest after rain. **Joschuari ($$$)**, plummy, spicy, and peppery, is 100 percent Blaufränkisch. And **Cecilia ($$$)** is a hazy copper-hued rosé, a touch reductive, made from a field blend of red and white varieties.

ALEXANDER & MARIA KOPPITSCH • BURGENLAND

[organic / biodynamic / natural]

Sometimes you get lucky. If someone actually wanted to *pay* Dua Lipa to post about a wine on Instagram, it would probably run them a few hundred thousand dollars. But when Maria Koppitsch tells the story of how the pop star came to post one of their bottles, she just laughs. "A winemaker we know asked us, 'Come on, Maria, how much did you pay?' I said, 'Are you crazy? We couldn't afford something like that!' She just loves natural wine; she's been a great promoter for it. A sommelier in Paris poured her our Lemon and she just decided to post it. Total luck," Koppitsch says. "But the *most* lucky thing is that Alex and I met each other."

That happened in the small town of Neusiedl am See, at the local club, "which is where a lot of marriages around here end up coming from," she says. Alexander Koppitsch's family has farmed in the area for around five hun-dred years. His grandfather sold wine to local residents, though he also started raising chickens in order to make some money year-round, selling wine over the counter along with eggs. "People would come by with a *doppler*, a two-liter bottle, buy some eggs, and fill the bottle up."

Alex worked for five years at Weingut Pittnauer, making natural wine and farming the vineyards biodynamically. When his father retired in 2010, he returned to take over his family vineyards together with Maria. Together they switched the viticulture to organic and biodynamic. "What we believe is essential about being a farmer is the connection to your land and your vines," she says. "We do everything by hand. Alex puts the biodynamic preps in a bucket, then sprinkles them on the vines with a brush. His father always jokes that he looks like a priest."

The Koppitsches make a varying number of wines each year. "All of them circle around this term, 'soil,'" Maria says. "The fun wines, which are about texture—they're on sand and gravel." The light-bodied, breezy **Koppitsch Homok** ($$), a white, the rosé **Koppitsch Rozsa** ($$), and the red **Rét** ($$), for instance, "are about the spirit, the vibe of our whole place—Neusiedlersee is a fun region. People come here for sailing, cycling, and so on."

The Perspektive wines, such as the energetic, grapefruit-and-herbs **Perspektive Weiss** ($$), a blend of Chardonnay and Weissburgunder, are from vines grown in the limestone hills nearby, "and are about that rock type, the purity and precision it gives you." Also look for the peppery, lively **Perspektive Rot** ($$), which blends Blaufränkisch and St. Laurent.

Aeon ($$$), a white blend of Weissburgunder and Grüner Veltliner, is made in small amounts from their two-thirds-acre Seefeld vineyard, the family's original property. Then there's **Touch** ($$), a skin-contact white, which takes Welschriesling and combines it with a 1930s *Gemichster Satz* field blend. "We thought it would be fun to combine them," Maria says.

Abendrot ($$) is a co-fermented, copper-hued blend of all six varieties the Koppitsches grow on the limestone hills. Then there's the changes-with-the-vintage, magnum-only (**When Life Gives You) Lemons** ($$$$), most recently made as a carbonic fermentation Pinot Noir. It comes each year from whatever single barrel Alex and Maria decide is most "lemon-worthy." And Dua Lipa loves it.

WEINGUT LOIMER • KAMPTAL

[certified organic / certified biodynamic]

Fred Loimer's winery is a jet-black cube, built above a 150-year-old cellar, on the outside of the small town of Langenlois in Kamptal. In essence it's a statement on his part about the play of the modern against the traditional in wine; it's also stylistically in keeping with the purity of the wines he makes.

Loimer took over running his family's winery in 1997. His early wines were characteristic of the Austrian style at the time. "We're a cold climate region. When I started, back in 1988, we were always searching for ripeness. But in 1992 the climate seemed to jump—that was one of the first warmer years. Suddenly it was very easy to reach 14 percent alcohol, even with Riesling. These riper wines started to get critical attention, and soon all of Austria was trying to do them. But then 1998 was the turning point for me. I just didn't like the wines; they were *too* big. So, in 1999, I started going back to that older style, lighter and more elegant."

He adopted biodynamics in 2006. "My generation was the one that brought in all the technology—the cultured yeasts, the enzymes, the fining and filtering—and this was my reason to change to biodynamics," he says. "At first, it really wasn't to be green or save the environment; it was the style of the wines, which I thought were getting boring. They were the same all over the world. Then, in 2005, I was talking with a biodynamic consultant—some friends and I were taking classes from him. We talked about farming the whole day, and that evening I decided to change. It was completely clear." Not only did Loimer adopt biodynamic practices himself, with several other winemakers he founded respekt-BIODYN, a biodynamic certifying organization. "Certification is important, because people have to be certain that what you're telling them is really what you are doing."

Now, more than fifteen years in, he's convinced of the value of this approach. "For me, the only way to make wine is to have respect for nature. There's no need for so many fungicides, fertilizers, pesticides, and herbicides. Soil life is the key. Spraying herbicides all over the soil is not a way to survive, for crops or for humans," he says. "The soil is the most important resource we have, not just for farming but for mankind. Nature works with a combination of plants and animals to build soil life. When you walk on it, you're walking on life from millions of years. There's more life *in* the soil than there is above the soil." If you don't preserve that life, Loimer feels, you've lost the soul of farming.

Fred Loimer makes some of Austria's finest Grüner Veltliners and Rieslings, at a wide range of prices. His winemaking is broadly non-interventionist, and he also has his line of "mit ACHTUNG" natural wines, fermented slowly on the grape skins in wooden casks and bottled unfiltered. The spicy, herb tea–scented, lightly tannic **Loimer Gemischter Satz mit ACHTUNG ($$)**, a field blend of Grüner and Roter Veltliner, Weisser and Roter Riesling, Welschriesling and Traminer, is a good example.

The **Loimer Lois Grüner Veltliner ($)** is one of the great deals in Austrian whites. It's lively and fresh, and made entirely with estate fruit. His **Langenlois Kamptal Grüner Veltliner ($$)** is meant as a portrait of the Kamptal region, and is more complex, with green apple, grapefruit, and classic Grüner vegetal notes (fresh pea shoots are a common description). The **Langenlois Kamptal Riesling ($$)** is equally appealing, a palate-whetting mix of lime and mineral flavors. The **Terrassen Grüner Veltliner Reserve ($$)** is concentrated and savory, thanks to long aging on fine lees.

There are a number of single-vineyard premier cru Loimer wines, all excellent. Look for the concentrated, apricot-inflected **Seeberg Riesling 1er ($$$)**, from vines up to sixty-five years old—"the oldest we have," Loimer says—fresh, peppery **Kaferberg 1er Grüner Veltliner ($$$)**, from a vineyard whose name translates as "Beetle Hill," and the creamy, citrusy **Spiegel 1er Grüner ($$$)**. Lastly, there's his **Heiligenstein Zöbing 1er Riesling ($$$)**, from what is probably the most famous Riesling site in Kamptal, and possibly all of Austria. "Heiligenstein was mentioned on labels and restaurant lists a hundred and twenty years ago," Loimer says, "a time when only village names were ever mentioned. The reason is the site. It's a hill standing alone by itself, and unusual because instead of loess or gneiss, it's sandstone. It's completely different from the rest of Kamptal, and much older. It gives an entirely different saltiness and minerality to the wines, which are always very silky, very fine, very elegant. They're never *loud.*"

SEPP MOSER · KREMSTAL AND BURGENLAND

[certified organic / certified biodynamic]

In many ways, the wines that Nikolaus "Niki" Moser is making today, together with his daughter Kathi and her husband, Jan, are not that different than the wines that were made in the thirteenth century from the church vineyards that his ancestors cared for: no enzymes, no yeast nutrients, no chemical stabilization, no winemaking additives, only natural yeasts, and minimal if any sulfur.

This is a family business. Kathi Moser says, "It's my father, me, and my husband, at least in the winery." (Niki's wife, Andrea, handles hospitality and Kathi's sister Mariana runs the family's store and restaurant, which focus on organic products from artisanal Austrian farmers and producers.) After generations of growing grapes, the family started producing their own wines in 1848. In the 1980s, Niki's father, Sepp, added sixty-seven acres in Neusiedlersee in Burgenland to the sixty acres of vines on the family's historic property

in Kremstal, and in 2000, Niki took over running the estate.

Farming has been biodynamic since 2005. "My father was interested in converting since the 1990s," Kathi says, "but at first there weren't many people to learn from in Austria. Then there was a big wave of people moving into biodynamics from 2003 to 2006, and we were part of it."

Sepp Moser produces two ranges, one more classical and one made with zero sulfur. "We don't call the no-sulfur wines 'natural' so much as 'puristic,'" Kathi says. "My father tasted a number of Slovenian wines in 2005 made this way, and he decided to try it himself. He was making natural wine before natural wine became cool." Both the classic and the "puristic" wines are effectively low-intervention—the Mosers' dislike of winemaking additives and adjuncts carries throughout—but the puristic wines are also made with zero filtration and zero sulfur.

The **Sepp Moser Von den Terrassen Grüner Veltliner ($$)** is a classic expression of this grape, with vivid acidity supporting crisp, tree-fruit flavors.

The **Von den Terrassen Riesling ($$)** is equally true to its variety, with green apple fruit and a flinty finish. Both are serious bargains. There are several single-vineyard Rieslings and Grüners; all are very good. The **Ried Gebling Riesling ($$)** suggests a cornucopia of tart apple and citrus fruit all firmly brought together by fine acidity. The **Ried Hedwighof Zweigelt ($$)**, from the family's Burgenland vineyards, offers vivid, tart red fruit flavors.

Then there are the "puristic" (i.e., natural) wines. The hazy gold **Minimal Grüner Veltliner ($$)** suggests orange peel and toasted nuts, with an alluring density of flavor. The **Diagonal Sauvignon Blanc ($$)** smells of passion fruit and the naturally occurring thiol 4-MSP, which if you're feeling positive smells like boxwood and if you're feeling negative smells like cat pee (passion fruit is actually a different thiol known as 3MHA). Either way, it's a funky but compelling aroma that in this wine leads into surprisingly ripe and definitely delicious apple and lemon-curd flavors. Lastly, there's the **Astral Muscat Ottonel ($$)**, a floral, electrically tangy, dry Muscat.

NIKOLAIHOF • WACHAU

[certified organic / certified biodynamic]

The oldest winery in Austria, Nikolaihof, was first a Celtic holy place, then a Roman fortress until AD 511. Then the Romans left, and, Nikolaus Saahs says, "after that, the history is unknown until AD 777, when a monastery was founded near here."

Venture down into the oldest part of the winery's cellars and you're standing in a room built more than eighteen hundred years ago. It was a wine cellar back then, and it is a wine cellar now. "A room used for eighteen hundred years for the same thing," Nik says. "And that was wine. I'm just a small part of the history of this house, and I know it. A thousand years of history and I'll be here maybe seventy years? That's nothing."

The Saahs family bought Nikolaihof in 1894, "really just as a place to live in and to farm," Nik says. They ran it from the early 1900s until the end of World

War II, when the Russian army occupied the property, and then recovered it after the war. "When my father inherited it in 1960, there were no animals anymore. The Russians took all the horses in 1945, and also destroyed most of the original casks—they shot them full of holes."

He adds that his father had no money in the early sixties to buy the chemical fertilizers and pesticides that everyone was using, and once he did

> *"How astounding to be here in a room where eighteen hundred years ago someone was filling a cup with wine, and here I am doing the same thing."*
> —Nikolaus Saahs

have some spare cash, he used that to buy land instead. In 1971, Nik's mother pushed them to start working biodynamically, well before most people even knew what biodynamics was. "Having no money at the right time can be very important," Nik says philosophically.

The family owns about fifty-five acres of vineyard, but they don't grow only grapes—herbs, fruit trees, flowers, and beehives all have a place here.

(Christine Saahs, Nik's mother, is an acclaimed chef, and the winery restaurant uses produce from the estate.) The terraced vineyards grow Grüner Veltliner and Riesling, plus tiny amounts of Weissburgunder, Malvasier, Neuburger, and Chardonnay.

I walked with Nik Saahs in the family's Im Weingebirge vineyard on a cool November day. The Danube rolled along below us, wide and languorous. Nearby, the family's dachshund, Lumpi, raced around, hunting for *ertseizel*—prairie dogs. Recently, Nik said, about ten feet of one of the terraces had broken, and it had taken three people over three weeks to fix it. "It doesn't make much economic sense. But if one wall breaks, then the next wall breaks, and then the whole thing is gone." He added, "Anyway, when I buy new land now, I will not earn money from it; my kids will earn money from it." Watching the dog go tearing off again, I asked why he was named Lumpi. Nik Saahs shrugged. "He's the sixteenth Lumpi. You'd have to ask my great-great-grandfather." The wind rustled through the wild thistles growing near the vine rows. Generations come, generations go.

The **Nikolaihof Hefeabzug Grüner Veltliner ($$)**, sourced from vineyards around Mautern, is fermented and aged in stainless steel and is precise and lightly stony. The **Zwickl Grüner Veltliner ($$)** is essentially the same wine but unfiltered, with sediment in the bottle; shake it lightly before pouring to distribute the sediment evenly. The Im Weingebirge vineyard dates back to the fifth century, and the **Im Weingebirge Federspiel Grüner Veltliner ($$)** is both flinty and creamy at once; the **Im Weingebirge Smaragd Grüner Veltliner ($$)** gains substantial richness and ripe apricot notes from the riper grapes used for Smaragd wines; it's impressively powerful, and hard to resist. The **Vom Stein Federspiel Riesling ($$)** is tart and steely, with a kind of laser-like incisiveness. Also, if you're feeling flush, look for the winery's **Nikolaihof Vinothek Riesling ($$$$)**, which is aged in 3,500-liter old oak casks for sixteen years before it's released. It's stunningly intense and lasting, always amazingly alive despite the lengthy aging.

WIENINGER • VIENNA

[certified biodynamic]

Though he makes all the usual-suspect Austrian varieties, Fritz Wieninger is more famous as a standard bearer for *Gemischter Satz*, the traditional Viennese white field blend of grapes—up to twenty different varieties—grown, pressed, and fermented together. He's also part of the ongoing renaissance of Viennese winemaking. His vineyards and cellar lie within the city limits, in Vienna's 19th and 21st districts. Nor is this a single, tiny, urban vineyard: Weininger farms 173 acres of vines in two separate locations.

Growing up, Wieninger worked at the family *heurige*, or wine garden, serving the wines his mother made. (She was one of the first women to graduate from the renowned enology college at Klosterneuburg.) "I was trained very technically, and believed in the modern developments in agriculture as my teachers at winemaking college taught me," he says. "But 2005, a difficult year, showed me that with our conventional farming methods we'd gotten into a dead-end street. I was seeing in the vineyards how wrong the impact of spraying was. And I was looking for a way out."

A friend who worked with biodynamics helped Wieninger switch a small portion of his vineyard over. "I had absolutely no idea what he was doing, but I wanted to see how the vines would be, how the grapes would be, and most importantly, how the wine would be. And after two years, I had wines of more character, that were more interesting. So, I asked myself, is that the direction you want to go? And I thought, yes. Let's get certified.

"And look, Rudolf Steiner—this is a guy you cannot understand. He's impenetrable. But the seminars I took about biodynamics opened my eyes," Weininger says. "It wasn't as esoteric as I had thought. It was more about working with nature in the right way."

Fritz Wieninger makes two Grüner Veltliners (at least that are imported to the U.S. currently), the straightforward **Wieninger Vienna Hills Grüner Veltliner ($$)** and the spicier, more focused **Nussberg Grüner Veltliner ($$)**, the latter from a steep hill of vines overlooking downtown Vienna. His **Vienna Hills Riesling ($$)** is zesty and bright. There's also a floral, cherry-plum **Pinot Noir Select ($$)**.

Wieninger's most compelling wines are his *Gemischter Satz* blends. The basic **Wiener Gemischter Satz ($)** blends eleven different varieties into a springy white full of citrus and floral notes.

His **Gemischter Satz Ulm Nussberg ($$)** comes from the hill of the same name, and includes Weissburgunder, Neuburger, Welschriesling, Grüner Veltliner, Sylvaner, Zierfandler, Rotgipfler, Traminer, and Riesling. It's richer and more luxuriously textured, with more stone fruit and mineral characteristics. The more high-toned **Gemischter Satz Rosengartl Nussberg ($$$)** comes from a parcel of vines that produced one of the city's most sought-after wines in the days of the Hapsburgs, an old mixed planting of five varieties: Grüner Veltliner, Weissburgunder, Neuburger, Traminer, and Riesling.

PRODUCERS PROFILED IN THIS CHAPTER

Gut Oggau

Alexander & Maria Koppitsch

Weingut Loimer

Sepp Moser

Nikolaihof

Wieninger

OTHER AUSTRIA PRODUCERS TO LOOK FOR

Paul Achs

Markus Altenberger

Judith Beck

Biokult

Christina Wines

Heinrich

Hirsch

Jurtschitsch

Meinklang

Maria & Sepp Muster

Barbara Öhlzelt

Bernhard Ott

Claus Preisinger

Pittnauer

Sattlerhof

Stågard

Tement

Christian Tschida

Umathum

GERMANY

G ermany is the only major European wine producer whose identity is tied to one specific grape variety: Riesling. It accounts for a quarter of the country's vineyards, but weighs far greater than that in terms of history, reputation, and acclaim. Nearly one hundred grape varieties are planted across Germany's vineyards, some in quite large amounts (thirty thousand acres of Müller-Thurgau, anyone?), but the long German wine story begins and ends with Riesling.

That's been true for many centuries. The first documented mention of Riesling in the country dates to 1435, in an invoice from a winery in Rüsselsheim to Johann IV, the Count of Katzenelnbogen, for "six vines of Riesling." The price was 22 shillings. From the Count's lands, Riesling spread down the length of the Rhine (up until the Thirty Years' War, which decimated the country and killed off almost a third of its population; during that era, wine became substantially less important than simple survival).

Yet the grape survived, and thrived. (The oldest Riesling vineyard extant today dates from 1720, at Schloss Johannisberg in the Rheingau.) Today German Riesling is made in a vast range of styles, under a labeling nomenclature that is either beautifully specific or totally baffling, depending on how you look at it. Regardless, there are five main regions for Riesling, most of them in river valleys: Mosel, Rheingau, Rheinhessen, Nahe, and Pfalz. The wines range from intensely tart and dry to unctuously sweet, from lacy and delicate to stern and powerful, from fruity and jubilant to stony and austere. Riesling is one of the great white grapes of the world, and its range of expression and transparency to terroir are unmatched. (Also worth noting: Germans drink more dry Riesling than sweet. By a lot. The myth that all German Riesling is sweet is exactly that: a myth.)

German winemakers also make other excellent whites, from Silvaner, Kerner, Weissburgunder, Scheurebe, and others; and, surprisingly, Germany is also the world's third-largest producer of Pinot Noir. German Pinot finds its best expression in Baden, Franken, and the Ahr—Baden, with its limestone soils, tends to make Pinots that are more Burgundian in style; Franken, lighter wines off sandy soils; and the Ahr, with its rocky, schist-based soils, more powerful, intense wines. There are more than twenty-seven thousand acres of Pinot Noir in Germany, and the best wines are brilliant. Unfortunately, outside of German wine stores, they can be hard to find.

About 9 percent of the country's vineyards are certified organic, and the country also has the fourth highest number of Demeter-certified biodynamic estates world-wide. But the ecological issue that most concerns German winemakers is climate change. It's true that rising temperatures have brought some benefits; a general warming trend has meant that in particularly cold places like the Mosel, years that would have simply never produced ripe grapes—not that uncommon fifty years ago—are a rarity. "We don't have to fight to get fruit ripe every year," Philipp Wittmann of the Rheinhessen's Weingut Wittmann says. But he acknowledges that this could easily become a problem, too. "We have to look at the future as well. In the past few years we've also started buying some vineyards in the highest parts of the hillsides, where it's cooler."

At Weingut Fritz Haag in the Mosel, Oliver Haag says, "When I started twenty years ago—almost twenty-five—they taught us at viticulture school how to increase ripeness. Last year, I went to a presentation by the same professor who taught that class, about how to control ripeness and *lower* the alcohol. Everything is changing." The problem with climate shifts is that not only temperatures shift, weather patterns overall do. Plus, as winemakers all over the world now report, violent, unpredictable weather swings are more and more common. "It's getting very, very challenging," Haag says. "It used to be we'd have one unusual vintage, and ten normal ones. Now it's just the opposite."

GEORG BREUER • RHEINGAU

[certified sustainable / organic]

Theresa Breuer took charge of the historic Georg Breuer estate in Germany's Rheingau in 2004, when she was only twenty years old. Her father, Bernhard, a living legend in the region, passed away suddenly in his late fifties, just as she was about to enter the enology program at Geisenheim University. She felt there was no choice but to return and continue his work, though she says she had no clue what to do. But with the help of her mother and uncle, she has kept Breuer among the top echelon of German wine producers, and the wines today are as good as they've ever been, if not better.

Rudesheim, where Breuer is located, is truly a village full of vineyards (while the village itself was bombed almost to nonexistence during World War II, actual vineyards were not targets). Bernhard Breuer, Theresa's father, expanded the family holdings from an initial seventeen to nearly seventy acres, and also helped found an organization focused on dry Rheingau Riesling, Charta. "My father felt there needed to be dry Riesling from Germany all over the world," Theresa says. "He felt he was given a unique chance for this tiny region to set the mark for dry Riesling. He was only fifty-seven when he passed away, but he prepared a great heritage for me—fantastic vineyards and a fantastic team. That allowed me to follow in his footsteps, and create my tiny ones next to his."

The Rheingau is small, but its wines are more influential than its size might suggest, partly thanks to vintners like Theresa Breuer. Today she farms 104 acres of organic vineyard in Rüdesheim, Rauenthal, and, most recently, Lorch. The winery is also part of the German AmBiTo project, which seeks to expand biodiversity in German vineyards.

The two baseline Breuer wines, the **Georg Breuer Charm Riesling ($$)** and **Sauvage Riesling ($$)** are excellent introductions to Rheingau Riesling. Charm is made in a slightly off-dry style, Sauvage in a dry style. The next step up are the "village" wines: the **Rüdesheim Estate Riesling**

Trocken (\$\$), **Rauenthal Estate Riesling Trocken** (\$\$), and **Lorch Riesling Trocken** (\$\$). Theresa Breuer says, "Rüdesheim is entirely south-facing; it makes shiny, pure wines that carry, for me, what Riesling is about. Rauenthal is on different slate—light in color and very fragile. If you try to crack it, it will actually fall apart. It brings an almost salty character to the wine, and a more inviting, fruity style. Lorch has *very* cold mornings, then warm afternoons. You get rich fruit flavors, but also very pure minerality and delicate acidity."

The **Terra Montosa Riesling Trocken** (\$\$) is sort of a second wine to the winery's grand crus, but is entirely impressive on its own, vivid and stone fruity and intense. Then there are five grand cru wines, all stellar, all dry, and all fairly pricey though not brutally so. Perhaps the most compelling are the three from Breuer's home base of Rüdesheim, the spicy **Rüdesheim Berg Roseneck Riesling** (\$\$\$), powerful and stony **Rüdesheim Berg Rottland Riesling** (\$\$\$), and the top of the trio, the complex, concentrated **Rüdesheim Berg Schlossberg Riesling** (\$\$\$\$).

CLEMENS BUSCH • MOSEL

[certified sustainable / certified biodynamic / natural]

It's a good marker of Clemens Busch's unwillingness to abide by the rules that after five generations before him of winemakers all named Clemens Busch, he named his son Florian. Busch took over his father's small estate in Pünderich in 1972, at the border where the Middle Mosel becomes the rougher and more remote Lower Mosel. The old family house, where Busch and his wife, Rita, live, sits directly on the Mosel's banks, looking across to the vineyards of Marienburg.

Initially Busch inherited five acres of vineyards from his father. Over the years he's slowly built that to some forty acres, all on Marienburg's rocky slopes—something that probably would have been impossible but for a viticultural shift in the 1980s, when vintners, tired of the expense and difficulty of farming steep vineyards carved right out of rock (and similarly tired of trying to sell Riesling), shifted toward growing Pinot Noir on the nearby flatlands. Busch cobbled together his holdings from dozens of local growers, at prices that today would be unimaginable.

Busch quit using herbicides in 1976, and in 1984 converted to organic farming. Later he moved to biodynamics, and joined the Austria-based biodynamic Respekt-BIODYN group in 2015. He was also one of the earliest natural winemakers in Germany, and has had a significant influence on that movement there. His wines are made solely using spontaneous fermentation with natural yeasts, and most are aged in traditional thousand-liter wood *Fuders*. All additives are strictly forbidden, pumping is kept to a minimum, sulfur is minimal to none, and any movement of the wines is determined by the phases of the moon.

For anyone used to traditional Mosel Rieslings, the Clemens Busch wines are an eye-opening experience. They flirt with oxidation, and are often full-bodied, even powerful—very different from the Mosel's usual transparent delicacy. In a way, they make a statement about the Mosel's potential: that the dominant paradigm isn't always the necessary one, and that Riesling can show even more sides than its already multifarious personality might suggest.

The basic **Clemens Busch Riesling Trocken ($$)** is, like most of the Clemens Busch wines, fully dry. It comes from a mix of old and younger Marienburg vines. The next step up are two soil-specific Rieslings, the **Riesling Vom Grauen Schiefer ($$)**, from gray slate soils, and the **Riesling Vom Roten Schiefer ($$)**, from red slate. The former is linear and laser-sharp, an austere combo of rock dust and lemon essence; the latter, rounder and spicier, with white peach notes. They're a great study in how Riesling shows, so very clearly, the type of soil its vines are rooted in. Busch mostly makes dry wines, but his **Riesling Marienburg Kabinett ($$)** shows that his talents aren't limited to that realm: juicy and mouthwatering, it's vivid with peach-pear fruit and crisp sweetness. There are also several *Grosses Gewächs* (grand cru) wines, among them the **Riesling Marienburg GG ($$$)**, from the family's original five-acre plot of vines, and the **Riesling Marienburg Rothenpfad GG ($$$)**, from the red-slate, iron-rich vineyard of the same name. Though similar in character, the first is more approachable, more succulent; the second, Busch's top wine, is a remarkable Riesling, powerful and intensely aromatic, a wild interplay of warm spices and stony minerality.

MAXIMIN GRÜNHAUS / VON SCHUBERT • MOSEL

[sustainable / organic]

How do you measure time with wine? Each year another vintage; they add up. Is three years old for a white wine? Five? Is a twenty-year-old German Riesling an old wine? If you're a member of the Von Schubert family, and your ancestor Carl Ferdinand Freiherr von Stumm-Halbert bought the Maximin Grünhaus estate in the Ruwer Valley in 1882, does that mean you've been there a long time? Possibly. But maybe not, when the *new* part of the cellar where you work dates from 1630.

All good things to think about when you open a bottle of Maximin Grünhaus Riesling and take a sip. The original cellar at Grünhaus dates back more than a thousand years, and the Von Schuberts have records from AD 1000 that document grape-growing at their Abtsberg vineyard. It's visible from the gates of the property, rising steeply just across the road.

I remember Carl von Schubert hosting a lunch at Grünhaus a while back. He served wild boar stew. "I used to shoot about three boar per year in the vineyards," he told me. "Now it's about thirty. Perhaps it's to do with global warming. We at Grünhaus suffer a lot from wild boar."

"They destroy the vines?"

"They love the sweetest grapes. But if they get into the vineyard, they have to risk ending their lives as sausage."

Carl stepped back in 2015, and the estate is now run by his son Maximilian, the sixth generation of Von Schuberts to live here. The wines are as good (or even better) than they've ever been.

The Ruwer, the tributary of the Mosel along which the Grünhaus vineyards lie, is known for delicate, filigreed Rieslings, extremely age-worthy despite their seeming weightlessness. The Grünhaus estate has three vineyards. Abtsburg, or the "Abbott's Mountain," is the oldest; when the Abbey of Maximin owned Grünhaus, the Abtsberg wines were solely for the abbott's table. Next over is Herrenberg, which provided wine for the second rank of monks, who sat next to the abbott. Abtsberg is primarily blue slate; Herrenberg primarily red. Then there's Bruderberg, planted with a selection of old clonal material on soil that's essentially the same as Abtsberg.

The vines average forty-five years of age, and are farmed without pesticides or herbicides. They're harvested by hand—a tractor would literally tumble down the slope, which in Abtsberg reaches seventy degrees. Max von Schubert and longtime winemaker Stefan Kraml use only indigenous yeasts. "Cultured yeasts can really drive a wine far away from its home soil," Max says. "With wild yeasts it's more like a marathon—hundreds of different people line up at the start, and you don't know who will win."

There are a tremendous number of Maximin Grünhaus wines, despite there only being three vineyards: basic estate Rieslings, Prädikat bottlings (*Kabinett, Spätlese, Auslese*), *feinherbs*, late releases, dry *Grosses Gewächs* wines, *eiswine, beerenauslese,* and *trockenbeerenauslese* . . . on it goes. Many of these do not come to the U.S. Of the ones that do the **Maximin Grünhaus Riesling Maximin ($)** is a true bargain, and for not that much more, so is the dry, fragrant **Maximin Grünhaus Schloss Riesling ($–$$)**.

The **Maximin Grünhaus Grünhäuser Riesling ($$)** is also made in a dry style. A blend from all three of the estate's contiguous vineyards, it's a liquid portrait of this secluded section of river valley. Then there are the Abtsberg and Herrenberg *Grosses Gewächs, Kabinett,* and *Spätlese* Rieslings. In general, the red slate wines of Herrenberg, such as the **Maximin Grünhaus Riesling Herrenberg GG ($$$)**, tend to open up earlier, and are fruitier from the beginning. The Abtsberg wines, such as the **Maximin Grünhaus Riesling Abtsberg GG ($$$)** or the **Maximin Grünhaus Riesling Abtsberg Kabinet ($$)**, have a more focused slate stoniness and open more slowly over time. Max von Schubert says, "For me Herrenberg is classically spicier, often more approachable when young than Abtsberg. Abtsberg is more mineral; more salty, a bit more elegant and straight. It's a great vineyard. Looking out in the morning, it calms me down and drives me crazy all at once."

FRITZ HAAG • MOSEL

[certified sustainable]

Wilhelm Haag, who passed away in 2020 at age eighty-three, was a legend in modern German wine. His determination to uphold the reputation of Riesling as one of the world's great wines and his focus on estate-grown, high-quality wines at a time when much of German wine production was shifting toward industrialization had an incalculable effect on the renaissance of German wine that started in the late 1980s. (He was also a founder of the VDP, Verband Deutscher Prädikatsweingüter, the primary German association of top wine estates.) He was tirelessly energetic, both as a winemaker and a promoter of Mosel wine. "In German, we'd say 'You could put him out the back door and he'd be back in the front door in the next second,'" his son Oliver Haag says. "I miss being in the cellar with him, philosophizing about wine. He was brilliant at making you feel his passion, his idea of how to make a wine."

The Haag estate is located in Brauneberg, a town named for the massive brown-gray slate slope that rises behind it. Oliver Haag farms seventy-two acres of vineyard, sustainably, with some organic practices. "No pesticides, no insecticides, and our fertilizer is organic material. We hand-pull leaves to protect against botrytis; we harvest everything by hand. It's extremely expensive, but a machine can't make a decision about which grapes are the best quality. We're using solar energy to produce almost all our own energy. Even small things—we don't use the special *Grosses Gewächs* bottle for our top wines; ours weighs 25 percent less. Transporting wine has more carbon footprint than any other part of the business. You do a lot of small things to protect nature, and it adds up."

The balance of tradition and change is key at Haag. The world is changing;

climate shifts alone necessitate being flexible. "I spoke to my father's old vineyard manager not long ago," Oliver Haag says. "He used to start harvesting at the end of October, the beginning of November. Now we start at the middle of September. And weather is more extreme—you'll have extreme dryness, for example, then a tremendous amount of rain in one hour, which just runs off. It used to be we got one unusual vintage, and ten normal ones. Now it's almost the reverse. It's very,

very challenging." But some things don't change: the vines on the steep slope of the Brauneberg still make extraordinary wine. "What I love personally is just to go up there without a cellphone," Haag says. "Or even on a tractor, with a little bit of music. Not cutting the grass, just flattening it, looking out at the village— to be in this stressless situation, doing some simple work, with this view from the top of the Brauneberg to the castle of Bernkastel, on a sunny day, it's just fantastic."

There are quite a few Fritz Haag wines once you get into different Prädikat designations, from *Kabinett* up to *Trockenbeerenauslese*. The **Fritz Haag Estate Riesling ($$)** and **Estate Riesling Dry ($$)** both have the filigreed acidity and purity that are hallmarks of the Haag wines; the former is lightly off-dry, the latter completely dry. The **Brauneberger Riesling Trocken ($$)** comes 75 percent from the Brauneberger Juffer vineyard and 25 percent from the Brauneberger Juffer Sonnenuhr vineyard (Juffer surrounds the smaller Juffer Sonnenuhr on three

sides) and adds more complexity and depth, keeping to a dry style. The single-vineyard **Brauneberger Juffer Riesling Kabinett ($$)** shows among other things how brilliantly a moderate amount of sweetness balances the laser-like acidity of great Mosel Riesling. The **Brauneberger Juffer Sonnenuhr Riesling Trocken GG ($$$)** is the estate's top dry wine. Juffer Sonnenuhr is lethally steep—up to an 80 percent grade in some places—and Haag's wine from it is a thrilling dry Riesling, chiseled and stony but with layers of flavor.

SYBILLE KUNTZ • MOSEL

[certified organic / certified biodynamic]

Sybille Kuntz's grandfather was a wine broker in Lieser, the same town where she lives and works today; her father had a small bottling company and made *Fuder*, the large wooden vats traditionally used here for winemaking. Wine was their business, "and when my parents couldn't pay for my university studies, I decided to open a wine shop to finance them," Kuntz says. That shop proved crucial for her wine education. "I tasted wines from all over the world. At the time, Mosel wines were all light and sweet, and I realized that it must be possible to make a different style of Riesling."

Kuntz started making dry Riesling in the Mosel, following her own interpretation of how these wines could taste. "My wines were the exact opposite of what my father made—bone-dry, more power, a different style. But he had to make lots of wine to help support our family. For me it was important to make less wine, and have better quality."

Kuntz started with the tiny, one-acre vineyard she purchased from her parents in 1984. Gradually she purchased more vineyards, and in 1990 she began to farm organically. "I wanted green cover crops, and flowers, and other growers then all just thought I was stupid. At one point I wanted to rent a vineyard from an older vintner, and he simply refused. He said, 'Your soil is not clean.' Clean!" she scoffs, still annoyed. "There was nothing *alive* in his vineyard—no grass, nothing."

For her winemaking, Kuntz says, "We don't add anything. This is pure nature. No fining, no yeasts, nothing. People use these things because they want to make sure the wine will be clear, and they take the easiest way and use chemicals. For me, if the wine is made from vineyards that are farmed well, then the grapes are stable and the juice is stable, and the wine will do everything it needs to itself."

Kuntz's wines are incandescent expressions of dry Mosel Riesling. The **Qualitätswein Trocken ($$)** comes from "younger" vines—in quotes because younger for Kuntz means forty years of age or so—and is racy and vivid. Her **Kabinett Trocken ($$)** is made with riper grapes from vineyards in Lieser Schlossberg, Rosenlay, Niederberg-Helden, and the Pauls Valley. Her **Spätlese Trocken ($$–$$$)**, another step up the ripeness ladder, is a focused, intense white, and her **Auslese Feinherb ($$$)** is made from grapes harvested at the point where they are dark gold, and wrinkled and shrunken due to botrytis. Very faintly off-dry, the wine is perfumed and com-

plex. Recently, Kuntz has also been making a skin-contact **Orange Riesling Trocken ($$)**. It was her vineyard manager's idea, and at first Kuntz was skeptical. "We tasted all these horrible orange wines, and I told him, please, no! But we tried it anyway. The first vintage was six months on the skins, which was a little much. We reduced the skin contact to three weeks, and now it tastes more like a Riesling, not just of grape skins."

DR. LOOSEN • MOSEL

[sustainable]

The most iconic object in the Mosel wine region is undoubtedly the ten-foot stone sundial perched mid-slope in the precipitously steep Wehlener Sonenuhr vineyard. Ernst "Erni" Loosen knows it well—in addition to the acres of Riesling he owns there, the sundial was a gift from one of his ancestors to the village of Wehlen, a kind of signifier that this particular slope actually got enough sun back then to produce ripe grapes. That's less of an issue now, thanks to global warming. But the sundial still stands.

The Loosen estate came into being

when Erni Loosen's great-great-grandfather married into the even longer-established Prüm family. "He married the older daughter first, she died, so then he married the younger daughter," he says with a shrug. Erni Loosen himself had no plans to go into wine, but when his father fell ill in 1986, he came back from college to run what the older man, a lawyer and politician, had more or less considered a hobby—nineteen acres of vineyard that produced more debt each year than profit. Two years later, in 1988, Loosen's mother said that she planned to sell the winery if none of her children stepped up to run it. Loosen's siblings essentially volunteered him for the job, with the argument that since he had an archaeology degree, he was never going to have a job anyway, and none of them intended to pay his bills if he went on welfare.

Loosen started working sustainably, with some organic practices, the day he took over. He's also lost none of his irrepressible, ex-hippie, contrarian energy, while at the same time remaining a staunch defender of classic Mosel Riesling. He now farms about one hundred acres of vines that average 60 years of age (the oldest are more than 130 years), and for many years he has been making some of Germany's most evocative and site-expressive Rieslings.

Dr. Loosen's two entry-level bottlings, the dry **Dr. Loosen Red Slate Riesling ($$)** and the off-dry **Dr. Loosen Blue Slate Riesling ($$)**, are exemplars of the two distinctive soil types of the Mosel: "Blue slate is always the charming ballerina; red slate is the muscular mountain climber," he says. There's also a brisk, sparkling **Riesling Sekt Extra-Dry ($$)**. Loosen makes an enormous number of both fruity (i.e., with residual sugar) and dry Rieslings from any number of famed vineyard sites. There are far too many to describe them all, but a few highlights include his **Berkasteler Lay Kabinett ($$)**, from the vineyards that lie between the estate house and the town of Bernkastel; an **Ürziger Würzgarten Kabinett ($$)** that fully expresses the classic spice-box characteristics of that vineyard; and racy, grapefruit-zesty **Wehlener Sonnenuhr Spätlese ($$$)**, whose sweetness is perfectly balanced by its electric acidity.

For dry wines, look for the stony, concentrated **Graacher Himmelreich Alte Reben GG ($$$)**; the smoky, lime-zesty, vivid **Erdener Treppchen Alte Reben GG ($$$)**; his effortlessly graceful **Wehlener Sonnenuhr Alte Reben GG ($$$$)**; and the sublime (albeit pricey) **Erdener Prälat Alte Reben GG Réserve ($$$$)**. The latter, from a single four-acre vineyard, stays for two years on its lees in large old oak casks, the traditional thousand-liter *Fuders* of the Mosel, and a further two years in bottle before release.

SHELTER • BADEN

[organic]

Shelter, owned and run by winemaker Hans-Bert Espe and his viticulturist wife, Silke Wolf, is in Baden, in the Breisgau district. There, Espe says, "The cold winds in the Black Forest during the night flow down and cool our vineyards." The result is a microclimate that's ideal for elegant, expressive Pinot Noir, or Spätburgunder, as it's called here.

Espe and Wolf named their winery after the abandoned concrete air-raid shelter where they started making wine, which was built during the post–World War II era for Canadian troops stationed in Germany. "In the next shelter over was a Hell's Angels chapter," Espe says. "Our first summer, they had a huge party with hundreds of bikers. Silke and I had to drive through in the evenings because we were harvesting grapes, and they'd take flashlights and look in the car to make sure we weren't police."

The couple's twelve-acre vineyard lies in a side valley a few miles away. The landscape is typical of the region: small terraces of vines on the hillside, forest above, cornfields below. In the fall, the vine leaves turn colors, yellow and scarlet and green. Beyond the cornfields that lie below the vineyard, just as the land starts rising, are a scattering of beech trees; then dark pines on the far hills.

No herbicides or pesticides are used in the vineyard; all harvesting is by hand; and, as Espe has said, "We renounce pumps and filters. Our 'pump' is the hard work and patience is our 'filter.'" The result is delicate, nuanced Pinots that may take some effort to find, but that are unquestionably worth the search.

The affordable **Shelter Lovely Lilly Pinot Noir** ($$) suggests autumn leaves on the nose, and is light-bodied and appealingly drinkable. The middle-tier **Shelter Spätburgunder** ($$), aged in old oak for fourteen to sixteen months, is medium-bodied with soft tannins, toasted spice, and dark raspberry flavors. The top wine, simply labeled **Shelter Pinot Noir** ($$$), is a barrel selection of the best lots from each vintage, with lots of aromatic depth, hints of fresh and dried herbs, and racy dark raspberry flavors, ending savory rather than fruity.

WASENHAUS • BADEN

[organic]

Wasenhaus is a tiny operation. Two young German guys, Alex Götze and Christoph Wolber, run it out of the barrel-crammed back section of a mothballed 1950s co-op winery on a back street in the town of Staufen, south of Freiburg. They're Pinot Noir specialists. Both have worked in Burgundy (Götze worked with Pierre Morey, and is still the vineyard manager for Domaine de Montille; Wolber worked at Domaine Leflaive and Comte Armand); they met in enology school there, and at some point, looked at each other and said, "Why aren't we making wines in Germany?"

Staufen is located right where the Black Forest falls into the Rhine River plain. Wolber says, "What you have here are higher mountains at your back that bring cooler air down; that's why apples from the mountains are more expensive, and it's also why the wines are so fresh. We also have a bigger diversity of soil than Burgundy does. Limestone, but also granite, gneiss, and volcanic soil."

But growing grapes here is not for the faint of heart. When I visited the Bellen vineyard with Christoph Wolber, my only question was "How the hell do you *farm* this place?" About a foot from where I was standing, the land plummeted straight off the road down to trees and a stream below. Looking at the rocky slope, I could see Pinot Noir vines clinging precariously to it. Wolber laughed. "Right? The guy who owns it, his son nearly pitched over the edge one time in his car—he was hanging right there by two wheels," he said, pointing to a spot about three feet from where I was standing. "The owner told me after that, 'You want it, it's yours. I'm never farming this damn place again.'" Now the two young winemakers pay fifty euros a year (plus an annual glass of schnapps) for the right to farm the land. Looking down over his potentially lethal vines, Wolber shrugged. "Sure, it's a crazy place. But it makes great wine."

The Wasenhaus wines skew toward the low-intervention school of natural yeasts, no sulfur, and organic viticulture—they are, if you like, natural without being "natural." Wolber says, "We like to make clean, fresh wine, not super-fruity wine. If the wine is alive and light, I'm happy."

The **Wasenhaus Grand Ordinaire (\$\$)** is Wolber and Götze's version of a "nouveau" red, made with whole clusters and carbonic maceration, juicy, buoyant, and light-bodied. The **Wasenhaus Spätburgunder (Pinot Noir) (\$\$)** is a blend from all the vineyards they work with, vivacious and red-fruited, with lots of cranberry and raspberry character. There are several single-vineyard Pinots. One standout is the **Wasenhaus Vulkan (\$\$\$)**, from volcanic soil in Kaiserstuhl, joyously floral, with bing cherry and savory spice; it's got a kind of beautiful transparency. Another is the **Wasenhaus Bellen (\$\$\$)**, from the extraordinarily steep vineyard mentioned above. Ultra-fine in texture, with gorgeous depth of flavor, it's a beautiful Pinot. There's also the **Wasenhaus Gutedel (\$\$)**, a fiercely mineral, low-alcohol white made from Chasselas.

NIK WEIS—ST. URBANS-HOF • MOSEL

[certified sustainable / organic]

In another life, Nik Weis might be making shoes. "My grandfather was a trained shoemaker—a *meister*, the highest level of the craft." But Weis's grandfather also grew grapes and made wine, and after World War II ended, he founded the first privately held vine nursery in the Rhineland Pfalz. "He stopped the shoemaking," Nik says. Just as well that was the result, because the wines Nik Weis makes today are remarkably good.

In 1947, the Weises started off with a little under four acres of vineyard land, Nik recalls. "In those days, peasant families didn't have huge holdings. Twelve acres meant you were a wealthy vintner." Piece by piece they purchased more land, and today Nik Weis owns about a hundred acres of vineyards, along with a nursery his grandfather founded.

Weis farms with both organic and sustainable methods. "What we do includes organic treatment of our vines—nettle teas, valerian teas. We don't use any systemic products, ever. I say, 'Our vines don't take pills, they only get potions.' No fertilizers, only compost. And for cover crops we use thirty different herbs. What we're doing is creating a soil biome, which is something that wasn't done in the Mosel. The rule here was *clean* soil, but we want an ecosystem to develop in the vineyard to help the vine. Insects, microorganisms, animals— you'll never get that with clean soil."

Weis recognizes that there's a balance to be found between what nature offers in its unedited, uncontrolled, wild way and what humans do *to* nature as farmers. "Agriculture means man does something with nature. If the wind blows through a hollow tree in a forest and makes a tone, is that music? No. If a man goes in and cuts down the tree and makes a perfect violin that can make music, that's not pure nature but it *is* a wonder. It's the same with making wine. If you have a vine growing near the river delta and the grapes fall off, land in a hole, and ferment, it's technically 'wine,' but is it good? No. So you work *with* nature to raise the vine in the best way, to produce much better fruit than it would alone in nature, which then makes something astounding."

Weis makes a plethora of wines. Of them, the **Nik Weis Urban Riesling** (\$) is a stellar value, fruity, lightly off-dry, and full of life. "It's a good representative of what the Mosel does," he says. "It unites two things: quaffability, so you can guzzle a lot of it, and that certain intellectual sophistication that Mosel Riesling can offer." His **Estate Riesling Bottled from Old Vines (\$–\$\$)** comes partly from vines his grandfather planted and partly from older vines in other vineyards. It's very lightly off-dry, but with such brilliant acidity that you don't even notice. The sparkling **Cuvée Clara Brut (\$\$)** is made from Chardonnay, Pinot Noir, and a touch of Riesling; think quince and citrus and minerals. And his **Laurentiuslay Riesling Grosses Gewächs (\$\$\$)** has that stony nobility that great Mosel Rieslings so often have. Smelling of crushed rock, lime zest, and green apples, it's austere, savory, and a little bitter in the best way.

WEINGUT WITTMAN • RHEINHESSEN

[certified sustainable / certified organic / certified biodynamic]

The Rheinhessen is complicated. It's the biggest wine growing region in Germany, with a vast range of climates, exposures and soil types, and it has both large, industrial producers, making vast amounts of Müller-Thurgau and Dornfelder for German supermarkets, together with ambitious, small producers such as Weingut Wittmann. "It's always tricky when you have very different quality levels under one regional name," Philipp Wittmann notes. "Maybe we should say we have a very diverse region, which happens to have a small club of fine wine producers—and then a lot of *young* winemakers, who've changed the direction of their family estates. Unfortunately, my hair is getting gray. I'm not one of the young guys anymore!"

Wittmann's family has been growing grapes and making wine in the small town of Westhofen for more than 350 years. For most of that time, they were classic, old-school, European farmers, planting vines but other crops as well. "It developed over time that we focused on wine," Wittmann says. "Looking back, our cellar was built in 1829; the oldest wines we still have are from the 1921 vintage. But the shift to focus solely on wine came in the 1980s."

The Wittmann vineyards have been certified organic since 1990. What prompted Philipp Wittmann to then move to biodynamics was climate change—drier years, more heat—and trying to determine what he might do in the vineyard to compensate. "The key point was balance in the vineyard. We decided to go 100 percent into biodynamics after 2003, which was an incredibly hot year." (Across Europe, 2003 had the hottest summer temperatures since 1540. More than thirty thousand deaths were attributed to the heat.)

Wittmann says, "What we do is a kind of gardening. It's very intense work in the vineyards—a lot of hours per acre, a lot of handwork. We're really wine farmers, in a positive and intense way. And with biodynamics, one thing you work on is little trigger points. Some of the results only appear after a long period of time—you can't say after one or two years, 'Oh, this is the difference between organics and biodynamics.' But today, one thing we know is as a result we have healthy vines and ripe fruit straight through the entire growing period. It also changes your appreciation of the vines. I'm a runner, and when I walk through the vineyards, there's the fresh air, the sense of everything around you being healthy—it's a kind of feeling of freedom."

Weingut Wittmann owns sixty-two acres of vines in the southern Rheinhessen. Philipp Wittmann says, "It's crucial for me that all of our wines, from the estate Riesling to the *Grosses Gewächs* wines, have the same fingerprint: biodynamic growing, spontaneous fermentation, big oak casks. The basic wines have to be comparable to the top wines, just in a smaller version."

Wittmann's affordable 100 Hills line uses contracted fruit from other certified organic growers together with estate fruit. Look for the zesty **100 Hills Dry Riesling ($)** and the stony-fruity **100 Hills Dry Pinot Blanc ($)**.

The **Wittmann Estate Riesling Trocken ($$)** is, year in and year out, one of the best values in dry German Riesling that can be found, racy and stony and entirely delicious. There's also a transparent, ruby-hued **Estate Spätburgunder Trocken ($$)**, full of fresh red Pinot Noir flavors. The **Westhofener Riesling Trocken Aus Ersten Lagen ($$–$$$)** comes from satellites of the grand cru Morstein vineyard, "so it's kind of a premier cru level," Wittmann says. It's stony and emphatic, completely dry, beautifully structured. Finally, there are the dry *Grosses Gewächs* wines. There are four, but the two more important are the **Kirchspiel Riesling GG ($$$)** and the **Morstein Riesling GG ($$$)**. Wittmann says, "They're not so different, if you look only at the soil, which is limestone. But Kirchspiel is east-facing; you get more early-morning sun. Morstein is south-facing, at a higher altitude. With Kirchspiel you always get into these spicy, green aromatics and flavors, and Morstein has more intense, yellow peach flavors, and more power."

PRODUCERS PROFILED IN THIS CHAPTER

Georg Breuer

Clemens Busch

Maximin Grünhaus / Von
  Schubert

Fritz Haag

Sybille Kuntz

Dr. Loosen

Shelter

Wasenhaus

Nik Weis—St. Urbans-Hof

Weingut Wittman

OTHER GERMANY PRODUCERS TO LOOK FOR

A. J. Adam

J. B. Becker

Christmann

Max Dexheimer

Enderle & Moll

Julian Haart

Immich-Batterieburg

Franz Keller

Weingut Keller

Koehler-Ruprecht

Kruger-Rumpf

Peter Jakob Kuhn

Peter Lauer

Markus Molitor

Ökonomierat Rebholz

Reichsrat Von Buhl

Schäfer-Fröhlich

Schlossgut Diel

Selbach-Oster

Stein

Von Winning

Weiser-Kunstler

Wöhrle

SLOVENIA, GEORGIA, AND LEBANON

Sighnaghi, Kakheti Valley, Georgia

SLOVENIA

Slovenia's vineyards produce an abundance of white wines—from familiar varieties, such as Sauvignon Blanc and Pinot Grigio, and from less familiar ones, such as Ribolla Gialla (called Rebula), Vitovska Grganja, Zelen, and Pinela. They also produce surprisingly good reds from Pinot Noir, Cabernet Sauvignon, and Merlot, along with native varieties such as Teran. And while pretty vineyards don't necessarily produce good wine, Slovenia's happen to be gorgeous. In the Brda subregion, which borders on northern Italy's Collio, the landscape of rolling hills and stands of oak trees is painted with vine rows, then broken up by small towns of white terra-cotta buildings. Farther south, in Kras, the terrain grows rougher, here and there a ruined castle looming over the winding roads. Along the Austrian border, in the Podravje region, the Alps rise in the distance.

That Slovenian wines make it to the U.S. at all is surprising. The country is one of those middle European football states, booted from empire to empire over the centuries. When Hemingway was driving ambulances on the Italian side of the border, Slovenia was part of Austria-Hungary. During World War II, the Italians, Germans, and Hungarians divvied up the place; after World War II, it ended up as part of Yugoslavia. Finally, when Yugoslavia disintegrated, the Slovenians found themselves autonomous once again. They took a deep breath, then they joined the EU. Not that vines care about politics: they go on producing grapes, no matter who's in power.

MOVIA • SLOVENIA

[organic / biodynamic]

"You know Hemingway," Ales Kristancic says. "*He* drank a lot of Movia wine."

Like many good storytellers, Kristancic has a breezy approach to facts. Still, this claim seems plausible. Dobrovo, the Slovenian town where Movia is located, is only about eight miles from the events portayed in Hemingway's *A Farewell to Arms*. But is an implied endorsement from Ernest Hemingway a reason to care about Movia's wine?

More reason is that Kristancic, one of the first Slovenian winemakers to garner international attention, is devoted both to organic farming and to creating wines that are deeply expressive of their place of origin. He practiced low-intervention winemaking before it was really a term; and while he's aligned with what has become the natural wine movement, he has very much forged his own independent path.

Kristancic is thoughtful, extravagant, and opinionated; both genuine and a complete showman; intensely focused and unpredictable all at once. If you plan to visit his winery, it's just

as likely that he'll decide en route that a field trip down to Croatia is a better idea. Plan to leave Movia with him at 9 a.m. in order to get to Ljubljana, Slovenia's cosmopolitan capital city, and—after he's agreed that this is an exceptional plan—you'll find yourself blending Pinot Noir with him for several hours in the Movia cellars instead.

Conversation is equally disorienting. This isn't because Kristancic's native language is Slovenian, but because his language is Ales Kristancic. To wit, cigarette in hand: "I need critics! I don't need this *wow-brow shikimiki zak-zak!*" Roughly translated, that means, "Hey, I need actual critics, not a bunch of useless hipster yes-men."

But unpredictability and a language spoken by only one person on earth can make for an entertaining time. During dinner at Movia he will hold court, saying things like "You have to walk on the edge. Forty-eight good barrels, two bad barrels, because the good wine is just, *zak*," indicating with the edge of his hand the line between brilliant and disastrous. "The famous winemaker Michel Rolland, he does not know this. If he brings this idea to Petrus, they will kill him. *Then* they will fire him." He laughs uproariously.

This is classic Kristancic. He walks a line between gnomic and insightful. "There are millions of things we know, but it is *good* that we do not know everything about wine." Or "More risk, more passion," balancing the two qualities in his palms. "More good, more bad. You play with fire on the hay, *zak-zak-zak, paf!* But only sometimes!"

Movia's wines are, unsurprisingly, full of personality. The **Movia Exto Gredic ($$)** is a minerally, almost oily Sauvignon Vert that's vividly flavorful. **Sivi Pinot Grigio Ambra ($$),** copper-orange in hue, receives ten days skin contact, giving its orchard-fruit flavors a textural (but not quite tannic) depth. **Rebula ($$)** is the Slovenian name for Ribolla Gialla; Movia's is apple-accented with fresh herb notes. The **Veliko Belo ($$$)** is the top white, a blend of Ribolla, Sauvignon Blanc, and Pinot Grigio that's full-bodied, complex, and lingering. There's also **Lunar ($$$),** which Kristancic describes as "Ribolla produced in a special way. We destem the berries, put in a special barrel, and do nothing more. Then the second time, with a tube, we decant the wine. It's just Ribolla and its expression. *Zak!*" Luminous orange in hue, oxidative in character, tannic from skin contact, and full-bodied, it was groundbreaking when it first appeared in 2001, and is still fascinating today.

For reds, there's a remarkably not-odd **Cabernet Sauvignon ($$$),** structured and elegant, with dark berry flavors. The **Modri Pinot Noir ($$$)** is transparent ruby, with layers of fine, red-cherry fruit and supple tannins. The counterpart to the white Veliko is the **Veliko Rdeče ($$$),** with Merlot, Cabernet, and Pinot combining to produce a silky, full-flavored, spicy red.

Kristancic's most idiosyncratic wine may be the minerally, sparkling **Puro ($$$).** It's bottled undisgorged—i.e., with the now-dormant yeast lees that helped produce the wine's bubbles still in the bottle. To get rid of all that dead yeast, it's suggested that one should open Puro while holding the bottle upside down and partly underwater. Some might consider this problematic for potential wine buyers. Kristancic, no.

GEORGIA

Tasting traditionally made wine in Georgia—which means wine fermented and aged in clay amphorae, or *qvevris*, that have been buried in the earth, wine without industrial yeasts and without additives, wine as simple and mysterious as wine can be—can feel like taking a trip back through eight millennia to the earliest origins of winemaking. Nestled between the Greater Caucasus and Lesser Caucasus mountains, Georgia forms a bridge between Asia and Europe. Over the centuries, invaders have swept through it: Persian, Greek, Roman; Turks, Mongols, Russians. And through all that, Georgians have gone on making wine.

The oldest evidence of winemaking in the world can currently be found at a site about thirty miles south of Georgia's capital, Tbilisi, called Gadachrili Gora. Here, archaeologists discovered chemical traces of ancient winemaking in pottery shards dating back to 5980 BC. It's transporting for anyone who loves wine to stand in the long grass next to the site, in the stiff breeze that almost always seems to blow, and to contemplate the fact that eight millennia ago, a Neolithic villager standing in the same spot was probably among the world's first winemakers.

Georgia's climate is largely continental except for the warmer, more humid areas near the Black Sea (home to more than 185 species of fish, "but," as one Georgian winemaker told me, "we only like trout"). There are eleven wine regions in the country and more than five hundred different grape varieties, though only a few are still used, primarily the white varieties Rkatseteli, Kisi, Mtsvane, and Chinuri, and the red Saperavi.

Georgia's traditional wines have had far more influence than could ever seem possible. For them, grapes—their skins, pulp, seeds, and stems—go into a *qvevri*. The *qvevri* is sealed, the yeasts on the skins of the grapes do their work, and between three and six months later, the *qvevri* is opened. Skins, stems, and seeds are ladled out, and the wine is moved to another *qvevri* to age until it's ready. The rediscovery of this minimal-intervention, amphora-based approach to winemaking, first by winemakers in Italy's Friuli region and later throughout the rest of the wine world, helped launch the trends both of orange wines and natural wines, and in many ways has made winemakers everywhere question their previously assumed reliance on technology.

It would be a lie to say that Georgian wines are easy to find in the U.S. But more and more are being imported, and there's no question they're worth the search. Their distinctive character takes some getting used to, but these are truly artisanal wines, and drinking them is a way of tasting the origins of wine itself, captured in the present in a bottle.

BAIA'S WINE · IMERETI

[organic / natural]

Baia Abuladze was twenty-two when she started her namesake winery together with her sister Gvantsa and her brother Giorgi. This was a wine startup the Georgian way. "We were going back and forth between Tbilisi and Obcha, and we'd saved up five thousand *lari* to buy bottles and this machine to bottle the wine out of *qvevris*," she says. "We'd put thirty or forty bottles in big bags, and we'd take the train at four a.m. into Tblisi, with four or five of those bags—that train is still my nightmare! Then we'd take a taxi to our flat, and walk the bags of wine up five floors. *Then*, it was time for delivery. We'd go into restaurants, and people would say, 'Where's your car?' And we were like,

'We don't have one.' We just had bottles of wine in our backpacks." That was in 2015. Today Baia and her siblings make about twenty-five thousand bottles per year. "We went from almost nothing to this. It makes us so happy," she says.

Georgia has no lack of stories about winemakers who fought hardship and won. "All the vineyards in our area were ripped up by the Soviets," Baia says. Essentially, the Soviets got rid of any grape varieties that weren't high-yielding or were problematic to farm, replacing them with ones that could be used for massive industrial-production wines. "Before the Soviets, there were lots of different grapes and lots of wine. It was a barter economy—you'd take the wine in jugs, or in a goatskin over your shoulders, to trade for corn, or oranges. My grandmother did that. But even during the worst years, she and my grandfather were happy—there's something in Georgia where people endure tough times, but they are always happy."

Baia, Gvantsa, and Giorgi make natural wine, but traditional Georgian winemaking *is* natural wine. She laughs if you talk about the natural wine movement in France and the U.S.: "We don't want to be arrogant, but guys, in our tiny village there are about two hundred families and they are *all* making natural wine."

The **Baia's Wine Krakhuna ($$)** comes from a grape whose name means "crisp" in Georgian. The flavors suggest melon and lemon, with a little bit of tannic bite from skin contact. **Tsitska-Tsolikouri-Krakhuna ($$)**, a blend of those three grapes, fermented on skins for fifteen days in *qvevris*, suggests persimmons and apricots, with more tannic body. With *qvevri* wines, Baia says, they dip out the wine after fermentation using a paper filter, "otherwise you'll have seeds and skins in the wine."

The **Baia's Wine Dzvelshavi ($$)** is a pale, transparent red, with tangy, lemony acid and red berry fruit. "There are maybe twelve acres of Dzvelshavi in the whole country," Baia says. "We planted about three and a half of them." The spicy **Gvantsa's Wine Otskanuri Sapere ($$)** is, like several of the reds, labeled with Gvantsa's name rather than Baia's. Gvantsa says, "Red grapes weren't traditional for our family, so Baia decided to put my name on those wines, in case they didn't work!"

PAPARI VALLEY WINERY • KHAKETI VALLEY

[organic / natural]

As William Faulkner wrote, "The past is never dead. It isn't even past." He might as well have been writing about the country of Georgia. At Papari Valley Winery, owner Nukri Kurdadze says, "During the Soviet era, our tradition of using *qvevris* was almost extinguished. There were only twenty or thirty families still working this way by the time that period ended." That Georgian grape varieties like Rkatseteli and Saperavi survived is somewhat of a miracle, too. "Georgian grapes survived because of Georgian farmers," Kurdadze says. "We're rebellious people. Always ready to fight." Kurdadze, who's in his sixties, is a first-generation winemaker. A physicist by training, he was born in Tbilisi and later worked in Moscow during the 1980s.

After the collapse of the USSR, he worked for a time in Europe for several large wine brands, then came home to found Papari Valley with his wife, fellow winemaker Keti Gurabanidze. He farms organically, hand-harvests his fruit, uses only wild yeasts, and says, "We still don't know

the entire potential of Saperavi and Rkatseteli, or really any of our native grapes. They were planted here long, long before the Soviets ever set foot in Georgia."

The past is never past. Over a glass of Rkatseteli, Kurdadze says, "In 1921, when our country was forced to join the Soviet Union, Keti's grandfather had twenty siblings. Seventeen were boys. All were killed but two. Her grandfather Alexander's nickname was 'Handsome.' The Soviet military would have shot him, too, but he escaped to Tbilisi—and because he was so handsome, he got cast in a Georgian film. After that, all the ladies were in love with him, and so they couldn't kill him!" A great story; Kurdadze smiles. But then he says, "The only word I can use to describe how I felt when the USSR fell is happiness. I never believed it could collapse. I could not imagine that this monster could die when it did. I can survive any kind of hardship myself, but my only dream is that what happened during the Soviet time never happens again for me or for my children."

"For me," Kurdadze says, gesturing as though he is pushing down into the earth, "*qvevri* wines are *deeper.*" That feels true of the **Papari Valley Rkatseteli ($$)**, amber-hued, tannic, almost viscous, with tangerine and dried apricot notes and a bassline of earthiness; it tastes excavated, not grown. His **Saperavi 3 Qvevri Terraces ($$)** recalls black plums and black pepper, juicy and dense, ending on prickly tannins.

SHAVNABADA • KARTLI

[organic / natural]

Here's the legend: In 1795, when the Persian army was encamped outside Tbilisi, every night a man on a horse wearing a black sheep's wool cloak would appear amid the sleeping troops and kill dozens of them, then vanish. This, the legend goes, was St. George, the savior of the country; his cloak was named Shavi Nabadi in Georgian. Hence the name of Shavnabada mountain, the monastery atop it, and, today, the wine made by the monks who live here.

Brother Markus, the bearded young monk in charge of winemaking, says, "We don't make a lot of wine. We're not a tourist-oriented cellar. If you show your wine to too many peo-ple, the wine understands, and leaves."

At Shavnabada wine is spiritual. Brother Markus again: "We don't filter our red wine or use any additives—that's not a respectful thing to do to wine. It's the blood of Jesus Christ."

The monastery, which dates from the 1100s, is quiet. Only eleven monks live here, and the mood is respectfully silent; you're as likely to hear the wind creaking in the trees or a solitary bird singing as you are to hear someone speak. But Brother Markus isn't averse to discussing the Shavnabada wines.

He learned winemaking from a Georgian biologist who had retreated from society. "He'd had a hard life. His son had been killed by the KGB, so he left Tbilisi and moved to the country. When I met him, he treated me as if I were his son. He knew all the grasses, all the herbs in the forest, the trees, the vines . . . but now his knowledge is gone, except for what I can carry on."

In the cellar, the monastery's *qvevris*—seven feet tall, holding four hundred gallons each—are buried in the earthen floor. A two-hundred-year-old vat made from a single piece of a linden tree trunk fills part of the room. Brother Markus prefers that you don't spit when you taste, which, if you believe that wine is tied directly to God, seems an entirely reasonable request. The thought-provoking aspect of tasting wine at Shavnabada is that even if you are not religious, you can't help but feel the tie that wine has to spirituality. "Our purpose as monks is to make people happy," he says. "It's not to make money. We put our soul and our heart into our wine, and that's why it's different. God is always present in this process." When asked if he ever thinks about people thousands of miles away drinking his wine, he adds, "There is a God, and God is everywhere in the world. We don't have to see each other to have that connection."

Shavnabada makes three wines. Its **Mtsvane** ($$), a white variety, spends up to thirteen years in *qvevris* before release. The color of burnished wood, it smells lightly sherried, and tastes of nuts, toasted nut skins, and smoke, the tannins from the grape skins present but not aggressive. The monastery's **Rkatseteli** ($$) is thrillingly savory, all toasted twigs and beeswax and light honey notes, with quite substantial tannins (both these wines are aged on skins, as is typical for traditional Georgian whites). The red **Saperavi** ($$) is dark and rich with black currant notes, very dry and quite tart in a bracing way; it's aged before release in bottles rather than in *qvevris*.

LEBANON

Lebanese winemakers would like people to stop talking about their wines in the context of war. As Faouzi Issa at Domaine des Tourelles says, "Politics is a problem everyone has. Only Lebanon has problems? There are problems all over the world."

Nevertheless, from the mid-twentieth century until now, Lebanon has been a more complicated place than many others to make wine. (But then, from 1913 straight until 1945, France was complicated, too—perspective helps.)

So give the war story a rest. "It's passé," Marc Hochar at Chateau Musar says. "What we'd like to do is get people to focus not just on war but on the quality of Lebanese wines and the unique nature of the terroir we have here." That terroir is principally the Bekaa Valley, a flat plain surrounded by mountains, high up in air that's brilliantly clear. It is an ideal place to make wine, as any Lebanese winemaker will tell you—three hundred plus days of sun a year, dry weather but also enough rain to keep your vines growing, native varieties that grow nowhere else, and centuries of history balanced against traditions borrowed from the French during their occupation between the two world wars. The Phoenicians made wine here six thousand years ago, and in the city of Baalbek, in the Bekaa Valley, you can visit the second-century temple to Bacchus, commissioned by the Roman emperor Antoninus Pius. In modern history, the two oldest currently operating wineries in Lebanon (Tourelles being one of them) date back to the mid-1800s.

Nowadays there are more than eighty wineries in Lebanon. There's political unrest at times, as well as other disasters, like the massive explosion that destroyed part of Beirut's port in 2020, injuring thousands of people and killing over 200. But the real story of Lebanese wine doesn't lie in the country's troubles. Instead, it's how good Lebanese wine can be. Besides, Faouzi Issa says, "We come from an exciting country. It's full of history, civilization, culture, problems, conflict, contradictions. Throw a bottle of Lebanese wine into a dinner, you'll extend the dinner an hour. Trust me. This is our strength!"

CHATEAU MUSAR • BEKAA VALLEY

[certified organic]

Chateau Musar is unquestionably the most internationally famous Lebanese winery. That recognition—for both Musar and to some degree the wines of Lebanon, period—can be chalked up to Musar's indefatigable, incredibly charismatic Serge Hochar, who passed away in 2015. Erudite, iconoclastic, charming—no one who ever met Serge Hochar ever forgot him. Today his work is continued by his sons Marc and Gaston and nephew Ralph.

Though Serge Hochar created Musar as it is today, the winery was founded by his father, Gaston, in 1930. Gaston Hochar never intended to work in wine; his family planned for him to become a doctor. But, Marc

Hochar recalls, "When my grandfather went to France to study medicine, he fell in love with wine. And when he came back, he said, 'OK, I'm going to start a winery.' Between World War I and World War II, you had the French army stationed in Lebanon, and they wanted wine, so it wasn't a bad idea—some years we would sell the soldiers our entire production."

Serge Hochar joined his father's winery in the late 1950s, but he set a stipulation: he would only work there if he could control the winemaking. "My father was a big character, a big personality, with very strong views—it's not that he wanted to get rid of his own father, but his feeling was 'Why should we do things the French way? Why shouldn't we do them the Lebanese way? Let's make wine how the Phoenicians did, a long time ago,'" Marc Hochar says. That meant concentrating on native Lebanese grape varieties as well as French ones, and also going against winemaking and grape-growing trends at the time. "In that era, people in wine were discovering the chemistry behind wine, and the more they understood the technical side, the more they wanted to control it," Marc says.

Hochar went the other direction: no additives, only local yeasts, minimal sulfur, and organic grape growing, though this was before the word "organic" was in common use. He was proud of aspects of his wines that more technically driven winemakers would dismiss as faults; as he said at one point, "If my wines had no volatile acidity, they wouldn't be Musar. I would stop making them. End of story." In essence, he was an early influencer of what became the natural wine movement, though he was definitely not part of it. Serge Hochar was not one to join movements. For him, Musar's wines stood alone, sui generis.

For many years Musar's story rested on the fact that Serge Hochar made wine continuously through Lebanon's fifteen-year civil war, which ended in 1990. Israeli tanks drove through his vineyards; he was stopped at machine-gun point by execution squads more than once; he told stories of drinking his wine in his Beirut apartment with shells falling on the city around him. But Musar's history extends before and after that period, and will continue into the future, even if Serge Hochar is no longer guiding it. In a way, the story of Chateau Musar resembles something Hochar said about his wines: "Musar has this ability to always be changing. You think you know it, you grab it, and then it is gone. It is like your life."

Chateau Musar's three most affordable wines are the **Musar Jeune Blanc** ($), a tartly apple-inflected blend of Viognier, Chardonnay, and Vermentino, the **Musar Jeaune Rosé** ($), floral and berry-scented, and the **Musar Jeune Rouge** ($), a medium-bodied, earthy blend of Cinsault, Syrah, and Cabernet Sauvignon. **Hochar Pere et Fils Rouge** ($$) is the middle tier—a single-vineyard blend of Cinsault, Grenache, and Cabernet Sauvignon that's more robust than the Jeune, but not as complex and age-worthy as the Chateau Rouge.

The remarkable **Chateau Musar Blanc ($$$)** is a blend of the Lebanese varieties Obaideh and Merwah. Serge Hochar always felt this wine could age even longer than his top red; old vintages, if you can find them, bear that out. Young vintages—so to speak, since the wine is usually released after six years aging or so—are lightly oxidative, balancing honey and citrus flavors. There's really nothing like Musar white in the rest of the wine world. As Serge liked to say, "It is a wine that will blow up your mind."

The **Chateau Musar Rosé ($$$)** is only made in years that seem right for it, and is effectively the white with a small amount of Cinsault. **Chateau Musar Rouge ($$$)**, like the Chateau white, is utterly distinctive, a savory, earthy blend of Cinsault, Carignan, and Cabernet Sauvignon. Serge Hochar liked to say that each vintage of Musar was dominated by either Carignan or Cabernet. Carignan years tend to be spicier and suppler, Cabernet years more structured and powerful. But as he also said in 2012, about his 1995 vintage, "The 1995 is more of a Cabernet-Cinsault year—but this is an opinion, and my opinion is always wrong. What can I say? I've been making wine for fifty years. I know how to make wine. But I know less and less *about* wine by the minute."

DOMAINE DES TOURELLES · BEKAA VALLEY

[organic]

Faouzi Issa has a lot to say about people's perceptions of Lebanon. "I was in Norway, right after the 2020 explosion at the port in Beirut. In Oslo, doing this big tasting. I was being very positive—I was frustrated, yes, and angry; we all lost friends or family in that explosion—but I was hiding those emotions. And one guy said, 'Listen, man, you don't really sound credible being so positive and happy. Where's that source of positivity?' And I told him, 'Listen, we have all the problems of the world in one dish in

Lebanon. But we wake up in the morning with blue sky, fresh air, the sound of the birds, the seasons that give us amazing fruit—this is what can fill the empty part of the glass. While you, in Norway, you have the best system, a lot of resources, and a lot of money, but you have six months where you wake up and it's dark. You have all the money in the world, but you wake up with darkness? Fuck that life, man!'"

Issa's energy is so contagious, and his wit is so sharp, that no matter what he says you find yourself either nodding in agreement or laughing. For instance, he loves Cinsault. A decade ago, he started making a 100 percent Cinsault. The grape is seen in France as not being of particularly noble standing. Issa puts it this way: "When I started making my Cinsault, most of the winemakers in Lebanon were still French. I don't know what's wrong with French people. They hate Cinsault. Even if they taste a good Cinsault, they still think Cinsault is their *piss en vin*. They pee on the wine. But we gave Cinsault the best climate, we gave it altitude, which is not available in France, we gave it bush vines, gravel soil, three hundred and twenty days of sun, all the care that Cinsault never had. And here, it competes with

Pinot Noir; it has the roundness, the cherry fruit, the spices. Fah! French people."

Domaine des Tourelles was founded more than 150 years ago in the Bekaa Valley. It was the first winery to sell bottled wine in Lebanon (before, wine was only sold in casks), and is a beautiful place, largely untouched over its century and a half of existence. Issa's family bought it in 2000. Issa had been studying and then making wine in France, but in 2008 his father asked him to come back and run the winery. He told his father he would do it, but only if he could run the winemaking on his own.

Issa's ambition was to return the wines to what Lebanese wine had been in the 1950s and '60s. "I hate to say it, but technology didn't improve wine. Starting sixty years ago, you get thousands of enzymes, manufactured yeasts, fertilizers, everything, all these technological additions. But I've tasted great wines from 1947, 1927, 1925, 1962—those wines are still alive, still young, amazing. Wine is ninety percent terroir, and good terroir doesn't need any chemical interventions or industrial products."

Issa farms organically and works solely with native yeasts and minimal intervention. "You talk to a winemaker and he says, 'I'm adding thirty grams of this enzyme to improve the color.' Seriously? Come on, man. If you go by the textbook, the profession of winemaker is the most boring job in the world. But when you go wild, using your balls and being adventurous, using native yeasts and old vines and organic viticulture, using your nose—that's exciting. You don't need eight years of fucking microbiology to make good wine. I have all these books in my office from my degree and I never open one of them."

Domaine des Tourelles makes a wide range of wines from its ninety-eight acres of vines. For whites, the floral, lightly honeyed **Domaine des Tourelles Blanc ($$)** is a blend of Viognier, Obaideh, Chardonnay, and Muscat. There's also a brisk **Merwah Obaideh ($$)**, a blend of the two classic Lebanese white grapes. "Merwah is grown at high altitudes next to cedar trees—lots of minerality and saltiness, but also ripe apple and fig," Issa says. Also, there's a lively **Rosé ($$)** from twenty-five-year-old Cinsault, Tempranillo, and Syrah vines.

In terms of red wine, the **Domaine des Tourelles Cinsault Vieilles Vignes ($$)** should not be missed. From low-yielding, seventy-plus-year-old vines, it's packed full of flavor but energetic and vivid, and remarkably affordable given what it offers. Issa's **Carignan Vieilles Vignes ($$)** is equally appealing. There's also the **Marquis de Beys Cabernet Sauvignon ($$)**, a bigger, bolder-style red. About his **Syrah ($$)** he says, "I love Syrah in the Bekaa Valley. It gives you such big, beautiful, silky wines." That's exactly what this one is.

PRODUCERS PROFILED IN THIS CHAPTER

Slovenia

Movia

Georgia

Baia's Wine   Shavnabada
Papari Valley Winery

Lebanon

Chateau Musar   Domaine des Tourelles

OTHER SLOVENIA, GEORGIA, AND LEBANON PRODUCERS TO LOOK FOR

Slovenia

Guerila Wines   Edi Simcic
Matic   Marjan Simcic

Georgia

Anapea   Nikalas Marani
Iago's Wine   Orgo
Lagvinari   Pheasant's Tears

Lebanon

Adyar   Massaya
Ixsir   Mersel

THE UNITED STATES

CALIFORNIA

Hirsch Vineyards, Sonoma Coast

O nly about a third of adult Americans drink wine (what the other two-thirds occupy their lives with is a total mystery). But that one-third adds up to about 79 million people, a group larger than the total population of France. And what those 79 million wine drinkers drink most is California wine.

California makes more than 80 percent of all U.S. wine—on its own, the state is the fourth-largest wine producer in the world. Its vineyards, all blessed in one way or another by that rich California sunshine, stretch across 147 American viticultural areas (AVAs) from the Ramona Valley, east of San Diego, to Seiad Valley, next to the Oregon border. (Admittedly, Seiad Valley has only three acres of vineyards and one defunct winery, but it's still an AVA.) Some of these are obscure, but some are world famous, and the most notable is Napa Valley. Napa is home to California's greatest Cabernet Sauvignon land (as well as California's highest wine prices); it also, despite its vaunted reputation, makes only about 4 percent of California wine.

So what *is* California wine? Is it powerful Cabernet, rich in tannins and ripe, dark fruit? Is it lush, oaky Chardonnay? Russian River Pinot Noir, with its black-cherry-and-cola signature? Central Coast Sauvignon Blancs that lean toward melon and sweet citrus rather than New Zealand's green-pepper intensity? Spicy, layered reds from hundred-year-old mixed variety vineyards planted by Italian immigrants well before Prohibition? Funky natural wine from Bay Area urban wineries? Biodynamic wine? Industrial mass-market wine? Wine in boxes? Wine in cans? Thousand-dollar bottles of Screaming Eagle Cabernet? Bulked-out tanks of smoke-tainted plonk destined for four-buck jugs on a supermarket bottom shelf?

The answer is yes. Unlike France or Italy or any other European country, California is defined by its *lack* of centuries-old tradition. Identifying California's terroirs is still an ongoing project; some are fully explored, others wait to be discovered. Partly that's thanks to Prohibition, which, when it was ratified in 1919, effectively wiped out the U.S. wine industry. Before 1920, there were twenty-five hundred commercial wineries in the U.S. Fewer than one hundred survived (there were two routes to avoiding extinction: sacramental wine, and wine grapes for "personal consumption").

The rebirth of California wine began in the late 1940s and 1950s, and took off in the late 1960s—a signal moment was Robert Mondavi's founding in 1967 of the first new Napa Valley winery since Prohibition. (That's also the first year since Prohibition where consumption of table wine in the U.S. surpassed that of dessert wine.) With ups and downs, there's been a steady incline in both consumption and reputation ever since.

Today, California wine is a $44 billion industry, but only a small percentage of that cash goes to independently owned, responsibly farmed wineries driven to make wines that express their specific terroirs. A small number of very, very large companies sell most of the California wine in the U.S.; there are a lot of bottles out there that probably bear more kinship to White Claw than they do to white Burgundy. Even so, there are hundreds of small and even not-so-small wineries and winemakers making ambitious, expressive wines, and more and more vineyards looking to sustainability, organics, biodynamics, and regenerative farming. (Fully 55 percent of California wine grape acreage is certified sustainable today, according to the industry trade body the Wine Institute. That is a bit of a mixed bag of a statistic—most California sustainable certifications allow for the use of glyphosate [Roundup], for example—but it's probably a fair argument that being sustainable is at least better than *not* being sustainable.)

Because the state is so damn *big*, the style of California wines is impossible to nail down, especially as successive waves of change in tastes crash onto its shores. Love for the oaky, buttery Chardonnays of the 1990s and 2000s has been receding as an interest in brighter, less unctuous versions grows. Ultra-ripe, high-point-scoring cult Cabernets are giving way to styles that hearken back to the more focused, streamlined wines of the 1960s and 1970s. Alternative varieties are in vogue, particularly among younger winemakers (and drinkers): low-alcohol, Alpine-style reds made from Trousseau, Poulsard, and Mondeuse; whites from northern Italian varieties such as Timorasso, Vermentino, and Ribolla Gialla. Because there are no European rules about what varieties can be grown where, if you can think of it, then someone in California has probably planted it.

The European natural wine movement has also made inroads in California, with producers like Broc Cellars and others. The easiest avenue that young, non-wealthy winemakers have available to them in the state is to skip the whole capital investment of building a fancy winery and (even more so) of buying vineyard land. Instead, they join up with some like-minded friends in a cooperative warehouse winemaking space, and DIY things on a shoestring budget. The number of ambitious wine brands that have started this way is hard to count, and that's no real surprise when vineyard prices in Napa Valley have hit $900,000 an acre. No tech billions? No vineyard for you. But that isn't stopping a lot of very talented young people.

Independent, environmentally aware producers making irresistible wines can be found in every wine region in California, from the long-established—Spottswoode, in Napa Valley, which has a history stretching back to the 1800s, was the first winery in the appellation to certify its vineyards organic, in 1985; today, under Beth Novak's leadership, it's also at the forefront of climate-change awareness in the wine world— to the super-recent. The San Luis Obispo AVA (or "SLO Coast," as locals call it) was only approved in 2022, yet rule-breaking winemakers like Gina Giugni of Lady of the Sunshine and husband, Mike Giugni, of Scar of the Sea had already staked out their place there, farming biodynamically and making some of California's most exciting wines.

New or old, startup or long-established, all of these producers have to contend with climate change. Intense heat spikes in August and September are the norm rather than the exception now, with temperatures in the 2022 harvest season reaching all-time highs above 114 degrees in both Sonoma and Napa. Add to that the growing threat of disastrous fires—the 2017 wine country fires were the second most destructive in California history, and smoke from fires in 2020 ruined grapes for many Napa Valley producers—as well as drought concerns, and there's a lot of justifiable nervousness among grape growers in the state. But farmers are a tough bunch, and passion runs high in wine. And every effort helps. Climate issues are a global problem, impossible to solve on a local level, but as Tablas Creek's Jason Haas says, "agriculture, even at our level, has the potential to be part of the solution to these big picture problems."

THE NORTH COAST

California's North Coast contains the state's most famous wine-growing appellations, Napa Valley and Sonoma County, along with dozens of others. Essentially, it includes all of the vineyard land north of San Francisco up to the northern border of Marin County, and from the Pacific Coast to the mountains that form the western border of the warm, inland Sacramento Valley—a rough rectangle of some 3 million acres, incorporating all of Mendocino, Lake, Sonoma, Napa, Solano, and Marin counties.

This is the golden heartland of California wine, and is where the industry both came back to life in the decades following Prohibition and later, in the 1970s, proved itself capable of making wines that could challenge the best in the world (and win). The key is the region's proximity to the cold Pacific, which moderates California's baseline warmth and provides coastal breezes and morning fog, especially in places where rivers cut through to the coast, as in the Russian River Valley. The resulting dramatic shift between day and nighttime temperatures during growing season gives cool-climate grapes like Pinot Noir and Chardonnay the ability to make energetic, terroir-expressive wines. The warmer, more inland sections of the appellation (Napa's valley floor or Lake County for instance) are equally ideal for Cabernet Sauvignon, Merlot, and similar Bordeaux varieties, as well as Zinfandel and Rhône varieties such as Syrah.

BEDROCK WINE CO. • SONOMA

[sustainable / organic (Bedrock Vineyard)]

Morgan Twain-Peterson comes by his commitment to California's historic vineyards honestly. His father is Joel Peterson, the founder of Ravenswood Wines, which, along with Ridge, probably did more to captivate wine drinkers with the potential of old-vine Zinfandel than anyone else (Ravenswood is now owned by Gallo). So, essentially, Twain-Peterson grew up surrounded by ancient vines.

He founded Bedrock with his longtime friend Chris Cottrell in 2007 in a converted chicken coop and goat paddock outside the town of Sonoma. An inauspicious start, possibly, but over time Bedrock has become one of the state's premier sources for evocative red wines made from historic vineyards and ancient vines. Twain-Peterson is also cofounder of the Historic Vineyard Society, a nonprofit established in 2011 to promote the idea that California's oldest vineyards have cultural value beyond simply being sources for grapes, and to help keep those vines in the ground.

"The post-*Sideways* period, from 2005 on, was really terrible for old-vine Zinfandel and Petite Sirah in the Russian River Valley," Twain-Peterson says. "All these farmers suddenly said, 'Hey, I can get five thousand dollars a ton for Pinot, I'm ripping this old stuff out.' Barbieri, for instance, that's gone. It was planted in 1905 and was the most genetically diverse vineyard out there, but it was ripped out and planted to Pinot Noir."

Bedrock is based at the Bedrock Vineyard, which Twain-Peterson co-owns with his father, Joel. Vines first went in the ground here in 1854, and were replanted following California's first phylloxera epidemic in 1888 by Senator George Hearst (father of publishing magnate William Randolph Hearst). The owner prior to Hearst, Twain-Peterson notes, was so ready to throw in the towel after losing all his vines to phylloxera that, upon getting rid of the property, he wrote in his diary, "Glory Hallelujah! Sold the vineyard, moving east! Bought my wife a diamond ring!"

Those vines Hearst planted are still thriving at Bedrock, 135 years old and still producing grapes—a mix of about twenty-seven different varieties, as was typical at the time. Not that the place was in perfect shape when Twain-Peterson took over. The previous owner, he says, "was a bit of a nozzle-head, trying to get four to five tons per acre off this place." The entire vineyard is 119 acres, with 33 acres of ancient vines from the original 1888 planting. There are 16,279 vines total—Twain-Peterson knows, because he has mapped every single one of them.

The rest of the vineyards Bedrock works with follow the same model: ancient vine, mixed plantings that somehow have weathered changes in taste and the passage of decades, and are still thriving. Twain-Peterson makes his wines using indigenous yeasts and no winemaking adjuncts or additives, and handles them as little as possible throughout the process. But he isn't by any means in the noninterventionist, natural wine camp; as he writes, "wine by definition is a result of manipulating a natural process to create something delicious."

Bedrock releases a large number of wines each year from a bewildering array of vineyards up and down California (but mostly in Sonoma County). To start, there's the **Bedrock Old Vine Zinfandel ($$)**, which comes from nearly a dozen different vineyards and is predominantly Zinfandel plus a plethora of other varieties. It's dark and juicy and entirely delicious. The **Bedrock California Syrah ($$)** is also a multi-vineyard blend, darkly brooding with glimmers of peppery spice. **Ode to Lulu ($$)** is an alluring rosé largely made from old-vine Mataro (Mourvèdre).

Of the many single-vineyard wines that Twain-Peterson makes, the **Monte Rosso Zinfandel ($$$)**, from a block of vines planted in 1886, is ebulliently aromatic and peppery. The **Evangelho Heritage Wine ($$$)** comes from a vineyard planted in the 1890s in Contra Costa County that is somehow wedged between a PG&E plant, a Burger King, and a motel that rents rooms by the hour. Of course. It's a field blend of Zinfandel, Carignan, Mourvèdre, and other grapes (*many* other grapes), full of savory, intense red-fruit flavors. **Old Hill Ranch Heritage Wine ($$$)** comes from the Old Hill Ranch vineyard, which Twain-Peterson thinks "is the greatest old-vine site in California." Darkly intense but never weighty, it has layers of flavor that unfold as it gets air (or time in a cellar). Twain-Peterson's flagship wine is the **Bedrock Heritage Wine** (**$$$**), which comes from the original block of vineyard planted in 1888, and is a blend of Zinfandel, Carignan, Mataro (Mourvèdre), and twenty-odd other varieties. It's both concentrated and finely detailed, its wild berry fruit accented by floral and spice notes—a vivid expression of over a century of California's vinous history.

BROC CELLARS · BERKELEY

[organic / natural]

Chris Brockway grew up in Nebraska, but he was fascinated by wine, he says, partly thanks to working in restaurants through his early twenties. College then provided a philosophy degree. "Which is great, but what do you do with your life? People were like, 'You're always talking about wine, why don't you become a winemaker?'" So he packed up his car, drove to California, and entered the enology program at Fresno State.

Learning to make wine is one thing; learning what wine you really want to make is another. "The learning process is also learning what you don't want to do," he says. "By 2005 I was trying to *unlearn* a lot of things. At the time there wasn't a lot of reference for what I was after."

What Brockway was after proved to be a California interpretation of the European natural wine movement. He'd been making wine for other people, but he didn't particularly like the wines he was making. "There were a lot of monolithic wines then, and this box you had to fit into. Back then, someone would say, you can't make a naturally fermented white wine! You have to inoculate, use commercial yeast. And I'm thinking, you can't? Because people used to, for thousands of years."

Brockway started Broc Cellars in 2006 in an industrial warehouse space in Berkeley, with no money and no employees other than himself. "I thought, 'If I'm going to go out of business, I might as well make wines I like and go out that way.'" "Natural wine," as a term, wasn't much in use, and there were only a small handful of California wineries working in that vein. He adds, "You know, our website says natural wine, but yes and no. It gets a little complicated. If you do a strict definition of natural, it's organic, and native fermentations, and *nothing* added. But we have some no-sulfur wines and some with a little added. I don't want to be locked into a definition, or a caricature."

Some of Brockway's mainstays include his effervescent, lemony **Broc Cellars Sparkling Chenin ($$)**, an easy-to-drink sparkler, and his **Nouveau ($$)**, a transparently scarlet, light-bodied blend of Valdigüe, Orange Muscat, and then a whole host of other varieties. It's floral and tingly, with light berry flavors; a great one to chill down. The **Amore Rosso ($$)** is a quirky, juicy, entirely delightful blend of Barbera, Dolcetto, and Sangiovese, lightened by a little Negroamaro Rosé. **Vine Star Zinfandel ($$)** has peppery strawberry flavors with a tea-leaf savoriness. It's a blend from the Arrowhead and Buck Hill vineyards in Sonoma County (Sonoma Valley and Fountain Grove AVAs respectively). "Arrowhead gives all these unusual Zin characteristics, black tea and black pepper and celery seed," Brockway says. The **Broc Cellars Nero D'Avola ($$)** comes from Fox Hill and is alive with grippy blackberry flavors; in Gaelic, *broc* means "badger," hence the badger on the label. "It's our spirit animal," Brockway says.

BUCKLIN OLD HILL RANCH • SONOMA VALLEY

[organic]

The story of Bucklin is the story of Old Hill Ranch, and the story of Old Hill Ranch is the story of California wine. In many ways Old Hill Ranch is a vineyard preserved in amber, a picture of the viticultural California that was, and that, in tiny patches here and there in this enormous state, still ekes out an existence, fighting time, trends, and, more often than not, the rapacious interests of real estate developers.

William McPherson Hill first planted the vineyard in 1852. He was a Gold Rush entrepreneur, and among other things the first person to sell peaches in Northern California. (They ran $2 apiece, or roughly $30 today.) Over the years, Hill planted more than fifty-three different varieties (Grenache, Chasselas, French Colombard, Tannat, Trousseau, Alicante Bouschet, you name it) but predominantly Black St. Peters, today known as Zinfandel.

In the 1950s, after the death of Kate Donohue Hill, Hill's daughter-in-law and last surviving heir, the ownership of Old Hill Ranch, as it came to be known, took some odd turns. Will Bucklin, whose family owns Old Hill, says, "In the fifties, the woman who owned it was a real estate agent—she wanted to rip it out and build houses. But then one year she had a Christmas tree with candles in her house, and burned the place down. She moved off the property in the sixties and rented it to a Gurdjieffian commune. It was kind of a dump site while they were here; a bunch of old cars, dead refrigerators, and plumbing equipment, vines covered in poison oak and blackberry bushes and coyote brush." The commune residents sold some of the grapes to local wineries and vinified the rest, which helped fuel Dionysian parties that went on for days. Welcome to California in the Aquarian age. But as the hedonism of the sixties guttered into the disillusionment of the seventies, the owner raised rents and the party ended.

In 1981, the ranch was bought—rescued, really—by Otto Teller. Teller was a Jaguar-driving, ascot-wearing, fly-fishing, World War II–veteran organic farmer and conservationist. He was, as Bucklin recalls, "stubbornly progressive in his approach to farming." Teller refused to use chemicals to revive the old vineyard, instead spraying the vines with liquified kelp as a fertilizer; he also refused to irrigate, since he felt it depleted the watershed. "He was a big proponent of dry-farming, and he was a big proponent of wildlife-friendly farming, too—he only ever got about a quarter to a half ton of grapes per acre here, because the grapes were being eaten by the local animals," Bucklin says, standing amid Old Hill's gnarled vines.

Bucklin is Otto Teller's step-grandson. Today he farms Old Hill under the same principles (albeit with somewhat less sacrifice to the appetites of local deer, gophers, and other critters). No herbicides, no tilling; extensive use of compost; essentially, pure organic viticulture and low-intervention winemaking carried out by, as Bucklin refers to himself, a "cantankerous contrarian who believes strongly in progressive agrarian principles." The ancient vines here are the same patchwork of varieties that McPherson Hill originally planted, because they're the same vines. Bucklin knows what most of them are; a few remain ampelographical mysteries. As he says about Old Hill, "The unknown is part of its charm."

Will Bucklin and his family make a number of wines from the property. (They also sell grapes to Morgan Twain-Peterson at Bedrock Wine Co., among many others.) Quantities are small, so the best way to find them is to contact the winery directly. The **Bucklin Old Hill Ranch Mixed Whites Field Blend ($$)** blends Muscat, French Colombard, Chasselas, and a host of other white grapes for a surprisingly light-bodied, lightly spicy white. **Old Hill Ranch Bambino ($$)** comes from vines planted in 2000 (even the hardiest old vines eventually fail; when they do, the Bucklins replant). It's a bright, juicy, predominantly Zinfandel blend, made with indigenous yeasts and aged in neutral oak. **Old Hill Ranch Mixed Blacks ($$)** gets its name from an old farmers' term for all the red grapes that weren't Zinfandel; it's mostly Grenache and Alicante Bouschet, along with thirty or so other varieties, and brims with spicy, dark cherry fruit, rich and luscious. Then there's the heart of the whole endeavor, the **Old Hill Ranch Ancient Field Blend ($$)**, from the vineyard's original 1880s vines. It's roughly 65 percent Zinfandel, together with dozens of other red varieties. Brambly, spicy, assertively intense, with peppery blackberry flavors, it's not only a delicious wine but also a portrait in a bottle of California's history.

CARLISLE WINERY • RUSSIAN RIVER VALLEY

[certified sustainable]

"I started with five gallons of Zinfandel in my kitchen," Mike Officer says. That was in 1987. Over the next several years, Officer made a barrel of Zinfandel each vintage with the help of his friends and his wife, Kendall, and eventually he and Kendall moved to Sonoma County to be closer to the source of his fruit. That's when a fascination with Sonoma's old-vine vineyards took hold of him; it remains the driving passion behind Carlisle Winery. "There's something special, even magical, about those ancient, twisted vines with their long roots and deep histories," Officer has written.

Anyone who's walked among the vine rows in a hundred-year-old vineyard has felt, unless they have a stone for a heart, something of what Officer is talking about. But if you don't have access to ancient vineyards, the Carlisle wines are the next best way of getting there.

The Carlisle (formerly Pelletti) vineyard itself was planted by Alcide Pelletti in 1927. Pelletti was part of a multi-decade wave of immigrants who escaped the brutal poverty of rural Italy for California. Sonoma's historic vineyards are an encyclopedia of Italian names: Pelletti, Belloni, Forchini, Giovanetti, Pagani . . . the list goes on. About Pelletti/Carlisle, Officer says, "Originally it was all just oaks here, but

---

> **"Don't let dogma get in the way of good wine."**
> —Mike Officer

Al just went down to the local hardware store and bought some dynamite and blew all the trees out." (There are rules about that sort of thing these days.) "It's about eighty-seven percent Zin, and the rest is thirty-nine different varieties, including ten white varieties. We've got a fair amount of Peloursin, a good amount of Tempranillo—it's crazy if you look at the map. And there's some pretty strange shit planted here, too . . . Criolla Mediano Dos, Grand Noir de la Calmette . . . we just pick everything and co-ferment it together. There's only one vine we haven't identified."

Officer also works with more than twenty old-vine properties throughout Sonoma County, and a couple in Mendocino and Paso Robles. "The history is what makes these vineyards so great—that, and they make great wine, of course." His wines are full-bodied and potent; Zinfandel in particular needs fairly full-on ripeness to really express itself.

This leaves the Carlisle wines somewhat at odds with the trend toward lighter, less fruit-forward wines, but richness is what these old vineyards give. Plus, Officer says, "I really don't give a rat's ass what the alcohol is. Do I find the wine pleasurable? Is it balanced? What the final numbers are, I really don't care. I just leave it to my palate to say yay or nay. Ultimately, all we can do is keep our heads down and try to make wine we believe in."

Of Carlisle's white wines, look for **The Derivative ($$)**, a blend of Semillon planted in 1886, Muscadelle planted in 1920, and Palomino planted in 1985, plus some ancient Colombard from the Mancini Ranch Vineyard. "It 'derives' from the old California 'hock' wines, which were blends of white grapes," Officer says.

For reds, Officer's first love was Zinfandel, and he makes some of the most expressive versions around. There are more than a dozen, but look first for his silky, spicy, red-fruited **Carlisle Winery Sonoma County Zinfandel ($$)**, a reliable steal. A step up is the **Piner-Olivet Ranches Zinfandel ($$)**, which blends fruit from five of his favorite old-vine sites in the Piner-Olivet area of the Russian River Valley.

His single-vineyard wines are all excellent. The **Montafi Ranch Zinfandel ($$–$$$)**, 87 percent Zinfandel, together with ten other varieties, comes from a vineyard planted in 1926. "It always displays a note of eucalyptus in the aroma," Officer says. "The winds blow the oils from the eucalyptus trees around the vineyard onto the grapes. If you make a wine from the block nearest to them, it smells like a bag of Andes chocolate mints." The **Carlisle Vineyard Zinfandel ($$–$$$)** suggests boysenberries and blackberries, its saturated flavor lifted by citrusy acidity. His **Papera Vineyard Zinfandel ($$$)** is 96 percent Zinfandel with a touch of Carignan, planted in 1934. It's dark, rich, and dense, classic Zinfandel, mouth-coating and full of black raspberry–black cherry fruit.

Of the Carlisle Rhône variety

wines, standouts include the potent **Papa's Block Syrah ($$)** and, without question, the **Two Acres Red Wine ($$)**. The latter comes from a two-acre vineyard of Mourvèdre planted in 1910, that Officer remembers as "being on the brink of death when we took it over. I found it in 1996 on my bike—it was all overgrown with weeds and poison oak and trees, and I thought, 'What a shame, someone's letting this vineyard go to waste.' I also thought, 'I know what Zinfandel looks like and this sure doesn't look like Zin.'" A formidable red, it's packed with dark cherry and cured meat flavors, with a lush texture.

COBB • SONOMA COAST

[certified sustainable]

Ross Cobb makes pinpoint-precise Chardonnays and Pinot Noirs from the far reaches of the Sonoma Coast, both from his own Coastlands and Doc's vineyards and from a smattering of other small, excellent sites farmed with similar care.

Coastlands was planted in 1989 by his parents David, a marine biologist, and Diane, a graphic designer and artist. It's been dry-farmed to save water and push the vine roots deeper into the earth since day one, with the result that "even during the crazy heat wave we had in 2022, we didn't need a drop of irrigation," Cobb says. "My dad also registered it sustainable back in 1991. We don't use any herbicides, and we've been doing no-till farming both at Coastlands, and then Doc's, which we picked up next door. No discing. No fertilizer or compost. It's truly, fully sustainable. Even with biodynamics, if you add compost and you don't have the cows on your own property, you're not being truly sustainable."

David Cobb was a longtime gardener—Ross recalls that wherever they lived they always had gardens, "so the vineyard was kind of a natural second career for him and my mother. They did all the pruning and picking and tractor work themselves. It was a lot of work. And you're not exactly rolling in cash as a grower when you're only getting 1.5 tons of grapes per acre." Vineyards as close to the Pacific Coast as Coastlands almost always yield minimal amounts of fruit, but the quality and focus of the wines that result can be remarkable.

Today David Cobb is retired (Diane Cobb passed away in 2006); Ross Cobb bought the land from his father in 2020. "I was able to give him fair market value for it, so now he's got a comfortable retirement—he's eighty-four—and I've taken over the whole operation." Cobb lives on the property with his wife and daughter, surrounded by vineyards, and the gardens his father planted. "Those were done sustainably as well—no fertilizers, no irrigation. You know, our well sits right below the vineyard," he says, "which means anything put onto the soil or vines is going to go *into* the well. Long-term health—not poisoning yourself or your family, for instance—that's also kind of a big part of sustainability."

Cobb makes anywhere from ten to fifteen different wines each year from his own fourteen acres of vineyard and from other far coast sites. The winemaking is hands-off but not extremely so: "I don't call it natural, because truly natural would mean that I don't show up for work and the wines just make themselves while I'm sleeping in!"

The Cobb wines are impeccably made, transparent expressions of place, pure and focused. Of the various whites, his stony, green apple-y **Cobb Cole Ranch Riesling ($$)** and the medium-bodied, savory **Doc's Ranch JoAnn's Block Chardonnay ($$$)**, which comes from a single acre plot of vines, are both highlights. But the primary focus is Pinot Noir. Start with the **Coastlands Vineyard Pinot Noir** ($$$), graceful and full of crisp red fruit and black tea notes. **Diane Cobb: Coastlands Vineyard Pinot Noir ($$$)** comes from a block planted with eighteen different clones of Pinot Noir. The very first Cobb wine came from that block: "I made a hundred and eighty cases, and I presented the wine to my father and mother, and said, 'Hey, this is what I made from that weird experimental block we planted.' And it was so good they offered to go into business with me.'" The **Wendling Vineyard Pinot Noir ($$$)**, full of foresty-savory character, comes from an organic/biodynamic vineyard at the far western edge of Anderson Valley. And the **Doc's Ranch Swan & Calera Selection Pinot Noir ($$$)** is electrically vivid, all taut red fruit and spice.

CORISON • NAPA VALLEY

[certified sustainable / organic]

Never underestimate chance. When Cathy Corison was at Pomona College, she was teaching a trampoline class for fellow undergraduates (she was a varsity diver, and divers practice a lot on trampolines). Next to the sign-up table for her class was one for a wine appreciation class. "On a whim, I put my name on the top of the list. It's crazy. There's no explaining it. I grew up in suburban Southern California. We weren't a wine-drinking family. My dad would never spend more than $8 on a bottle of wine. Gallo Hearty Burgundy, that was it."

From a chance interest in a wine appreciation class to a career as one of Napa Valley's most respected and influential winemakers, via trampoline; not exactly the typical route. "But that class just grabbed me by the neck and ran with me," she says. From Pomona, Corison went on to a master's degree in enology from UC Davis. "Not because I wanted the piece of paper, but I felt like I needed it. Women didn't make wine in those days." (Nor did they dive—she was on the men's team at Pomona.)

When Corison got to Napa in June 1975, she says, "It was just exploding. The place was buzzing with energy. And I was that girl who just wanted to make wine, against all odds. My major professor at Davis even sat me down to make sure I understood that I would probably never get a winemaking job in Napa Valley."

The professor was wrong. It took two years, but Corison got an internship at Freemark Abbey in 1978. At first the owners wouldn't let a woman in the cellar. She says, "I always had a big wrench in my pocket, because a couple of the guys loved to tighten things down so tightly that I couldn't get them undone. I put up with a lot. But I just kept telling myself, I'm going to leave these guys in the dust."

From Freemark Abbey to a now-defunct winery on Spring Mountain, and from there to Chappellet, where Corison spent ten vintages. It was demanding, exhilarating, and extraordinarily fulfilling, Corison found, and the wines she made at Chappellet were greeted with acclaim, but in the end she left. "The only way I can describe it is that there was a wine inside of me that needed to get out. I was looking for something a little brighter than what those vineyards were giving me. I love wines that have a life force, a vibration. Cabernet is always going to be powerful—no matter how you grow it, how you pick it, how you make it, it's powerful. But it's way more interesting to me at the intersection of elegance. The wines of the world that I loved were always both powerful *and* elegant."

The wine she wanted to make was fully formed in her mind. Cabernet

---

"That's where wine sits for me, between heaven and earth. Though, you know, I don't say heaven. I'm not a religious person. But it sits between earth and sky, if you don't manipulate it."
—Cathy Corison

Sauvignon from Napa Valley's Rutherford Bench, power and elegance to-

gether, aromatic, long-lived, "and that's what I've been doing ever since. Thirty-four vintages now, in this barn where I work. I'm trying to do exactly the same thing every year, but I hope I'm better at it three decades later than I was when I started."

Corison sustainably farms her Kronos and Sunbasket vineyards in Rutherford (she uses organic methods as well but is not certified), and for her Napa Valley Cabernet she buys grapes through long-term relationships with growers in other parts of the valley. She utilizes solar power for most of the winery's electricity. And she has also continually remained true to her initial vision, regardless of how ripe, black, and massive most Napa Valley Cabernet became during the late 1990s and the first decade of the 2000s. Today, rather than seeming outliers, her wines instead define for many young vintners what Napa Cabernet actually ought to be.

The **Corison Napa Valley Cabernet Sauvignon ($$$$)** is her flagship wine. "Cabernet can grow a lot of places and make beautiful wines," Corison says, "but with the Rutherford Bench, I look for that full range of Cabernet

flavors, cherries to cassis to blackberries. Grow it right and pick it right and all those flavors can be in the glass at the same time." Her **Kronos Vineyard Cabernet Sauvignon ($$$$)** comes from fifty-plus-year-old vines planted adjacent to the winery in Rutherford. The vineyard is named after one of the Titans of Greek mythology, the sons of heaven and earth. The old vines give the wine more concentration than her Napa Valley Cabernet; it's inky and intense, and able to age for decades. The **Sunbasket Vineyard Cabernet Sau-** **vignon ($$$$)** comes from a vineyard Corison long used as a component for the Napa Valley wine, before buying it in 2015. She also makes a tiny amount of Sunbasket Cabernet Franc, a Rosé made from Cabernet, and a Gewürztraminer, all of which are only available directly from the winery.

CRUSE WINE CO. • SONOMA COUNTY

[organic]

Michael Cruse's Monkey Jacket Red sums up what might be called the world of "alt-California" wine. There is no Cabernet or Pinot or Chardonnay here, no new oak barrels, none of the velvet-black richness of grapes grown to over-the-top levels of ripeness. Instead, Monkey Jacket is an offbeat mix of Valdiguié, biodynamic Petite Sirah, old-vine Carignan, and a little who-knows-what's-in-it red field blend, partly fermented whole-cluster, and aged in old oak barrels and concrete tanks. It's a bolt of pure, electric, jangly fruit that actually tastes about as California as you can get.

And about that name: "I was working on finances all night long, trying to figure out how to make this work, and had little kids, and was trying to stay awake," Cruse says. "And I'd listen to music. I grew up listening to punk bands, but that wasn't lightening my mood any. What I ended up finding was this old sea shanty called 'Banks of Newfoundland,' about guys who'd pawn their monkey jackets—what sailor's jackets were called in the 1800s—for women and booze, and then die of hypothermia. Great!"

Cruse also falls into the alt-Cali wine world by virtue of not being loaded with tech money, or being born into an already established wine family. "My family's kind of blue-collar. My dad worked for a trucking company when I was a kid." Cruse, though, had an aptitude for science, and ended up studying biology in college, where an inspirational lecture by Terry Leighton of Kalin Cellars (winemaker, but also microbiologist at UC Berkeley) nudged him toward wine. That, and not having a job: "I really came to winemaking from the 'hey, I can make eighteen dollars an hour driving a forklift doing this' point of view."

Today Cruse has a reputation as one of California's most talented sparkling wine makers as well as an iconoclastic producer of eminently drinkable, offbeat wines from varieties outside of California's mainstream. He's also strongly committed to organic practices. "We only work with vineyards that are organic or are actively transitioning to it," he says. He follows a similar approach in his winemaking: minimal sulfur; no added acid, yeast, or nutrients; no high-tech intervention. Beyond that, though, there are no rules.

From his warehouse winery in Petaluma, Michael Cruse makes a host of sparkling wines in almost every style: "I started doing a little *pét-nat*, then traditional method, then a little sparkling Valdiguié . . . then the wheels came off the wagon, so to speak." The *pét-nats* aren't funky-natty juice, though; Cruse is a precise winemaker with a scientific background, and even his more experimental wines are grounded in that. The **Cruse Wine Co. Tradition ($$)** is typically about 75 percent Chardonnay and 25 percent Pinot Noir, dry and savory with a kind of fresh pastry-plus-chamomile note. His **Tradition Rosé ($$)** offers pretty red berry flavors with lime-zesty acidity. **Reserve Cask ($$$)** is more complex, its flavors long and lasting, full of juicy citrus, autolytic yeast notes, and creaminess. The pale pink **Sparkling Rancho Chimiles Valdiguié ($$)** is a *pét-nat*, tart and driving up front and resolving into peach-watermelon flavors.

Of the still wines, depending on the year, there's a floral **Rorick Vineyard Chardonnay ($$)** from the Sierra foothills; a crunchy, crushable, 100 percent carbonic fermentation **Valdiguié Nouveau ($$)**—Cruse bears some responsibility for the mini-renaissance of California Valdiguié—a firmly tannic **Alder Springs Vineyard Tannat ($$–$$$)**, and many others. The **Monkey Jacket Red ($$)** appears every vintage. Though the varietal composition changes somewhat with each release, it always retains its boisterous, bright, California-sunshine character.

DREW WINES • ANDERSON VALLEY

[certified organic / biodynamic / regenerative]

To drive to Jason Drew's winery, hidden along the Mendocino Ridge in the western reaches of the Anderson Valley, is to get a reminder of how much of this remote part of California is still undeveloped. The road, Highway 128, winds through coastal redwood forests, tracking along the Navarro River. Sometimes the sun shines through the branches, sometimes you're passing through an arboreal twilight even in the middle of the day. It's intensely quiet. At times the landscape breaks open into apple orchards and vineyards, or into vineyards that once were apple orchards, which is the case at Drew.

The property was a certified organic apple farm in 2004 when Drew and his wife, Molly, bought it. "Our intention was always to farm organically," he says, "so that made things a lot easier. It's safe to say our place has been organic for at least twenty-five years." There are still plenty of apple trees on the property, covered with white blossoms in May, with the Pacific glinting through a notch in the hills. "When we first moved here, we had to clear some of the land. Then I had to feel the climate, let the ground lay fallow for at least two years before planting—and that was a good thing," Drew says. He planted Pinot Noir and Chardonnay, and now farms using some biodynamic principles. "Biodynamics forces me to look upward and outward more than inward," he says. "I've always said it takes about five years to *begin* to understand a vineyard. But I'm not married to biodynamics, and the farm isn't certified."

Their home vineyard is called Faîte de Mer Farm, which translates as "sea ridge," because the proximity of the Pacific is key here. "Since the soils are all ancient ocean floor, and since we're the most westerly vineyard in Mendocino County, at just three miles from the coast, we thought it was fitting." Faîte de Mer is eight—soon to be ten—acres of vines, along with ten acres of heirloom apples, a small truffle orchard, and a small olive grove. The Drews also make wine from several other high-altitude vineyards in the Mendocino Ridge and Anderson Valley AVAs. "I like that our wines don't just shout fruit, fruit, fruit," he says. "You get the ocean breeze, the coolness, that saline intensity in them."

The **Drew Anderson Valley Chardonnay ($$)** comes from the Valenti and Cloud Ridge vineyards, and with its wet stone, lemon curd, and pear flavors recalls Puligny-Montrachet through a Mendocino lens. The **Suitcase Albariño ($$)** got its name because the vines were a suitcase selection (literally, cuttings smuggled back in a suitcase) from Morgadío in Spain's Rías Baixas region. It's tart and tingly and entirely refreshing. The **Viognier Valenti Ranch ($$–$$$)** expresses the variety's round, mouth-filling nature, but there's also a kind of salty lime briskness that balances the richness.

Drew's reds are some of the most expressive California Pinot Noirs and Syrahs to be found, vivid expressions of their home vineyard and the other small growers that Jason Drew works with. The floral **Drew Fogeater Pinot Noir ($$$)** is a blend of fruit from vineyards in Anderson Valley's Deep End—Morning Dew, Wendling—as well as their estate fruit. "The idea is to express the Anderson Valley," Jason Drew says. "The forests, the coasts, the red fruits." He also makes a single-vineyard **Wendling Vineyard Pinot Noir ($$$)**, high-toned and electric. There are three vineyards from the Drews' own Faîte de Mer Farm. The **Faîte de Mer Farm Pinot Noir ($$$)** has a faint whiff of oak, soft blue-red fruit, and a truffle note that Drew says is a signature of the site. The **Estate Mid-Slope Pinot Noir ($$$)** comes from three separate blocks on the farm. It's more powerful than the Faîte de Mer, with a kind of fragrant, black raspberry character. The **Estate Field Selections Pinot Noir ($$$)** is darkly floral and slightly wild, luscious but also structured. "Field Selection is some of our best blocks, with heritage selections of Pinot playing a leading role. I love the character of the fruit in it," he says. "Earthy, truffley, loamy, dark but still red." His **Valenti Ranch Syrah ($$$)**, from a windswept, high-elevation vineyard six miles from the coast, smells of fresh-cracked white pepper. It's inky and intense, the aroma lifted by a small percentage Viognier that's co-fermented with the Syrah, full of cured meat and bacon flavors, and hints of violets.

FROG'S LEAP VINEYARDS • NAPA VALLEY

[certified organic]

John Williams delights in being outspoken. (He's also very funny.) Ask him about irrigation, for instance: "When I got here in 1975, *all* the vineyards were dry-farmed. All the great early Cabernets, the Inglenooks and so on, were. This idea that you can't grow grapes in Napa Valley without irrigation? Well, that's just horseshit."

Williams has been farming organically for more than thirty-five years now, and is, as he says, "on that regenerative ag path, too." Frog's Leap grows fifty other crops in its gardens and orchards besides grapes, and Williams maintains an extensive natural habitat around the vineyards (as well as an employee crop-sharing program; someone has to eat all that produce and fruit). The additional crops allow him to keep his vineyard workers employed throughout the year, "and from a social equity point of view that's crucial."

Frog's Leap's rebuilt farmhouse was the first LEED (Leadership in Energy and Environmental Design)–certified winery building in California; entirely made with recycled wood, it utilizes geothermal wells (under the parking lot) for cooling, along with enough solar power to cover all its electricity needs. Frog's Leap has grown over the years—Williams acquired the fifty-two-acre Rossi Ranch vineyard in 2007, and also has another fifty-two acres on another nearby site—but his focus on organic viticulture hasn't wavered. "Life below the ground is very intense, and this is why you farm organically," he says. "We invite life back *into* the system, rather than stamping life out of it. You know, the average vine life in Napa is down to seventeen years. Because without healthy soil, you don't have healthy vines. With conventional agriculture, you cut the vine's head off, poison the soil where the roots are, kill all the plant and insect life in the vineyard, and dose the vine with steroids—is it any wonder vines like that can't get naturally to real ripeness?"

Frog's Leap's wines are widely available. The **Frog's Leap Napa Valley Sauvignon Blanc ($$)** is reliably appealing, full of grapefruit and lemon flavors, fresh and zesty. There's also the **Sauvignon Blanc Concrete Aged ($$$)**, made from the winery's best Sauvignon blocks, fermented in concrete eggs, and given lengthy lees contact. It's a tingly, zesty, complex wine, with layers of citrus flavor and usually a light honey note. The winery's **Shale & Stone Chardonnay ($$)** comes from fruit grown by Truchard Winery (certified sustainable but not organic). "We used to just say 'Napa Valley Chardonnay' on the label," Williams says, "but it kept getting returned because it wasn't 'Napa Chard' enough." It's crisp and bright, with a kind of linear intensity.

The **Frog's Leap Napa Valley Zinfandel ($$)** is the wine that first brought Williams wide attention, and it remains a model for the variety: generous raspberry-boysenberry fruit, plush tannins, a fragrant herb note, brambly spice. The winery's lively **Heritage Blend ($$)** comes from a kitchen-sink mix of old interplanted varieties at Rossi Ranch: Charbono, Valdiguié, Petite Sirah, Mourvèdre, Carignan, and Riesling. And the **Estate Grown Cabernet Sauvignon ($$$)** is a stellar deal compared to many Napa Cabernets that cost much, much more. Dusty red and black fruit, tongue-coating (but not biting) tannins, lasting flavor—it's hard to argue with.

GRGICH HILLS ESTATE • NAPA VALLEY

[certified organic / certified regenerative]

Grgich Hills Estate is in Rutherford, the heart of Napa Valley, but its roots stretch back to Yugoslavia before the Second World War. As a boy, founder Miljenko "Mike" Grgich lived in the tiny town of Desne, on the Dalmatian coast. "His parents grew their own food," his nephew Ivo Jermaz says. "They grew grapes, made wine. As a kid, Mike was a shepherd—sheep and goats and one or two cows. There were no herbicides, no pesticides, nothing." Jermaz also grew up in Croatia, "and in the sixties and seventies, when I was there, my grandparents and my father farmed the same way. That's what we grew up with."

Grgich went on to a storied career (the 1973 Chateau Montelena Chardonnay he made triumphed over some of the greatest wines of France in the now-famous "Judgment of Paris" tasting in 1976) and cofounded Grgich Hills in 1977. Jermaz joined him in 1986, starting out as a barrel washer at the winery; he now oversees the viticulture and winemaking for the entire 366-acre estate. "When I first joined, it was a one-man show here," he recalls.

"Mike was traveling six months a year; he had no time for farming. When he bought 205 acres in American Canyon in 1997, he said, 'Ivo, I trust you to develop this land, to plant vineyards here.' That was scary as hell—I didn't know anything about farming! But I realized that the magic of a wine is never in the winery. It's always in the vineyard. So immediately I tried to learn how to grow the best possible grapes."

For Jermaz that meant, among other things, stopping the use of fertilizers and systemic herbicides. By 2003 the entire estate was certified fully organic. And in 2023, Grgich Hills became one of the first Regenerative Organic Certified estates in California. "Despite our organic farming, I felt there were missing components," Jermaz says. "The holy grail of regenerative farming is the microbial life in the soil, and my frustration with organics was, basically, why is the microbial life in *my* soil developing so slowly?"

The big revelation for Jermaz was not tilling. He now keeps a permanent cover crop of fifteen to twenty different species of plants, and four thousand sheep graze and fertilize the property every February and March (then they leave; if they stick around after budbreak, they tend to nibble off the tender grape buds, which are tasty, if you're a sheep). "It's a huge problem with agriculture today," Jermaz says. "Most soils are completely bare. When I see that, I know the soil is naked, thirsty, hungry, and running a fever."

The Grgich wines are all made

> *"You want to make a wine that's the same every year? Why? That's Coca-Cola."*
> —Ivo Jermaz

---

with native yeast fermentations, something Jermaz feels strongly about (he feels strongly about a *lot* of things—if you want to get fired up, sit down with him and talk about the environment). "People use these godforsaken systemic fungicides, which kill all the native yeasts on the grapes. Of course you have to inoculate—you killed everything! People believe, oh, yeast is yeast. This is nonsense. Commercial yeast produced in a laboratory has nothing to do with what natural yeast is. You put commercial yeast in a tank, you have to feed it, put a crapload of nitrogen in—it's like having three nice logs in your fireplace, then pouring gasoline over them. You don't need that much power. Our fermentations take two to three weeks, but the result is always superior wine."

All the Grgich wines—there are quite a few—are made from estate fruit. The **Grgich Hills Sauvignon Blanc Fumé Blanc ($$)** is reliably one of Napa Valley's best, lightly green peppery, with citrus-melon flavors and subtle oak notes. The **Napa Valley Chardonnay ($$)** avoids the fleshiness that Napa's climate sometimes gives to Chardonnay by not going through malolactic fermentation; it's bright and zippy. The **Miljenko's Se**lection Chardonnay ($$$)** adds additional complexity.

The winery's **Napa Valley Zinfandel ($$)** comes from a thirty-five-acre vineyard above Calistoga, and is usually a standout in the lineup: brambly red fruit, dried herb-spice notes, rich but balanced. The cassis-scented **Napa Valley Cabernet Sauvignon ($$$)** isn't inexpensive, but it's a lovely wine, and for Napa Valley Cabernet, a bargain. The winery's top Cabernet, the **Miljenko's Selection Old Vine Cabernet Sauvignon ($$$$)**, comes from vines in Yountville planted in 1959 (some of the oldest Cabernet in Napa Valley). It's a powerhouse, with lots of dark fruit and muscular tannins, deserving of some time in a cellar.

HALCON ESTATE • MENDOCINO

[certified organic]

Halcon is one of the more exciting single-vineyard, single-wine projects to come along in California for a while. The 162-acre vineyard, acquired in 2021 by wine entrepreneur Baron Ziegler and winemaker Pax Mahle (of Pax Wines), isn't well known, but to a small coterie of Rhône-loving winemakers it has long been seen as one of the best Syrah sources in Northern California.

The former owners planted fifteen acres of vines in 2005 in a windy, high-elevation site in Mendocino's Yorkville Highlands, a place that because of its altitude has temperatures that roughly mirror those of the northern Rhône. That makes for excellent cool-climate Syrah, but also, unfortunately, makes farming risky. Mahle says, "In 2021, Baron and I harvested twenty-one tons of absolutely perfect Syrah from Halcon. In 2022,

we got .7 of a ton, total. Frost wiped the vineyard out. Then the small but still pretty good-looking crop we had after that got decimated by the massive heat event that hit California that September. The vine canopies were just too underdeveloped to protect the fruit."

Nevertheless, the two are forging on, in an attempt, as Ziegler has said, "to make the Pierre Gonon of Northern California," citing the cult-favorite St.-Joseph producer (whose wines were once relatively affordable, but now sell out instantly at $175 a bottle or more). Halcon will produce a single-estate wine, though Mahle says, "In really exceptional vintages we may select out a special reserve Syrah bottling." Farming is organic, and the plan is to transition in the next few years to biodynamic.

Halcon currently makes one wine. In its initial vintage, the **Halcon Vineyard Syrah** ($$$), notes of violets and white pepper lift from the glass. The wine is powerful but focused, all blue fruit and spice, with a hint of cured meat on the finish. It tastes like Côte Rôtie seen through a California lens, or, simply, first-class Syrah from a top-level, cool-climate California vineyard.

HIRSCH VINEYARDS • SONOMA COAST

[organic / biodynamic]

Often people ask David Hirsch, "How the hell did you ever *find* this place?" It's a fair question. Even today, getting to Hirsch Vineyards requires heading out to Highway 1 on the edge of the Pacific, turning north at Jenner where the Russian River flows into the sea, and then cutting inland on a road that climbs and winds and eventually becomes dirt. You bump along over a cattle guard or two, past some bemused cows, back through the evergreens,

> *"Our wine is real wine from a real place made by real people. That came out of this site, this place. It wasn't some cozy, clever marketing riff or sound bite."*
> —David Hirsch

and finally you reach your destination. This is the far Sonoma Coast, much of it still forested and wild. Hard to get to now; in 1980 the middle of nowhere. Hirsch says, "I didn't find it, it found me."

The land Hirsch found was an old sheep ranch. He bought it, moved there. No desire at all to be a grape grower. But when his viticulturist drinking buddy Jim Beauregard came to visit, they were walking around one of the pastures when Beauregard turned to him and said, "You plant Pinot here and this will be a world-famous vineyard." A few months later, Beauregard returned with a thousand young Pinot vines. Hirsch planted them. Beauregard was right: Hirsch now *is* a world-famous vineyard. Hirsch says, "And to this day, you know, forty years later, I still haven't been able to get out of him how he knew that."

Hirsch and his daughter Jasmine work together, farming seventy acres of vines on this eleven-hundred-acre property (Jasmine Hirsch is the winemaker). "And in those seventy acres that do have vines, we have sixty different blocks," Hirsch says. "It's a very complex site because the San Andreas Fault runs through it, and because of the intense soil erosion from unregulated logging and overgrazing before we got here. There used to be four to five feet of topsoil here from millions of years of forest composting, but that's all gone. If it was still around, we wouldn't be growing grapes here, we'd be growing mushrooms."

Farming is organic and biodynamic. David Hirsch says, "Over time I started to realize, along with many other California grape farmers, that what we can see aboveground is really a function of what's happening belowground. Beyond that, the beautiful thing about biodynamics or any other holistic approach to farming—anything that focuses on the quality and the values of a place and tries to include everything, from the soil, to the earth, to the core, to the solar system, the sun, the moon—is that the more that you include, the more possibility *you* have of entering into the dynamic. The 'bio' of biodynamics is pretty straightforward. Any decent farmer can get it. It's the 'dynamic' part that's the mystical side."

Both father and daughter live on the property; it's big enough to be close to your family but not too close. But even in an idyllic place, farm work is dangerous. In 2014, David Hirsch was nearly killed in a freak tractor accident. It put him in the hospital for almost a year, and left him permanently in a wheelchair. But he still oversees all the viticulture, and his will and passion come through whenever you talk to him; it's impossible not to be inspired when he speaks about land, and place, and how wine can communicate the essence of where it's from. Though definitely not all wine: "Too many people in our business think of a vineyard as an asset. Then there's a handful of us who realize that land—a farm, a vineyard—is not an asset, it's something that's incredibly, immeasurably valuable.

"I remember one time Ted Lemon [of Littorai; they're good friends] gave a talk to a bunch of winery owners, and the subject was 'Can California Chardonnay approach the quality of Burgundy?' Ted made a point which was really poignant, that his experience in Burgundy was all about scale. The people he knew there, they made all of their decisions around the kitchen table. They were able to go out to their vineyards on a bicycle or by walking if they needed to. And all the key decisions about what to plant, when, where, how to do the wine growing, were made right there. So, giving this talk, he looks around the room and says, 'How many of you live in the place where you farm? How many of you actually get out to the fields every day, every week, every month?' There was just silence."

There are no tricks to the farming at Hirsch or to their wines. "People say, 'How do you manage to produce this quality of grapes and wine?' and the answer is really simple," David Hirsch says. "We get up every morning and we go to work. We don't have any magic bullets. We don't have any killer concepts. We discover the answers to our challenges every day."

Jasmine Hirsch says of the wines, "We approach our vineyard in two ways. The whole property, which is like a village in Burgundy; but then you can zoom in to parts of the vineyard. Our San Andreas cuvée is a macro look at the whole of Hirsch. Then we do four or five wines that are single parcels." The **Hirsch Vineyards San Andreas Pinot Noir ($$$)** has what might be called the Hirsch signature—raspberry-and-violet aromas, lasting dark raspberry flavors, and a light earthy note underneath them; also, that far coast, cold-climate lift and energy.

(There are two more casual Pinot bottlings, the **Bohan-Dillon Pinot Noir** [$$], which is the only wine for which the Hirsches use any outside fruit, and the **Family Blend Pinot Noir** [$$], which is only available direct from the winery. Both are juicy, bright, and delightful, albeit a little less complex and layered than San Andreas.)

Of the single vineyards, the **West Ridge Pinot Noir ($$$)** comes from a single block on clay soil that's "so dense it's like rock," Jasmine Hirsch says. "These vines have leaf-roll virus, so they always produce this delicate, fragile, super-aromatic, mysterious wine." **Block 8 Pinot Noir ($$$)** comes from a second patch of vines on very different soil that's high in iron oxide. "It's more powerful and in your face. But you can walk from West Ridge to Block 8 in two minutes. That's the San Andreas Fault for you." The **Reserve Pinot Noir ($$$)** is both a selection of specific blocks and the best barrels from those blocks. "For me a reserve should be from the vineyard. I look for parcels that have that greater intensity," she says.

There's also a small amount of excellent **Chardonnay ($$$)** from a tiny section of windblown vines. It's a steely white that opens to creamy, lemon-inflected fruit, reminiscent of top-quality Puligny-Montrachet. Or perhaps it's the other way round—maybe Puligny-Montrachet really resembles great Sonoma Coast Chardonnay. But don't try telling people that in Burgundy.

HONIG WINERY • NAPA VALLEY

[certified sustainable]

In 1964, Louis Honig, a San Francisco ad man, bought sixty-eight acres of former ranchland in Rutherford, smack in the center of Napa Valley. At that time Napa land wasn't in high demand, and he paid only about $1,000 an acre for it. But the Honigs didn't start making wine until 1980, and when they did, they decided to focus on Sauvignon Blanc, mostly because no one else was making it. The first vintage was two hundred cases total, vinified in an old tractor barn on the property. What the Honigs didn't realize was that the reason no one was making Sauvignon

Blanc was because no one was *buying* Sauvignon Blanc.

Enter Michael Honig, Louis's grandson. He was in college, but was a terrible student; skipping class to go skiing will do that. Since the winery was floundering, Honig's father offered him an out: leave school, and take over running the place. As Honig recalls, his father said, "Look, you're failing, so why not?" Honig wasn't confident about this prospect. "I don't think I'm going to be very good at this," he replied. His father shrugged: "Well, it's not like the business can get much worse."

That was in 1984; Honig was twenty-two. That first year, he sold the family's Sauvignon Blanc door-to-door in San Francisco stores and restaurants, and delivered the wine in the back of his station wagon. That work paid off over time, and today the Honigs make roughly seventy thousand cases of wine a year (about half estate; for the other half, the winery only works with sustainable growers).

Honig has been, with his wife, Stephanie, an early adopter of sustainable and socially responsible practices. They run the winery on solar power, feeding the excess generated by fifteen hundred or so solar panels back into the energy grid. In the vineyard, among other sustainable practices, they've pioneered the use of "sniffer dogs," who can detect the presence of mealybugs (a common pest) by tracking their pheromones. Lighter weight glass bottles lower the winery's carbon footprint; there's also a project in the works to use worms to clean and filter the winery's wastewater. "As a generational business, our biggest asset is our land," Michael Honig says. "If we don't care for it properly, we won't have a legacy to pass down."

The zesty **Honig Napa Valley Sauvignon Blanc ($$)** is the winery's largest-production wine by a long shot (people eventually caught on to the idea of drinking Sauvignon). Recently the Honigs stopped using foil capsules on the bottles; they effectively serve little purpose other than decoration, and just end up in landfills. The **Napa Valley Reserve Sauvignon Blanc ($$)** comes from the Honig estate vineyards; a portion is fermented in new French oak barrels, giving it a creamier texture and vanilla-spice notes. Their **Napa Valley Cabernet Sauvignon ($$$)** remains an excellent value in a region where prices are climbing ever higher. It combines estate and purchased fruit for a cassis-inflected, elegant red.

IDLEWILD • SONOMA COUNTY

[organic / regenerative]

Sam Bilbro and his Idlewild Wines are a good example of why it can be very hard to label how people grow grapes once you get past conventional, chemical-based farming. His own term is "holistic farming," which seems as good as any, but then what *is* holistic farming?

Bilbro laughs. "I oversee three vineyards, and farm about a hundred and sixty acres that I've converted from conventional to organic/regenerative-based programs. It's tricky. I think we sometimes use one or the other of the various words out there, but none of them really talk about everything we're trying to do." That includes ensuring that all vineyard workers receive minimum wage and access to health care; replanting only with drought-resistant rootstocks, in anticipation of climate change issues; replenishing soil via compost, manure, and cover crops, and working no-till if possible; using worm-composting and organic compost teas to help fertilize and also create greater microbiotic life in the soil; zero herbicides; and, as of 2023, high-density sheep grazing to "mow" cover crops, fertilize, and break up soil (sheep's hooves function as a very light form of tilling). Bilbro says, "I use the word 'holistic' since I'm trying to look at the big picture in a natural way."

Though Bilbro grew up in a wine family, he didn't plan to make wine at all. "I always loved being with my dad in the vineyard, cellar, garden, and kitchen, but I just never felt the love for actual wine the way he did. Then, towards the end of college, while I was playing in a crappy punk band, I had my first sip of Barbaresco. It was like a lightning rod. Suddenly, I saw all those childhood memories through a new lens—it made me fully fall in love with wine again."

Bilbro makes wine from Piedmontese grape varieties on California terroir, which puts him in that realm of California vintners pushing at the boundaries of what we think of as "California wine." The best introduction to his work is his floral, citrusy **Idlewild Flora & Fauna White**

($$), a light-bodied blend of (usually) Arneis, Muscat Canelli, Cortese, Erbaluce, and Favorita; and its crisp, cherry-scented counterpart **Flora & Fauna Red ($$)**, made from Dolcetto, Barbera, Nebbiolo, and Freisa. (There's also a quite good **Flora & Fauna Rosé [$$]**.) Of the others, standouts include an almond-scented, focused **Arneis ($$)**; a rambunctious, floral, red-fruited **Freisa ($$)**; and a **Nebbiolo ($$–$$$)** that's one of the few outside Piedmont that actually does taste like Nebbiolo.

KEPLINGER WINES • NAPA VALLEY

[sustainable]

Helen Keplinger sources grapes from distinctive vineyards throughout California for her eponymous brand. (Her day job continues to be consulting for a number of high-end Napa Cabernet producers.) Keplinger mostly focuses on Rhône varieties: Grenache, Syrah, Mouvèdre, Petite Sirah, Viognier. And when you talk to her, it's clear that earth and rocks are things she's passionate about. When she first went to visit Ann Kraemer's famed Shake Ridge Vineyard in the Sierra Foothills, she says, "Just driving out there and being blown away by these super-red soils and granite outcroppings, it was just thrilling—wild and visceral and incredible." Of course, that isn't unusual for a winemaker.

There are not many other people who get quite so excited about dirt.

"I think my sensibility comes from my mom, of having beautiful fresh ingredients in a garden and taking those, with minimal dressing up, and making something delicious," she says. "It's the same principle with winemaking. Start with a site that's compelling and that will make a wine that's intense and special and has a distinct voice of that site, do the work in the vineyard to farm for that intensity and complexity, then take the grapes into the winery and try to honor everything that was done in the vineyard. You never master that process; you're always learning, and you can always improve."

Keplinger makes wine from vineyards mostly in Napa Valley and Sonoma County and also Shake Ridge in Amador County. "All the vineyards I work with are farmed sustainably," she says, "and a good portion organically. And the ones that aren't organic, every year I ask if we can switch over."

The Keplinger **Eldorado ($$$)** is a rich but focused white blend of Viognier, Roussanne, and Grenache Blanc from Shake Ridge Vineyard, a kind of echo of white Hermitage in a California way. **Lithic ($$$)**, also from Shake Ridge, blends Grenache, Mourvèdre, and Syrah into a heady, full-bodied, spicy red. **Mars ($$$)** is a similar blend but from Sonoma County rather than Amador, more red-fruited and taut. **Sumo ($$$)** is one of California's top Petite Sirahs, powerful and peppery, full of blue and black fruit, its aroma lifted by the inclusion of a small amount of Viognier in the blend. **El Diablo's ($$$)** dark berry flavors finish on white pepper notes; it's 100 percent Grenache from the El Diablo Vineyard in the Russian River Valley. **Basilisk ($$$)** is a different take on Grenache, though also from Russian River; it's silkier, all raspberry-strawberry flavors that glide across the palate. (Helen also makes **Vermillion [$$]**, a spicy, affordable, kitchen-sink blend of Grenache, Syrah, Mourvèdre, Cabernet, and other grapes from a host of different vineyards, which she sells under its own label rather than as Keplinger.)

KUTCH • SONOMA COAST

[organic]

Jamie Kutch has made a name for himself with terroir-expressive, eloquent Pinot Noirs sourced from primarily some of the Sonoma Coast's top vineyards (the Santa Cruz Mountains AVA is in the mix as well). But talk to him these days and you're likely to catch him while he's pulling weeds by hand from around the rootstock he's planted at his newly planted Kutch Vineyard outside Sebastopol.

The latter represents the fulfillment of a long-standing ambition. Kutch was in New York City in 2005, working in finance, and, he says, "I was just burned out on the chase of the dollars, the Wall Street rat race in New York City. I was a trader, and I'd spend my days on the trading desk staring at two or three computer screens. But during lunch I'd get on the wine chat boards; that was when my day was alive. I got to talking with Michael Browne [cofounder of Kosta Browne] and he said, "Come out! Make wine, I'll help you. And I basically just jumped on a plane and headed to California and completely changed my life."

The vineyards Kutch works with are all farmed organically, and the new estate vineyard will move beyond that. "It will be both organic and regenerative," he says. "Very similar to biodynamic without the strict rules. We're already employing cover crops, working no-till, raising worms for vermicompost and vermicompost teas. As the vines get established, we'll bring in chickens and tow a chicken-trailer through the vineyard; eventually sheep. I'm also aiming for massive diversity—we didn't plant vines fence-line to fence-line. We have an apple orchard, a vegetable garden, a pond for frogs and flies and gnats—the gnats get eaten by swallows—and avocado, cherry, and plum trees. Native bee boxes. The better off the vineyard is, the more you end up in total synchronicity with nature."

This makes it sound like Kutch's project is vast; it's actually only 12 acres, with 6.5 acres of vines, not far outside Sebastopol. But small doesn't necessarily imply limited, as the documentary *The Biggest Little Farm* makes clear, which Kutch cites as an influence (an aside: great movie, watch it). "It seems like the food world is often ahead of wine in the thought process about living soil," he says, referring to the movie, and the path followed by Apricot Lane Farms in it. "You see the transformation of dead soil into living soil, and it's truly amazing. But it can happen. You have a bin of half a million worms, eating compost or cow manure, and basically their poop is like black diamonds—millions upon millions of healthy bacteria and microorganisms. Put that into the soil, and the vines become happier, stronger, greener."

Small can be vast, in fact. And small can also equal independence: "We have no investors. I've never taken money from anybody, and I've saved my whole life for this," Kutch says. "My wife, Kristen, and I bought this land in 2021. We're going to live here, and I think down the line we'll probably die here. Right now, it's hard to tell the story, because we're right at the beginning. But it will happen."

Kutch currently makes a range of Pinots and Chardonnays from the five organic vineyards he sources fruit from; the Kutch Vineyard won't produce a crop for another few years. Of the whites, the **Kutch Sonoma Coast Chardonnay ($$)** is a refined expression of the crisp focus that Sonoma Coast fruit offers; for more stony intensity, look toward the **Trout Gulch Vineyard Chardonany ($$$)** from the Santa Cruz Mountains.

Of the reds, the **Sonoma Coast Pinot Noir ($$)** paints a good picture of Jamie Kutch's style: restrained but not attenuated, with lifted aromatics, vibrant red fruit and a hint of spice. The aromatic, complex **Falstaff Vineyard Pinot Noir ($$$)** comes from a cold, foggy site eight miles from the Pacific; a high-toned red that vibrates with energy. The **McDougall Ranch Pinot Noir ($$$)** offers a contrast: darker fruit, more power, more savory. There are several more, both Chardonnays and Pinot Noirs; the best way to find them is to contact the winery directly.

LITTORAI • SONOMA COAST

[organic / biodynamic / regenerative (estate vineyard) / sustainable or organic (other vineyards)]

"When I got started," Ted Lemon says, "the bigger, bolder style of California wine was in ascendance." That was in the early 1990s. But big, bold wines were not what Lemon wanted to make. He had worked in Burgundy, and wanted to bring Burgundy's focus on wines that expressed place to bear on Californian terroir; to make wines that were nuanced and expressive, from cool-climate vineyards in the Pacific-influenced far reaches of Sonoma and Mendocino.

That he was able to contemplate doing this at all was serendipitous. A fall spent working the harvest at Domaine Dujac after he graduated from college had led to an impressive Burgundy education, with time spent at Georges Roumier, Bruno Clair, and Domaine Parent, and finally a role as winemaker—at age twenty-five—at Domaine Guy Roulot. But chance definitely played a role: "I was taking a wine appreciation class in Dijon, and the instructor said, 'You seem awfully interested in this, if you ever want to work a harvest, let me know.' I had no connections. It was strike out after strike out, but I knew that Jacques Seysses at Dujac had married an American woman. I literally cold-called him from a phone booth in Dijon. If he hadn't answered, I might be a teacher of French literature somewhere. That's a horrifying thought."

Lemon and his wife, Heidi, founded Littorai in the early 1990s. By 2003, they were able to purchase thirty acres of land on a hilltop between Sebastopol and Freestone. "The question then is how are you going to farm," Lemon says. "I was done with conventional farming. I'd seen the shortcomings. You're always adding more additives. It's a merry-go-round."

Over time what he has landed on is an approach he calls "generative agriculture." It borrows from biodynamics, permaculture farming, and agro-ecology, but Lemon isn't inclined toward any kind of certification. It also specifically looks at the role of humans in the context of their relationship to the environment. As Lemon says, "Who believes we're going to regenerate the world of 1800 anytime soon? We aren't going to—we can't—return to that."

Lemon uses only natural materials and estate-produced compost for his farming; vineyards he sources from other than his own are similar in philosophy (about 85 percent are biodynamic, the other 15 percent organic). Though, as he says, "A lot of biodynamic farmers get lost in the ideas. You lose the idea of good peasant farming."

Most recently, in his estate Pivot Vineyard, he's planted native trees and plants throughout the rows. Typical viticulture would regard these as competitors with the vines. But what Lemon notes is that old-growth forests, for instance, naturally bring countless plant species into balance; they're ecological realms that work on interdependence. "I've grown to appreciate in life how the most innocent, childlike questions are the most important. So I wondered, what does the forest know that I don't? Because it's in a state of ecological equilibrium." That's what he's working toward on his own property. "It's still a vineyard in the traditional sense," he says, standing at the top of one rise, looking past the vines to the green wall of trees beyond. "But I've tried to bring back native species among the vines."

He adds, "I finally realized that the detours were the path. Our limitations in terms of managing the animals, harvesting too early, all of that is the path. You never finish learning. And the big lesson to me was this idea of trying to generate a different relationship to the land."

Littorai makes some of California's most beautifully expressive Chardonnays and Pinot Noirs. There are quite a number, from a dozen different vineyards, including the Lemons' own Pivot Vineyard. All are hotly sought after by collectors and sommeliers, but can be found in stores with some hunting, particularly the graceful **Littorai Sonoma Coast Chardonnay ($$$)** and the equally expressive **Sonoma Coast Pinot Noir ($$$)**, both of which come from fruit that did not quite make the cut for the single-vineyard wines.

It's hard to pick favorites here, because Lemon's wines are so good across the board, but of the whites, the **Littorai B.A. Thieriot Vineyard Chardonnay ($$$$)** is stellar. "It's the most in the citrus realm of my Chardonnays," Lemon says. The **Heintz Vineyard Chardonnay ($$$$)** is "the most 'California'—the most tropical, for lack of a better term." The **Tributary Vineyard Chardonnay ($$$$)**, from a four-acre plot that was the Lemons' estate vineyard before they bought the land where they are now, "always has a little more mid-palate richness."

Of the Pinots, the **Littorai Savoy Vineyard Pinot Noir ($$$$)** mingles floral notes with a bolt of crunchy redberry fruit, becoming savory toward the end. "It always ages, and it's always consistent. It may not be the sexiest, or the most tannic, but it always goes uphill." The **One Acre Pinot Noir ($$$$)** is both deeper and more tautly focused, spicy up front. "For this wine, I always think about rose petals. Richer, but more savory than Savoy. And the tannins kick in at the end." The **Pivot Vineyard Pinot Noir ($$$$)**, from the Lemons' home property, plays dark,

sweet fruit against a light herbal character. "To me it's marked by this almost green, blackberry-cane note," Lemon says. "And the acidity always *feels* more pronounced than the numbers indicate." For me, that appealing, subtle greenness also serves as a reminder that yes, wine really does come from the fruit of a plant.

LONG MEADOW RANCH • NAPA VALLEY

[certified organic]

In addition to growing grapes for wine, at Long Meadow Ranch the Hall family farms organic artichokes, beets, tomatoes, cardoons, watermelons, and a host of other crops; raises chickens for eggs; grows olives for olive oil; keeps bees for honey; produces grass-fed beef from 350 head of cattle; and breeds horses, which seem to be about the only things Long Meadow produces that people aren't allowed to eat. (The Hall family also owns Farmstead restaurant in St. Helena, where a lot of that produce goes.)

All farming at Long Meadow is certified organic. "My mother was an organic-farming pioneer in the 1940s,"

founder Ted Hall says. "I grew up on a small farm in western Pennsylvania. Sadly, 'organic' has often become a political statement, but it's been a motivating part of what we've done here at Long Meadow since the beginning. And it's as much a system of thought as it is about the produce."

Long Meadow's wines are old-school Napa: lower in alcohol and more streamlined, less buxom, more aimed at being appealing partners for food at a meal. "We rejected the idea that we're supposed to be making gladiators for spit-bucket contests," Ted Hall says.

The Halls grow grapes on 150 acres of vineyard in Napa and Anderson valleys, and though Long Meadow is certified organic, the Halls term their approach "full-circle farming." Integration of the different agricultural aspects is key: pumpkin vines and dead tomato plants go into compost, for instance, as does vegetable water (a high nitrogen by-product of olive oil production, which Hall calls "magic fuel" for composting). Chickens provide eggs, but also manure for compost. Solar power is used for both winery and residential needs. Hall is also firm that organic farming is cost-effective: "This is not philanthropy for foodies. I farm organically because it results in higher quality and lower cost."

Long Meadow makes a wide variety of wines; the following four stand out. The **Long Meadow Ranch Anderson Valley Chardonnay ($$)** comes from the family's estate in the Deep End of Anderson Valley. It's classic cool-climate Chardonnay, lightly floral on the nose, with brisk acidity and citrus-driven flavors. The family's **Anderson Valley Pinot Noir ($$)** follows a similar vein: pomegranate-tart, with a lightly savory finish. The **Napa Valley Cabernet Sauvignon ($$)** blends fruit from the family's mountain and Rutherford vineyards, and hews to the less-extravagant style that both Ted Hall and son Chris Hall (who now oversees the wine side of things) favor. The **Rutherford Estate Cabernet Sauvignon ($$$)** has more depth and power, but its black cherry and currant flavors never become heavy.

MASSICAN • NAPA VALLEY

[certified sustainable / organic / certified organic (depending on vineyard)]

Massican is the brilliant, offbeat, always intriguing brainchild of winemaker Dan Petroski. For fourteen years now, Petroski has been making compelling, finely focused white wines from northern Italian grape varieties in Napa Valley—unusual right there— as well as spinning off endless projects and platforms from his seemingly never-sleeping mind. I've literally never reached out to him, by phone, by text, by email, and not gotten a response almost instantly—ten a.m., five p.m., midnight, two a.m., five a.m.—it's uncanny. Vermouth, beer, NFTs, think-tank meetings about global warming and wine, about natural wine, about the future of Napa Valley, plans for a bar in the metaverse (still not sure what that meant)—it's all quite dizzying, and very impressive. Perhaps the man is a brilliant android, because it's very unclear how one human could manage all this.

And regardless, it all does go back to the wines. Petroski has a gift for making evocative, nuanced whites that go against the usual ripe Napa Valley model. He sources from a number of vineyards, leaning organic, at the very least sustainable: "Of my current lineup, two are certified organic, four organic and not certified, and then five certified sustainable," he says. He's also been a crucial player in bringing the conversation about climate change to bear on Napa Valley wine. He says, "I've gotten a lot of shit for talking about the possibility of Napa Cabernet going away due to climate change. But the actual Cabernet mindshare is a very modern phenomenon here in California, so don't discredit yourselves and your own talent to say, 'Oh, we only need to be making Cabernet here.' We're going to grow great, delicious wines in this Valley for a very long time. It'll be a bump in the road to convince someone that they have to pay $200 for a Napa Valley Touriga Nacional in a bottle [a more heat-resistant varietal]." He adds, simply, "The future of agriculture here is understanding and dealing with climate change."

The **Massican Annia** ($$) is a tingly, floral blend of Ribolla Gialla, Tocai Fiulano, and Chardonnay, a great wake-you-right-up white (should you find yourself drinking wine in the morning). **Gemina** ($$), a fifty-fifty combo of Greco and Falanghina, takes inspiration from Campania and its citrusy, stony white varieties. Petroski's **Sauvignon Blanc** ($$) is a fresh bolt of lemony-grapefruit flavor with shimmering acidity. Lastly, he also makes an elegant, stone-and-citrus **Chardonnay** ($$–$$$) from the Hyde Vineyard.

MATTHIASSON • NAPA VALLEY

[organic / certified organic (depending on vineyard)]

Though their winery has been going for twenty years now, Steve and Jill Matthiasson's history with farming stretches back before that. They met in graduate school at UC Davis, where Steve was studying organic viticulture and Jill was working for a nonprofit helping sustain family farms in California and get healthy food to children. "We're idealistic people," Steve says simply. Essentially, they both realized they could have careers in agriculture helping people focus on sustainable and organic farming, whether for grapes or other crops. Though, Jill adds, "Organic is not like you're here and you're done. It's not an endpoint. It's more a place to start."

Matthiasson, the couple's eponymous winery, started in 2003. Today they own three vineyards in Napa Valley, and rent eleven others that they farm themselves. In their home vineyard, directly behind their house in the Oak Knoll District, they've also planted more than 200 fruit trees (the preserves they make, which are sold to their winery mailing list customers, are stellar) and 150 olive trees, along with other vegetables. They're similarly planting hedgerows at the Phoenix Vineyard behind their winery. Walk that vineyard with the Matthiassons, and it's hard not to notice the difference between their soil and that of the vineyard adjacent to them, which is farmed conventionally. "Yeah, that side is out of the *Lord of the Rings*," Steve says. "The soil is hard as rock—not a good thing." The Phoenix soil is dark and crumbly, and smells sweet. It, too, used to be fairly lifeless, but, he says, "You can transform a vineyard that's been chemically managed. You can bring it back to life. All we've done here besides prune the vines properly is letting the grasses grow, and using compost to prime the pump, so to speak."

"Essentially," Jill adds, "we're trying to make this place a hospitable place for as much life as possible."

Matthiasson's farming is organic, tailored to each site they work with. Cover crops and hedgerows of native plants and flowering bushes help with carbon sequestration and make the vineyards a "good bug" habitat. They also get all their power from renewable "deep green" sources, use for their bottles low-weight glass made from 100 percent recycled material, and tie their vines with biodegradable hemp rather than with plastic. Also, both of the Matthiassons feel that how workers are treated is a key part of any beneficial farming method, so they employ their vineyard employees year-round (unusual in vineyards), provide healthcare and 401(k) plans, and fund training opportunities for them for ESL and viticulture classes (and chemistry classes for cellar employees).

Their winemaking practices are low-intervention. What Steve Matthiasson looks for in his wines, he says, is "energy—our wines are for food. So, generally, all of our wines have a lot of lift, vibrancy. I'm not looking for weight." That sensibility derives from an early trip he took to Friuli, where, he says, "I realized, tasting these Friulian whites, that you didn't have to throw out richness to have freshness. You can have both in the same wine."

There are quite a few Matthiasson wines, but not all are made in every vintage. Regulars include the vividly crisp **Matthiasson Linda Vista Vineyard Chardonnay ($$)**, which comes from certified organic vines behind the Matthiassons' home in Napa's Oak Knoll District. The **Lost Slough Vineyard Chenin Blanc ($$)** comes from the Clarksburg area, and is similarly bright, with pear-citrus fruit. The **Matthiasson Vineyard Ribolla Gialla ($$–$$$)** expresses all that stony minerality that drew Steve Matthiasson to the variety in the first place. "George Vare was given a few sticks of the Ribolla budwood from Josko Gravner in 2001, and grafted it into his own vineyard, which I was managing. Jill and I

fell in love with the variety in the process, and immediately grafted the variety into our own vineyard when we purchased it in 2006."

For reds, the spicy, leafy **Matthiasson Vineyard Cabernet Franc ($$$)** usually comes in at a very modest alcohol level, 12 percent or so—a great red to chill down in the summer. The **Grenache/Syrah/Mourvèdre Helen's Gate Vineyard ($$$)** is a co-fermented field blend of those three varieties, from a vineyard in Napa Valley's Rutherford District. It's earthy, with lively red fruit and peppery notes. The **Matthiasson Napa Valley Cabernet ($$$)** is, like all of the couple's reds, in a more lifted, elegant style, with red cherry and graphite accents; the **Phoenix Vineyard Cabernet Sauvignon ($$$)**, which comes off of unusual (for Napa) marine shale soils, is distinctively fragrant and blue-fruited; it's unlike any other Napa Cabernet I've had.

NAVARRO VINEYARDS & PENNYROYAL FARM • ANDERSON VALLEY

[sustainable (Navarro) / sustainable + regenerative (Pennyroyal)]

It's lucky for the wine-drinking world that, back in 1974, Ted Bennett and Deborah Cahn decided they'd rather make wine than sell stereos. Bennett traded in his share in a number of Bay Area audio stores for a life in the remote reaches of California's Anderson Valley. Cahn, a graduate student in literature who'd been helping him write ad copy, was all for the idea. "We were influenced by the back-to-the-land movement of that era for sure," Cahn says. "I thought we were simplifying our lives—that turned out to be a joke!"

Bennett and Cahn penciled out that they could either buy about fifteen acres in Napa Valley or nine hundred in the Anderson Valley. They went for the latter, purchasing an old sheep ranch nineteen miles from the ocean; on a clear day, standing amid the vines in their upper vineyards, you can see the Pacific in the distance.

Bennett and Cahn and their children Sarah Cahn Bennett and Aaron Cahn Bennett farm about ninety acres of sustainable vineyards, growing Gewürztraminer, Pinot Noir, Chardonnay, Riesling, Pinot Gris, and Muscat. Flowering cover crops grow in the vineyard rows, while a flock of sheep plus chickens and geese keep those cover crops from taking over, and help fertilize the vines along the way. Sustainability efforts also extend to being one of the first certified fish-friendly wineries in the U.S.—good if you're located along a river that flows into the sea—and to making sure vineyard workers have permanent, full-time jobs rather than relying (as many wineries do) on migrant labor. Cahn says, "We don't use herbicides or pesticides.

We do use some sulfur in the vineyard, because we have to be wary about rot. We'll use peppermint oil, too—Ted calls it a 'hippie solution,' but it works."

(Cahn and Bennett's daughter Sarah Cahn Bennett started Pennyroyal Farm, twelve miles away on the other side of Boonville, in 2008. It's both a creamery and a winery, with twenty-three acres of regeneratively farmed vines and cheeses from 150 goats and sheep. "The goal was really to just make some cheeses to pair with our wines," Cahn Bennett says, "not to take over the cheese world. But the cheeses have done crazily well.")

There's a kind of honesty and unpretentious directness at Navarro and at Pennyroyal, as well as in an investment in the community that goes beyond just the winery. Sarah Cahn Bennett, for instance, supplements her wine- and cheesemaking as a volunteer emergency medical technician. "It's important to be part of this place," she says. Deborah Cahn echoes that sentiment: "There's a different kind of integrity or connection when you grow the grapes here in the community, when your kids go to school here, when you're involved. Some of the old-timers we adored out here are now just brands. But we're still here. I'm in my seventies, Ted's in his eighties, and both our kids are in the business. And there are six grandkids, aged five to fourteen, who already like to hang out at the crushpad. The winery is literally fifteen feet from our homes. That's what gets me about absentee owners—we literally walk through our vineyard every single day."

Navarro's and Pennyroyal's wines are primarily sold direct (see the websites, or go visit—both are wonderful places). The flagship **Navarro Vineyards Dry Gewürztraminer ($–$$)** is one of California's most distinctive white wines, exotically floral and tasting of lychees, kumquats, with a broad, warm spiciness. The winery's **Méthode à l'Ancienne Pinot Noir ($$)** is always delicate and fragrant, full of bright red fruit, with light but firm tannins. The slightly pricier **Deep End Blend Pinot Noir ($$)** is a blend of the winery's top Pinot lots, and has a bit more depth and structure. The **Chardonnay ($$)** is a model of balanced, all-things-in-moderation California Chardonnay. Year in and year out, it's a steal. There are many other Navarro wines in the portfolio, all worth trying.

At Pennyroyal Farm the tart, green apple-y **Brut Rosé ($$)** is a total pleasure to drink, particularly with some of the Pennyroyal goat cheeses. The same could be said of the unusual **Anyhow Blanc** ($$), a blend of Chardonnay and Sauvignon Blanc that ties together the richness of Chardonnay to the grapefruity zip of Sauvignon unexpectedly well.

NEAL FAMILY VINEYARDS · HOWELL MOUNTAIN

[certified organic / certified biodynamic]

Mark Neal started driving a tractor when he was eight. That's not entirely unusual for a farm kid, but it *is* unusual to take out a loan from your father to buy that tractor at age nine, and pay it off fully at fourteen. That's especially unusual in Napa Valley, though in the 1960s, when this happened, Napa was a far more rural place than it is now. Drive down Highway 29 today, and it's very hard to imagine that most of what you're passing was once almost all prune trees and walnut orchards.

Jack Neal, Mark's father, was a medic on the front lines in the Korean War. He and his wife, Athene, moved to Napa Valley in the early 1960s, then started a vineyard management company in 1968, which today Mark Neal owns and runs. It's not a small operation, and it's particularly significant in that Neal farms more organic acreage than anyone else in the Valley—some 840 acres for eighty different clients, more than 700 of which are also biodynamic.

"I was doing earth-moving for my dad when I was twelve—my mom would invent Greek holidays to get me out of school—and I started making wine with him when I was fifteen. And I grew up around organic farming," Neal says. "My grandmother's family was from Crete, with vineyards and olives, farming traditionally. I remember my grandmother would say, 'Jack, you're planting vines at the wrong time, it's not with the moon.' She also made compost piles, turning them, for my mother's garden. It was hard to figure out what they were doing, because it was always Greek-English-Greek-English back and forth, but that was my foundation."

Neal owns his family's original vineyard in Rutherford plus his home vineyard, hidden away on Howell Mountain. Both are certified organic and biodynamic, and he dismisses the idea that organic viticulture is more expensive, a common argument against implementing it. "It isn't, because once you get it established, the system maintains itself," he says. "Look, if you use weed killers—vines have roots, too—you're adding a stress index, and then you need fertilizers. Once you get that hamster on the wheel, you're in: more systemics every year, around and around. Organics takes some time, but you really just need that first year. When you take the needle out of the vine from that systemic IV, the vine needs a year to come out of shock—it's like the vineyard is saying, 'What did you do to me???' But it works."

But it frustrates Neal that organic viticulture doesn't have as much hold on the public imagination as, say, organic lettuce. The key, he feels, is making people aware of how the grapes for the wine they're drinking were farmed. He recounts a story: "My first science project was in second grade at St. Helena Elementary. The teacher told us to put a couple of celery sticks into a glass of water, and then we put some red dye in the water. When we got to school the next morning, the celery had turned the color of the dye. He asked us, would we eat that red celery? The moral of that story was drilled into me from day one: Know your farmer. Otherwise, who the hell knows what you're eating." Or drinking.

Neal's winery is at his Howell Mountain property. There, he makes a number of wines from both Rutherford and Howell Mountain fruit. Most are red, but one white to look for is the creamy, lime-inflected **Neal Family Vineyards Rutherford Dust Vermentino ($$)**.

The **Neal Family Vineyards Napa Valley Cabernet Sauvignon ($$$)** blends fruit from both the Rutherford and Howell Mountain vineyards, and is made in an elegant style, with spicy red currant fruit. For a bit more power and depth, there's also the **Rutherford Dust Cabernet Sauvignon ($$$$)**, which, true to Rutherford form, does display that telltale dusty note along with its dark, polished fruit, and a firmly structured, age-worthy **Howell Mountain Cabernet Sauvignon ($$$$)**.

PAX WINES • SONOMA COAST

[sustainable / organic (majority of vineyards)]

Anyone who doubts the effects of climate change on growing grapes for wine should talk to Pax Mahle. Together with his wife, Pam, Mahle has been making expressive Syrahs and other varieties from top cool-climate sites for nearly a quarter of a century now. But he says, "The current climatic issues we have been dealing with mean that we've been losing entire crops in recent vintages, either from frost, heat, or smoke." In 2021 the Mahles bottled four Chenin Blancs from four different appellations; in 2022, due to unseasonal frost damage, they were only able to bottle two, and one of those was only a single barrel of wine. In 2022, from the five vineyards they use for Gamay Noir, they were able to salvage the fruit from one. "Two were lost to smoke damage, two to frost," Mahle says. "We make our Sonoma Hillsides Syrah only in exceptional years, but there won't be a 2022 of it regardless of the quality of the vintage, thanks to smoke."

Over time, the Pax winery has also become a kind of incubator space for similarly minded, young, independent winemakers; there's a lot of lively energy there at all times, presided over by the Mahles. "And we do our best to source from only organic vineyards," Mahle says. "We may start working with a vineyard that isn't, but our intention is to convert them. After working with someone for a year or two, making slow changes, you get to a point where it's 'Wow, you're organic, and we didn't even have to make a big deal about it.' Regardless, our long-term sources and vineyard-designated wines are all organic."

Among the Pax wines to look for are several Chenin Blancs (depending on vintage). The **Pax Buddha's Dharma Chenin Blanc ($$)** comes from vines planted in 1944 just north of Mendocino's City of Ten Thousand Buddhas monastery, and is floral and stonily intense; his **Alder Springs Vineyard Chenin Blanc ($$)** is typically rounder, with more green apple notes. There's also a delicate **Trousseau Gris ($$)**, as crisp and thirst-quenching as Rosé gets.

For reds, the light-bodied **Alta Monte Gamay Noir ($$)** comes from two vineyards (one Sonoma Coast, one Russian River) and has a deft interplay of red and blue fruit; the **Bearg Ranch Gamay Noir ($$)** is luscious and silky. The easiest Syrah to find is the **Pax North Coast Syrah ($$)**, a stellar deal blended from a number of vineyards Mahle regularly works with. His **Sonoma Coast Syrah ($$)** is all cold-climate sites, spicier and leaner than the basic north coast wine. The **Pax Alder Springs Syrah ($$$)** comes from the first vineyard he ever worked with; it's floral and full of savory blue fruit, and the **Sonoma Hillsides Syrah ($$$)**, inspired by the wines of St.-Joseph in the Rhône, blends fruit from his best sites. The latter, particularly, is terrific stuff—layered, complex, savory, and full of energy. As Mahle says, a bit confrontationally but with total accuracy, it's not your "standard run-of-the-mill Syrah, shapeless with the blubber, oak, and extraction that many people wrongly confuse with quality."

PEAY VINEYARDS • SONOMA COAST

[certified sustainable / certified organic]

"Cold air moves like a molasses river," Nick Peay says, talking about growing grapes on the far Sonoma Coast. This is not an easy place: even the height of summer's warmth is checked by cold wind funneled in off the Pacific. The Peays are happy when they get two tons of grapes an acre off their land. (The average in Sonoma County is close to double that.) Some years, they get less than a ton. "If not frost, then it's poor flowering," Nick's brother Andy Peay says. "It happens every three to four years. It's hell on a business model."

But this is where they need to be to make the wines they want to make (together with Nick's wife, winemaker Vanessa Wong). Finding their land, back in the mid-1990s, was the result of a form of prospecting. Sonoma's far coast was almost entirely undeveloped then. The Peays consulted USGS survey maps, looking for breaks in the coastal ridges where land good for vineyards might lie, trespassed on logging roads, avoiding foresters working for the logging companies, and quizzed local real estate agents without letting on they were looking for vineyard land. ("The price immediately goes up," Andy says.) The search was complicated by the fact that most of the farming going on in the area was, at that time, illegal. "At one point I was camping on the Lost Coast in Humboldt County, and from the beach I could see this vineyard maybe half a mile in," Andy Peay recalls. "I hiked in to check it out, and these two ragged-looking guys appeared and said, 'What you want?' I was like, 'Well, I saw the vineyard from the beach.' They gave me the once-over and one of them said, 'We're bottling our sparkling behind this shed, you want to check it out.' At this point I'm figuring, OK, this is the part where I get killed, because this is *clearly* a front for a growing operation. Which it was, but they actually were making wine, too. Five old hippies in tie-dye hats. They handed me a glass and a joint, and that was pretty great."

Finally, the Peays found an old sheep ranch on top of a fog-shrouded hill, four miles from the Pacific, for a price they could scrape together. There were zero neighbors. "Being first is nice in terms of what you pay," Andy says. "Five years later, prices here were up tenfold. And recently it just went completely crazy."

Today the Peays have fifty-three acres of vines. Andy is the business side; Vanessa, the winemaker; Nick, the viticulturist. Farming has been organic from the start, and they use regenerative practices as well: no tilling, sheep in the vineyard in the spring to manage ground cover, compost from their own stems and seeds. It's rewarding: "We're twenty vintages in, the vineyard's better than it's ever been, and the wines are better than they've ever been," Andy says. But it's hard work, and it doesn't allow for much rest: "When Nick broke his leg in 2021, it took him a month before he could strap a block onto his foot and then strap his leg onto the tractor. But then he was out there. It was the middle of fruit-set. You don't get to stop."

The Peays make thirteen wines under the Peay Vineyards label, and an additional four under their more affordable Cep brand, which uses fruit that doesn't quite make the cut for the top wines (or else comes from a long-term contract with the organic Hopkins Ranch vineyard). Some highlights of the Cep line include the lively, light-bodied **Cep Rosé of Pinot Noir ($$)** and the **Cep Vineyards Sonoma Coast Estate Pinot Noir ($$)**, a silky red that ought to cost more than it does, given its quality.

The **Peay Estate Chardonnay ($$$)** has a savory, flinty edge to its overall pear-plus-lemon-cream character, and the **Peay Viognier ($$$)** is round and supple, yet with a crisp snap of acidity that keeps it from becoming flaccid. The winery's **Sonoma Coast Pinot Noir ($$$)** is a superb overall picture of what the estate vineyard can produce. The more delicate **Scallop Shelf Pinot Noir ($$$)** comes mostly from Pommard clones on the site; a different blend, the **Pomarium Pinot Noir ($$$)** tends to be darker and more earthy. Peay's Syrahs were some of the early examples of the heights that cool-climate Syrah can reach in California, and are still uniformly excellent. The **La Bruma Syrah ($$$)** is particularly compelling, with cool blue fruit, floral notes, and a peppery, high-toned finish.

RIDGE VINEYARDS • SANTA CRUZ MOUNTAINS / DRY CREEK VALLEY

[certified sustainable / certified organic]

Ridge Vineyards has been at the forefront of both responsible viticulture and winemaking for many years, and has also been instrumental in bringing attention to California's old-vine, heritage vineyards. Paul Draper, Ridge's former longtime winemaker and CEO (he remains chairman of the winery's board), is a monumental figure in California wine, widely influential and respected, if less well known to people outside the wine business than a figure like Robert Mondavi. Head winemaker John Olney and vineyard manager David Gates are continuing the work Draper started, and making some of California's best wines in the process.

The winery's history stretches back to before 1900, when a San Francisco doctor named Osea Perrone bought a large parcel of land near the top of the Monte Bello Ridge in the Santa Cruz

Mountains, west of what's now Cupertino. He planted vines and built a limestone winery, naming it Monte Bello; its first vintage was in 1892. The modern era starts with three Stanford Research Institute engineers, who bought the property as a weekend retreat. One of them, Dave Bennion, made a half barrel of Cabernet from it in his garage in 1960, which proved to be so good that the trio started making wine commercially.

Ridge makes one of California's great Cabernets, Monte Bello, from that original property, but over the years it has become possibly even more well known for its championing of Zinfandel. As John Olney says, "The founders went out looking for Cabernet around California, but there really wasn't much Cabernet planted—instead they found all these old field blends." Back then, the fruit from those vineyards mostly went into mass-market reds—Gallo's "Hearty Burgundy" and the like. Bennion, his partners, and later Draper (who came on in 1969 as winemaker), saw the hidden potential of those old vines. Ridge's first Zinfandel came from a nineteenth-century vineyard a bit farther down the Monte Bello hill; the winery's now-signature Geyserville Zinfandel (now simply called Geyserville) saw its first vintage in 1966.

> "With these old vineyards the stories are endless, and they are all true."
> —David Gates

David Gates, who started managing Ridge's vineyard program in 1989, says, "For me old vineyards are this window into old California. Most of the people in wine here in the early 1900s were immigrants; they came from a history of farming in Europe that included grapes and wine. It was really part of the day, part of food, something you had with your meal. These old vineyards kind of wrap all that up, and of course a lot of them—Lytton Springs, for example—make great wine, too."

All of the estate vineyards, which make up three-quarters of the fruit Ridge uses, were certified organic as of 2022. (Ridge is the largest grower of organically certified grapes in both Sonoma County and in the Santa Cruz Mountains AVA.) The winemaking is "pre-industrial," a term Draper coined. Essentially the idea is to follow nineteenth-century winemaking techniques, but use modern-day analytical tools to anticipate potential problems. So: no commercial enzymes or nutrients; malolactic fermentation that occurs naturally; wine clarity only through settling and racking, with fining, if absolutely needed, done only with egg whites; minimal sulfur; and all natural yeasts. Olney says, "Commercial yeast, you put it in, it just ferments everything dry, no matter what. It's very predictable, but the wines are less interesting. But if you're going to make wines in a natural, hands-off fashion the way we do, there's inherent risk. You really need a lab to see what's potentially going on, to alert you to a potential problem.

We're minimal intervention, not *no* intervention."

Ridge also lists ingredients on all its wine labels. Olney says, "From 2011, Paul really wanted to show everyone exactly what was in each bottle. The ingredient labeling we do is a way of saying that if you've got the right terroir, the right grapes, and you're farming them correctly, you shouldn't be relying on Mega Purple and enzymes, and all those other things that get sprinkled in."

To cover all the Ridge wines would take several pages, but a few qualify as do-not-miss-no-matter-what bottles. The two anchors of the Zinfandel-based wines are the **Ridge Lytton Springs** (\$\$–\$\$\$), from one-hundred-plus-year-old Zinfandel vines in Dry Creek Valley interplanted with Petite Sirah, Carignan, Mataro, and Grenache, and **Geyserville** (\$\$–\$\$\$), which draws on even older vines—the "old patch," planted more than 130 years ago—together with some not-quite-as-ancient vines planted in the 1960s. Geyserville, made from Zinfandel with Carignan, Petite Sirah, Alicante Bouschet, and Mataro, tends toward more red fruit and more acidity; Lytton, darker, blacker fruit, and more

brambly spice. Also look for the peppery, black-fruited **Benito Dusi Ranch Zinfandel** (\$\$), from a vineyard south of Paso Robles planted in 1920, and the boysenberry-rich **Pagani Vineyard Zinfandel** (\$\$\$), from a vineyard whose two sections were planted in the 1890s and mid-1910s. But there are many others.

Ridge also makes excellent Rhône variety wines, like the red-fruited, Carignan-based **Evangelho** (\$\$), from the Contra Costa County heritage vineyard of the same name, and a few white wines, such as the vivid, citrus-tropical **Halter Ranch Grenache Blanc** (\$\$) and its exceptional **Monte Bello Chardonnay** (\$\$\$), about which Olney says, "In terms of style, we try to skate this fine line between a fairly rich white that will have the ability to age, and picking early enough to maintain fresh acidity." There's also a quite good and more easily findable **Estate Chardonnay ($$)**.

And then there's Cabernet Sauvignon, where the Ridge story started. The **Ridge Estate Cabernet Sauvignon ($$$)** is polished and complex in every vintage; a go-to California Cabernet. And the simply named **Ridge Monte Bello ($$$$)** is one of the benchmark Cabernets of California, complex, layered, always expertly balancing power with precision. It can age effortlessly for decades.

SANS WINE COMPANY • NAPA VALLEY

[organic / natural]

Sans comes in cans. The brainchild of Gina Schober and Jake Stover, its premise is simple: source organic grapes, make wine from them in a natural, noninterventionist way, and sell the resulting juice in cans. The company's slogan, "sans chemicals, sans additives, sans pretense," pretty much says it all.

The inspiration came from a river, specifically the Russian River as it flows through Guerneville. Stover at the time was planting a vineyard for a client near the coast, and took Schober along with him for a visit. She says, "On our way back, I saw people out on the river, floating along on inner tubes, and it hit me: *canned wine*. I thought of all the people I knew who loved wine, and how if they were out there on the river, what would they drink?" She turned to Jake and told him they should make canned wine. He told her she was crazy. She said, "Well, what if we made high-quality wine in cans, utilizing our knowledge of winemaking and farming and the wine business, and did it in a noninterventionist way?" He said, "Hm—maybe you're *not* crazy." By the time they got back to town, they'd laid out the basic idea for Sans.

As of 2022, all of the fruit for Sans's wines was certified organic, and the winemaking takes place at an organic facility, using effectively no sulfur. "We're also working on a program to provide incentives for growers to transition to organic certification,"

Schober says. "It's tough, as you can imagine, to try and build Sans and also find enough certified organic fruit. Especially given frost, fires, droughts, and so on. But that's what we're trying to do."

Canned-wine skeptics may scoff, but the Sans wines are remarkably good (and you can drink them while floating down a river). The lightly hazy, apple-y **Sans Wine Company McGill Vineyard Riesling ($)** is a tart pleasure; so is the citrus-tropical **Finley Ranch Sauvignon Blanc ($)**. The company has probably gotten the most attention for its **Poor Ranch Vineyard Carbonic Carignan** ($), a vivacious, faintly tingly red that deserves to be chilled down; it's a no-brainer for the summer. The **Poor Ranch Vineyard Zinfandel ($)**, from vines planted in 1952 in Mendocino, is more robust and dark-fruited, but still has impressive lift and vibrancy. These are utterly unpretentious, fun wines, sold in cans, that come from organic grapes and a very talented winemaker—what's not to like?

SCHERRER WINERY • RUSSIAN RIVER VALLEY

[sustainable]

Fred Scherrer's wines live in that odd no-man's-land of being loved by the few who know about them, and not known by many, many people who *would* love them, if only they knew. Which is odd, given that the Scherrer family has been growing grapes continuously on the same land since 1899, something very few California vintners can claim.

Those old vines were planted by Scherrer's grandfather, also Fred, in 1912. He was a farmer, not a winemaker, mostly growing plums for the thriving prune business (now long gone), along with other crops. The family ate what they grew, and what wine the first Fred Scherrer made was for family consumption: a couple of barrels they'd draw from, into a pitcher or jug.

The younger Fred Scherrer got interested in wine in the 1970s, first doing home winemaking while still a teenager, then getting an enology degree from UC Davis. Scherrer Winery's first vintage was 1991, using fruit from the family vineyard and others in Sonoma County. "Up until my dad's passing we conventionally farmed, albeit in a pretty 'soft' way," Scherrer says. "Afterwards, I inherited a lot of his duties at the vineyard—on top of running my winery!—including pest control. We're now working sustainably, transitioning into certification, and using some organic learning as well. Before World War II we farmed organically there anyway, though there were some consequences in high pressure mildew and rot years."

Scherrer has always released his wines with a little more age than most California producers. Recently, he says, "We've been drifting towards much more time. The texture benefits immensely—I feel like I'm just seeing some of the tip of this iceberg, a decade from starting to work this way. There are no fancy, high-tech winemaking tricks employed on my wines. But they do speak to the value of a long time in barrel on lees."

And, with his Zinfandel, they speak to the value of old vines: "They bring wisdom to the whole. They're subtle, nuanced; it's all about subtlety. And those characteristics don't blend out—they go a lot further than they should. I don't understand it, but I accept it."

Fred Scherrer makes his wines in an old apple-packing warehouse just outside Sebastopol. The easiest way to get them is to contact the winery directly, as they don't often appear in stores. There are quite a few of them, too, but here are some highlights. The **Scherrer Winery Scherrer Vineyard Chardonnay ($$)** is a brisk, bright interpretation of the grape, a surprise from the warm Alexander Valley. Fred makes a number of Pinot Noirs from different vineyards in the area; his red-fruited, elegant **Sonoma County Pinot Noir ($$)** draws on many of them. The **Russian River Valley Pinot Noir ($$$)** has darker fruit and hints of cola—classic for that AVA. Scherrer's **Old and Mature Vines Zinfandel ($$)** has been for many years one of my favorite California zins. Many of the vines in the Scherrer Vineyard date from 1912, and that maturity plays out in its complex dark-berried fruit and savory, foresty notes. There's also an excellent cassis-scented **Scherrer** **Vineyard Cabernet Sauvignon ($$$)**, its flavors polished and long.

SPOTTSWOODE • NAPA VALLEY

[certified organic / certified biodynamic]

Spottswoode is part of the remarkable group of Napa Valley wineries that came to prominence in the early 1970s, though its story actually starts much, much earlier. It was founded in 1882 by a German immigrant to California, who called it Lyndenhurst; in 1910, after several changes in ownership, it was sold to a woman named Susan Spotts, who renamed it in honor of her late husband. The modern-era story starts in 1972, when a San Diego doctor named Jack Novak and his wife, Mary, decided they wanted to raise their children in a rural setting (Napa Valley was rural then; today it is still agricultural, but hardly rural). They sold everything, moved in, and started to make wine. At that time the forty-five-acre estate was planted with an oddball mix of Petite Sirah, Napa Gamay, French Colombard, and Green Hungarian.

Jack Novak died before he could ever see his dream to full fruition, but his wife, Mary, persevered. Before his death, she and Jack had planted Cabernet, and those vines propelled Spottswoode to the top echelons of Napa Valley. Novak, a woman whose graciousness and elegance sometimes caused people to underestimate her willpower, oversaw Spottswoode with the help of her daughters until she passed away in 2016. Today Spottswoode is still owned by the Novak family, with Mary's daughter Beth Novak Milliken in charge. (Aron Weinkauf, who joined in 2006, is the winemaker and vineyard manager.)

Over the years, the Novaks have been at the forefront of environmental awareness in Napa Valley. Spottswoode became the first organically farmed vineyard in Napa Valley in 1985; Novak and Weinkauf went biodynamic in 2006. Native cover crops grow in the vineyards, which are also filled with insectaries, apiaries, and bird boxes. The winery relies on solar power; over time the Novaks have reduced water usage during harvest by half; and recently the winery switched to lighter glass bottles to reduce emissions from shipping. Novak, who is on the board of the nonprofit International Wineries for Climate Change, says, "At a basic level, sustainability in general is all about the resilience of the soil and the vines. If we as humans take care of our health, we should be more resilient to stress and disease. This is the same principle behind organic and biodynamic farming—building systemic resilience. With climate change, this is something we need more than ever. It's not just a Napa Valley issue; it's a planetary issue."

The **Spottswoode Napa Valley Sauvignon Blanc ($$)** comes from a mix of estate and purchased fruit from Napa Valley and Sonoma mountain (all sustainable, and most certified organic). It's an example of the heights that California Sauvignon Blanc can reach: impeccably balanced between citrus and orchard fruit, long and lightly stony on the finish. The winery's **Lyndenhurst Cabernet Sauvignon ($$$)** also draws on estate plus purchased fruit, the majority of the latter certified organic. It's full of blue and red fruit flavors, often with a tobacco and spice note. The **Spottswoode Estate Cabernet Sauvignon ($$$$)** is one of Napa Valley's definitive wines; if you want to know why this place became so famous for Cabernet, you can't do better than to start here. Layered and rich, powerful and elegant at once, it's able to age for decades in a cellar. Year in and year out, it's a brilliant red wine.

STONESTREET WINES · ALEXANDER VALLEY

[certified sustainable]

There's no talking about wine in California without talking about the Jackson family. Jess Jackson was a titanically influential figure, and Kendall-Jackson's mega-selling Vintner's Reserve Chardonnay remains the best-selling white wine in America after many, many years of holding that title. Vintner's Reserve isn't the kind of wine that's the subject of this book—though, for a wine made in the millions of cases, it is more thoughtfully wrought than people might think. But Stonestreet is a different case, partly because it is Barbara Banke's (and was Jess Jackson's, before he passed away) home.

Banke was married to Jackson until his death and is now the head of both the family and their vast wine empire (the word is not an exaggeration). But home is where the heart is, as the saying goes, and that's Stonestreet. Banke lives on the property, as did her daughter Julia until her house was destroyed in the 2019 Kincade Fire, which burned through seventy-seven thousand acres throughout northern Sonoma County. Son Chris Jackson, who oversees Stonestreet Wines, lives nearby. ("My role is being the custodian of the mountain," he says.)

The estate covers fifty-one hundred acres on Alexander Mountain, but less than a fifth of those acres is vineyard. The rest has the natural biodiversity of the area: native plants, forest, animal life. The farming is certified sustainable. Jackson purchased the property in 1995, and as Chris Jackson says, "My

father happened to buy great vineyard land before the market realized what great vineyard land was worth." Not that the location was unknown: the previous owner, Ed Gauer, had grown grapes there since 1972, planting at a time when prunes were still more of a cash crop than wine grapes in Sonoma County. (Helen Turley's Gauer Ranch Chardonnays for her Marcassin label were hotly sought after by wine collectors in the 1990s.)

The Jacksons have become a major force in sustainability initiatives not just at Stonestreet but throughout the wine world. Together with Familia Torres in Spain, they founded the International Wineries for Climate Action organization in 2019. Group members pledge to reach net-carbon-zero status by 2050 (in Jackson's case, the goal is to cut their carbon footprint by 50 percent by 2030 and reach climate positive status by 2050, without purchasing carbon offsets, a common workaround). Taken together, the family's properties are the largest generator of solar power in the U.S. wine industry, and water conservation measures—recycling, UV tank sanitation, rainwater harvesting—are standard. Bottles, of which Jackson Family Wines obviously uses a lot, are 50 percent recycled glass and have been weight-reduced to lower their carbon footprint. The family is also part of the United Nations carbon-recovery Race to Zero campaign.

So while Jackson Family Wines does make a mind-boggling amount of wine overall, the family is also working to mitigate climate change on a vast scale. The amount of greenhouse gases released into the atmosphere by the wine industry doesn't remotely compare to what's produced by aviation, automobiles, or even cows (livestock accounts for 14.5 percent of global greenhouse gases). But every little bit helps, and if more of the world's largest wine companies followed the Jacksons' lead, that would, inarguably, be a good thing.

Stonestreet makes a bevy of wines that express the intricacies of this large estate's range of terroirs. The **Stonestreet Estate Sauvignon Blanc ($$)** leans into the fruit of Sauvignon, rather than its herbaceous side, with a lemony pop of acidity. The **Estate Chardonnay ($$)** is a blend from different sites around the mountain, full of orchard fruit flavors and warming spice notes from a moderate level of oak. The **Estate Cabernet Sauvignon ($$$)** has firm, mountain-vineyard tannins framing its red and black fruit flavors; it's an impressive, ageworthy red for the price.

Where the estate sings are its single-site wines, particularly its Chardonnays. There are plenty. High points include the lemony, minerally **Broken Road Chardonnay ($$$)**, planted on gravelly sand-loam at eighteen hundred feet elevation, the flinty **Gravel Bench Chardonnay ($$$–$$$$)**, on gravel at fifteen hundred feet, and the luscious but focused **Upper Barn Chardonnay ($$$$)**, on loam at eighteen hundred feet. The latter is one of California's top Chardonnays, year in and year out, and ages beautifully.

Highlights among the single-site reds include the **Bear Point Cabernet Sauvignon ($$$$)**, which comes from the back side of the mountain and is unusually spicy and peppery, with blue- and blackberry fruit. The single-site Cabernets here tend to be powerful, tannic, muscular wines; Bear Point is usually the most open on release. **Christopher's Cabernet Sauvignon ($$$$)** is the top red from the estate, and can be brooding and somewhat unforgiving when young. Given time, that intensity unfurls into layers of dark fruit, stony mineral notes, and dried-herb flavors.

PRODUCERS PROFILED IN THIS CHAPTER

Bedrock Wine Co.

Broc Cellars

Bucklin Old Hill Ranch

Carlisle Winery

Cobb

Corison

Cruse Wine Co.

Drew Wines

Frog's Leap Vineyards

Grgich Hills Estate

Halcon Estate

Hirsch Vineyards

Honig Winery

Idlewild

Keplinger Wines

Kutch

Littorai

Long Meadow Ranch

Massican

Matthiasson

Navarro Vineyards &
    Pennyroyal Farm

Neal Family Vineyards

Pax Wines

Peay Vineyards

Ridge Vineyards

Sans Wine Company

Scherrer Winery

Spottswoode

Stonestreet Wines

OTHER NORTH COAST PRODUCERS TO LOOK FOR

Arnot-Roberts

Barra Family / Girasole

Bee Hunter

Big Basin Vineyards

Ceritas

Dashe

Dehlinger

Donkey & Goat

DuPuis Winery

Failla

Thomas Fogarty

Hanzell

Hendry

Inman Family Wines

Jolie-Laide

Keller Estate

Limerick Lane

Lioco

Marine Layer
Newfound Wines
Occidental
Once & Future
Porter Bass
Porter Creek Vineyards
Radio-Coteau
RAEN
A. Rafanelli Winery
Ramey
Read-Holland
Reeve
Ryme
Scribe
Shannon Ridge
Robert Sinskey Estate
Smith-Madrone Vineyards &
  Winery
Leo Steen
Joseph Swan
Trefethen Family Vineyards
Vallette Wines
Winery Sixteen 600

THE CENTRAL COAST AND BEYOND

California's Central Coast region covers a vast amount of land from San Francisco down to Santa Barbara, running north to south a distance of some 280 miles, and stretching inland from the Pacific coast to the borders of California's Central Valley. Some of California's earliest vines were planted here in the late 1700s by Padre Junípero Serra, a Spanish priest, as he established a chain of missions that would eventually stretch from San Diego to what's now Sonoma County. (The first actual commercial winery started even farther south, in 1834 in Los Angeles, where the city's Union Station is now.)

Because the Central Coast is so big, and its wine regions so varied, it's almost impossible to generalize about its wines. In places like the Sta. Rita Hills where valleys cut east-west to the ocean—atypical for California—the cold influence of the Pacific makes the land ideal for Pinot Noir and Chardonnay, and Syrahs that recall those of the northern Rhône. Head inland to appellations like Santa Barbara County's Happy Valley or to Paso Robles, and Bordeaux varieties thrive, as well as warmer-climate varieties such as Zinfandel. Numerous old-vine plantings of Zin, Carignan, and Mourvèdre (or Mataro, as it was once known in California) still exist in Contra Costa County, east of San Francisco Bay. And California's "Rhône Ranger" movement got its start in the Central Coast in the 1980s, when adventurous winemakers started bringing Rhône varieties like Syrah and Grenache to wine lovers' attention.

Beyond the Central Coast, California winemakers have long made wine in the Lodi and Sierra Foothills regions (the latter of which contains AVAs such as Amador County, Eldorado, Fair Play, and Fiddletown). Quality in the past was mixed, but younger talents have been investigating the region in recent years and making some striking wines—its lower land costs are a draw, as are its lower living costs compared to the Bay Area and the famed wine regions north of it.

BECKMEN VINEYARDS • SANTA BARBARA COUNTY

[certified biodynamic]

Steve Beckmen was an early adopter of biodynamics in California's Central Coast, switching his 125-acre Purisima Vineyard in Ballard Canyon over in 2002. "I heard about biodynamics around 1994, 1995, the same time we started the winery, but the big influence was meeting [the biodynamic consultant] Philippe Armenier. He was really the guy who showed us how we could do it over a large number of acres. And there's no question it's worked."

Beckmen says, "I liked the idea of having a coherent system, instead of just reacting to everything, which seemed like what we were doing then as farmers. I also had newborn children, and we were living on the vineyard property—still do—and I didn't want them exposed to systemic chemicals or anything. Same for my workers and crew."

Beckmen doesn't come from a wine family. His father, Tom, though born on a farm, founded the electronic music company Roland US, more or less creating the market for electronic keyboards in the U.S. (and resulting in many stoned 1970s teenagers being mind-blown by endless rock synthesizer solos). Steve Beckmen started playing both piano and guitar at age five, and assumed he'd be a musician. But when he moved to California to start Beckmen Vineyards with his father, that more or less faded: "Being a musician and being a winemaker don't go together very well—winemaking pretty much destroys your hands."

His most recent project, starting in 2018, is a series of wines called Ingredient, which are made in the nonintervention style of natural wines. "I have a fascination with historical things, and trying to make really good wine without the conveniences of modern winemaking intrigues me. Also, I'd made five or six trips to northern Italy, and just got attracted to the tradition of skin-contact whites there. I guess my dream is to be Josko Gravner at some point in my life! OK—maybe not *be* him, but at least make wines that are similar in a way to his."

Beckmen concentrates on Rhône varieties at his Purisima Vineyard. "Ballard Canyon is warm, but it acts more like a cool place. It gives acidity and focus to warm-climate wines." The tropical-fruited **Beckmen Vineyards Purisima Mountain Vineyard Sauvignon Blanc ($$)** is fermented in stainless steel but aged in clay amphorae. The **Purisima Mountain Vineyard Viognier ($$)** benefits from Ballard Canyon's gift for sustaining acidity; it has the peachy lushness of Viognier, but avoids becoming flabby.

For reds, the juicy **Cuvee Le Bec ($$)**, a blend of Syrah, Grenache, Mourvèdre, and Counoise, is a great introduction to Beckmen's wines. The **Estate Grenache Los Olivos District ($$$)** is rich with kirsch–black cherry flavors; the **Purisima Mountain Grenache Libre ($$$)** comes from two small blocks of vines and is deeper and more complex. Beckmen's **Purisima Mountain Vineyard Syrah ($$)** has long been a go-to for Central Coast Syrah, full of blackberry and black pepper character; the **Purisima Mountain Vineyard Block Six Syrah ($$$)** is savory and gamey, equally impressive if not more so, and comes from the first section of vineyard that Steve Beckmen converted to biodynamics, back in 2002.

Look also for the **Ingredient Sauvignon Blanc ($$$)**, fermented and aged on skins for ten months in amphorae, and the **Ingredient Syrah ($$$)**, which also ages for ten months on the skins, then a further year without, all in amphorae. The fruit for the latter is from Block 6 of Purisima Mountain, making it a fascinating contrast—earthier, lighter in alcohol, more floral—to the regular bottling from that block.

DOMAINE DE LA CÔTE / SANDHI / PIEDRASASSI • STA. RITA HILLS

[organic (Domaine de la Côte); sustainable or organic (Sandhi, depending on vineyard); organic or biodynamic (Piedrasassi, depending on vineyard)]

Roadside scenery in the windswept agricultural town of Lompoc includes an air force base, a federal penitentiary, and, these days, endless rows of plastic-sheathed hoop sheds for cannabis production. But Santa Barbara County's Santa Rita Hills AVA, one of California's best places for cool-climate Pinot Noir, Chardonnay, and Syrah, is only ten miles away, and hidden inside a small Lompoc warehouse complex on a street with the romantic name of Industrial Way are some of the best boutique wineries on the Central Coast—among them the conjoined producers Domaine de la Côte, Sandhi, and Piedrasassi.

Don't let the street name fool you: these are not, in any way whatsoever, industrial wines. Instead they're the products of a pair of prodigious wine talents, Rajat Parr and Sashi Moorman. Both started in the restaurant world. Moorman worked as a cook in Washington, DC ("I cleaned squid for hours"), then moved to California and became assistant winemaker at Ojai Vineyards. Parr came to the U.S. to train as a chef but got sidetracked by wine while working as a server in San Francisco; he eventually became one of the most respected sommeliers in the world. The two started making wine together in 2007, and now co-own Sandhi, which concentrates on Chardonnay, and Domaine de la Côte, focused on Pinot Noir, together with a third partner; a third project, Evening Land, is in Oregon. Piedrasassi, devoted to Syrah, is Moorman's solo project.

Moorman oversees the winemaking and farming; Parr is more the face of the brands, though the two work closely together. Domaine de la Côte's vineyards are farmed organically, as are the thirty acres on that property that go to Sandhi. But Moorman is mixed about people's reliance on the word "organic" as a label. "Steve Matthiasson once told me, 'People ask me all the fucking time, do you farm organically or biodynamically? No one asks me if I give my workers health insurance.'

That's the problem right there. It's *all* about health. We don't use anything in our vineyards that would be harmful for our workers, and we don't use anything that would be harmful to our customers—the point is not so much about the farming practice itself, but overall health."

He adds, "This question of what you use is holistic. It's not just the vineyard, it's the winery, too. And as a winegrower, even if you don't live at the vineyard yourself, you've got people working there. If you're farming with really nasty stuff, it means you don't give a shit about the people working for you. Something that really frustrates me on the organic side is most people use copper. Copper is an organic material, sure; but so is plutonium. You could put plutonium in your vineyard and still qualify as organic. So, with copper, there's plenty of evidence that it's dangerous, plus it just builds and builds in your soil. After a hundred years you've built up real toxicity.

"Anyway, for me, it's more taking a global perspective. Are you promoting biodiversity in your vineyards? Are you promoting biomass and microbial life in your soil? If you are, then that means unequivocally that you're using organic practices. It's about getting to the actual illness rather than just treating the symptoms."

Moorman and Parr's wines lean to the more transparent, shimmering side of the wine spectrum, and are made with native yeasts and a good amount of whole-cluster fermentation. "The Pinots and Syrahs that Raj and I fell in love with all came from places where they weren't getting fully ripe—wines like old-school Barolo and Burgundy and Cornas and Côte Rôtie. Energy, freshness, finesse—these are all words trying to describe what it means to be drinking a wine that's just a little underripe. And Domaine de la Côte is a really special place because the Pinot there doesn't get fully ripe—it gets *just ripe enough.*"

When Moorman planted the Domaine de la Côte estate vineyard in 2007, he told me at the time that it was going to be a risky endeavor; it's so close to the Pacific Coast that he wasn't sure whether "just ripe enough" was even going to happen. Happily, the risk paid off. The **Domaine de la Côte Sta. Rita Hills Pinot Noir ($$$)** combines fruit from across the estate and is a great introduction to the property's wines. There are five single-site Pinot Noirs; all are excellent. **Memorious ($$$$)** is generally the most delicate and floral. **Bloom's Field ($$$$)** keeps that rose-petal character but adds a little more intensity and power, though never losing its innate finesse and transparency. **La Côte ($$$$)** is the deepest and most structured (again, still in a very lifted and graceful mode). Look also for the **Sous le Chêne** and **Siren's Call Pinot Noirs**. The single-site wines particularly are made in small amounts and are highly sought after; they definitely take some searching, or else get on the winery's mailing list.

Sandhi concentrates on Chardonnay. The **Sandhi Sta. Rita Hills Chardonnay ($$)**, which is made primarily with estate fruit from Domaine de la Côte, is a stellar example of this AVA's cool-climate snap and precision, for a modest price. The **Sanford & Benedict Vineyard Chardonnay ($$–$$$)** comes from an iconic site—it was the first vineyard planted in the Sta. Rita Hills, back in 1971—and is a little richer, with a zesty, bright citrus character and plenty of minerality. The **Rinconada Chardonnay ($$$)**, from the first certified organic vineyard in the AVA, is a bit fuller and rounder, but still retains the basic energy that drives all of the Sandhi wines.

Piedrasassi is about Syrah. "I hate using this phrase, but it's truly a passion project," Moorman says. "You can't be in the Syrah business and think you're ever going to have a really successful winery." Profitable or not, these are thrilling cool-climate Syrahs. The **Piedrasassi Sta. Rita Hills Syrah ($$)** is peppery and savory, full of vibrant blue-red fruit; it comes from the Patterson and Casa Casera vineyards. The **Santa Maria Valley Syrah ($$)** is from the X Block (biodynamic) and Z Block (sustainable) at the Bien Nacido Vineyard. It's more generous than the colder-climate Sta. Rita Hills wine, but still has vivid spice and herb characteristics. The **Arroyo Grande Valley Syrah ($$)** uses fruit exclusively from the Rim Rock Vineyard (organic); it reveals more blue fruit and white pepper, with a distinct hint of violets.

FORLORN HOPE • SIERRA FOOTHILLS

[organic]

At Forlorn Hope, Matthew Rorick makes wonderful, unclassifiable wines from his steep, rocky vineyard in the Sierra Foothills. Asked if he sees himself as a natural winemaker or a conventional winemaker, he says, "I guess there's a little of both, but I largely don't care. I've never positioned myself as a natural winemaker. It's crept into our story a little, because people say, 'Hey, Forlorn Hope! That's natural!'"

Unclassifiable seems right for a guy who got out of high school and made a decent go of it as a professional skateboarder, only to realize that skateboarding wasn't perhaps a recipe for the rest of life. He joined the navy—"Mostly just to spite my mom, like, 'Hey Mom, I'm not going to college, hahahaha!'" he says. "I was being a jackass"—and spent a few years repairing submarine telescopes, then got out, studied literature, and finally went to UC Davis to study enology and viticulture.

The love of wine was instilled by his grandfather. "I lived with him after I got out of the navy. He loved wine and loved to cook, and he had a cellar full of bottles. A lot of my inspiration came from just sitting around the table with him—we'd be drinking a glass of something, and he'd be telling me about visiting that place, being at the winery, meeting the winemaker. It was completely fascinating. That handful of years I lived with him were amazing."

Several years working for other wineries in California and around the world taught Rorick the practical aspects of making wine, but eventually he started to wonder why he simply didn't *like* some of the wines he was making. "I asked myself what wines I did like—and I went back to the European wines and late sixties and seventies California wines I'd had with my grandfather. Wines that were more balanced, less ripe and extracted. That was the genesis of Forlorn Hope."

For the first several years, Rorick bought fruit from other growers, but it nagged at him; he wanted to grow his own grapes. "I was emulating all these European producers, but I wasn't doing my own farming. So I thought,

'Maybe I can find a two- or three-acre vineyard up in the Foothills.'"

He ended up with 350 acres of land and 75 acres of vineyard. "My three cousins, who are like sisters to me, were like, what if we invested, made this into a family thing in Granddad's memory." Several years later the cousins wanted out; wine was more work than they'd anticipated. "Somehow, I found a lender. Which itself is crazy. But that's how I went from 'it might be nice to have three acres to farm' to 'I have seventy-five acres of vines and I am in *completely* over my head.'"

Somehow, Rorick has made it work. He's also farmed organically since the day he took over the vineyard. "It's out of respect for the land, a concern for the way we live on the planet, and, you know, just being worried about what we put in our bodies. The big issue here is weed control—with the star thistle up here, Roundup is literally the only thing that can tackle it. Or goats. But goats like to eat vines, too. I had to ask myself, 'Do I want to drink wines where the soil has been treated with glyphosate, or do I want to just suck up the cost and do it all by hand?' I chose the latter."

Ask Rorick how many wines he makes, and he'll laugh and say, "I have no idea!" But everything he does make (with one exception, his Nacré Napa Valley Semillon) comes from his own vines. Some are made with minimal use of sulfur; some with none. All are spontaneously fermented with ambient yeasts. Rorick says, "It's funny, because so many of my Davis classmates think I'm completely unhinged, and then I'll get some natural winemaker who'll say, 'Oh, he's a conventional winemaker.' If I get asked, the only thing I can say is, well, it depends on your definition of natural, I guess."

The **Forlorn Hope Queen of the Sierra White ($$)**, **Queen of the Sierra Rosé ($$)**, **Queen of the Sierra Amber ($$)** (an orange wine), and **Queen of the Sierra Red ($$)** are made every year and are the most easily found of Rorick's wines. Each is a picture of the whole property in a given year (the red, for instance, might include Barbera, Trousseau Noir, Graciano, Zinfandel, and Mondeuse one year; another year the blend might change).

The citrusy, salty, varietal **Forlorn Hope Chenin Blanc ($$)** is a regular presence; same for his pale ruby, aromatic **Grenache ($$)** and his even more transparent, peppery, cranberry-scented **ODB Trousseau ($$)**. There are many one-off or ir-regularly produced wines as well, which honestly is part of the fun. Rorick says, "You can have some fun and irreverence with wine, and still be serious about what you're doing." Examples include the **Abandoned**

Bicycle Muscat ($$), which is aged for five years before release, the **Rom Belkving White Zinfandel ($$)**—crisp and dry, not a typical white Zin at all—or the lime-zesty **Amerikan-ischen Kobold Riesling ($$)**. Best way to find them? Get in touch with the winery directly, though they do pop up here and there on indie wine store shelves.

KINGS CAREY • SANTA BARBARA COUNTY

[sustainable or organic (various vineyards)]

James Sparks grew up in a Mormon family in Idaho, left the church, moved to Los Angeles to be in a rock band, then followed his fellow band mem-ber and brother-in-law up to the Santa Ynez Valley and started helping out at a winery. Maybe not the *usual* path, but in Sparks's case, it worked.

After a stint at Dragonette Cel-lars, Sparks became the winemaker for Liquid Farm in Los Olivos, a day job he still holds. Along the way, he launched Kings Carey with his wife, Anne Ferguson-Sparks.

Sparks is a thoughtful, deft wine-maker with a gift for making expressive

but not flashy wines. He doesn't have his own vineyard land or winery—for those things, wealth and lots of it is the usual requisite. But he works with sev-eral top-flight Santa Barbara County vineyards, all chosen both for quality and for a certain level of trust with the vineyard manager in each case: more than certification of one form or an-other, it's a question of whether the person farms in a conscious way, think-ing about growing grapes in a manner that respects the land and allows the fruit to express place. As Sparks notes, it really comes down to the fine de-tails. "There are organic vineyards, for example, that irrigate like there's no tomorrow—which counteracts on a larger level the good they might be doing with an organic program." But as a general rule, Sparks tries to work with vineyard managers to move things toward organic practices, if they aren't there already.

Sparks only makes five hundred or so cases of Kings Carey each year (though substantially more at Liquid Farm, itself well worth checking out), so the easiest way to track down his wines is to get in touch directly. The lemon-zesty **Kings Carey Semillon ($$)** comes from the Star Lane Vineyard in Happy Canyon; it's the only vineyard he currently works with that is not farmed organically, though it is certified sustainable. The **Mar Farm Chardonnay ($$)** offers pure, bright, vivid citrus flavors; it's a good example of Sparks's light, minimal-intervention touch in the winery. His **Grenache Rosé ($$)** from the organic Spear Vineyard is lively and low in alcohol (usually around 12 percent). Then there are two Kings Carey Grenaches: the pale red, light-bodied **To Market Grenache ($$)**, a good candidate for chilling down in the summer, and the flagship **Kings Carey Grenache ($$)**. Also from the Spear Vineyard, this is regularly one of the best Grenaches in California, though it remains under most wine lovers' radar; it's an incredibly silky, pure expression of this variety, its flavors complex and lasting and deserving of more attention.

LADY OF THE SUNSHINE / SCAR OF THE SEA • SAN LUIS OBISPO

[certified organic / certified biodynamic / regenerative / natural]

Mikey and Gina Giugni share a life, a winery, and a vineyard, but make wine under two names. Scar of the Sea is his, Lady of the Sunshine hers. Drawing the line between them is difficult, because they both help out on each other's wines, but to make a fairly accurate call, Gina's Lady of the Sunshine wines are a bit more classic in nature, and Mikey's Scar of the Sea wines lean a little more in a natural wine direction. But their philosophies align. "The words 'sustainable,' 'organic,' 'biodynamic,' 'regenerative' are all key words for us," Mikey Giugni says. "And we're also big proponents of certification, in a world plagued by greenwashing."

"Certification is authenticity through accountability," Gina adds. "Plus, it creates a community of resources for other people and farmers, too."

Scar of the Sea came first. Mikey Giugni started the brand in 2012. He'd been making wine in Tasmania, "and at the end of the vintage I was cruising around the island, surfing and camping. I came across this old church one day with a stained-glass window that said 'Scar of the Sea.' It was such a great name, so that's what I named the winery. Later, back in the U.S., I couldn't find any mention of the church on the internet, which was weird. And at one point my brother looked at the photo I'd taken of the window and said, 'You're a fucking idiot, dude. It's *star*, not scar.'"

Such is the haphazard nature of inspiration—and what the hell, it really *is* a great name for a winery. Scar of the Sea's wines are not stratospherically priced, intentionally. "I want my wines to be accessible and affordable. A bottle might be thirty-six dollars, but that's sort of our upper range—not unreachable." With Lady of the Sea, Gina follows the same sensibility.

She grew up on a biodynamic farm in the Sierra Foothills, her parents having stepped out from the mainstream of California life quite a while back. "At a certain point, I started asking myself, 'Why does my family do it this way, and our neighbors don't?' That's what drew me in. Then, when I turned twenty, I fell down the wine rabbit hole."

The heart of both efforts is the Chêne Vineyard in Edna Valley. Though the Giugnis don't own the land, they have carte blanche to farm as they want, which for them means biodynamics, native cover crops, chicken tractors for both pest control and manure, and zero chemical inputs. Walking the vineyard, it's impossible to miss their connection to this land; they talk about it as if it were part of their family. But there's lightness, too: "Our focus has been regenerative agriculture and biodynamics, but not taken so seriously that it's not fun," Gina says. "Still, some of the local farmers definitely find it a little strange. We asked the folks across the road if they'd let us have the manure from their cows, and they were like, 'What? You want our *poop?*' We told them, 'Yes, we really, really do.' So, they sort of shrugged and said, 'OK. You're weird, but sure, you want a bunch of cow crap, take it.'"

In addition to Chêne, the Giugnis source from other organically and bio-dynamically farmed vineyards on the San Luis Obispo coast and in Santa Barbara County, as well as from Gina's family's farm. "We stopped buying from growers who were disconnected from their vineyards," Mikey says. "We want to buy from people with real connection to their land. If I'm buying ten thousand dollars of grapes, I want that money to stay in our farming community. You have power with where you spend."

The **Lady of the Sunshine Chêne Vineyards Chardonnay ($$)** is lime-salty, deeply mineral, but with an underlying richness. Gina's **Lady of the Sunshine Chevey ($$)**, a nod to Cheverny in France's Loire Valley, blends Chardonnay and Sauvignon Blanc with surprising success: the Sauvignon gives zippily fresh grapefruit flavors, the Chardonnay body and a stony note. The whole-cluster fermented **Chêne Vineyards Pinot Noir ($$)** is full of earthy dark berry flavors, with fine-grained tannins and a light coffee-toast note from the stem inclusion. Finally, her **Primitivo ($$)** comes from her family's vineyard, located, Gina says, "where the oaks start to transition into sugar pines and ponderosas." It's round and sweetly ripe despite the fact that it's also very low alcohol (about 12 percent). "Blueberry-pie bramble," is the way she describes it.

With Scar of the Sea, Mikey Giugni makes a wide range of wines. A few highlights: his smoky **Scar of the Sea Bassi Vineyard Chardonnay ($$)** gets its struck-match aromatics from the reductive winemaking approach he uses here; it's intense in the best way, full of juicy acidity. The **Vino de los Ranchos Pinot Noir ($$)** uses organic grapes from the Santa Maria Valley and is brisk and earthy, with a raspberry and tomato-skin character. Sharply peppery, savory, and lean, the **Bassi Vineyard Syrah ($$)** is "as coastal as you can get," Giugni says. Bassi is only a mile from the Pacific, which shows clearly. There are others, all worth looking into. Also don't miss Giugni's ciders (available directly from the winery), which offer him freedom for some offbeat experimentation. Particularly tasty? Newtown Pippins co-fermented with Sauvignon Blanc and lime leaves. "Our beach-time jungle juice," he calls it. Who says there have to be rules?

MELVILLE WINERY • STA. RITA HILLS

[sustainable / organic]

Fish emulsion. "It's really thick, like motor oil," Chad Melville says. "And it smells beyond nasty. I get it on my fingers and I can't get it off for days. But it's incredibly rich in amino acids, and it brings this glow to the vineyard, and protection, and health—it gives this amazing energy to the plants. Ask native Americans why did they bury fish in their farming land? Because it works."

The Melville vineyard covers 120 acres in the Sta. Rita Hills appellation of Santa Barbara County. Chad Melville's father started Melville in the early 1990s, after he fell in love with Pinot Noir (it happens). Chad Melville joined in 1997, when he was four years out of college. "I'd been exposed to farming early on, but until I was twenty-three or twenty-four, being a farmer to me just meant being bored and sweaty and sticky. Then I started tasting wines out of barrel, and the farming all started to make more sense. OK. Now I get it. *That's* why we do this."

Melville is entirely organic, but it isn't always easy in this coastal region. "Where we are is perfect for mildew," Melville says. "If we didn't have the wind off the ocean, no one would be growing any grapes here. We use organic sprays, but we also have to get in and open up the canopies, pull the leaves away from the fruit zone by hand. It's a lot of work, and it's expensive. Plus the fish emulsion! It's all about prevention, prevention, prevention."

These difficulties have not in any way dissuaded Melville that farming the way he does is the right thing to do, both for his wines and for the overall ecosystem. "If we're going to have an honest relationship with the land, that has to be about respect—for the earth, the ocean, the mountains. I could never do anything disrespectful to the soil and look Mother Nature in the eyes again."

And Melville's approach is also about flavor, and making the best wines possible. Living soil, which keeps the vines' uptake of both macro- and micronutrients robust, is key, he feels. "We've all had this experience where you bite into a peach, and it's soft, and there's sweetness, but there's just no flavor. It's exactly the same with grapes. We take soil samples and leaf samples twice a year, because we want to see whether what's in the soil is being taken in by the vines. It's like looking in the refrigerator, and then seeing what the vine is taking from the refrigerator. But if the soil isn't alive, it's like the refrigerator has a lock and chain on it."

The **Melville Estate Chardonnay** (\$\$) often has a faint honeysuckle note to its dried-pineapple and citrus fruit. The **Estate Pinot Noir** (\$\$) is crisp and floral, with lots of blue fruit flavors. "When I smell that blueberry character, that's like 'Ding! Ding! Ding! Santa Rita Hills!'" Melville says. "Ripe fruit wrapped around vivid acidity." The **Melville Terraces Pinot Noir** (\$\$\$) is from a section of vineyard that looks due west toward the ocean. It's higher-toned, more red fruit, and peppery on the finish. The **Block M Pinot Noir** (\$\$\$) is darker, still elegant but more powerful. "It's got a lower rumble," Melville says. "More bass. Terraces is more lifted and pretty." The **Estate Syrah** (\$\$) is classic cool-climate Syrah, savory, floral, with lots of black pepper notes. Melville's **Donna's Vineyard Syrah** (\$\$\$) amps up the intensity from the estate, adding some savory black-olive and cured-meat characteristics. "You go into this vineyard when it's ready to be picked and squeeze a berry, your fingers will be stained for two days."

PISONI VINEYARDS • SANTA LUCIA HIGHLANDS

[certified sustainable]

There's a common saying about vineyards, which is that stress is good for wine grapes—a stressed vine gives fruit with greater character, more substance. You have to assume this is what Gary Pisoni is talking about when he says that he likes to "put the grapes' balls to the wall." Even at seventy, Pisoni is robustly larger than life, a guy who grew up in a vegetable-farming family in the Salinas Valley and played football for the local high school, then fell in love with wine on a sales trip to Puerto Rico with his parents. "I was eighteen or nineteen. We were at a dinner at a restaurant, and I saw this sommelier open a wine, pour it in his tastevin, and swish it around, taste it, slurp it, and I thought, 'Man, I want to do *that!*'" Pisoni started making wine in his garage in 1975, then in 1982, on land that no one remotely thought might be suited to vines, he planted what is now one of California's greatest Pinot Noir vineyards. He's a Falstaffian figure, with a booming voice, huge personality, mane of curly hair, and penchant for Hawaiian shirts. Barrel around his property with him in his ancient jeep,

which looks like it might be a relic from World War II, and he'll yell as you bounce over ruts and stones, "Intensity!! I love intensity!!!"

For all the bluster, Pisoni is a great farmer. He's now passed on most of the day-to-day work to sons Mark (vineyards) and Jeff (winemaking), but is by no means retired. And that intensity in the wines is still present, though it's leavened by bright acidity and beautiful clarity. Jeff Pisoni says, "People have associated us with power and intensity forever, but we do farm to build some finesse in with that."

The Pisoni vines lie on a steep bench of land on the southern edge of the Salinas Valley. The farming is meticulous and always has been, with Gary and now Mark working to balance the warmth of the Santa Lucia Highlands with the frequent cold ocean wind off Monterey Bay. That combination, together with the site's shallow, decomposed granite-and-clay soil, produces Pinot Noir that has richness and amplitude but also a fine line of firm acidity and vivid red-fruit flavors.

The land is certified sustainable, and Mark also draws on organic and biodynamic methods. "If the whole ecosystem's healthy, then the soil will be healthy," he says. "I just call it good farming. We also completely stopped using herbicides and chemical fertil-izers. We don't fertilize with anything except compost that we make on the farm, and we also planted a lot of fruit trees to increase biodiversity. I love going up and eating an apple or fig right off the tree. It reminds me what a special place this is, every time."

The Pisonis make one wine from their vineyard under their name, the **Pisoni Pinot Noir ($$$$)**. It keeps to the model that Gary Pisoni established: power but also focus, with rich red and blue fruit flavors, chewy tannins, and floral notes. It's a benchmark California Pinot Noir.

The family also makes other wines under their Lucia and Lucy labels, which are easier to find (demand for the Pisoni Pinot far outstrips pro-duction). The **Lucy Rosé ($$)** is 100 percent Pinot Noir, and $1 from every bottle sold is donated to breast cancer research; similarly, $1 from every bot-tle sold of the **Lucy Pico Bianco ($$)**, a crisp blend of Pinot Gris and Pinot Blanc, goes to ocean conservancy re-search. The **Lucia Santa Lucia High-lands Estate Cuvée Chardonnay** ($$–$$$) balances crisp green apple and rounder pear notes against mod-est vanilla oak. The **Soberanes Vine-yard Chardonnay ($$$)** is lemony and stony, a little more high-toned overall. For Pinots, the **Lucia Santa Lucia Highlands Estate Cuvée Pinot Noir** ($$–$$$) again is a blend from the family's three vineyards (Pisoni, and then Garys' and Soberanes, which they co-own with grower Gary Franscioni) with ripe, black cherry flavors and plenty of spice notes. The **Garys' Vine-yard Pinot Noir ($$$)**, from a foggy, windy site, offers more depth of flavor in a similar vein. There are also two Sy-rahs: the dark-fruited **Garys' Vineyard Syrah ($$$)** and the more peppery, sa-vory **Susan's Hill Syrah ($$$)**, which comes from a single small plot of Syrah vines at the Pisoni Vineyard.

SANDLANDS / TURLEY WINE CELLARS •
LODI AND NAPA VALLEY

[organic or certified organic (depending on vineyard)]

Tegan Passalacqua is one of California's most respected proponents of old, forgotten, historic California vineyards. He's a Napa Valley native, but not from a winemaking family—his father drove a cement truck for thirty-two years. Passalacqua says, "He poured foundations for a lot of wineries in Napa, but that's about it." But vineyards caught Passalacqua's interest, and after getting a bachelor's degree in public health, he shifted into wine.

For Sandlands, Passalacqua specializes in affordable wines from vineyards he's passionate about. He's also the longtime winemaker for Turley Wine Cellars, the much-acclaimed producer of (primarily) old-vine Zinfandel, founded by owner Larry Turley in 1993. The two wineries share a focus on vineyards that are part of California's cultural history. Stylistically, Passalacqua's Sandlands wines are lighter-bodied and zippier than Turley's, which tend toward a richer, riper style.

For Passalacqua, these vines aren't merely old but historic, with a value that extends far beyond the per-ton cost of their grapes. "They remind me that what we do is agri*culture*," he says, "instead of agri-business."

In a sense, Passalacqua is a vineyard prospector. Antioch, California, he says, "is full of little plots. I've stopped by almost all of them. Some have called me back, some haven't." In Fiddletown in the Sierra Foothills, he'll tell you, the notary public is the woman to know, at least regarding vineyards, "because all the foreclosures have to be notarized." In Lodi, he managed to scrape up enough money to buy the Kirschenmann Vineyard back in 2012, nearly a hundred years after its vines first went in the ground. Initially, Passalacqua couldn't afford the asking price. He left the first meeting with the owner disheartened, convinced the fruit would either end up in some anonymous blend or, worse, that the vines would be ripped out.

But then he got a call the next day saying she'd lower the price. "I was driving to work at seven a.m., and she said, 'When you left yesterday, I knew that my grandfather, my father, and my brother would want you to own that vineyard.' I couldn't believe it. She was seventy, and her children weren't interested at all. Something just clicked in her that I would take care of her family's property."

At Turley, Passalacqua makes more than fifty different wines; at Sandlands, he makes about six. All vineyard sources are farmed organically. The only hitch with the Sandlands wines is that they're made in very small quantities—a few barrels here, a few there. (Best strategy, get on Passalacqua's mailing list.) The simply named **Sandlands Lodi Red Table Wine ($$)** is a blend of Cinsault from the Bechthold Ranch (planted 1886), Carignan from the Spenker Ranch (1900), and Zinfandel from Passalacqua's own Kirschenmann Vineyard (1915). It's bright and juicy with crunchy red fruit, one of those "how did my glass get empty so fast?" wines. The **Sandlands Cinsault ($$)** explores the fragrant side of this Rhône grape variety, violet-scented, delicate, and very low in alcohol (12 percent or so). Passalacqua's **Sandlands Chenin Blanc ($$)** recalls the linear, laser-precise wines of Loire producers like the late Jacky Blot more than it does typical California Chenin.

From Turley, the robust **Old Vines Zinfandel ($$)**, sourced from fifteen to sixteen different vineyards, is an excellent introduction. Among the other Turley wines (many of them available only to mailing list customers), look for the **Duarte Zinfandel ($$$)**, a dark, silky blend of grapes from three ancient Contra Costa vineyards—Evangelho, Del Barbi, and Mori. The Turley **Dogtown Vineyard Zinfandel ($$$)** comes from one of Passalacqua's favorite Lodi sites, planted in 1944. Minty, chocolatey, and rich with black cherry fruit, it's a hedonistic pleasure. There are many, many other Turley wines, but keep an eye out for the **Turley Hayne Vineyard Petite Sirah ($$$)**, a remarkable wine from a variety that too often produces blunt, sledgehammer-ish reds. Intense, inky, and able to age for decades, the Turley version is one of California's iconic wines.

TABLAS CREEK • PASO ROBLES

[certified organic / biodynamic / certified regenerative]

In 2020, Tablas Creek became the first winery in the U.S. to earn Regenerative Organic Certified status. The program looks at every aspect of a farm: soil health, carbon capture, biodiversity, animal welfare, and farmworker fairness. Proprietor Jason Haas says, "We felt this was kind of the gold standard for wine and agriculture, and if we got certified, it would help to build awareness."

What's notable about Haas's efforts is they're done at scale. Tablas isn't tiny. Haas farms 125 acres of vines and makes more than sixteen thousand cases of wine per year—not so big in commercial wine terms, but very big in the organic/biodynamic/regenerative realm. Haas says: "Regenerative organic methods give agriculture the ability to be a part of the solution to big-picture problems like climate change, resource scarcity, and inequality—and since roughly 30 percent of the earth's land mass is used for agriculture, those problems aren't solvable without getting agriculture on board."

As you walk through the vineyards here, the place feels deeply *alive*. Sweet pea, purple vetch, oats, clover, and daikon radishes flourish between the vine rows (there are reasons: pea and clover are legumes and help provide nitrogen; vetch keeps erosion down; oats add biomass; the daikon plants act as soil aerators). Three hundred sheep graze the property, producing about 750 pounds of manure each day, which they spread into the soil with their hooves; three formidable mastiffs, Adelita, Bjorn, and Osa, guard the sheep against coyotes and mountain lions. Haas and his team pull fallen logs from the surrounding forests to make biochar. "It helps short-circuit the carbon cycle," he says. "You're essentially making a natural form of charcoal that keeps carbon in the soil. A big part of what differentiates regenerative ag is that you use natural processes to mimic what would happen in a wild ecosystem."

Tablas Creek has been organic from its inception. When Jason Haas moved it to biodynamics, "it was spurred by trying to eliminate outside inputs. It's great to be using organic fertilizer, but can we make that here, not ship it in? So, sheep. We started with our flock in 2013, then had to hire a shepherd in 2016—sheep are good at a lot of things, but not designing plans and executing them."

The shift to regenerative came about when Tablas Creek's longtime winemaker, Neil Collins, was at a dinner with Yvon Chouinard, the eco-activist founder of the brand Patagonia. They started talking about regenerative agriculture, and Chouinard mentioned a pilot program for winery certification that the Regenerative Organic Alliance had started.

Haas realized that much of what he was already doing fit the regenerative program. "A lot of it comes straight from biodynamics," he says. "But both organic and biodynamics are very focused on farming. Regenerative certification requires you to be audited to show you're reducing your use of limited resources like water and energy; you have to actually measure the carbon content in your soil, for instance. You also have to show that your animals are treated well, and it adds something not really touched by other certifications, which is farmworker fairness. Not just showing that you're paying a living wage and that your workers are safe, but that their feedback is actually sought after and acted upon."

Regenerative farming, Haas says, has the breadth of sustainability, plus the rigor of organics and biodynamics. "But it also sidesteps the whole mysticism-astrological-signs-cosmic energy part of biodynamics, which I find pretty dubious. The certification program isn't solely for vineyards, but we were in a position to be the first winery. And I thought, 'If we can have a role in spreading the word about regenerative farming, then that's completely worth doing.'"

The Paso Robles AVA is warm and dry, to say the least—as Haas says, "It can be a hundred and five, and there will be times you'll see nothing but blue sky for months. It can feel like living on the surface of the sun." But the proximity of the Pacific Ocean allows Tablas Creek to make warm-climate wines that still retain acidity and have structure and tension. The most affordable are the **Patelin de Tablas ($$)** wines, but because they are made from sourced as well as estate fruit, they are not certified organic/regenerative, unlike the estate wines. "Unfortunately, you can't make a twenty-five-dollar wine from grapes it costs you five thousand dollars a ton to farm," Haas observes. His hope is that one day he'll be able to reduce farming costs to make that equation more workable.

The rest of the Tablas Creek wines—there are fifteen to twenty each vintage—all come from the estate vines. The **Tablas Creek Côtes de Tablas Blanc ($$)**, a Viognier-based white blend, melds the richness supplied by Paso Robles's generous climate with tangy acidity and light, saline mineral notes. There are also a large number of varietal white wines. Highlights include a lime-scented **Vermentino ($$)**, a **Marsanne ($$)** full of melon and faint honey notes, and a crisp, minerally **Roussanne ($$)**. The top white is the complex **Esprit de Tablas Blanc ($$$)**, a blend of Roussanne, Grenache Blanc, Picpoul, and Clairette Blanche modeled on Châteauneuf-du-Pape Blanc.

For reds, there's the **Côtes de Tablas ($$)**, which blends Grenache, Counoise, Syrah, and Mourvèdre for a brambly, spicy red with enough structure to age, plus a profusion of single-variety bottlings. All of these are good, particularly the ruby-hued, expressive **Grenache ($$)**, an earthy, slightly feral **Mourvèdre ($$)**, and what is certainly the only varietal **Vaccarèse ($$)** made in the U.S., and possibly in the Rhône as well. If you happen to be at the winery, also look for **En Gobelet ($$$)**, an intriguingly herbal, peppery, unusual blend of Grenache, Mourvèdre, Syrah, Counoise, and Tannat (it's only sold through the tasting room). Finally, there's Tablas Creek's flagship red blend **Esprit de Tablas ($$$)**, which is modeled on the great wines of Châteauneuf-du-Pape. Powerful and complex, it has layers of dark fruit and spice flavors, sometimes with a savory, appealingly gamey note. It also has that rare capacity to drink beautifully on release or age for a decade or two in a cellar.

THACHER WINERY • PASO ROBLES

[organic]

Sherman Thacher started his fermentation career in the early 1990s, brewing beer at Los Gatos Brewing Company in Northern California. Today he's making wine on the central coast, in the Adelaida District of western Paso Robles. Thacher Winery, which he runs with his wife, Michelle, focuses on what he terms "expressive varietals"—Cinsault, for instance, or Valdiguié—made in a bright, less extracted, less weighty style.

The winery is on a former horse ranch; its hundred-year-old white barn, with "KR" painted on it in huge letters (for Kentucky Ranch), still stands. Thacher's five-acre estate vineyard and his Homestead Hill vineyard in the Willow Creek District are both farmed organically, but are not certified. "Our ranches have been using all organic sprays for about five years. I can go to Tractor Supply and buy a sprayer for three hundred dollars and blast the vineyard with Roundup or whatever, and it'll look perfect, but what's the point of that?"

He adds, "It does take a while to get there, though. I bought, what, forty tons of organic cow shit this year? We work as responsibly as we possibly can. It makes sense. It's farming consciously. But I'm not grinding up horns to put down gopher holes and whatnot." (In other words, no biodynamics here.) Thacher also buys fruit from several other Paso Robles vineyards, keeping to places that suit the style he's after: lighter, fresher, crisper. That does mean picking in some cold, windy locations—his Thacher Cabernet Sauvignon, for instance, comes from an old, head-trained vineyard in a location the longtime owner refers to as "pneumonia canyon."

Thacher's winemaking leans low-intervention without heading into full natural-wine territory. "Our wines are on the leaner side," he says, "so we don't have to add acid, water back, or any of that." Native yeasts are used for all fermentations. Recently, he has also started making cider, from heirloom variety organic apples he grows on the property.

The appealing **Thacher Sparkling Viognier ($$)** has yeasty, honeyed aroma, round citrus flavors, and dusty spiciness. The winery's **Chenin Blanc ($$)**, from fifty-year-old vines, is fermented both in amphorae and old oak barrels; it's full of bright apple-quince notes. Thacher's signature red is a buoyant, light-bodied **Cinsault ($$)**, floral and red-fruited and perfect for chilling down. Thacher uses whole-cluster fermentation for it: "We get really nice spice from the stems— that distinct white pepper character." His **Valdiguié ($$)** is peppery and leafy on the nose, full of juicy fruit and light tannins. "When we started doing this, no one wanted Valdiguié," he recalls. "Farmers couldn't give the grapes away. Now everyone wants it. People are all over it like spider monkeys." Finally, **Controlled Chaos ($$)** is a meaty blend of Mourvèdre, Zinfandel, Grenache, and Counoise with plenty of spicy, dark-berried flavor. In the choice of name, it gives a fair picture of the vibe of the winery, too. (Side note: Thacher's assistant winemaker Daniel Callan also makes an excellent, affordable, juicy blend of Valdiguié, Cinsault, and Negrette for his own Slamdance Koöperatieve label. Seek it out.)

A TRIBUTE TO GRACE • SANTA BARBARA COUNTY

[sustainable or organic (depending on vineyard)]

Around 2013, I was in a wine store in Napa Valley, looking for something to bring to a friend's house. The owner pressed a bottle I'd never heard of into my hands: A Tribute to Grace Grenache. "This is the best Grenache being made in California," he said. "You *need* to try it." My immediate thought was, 'Well, the best Grenache being made in California isn't that high a bar, but what the hell.' A few hours later, I took a sip, and thought, "Fuck me, this *is* the best Grenache being made in California."

There's one wine that people who love Grenache love more than any other, and that's the elusive and extraordinary and extremely expensive Château Rayas, one of those rare wines that when you taste it seems somehow to have been beamed in from some other, more radiant plane. A Tribute to Grace is the only California Grenache that's ever reminded me of it. But that's what Angela Osborne, A Tribute to Grace's owner and winemaker, has in mind. "When I first tasted Rayas, that made me realize the style of Grenache I wanted. That ethereality! Who doesn't want the ethereal?"

Osborne grew up in New Zealand. While she was in film school there, she worked in a wine shop. "I learned the storytelling of wine before I ever made any," she says about the experience. But she had no plan to pursue wine, until her film career was hijacked when a friend suggested she move to California to work harvest in 2002. Restlessness then led to three years in London, but wine kept nagging at her, and in 2006, "I came back and thought I would work and figure out how to start this crazy dream."

She got a job at a wine shop in Santa Barbara, and that Thanksgiving a group of winemakers came to pour. When she mentioned her desire to make wine, one of them said, "Well, what are you waiting for? You can piggyback on my vineyard contract and use my winery to make it." Osborne's first vintage was 2007.

Osborne falls into the "force of nature" realm of personality; she's magnetic, for one thing, and talking to her,

---

"Who doesn't want the ethereal?"
—Angela Osborne

---

it's hard to imagine that she ever *wouldn't* make wine. Her initial wine, and still the anchor of her portfolio, comes from an obscure vineyard tucked high up in the hills in a remote eastern corner of Santa Barbara County called Santa Barbara Highlands. "You get to the top, and it's just a moonscape," she says. "It's dry and empty and full of tumbleweeds. And this incredible intensity of light, which reminds me of New Zealand." It's a great Grenache site. She's added others since: "My dream was to make three single-vineyard Grenaches. But a few years in, I started to expand—laterally, which is pretty much what you have to do when you work with only one variety."

Osborne's winemaking is straightforward: "I don't use machines. Only a destemmer and a press. Foot-treading every day. And some good music." The vineyards she buys fruit from are mostly organic, and at the very least sustainable: "We pay extra to do all our vineyard work with manual labor and no horrible spraying. The only herbicide we use is . . . well, a hoe." This approach produces what she wants in her wines, "the expression of Grenache I resonate with the most. Sandalwood and frankincense and myrrh, which create a framework around that floral rose and slow-cooked rhubarb character. It feels very otherworldly. And it has a lot of personal meaning for me. And this very quiet power."

The personal meaning of those aromas ties in with her winery's name. Grace Ingrid Frear Brookes was Osborne's grandmother. Osborne spent every Thursday night with her when she was growing up; some of those Grenache spice scents recall her childhood. Grace Brookes passed away in 2013. "She lived to be ninety-one years young," Osborne says. "She passed when our firstborn was just ten days old. My husband and I were in New Zealand to give birth, so the divine circle of life was a very poignant experience for me. She was admitted to hospital in Hamilton, we rushed down, she met my son for the first time, proclaimed 'isn't he worthwhile,' and passed into a sleep an hour later that she didn't awake from." And yes, Grace Ingrid Frear Brookes did get to enjoy a glass now and then of her namesake wine.

Of Osborne's many Grenaches, the **Tribute to Grace Santa Barbara Highlands Vineyard Grenache ($$)**, year in and year out, offers a kind of light-on-water transparency that's saturated with flavor despite its deceptive weightlessness. Her **Besson Vineyard Grenache ($$$)** comes from a vineyard planted in 1910 near Gilroy, on sandy soil (Grenache tends to be more delicate when planted on sand than when planted on granite- or clay-based soils). Sweet berries, violets, lots of blue-fruit notes.

It's denser than the Santa Barbara Highlands, but still lithe rather than weighty. The **Shake Ridge Ranch Grenache ($$$)** comes from grower Ann Kraemer's organic vineyard high up in the Sierra Foothills—it's sultry, red-fruited, and lasting. Lastly, the **Provisor Vineyard ($$$)** from Dry Creek Valley in Sonoma County is the most full-bodied of Osborne's wines with darker roast-plum and olive flavors; it's the one that most expresses California's familiar warmth and generosity.

TWO WOLVES • SANTA BARBARA COUNTY

[certified organic]

Alecia Moore is a musician—a good portion of the world knows her as P!nk—but, she says, "wine is my second career." And when not pursuing her first career as a singer, she's either out in the vineyards or in her winery in Santa Barbara County, topping off barrels, pruning vines—all the typical activities of a small-estate vigneron—together with her assistant winemaker Alison Thomson.

Moore didn't grow up with wine. She grew up in Doylestown, Pennsylvania, got kicked out of the house when she was fifteen, dropped out of school, and devoted herself to music—but as a touring musician in her early twenties she discovered, and fell in love

with, Châteauneuf-du-Pape. That led to an unlikely quest: "I was in Paris on tour, and I was bored and just thought, 'I have to find this Châteauneuf-du-Pape place.' So I took the train to Avignon, and actually ran out of money while I was there—I ended up singing for cheese sandwiches on a street in Avignon. I think I sang Edith Piaf."

There are a lot of ways to fall in love with wine; whatever the route, the destination is the same. "All of a sudden, when you start to love wine," Moore says, "it teaches you to pay attention to life. To pay attention to your food, for instance, where it comes from, what things smell like. Like, 'Why do I not know how to describe the difference between the flavor of a lemon and a lime?'"

Moore makes wine at her Two Wolves vineyard, a little more than twenty-five acres of certified organic vines in the Santa Ynez Valley, in two parcels (Two Wolves vineyard and Right Left vineyard; they're a quarter of a mile or so apart, both on the estate). It's a warm wine region, and the wines reflect that: they're rich and robust, but with a firm spine of acidity that keeps them fresh. Moore lives at the vineyard with her husband and children, one key reason, she says, that working organically was important to her.

All of Moore's wines are made in fairly small quantities. Her **Two Wolves Sauvignon Blanc ($$)**, fermented in two cement eggs ("Edgar" and "Althea"), has the fresh melon character of warm-climate Sauvignon, with some vibrant lemon-grapefruit zip. There's also a textural, funkily expressive, skin-contact **Semillon ($$)**, full of quince flavor and a modest amount of skin tannin; it's a great cheese wine.

For reds, Moore is one of the few producers in California to make a varietal **Graciano ($$$)**, more usually found as a blending variety in Spain's Rioja. The Two Wolves version is done with carbonic maceration, making for a brightly juicy, cherry-inflected, highly chillable red. The winery's **Syrah ($$$)** is dark and intense, translating inland Santa Barbara County's heat into a powerful, spicy wine; the **Cabernet Sauvignon ($$$)** is similarly powerful, with plenty of blackberry fruit and tongue-gripping tannins. It's one to age, though it's eminently drinkable on release. Her **Petite Verdot ($$$)**, another variety more often used for blending, is ultraviolet purple in hue, with spice and fresh herb notes, leaning to the savory side. But for me, the best of the Two Wolves reds is the **Cabernet Franc ($$$)**, which seamlessly balances the varieties herbal-tea-leaf pepperiness against ripe, dark fruit. It's a remarkable expression of the variety.

VILLA CREEK / MAHA ESTATE • PASO ROBLES

[certified biodynamic]

Cris Cherry and his wife, JoAnn, moved to Paso Robles in 1996 and opened their restaurant, also called Villa Creek, in 1998. His wines, Chris says, "started as a house wine project, with all these growers and vintners we knew. It was just going to be a barrel at first, but that grew into seven." Today Villa Creek and MAHA make about three thousand cases of wine, while the restaurant—which garnered plenty of acclaim over the years—closed in 2017. It took a while to shut it down. Jo says, "We thought, 'Wow, we're winemakers now. So . . . how do we get rid of this restaurant?'"

From the start, the Cherrys' plan was to use fruit only from certified organic vineyards. When Cris and Jo purchased their own land—"We have a mortgage on it," she says. "It's not like we inherited it; we haven't been here three hundred years"— they started off farming organically and switched to biodynamics in 2012. "The learning curve is a bit of a challenge," Cris says, a modest understatement. "But it's fun, and it's interesting. We're constantly learn-ing more and more. Part of our inspiration was a quote from Michel Gassier, in the southern Rhône. He told me, 'There are lots of great wines that come from vineyards all over the world, but the best wines I have ever put in my mouth come from vine-yards farmed biodynamically.'"

Jo adds, "It's a lot like raising a child, growing vines this way. You want to give them the best start pos-sible, and that's not by giving them a lot of drugs."

Cris Cherry's winemaking draws on his experience as a chef, at least in terms of overall approach: "Much like good cooking, good winemaking is more with less. More with more is easy. Nuance is what's elusive. Coming from a restaurant, if you have great in-gredients, that's enough. What's on the steak? Salt and pepper. That's it. Noth-ing else. Same with grapes." The Villa Creek wines concentrate on Syrah and Grenache, typically use a fair percent-age of whole-cluster fermentation, and come from both the Cherrys' own es-tate vineyard and from organic and/ or biodynamic vineyards in the region.

Their MAHA wines, made similarly, come solely from their biodynamic estate (the winery itself is also certified biodynamic).

Villa Creek Rocks & Flowers ($$) is the winery's most affordable red blend, a fragrant, luscious, dark-fruited, softly tannic red made from Grenache, Syrah, Mourvèdre, and Carignan. The Cherrys' **Garnacha ($$$)** is all spicy raspberry and raspberry liqueur flavors, supple and graceful. (Side note: since the Cherrys use the Spanish pronunciation for the name of the winery, [i.e., *vi-ya* not *vil-la*], they also prefer to use the Spanish names for grape varieties.) **Avenger ($$$)** blends Syrah with smaller percentages of Grenache and Mourvèdre. Cris says that he prefers that his Syrahs lean toward "rocks and flowers, rather than being big and super-textured," and that's true here. The **James Berry Vineyard High Road ($$$)** ups Mourvèdre to the dominant position, and brings that variety's aromatic, meaty savoriness to the wine's black pepper and black cherry flavors; it does a good job of being irresistible no matter the vintage.

The MAHA wines are smaller production and most easily found direct from the winery. **Backlit ($$$$)**, peppery, full-bodied, and intense, is about a third Petite Sirah, the rest Mourvèdre, Grenache, and Carignan. **Understory ($$$$)** is more an expression of Grenache (about three-quarters, depending on the vintage): ruby red in hue, with silky red and blue fruit flavors. But the standout may be the sole white, **Before Anyone Else ($$$$)**, one of the only 100 percent Clairette wines in California (or even in the Rhône for that matter). Pale gold, complex, and flavorful (think tangerine, lemon, minerals, and a little toasted nut character), it's an excellent look at the potential often still hidden in Paso Robles for truly impressive white wines.

PRODUCERS PROFILED IN THIS CHAPTER

Beckmen Vineyards

Domaine de la Côte / Sandhi /
   Piedrasassi

Forlorn Hope

Kings Carey

Lady of the Sunshine /
   Scar of the Sea

Melville Winery

Pisoni Vineyards

Sandlands / Turley Wine Cellars

Tablas Creek

Thacher Winery

A Tribute to Grace

Two Wolves

Villa Creek / MAHA

OTHER CENTRAL COAST AND BEYOND PRODUCERS TO LOOK FOR

Adelaida

AmByth Estate

Birichino

I. Brand & Family /
   Marea

La Clarine Farm

Dragonette Cellars

Edmonds St. John

Foxen

Grimm's Bluff

Kukkula

Paul Lato

Liquid Farm

Oceana

Popelouchum

Clos Saron

Seasmoke

Site

Talley Vineyards

Tatomer

Tyler

OREGON

Sokol Blosser's estate vineyards, Willamette Valley

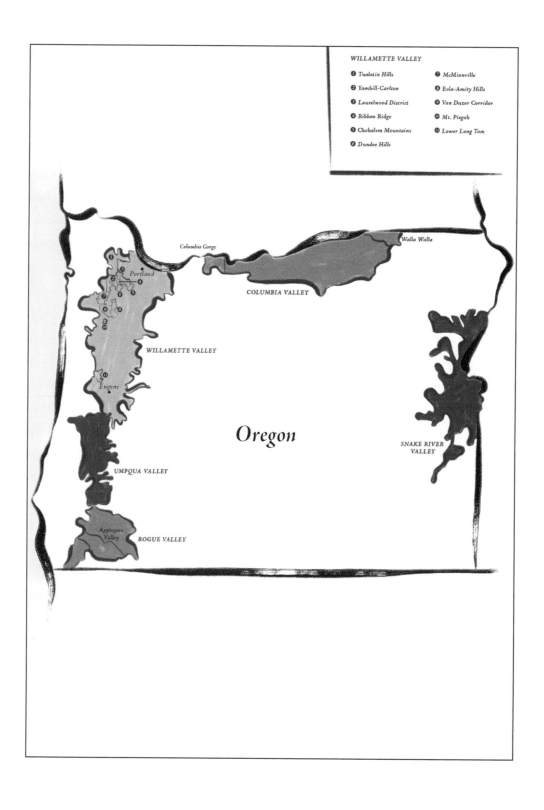

WILLAMETTE VALLEY

❶ Tualatin Hills
❷ Yamhill-Carlton
❸ Laurelwood District
❹ Ribbon Ridge
❺ Chehalem Mountains
❻ Dundee Hills
❼ McMinnville
❽ Eola-Amity Hills
❾ Van Duzer Corridor
❿ Mt. Pisgah
⓫ Lower Long Tom

Columbia Gorge

Walla Walla

Portland

COLUMBIA VALLEY

WILLAMETTE VALLEY

Eugene

Oregon

SNAKE RIVER
VALLEY

UMPQUA VALLEY

Applegate
Valley

ROGUE VALLEY

t takes an interesting state to devote almost two-thirds of its vineyard land to a variety often referred to as "the heartbreak grape." But Oregon *is* an interesting state. Leaving aside news media reports of far-left Antifa activists battling it out with far-right paramilitary goons in the streets of Portland (honestly a place where most residents just want to start the day with a really excellent cup of coffee, and kind of wish it weren't raining), it's the one wine-producing state in the U.S. whose identity is inextricably tied to a single variety: Pinot Noir.

Though plenty of other varieties grow here, too, Pinot has made Oregon's name, and the state is entirely suited to it. The Willamette Valley, stretching south of Portland some 150 miles, is one of the coolest wine growing regions in the U.S., but that's a moderated coolness; the valley is protected from the cold Pacific by the Coast Range in the west, and from eastern Oregon's heat by the Cascades in the east. Summer days are warm, summer nights brisk, the growing season is long, and the combination of volcanic, sedimentary, and windblown loess soils—legacies of the Missoula Floods that occurred some eighteen thousand years ago—make it Pinot heaven.

Not that people always knew that. When Eyrie Vineyards' David Lett planted the first Pinot Noir vines in Willamette in 1965 (followed a few months later by Charles Coury), everyone assumed the place was too wet. As Myron Redford of Amity Vineyards has said, "Lett and Coury had been told the rain would wash them out, they would grow fungus between their toes, it would rot their clothes off, and there was no way in hell they would be able to grow great grapes up here." Lett, who happened to arrive during the legendary Christmas floods of 1964, when torrential downpours submerged sixty-one thousand acres of the valley, was understandably disconcerted to find his promised land under water, but he planted anyway—and found exactly what he'd thought would be the case from research he'd done while studying viticulture and enology at UC Davis. Once-in-a-century flooding aside, rain in Willamette was mostly a problem during the winter. The actual growing season was nigh-on perfect for Pinot Noir.

As Lett's son Jason says, "There's a narrative that people showed up in Willamette in hippie vans and sort of looked around like, 'Whoa, man, what can I do here?' But in fact, there was a lot of intellectual specificity to what my dad and people like him were trying to do, and they were adamant about the quality they were trying to achieve. None of the people who came here initially were aiming for the middle." Those people included other pioneers, like Dick Erath, Charles and Shirley Coury, Dick and Nancy Ponzi, Susan Sokol Blosser and Bill Blosser, and David and Ginny Adelsheim, all of whom started wineries around 1969 to 1971. That was the liftoff era for Oregon wine.

Hippie-driven or not, Oregon viticulture also has a long history of sustainable, organic, and biodynamic farming. Most of its nearly one thousand wineries are small and family-owned (70 percent produce fewer than five thousand cases per year), and the state itself has a lengthy history of environmental awareness. Fifty-two percent of the certified biodynamic vineyards in the U.S. are in Oregon (despite the fact that the state only makes about 1 percent of U.S. wine); and almost a third of the wineries in the state are certified sustainable by its long-running LIVE program, which started in 1995. On top of that, many more vintners farm with sustainable, organic, or biodynamic practices without being certified.

Other varieties grow here besides Pinot Noir. Oregon Pinot Gris and Chardonnay can be superb, and Syrah grows particularly well in the southern Umpqua, Rogue, and Applegate valleys. While some of the founding families have since sold to investors or larger winery groups—Erath, for example, is now owned by Washington's Chateau Ste. Michelle, and Ponzi was recently purchased by Champagne Bollinger—Oregon remains a magnet for young, independent winemakers driven by a passion for making terroir-expressive, responsibly farmed wines.

ANTIQUUM FARM • WILLAMETTE VALLEY

[organic / regenerative]

Stephen Hagen is a farmer who happens to make wine. At Antiquum Farm, in the far southern reaches of the Willamette Valley, he practices what he refers to as grazing-based viticulture. "It takes things several steps further than organics or biodynamics," he says. "It's about having an extremely diverse scope of life in the vineyard. In a way, the gut fauna of all these animals is a kind of inoculant for the soil."

At Antiquum, "these animals" include a hundred head of sheep, a passel of kunekune pigs, geese, fifty or so turkeys, a whole lot of chickens, and six dogs who keep all of those animals from being picked off by local hawks, eagles, mountain lions, and black bears. "At the peak of the season, this farm is a loud, messy, vibrant thing," Hagen says, happily. A big, bearded guy, he thoroughly looks the part of a man who'd be comfortable around a certain amount of agricultural chaos.

Hagen keeps livestock, of one kind or another, in his vineyard year-round, moving the animals fifteen to seventeen times a year. That keeps the cover crop between the vines in a constant fast-growing state, which helps create more biomass in the soil. "Every time you graze, you create a die-off of the root structure. It's composting, but without the big pile, without the cows. Rotational grazing creates a buzz and hum of microbial action in the soil. And you're doing it in the absence of herbicides, in the absence of tillage—all those human inputs that change and homogenize the soil's microbiome."

"Conventional farming tends to be predictive: if this is happening, I do this, and then I get this. But that approach doesn't provide deeper answers to what's really going on."
—Stephen Hagen

This is all, Hagen says, toward making the vineyard a more emphatically alive and expressive place. His approach dovetails with recent thinking about terroir overall, which is that in addition to the overtly identifiable aspects of place—whether you're on limestone or clay, or the angle of exposure to the sun—the microbiome of the soil itself drives a lot of what we think of as site character in wine. "What we've seen bear out in our wines is that these microbial populations shift, even in a small area. So our six-acre vineyard of Pinot Gris has three totally different ripening patterns. Same soil, same farming, but the wines don't taste the same."

Hagen is a local kid. "I grew up over the ridge and just down the road, four or five miles from where we are. I trespassed all over this place—in the seventies and eighties I had a pretty feral childhood out here, hunting, fishing, roaming around. By the time I was ten, my parents gave me a twelve-gauge shotgun and a horse, and pretty much turned me loose."

Being part of the local community gives him a sense of belonging there, living amid 120 acres of forest and 20 acres of vines that comprise Antiquum. "That history informs my farming decisions. When my wife, Nikki, and I bought the property, we knew nothing about wine, we knew nothing about vineyards, and we started for all the wrong reasons—we thought it would be really pretty and really romantic! Really ignorant was more like it. But part of that was thinking, 'If we're actually going to do this, if we're really going to drill into the concept of terroir and make wines that express that, then we have to find a way to farm this place that's self-contained.' Now I take just as much pride in the terroir of my chickens, or my eggs, as I do with my wine. They're all equally important. The vines—not to sound too hippy-dippy about it—are part of a community."

The **Antiquum Farm Daisy Pinot Gris ($$)** comes from the center portion of Hagen's six-acre Pinot Gris vineyard; it's fresh and tart up front, shading into rounder stone-fruit notes. **Aurosa Pinot Gris ($$)** is fermented on its skins for a brief time, giving it a toasty, savory character and a rose-gold hue. "I love the hibiscus and rosehip-tea character of the tannins,"

Hagen says about it. **Alium Pinot Gris ($$)** gets far more skin contact—forty days—and is more copper-rose colored, with floral notes and lightly tannic berry and pepper flavors. "We make it exactly as if we were making Pinot Noir." The **Juel Pinot Noir ($$–$$$)** is a cross-representation of the whole site. It's floral and full of dark berry fruit bolstered by electric acidity. **Passiflora Pinot Noir ($$$)** comes from the highest portions of the vineyard and is taut and high-toned. The **Luxuria Pinot Noir ($$$)** by contrast "is the deep, dark, brooding, Barry White–note Pinot," Hagen says. Lots of spicy dark cherry flavors here, and savory earthiness.

BERGSTRÖM VINEYARDS • DUNDEE HILLS

[certified organic / biodynamic]

If you're in need of a good triumph over adversity story, John Bergström's is hard to beat. Bergström grew up in a communal household in rural Sweden in the 1930s, six families living in the same house. They hunted moose, fished, and farmed potatoes, made all their own clothes, and when Bergström was age twelve, his parents told him they wouldn't pay for his education anymore. He took out a loan to buy an ax and a saw, and got work in a logging camp. "But he read a lot," his son Josh says, "and he had this American dream of moving here." Serendipity stepped in: his aunt and uncle in the U.S. sent a letter to Bergström's cousin, offering to sponsor her, but the prospect scared her. John Bergström went instead, boarding a steamer at age seventeen. He arrived in New York, flew directly to Portland, Oregon, entered high school

not knowing a word of English, and graduated as the student body president. College and medical school followed, and later a career as a surgeon. Then, Josh Bergström says, "around 1996 he wanted to retire and move out to the country. He found a fifteen-acre piece of land in the Dundee Hills— it had been a hazelnut and black walnut orchard—and bought it on the spot."

Wine might never have entered the picture but for the day the elder Bergström came across a guy on his land picking mushrooms, who said, "Amazing land you've got for mushrooms here. It'd be an amazing place for a vineyard, too." The mushroom-hunter turned out to be Dick Erath, one of the founding fathers of Oregon wine. "My dad called me and said, 'What if we started a vineyard together?'" Josh Bergström recalls. The younger Bergström was in college at the time. "I remember hanging up and going to buy a corkscrew, a glass, and a bottle of Cristom Pinot. I tasted it, called him back, and said, 'Yeah, seems like a great idea.'"

The deal was simple: John Bergström would plant the vineyard, and Josh Bergström would learn how to run it. That required a course of study in Beaune, France, "where I met my wife, Caroline," Josh says. "We fell in love, were engaged three months later, and started Bergström Vineyards. I was the first tractor driver, she was the first salesperson, and we would hand-hoe the entire vineyard. We'd put cases of wine in the car and call on accounts all over the state. While raising kids. And running a business."

Today Bergström owns seventy acres of estate vineyards across five different Willamette Valley sub-appellations. All of it has been farmed biodynamically from the beginning. Bergström recalls meeting Pierre Morey and Anne-Claude Leflaive—biodynamic pioneers in Burgundy—"who were incredibly inspiring. I wasn't an ecological warrior; at the time I just wanted to make better wine. But when I got back, I realized that whatever is on the vine or in the sap stream is going to end up in the wine. Same as coffees, teas, jams, jellies. *Exactly* the same. And knowing we were creating a family business, and wanting to drink our wines with people we loved, we decided we didn't want to poison them."

Bergström isn't enchanted with Demeter, the organization that oversees biodynamic certification: "I was certified, but I stopped. Every year they treated us like terrorists. 'You sure you didn't cheat? You sure you didn't break the rules?' And then I bought four ATVs, and they said, 'You didn't ask permission from us to buy those,' and I was like, 'Fuck off.'" But he's invested in the practice itself: "It has that voodoo mysticism aura around it, sure. But it makes the soil better, more alive; our vines are incredibly healthy; we harvest a week earlier than our neighbors; and if you walk into our vineyard, there's noise—birds, insects. You go to a chemically farmed vineyard and it sounds like a graveyard. Total silence."

Bergström's Chardonnays are among the best in Oregon. The **Bergström**

Old Stones Chardonnay ($$$) offers flinty reductive notes leading into citrus and stone fruit flavors. "The name is to remind people that even though the Oregon wine industry is only sixty years old, we're growing vines on soil that's sixty million years old," Josh Bergström says. The more floral **Le Pré du Col Chardonnay ($$$)** comes from the vineyard of the same name in the Ribbon Ridge AVA. Bergström's top white is the **Sigrid Chardonnay ($$$$)**, which comes from the oldest vines in three of the five estate vineyards. "It has that tension and vibrancy and marine salinity that Old Stones has, but then an added layer of texture," Bergström says. (There are several other Chardonnays as well.)

The many Pinot Noirs are equally impressive. The entry point is the **Cumberland Reserve Willamette Valley Pinot Noir ($$)**. "Even though it's our most affordable Pinot, it's the hardest to make," Bergström says. "It's supposed to represent our style, trying to capture the savory side as well as the fruit side." Think wild berries, chewy tannins, spiciness. Bergström's **Silice Pinot Noir ($$$)** comes off of sandy soils in the Chehalem Mountains AVA, and is lithe and bright, with vibrant red fruit flavors. And the **Bergström Vineyard Pinot Noir ($$$)** comes from the family's original acreage in the Dundee Hills. "The soil there is an amalgam of fifteen different lava flows over twenty million years—it gives you this sanguine, iron, grilled meat note, then this minty thing afterward. It's our most powerful Pinot, but has the most elegant tannic structure."

BIG TABLE FARM · YAMHILL-CARLTON

[organic / regenerative]

"There's actually no practical farming benefit to using horses," Clare Carver says, looking at her two draft horses, Huston and Hummer. "I mean, people talk about, 'Oh, well, horses use less fossil fuel.' But that's bullshit, because you have to put the horses in a trailer and haul them up to wherever you need them, and there goes all your fossil fuel savings. But one thing horses do is make you slow down and pay attention. I think that's one of the huge problems with the direction of our culture, that it's all headed towards less and less being in the moment, and more and more kind of racing around answering texts and speeding through things, in a weird way. A horse definitely won't answer your texts."

It's true. Neither Huston nor Hummer seems remotely inclined to pick up an iPhone and start texting, though you get the sense they'd happily step on one. Big Table Farm is seventy acres of forest, grazing land, vines, sheep, cows, pigs, goats, chickens, bees, and horses (those two), along with a dog (Levi), a couple of cats, and Big Table's owners, Clare Carver and Brian Marcy. It's a working farm as well as a winery, using organic and regenerative practices. The chickens and pigs help fertilize the land—in a "chicken bus" and "winnepigo," both of which Marcy built—and rotational intensive grazing helps build the soil and sequester carbon. (Also, the laying chickens provide eggs; the pasture-raised chickens, the pigs, the sheep, and the cows provide meat; vegetables grow in the gardens; and dinners at the namesake big table, which are frequent, almost exclusively draw on ingredients grown here.) Carver is the farmer; Marcy the grape grower and winemaker.

The couple were living in Napa Valley, where Marcy had been a winemaker for nearly a decade, before they decided in 2006 to move to Oregon. "We had a garden on every inch of the lot of the house we were renting there, we had backyard chickens and fruit trees, I was canning and doing all this stuff, and Brian was helping other people make wine. And I think both of us knew we wanted to expand as humans, you know?" Carver says. "Not just in terms of our physical space, but in terms of what we could accomplish; we just needed more space, physically and spiritually." Oregon proved to be the answer. Land was far cheaper than in Northern California, and Marcy had been making Pinot Noir and Chardonnay anyway.

Big Table is now both a successful farm and a successful winery, its wines made with fruit from like-minded Oregon growers (Carver and Marcy planted their own vineyard on the property in 2021). Brush and invasive scrub from the land cleared for the vineyard was converted to biochar, using a conversion system that doesn't release smoke into the atmosphere, and the biochar was then added to Big Table's compost piles to be worked back into the soil. Their first wines from those vines will probably appear in 2026. "Normally you'd have good fruit three to four years from when you plant, but we're working no-till and that makes it more like five to six," Carver says.

Some bumps along the way have been dire, as in 2020 when smoke from nearby wildfires rendered much of the Willamette Valley's Pinot Noir harvest unusable; some, on the other hand, have been simply absurd. Early on, Carver says, she was feeding one of her cows apples out of a bucket, "and she put her head in the bucket, and the handle flipped over and looped behind her ears. So now she's got a bucket on her head and she can't see, and I've got this frightened cow running around, who won't let me catch her to get the bucket off her head. At one point she was running blindly, and I jumped in front of her, legs apart, arms apart, like, 'Josephine, stop!' And she ran right over me. I completely got trampled, but I was fine. But, yeah, lesson learned: never jump in front of a running cow with a bucket on its head."

Carver and Marcy currently make wines from a range of sustainable and organic Willamette Valley vineyards. All wines are made without any adjuncts or additives, minimal sulfur, and with "whatever yeast blows in the door," as Marcy says. The **Big Table Farm Yamhill-Carlton Chardonnay** (\$\$) is a snapshot of their home AVA, juicy and racy all at once. **Wild Bee Chardonnay** (\$\$) incorporates fruit from all seven of the growers they work with across the Willamette Valley; it's similar in style but perhaps a bit softer on the palate. The **Elusive Queen Chardonnay** (\$\$\$) is the top Chardonnay, a selection of the winery's top barrels, floral, complex, and alluring on release but worthy of aging for several years. There's also a skin-contact **Pinot Gris** (\$\$), pale rose in color and faintly tannic.

There are several Pinot Noirs, starting with a fine-tuned **Willamette Valley Pinot Noir** (\$\$) and Marcy's spicy, silky **Yamhill Carlton Pinot Noir** (\$\$). Single-vineyard wines include a delicate **Cattrall Brothers Vineyard Pinot Noir** (\$\$\$); an old-vine **Sunnyside Vineyard Pinot Noir** (\$\$\$), full of wild berry flavors; a black cherry–ish **Pelos Sandberg Vineyard Pinot Noir** (\$\$\$), from a somewhat warmer site, and several others. Syrah lovers should also look for the **Funk Estate–The Rocks Syrah ($$$),** dark-fruited and intense, with olive and black pepper accents.

BRICK HOUSE VINEYARDS • RIBBON RIDGE

[certified organic / certified biodynamic]

"If you're standing on the dirt," Doug Tunnell says, "you're standing on the roof of a whole kingdom of microbes." Tunnell is the owner and winemaker of Brick House Vineyard, one of the early adopters of organic and biodynamic viticulture in the Willamette Valley. "As far as I'm concerned, biodynamics is all about bugs. The microbes, which are so important for

---

"Happy microbes, happy vines, happy grapes, happy wines, happy people."
—Doug Tunnell

---

feeding our plants, and bringing better balance to our fruit and our wine."

Making wine is Tunnell's second career. Through the 1980s, he was a foreign correspondent for CBS News, working in places as far afield as Bonn, Paris, London, and Lebanon. But he's a Willamette Valley native, and he re-turned to Oregon with an eye toward making wine. Once he got there, a friend told him to look at a farm outside Newberg, "and I didn't even get down the road from the gate to the actual driveway before I'd agreed to buy it. Came out here, saw it, bingo." There weren't any vines on the property, just hazelnut trees, pastureland, and a moribund fruit orchard; Tunnell planted vines the next year. From day one he made a decision not to use any synthetic chemicals at all. "Organics was largely because of having grown up around here. My family house was close to the Willamette River, and me and my friends were all river rats as kids—we had boats, went fishing. But I saw firsthand that it was a very polluted river. And as an adult I thought, 'If I'm going to be farming in this watershed, I don't want to contribute to that.'"

He started studying biodynamics

in 2002, and became fully certified by 2005. "These are methods and techniques and concepts that farmers have used for thousands of years," he says. "Through biodynamics we feel we can enhance the plant's ability to photosynthesize, and also enhance the soil to feed those microbes that deliver nutrients to the plant's root system." As well, he points out, in conventional farming the farmer stands outside of the ecosystem of the farm. With biodynamics "the hand of man, the farmer, his family, their dogs, they're all a part of this whole. I don't stand outside the land and assess it; I grow the grapes and make the wine as part of this little world of our farm. As a human, you're just part of it."

Tunnell's farm covers forty acres, but only twenty are planted with grapevines. Biodiversity is a key part of the focus; for a new vineyard he's contemplating on the property, Tunnell is planning to interplant plum trees with the vines. "It's a wild plum species we think will do really well." He adds, "I'm absolutely convinced that a more natural approach to viticulture delivers better wine. It's a more transparent product, something that you can be really proud to have people taste, and I think people can discern the authenticity of the wines as a result."

All of the Brick House wines come from the biodynamic estate vineyard, and are made in the ninety-year-old horse barn that Tunnell converted into a winery. The **Brick House Ribbon Ridge Chardonnay** ($$) is deeply flavorful, with orchard and citrus fruit nuances, and a light toasty note from oak. **Cascadia Chardonnay** ($$$) is a reserve selection from the top barrels.

Tunnell was an early proponent of Gamay in Oregon, a variety that is now seeing a kind of micro-movement among small, nontraditional vintners. His vividly purple **House Red Gamay Noir** ($$) is a juicy, slightly rustic steal. Depending on the vintage, there can be several Pinot Noirs, but consistent releases include the floral, cherry-raspberry **Select Pinot Noir** ($$), as the name suggests a selection of barrels out of the entire vintage, and the similarly red-fruited but spicier **Dijonnaise Pinot Noir** ($$), from the Dijon clones of Pinot in the vineyard.

BROOKS WINERY • EOLA-AMITY HILLS

[certified organic / biodynamic]

It's impossible to talk about Brooks without talking about its founder, Jimi Brooks, even though he's been gone for almost two decades now. A big, long-haired, larger-than-life guy with an ouroboros serpent tattooed on one shoulder—it now lives on the winery's labels—he looked intimidating but was, as fellow vintner Josh Bergström says, "like a big teddy bear. And really magnetic. He drove a Unimog, this enormous army vehicle, loved Russian gypsy music, and loved to cook. But the food never came out until after midnight—he'd say, 'I'm going to roast a whole goat,' but the goat wouldn't be finished until one a.m." His sister, Janie Brooks Heuck, recalls another winemaker's reaction the first time he met her brother: "Jimi showed up unannounced at Ken Wright's house one night, and Ken said later, 'I opened the door and there's this huge guy I've never seen before, in a long leather trench coat, and all I can think is, 'Is he going to kill me?'"

Image aside, Brooks was a prescient winegrower. When he graduated from college, he bought a one-way ticket to Europe, where he "taught English, cleaned brothels, you name it," Janie Brooks Heuck says. Eventually he found a job at a biodynamic vineyard in Beaujolais. Soon he knew what he wanted to do, and he knew how he wanted to do it. In 1996, he moved back to Oregon, started as a vineyard manager at WillaKenzie Estate, and then founded Brooks. "He told me, 'I'm going to restore the reputation of dry Riesling in Oregon,'" Brooks Heuck says, and that is what he more or less did. Then, in 2004, standing in his kitchen one morning making coffee, he had an aneurysm and died instantly. He was thirty-eight.

Brooks Heuck recalls when it happened. "I got up to Brooks the night he died, and got to his house and there were at least fifty people here. It was the middle of harvest, and all the growers were like, 'We'll take care of the wine side, you do the business.' I had no idea what it even meant—I was a stay-at-home mom! All his friends pitched in and made the 2004 wines, and then, in May of 2005, his friend Chris Williams said, 'If you want to continue

Brooks, I'll come be your winemaker.' I was standing in the driveway at my house when he called."

Two decades later, Brooks is going strong, Williams is still the winemaker, and Janie Brooks Heuck is its managing director. The eighteen-acre biodynamic estate vineyard provides about 20 percent of the grapes for the Brooks wines. The rest is farmed under long-term lease, "all of it either certified organic or biodynamic," she says. The winery also participates in the 1% for the Planet project (1 percent of gross sales are donated to environmental causes). "It still has Jimi's sensibility," his sister says, "just instead of making twenty-five hundred cases of wine a year, we're now making twenty-five thousand."

Jimi Brooks would have approved of the number of Rieslings that his namesake winery makes—a dozen or more, depending on the vintage. A few to look for include the lightly off-dry **Brooks Estate Riesling** ($$), the lemony, zesty **Ara Riesling** ($$), and the honeysuckle-scented **Willamette Valley Riesling** ($$), which is the most widely available by a good measure. Other whites include a juicy, potent **Estate Pinot Gris** ($$) and one of the better Oregon Alsace-style blends around, the winery's **Amycas White Wine** ($$), all stone fruit and spice flavors.

For reds, start with the blue- and red-fruited **Brooks Willamette Valley Pinot Noir** ($$), which is delicious and also a bargain as far as Willamette Valley Pinots go. Smaller-production wines include the lighter-bodied, fragrant **Janus Pinot Noir** ($$), the tea-leafy, cherry-scented **Rastaban Pinot Noir** ($$$)—one of the first Pinots that Jimi Brooks produced, and named after a star in the Draco constellation—and an elegantly structured and floral **Old Vine Pommard Clone Pinot Noir** ($$$) off the estate vineyard.

CRISTOM VINEYARDS • EOLA-AMITY HILLS

[organic / biodynamic]

"Everything about Cristom's beginning was about looking for a good piece of soil," Tom Gerrie says. His parents, Paul and Eileen, were Pittsburgh-based wine lovers, and wanted to start the next chapter of their lives growing grapes and making wine. In 1991, at the International Pinot Noir Celebration (IPNC) in McMinnville, Oregon, they were introduced to Mike Etzel of Beaux Frères (now owned by billionaire François Pinault's Artémis Domaines); they became friends, and soon Etzel found them the piece of land that became Cristom. Gerrie says his father's background was "petroleum engineering, he worked with geologists; there was something about that ground that spoke to him."

Cristom was founded in 1992, at the start of the second wave of wineries in the Willamette Valley, in company with Domaine Drouhin, Argyle, Beaux Frères, Chehalem, and others. "We were about the seventy-fifth winery in the state," Gerrie says. "Now there are more than a thousand."

Tom Gerrie was eight when his family moved west. "Some of my early memories are watering baby vines with a long, long hose hauled over from a tank truck." Initially, the elder Gerries farmed conventionally, but working in 2004 with Etzel, who farmed biodynamically, changed their son's views about viticulture. "I just had this tremendously profound connection to the way Mike farmed," Tom says. "Building compost piles, turning them the next year, getting the compost into the vines, seeing the richness of that, how it was filled with life—that was like, yes, *this* is what needs to be feeding back into the soil, not just for the vines but for this entire property. I wasn't really able to put it into words, but I knew I wanted Cristom to be in a place where it would be a healthier, more vibrant, more ecologically diverse, more sustainable ecosystem for whoever came after me."

Cristom has been biodynamic for several years now, but is not certified. "We're renegade biodynamicists and intentionally so," Gerrie says. "We're trying to pull together different farming paradigms, whether it's permaculture or organic principles or biodynamics; I'm looking for that Venn diagram place where they all meet."

Has this full-on dedication to renegade biodynamics—if that's what to call it—made a difference? Gerrie gives one personal example: "There's a pear tree down by the vineyard house, and I didn't even know it was a pear tree. It hadn't fruited once in my life. But now it has this crazy abundance of fruit, because there are chickens and sheep around it, working their manure back into the soil. We're putting life back into our soil every single day. Everything here will be healthier for it. And it's not just one pear tree; it's ninety acres of vines, and another one hundred and fifty of forests and fields. A place. A whole ecosystem."

Cristom focuses on seven wines, five of which are solely from the estate. The other two, the **Cristom Vineyards Eola-Amity Chardonnay ($$)** and the **Mt. Jefferson Cuvée Pinot Noir ($$)** also use fruit from other growers. "We try to work with people who believe what we believe, or at least are willing to shift or make changes toward working organically," Gerrie says.

The single-vineyard wines come from the ninety acres of estate vines. The **Louise Vineyard Chardonnay ($$$)** balances between citrus and tropical fruit, rich but lifted by fresh acidity. The **Louise Vineyard Pinot Noir ($$$)**—all of the vineyards on the property are named for family matriarchs, except for the Paul Gerrie Vineyard—comes from the oldest vines on the property. The **Eileen Vineyard Pinot Noir ($$$)**, from a higher elevation, tends to be more delicate and floral, with vibrant red fruit. The **Marjorie Vineyard Pinot Noir ($$$)**, from what were the original vines on the site (since mostly replanted due to phylloxera) has more blue fruit and spice. Finally, the **Jessie Vineyard Pinot Noir ($$$)**, from an extremely steep, volcanic soil site, is more concentrated and intense, though still remarkably elegant. There are a number of other small-production wines, but they are mostly available only through the tasting room or Cristom's wine club.

DAY WINES • DUNDEE

[organic or biodynamic (depending on vineyard) / natural]

"It's my job to do what I want," Brianne Day says. "The first year we made Tears of Vulcan, I'd been drinking a lot of textural, skin-contact whites from Sicily. What could I do from that in Oregon? And right around then I saw Black Sabbath in concert, so I gave it a kind of metal name. And I told the label designer, there's always all these

---

"Whether you're making natural wines or conventional wines, following dogma blindly leads to flawed wines."
—Brianne Day

---

naked chicks on the labels of natural wine. The hell with that. Can you make me a shirtless, volcano-god-guy label?"

Day got what she wanted. Tears of Vulcan is an orange-hued, skin-contact blend of Viognier, Pinot Gris, and Muscat from two organic vineyards in the Willamette Valley's Chehalem Mountains, and it's a great example of Day's approach. (And yes, there is a shirtless volcano-god-guy on the label.)

Day's family came to Oregon from Nebraska during the Great Depression to pick fruit. "I'm fourth-generation Pacific Northwest," she says. "I'm an American girl, and there are aspects of this place—the forests, the mountains, the vineyards—that I really love. I want to make wines from here. Not ones that pretend to be from France."

Her wines lean to the natural side, but not rigidly. "We're native yeast, native malo, but I think sulfur is useful. I don't like volatile acidity and I don't like mouse, and sulfur is the best way to deal with those things." ("Mouse" or *gout de souris* is a flaw in some natural wines—specifically the presence of three tetrahydropyridines, if you want to get geeky about it—that make the wine taste, well, like a mouse cage.) "I hear people say they never, ever use sulfur," Day says, "and I'm like, 'There's no sulfur in your winery? None? You don't even sulfur barrels for storage? Are you *looking* for a Brett infection?'" (Brettomanyces, or "Brett," is a yeast that can produce off-aromas in wine, or that, if you are firmly in the natural wine camp, is just fine.)

Day is sharp and opinionated, a rule-breaker by nature. That kind of energy can be magnetic or annoying (sometimes both). She has the magnetic without the annoying; plus, she makes you laugh. Though she studied winemaking, she says, "I never finished. I did all the winemaking courses, but then I was sitting in this required marketing course and listening to the instructor say, 'Your label always needs to have this, and always needs to be consistent, and your brand needs to be . . . ,' and I thought, nope, never, not doing that. So I quit!"

And started a winery, of course.

Day works in a former vitamin-packing warehouse outside Dundee—"It smelled like D vitamins in here when I bought this place, and it smelled like vitamins for a long time afterward. Thankfully, not anymore"—and makes an abundance of wines that range from the relatively traditional to the definitely unexpected. Her textural, apple-lemony **Day Wines Vermentino ($$)** is on the more traditional side. The **Belle Pente Vineyard Chardonnay ($$)** is vivid and fresh, an Oregon wine that hints at Chablis character. "The marine sediment in that vineyard gives you such savory, umami character," she says. The orange-hued **Tears of Vulcan ($$)** is floral, tangy, and also full of savory, umami notes. There's also the more affordable **Vin de Days Orange ($$)**, a blend of Gewürztraminer, Müller-Thurgau, and Pinot Gris, with its spicy, tangerine-lime fruit. (There are several Vin de Days wines, all good, and all priced around $25.)

The red **Infinite Air Castles ($$)** is a strawberry-suggestive, lively mix of Gamay and Dolcetto. "Blending them made sense to me—they're not the snooty grapes of those regions, Burgundy and Piedmont; they're humble and easygoing," Day says. About her peppery, floral **Mondeuse ($$)**, she says, "It's cool how varietally on point it is, plus I love light-bodied reds."

Her **Johan Vineyards Pinot Noir ($$$)** is full of dark cherry flavors with fresh herb and tea-leaf accents: "It has a real evergreen-woods spiciness," Day says. "It smells to me like the Oregon mountains—speaking as a person who spends a lot of time in the Oregon mountains." **Hock & Deuce ($$)** uses Syrah from the Applegate Valley for a rich, dark, savory red. **100 Years** a Lady ($$), a zippy, raspberry-rich Pinot Meunier, "was named for my grandmother's one hundredth year. I gave it to her before she passed away at a hundred and one." The name of Day's alluringly cassis-scented **A Peridot** Afternoon ($$), which is Syrah plus a small percentage of Viognier, is similarly family-based. "It references my kid. I had him on August 11 at 4:23 in the afternoon. Three weeks before harvest. And I'm a single mom. We did it!"

ELK COVE VINEYARDS • YAMHILL-CARLTON

[certified sustainable / organic]

Elk Cove is one of the few first-generation Willamette Valley Pinot Noir producers still in family hands, and it seems as though it will remain that way. Anna Campbell, daughter of founders Pat and Joe Campbell, says, "We joke that we're definitely staying family owned, if only because our family is so fertile."

Today the Campbells, led by Pat and Joe's son Adam, farm more than four hundred acres of vineyard (Anna is Adam's sister). The vineyards are certified sustainable and salmon safe. "We actually farm organic," Adam Campbell says, "but we don't certify. We could *get* certified, but is it worth the time and money? I'd rather spend that money paying our workers more. Anyway, when we talk about the things that matter to us, certification is pretty far down the list."

What does matter is continuing a family legacy for site-specific wines grown and made where the Campbells live. Joe Campbell, an Oregon native, didn't think he was going into farming: he was at medical school in the late 1960s at Stanford; his wife, Pat, at the time was working at a jazz club in San Francisco. But a bottle of red Burgundy they splurged on at a restaurant one night lodged in their minds, and when they returned to Oregon, they couldn't shake the idea of planting grapes. They first lived in a trailer on the property they'd bought, then in a house on stilts in the trees (it was the 1960s, after all), which they built themselves, largely with salvaged wood from an old logging flume.

"My dad was self-taught as a winemaker," Adam Campbell recalls. "I learned by working right alongside him when I was a kid." He points out that for great wine, there's no need for high-priced consulting winemakers, or investment banking fortunes; instead, what's crucial is good land, a propensity for hard work, and the willingness to learn every year. "Look, the best Pinot Noir in Oregon could be made next year in someone's garage. I wouldn't even be surprised."

The affordable **Elk Cove Estate Pinot Gris** (\$\$), year in and year out, is a standout among a sea of pleasant but sometimes innocuous versions of this Alsace variety. The **Estate Pinot Blanc** (\$\$) is a perfumed white with a chalky texture. "It ripens later than Pinot Gris, so you have to be more careful with it," Campbell says.

The winery's modestly priced **Willamette Valley Pinot Noir** (\$\$) uses estate fruit from all six of their vineyard sites. With its round, dark cherry fruit and silky tannins, it's a good intro to Campbell's style. There are quite a number of single-vineyard Pinots, all of them distinctive. The **La Bohème Pinot Noir** (\$\$) comes from the original estate planting in Yamhill-Carlton. It ratchets up the darkness of the fruit compared to the Willamette Valley bottling in most vintages, but remains streamlined and elegant. The **Roo-sevelt Vineyard Pinot Noir** (\$\$\$) is fragrant and more red cherry–leaning. It's the sister wine to La Bohème, from a south-facing slope near the winery, with a creamy texture despite its firm tannins. "It's always a little bigger and more muscular than La Bohème," Campbell says. The **Five Mountain Pinot Noir** (\$\$\$), from the Laurelwood AVA, is spicy and lifted. "It always has this black pepper quality that I like," Campbell says. **Mount Richmond Pinot Noir** (\$\$\$) uses fruit off their two-hundred-acre vineyard on marine-sediment soil in Yamhill-Carlton, and has sweet, dark cherry flavors, toasty notes, and firm tannins. "Mount Richmond is our most classic Yamhill-Carlton site," Campbell says. "We basically planted ten acres there every year straight for twenty years. Apparently, that's just how we do things."

THE EYRIE VINEYARDS • DUNDEE HILLS

[certified organic]

Funny thought, but if David Lett hadn't skipped a medical school interview and instead driven by Napa Valley's Souverain Winery one cold, wet day in the 1960s, Oregon might not now be known for Pinot Noir. Lett, who passed away in 2008, was the first person to plant Pinot Noir in Oregon's Willamette Valley. Before that, though, he had to figure out that he wanted to be a winemaker.

"My dad was from the great wine-producing state of Utah," Jason Lett jokes. "He grew up one of the few nonobservant Mormons in his town. He was supposed to go to medical school—my great-grandfather was very 'the first male heir born shall go to medical school!'" Lett dutifully interviewed at twelve medical schools and hated the whole idea. Then, the day he drove by Souverain, he saw a man standing outside wearing a slicker, washing barrels, and thought that looked interesting. "My father stopped to talk to him, and by the end of the day he'd found out what he wanted to do with his life."

David Lett was one of six members of the 1964 graduating class in viticulture and enology at the University of California at Davis, "right at the beginning of people in the U.S. looking at wine as something other than what you drank out of a paper bag while sitting on the sidewalk on skid row," Jason Lett says.

In addition to his degree, Lett came out of Davis with a love for Pinot Noir. He started looking around, and settled on three places he thought he might be able to plant Pinot successfully: the Minho Valley in northern Portugal, the South Island of New Zealand (prescient), and Oregon. "Which was where he settled," his son says. "Usually people find a place, then figure out what will grow there. Willamette Valley is the only wine region I can think of that's been purposefully selected for a specific variety, rather than the other way around."

Using his father's horse trailer Lett brought up to the Willamette Valley three thousand Pinot cuttings from UC Davis's test nursery. He and his wife, Diana, arrived, as it happened, right after the still-legendary Christmas floods of 1964, which put almost sixty-one thousand acres of the valley underwater. Diana once recalled him saying, "Damn! They told me Oregon was wet, but this is really bad!" Nevertheless, after the floods had receded, the Letts put their Pinot vines in the ground. It changed the course of wine in Oregon.

The Eyrie Vineyards' first vintage was 1970. Lett made it in a former turkey-processing plant in McMinnville, which remains Eyrie's winery to this day. Jason Lett, who was born in 1969, was there from the start. "My mom was away some of the time, and Dad would spend all day out picking grapes and all night making wine, and taking care of a three-year-old while he was doing it. But the way he took care of me was by giving me a job. 'Here, throw these clusters into the destemmer one at a time.' That kind of thing kept me busy for hours, and happy, because I was there with the big guys."

David Lett passed away in 2008. Today his son makes some of the most elegant, thoughtfully realized wines in Oregon, building on the foundation his father laid.

"We farm agrodynamically," Jason Lett says, with the kind of light edge of humor that often marks his tone. "At least that's what we call it. My father was farming organically in the 1960s. Farmers here scratched their heads a lot over Dad, absolutely." The elder Lett also started doing no-till farming early on, partly for practical reasons; Oregon winters are wet, and "all that cover crop drinks up the water and keeps your fields from turning into the Marne Valley in World War I," Jason Lett says. "When I was in college, I read *One Straw Revolution* by Masanobu Fukuoka, and that was when I was like, right, Dad's on this whole *other* thing. Very intuitively based, no certification, no licensing program—and now everything he's doing is getting branded as regenerative. He's the hippest cat in the classroom today."

Lett keeps some jars of soil in Eyrie's tasting room. They're the same type of soil, but one jar's soil is organic, one was conventionally farmed, and one was "blasted with chemicals by the road authority—the county came by and sprayed some sort of horrendous crap on it twenty years ago and nothing's grown there ever since." In the jar from Eyrie's organic vineyards, the soil is loose and full of air: "Healthy soil is about 30 percent air, and those channels store water, allow roots to grow," Lett says. "I can sink a shovel into that, no problem."

The jar of soil the road authority treated is dense and dead. "This soil?" Lett asks. "You'd have to hit it with a pickax to get anything out of it."

Eyrie farms sixty acres of vines in five separate estate vineyards in Oregon's Dundee Hills. **The Eyrie Vineyards Pinot Gris Estate ($$)** is aged longer on its lees than most Oregon versions, giving it greater texture and depth. The **Chardonnay Estate ($$)** is a stellar example of Oregon Chardonnay for a relatively modest price, aged entirely in neutral French oak. A buy-it-by-the-case purchase if there ever was one. The **Pinot Noir Estate ($$)** is a blend from the estate vineyards and is a benchmark Willamette Valley Pinot: elegant and lifted, with fresh red fruit and herbal notes (it also ages beautifully). Lett also makes a large number of smaller-production, single-vineyard Pinots, as well as limited releases of other varieties. A few not to miss include a crisp, lemony **Melon de Bourgogne Estate ($$)**, made from vines that David had been told were Pinot Blanc when he planted them, an ethereal, spicy, red-fruited **Trousseau Estate ($$)**, and the **Pinot Noir The Eyrie ($$$)** from the original Pinot Noir vines that David Lett planted in 1965. It's a beautiful Pinot—fragrant, complex, and as a bonus, loaded with historical significance.

HIYU WINE FARM • COLUMBIA GORGE

[organic / regenerative]

Hiyu Wine Farm represents a new—or perhaps very old—approach to winemaking. Founded in 2010 in Oregon's Hood River Valley by Nate Ready, a former master sommelier, and China Tresemer, Hiyu is a thirty-acre polyculture farm, with gardens, pastureland, pigs, cows, chickens, and ducks. And, yes, vineyards, here planted with more than 107 different grape varieties.

"The inspiration for Hiyu was that China and I had been learning about farming, and eventually we felt this need to have our own piece of land," Ready says. "We'd made a lot of trips to Europe, and were very interested in the kind of place where raising the animals, growing the food, making the wine, and consuming those things all happened in the same location."

Ready effectively creates his wines in the vineyard: the Hiyu property is divided into half-acre blocks, each planted with a field blend representing a different region or historical moment. One wine might come from a block planted with fifteen southern Mediterranean varieties—"Assyrtiko plus a bunch of southern Italian grapes, Fiano, Falanghina, others. We were trying to understand what would happen if we planted grapes that have high acidity in a Mediterranean climate in an Alpine climate, which is what we have." (Essentially, there's a theoretical underpinning to most of the wines Ready makes.) Another, Falcon Box, is from a parcel planted to what a field blend of grapes on the hill of Corton in Burgundy might have looked like prior to the 1870s phylloxera epidemic. "It's the idea of going back to a time when all these different genetics were in the same place, and there was all this potential complexity to play off," he says.

The farming falls into the organic/regenerative/Fukuokan realm. No tilling; vegetation is controlled by the farm's animals, who live among the vines. Sulfur, which is allowed in organic viticulture, isn't used. Instead, Ready and Tresemer use natural treatments like cinnamon oil or herb teas. Eighty different varieties of grapes are grown; all the varieties in each plot are harvested and co-fermented together using ambient yeasts; no new oak is used, no fining, no filtering, and only a homeopathic amount of sulfur (5ppm) at bottling. Some wines are aged for a couple of months; some for as long as ten years. There's no template, no recipe—Ready and Tresemer decide the approach for each wine on its own. Unsurprisingly, quantities are small: fifty to one hundred cases of each wine.

"A lot of what we were trying to do here when we started was to address the state of American wine at the time. I felt that wines at the apex of quality weren't as moving or magical as when I tasted these authentic wines coming out of Europe. One thing I could point to was that, for those wines, the person doing the viticulture is the person making the wine and is the person living on the property. You can't make a direct correlation as to why that's different, but when you taste the wine, you feel it. We felt this need to start a project in a place where we were personally farming and touching every single grape. It all becomes part of the same spirit."

The Hiyu wines are deeply distinct from one another, though they are clearly linked by winemaking approach and location. The hazy-gold, peppery **Hypericum Spring Ephemeral ($$$)**, which receives five days of skin contact, comes from a half-acre block planted with more than fifteen southern Mediterranean varieties. "The lemon-tangy, herbal **Falcon Box ($$$)** is a savory blend of Chardonnay, Pinot Gris, Aligoté, Melon de Bourgogne, and a host of other interplanted varieties, all from a single block. **Columba ($$$)**, made from a palette of Spanish varieties—Albarino, Arinto, Macabeo, Verdelho, and others—has an earthy, almost beery nose, then tingly flavors of grapefruit, grapefruit peel, and green apple. **The May ($$$)** is a whole-cluster, co-fermented blend of Pinot Noir and Pinot Gris that spends anywhere from thirty to seventy days on skins. It's very *green* in character, with lots of stem character, smoky dark berry flavors, and lots of presence: unusual and fascinating. **The Crataegus ($$$)** combines Syrah, Teroldego, Mondeuse, Lagrein, Marzemino, Viognier, and a variety of other grapes for a mossy, dark-fruited, earthy red that's nevertheless tart and bright (and only around 11.5 percent alcohol). There are many more, as well as the winery's more affordable Smock Shop wines. All, realistically, will take some hunting to find—the best approach is to contact the winery directly.

MARTIN WOODS • MCMINNVILLE

[sustainable or organic (depending on vineyard)]

The long, winding, gravel road leading to Evan Martin's ramshackle house-cum-winery dives deeper and deeper into oak and cedar and Douglas fir, the trees soon encroaching on the road, moss hanging from the boughs, leaves above darkening the Oregon sun. "A sommelier in Colorado put me on her list as Martin *of* the Woods rather than Martin Woods," he says. "I never said anything, because it's kind of accurate."

Martin, a long, lean fellow in his late thirties, doesn't come from wine. He grew up in the Midwest, went to Colorado for college, moved on to Seattle to study philosophy, and there, he says, "got romanced by this idea of traveling the world through a bottle of wine." A couple of semesters at Walla Walla Community College for viticulture, then more wandering, and then work as a sommelier in Santa Fe. But finally, "I wanted to get back into production, so I landed a harvest gig." The result, ten years down the road: a house on a remote hilltop, barrels and tanks filling the first floor, a life making wine. "A lot of winemaking is really physical—the long hours, all that work. But I like that. I like harvest time. It's the time when you turn off the administrative brain. All there is is the vintage. It's clarifying."

Martin sources grapes from sustainably and organically farmed vineyards around the Willamette Valley, focusing on higher-elevation, cooler spots. His goal, he says, is to make wines that are "alive, and real, and un-fucked-with. It's accurate to say I make wine for wine geeks," he says. "Because that's who I am."

Among Evan Martin's wines, look for the **Martin Woods Hyland Vineyard Riesling ($$)**, a standout New World expression of this variety (one of the best in the U.S., certainly). From vines planted in 1973, it's either dry or not depending on the vintage, and has lasting flavors of apple, tangerine, and (often) wildflower honey. "I'd say it humbly, but I think Hyland is one of the best Riesling sites outside Europe," Martin says. His **Havlin Vineyard Grüner Veltliner ($$)**, from a cool location in the Van Duzer corridor, suggests grapefruit peel and white pepper. The **Havlin Vineyard Chardonnay ($$)** ages for twenty-one months in a combination of Oregon and French oak, none of it new. It's a delicate, evocative wine with ginger and crisp pear notes. The **Yamhill Valley Vineyard Chardonnay ($$)** has a more earthy character, with a little reductive-winemaking flinty snap and layered citrus flavors.

Martin's Pinot Noirs are transparent in both hue and character, wines that float across the palate rather than thud into it. The **Hyland Vineyard Pinot Noir ($$$)** has bright red cherry and rhubarb notes, light but with plenty of depth; the **Jesse James Vineyard Pinot Noir ($$$)** is floral and savory, with a green peppercorn note. "I like that idea of Pinot showing a range of shades from green to red, red, red and then to black—like an Ansel Adams photograph, with white and black and then all those infinite shades of gray." The **Bednarik Vineyard Pinot Noir ($$$)** from the Tuluatin Hills follows a similar line, with lots of texture but still an enviably weightless quality.

MAYSARA WINERY • MCMINNVILLE

[certified biodynamic]

Maysara, in Oregon's Willamette Valley, is a peaceful place. The vineyards roll across the hills, broken up by pastures, meadows, forest. Blue chicory flowers toss in the wind. "For thousands of years," Moe Momtazi says, "chicory was used as a medicine, for hundreds of ailments. In our old country, they'd make a spirit with it."

Momtazi's old country is Iran. Maysara, which he founded in 1998, may be peaceful, but his and his wife, Flora's, journey here was anything but. The couple escaped from Iran in 1982, a few years after the Islamic revolution. "My wife was eight months pregnant," he recalls, "and we were on the backs of motorcycles, with drug smugglers taking us out. We went through the mountains into Pakistan, which was terribly hard. I'm really glad we didn't get killed there."

From Pakistan they made it to Spain, and from Spain to Mexico and eventually Dallas, where they filed for political asylum. "Sometimes when you are desperate you need to believe in something," he says. "During that hardship, I decided that whatever country accepted us, I would do something good for it. It's a kind of thankfulness." That decision led to Momtazi's embrace of biodynamics at Maysara—of farming in a way that benefits the environment in the place he now calls home.

"We're determined to work with nature," he says. "We don't bring anything in from the outside. Conventional farming not only destroys the soil, but it also kills creatures. For instance, we have osprey here, and bald eagles and falcons. We've stocked the ponds with trout and bass to keep the raptors here, because they help keep away the migratory birds that eat grapes. We've planted a lot of fruit trees that have affinity with the vines, like white mulberry. And a lot of medicinal plants as well, besides the chicory—valerian, for instance, and roses for rose hips. Valerian teas help dehydrate things after rain, and rose hips have a lot of vitamin C, which can help raise sugar levels in grapes. And our winery building is ninety percent material from the property—wood, stones—and anything that wasn't off the property is recycled."

Momtazi is unusual in the biodynamic realm in that he's also a civil engineer and a trained scientist. "I studied modern physics: Einstein knew he could mathematically prove relativity, so he basically said, 'If you want to deny it, that's your decision. But I know relativity is true.' I feel the same about biodynamics. And I've always done experiments, to see for myself." At one point, he created two compost piles fifty feet apart, one that utilized biodynamic preps and one that didn't. One day, his vineyard manager called him over. "He's saying, 'Look at this! Look!'" Momtazi recalls. "And I go over and he holds up this shovelful of dirt, with worms just *dripping* off of it. The compost with the preps had so much more worm activity. So much more life. It was amazing."

The combination of scientific rationality and a belief in nature as something larger than what humans can understand is central to Momtazi's ideas. "Wine, in our culture, going back to the Zoroastrian times, was a very sacred thing," he says. "The sun was one of the gods, and wine was the liquid embodiment of the sun's radiance. And with food, my grandfather used to talk about how food is not just a stomach filler. He was right. Just in my lifetime, I've seen how the diseases we get are due to the bad food we consume." Momtazi looks out at his vines, at the green cover crops growing between them, at a raptor circling higher and higher on an updraft, and shakes his head: "How can you put poison in your food chain and then expect to be healthy?"

"How can you put poison in your food chain and expect to be healthy?"
—Moe Momtazi

Maysara has 260 acres of biodynamic vineyards: Pinot Noir, Pinot Gris, Pinot Blanc, and small amounts of Riesling. (It's one of the largest biodynamic vineyards in the U.S.) The wines are made by Momtazi's daughter Tahmiene in a hands-off, noninterventionist style. "We don't manipulate, and when you don't manipulate things, it takes them longer to evolve," Momtazi says. "You have to be patient. But then they become something really noble and unique."

The **Maysara Arsheen Pinot Grigio ($$)** is rounded and ripe, with nectarine and tropical fruit notes. **Autees Pinot Blanc ($$)** has a light, waxy spice note, not atypical of Pinot Blanc, with bright citrus flavors. **Jamsheed Pinot Noir ($$)** is dark and juicy, all cherry liqueur and earth notes. (It's named for a Persian legend: the ancient king Jamsheed could perceive his entire realm by peering into a goblet filled with wine.) The estate's two easternmost and two westernmost blocks go into the **Cyrus Pinot Noir ($$)**, which is in a more elegant and silky style than Jamsheed. Then there's the darkly spicy **Asha Pinot Noir ($$$)**, made with fruit from the original thirteen acres of vines that Moe Momtazi planted in 1998.

WALTER SCOTT WINES • EOLA-AMITY HILLS

[organic and/or biodynamic (depending on vineyard)]

Walter Scott Wines has rocketed swiftly to the top level of Oregon wineries largely on the strength of Ken Pahlow and Erica Landon's shimmering, age-worthy Chardonnays (not to dismiss their Pinot Noirs, which are also excellent). Yet for all the acclaim, this is a down-to-earth, family operation, making great wines out of a no-nonsense winery building off a farm road northwest of Salem.

Both Pahlow and Landon grew up in Oregon. Pahlow planned to become a physical therapist, "but got the wine bug, waiting tables in a restaurant. I did that for a while, then worked for a wine importer, and finally went knocking on Mark Vlossak's door at St. Innocent and got a job. And that was it." Landon also started in the restaurant business, largely in Portland. Pahlow recalls, "I used to sell her wine. Did that for five years. Then one Friday night we got together, and we've been together ever since."

The two emptied out their retirement savings and started Walter Scott in 2009. They moved to the winery where they are now in 2012, and today make around forty-five hundred cases of wine per year. "Now, twenty-three years in," Pahlow says, "I feel like I'm just getting started. No matter how long you've been making wine, you can learn one subtle thing in one vintage, and it can completely change your approach."

It takes about ten minutes of talking to Pahlow, probably less, to figure out that his influences lie in Burgundy. The domaines that have inspired him and Landon—Mugneret-Gibourg ("back when you could afford it!"), Roulot, Lamy—come readily as references when he describes their philosophy and approach. Echoing that, there's a quote from the OG Burgundy authority Remington Norman painted on one wall of the winery: "It is the details that make the difference between magic and mediocrity."

Detail, or possibly precision, is a signal aspect of the Walter Scott wines. Red or white, they're finely chiseled, with a purity of flavor and texture even in problematic vintages that's hard to match.

"The most important thing for us is to show off place," Pahlow says. "But we also talk a lot about the human aspect of terroir. The human aspect of terroir is massive. If we're going to put a vineyard name on a wine, the owner's personal energy needs to be in there." Pahlow and Landon contract for fruit with some of the best growers in Willamette, working only with organically or biodynamically farmed properties. "We had a couple who were more conventional, but we convinced them to change," Pahlow says. "I use Josh Bergström's motto: I don't want my kids growing up and drinking wines with industrial chemicals in them. So we source grapes at places like Witness Tree, for instance, where you can basically build a salad while you walk through the vineyard rows. They use legumes as cover crops—so many fresh peas!"

Pahlow and Landon's Chardonnays are mineral-driven, laser-focused wines made in the reductive style initially popularized by top Burgundy producers

Coche-Dury and Domaine Leflaive (one telltale sign is a kind of struck-match note, or *le matchstick*, as the French term it). Native yeasts are used for all wines;

minimal extraction is generally the rule, along with moderate use of new oak. The **Walter Scott Cuvée Anne Chardonnay ($$$)**, a barrel selection from most of the single vineyards they work with, is a great introduction. The **Koosah Vineyard Chardonnay ($$$)**, from vines at seven hundred to eleven hundred feet in the Eola-Amity Hills, is all lime blossom, bristly, tart acidity, and stony notes; it's "super-electric," as Pahlow says. The **Freedom Hill Vineyard Chardonnay ($$$)** is matchstick-flinty, savory, and smoky, somehow light but with plenty of body as well. The **X Novo Vineyard Chardonnay ($$$)** comes from an organic vineyard planted with more than twenty different Chardonnay clones. "Nine vintages in, we're still figuring it out," Pahlow says. "Kaffir lime is what Erica says it reminds her of." About the **Justice Vineyard Chardonnay ($$$)** Pahlow says, "it's definitely pushing the

level of reduction," and so it is: the intensely flinty, smoky nose leads to a powerful white with lots of peach and mint notes.

The Pinot Noirs are similarly impressive. Pahlow and Landon's lively **La Combe Verte Pinot Noir ($$)** is the most affordable cuvée. The **Freedom Hill Vineyard Pinot Noir ($$$)** is brightly floral, with zippy raspberry-cherry flavors. The **X Novo Vineyard Pinot Noir ($$$)** has peppery, penetrating aromas and rides high on your palate with bright red berry flavors and super-fine tannins. The **Soujeau Vineyard Pinot Noir ($$$)** comes from an incredibly rocky fifteen-acre site. Darker ruby in hue, it has an intense nose of dark red fruits, with saturated red and blue fruit flavors and, as always, that mysterious elegance and lift that seem to define Pahlow and Landon's wines.

SOKOL BLOSSER • DUNDEE HILLS

[certified organic]

Having crazy parents is not always a bad thing, it just depends on the *kind* of crazy. For instance, ask Alison Sokol Blosser how her family's winery got started, and she'll say, laughing, "Crazy parents! They really were—they had no farming background, no winemaking background, no business background, and they just thought it would be cool to grow something." That's definitely the good kind of crazy.

"So they thought, 'Why don't we start a vineyard?'" she says. "'It'll be interesting. And fun.' They had no idea what they were getting into—it was just 'Let's grow the grapes and then see if we can make this work.' And then my grandfather told them, 'Well, why don't you make wine from your grapes?' We later found out he had Alzheimer's, which explains something."

Sokol Blosser was part of the first wave of Willamette Valley wineries, along with Eyrie, Ponzi, Erath, Adelsheim, and others, all of whom first started making wine in the late 1960s and early 1970s. Many of those pioneers have since been sold to larger companies or to investors; Sokol Blosser, like Eyrie, remains family owned. Not that it's been easy.

"By 1990 things were pretty bleak—we had so much Top Ramen and canned Stagg chili for dinner, to save money—my father went back to his day job, and my mother started running both the winery and the vineyard," Alison Sokol Blosser says.

The vineyards were farmed sustainably for many years before the family switched to organic in 2002. Sokol Blosser was also the second winery in the world to become a certified B Corp, which assesses both social and environmental practices. "We're working with a lot of regenerative practices as well. On-farm composting, no-till agriculture. That's on about one hundred and twenty acres of vineyard, split between three sites."

Alison adds, "What we talk about internally with the team is that we make good shit *and* we give a shit. We want to make wines that people feel good about drinking, and that are responsible to the land. My parents were the impetus for that—my dad, who was in urban planning, was interested in sustainable development, and my mother was here on the farm. For instance, in 2002, we built a new barrel cellar, and my mother said, 'OK, we're going to get LEED certified [Leadership in Energy and Environmental Design].' That was a 25 percent greater cost, because at that time nobody knew what LEED certification was or knew how to do it, but we did it anyway."

Sokol Blosser's affordable, popular line of Evolution wines are fun to drink, but they are not made from estate fruit. As such, they can't be considered 100 percent sustainable or organic, but they're excellently made and bargain-priced, and from one of the Willamette Valley's signature names.

The estate wines all come from the winery's certified organic vineyards. For whites, look for the **Sokol Blosser Willamette Valley Estate Pinot Gris ($$)**, a textbook Oregon Pinot Gris that combines fruit from the winery's Eola-Amity Hills and Dundee Hills vineyards. The **Dundee Hills Estate Chardonnay ($$)** balances crisp citrus notes against warmer ripe apple fla-

vors. The **Blossom Ridge Sparkling Rosé of Pinot Noir ($$$)** comes from organic vineyards in Eola-Amity Hills and is a floral, red-berried, sparkling pleasure.

Pinot Noir is the focus for the reds, this being the Willamette Valley. The mainstay **Dundee Hills Estate Pinot Noir ($$)** has classic Dundee red cherry and earth characteristics. There are several single-site Pinots as well, all very good. Among them, the **Orchard Block Pinot Noir ($$$)** leans to the more delicate side, with fresh herbal notes and fine, soft tannins, whereas the **Watershed Block Pinot Noir ($$$)** tends toward more black cherry/cola notes and a fuller, richer texture.

SOTER VINEYARDS • YAMHILL-CARLTON

[certified organic / certified biodynamic]

Tony Soter's tasting room and winery is one of the prettiest places to taste wine in Oregon. It stands atop a small hill, looking out over a sweeping expanse of Willamette Valley vineyards, a thrillingly dramatic view that's somehow remarkably peaceful at the same time.

Both Soter and his wife and co-

founder, Michelle (who passed away in 2019), were from early on committed to ecologically friendly practices both in viticulture and in life. Soter was an acclaimed winemaker in Napa Valley during the 1980s as well as an early evangelist for organic farming; he was the winemaker at Spottswoode in 1985 when it became, partly through his influence, the first certified organic vineyard in Napa Valley. He continued those efforts for other consulting clients as well as at his own Etude Winery (which he sold to Beringer in 2000, in order to move to Oregon full-time).

Soter Vineyards was founded in 1997, and he and Michelle purchased Mineral Springs Ranch, where the winery is now located, in the early 2000s. The ranch is not solely a vineyard, and was very much Michelle Soter's life's work as much as it was her winemaking husband's. The garden she planted on the property was organic from day one, and now encompasses forty acres of vines, three acres of vegetables, and thirty acres of grains, as well as beehives, chickens, sheep, goats, and cattle. (All of the farm's products are used for the culinary program at the tasting room, easily one of the best on the entire West Coast.) The 240-acre property was certified biodynamic in 2016.

Though Soter was acclaimed for many years in Napa Valley for the Cabernets he made there (he consulted for heavy-hitter names such as Araujo, Dalla Valle, Viader, and Niebaum-Coppola, as well as Spottswoode), his passion has remained tied to the transparency and site-expressiveness of Pinot Noir.

The Soter wines are made in a renovated 1940s-era barn (the entire facility is certified carbon neutral). The most affordable is the **Planet Oregon Willamette Valley Pinot Noir ($–$$)**, made from sustainable fruit from a range of growers. Since its inception, for every bottle sold, a dollar has been donated to the nonprofit Oregon Environmental Council. The thirst-quenching **Soter Vineyards Origin Series Pinot Noir Rosé ($$)** and silky **Origin Series Yamhill-Carlton Pinot Noir ($$$)** also come from purchased fruit, organic for the Rosé, and sustainable or organic for the Pinot. Soter also makes a number of other Origin Series wines, all worth looking for.

Of the estate wines, the **Soter Vineyards Mineral Springs Brut Rosé ($$$)** is a bright sparkler that mingles cherry and citrus flavors. The **Mineral Springs Blanc de Blancs ($$$$)** is elegant and nuanced, a testimony to how the best Oregon sparkling wines can rival those of Champagne.

The red-fruited **Soter Estates Pinot Noir ($$$)** uses fruit both from the biodynamic Mineral Springs and two certified organic vineyards that Soter owns as well, Tarren Vineyard and Ribbon Ridge Estate. **Mineral Springs Ranch Pinot Noir ($$$)**, on the other hand, comes solely from the forty acres of vines lying along the Mineral Springs ridgeline, and is a concentrated Pinot full of dark berry flavors and tea-leaf notes. **Mineral Springs White Label Pinot Noir ($$$$)** is made only from the oldest vines on the property, and only in the best years. It isn't inexpensive, but for those who feel like splurging, it's a stellar bottle of Pinot Noir.

TRISAETUM • RIBBON RIDGE

[organic / regenerative]

One of the first things that James Frey was told when he started to plant a vineyard in the Willamette Valley was not to grow Riesling. Pinot Noir, sure. But Riesling? Forget it. "Everyone here said, just don't," he recalls. "Really bad idea. But Riesling was my first love, my family is originally from Alsace, and so I just decided whether it makes any money, whether it makes any sense, I want to make Riesling."

Frey came to wine by chance. A honeymoon visit to Napa Valley led to a passion for wine, both for Frey and for his wife, Andrea Lassa—the ethos, the agriculture, everything. Eventually they moved to Oregon, where they found a steep, rocky plot of land outside McMinnville, in the Willamette Valley, and planted a vineyard. Two years later they found another property in the Ribbon Ridge AVA, bought that, and planted a second vineyard. Since then they've lived on their land, growing grapes and making wine.

From the beginning they've farmed organically. Native plant life covers half their acreage, no herbicides are used, they avoid tilling, and grape skins and seeds are composted and returned to the vineyard. "It's trying to create a sustainable, regenerative agricultural system where the number of inputs we have to bring in are minimal," Frey says. "All these decisions, if you make them early on, it helps you enormously.

If you destroy what's already on the site when you start, it's very hard to get it to come back."

And Riesling? Frey makes eight different Rieslings each year. "Going back to that whole, 'you should never plant Riesling' thing?" he says. "Well, it kinda worked out."

All wines at Trisaetum come from Frey and Lassa's estate vineyards, and are made using native yeasts and as little sulfur as possible. Of the Rieslings, the **Trisaetum Ribbon Ridge Estate Riesling ($$)** is full of bright stone-fruit flavors and is made in a medium-dry style; the **Ribbon Ridge Estate Dry Riesling ($$)** is dry and intense, with a stony end. Both are excellent introductions to Frey's wines. **The Estates Reserve Dry Riesling ($$$)** punches up that intensity; it's a blend from all three of the Trisaetum estate vineyards.

For Pinots, one intriguing entry is the **Trisaetum Nuit Blanche White Pinot Noir ($$)**, made from Pinot Noir juice drained from the skins before any pigment can enter the wine. It's floral, delicate and lively, entirely appealing. The **Willamette Valley Pinot Noir ($$)** is a selection mostly from young vines; it's full of direct red fruit and fine-grained tannins. The **Ribbon Ridge Estate Pinot Noir ($$$)** and the **Wichman Dundee Estate Pinot Noir ($$$)** present two views of the Willamette Valley's differing terroirs; Ribbon Ridge is more substantial, with darker fruit, and the Dundee wine is more floral and lifted. There are several other Pinots in the portfolio as well, along with an ebullient, hard-not-to-like **Ribbon Ridge Estate Gamay Noir ($$)**.

PRODUCERS PROFILED IN THIS CHAPTER

Antiquum Farm

Bergström Vineyards

Big Table Farm

Brick House Vineyards

Brooks Winery

Cristom Vineyards

Day Wines

Elk Cove Vineyards

The Eyrie Vineyards

Hiyu Wine Farm

Martin Woods

Maysara Winery

Walter Scott Wines

Sokol Blosser

Soter Vineyards

Trisaetum

OTHER OREGON PRODUCERS TO LOOK FOR

Adelsheim

Analemma

Antica Terra

Apolloni Vineyards

Belle Pente

Bethel Heights

Bow & Arrow

Cameron Winery

Cooper Mountain Vineyards

Cowhorn Vineyards

Crowley

Division Winemaking Co.

Dominio IV

Et Fille

Haden Fig / Evesham Wood

Hamacher

Idiot's Grace

Illahe Vineyards

Johan Vineyards

King Estate Winery

Lavinea

Love & Squalor

Montinore Estate

David Paige Wines

Troon Vineyard

Winderlea

WASHINGTON

Bud Break at Cayuse Vineyards, Walla Walla

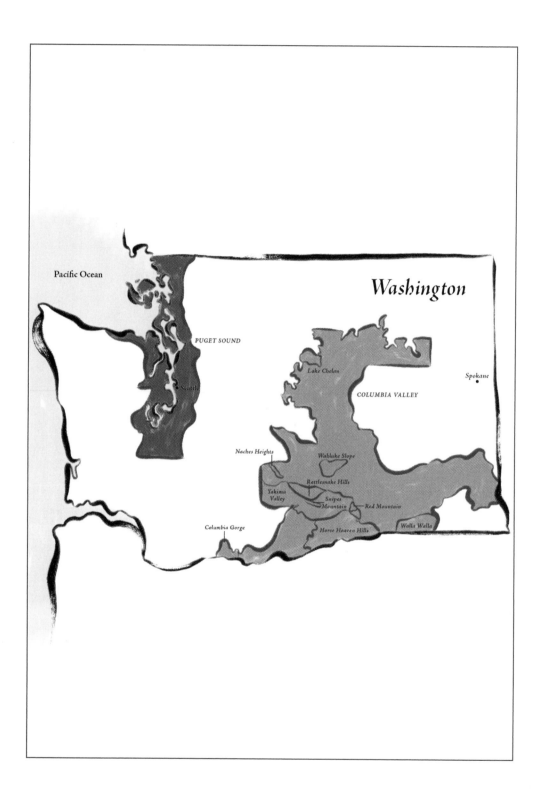

The first thing to know about Washington State wine is that the vast majority of it comes from east of the Cascades. Put aside any images of coastal Seattle, of tens of thousands of Microsoft and Amazon and Starbucks and Boeing employees stopping for a latte en route to work; eastern Washington is farm country. As Rick Small at Woodward Canyon Winery notes, "In Washington State you can get an ag permit to drive a grain truck at age twelve. You can't drive a car into town, but you can drive a grain truck in."

Most of that farming is apples, potatoes, and wheat, but wine grapes have been here a long time, too. The first grapes were planted in 1825 by traders working for the Hudson's Bay Company. Those almost certainly weren't used for wine—that started later, with German and Italian immigrants arriving in the state in the 1860s. That start got shut down by Prohibition, and the present-day Washington wine industry really didn't begin until the 1960s. Today Washington is the second-largest wine producer in the U.S. after California—though that's a very distant second. Taken together, all of the state's vineyards, some sixty thousand acres, are just more than what's planted in California's Sonoma County alone.

The vast Columbia Valley AVA encompasses 99 percent of the state's wine-producing vines. It lies in the rain shadow of the Cascades, covers a large portion of the central and southern parts of eastern Washington, and extends down into Oregon as well. It's effectively a low desert area, arid or semi-arid, warm and dry during the growing season and often bitter cold and windy during winter. The soil that all those vines grow on owes its character to the Missoula Floods, a series of cataclysmic events at the end of the last Ice Age, when vast glacial lakes broke through their ice dams to flood almost the entirety of eastern Washington—if you look down from a low-flying plane even today, you can see the broad ripples of land, like vast dunes, that the successive floods formed. And if you visit a winery in Walla Walla or Yakima, it's worth considering that where you are standing was once under about five hundred feet of water.

One Washington company—Chateau Ste. Michelle—makes far, far more wine than any other. It buys or grows roughly two out of every three wine grapes in the state, and makes more than 7 million cases of wine per year; Washington State *in toto* only makes 17 million. (In addition to its namesake brand, Ste. Michelle also owns 14 Hands, Columbia Crest, Canoe Ridge, Northstar, and several others; it's currently owned by a New York–based private equity firm.) And yet, amid the oceans of wheat that cover the center of the state, small-scale wineries are popping up everywhere. Between 2001 and 2019, the number of wineries in Washington grew from one hundred to more than a thousand. Attention has also landed not just on well-known regions like Walla Walla and Red Mountain, but newer names such as Snipes Mountain, Rattlesnake Hills, Royal Slope, and the Columbia Gorge (which extends onto the Oregon side of the Columbia River). As in California, many young, bootstrapping winemakers work out of urban winery locations in Seattle or nearby Woodinville. And while the state hasn't exactly been at the forefront of sustainable or organic viticulture, it did finally (in 2022) launch a statewide sustainability certification program.

CADENCE · RED MOUNTAIN

[sustainable]

Cadence, owned and run by husband-and-wife team Ben Smith and Gaye McNutt, makes some of Washington State's top Bordeaux variety wines and, in 2019, was finally able to switch to 100 percent estate fruit from Smith and McNutt's Cara Mia vineyard on Washington State's Red Mountain. Smith says, "It wasn't the easiest of decisions. We had twenty-year relationships with wonderful growers and vintners. But Cara Mia is ours; that's a wonderful feeling."

The couple have owned Cara Mia since 1997. They were on a weekend date out to Walla Walla, McNutt recalls, and were driving around Red Mountain (Smith was a home winemaker at the time; both were wine lovers). "We literally saw these for-sale signs stuck in the ground with a phone number on them, so we called. It was a really good price, and so we said, 'Why don't we buy some land?'" She laughs. "We weren't married, we weren't even living together. I figured, well, if things fall apart, we can just sell it. An accountant friend of mine told me, 'Good God, are you crazy? Don't do that.' But

by the next year we were married and had started the winery."

Smith, an engineer at Boeing, was a member of the semi-legendary Boeing Wine Club, which over the years has produced a surprisingly large number of home-turned-pro winemakers in Washington State. He'd been making wine in his garage for a number of years; taking the leap into starting a winery just seemed to make sense. "We still do the pinch-me thing every now and then that it worked out as well as it did," he says.

Their 8.5-acre Cara Mia vineyard currently gives Smith and McNutt all the fruit they need. Farming is sustainable. "We're not completely organic, and certainly not biodynamic," Smith says. "Some treatments, for instance, are safer for our crew and our vines than copper sulfate, which is the standard organic fungicide. Copper sulfate has a forty-eight-hour lag before the crew can even re-enter the vineyard. We use a soap instead if there are mold issues; it breaks down the surface tension so the spores don't puff out, and the vineyard guys can go back in in two hours rather than two days. But we try to avoid chemical treatments overall. There's no A10 Warthog that I'm calling in to hit the place with defoliants." (That's Smith's aviation-engineer background talking: the Thunderbolt II, known to troops as the Warthog, was a fighter plane built for ground support.) "Anyway, there are a lot of opinions out there about the best way to farm, and the reason for that is that no two places are the same," Smith says. "You can't farm Germany the way you farm eastern Washington. There are different pest pressures, different mildew pressures, different disease pressures—different everything."

The **Cadence Coda ($$)** is a roughly equal blend of Cabernet Franc and Merlot with a small amount of Petite Verdot; for under $30, it's a bargain, full of red and black cherry fruit and floral notes. (There's also a **Coda Rosé** [$$] that's an unusual, lively fifty-fifty blend of Petite Verdot and Cabernet Franc.) The **Cara Mia Vineyard Cabernet Sauvignon ($$–$$$)** is the only varietal wine in the lineup. Like all the Cadence wines, it leans toward elegance rather than weighty power; red fruit, taut tannins, lasting flavors. The two top wines are **Camerata ($$$)** and **Bel Canto ($$$)**, the former mostly Cabernet Sauvignon with roughly equal parts of Cabernet Franc and Merlot, the latter mostly Cabernet Franc, with a modest amount of Merlot. Camerata is a bit more powerful, perhaps, Bel Canto more aromatic and supple, but both are exquisite expressions of Red Mountain terroir.

CAYUSE VINEYARDS / NO GIRLS / HORSEPOWER • WALLA WALLA

[organic / biodynamic]

It's impossible to talk about Cayuse and Christophe Baron without talking about rocks. Specifically, *the* rocks, as in the Rocks District of the Milton Freewater AVA. Cailloux, Baron's first vineyard, was planted there. "A lot of people refer to the area as 'the rocks,'" he says, 'but I think I'm the only one who calls it the stones. It's ancient riverbed." It's also one of the greatest New World terroirs for Syrah. (And, despite providing fruit primarily for Washington wineries, the AVA itself actually lies right across the state border, in Oregon.)

Baron grew up in a Champagne-producing family in France. The family business was too crowded with relatives, so he departed for the U.S. Northwest. One day at lunch he showed a graper-grower friend some photos of Châteauneuf-du-Pape and the famous, flat stones or *galets* that cover the ground there. "I was saying, 'Look, in France, we grow vines in really stony land.' And my friend said, 'Well! I know a place near Walla Walla that's just like that. Littered with stones, like

the size of a fist.' And I said, '*This is it.* I'm planting Syrah right there.'"

Baron's initial 1998 vintage from Cailloux (called Cobblestone initially) launched him on a rocket-like climb to acclaim. Soon he planted his En Cerise vineyard a quarter of a mile away; others—En Cerise, Coccinelle, Armada, En Chamberlin—have followed. All have been farmed biodynamically since 2002. "We have never used forces of death in our vineyard, only forces of life, so from day one we were organic. Then we switched to biodynamic." He also makes the No Girls wines with his longtime co-winemaker (or "co-vigneronne") Elizabeth Bourcier, and his Horsepower wines. All operate under his Bionic Wines umbrella. (The Horsepower wines are literally that: horses are used for all the vineyard work.)

Though he makes exceptional wine, Baron doesn't consider himself a winemaker. "There's no winemaker at Cayuse. I'm a vigneron. A winegrower. A farmer. I just grow the best fruit possible, and then try to intervene as little as possible—sometimes in wine-making the ego can talk too much." That said, Baron is hardly immune to taking some pride in his accomplishments. Shortly after he released the first Horsepower Syrah, he says, "I saw my friend Louis Barruol of Château de Saint Cosme at a trade tasting, and he came over to say hi. I was pouring Cayuse, but I'd brought a bottle of Horsepower, which I had under the table. He'd never had it before. He tried it, he looked at me, and he goes like 'fuuuuuuck you.' He made my day. It was like, 'Holy cow, what have you created there?'"

The good news: all of the Bionic Wines (Cayuse, No Girls, Horsepower) are stellar. The bad news: everyone knows that, and there's a 15,000-person wait list to get on Baron's 4,500-person mailing list. However, a small amount goes to retail and restaurants, and can be found with some assiduous hunting.

The easiest to find, and the most affordable, is the **No Girls Double Lucky 8 ($$–$$$)**. Made from Grenache, Syrah, and Tempranillo, it's full of dark, sweet fruit and white pepper notes, and wildly overdelivers for the under-$50 price. Look also for the shimmering, savory **No Girls La Paciencia Vineyard Grenache ($$$$)**. The No Girls name, Baron says, celebrates that a woman makes these wines. "Every time there's a woman making wine, the wine world is better. The first woman to graduate from enology school in Burgundy, ever, was my aunt, in 1970. Fifteen years before that, women weren't even allowed in the cellars—it was felt they'd turn the wines bad! Completely crazy."

Of the Cayuse wines, the **Cayuse Cailloux Vineyard Syrah ($$$$)** gets a floral aromatic note from co-fermentation with a small amount of Viognier (traditional in Côte Rôtie). There's beautiful red and black fruit here and what Baron calls "attic dust—like in an old French attic." The **En Cerise Vineyard Syrah ($$$$)** is darker and more powerful, "a little more backbone, and more angular in a good way." **Armada Vineyard Syrah ($$$$)** tends to be more earthy, with a smoky-meaty note that recalls red Hermitage. There's also one white in the Cayuse lineup, Baron's **Cailloux Vineyard Viognier ($$$$)**, a silkily exotic white whose citrus-and-stone fruit flavors linger impressively.

The principal Horsepower wine is the **Sur Echalas Vineyard Syrah ($$$$)**, gamey, white peppery, and incredibly intense. "It's polarizing. Either you like it or you don't," Baron says. "But isn't that what wine's about? What's the point of trying to please everybody?"

LATTA WINES • SEATTLE

[sustainable]

Andrew Latta is a standout in the growing world of urban winemakers and wineries, a trend that's been expanding in California (Berkeley and Oakland), Oregon (Portland), and Washington State (Seattle). It's been fueled by young winemakers realizing that (a) you don't have to spend a fortune on wine country real estate to make great wines, and (b) the audience for your wines is probably in the city anyway. Latta, who grew up in Kentucky, got into the wine business working in restaurants before moving to Washington State to learn to make wine. A cellar rat job at Dunham Cellars in Walla Walla led to nine years making wines at K Vintners, which in turn gave him the vineyard connections he needed to launch Latta Wines in 2011.

Latta's focus is Rhône-variety grapes, sourced from sustainably farmed vineyards. But as he notes, "That word sustainability is nearly as nebulous—but maybe not as nefarious—as 'clean wine.'" Washington State, surprisingly, didn't have a sustainable certification program until a few years ago; one of Latta's partner vineyards, the Weinbau Vineyard, was one of the first through the process.

"Certified or not, I try to take a pretty sober look at the practices we employ across our sites," he says. "There's always a push-pull between what's best for the vine and the wine, the broader earth, the people doing the work, and the bottom line. As someone who physically applied elemental sulfur for years in a biodynamic vineyard—a chemical that's approved for all certified organic and biodynamic systems for fungal control—I can tell you that it's absolutely brutal to work with. Even wearing a full coverage spray-suit and respirator, the sulfur volatilizes off your body every time you take a shower for days afterward. That's unsettling. Also, it acidifies the soil pretty aggressively, and has to be reapplied every two weeks, or immediately after there's rain—that's a lot of tractor diesel."

Latta admits that he doesn't know where the perfect balance lies; but then, who does? The net-net, as they say, is that in the end "we try to be as organic and soft as possible. There's not a perfect solution, but as long as your answer to 'why' isn't 'because it's the cheapest,' you're at least trying." And there are other avenues toward helping the world as well. Not long ago Latta launched a series of affordable wines under the name Kind Stranger. Proceeds from them benefit the local Seattle charity Mary's House, which helps women and their children escape homelessness, and the International Rescue Committee.

Though Latta sources fruit from various sites in eastern Washington, the wines are made at the SODO Urban Works facility in Seattle. For whites, seek out the minerally **Latta Wines CB Roussanne Lawrence Vineyard ($$)**, a nod to the white wines of France's Alpine Savoie, or the more full-bodied **Lawrence Vineyard Roussanne ($$)**. Among the reds, the **Latta Latta GSM ($$)** is an appealingly priced, peppery blend of Grenache, Syrah, and Mourvèdre. The full-bodied **Upland Vineyard Mourvèdre ($$)** adds a gamey note to its dark-berried, licorice-accented fruit, and the earthy **Dana Dibble Syrah ($$)** is named for the third-generation farmer who owns the Freewater Rocks vineyard it's sourced from. The **Upland Vineyard Grenache ($$)** is a silky, impossible-to-resist mélange of strawberry and cherry fruit sparked with white pepper notes—it's one of Washington's best Rhône-style reds. There are others as well, among them the **Kind Folks Cabernet Sauvignon ($)**, a killer deal that also helps out people in need.

[sustainable]

Leonetti was Walla Walla's first bonded winery, founded by Gary and Nancy Figgins in 1977; it was also the first Washington State winery (along with Quilceda Creek) to become a so-called "cult" producer, with a waiting list to be on its mailing list, stratospheric scores from wine critics, and the allure of its wines necessitating a kind of treasure hunt in order to track them down. What's odd about that story is how counter it runs to Leonetti's beginnings.

The Leonettis started farming in eastern Washington in the early 1900s. Like many of their fellow immigrants, they made wine at home, to drink on a daily basis—it was simply a part of everyday life. Second-generation Virginia Leonetti married a Walla Walla local, Berle Figgins, and her son Gary grew up visiting his grandparents' farm outside town, seeing wine being made in the basement of their farmhouse. During an Army Reserve stint in the early 1970s, Figgins was stationed in California along with fellow Walla Wallan Rick Small (who went on to found Woodward Canyon Winery). The two of them spent weekends vis-

iting wineries, and once he was back in Washington, Figgins started making home wine as a hobby. That hobby led to planting a vineyard on his grandparents' old property, then the purchase of additional vineyard land, then a winery established in an old horse shed on the property, and finally the first Leonetti Cabernet Sauvignon—named in honor of his grandparents—in 1978.

The acclaim came later, and when it came, it was big. But if you walk Leonetti's vineyards with Chris Figgins, who started working with his father in 1996 and took over fully after Gary's retirement in 2011, you're quite aware you're talking to not just a winemaker but a farmer, someone with roots here that are even deeper than those of the vines. (Walla Walla is still a farm town, and for every acre of vines, there must be a thousand or more of wheat.)

Figgins says, "Our wines are neither certified biodynamic nor organic, but that's only the start of the story. Biodynamics itself is a belief system, not just a set of practices, and one with which I don't wholeheartedly agree." Even so, together with his longtime viticulturist

Jason Magnaghi, Figgins has borrowed strategies from biodynamics—compost piles than utilize the skins, seeds, and stems from winemaking, along with grass clippings and fallen leaves off the properties; brewing compost teas from earthworm castings, which are then fed into the vineyards' drip-irrigation lines to improve soil health. He's not inclined to follow organics rigidly, either. "I find organics to be too restrictive and harsher on the environment than our sustainability program," he says, noting—as many do—that copper, the approved organic treatment for fungal issues, is a heavy metal and toxic to the soil. "I won't let copper anywhere near my vineyards." Reducing water use, growing cover and companion crops to increase biodiversity and attract beneficial insects: "The end goal," Figgins has said, "is to run our business in a manner that ensures we can produce the same or better-quality wines generations from now, while doing our part to preserve our natural resources."

The Leonetti wines are highly sought-after by collectors, but they're out there. The wines from Chris Figgins's more recent, eponynous project, Figgins, are also excellent, and much easier to find. The **Figgins Estate Riesling ($$)** is stony and saline, a deeply refreshing, very faintly off-dry white. **Figlia ($$$)** is a full-bodied blend of Petite Verdot and Merlot, its dark fruit accented by olive notes. The **Figgins Estate Red ($$$–$$$$)** is primarily Cabernet Sauvignon along with Petite Verdot and Merlot; it's bigger, more tannic, and more luscious.

The **Leonetti Cellar Merlot ($$$)** is one of the best Merlots in the U.S., full of dark berry fruit and dried tobacco notes. The winery's **Cabernet Sauvignon ($$$$)** is a Walla Walla benchmark, with plenty of black fruit (blackberry, black plum) and dried herb notes. It's powerful but always remarkably balanced. The **Sangiovese ($$$)** is all high-toned red fruit lifted by fresh acidity that descends into fine-grained tannins and earthy notes. There are several excellent single-vineyard wines from Leonetti, but they're hard to get unless you happen to be on the mailing list; the same is true of the wonderful (but pricey) **Red Wine Reserve ($$$$)**, which comes from the best barrels in each vintage.

WOODWARD CANYON WINERY • WALLA WALLA

[sustainable]

Rick Small of Woodward Canyon Winery grew up in a farming family. He also happens to make some of Washington State's best Cabernets, and has for going on four decades now. The Smalls, like other longtime Walla Walla families, were wheat and cattle farmers. Small is deeply rooted here; even his winery's name comes from the school bus route that he took as a boy.

"We've had family land in Woodward Canyon for three generations now," he says. "On my mother's side I'm five generations here. I have four brothers in wheat and cattle." Small might have headed in that direction himself, but when he was in the Army Reserves in the 1970s, he started making homemade wine with fellow reservist Gary Figgins (founder of Leonetti Cellar). Those homemade wines led to bigger ambitions, and in 1981, Small founded Woodward Canyon, Walla Walla's second winery. (Figgins founded Leonetti in '77, edging Small out for the title of first winery by four years.)

Asked whether there were other vineyards around when he planted his vines, Small laughs. "Oh, no—this was all wheat, wheat, wheat, and everyone thought I was an absolute raving lunatic. Plus, I had long hair then. Now I have *no* hair, but I'm still a long-hair person." Even today, looking out across the eastern Washington landscape, the low, rolling hills, what you see are acres and acres of wheat, stretching to the horizon. Walla Walla is a significant place in Washington wine, but its vineyards are tiny dots in a vast ocean of grain.

"The thing is," Small says, "we could have had a wine industry here generations ago. But the Italian immigrants in the area tried planting Mediterranean varieties, and they just froze out. Particularly in the 1950s, Walla Walla had awful freezes—Alberta Clippers, they were called. Temperatures that went from seventy degrees to negative thirty degrees in a couple of days. During one, my dad was up in the mountains hunting, and he said it got so cold so fast that it froze the sap in the branches of the pines. Limbs were cracking and dropping right off the trees."

Woodward Canyon Winery lies at about 800 to 950 feet altitude, forty acres of vines dotted here and there with juniper trees ("native when Lewis and Clark were here," Small says). When he first started planting he had no water rights, so he had to haul water up in his truck, and because he had no power, he had no pumps, either. And there were massive rocks in the soil deposited when the glaciers left by the Missoula Floods melted, eons before. "Like huge ice cubes," Small says. "I had to dig those out. No wonder people thought I was crazy."

As he stands now amid his vineyard rows, a distant high-pitched yipping brings an annoyed look to his face. "Coyotes," he says.

Well. When it comes to problems, at least coyotes don't eat grapes.

"Coyotes? Oh, they'll eat grapes," Small says. "Absolutely. Especially Merlot."

Small's wines come mostly from his forty-one-acre, sustainably farmed Woodward Canyon vineyard, though he purchases fruit for his **Woodward Canyon Winery Washington State Chardonnay ($$)**. It's brightly zesty, with pear-pineapple flavors and light, toasty oak notes on the finish. The **Estate Cabernet Sauvignon ($$$)** is a picture of the entire vineyard, plummy and with lightly savory black olive and toast notes. The **Artist Series Cab-**ernet Sauvignon ($$$), one of Walla Walla's benchmark wines, tends to be lush with black cherry and black currant fruit, with a light aromatic mintiness. "There's a little herb, and a little more tobacco, in the Walla Walla Cabernet Sauvignon character," Small says. His **Estate Old Vines Cabernet Sauvignon ($$$)** is more cedary and spicy, the flavors a little wilder, with lots of tannic force.

PRODUCERS PROFILED IN THIS CHAPTER

Cadence

Cayuse Vineyards / No Girls / Horsepower

Latta Wines

Leonetti Cellar / Figgins

Woodward Canyon Winery

OTHER WASHINGTON PRODUCERS TO LOOK FOR

Abeja / Pursued by Bear

Avennia

Brook & Bull / Vital Wines

L'Ecole 41

Force Majeure

Gramercy Cellars

Kiona Cellars

Rasa

Reynvaan

Savage Grace

Sleight of Hand

Syncline

THE SOUTHERN HEMISPHERE

AUSTRALIA AND NEW ZEALAND

Moonrise, Cullen Wines, Margaret River, Australia

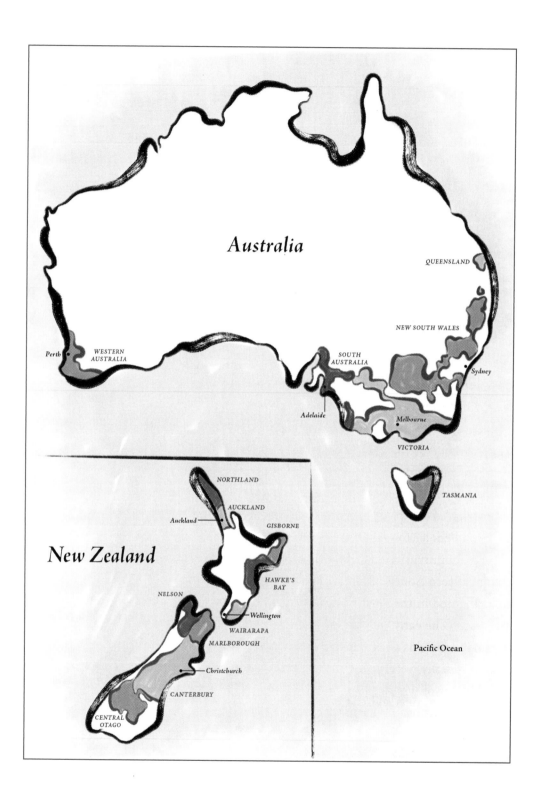

Australia

QUEENSLAND

NEW SOUTH WALES

Perth •

WESTERN
AUSTRALIA

SOUTH
AUSTRALIA

Sydney •

Adelaide •

Melbourne •

VICTORIA

TASMANIA

New Zealand

NORTHLAND

AUCKLAND

Auckland —

GISBORNE

HAWKE'S
BAY

NELSON

Wellington

WAIRARAPA

MARLBOROUGH

Christchurch

Pacific Ocean

CANTERBURY

CENTRAL
OTAGO

AUSTRALIA

The most important thing to know about Australian wine is that there is *far* more to to it than, as an Aussie winemaker said disparagingly to me once, "a bunch of ethanol-driven confectionary lolly-water." For many years, the U.S. was overrun with exactly that—inexpensive, super-fruity, high-alcohol Shiraz, often with cute "critter" labels. Those wines quite effectively obliterated in peoples' minds the idea that Australian wine could be complex, fascinating stuff, made by ambitious independent vintners, from regions all around this island continent. Also, Australian imports to the U.S. have been on an upswing in recent years even as the dominance in the market of cheap-and-cheerful Shiraz has declined, resulting in far more stylistic range and choice for anyone who wants to explore.

The country's wine history starts in the late 1700s, when ships bearing vine cuttings from South Africa's Cape of Good Hope arrived in New South Wales, to be planted in the governor's garden there; the first commercial wine appears in the 1820s. The early years of Australian wine weren't easy, not only because of the continent's origins as a penal colony; the climate was harsh, the grape varieties that arrived initially weren't suited to it, and, as another winemaker noted to me at one point, "most of what's in Australia will bite you, and some of it will kill you." Not exactly promising. The real birth of the industry lies with James Busby, a Scottish immigrant with viticultural training who brought cuttings of the classic French varieties over in stages—a small amount in 1824, followed by a vastly larger amount in

1832, from which he planted several hundred varieties (before giving up on Australia's job prospects and moving to New Zealand; regardless, he remains known as "the father of Australian wine").

Today wine grows everywhere in Australia except in the arid, empty outback. Cool-climate regions such as the Yarra Valley and Morning Peninsula in Victoria, Great Southern in Western Australia, and the Adelaide Hills in South Australia (as well as Tasmania) are sources for exceptional Pinot Noirs, Chardonnays, and Rieslings; Margaret River in Western Australia and Coonawarra in South Australia make world-class Cabernet Sauvignon and other Bordeaux varieties; Tasmania arguably produces the country's best sparkling wines; and of course there is Shiraz (Syrah) everywhere, and in every style, from the luscious, full-bodied versions of Barossa and the McLaren Vale to leaner, more savory styles from cooler areas. Among young winemakers there's a robust natural wine scene as well. The number of organic and biodynamic vineyards in Australia is growing, but they still remain a tiny percentage of the whole—nevertheless, progress is progress, no matter how small.

CULLEN WINES • MARGARET RIVER

[certified organic / certified biodynamic]

Vanya Cullen is one of the most influential winemakers in Australia, partly for her championing of eco-friendly vineyard and winemaking practices. And those practices stretch back to Cullen's beginnings in 1971, when her parents, Kevin and Diana, first planted their vineyard in Western Australia's Margaret River region.

From the start, the Cullens' reliance on chemicals for farming was minimal. The shift to organic viticulture happened in 1998, a joint decision between Vanya and her mother, Diana (at the time Diana was the winemaker; today, Vanya is both winemaker and estate director). A few years later, Vanya shifted to biodynamics, attracted by its holistic approach to the vineyard and its focus on giving back to the land in the context of what you take from it. Cullen's seventy-seven acres of vineyard became certified biodynamic in 2004 (a move greeted at the time with a drop in sales and in some cases active hostility; but sales more than recovered, and the hostility faded).

In 2006, Cullen Wines became Australia's first certified carbon neutral winery. What Vanya Cullen found, after several years of soil testing, was that strict biodynamic practices, intensive composting, solar panels to provide electricity, and other efforts (for instance, buying carbon credits to support tree planting in the Yarra Yarra biodiversity corridor north of Perth) had actually made their farming carbon-positive; Cullen Wines removes more carbon from the atmosphere than it emits. The Cullens also have five large biodynamic gardens on their property, which supply 90 percent of the fruits and vegetables used in the winery's restaurant—which, by the way, is excellent.

The **Cullen Dancing in the Sun ($$)** is a lively peach-citrusy blend of Semillon, Sauvignon Blanc, and Verdelho. A step up is the **Ephraim Clarke ($$)**, roughly two-thirds Sauvignon Blanc and one-third Semillon (percentages vary by vintage), it's vividly citrusy, with light cut-grass notes and a hint of spice from French oak. The winery's **Kevin John Chardonnay ($$$)** is one of Australia's top Chardonnays, from vines planted in 1976. Margaret River is a world-class region for Chardonnay, and this layered, complex wine shows it. **Amber ($$)**, a blend of Semillon and Sauvignon Blanc that ferments on skins for ten or so days, is sunset-hued and textural without being overtly tannic, with rounder citrus notes (orange, bergamot) and talc-like minerality.

Red Moon ($$) is a crisp, medium-bodied blend of Malbec, Petite Verdot, and a small percentage of Merlot; plenty of crunchy red fruit here, with moderate tannins. And the **Diana Madeline Cabernet Sauvignon ($$$$)** is regularly one of Australia's top red wines, full of deep, dark fruit but not massive at all, seamless and precise.

HENSCHKE • EDEN VALLEY

[organic / biodynamic (estate) / sustainable (purchased fruit)]

Henschke's history reaches back to the mid-1800s, and its Hill of Grace Shiraz is rightly recognized as one of the two greatest red wines in Australia (the other being the iconic Penfolds Grange). Yet under owners Stephen and Prue Henschke, the winery has also been at the forefront of sustainable, organic and biodynamic winegrowing in Australia.

The Henschkes farm 269 acres of vineyard primarily in South Australia's Eden Valley (they also own land in Barossa and Adelaide Hills). Their property is also devoted to native forests, grass- and bushlands, much of it restored over the years by Prue Henschke. (Stephen is the winemaker; Prue, the viticulturist.) Prue writes, "My philosophy is a holistic one— to ensure our created environment sits in a healthy balance with our natural landscape. I'd like to see the next generation inherit a fertile and sustainable land." That key understanding, of the man-made nature of a vineyard being in harmony with nature overall, and of humans being a part of the landscape rather than separate from it, is at the heart of her viticultural work.

The wines are, and have been for decades, among the best in Australia. (Note that the Henschkes also source grapes from other farmers, and not all of their more affordable wines are organic/biodynamic, though they are certified sustainable.) Nor has the winemaking here changed much, if at all, over the generations: gentle handling, not much fining or filtration, minimal sulfur use, no "cosmetic" adjustments.

The Henschkes make a plethora of wines, and though many do not get to every market around the world, a good proportion do. The **Henschke Julius Riesling ($$$)** is "based on early clones that came to Barossa. Most towards fifty years old. And some Geisenheim clones which are a bit more floral," Stephen Henschke says. The flinty **Lenswood Croft Chardonnay ($$$)** is certified biodynamic, as are all the wines from their Lenswood Vineyard, such as the supple, lovely **Giles Pinot Noir** ($$$). (The 2019 Ash Wednesday bush fires in the Adelaide Hills burned the Lenswood Vineyard to the ground, but it didn't destroy the vine roots. As of 2023, Prue Henschke will have about half the vineyard back in production.)

Henry's Seven ($$), from sustainable Barossa fruit, "started off as a trial for a Shiraz-Viognier," Stephen says. "The first thing we discovered was that Viognier really does brighten the perfume of Shiraz and gives it an almost umami character on the palate." The **Keyneton Euphonium** ($$$), named for the family brass band the family ran in the late 1800s, is a Barossa blend of Shiraz, Cabernet Sauvignon, Merlot, and Cabernet Franc, robust and spicy.

The winery's top wines are expensive, and in the case of Hill of Grace, stratospherically so. But they are worth mentioning. All are from the Henschke's home vineyard in Mount Eden. The **Mount Edelstone** ($$$$) is 100 percent Shiraz planted in 1912 and, Stephen Henschke says, has a character, particularly in cool vintages, that recalls "spicy plums—Prue describes it as being like rubbing fresh sage leaves around a peppercorn." The **Cyril Henschke Cabernet Sauvignon** ($$$$) is effortlessly balanced, a complex array of floral, herbal, and cassis flavors. Lastly, there's **Hill of Grace** ($$$$), a profoundly great Shiraz from vines more than 160 years old, rich and velvety but elegant all at once, incredibly long-aging . . . and it costs a fortune (about $800 a bottle). Mortgage your house? Sell your car? Regardless, if you get the chance to try it, don't let it pass you by.

JAUMA • ADELAIDE HILLS

[organic / natural]

Jauma's James Erskine first came to the Aussie wine-drinking public's attention with Natural Selection Theory, an avant-garde winemaking collective he helped found, which existed from 2010 to 2012. To give a sense, at one point the group was invited to participate in an exhibition of ephemeral art at a gallery in Adelaide. "We had a friend write a wonderful love poem and a vile hate poem," Erskine said. "I painted the poems by hand onto six-gallon glass demijohns filled with a blend of Cabernet Franc, Grenache, and other varieties. Half got the love poem, half the hate one." For three months, the love wine was displayed in a room where a recording played the love poem; in a different room, the hate wine was blasted with the hate poem. Finally, the wines were decanted into bottles for a tasting. "They were all sourced from the same original barrel," Erskine recalls, "but they were amazingly different. Love was so soft, so welcoming—yet fading fast. Hate was strong and steadfast, with a rich tannin line driving forward to infinity."

This is not exactly your standard approach to winemaking, but if you're chatting with Erskine, it somehow starts to make sense. Erskine, as owner and winemaker, and Fiona Wood, who handles the farming, run Jauma from an 1860s apple-picking shed, now crammed with barrels and the occasional cured ham (Erskine hangs them from the rafters), hidden away in Australia's Adelaide Hills. Lanky and ponytailed, Erskine is a former sommelier turned natural winemaker, and has been much more influential in the avant-garde side of Australian winemaking than his natural modesty would reveal. Erskine works with organic grapes, zero sulfur, zero other additions, native yeast, no new oak, no fining or filtration, and often extended skin-contact for white wines—natural, yes, though unconstrained might actually be the better word.

There's a wide range of Jauma wines, with a focus on Grenache. The **Jauma Hola Nuria ($$)**, a *pét-nat* sparkler made from Verdelho and a small amount of Muscat, is lightly spritzy and full of vivacious tropical fruit. **Why Try So Hard ($$)** is a rose-orange blend of Chenin Blanc with a little Muscat and carbonic-maceration Grenache. **Disco Special Red ($$)** is a brambly, tingly Shiraz/Grenache blend from McLaren Vale fruit; **Tikka the Cosmic Cat ($$)**, named after the winery cat, is a vividly purple, carbonic-maceration Shiraz, low in alcohol and appealingly chillable. **Like Raindrops ($$)**, possibly Erskine's most easily findable wine (though all will take some hunting; look to stores that specialize in natural wine), comes from forty-plus-year-old Grenache vines in McLaren Vale and Clarendon. It has a very faint CO_2 tingle, and ripe cherry flavors with a little cracked-twig character from 100 percent stem contact. If you want to dive headfirst into Australia's natural wine movement, there's no better place to start.

MAYER • YARRA VALLEY

[organic]

A couple of decades ago, it was easy to make an argument that Australia was the most significant wine-producing country incapable of producing worthwhile Pinot Noir. Vineyards were planted in the wrong place, and the wines they produced were often jammy, flat, and oaked to death, a kind of lumpen approximation of the shimmering delicacy that drives Pinot Noir's allure. There were some exceptions, but they were few and far between.

Today that's changed, and there are superb Pinots coming from a number of cool-climate Australian wine regions. Ask Yarra Valley winemaker Timo Mayer why that's the case, and he'll reply, "Because about twenty years ago a bunch of us woke up and asked ourselves, 'Why aren't we making wines we want to drink?'"

Mayer is a prodigiously bearded German expat who's been living in Australia for almost three decades now. Cheerfully blunt, he has a strong German accent spiced up with Aussie colloquialisms—he refers to his six-acre home vineyard as "the bloody hill" because, he says, "it's so bloody hard to farm the thing." His wines are made with 100 percent whole-bunch fermentation, because, he says, "it takes away that sweet fruit and takes you into the savory. I started working this way because I was so sick of that sweet fruit style. We all were."

Despite the proprietor's outspokenness, the Mayer wines tend toward elegance and transparency. Of them, the pale ruby **Mayer Yarra Valley Pinot Noir ($$$)** is aromatic, savory-spicy, and alluring. His **Yarra Valley Chardonnay ($$$)** is similar in approach: minimal oak, no finding, no filtration, flinty and citrusy and intense. About his **Yarra Valley Syrah ($$$)**, Mayer says, "It's purely about the perfume and the fruit. Not oak-fucked, not alcoholic, no dead fruit—that's what I'm after. We try to seek the savoriness."

TOLPUDDLE • TASMANIA

[organic]

Tolpuddle makes standout Chardonnay and Pinot Noir from fifty acres of organic vineyard in Tasmania's Coal River Valley. The winery is a partnership between Michael Hill Smith, whose family founded Yalumba—"so, six generations of intergenerational wine inbreeding," he says dryly—and his cousin and partner Martin Shaw. The two went into business initially in 1989 with their eponymous Shaw + Smith brand, but Tolpuddle is distinct from that.

"It's worth remembering that Tasmania is less than one percent of all Australian wine," Hill Smith says. "In volume terms it's absolutely insignifi-cant, but in quality terms it's *very* significant." He and Shaw took a trip there in 2011 and were blown away by the character of the wines. At one point, before a lunch at a local winery, they were tasting Chardonnay and Pinot Noir out of barrels. "And all the Chard we liked, we're like, god, what's *that*? 'Well,' the winemaker said, 'those grapes are from Tolpuddle.' And then the exact same thing happened with the Pinots. We thought, fuck, we'd better visit that! Drove over, saw it, lovely slope, planted beautifully, really nicely done. We looked at each other and wondered, should we try and *buy* this? It was just one of those random thought bubbles. Nine months later we owned fifty acres of vineyard in Tasmania—it was the most expensive lunch I've ever had!"

Hill Smith notes that they still had to do ten years' work to bring the site back into shape; they also began farming the land organically. "In Australia everyone at first thought organic was the loopy left, but now farming with organic or biodynamic principles, with or without certification, is much more common," he says. "I went to Littorai in California some years ago, and was really struck by Ted Lemon saying, 'you know, I didn't embrace this credo out of nowhere. It's that I woke up one day after years of conventional farming and thought, there has got to be a better way.' That's the heart of it, really. That's what Tolpuddle is about."

The **Tolpuddle Tasmania Chardonnay ($$$)** is one of the best Australian Chardonnays around. It has the distinctive matchstick-flint aroma of reductive winemaking, and is deeply savory with, as Hill Smith puts it, a "line of confronting acidity wrapped in quite intense flavor." The **Tolpuddle Tasmania Pinot Noir ($$$)** has dried leaf notes from whole-cluster fermentation; you'd think from the nose that it might be light and thin, but there's terrific spicy red fruit on the mid-palate, and a long, savory finish. (It should be said that the Shaw + Smith wines, with the exception of their popular, large-production Sauvignon Blanc, also come from organic vineyards—the **Shaw + Smith M3 Adelaide Hills Chardonnay ($$)** and the **Adelaide Hills Pinot Noir ($$)** are both impressive, and the single-vineyard **Balhannah Vineyard Shiraz [$$$]** is even better.)

PRODUCERS PROFILED IN THIS CHAPTER

Cullen Wines

Henschke

Jauma

Mayer

Tolpuddle

OTHER AUSTRALIA PRODUCERS TO LOOK FOR

Basket Range

BK Wine

Brash Higgins

Brokenwood

Commune of Buttons

Charlotte Dalton

Mac Forbes

Grosset

Lambert Wines

Lucy M

Moss Wood

Sami-Odi

Sam Viciullo

Unico Zelo

Yetti & the Kokonut

NEW ZEALAND

New Zealand faces an unusual problem in that its principal grape, Sauvignon Blanc, has been so successful that it eclipses people's awareness of all the other varieties that thrive in the country's vineyards (a problem shared with Argentina and Malbec). It accounts for 72 percent of what's planted here, and a whopping 86 percent of what's exported to the rest of the world. There's no arguing with success, perhaps, but anyone making Pinot Noir, Chardonnay, Riesling, Merlot, or Syrah here might raise an eyebrow at that assumption. What's also interesting is how rapid that climb has been—the first Sauvignon Blanc was planted in New Zealand in 1969. But then the country's entire wine history is recent, too.

Though grapevines arrived in New Zealand in the early 1800s, the nascent industry was more or less exterminated by a combination of oidium (powdery mildew), phylloxera, and fervent prohibitionists toward the end of the nineteenth century. It took until the 1980s for New Zealand wine to recover both in terms of quantity and quality—for example, in 1960 there were a total of 964 acres of vines in the entire country. In 1990, there were more than 12,000. Today there are more than 100,000.

The country has also been at the forefront of ecologically aware viticulture. New Zealand was the first country to launch a national vineyard sustainability program, and as of 2002, fully 96 percent of its vineyards are certified sustainable. About 10 percent of the country's wineries are certified organic. Since 2019, New Zealand has also had a carbon reduction certification program in place.

And yes, while there is a tremendous amount of New Zealand Sauvignon Blanc out there (some of it very good, and some as generic as a wine can be), there are also world-class New Zealand Pinot Noirs, from Central Otago, Waipara, Marlborough, and other regions; stellar Syrah, from Hawke's Bay and Auckland; top Chardonnays, from Auckland, Gisborne, and Marlborough; and many other varieties.

FELTON ROAD • CENTRAL OTAGO

[certified organic / certified biodynamic]

When Felton Road owner Nigel Greening first took over in 2000, he shifted the property to organics, and quite soon after made a further shift to biodynamics. "I'd worked a lot in my past life with the auto industry, and I'd been really horrified by the way that people in that business equated quality with zero defects. There was this generally accepted idea that if you had no defects, then you had a quality product. I thought, that's nonsense. You can have perfectly made rubbish. It's about the qualities that you put *in*, not necessarily the defects that you take out. And I felt with organics, it was more like zero defects; these are all the things you *mustn't* do. Biodynamics, with all its flaws and some of the slightly crackpot areas, was really a philosophy of 'here are the things you *should*

do' instead of 'here are the things you *shouldn't* do.' I liked that."

He's stayed on that path ever since, together with longtime winemaker Blair Walter. Together they've made Felton Road into one of Central Otago's most acclaimed wineries. Greening himself took one of those haphazard paths that sometimes leads to wine: studying biochemistry, dropping out to become a rock guitarist, achieving success as an advertising creative director, then leaving to become a winery owner.

Greening has an endlessly curious mind, and he's not dogmatic. "I'm not sold on all aspects of biodynamics, and that's fine. All of us get on or off the bus at different points, but we all share the same kind of passion for this ever-changing ecosystem of land. And thinking about what's going on in the ground is something that all organic farmers and all biodynamic farmers have in common. It's that lovely idea: be careful how you're stepping on my land, because you're not stepping on dirt, you're stepping on the roof of another kingdom. And it's a kingdom where one spoonful of soil has more organisms in it than there are people on earth. That's quite cool, right?"

The **Felton Road Bannockburn Chardonnay ($$)** and **Bannockburn Pinot Noir ($$)** are a great introduction to the winery's sensibility. Winemaker Blair Walter says about the Pinot, "Bannockburn is a blend of all four of our vineyards. It's our 'Bannockburn village' wine, in a sense." There's also an excellent, lightly off-dry **Bannockburn Riesling ($$)** and a dry, sprightly (and aptly named) **Dry Riesling ($$)**.

Of the various single-vineyard and single-block Pinots, Walter remarks that the **Calvert Pinot Noir ($$$)** "is a little more linear, mineral, austere," whereas the **Cornish Point Pinot Noir ($$$)** "is a bit more the Central Otago character of rich, round, perfumed fruit—soft, chewy tannins versus tougher tannins with the Calvert." The top-of-the-line **Block 3 Pinot Noir ($$$$)** and **Block 5 Pinot Noir ($$$$)** both come from the winery's home Elms Vineyard. Walter says, "Block 3 is typically spicier, more dried herbs, earthier, with rounder, broader tannins. Block 5 is more linear, darker fruit, dark cherry, stronger tannins."

GREYWACKE • MARLBOROUGH

[certified sustainable and/or organic (depending on vineyard)]

Kevin Judd knows Sauvignon Blanc. He was the founding winemaker at Cloudy Bay, where he effectively created the New Zealand style of Sauvignon Blanc that shot to world prominence in the 1990s. He departed in 2009, a few years after Cloudy Bay was sold to the massive luxury conglomerate LVMH, and started his own winery, Greywacke.

Judd changed his stylistic direction somewhat after leaving, though Sauvignon Blanc remains his focus, and is about 70 percent of what he makes. "With Greywacke, I steered away from that in-your-face, herbaceous style," he said when I met with him. "My Sauvignon is still a classic Marlborough wine, but a riper, more full-textured version of that." A large part of that comes from controlling the vine's inherent vigor: "Sauvignon grows like a weed, really. You can easily set fifteen tons an acre. I've seen fruit come in at twenty-plus tons." (Ideally, at least for good-quality wine, yields would top out at about five tons.) Judd uses wild yeasts for fermentation. "The concept of terroir involves a combination of the soil and climate of a wine region. We like to take that one step further and suggest that microflora is also in fact part of the terroir, the yeasts, the bacteria—they're all part." That sense of place is embedded in the name of the winery as well: the home vineyard is full of duck egg–sized pebbles of the hard gray sandstone called greywacke.

> **"I regularly meet people who say, 'Oh, I'm not really a fan of Sauvignon Blanc.' They almost whisper it, as if it were some sort of terrible secret."**
> —Kevin Judd

The **Greywacke Marlborough Sauvignon Blanc ($$)** still retains a touch of pepperiness, but it's more elegant and subtle than most New Zealand Sauvignons, with grapefruit peel and lime notes. Judd's **Marlborough Wild Sauvignon ($$)** is fermented in old oak barrels (mostly) using only wild yeast. "The juice just goes into the barrel and I don't do anything to it," he says. It adds a riper pineapple character, and a bit of resinous citrus peel. His **Marlborough Riesling ($$),** from a certified organic vineyard, is floral, zesty, and lovely; it's very lightly off-dry. He also makes a creamy, lightly off-dry **Marlborough Pinot Gris ($$)** and a vivid, distinctly spicy **Marlborough Pinot Noir ($$),** the latter with fruit from hillside vineyards in the Southern Valleys area.

KUMEU RIVER · KUMEU

[certified sustainable]

Kumeu River arguably makes New Zealand's greatest Chardonnays. It is also inarguably an unusual New Zealand producer because it does not make Sauvignon Blanc. "We dabbled in it for a little while, and then abandoned it," Michael Brajkovich says. "It became clear to us that Chardonnay was the best variety for us, under our cool-climate conditions."

Brajkovich's family arrived in New Zealand as part of a wave of Croatian immigrants in the early 1900s, who came to grow kauri gum, one of New Zealand's biggest exports at the time. It was a hard life, and eventually Brajkovich's grandfather gave it up to return to Croatia. But by the late 1930s, the Dalmatian coast—along with the rest of Europe—was facing the prospect of a ruinous war.

"He came back, because New Zealand was really the only other place he knew," Brajkovich says. "That was in 1938." There was no future in the gum fields, so using what little money they'd saved, the Brajkoviches bought eighteen acres of land "out near Kumeu," Michael Brajkovich says, "which was out near absolutely nothing at all. They didn't know it would be good for grapes; they bought it because it was cheap." That turned out to be a very smart purchase. Today Kumeu River has about a hundred acres of land, sixty of which are devoted to sustainably grown, dry-farmed grapevines.

Brajkovich's most affordable wine is the **Kumeu River Village Chardonnay ($$)**, its creamy, green apple flavors lifted by a light snap of reduction. The winery's **Estate Chardonnay ($$)** is lightly spicy from about 20 percent new oak and beautifully textured, with peach and apple notes.

There are also several single-vineyard wines. The **Coddington Vineyard Chardonnay ($$$)** is full-bodied and suggestive of orchard fruits, while the **Hunting Hill Vineyard Chardonnay ($$$)** is "more at the citrus end of the spectrum," Brajkovich says. **Mate's Vineyard Chardonnay ($$$)** comes from the original Chardonnay vines that Brajkovich's father, Mate, planted in the 1950s. "There's always a subtle earthiness in it that comes from vine age." Lastly, the chalky **Ray's Road** Chardonnay ($$$) comes from a vineyard in Hawke's Bay. (The winery's **Village Pinot Noir** [$$] and **Hunting Hill Pinot Noir** [$$$] are also well worth looking for.)

RIPPON · CENTRAL OTAGO

[certified organic / certified biodynamic]

There's a lot of competition for "most beautiful vineyard in the world," but Rippon, in Central Otago, has more than a fair shot at that title. From its vineyards, which slope down to a line of poplars on the shore of Central Otago's azure Lake Wanaka, the eye travels across the water to the snow-capped Southern Alps; it's a dramatic, picture-postcard setting that even Switzerland would have a hard time beating. Though none of that would matter if Nick Mills's wines weren't also so good.

The farm was first purchased by Mills's great-grandfather in 1912, but after his death the family had to sell the land to pay death taxes. At an auction a few decades later, though, the next generation was able to buy back the section that Mills now owns and farms. There were no vines on it at that time. That had to wait until Nick's father, Rolfe, who had seen vines growing on schist in the 1940s in Portugal, apparently thought to himself, "Well, that should work here!" (Rolfe served on submarines in the Atlantic during World War II; he visited Portugal on his way back from the war.)

Rolfe Mills passed away in 2000. "He was the dreamer—a visionary—but my mother created the business," Nick says. He joined in 2002 after studying enology in Beaune, France, a period that also included stints at Domaine de la Romanée-Conti and Jean-Jacques Confuron. "I was of two minds about coming home, but then I did come here—and thought, 'Doh, what were you thinking?' It's home. A place where your feet just start growing roots into the ground."

Rippon's thirty-seven acres of vineyards have been organic since the day Rolfe Mills planted the vines, and biodynamic since 2003. Talk to Nick Mills about that choice, and he'll note that vines don't metabolize minerals directly out of the soil, but instead use the microflora in the soil for that purpose; the soil has to be alive for that to happen. "Hence biodynamics. But also, working with vines is a meditative, spiritual thing."

Rippon makes over a dozen wines. All are superb, but there are two standouts to look for, both from the oldest vines on the property, whose roots have dug deep into the schist soil of the vineyard. The **Rippon Mature Vines Riesling** (\$\$–\$\$\$) is concentrated and stony, a kind of wake-up call to your palate— it has a purity that suggests the glacial waters of the lake that its vines overlook. The **Rippon Mature Vines Pinot Noir** (\$\$\$) is floral and full of concentrated blue and red fruit, but seemingly weightless; there are tannins here, but they glide past rather than grip your tongue.

PRODUCERS IN THIS CHAPTER

Felton Road

Greywacke

Kumeu River

Rippon

OTHER NEW ZEALAND PRODUCERS TO LOOK FOR

Bell Hill

Black Estate

Carrick

Dog Point Vineyard

Clos Henri

Huia

Millton Vineyards & Winery

Pyramid Valley

Quartz Reef

Seresin Estate

Two Paddocks

ARGENTINA AND CHILE

Finca Piedra Infinita Vineyard, Familia Zuccardi, Mendoza, Argentina

ARGENTINA

Argentina, like New Zealand, is one of those countries whose curse and blessing is to be identified with one extremely popular grape variety. Here it's Malbec. Argentine Malbec more or less saved the Argentine wine industry, but its ubiquitousness tends to obscure how much else is going on here, and how good some of that can be.

As with Chile and the United States, the first wine grapes arrived in Argentina in the 1500s courtesy of Spanish missionaries—if your plan is to convert a lot of people to Catholicism, you're going to need a lot of Communion wine. What they planted was mostly Listán Prieto and Muscat of Alexandria from the Canary Islands, which crossbred over time, adapted to their new environment, and became known as various forms of Criolla (País in Chile, Mission in the U.S.). It wasn't until the 1800s that more familiar French grapes arrived here, largely thanks to a French agricultural engineer named Michel Aimé Pouget, who had a mandate from the Argentine president in 1853 to source new grapes that would do well in Argentine soil. Among the varieties he planted was Malbec.

Short version: it did well. Argentina has about 75 percent of the world's Malbec (it long ago fell from favor in Bordeaux, its homeland). Almost 40 percent of Argentina's vines are Malbec, largely located in the country's most significant wine region, Mendoza. And wine drinkers love it—in Argentina's climate and soil, it thrives, making dark, robust wines, rich with flavor, that because of modest land and labor prices, remain impressively affordable. Nor is it limited to that: recently, a number of vintners have started exploring Malbec made in a less flamboyant, more restrained style (Sebastian Zuccardi at Zuccardi is at the forefront of this movement).

There are excellent wines in Argentina from other varieties as well, if one looks. Cabernet and Chardonnay, unquestionably, but also Pinot Noirs from Tupungato, the coolest part of Mendoza, and remote Patagonia; Torrontés from the high-altitude vineyards of Cafayete; even a few vintners exploring the possible potential of worthwhile wines from Criolla (this hasn't yet hit the excitement level of the País movement in Chile, but time will tell; also, Torrontés is technically a Criolla variety, but is well enough known that it really exists in its own category).

Organic viticulture has been slow to take off in Argentina, but that's changing. Currently about 23,000 of the country's 531,000 acres of vines are farmed organically (2022 statistics), but production is increasing rapidly.

BODEGA CHACRA • PATAGONIA

[organic / biodynamic / regenerative]

Piero Incisa della Rocchetta, the owner of Bodega Chacra, has a tattoo of a bee on his foot. Of course, a lot of people have tattoos. But most people don't have tattoos originally designed by Michelangelo for the coat of arms of one of their ancestors.

I noticed the bee tattoo one day when I was talking to him in the kitchen of his house in Patagonia, Argentina, where he lives when he's not in New York or, sometimes, Tuscany.

Incisa's reason for being in Patagonia is to make world-class Pinot Noir, but you quickly get the sense that another reason he's there is because Patagonia is about as far as you can possibly get from Tuscany, short of moving to Antarctica (and Patagonia isn't actually all that far from Antarctica). The day I was there, Incisa was cooking an al fresco lunch for the winery and vineyard workers at Chacra. This was a regular occurrence, and one that never could have happened back in Italy. There, a person with his background is far more constrained by the rules of society and class. He said as he cooked, "In Italy, once I went into the office at Sassicaia and said 'you,' to the estate manager." He meant that he'd used the familiar Italian "*tu*" rather than the more formal "*lei*." "I was reprimanded. I was told, no one in our family has *ever* said 'you' to an estate manager."

Incisa glanced out the window at some of his staff members, who were setting up tables on the lawn. "I'm not criticizing the Italian system," he said thoughtfully. "But it's not who I am."

Then who, exactly, is Piero Incisa della Rocchetta? Well, first he is an Incisa della Rocchetta, a scion of a noble Piedmontese family whose ancestry can be traced back to the eleventh century. Dante modeled characters on his relatives; Michelangelo, evidently, drew bees for them. Second, though he's distanced himself from it, his family owns Tenuta San Guido, the home of Sassicaia, the legendary Cabernet-based Tuscan red created by his grandfather Mario and shepherded to international acclaim by his uncle, the Marquis Nicolò Incisa della Rocchetta. Third, he's a charming guy—quick to laugh, philosophically inquisitive, and surprisingly modest. Fourth, and possibly foremost for him, he's someone making profound wine in the far, far reaches of Patagonia.

Often when people use the phrase "in the middle of nowhere," they're exaggerating. The Río Negro region of Patagonia, where Bodegas Chacra is located, really *is* the middle of nowhere. To get there, you fly to Buenos Aires, catch a four-hour connecting flight south to Neuquen, get in a car, drive for an hour down a two-lane highway, take a left, drive over gravel and dirt roads for another half hour, and then get out. What's here? The Río Negro itself; the corridor of fertile (more or less) land on either side of it that the English irrigated in the 1820s; the edges of the valley, lifting up to dun-colored, mesa-like cliffs; and then, on all sides, as Incisa says, "two thousand miles of nothing. Here you are really aware of how insignificant we are, how meaningless. We like to think we're so important, so indispensable, but we aren't."

Yet this remote part of Patagonia is a beautiful place. In the poplars surrounding his vineyard—planted throughout Río Negro because they grow extraordinarily fast and block the ever-present wind—flocks of vivid, yellow-headed parrots chatter maniacally at each other. The light is brilliant: Patagonia is so far south that the sun's luminosity razors the outlines of the trees against the sky. But it's not an easy place to make wine. In September, the winds can reach eighty miles per hour. Dust is omnipresent. Frost can wipe out whole crops. Plus, there are unexpected human problems: "The power goes out, the water goes out, they change the laws—you must be very persistent," Incisa says. It does seem that the Sisyphean nature of making wine here must actually hold some appeal for him. A challenge is a way of proving oneself. Sassicaia's shadow is substantial. Making his own wine in Tuscany would be impossible; making his own wine in Napa Valley or some other famous wine region would be predictable. Making wine in Patagonia? That's another story.

Not that long before he started Chacra, he says, an English entrepreneur bought vineyards not too far away. The man struggled along for a year, then, right during the middle of harvest, he vanished. Packed up, left the winery, and was gone. The workers had no idea what to do. The wine turned to vinegar in the tanks. "He simply disappeared. He just couldn't take it."

Incisa told me that story a few years before he himself slipped while standing on top of a winery tank. He fell fifteen feet to the stone floor of his winery, nearly killing himself. He broke multiple bones, was in a full-body cast for months, then in a wheelchair for several more months.

But he did not disappear. In fact, he says now that the accident helped clarify his life: it spurred him to leave his involvement with Sassicaia once and for all; it made him value himself in a different way. It gave him clarity, he says.

Making wine, if you come from a family with several hundred years of history doing exactly that, is never purely practical. Nor is it purely artistic. For Incisa, the social and communal are a necessary part as well. He credits both his grandfather and his uncle for this: "What both of them gave me is the need to understand the privilege you have, and the necessity of being in service to others." Thanks to this, Chacra feels as much a village as it is a winery. When he arrived, Incisa recalls, he had employees who lived in mud houses. Now many of them have their own farms. Call it another white-guy savior story, sure, but the net result is that a good number of people here aren't living in mud houses anymore.

"When I first came here, nothing made sense. It was nothing like what I was used to," Incisa says, looking out at the rows of vines, and the cliffs at the edge of the valley. In the foreground some of the staff are chucking wood into the outdoor clay oven that every Argentine farmhouse has. Empanadas will go in as soon as it's hot enough. "What I've learned is that in the end, it's this place and these guys," Incisa says. "Not me. I'm really irrelevant here. But if I can remove the anxiety of someone, a father, who's going to be kicked out of his home with his three-year-old daughter and wife, if I can give him work . . . that's better than any drug, better than any money."

Incisa farms Chacra's vineyards according to biodynamic practices. Winemaking follows a minimal intervention approach. He's also planted more than thirty-seven thousand trees on his land, more than four thousand lavender and rose bushes, and put in two hundred beehives. "And biodiversity came back," he says. "Raptors, armadillos, ladybugs, hares, all of it."

The Bodega Chacra Pinot Noirs are exemplary. The **Bodega Chacra Cinquenta y Cinco ($$$)** is fragrant and silky and comes from a single vineyard planted in 1954. **Treinta y Dos ($$$)**, beautifully textured with complex berry flavors, is again from a single small vineyard, this one planted in 1932. Then there's also a more transparent, floral version of Treinta y Dos that's made without sulfur, **Chacra Sin Azufre ($$)**. Incisa describes it as "an exercise to see how the wine would be if we never looked at an analytical sheet from the winery. We smell it, we taste it, we touch it—we do everything for it based on our senses alone." **Barda ($$)**, the least expensive Pinot Noir, is moderate in alcohol, red-fruited and bright. A lovely red wine, it also has the additional virtue of being much easier to find than the others. Incisa's latest project is a taut, minerally **Chardonnay ($$$)**, made together with Burgundy superstar Jean-Marc Roulot.

FAMILIA ZUCCARDI • MENDOZA

[organic]

Familia Zuccardi successfully rode the Argentine Malbec wave from the 1990s into the mid-2000s. But Sebastián Zuccardi, who joined the winery in 2002, found himself growing more and more dissatisfied with the *nature* of the wines they were making.

"I've made two good decisions in

my life," he says. "The first was that when I started, I decided to study viticulture. The second decision was that when I finished university, for seven years I did harvest with my family, but then I did harvests in Spain, in Portugal, in the U.S. And I came back to my father and said, 'We have to talk more about the *place*. That has to be our focus.' He said, 'Are you sure?' But this kind of change only happens in family companies. You can make decisions that aren't driven by shareholders or stock prices."

Sebastián's related decision was to try and pull Malbec back from the style that had popularized it around

---

"If you want to do less, you need to know more."
—Sebastián Zuccardi

---

the world: big, dark, almost overbearing wines, more inclined to bludgeon the palate into submission than seduce it. "This was around 2014. The idea of a great Malbec then was a super-

concentrated red, high in alcohol, lots of oak. But really ripe fruit all tastes the same. So, in 2014, I said, 'No more!' I wanted to talk about texture. 'I'll do a Malbec,' I thought, 'without sweetness and with a focus on texture.'"

That was his Concreto Malbec, a forerunner in a now-substantial movement among a group of younger Argentine winemakers to reclaim Malbec as a terroir-expressive, elegant variety. "To put change on the map you have to work together," he says. "We all have a great relationship. We share what we know, and *then* we compete."

The Uco Valley, where Sebastián concentrated his efforts, is a cool, high-altitude area. The wines there naturally have more nerve, more tension, brighter acidity and less hefty fruit. Sebastián also pulled back on the use of oak. "When I stopped buying barrels, my father said, 'Great! We're going to save a lot of money.'" He laughs. "But . . . no. Because I put all that money back into the vineyards."

Zuccardi's "A" and "Q" wines are affordable, regional bottlings that are impeccably made and hard to resist on a casual weeknight. The Poligonos wines—there are several—are the next step up, in

essence the equivalent of Burgundian village wines. The **Familia Zuccardi Poligonos Cabernet Franc San Pablo** (**$$**), for example, from vineyards near the town of San Pablo in the Uco Valley, is full of warm red fruit with green peppercorn nuances. The **Poligonos Malbec San Pablo ($$)**, with its black tea aromas, is precise and peppery.

Zuccardi's **Fosil Chardonnay ($$)** is one of the best Chardonnays of Argentina, and comes from a vineyard at thirty-two hundred feet, right up against the Andes. Lime zest aromas, bright peach and lime flavors, thrilling focus—it feels like drinking that cold, intense Andean sunlight. **Concreto Malbec ($$)** has, as Zuccardi had intended, great texture—it's a statement about what Malbec can be, rather than what it so often is. "For me it's blood, dark red fruit, rust, not sweetness, and then that dryness on the tongue," Sebastián says. "When you grow Malbec on limestone, as we do for this wine, you get this dry feeling—not hard tannins, more like licking a stone."

Zuccardi's *finca* wines are the apogee of the project, the equivalent of premier and grand cru vineyards (and priced accordingly). **Finca Piedra Infinita ($$$)** is a profound Malbec. "It means 'infinite stones,'" Sebastián says. "The vineyard is extremely stony—*huge* stones. I took out a thousand truckloads of stones in order to plant it, and those are what we used to build our winery." There's dark fruit here, and mocha notes, but the wine is powerful without being fat or sweet.

He also makes a series of natural wines at his family's Santa Julia winery, which itself has over 790 certified organic acres of vines. "I wanted to make some natural wines but in an intelligent way," Sebastián says (a statement that won't endear him to the natty wine clique). "In a sense the natural movement is like biodynamics, in that for many years, agriculture lost communication with the land, and biodynamics responded to that."

The Santa Julia natural wines use no sulfur during production, no manufactured yeasts, no filtering, and no fining—as little intervention as possible. The **Santa Julia Blanco Natural ($)** is a Torrontés with seven hours of skin contact. "You need that, because you need character—the taste of Torrontés is in the skins," Sebastián says. The **Santa Julia Natural Malbec "El Burro" ($)** has a slight but not unappealing reductive funk, and punchy blue- and blackberry fruit; it tastes direct and unedited. Regarding natural winemaking, and winemaking in general for that matter, Sebastián says, "We often taste every single one of our wines twice a day during fermentation, and then say, 'do nothing.' But to say 'do nothing' is a decision itself, of course."

PRODUCERS PROFILED IN THIS CHAPTER

Bodega Chacra   Familia Zuccardi

OTHER ARGENTINA PRODUCERS TO LOOK FOR

Andeluz	Passionate Wines
Domaine Bousquet	PerSe
Ernesto Catena	SuperUco
Catena Zapata	Ver Sacrum
Escala Humana	Zorzal

CHILE

Chile is dotted with vineyards throughout its lengthy snake-like sprawl down the western side of South America. The country is exceptionally narrow and exceptionally long—only 236 miles across at its widest point, but more than 2,600 miles from north to south. Vines thrive along most of that length, from the desertlike Elqui Valley in the far north to the cold Malleco Valley in the far south, planted on land between the peaks of the Andes and the endless Pacific Ocean.

Much of that vineyard land, more than five hundred thousand acres, is devoted to the wines Chile made its international reputation with: inexpensive Cabernets and Merlots made by large wine companies. That situation stretches back to the late 1800s, when Chile first made its presence known internationally in wine—the country has never been affected by phylloxera, so while Europe's vineyards were being decimated by the root louse, Chile could provide wine. (The concentration of ownership starts there, too; in that era, a handful of families owned the entire wine industry in Chile.) That prosperous moment dwindled as European vineyards were replanted, and for much of the century Chilean wine was in a kind of doldrums of indifferent farming, antiquated winemaking, and political turmoil.

The 1990s, post-Pinochet, saw Chile return to the world stage; being a provider of endless amounts of good-quality, affordable Cabernet, particularly, was an excellent role to play (nearly a third of Chile's vines are Cabernet Sauvignon). But that success as a value-wine source has obscured some of the more interesting aspects of Chilean wine. Cool-climate regions—whether northerly, like the Elqui Valley and Limarí, or immediately coastal, like the Casablanca Valley and the San Antonio Valley—can produce thrillingly precise Sauvignon Blancs and Syrahs that suggest the spicy savor of the northern Rhône (and, in a few instances, very good Pinot Noir). The far south—Maule, Itata, and Bio Bio—has seen a boom in young vintners exploring the wealth of dry-farmed, old-vine material there (many working with less interventionist winemaking approaches). Groups such as VIGNO, a collection of vintners focused on old-vine Carignan vineyards, and Almaule, similarly focused on old-vine País, have sprung up there as well. As is often the case, if you're looking for excitement, head to the fringes.

Despite Chile's generally dry climate, organic viticulture has been slow to develop here; it's probably a safe assumption that the dominance of large-scale industrial wine production in the country has been a damper on it. Roughly 7 percent of the country's vineyards are farmed organically, though that number has been rising. There is also a small but growing number of biodynamic pioneers, for instance Alvaro Espinoza at Antiyal.

ANTIYAL • MAIPO

[certified organic / certified biodynamic]

In 1996, though Alvaro Espinoza had been one of Chile's most acclaimed winemakers for many years, he wanted to make his own wine, one that would express both his own vision and the character of the Maipo Valley. He also intended that the vines for it would be farmed with organic, low-intervention agriculture (in a country where vast vineyards of conventionally farmed vines are common). That was the start of Antiyal, its name taken from a Mapuche word that means "sons of the sun." At the time, in Chile, organic and biodynamic viticulture were complete unknowns.

Espinoza has also focused on biodiversity, from the almond trees and cacti that dot his property to the chickens, horses, alpacas, sheep, and goats that are part of the farm as well. All the manure he needs for compost comes from his own animals; his feeling is that industrial agriculture has disrupted the natural balance of farming; crops and animals should both play valuable roles, each helping provide life to the other. His fifty-acre property sits in the foothills of the Andes, in a small valley at about twenty-six hundred feet altitude; the twenty-five acres of vines are planted to Cabernet Sauvignon, Carménère, Syrah, Petit Verdot, and Garnacha.

Espinoza's affordable Pura Fe wines all come from his estate, just as the pricier Antiyal wines do. The **Pura Fe Carménère ($$)** expresses the berry and black pepper nature of the variety, with characteristic green tobacco accents. **Pura Fe Cabernet Sauvignon ($$)** is riper and softer, its herbal notes shading more toward eucalyptus. **Antiyal Kuyen ($$)** is a concentrated, black-plummy blend of Syrah, Cabernet Sauvignon, Carménère, and Petit Verdot, ending on balsamic herb notes. **Antiyal ($$$)**, Espinoza's top wine, is usually about half Carménère, together with Cabernet and Syrah. It's powerful and filled with ripe red fruit, but there's fresh acidity there, too, keeping it lifted and vibrant.

J. BOUCHON • MAULE

[certified sustainable / organic]

Go down to the river's edge outside the small Maule Valley town of Mingre, and you'll see grapevines crawling up the trees. Go during harvest time, and you'll see workers on ladders harvesting those grapes. No one planted these vines. "We have a theory," Julio Bouchon says, "that birds ate the seeds from grapes and deposited them into the creek that flows down from the forest. Or else old prunings were tossed into the forest. All my life I saw these grapes hanging from the trees, but I never thought I would make wine from them. But this is our País Salvaje. It was also the first time we made wine in a natural style, and my father asked, 'Julio, do you think we'll be able to sell a single bottle of this wine?'"

País Salvaje is now the Bouchons' best-selling wine in the U.S., which says something about Julio Bouchon's vision (and also the changing, and much more adventurous, tastes of wine drinkers today).

Overall Bouchon makes a point of working exclusively with old vines, all in Chile's southern Maule region. "In 2013 we started rediscovering these vines that were abandoned. It's a sad story in some ways, but at the same time there are a lot of farmers in our area with beautiful, beautiful vineyards—farmed in the local way, just family farming for local consumption. These guys, you can rescue them, and rescue their vines by buying their grapes at a fair price. Young people here have been abandoning the region for the cities, because they can't survive on the money they get for bulk wine. But if you pay them enough, they *can* survive."

Bouchon is part of a movement of Chilean vintners working with old vines in under-recognized regions like Maule, often in noninterventionist or natural ways. He isn't trying to make first-growth Bordeaux here, or grand cru Burgundy. His wines are priced affordably, in fact for far less than they should be, given what they offer. But Bouchon is fine with that. "I think of wine as a party," he says. "Some wines, it's a party for lawyers, they're in black tie. Some wines, it's more a party for gypsies, they're all in colorful clothes, dancing. I like being at the second party."

The Bouchon family farms 395 acres of vines. The two principal vineyards are farmed organically, and a third, smaller one is sustainably farmed (these are not certified organic yet, but the Bouchons are working toward it). Bouchon works in an adobe-walled, clay-floored winery that dates from the early 1900s, and his winemaking approach leans toward low-intervention practices, though not in an extreme way. He makes three wines from the País (or Listán Prieto) grape. The **J. Bouchon País Salvaje Blanco ($)** is a copper-hued white, which is odd because País is a red grape; Bouchon found some of these wine vines were producing much lighter clusters than the rest, and decided to vinify them separately. His regular **País Salvaje ($)**, on the other hand, is red: all crunchy berries and zesty acidity. The strawberry-scented **País Viejo** ($$) comes from hundred-year-old vines growing in an actual vineyard, as opposed to in trees. And **Canto Sur** ($$) is a spicy, juicy blend of Carménère, Carignan, and old-vine País.

KINGSTON FAMILY VINEYARDS • SAN ANTONIO VALLEY

[organic]

Ask Courtney Kingston whether Pinot Noir is temperamental in Chile, and she'll say, as a winemaker would, "Oof. Yes. But it's also so expressive."

Kingston Family Vineyards, in Casablanca, has made its name on Pinot Noir. This focus wasn't originally in the plans. The family started here in the early 1900s, when Carl John Kingston left Michigan to prospect in Chile for copper and gold. Zero luck with that, but he did find a promising cattle ranch twelve miles from the Pacific. Today, while the view from the winery is of vines, Kingston says, "over the hill there are still thirteen hundred cows being milked twice a day."

It was her idea to plant vines, and to plant Pinot, specifically—the cool Casablanca hillsides seemed potentially ideal for it. (Her family's response was "Oh god, not another cheddar cheese project," a reference to an ill-fated plan of her grandfather's some years back.) Kingston's feeling was that if they could get Pinot right, it would get them off the "standard variety carousel," as she puts it, of inexpensive, mass-produced, Chilean Cabernets and Chardonnays that fill supermarket shelves. And, it turns out, she was correct.

Kingston farms 350 acres of organic vines. While Pinot Noir is the focus, the winery's **Cariblanco Sauvignon Blanc** ($) is a classic rendition of Casablanca Sauvignon, crisp and bright with passion fruit and citrus peel character. Syrah also benefits from the cool-climate terroir here. **Lucero** (\$\$), the more affordable, is peppery and smoky; **Bayo Oscuro** (\$\$\$), produced only in top vintages, is darker, more substantial, powerful. Finally, two Pinot Noirs, both at the top of the game in Chile. **Tobiano** (\$\$), all wild strawberry and herbs, is an easy-drinking pleasure. **Alazan** (\$\$\$), the top wine, shows the potential of Chilean cool-climate Pinot with its leafy dark berry flavors and layered, savory intensity.

DE MARTINO • MAIPO

[organic]

"Before 2010, we worked like all the other wineries," Sebastián De Martino says. "But in 2010 we decided to change—because we didn't *like* the wine we were making, honestly. I had none of our own wine in my cellar." The wines the De Martinos had been making up to that point fit the mold for Chilean wines of that era: soft, sweet, ripe, ink-dark, oaky, extracted. "Now we have no new barrels, no manufactured yeasts, some wines in *tinajas* [amphorae], and we've changed a *lot* of the management in the vineyard."

De Martino was founded by Pietro De Martino, who emigrated to Chile from Italy's Abruzzo region in the early 1900s. De Martino was in the construction business, but he fell ill; his doctors suggested retiring to the country. That inspired him to buy the property where De Martino now stands, south of Santiago in the town of Isla de Maipo. De Martino never saw his project succeed. He moved back to Italy and the winery was semi-abandoned until after World War II, when his nephew completed his work. Jump forward, and De Martino was an early adopter of organic viticulture in Chile, starting in 1998; it was also the first Chilean winery to become carbon neutral, in 2009.

De Martino's most fascinating wines are from the Legado project, which Sebastián De Martino started a few years back, and a line of single-vineyard wines from small growers scattered around southern Chile.

"Maipo is good for Carménère and Cabernet," De Martino says, "but I was interested in more than that. The idea was to take the right grapes from wherever they might grow, and bring them here to be vinified." As a result, he says, he drives more than forty-five thousand miles a year, working with small farmers under long-term contracts. He's also a member of VIGNO, the association of Carignan producers in the far south Maule Valley.

The **De Martino Legado Limarí Valley Chardonnay ($$)** suggests lime blossoms and citrus honey; it's a very alluring white. The **Legado Maipo Carménère ($$)**, from a vineyard near the winery, is herbal and savory. "If you don't get that tobacco and spice in Carménère, it's overripe," Sebastián says. "And if you wait for black fruit, Carménère has no personality and no acid." The **Legado Cabernet Sauvignon ($$)** is similar in style, toasty-smoky with a character recalling fire-roasted peppers and tangy red currant notes. "Very Maipo Valley," Sebastián says. To push the flavor envelope, look for the **Alto de Piedras Maipo Carménère ($$–$$$)**, which suggests toasted Indian spices overlaid on red fruit. It's almost always very low in alcohol. The **Limávida Maule Old Vines Field Blend ($$$)** is Malbec and a host of other varieties all planted in 1945. The aroma is a swirl of strawberry, cherry, earth, and leather; on the palate it's plush and dense, but somehow not at all heavy. The **Las Cruces Cachapoal Old Vines Field Blend ($$)** is also unusual: a balancing act between the darkness of Malbec and the herbaceous character of Carménère, tangy and tannic on the finish.

PEDRO PARRA Y FAMILIA • ITATA VALLEY

[sustainable / organic]

Pedro Parra is one of the most acclaimed soil scientists in Chile, if not the entire world of wine. But he had no actual plan to make wine himself. "I trained as a forest engineer. My family never drank wine. *I* never drank wine. And in university, my big interest was movies—except that at that time in Chile, there was no way to study movies. I was a musician, too, but that's not easy, either. So at age twenty-five, I was a guy who had nothing. But I got a scholarship to Montepellier in France to study geology, and one lucky day, I was sent to the campus in Paris, where they were studying terroir. I worked there for three or four months, and what that brought to me is this idea of holisticity, of all these elements coming together in wine."

This led to a PhD on terroir, and when he returned to Chile, Parra started making his own wines, ones, he hoped, that would have energy, minerality, freshness, and complexity. "At the

---

"I'm a scientist. But look: science is very square. It's two plus two equals four. And wine is never two plus two equals four."
—Pedro Parra

---

end of the day, the only place I found enough character and personality and tension in the wines was Itata. The only problem was that Itata was considered by everybody to produce the worst of the worst of Chilean wines."

Itata, in Chile's far south, was first planted in the 1500s, when Spanish conquistadors came and conquered the land. It's five to six hours away from Santiago, and its weather is entirely different from that of Maipo or Cachapoal: cloudy, humid, and cold. "The terroir it's most similar to is Barolo," Parra says. "The Barolo topography, with the granite soil of St.-Joseph or Cornas." There's no tradition of Bordeaux varieties here, either. Everything is País, bush vines, or more recently planted Cinsault. For most of its existence, Itata made local wines, sold around the region's small farming towns or drunk by the families who made them.

It took Parra several years to find the exact terroir he was looking for, and when he did, it took several more years to get his wines to express what he had in mind. "Pedro Parra y Familia started in 2013," he says. "That wine was undrinkable. In 2014, the fruit was better, but my winemaking was horrible, so that was undrinkable, too. I finally got some direction in 2015, and 2016 was OK, but 2017 was the real change, because I got control of the farming." For Parra the farming is the center of the story, and the soil is the soul of the farming. His deep understanding of the underground aspects of terroir has driven his consulting career (he has clients all over the world). One part of his focus is a terroir's geological character; another, the life in the soil itself. "The microbiology of that soil connects the vine's roots with the minerals in the soil," Parra explains. "It's like with music. If you don't have a connection, you can't play an electric instrument. If you are a lousy viticulturist, if you spray shit in your vineyards, you kill the microbiology. And if you do that, you kill the connection. No transmission, no minerality, no tension, no life, goodbye."

Parra's most affordable wines are his floral, wild strawberry–suggestive **Pedro Parra y Familia Vinista País ($–$$)**, the more structured **Pencopolitano Cinsault/País ($–$$)**, and his leafy, earthy, red-fruited **Imaginador Cinsault ($–$$)**, all of which hover around $20 a bottle. About Imaginador's name he says, "If you don't have imagination, you don't *move* in wine. Wine is about not having fear, and having imagination to do something different."

His single-vineyard wines, of which there are several, are mostly named after jazz musicians, for instance the minerally, incisive **Hub Cinsault ($$)**, named after the great jazz trumpeter Freddie Hubbard, and the precise, complex **Monk Cinsault ($$)**, which really does taste rather like Thelonius Monk's music sounds. But even if Parra does make his own wines, please don't call him a winemaker: "I hate that word, 'winemaker.' A guy who makes wine should be someone who knows his terroir, who knows how to play its music. That's all."

PRODUCERS PROFILED IN THIS CHAPTER

Antiyal

J. Bouchon

Kingston Family Vineyards

De Martino

Pedro Parra y Familia

OTHER CHILE PRODUCERS TO LOOK FOR

Emiliana

Garage Wine Co.

P.S. Garcia

Koyle

Laberinto

Luis Antoine Luyt

Matetic

Montesecano

Odfjell

Viñedos de Alcohuaz

SOUTH AFRICA

Hamilton Russell Vineyards, Hemel-en-Aarde

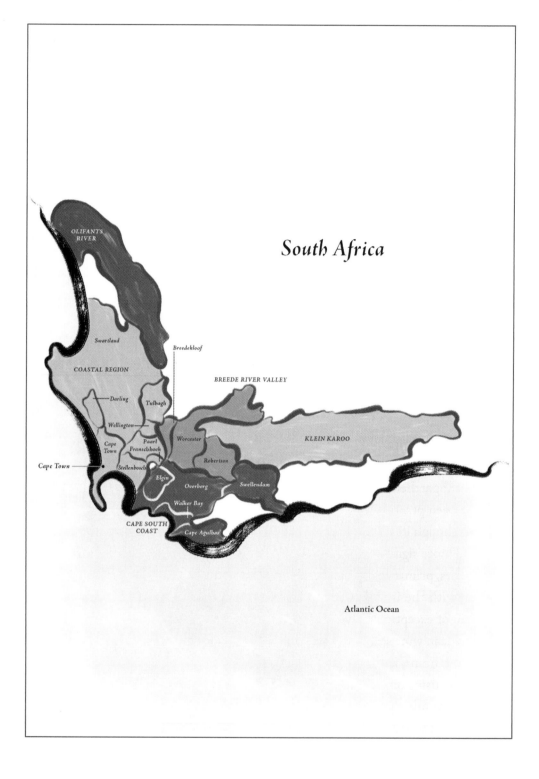

OLIFANTS
RIVER

South Africa

Swartland

Breedekloof

COASTAL REGION

BREEDE RIVER VALLEY

Darling

Tulbagh

Wellington

Worcester

KLEIN KAROO

Cape
Town

Paarl
Franschhoek

Cape Town

Stellenbosch

Robertson

Elgin

Overberg

Swellendam

Walker Bay

CAPE SOUTH
COAST

Cape Agulhas

Atlantic Ocean

South Africa's winemaking history stretches back to the 1650s, longer by a good stretch than that of the United States or Australia, thanks to a decision by the Dutch East India Company to establish a way station on the Cape of Good Hope. The idea was to resupply spice trade ships there with fresh provisions; the first governor of the Cape also had the thought to plant grape vines. Not very successfully—the Dutch have never been known for winemaking—but plant he did, and very slowly a wine culture came into being.

The twentieth-century history of South Africa's wine was marred by the country's racist apartheid policies from 1948 until the early 1990s (though segregation had long been practiced before that). Today, as apartheid recedes in time's rearview mirror—though its effects linger—South African wine is becoming internationally more and more significant. That visibility has been helped by a generation of young winemakers, primarily associated with the Swartland region north of Stellenbosch. Starting with the first Swartland Revolution event in 2010, a kind of multi-day bacchanal of exceptional new wines (and lots of partying), word spread that a new South African wine sensibility was on the rise: making wines without added yeasts, acids, and tannins, and without the use of technology like reverse osmosis to adjust alcohols; focusing on old-vine vineyards full of stellar Chenin Blanc, Syrah, Cinsault, and a bevy of other grapes (leaning heavily on Rhône varieties).

That's not to say there isn't excellent wine elsewhere in South Africa. Stellenbosch, spreading out from the city of Cape Town, is probably the country's premier wine region; producers like Hamilton Russell and others have long made intriguing reds and whites from cooler regions like Hemel-en-Aarde and Elgin; and there's a nascent natural wine movement as well, from young, irreverent talents like Craig Hawkins at Testalonga.

The wine industry as a whole has been extremely active in preserving biodiversity, establishing the Biodiversity & Wine Initiative to protect native species, in terms of both plant and animal life; there's also a sustainable program known as IPW (Integrated Production of Wine). Certified participants can use the "Integrity & Sustainability Certified" seal on their bottles—a strip of paper that winemakers have been known to refer to as the "bus ticket."

HAMILTON RUSSELL VINEYARDS • HEMEL-EN-AARDE

[certified sustainable / organic]

Anthony and Olive Hamilton Russell make some of South Africa's finest Pinot Noirs and Chardonnays from their estate in the cool Hemel-en-Aarde valley. Their vines lie a short distance from the Indian Ocean, near the old fishing village of Hermanus, on one of South Africa's most southerly sites, and that coastal proximity shows in the brisk snap of energy and taut focus in their wines.

Hamilton Russell was founded in 1975 by Anthony's father, a wine-loving advertising executive, at a time when South Africa was isolated from the rest of the world thanks to the apartheid regime's racially segregationist policies. Anthony, though, left South Africa to study business with no plans to ever return—he loathed the South African government's racist policies. But when Nelson Mandela was released from prison in 1990 and the Nationalist Party and apartheid crumbled, he came back, started working on the estate, and took over running it in 1991.

At that time the winery was planted mainly with Bordeaux varieties; it was also marginally profitable at best. "It seemed a bit of a financial albatross, and Anthony's father was getting tired of donating money to it," Olive says. "So, in 1994, Anthony bought it from him." Anthony also felt that the varieties his father had planted weren't suited to the site; after extensive soil research, he located 128 acres that were similar geologically to Burgundy's Côte de Nuits, and grafted them over to Pinot Noir and Chardonnay.

The Hamilton Russells have been organic since 2014, though they are not certified. "There are too many hoops to jump through," Olive says. "And we're not organic as a selling point; we're organic because it's what we want to do. We love that piece of earth we're on. So we hope that in one hundred or two hundred years someone—ideally our family, but someone—will still be making beautiful wine from it. And if we were to keep depleting the soil, that won't happen." They've also moved to no-till viticulture. "It stops erosion, and we get more water penetration," she says. "The pros far outweigh the cons, we've found. Though it is aging our viticulturist, Johan, very rapidly!"

The Hamilton Russells' South African wines set an early benchmark for Chardonnay and Pinot Noir there, and while they are now rivaled by some other producers, no one has surpassed them. The **Hamilton Russell Hemel-en-Aarde Estate Chardonnay ($$)** has a pretty nose of toast and stone fruit, with tart citrus flavors. There's a slight flinty hint of reduction, too, but it's subtle. Olive Hamilton-Russell says, "There's more and more a trend in the New World to ramp reduction up, to the point where it masks site. That's not what we're after." The **Hemel-en-Aarde Estate Pinot Noir ($$$)** is intensely savory, all spice and tea-leaf notes, with cranberry and raspberry flavors underneath. "In South Africa we get spice and structure effortlessly," Olive says. It's a wine that ages beautifully over time.

The couple also make two Oregon wines, from sustainable purchased fruit. The **Hamilton Russell Maple Grove Willamette Valley Chardonnay ($$$)** comes from the Maple Grove Vineyard near Monmouth, and is fragrant with the scent of lime blossoms; it's fuller and rounder than the South African wine. The **Zena Crown Eola-Amity Hills Pinot Noir ($$$)** is similarly richer in style than its South African counterpart, though still elegant and lifted.

MULLINEUX FAMILY WINES • SWARTLAND

[sustainable]

Chris and Andrea Mullineux grew up ten thousand miles apart, he in Cape Town, and she in the San Francisco Bay Area. But they both studied winemaking, and crossed paths in the South of France. "I was at Château Pibarnon in Bandol and she was in Châteauneuf-du-Pape, and we met at a wine festival," Chris says. (Basically the wine-world equivalent of a rom-com meet-cute.) He went back to South Africa to make wine, and needed help; Andrea came and worked with him for three years. They started dating, got engaged, "and a month before our wedding we said, 'Why not start our own thing?'"

That was 2007. A winemaking friend had told them about the up-and-coming Swartland region, north of Stellenbosch. Neither had family in the wine business, nor did they have much money, so they leased vineyards, and finally in 2013 got a bank loan to buy their own land.

"Swartland is intense," Chris says. "If you come during harvest, it's dry, it's hot, it's sunny—not an easy place to be. You'd think the wines would be monsters as a result, but they aren't. They're graceful, with freshness and energy." Where that starts, he says, is in the vineyards. "For that character, you need to work naturally. Don't feed the vines with fertilizer, don't use herbicides between the rows. We've got a dry climate, so moisture is critical. But building life in the soil is the way to do that, with cover crops, mulches, composts." The Mullineuxs keep a good portion of their land planted with fynbos, the native scrub of South Africa. "Corridors of fynbos, as an insectary—it's home to ladybugs and wasps and other beneficial insects. If we'd just planted vines, I'm sure we would have had an outbreak of something by now."

They live on the farm, and make their wines there. It's a good life, albeit sometimes isolated. But then, those in search of excitement can always head into Malmesbury, Swartland's main town. "If you need to get your tractor repaired, or something welded, it's a great place," Chris says. "Though honestly, other than that, there's not a lot there."

Of the baker's dozen wines the couple make, there are a few standouts. The rich but focused **Mullineux Family Wines Old Vines White ($$)** is Chenin Blanc from seventy-plus-year-old vines, blended with Clairette, Semillon Gris, and Macabeo. Their **Roundstone Vineyard Chenin Blanc ($$)** comes from younger vines at their home vineyard; it's stony and precise, with orchard fruit flavors. The spicy **Kloof Street Rouge ($)** comes from an affordable line of wines the Mullineuxs started a few years back. "But no compromises on the fruit or the winemaking," Chris says. The flagship **Mullineaux Family Vineyards Syrah ($$)** is full of red and blue fruit, ripe but balanced. "When I taste this wine, it's like looking at the whole of Swartland through the lens of Syrah," Chris says. The **Schist Syrah ($$$)** is powerful, with dark fruit and cracked pepper notes. "In Swartland you get a lovely fullness in red wines, but what really defines them are the tannins: firm but never rough, almost a chalky, sophisticated character." The **Granite Syrah ($$$)**, by contrast, is linear and savory, with higher acidity and more red fruit.

TESTALONGA · SWARTLAND

[organic / natural]

"My vineyards are surrounded by mountains," Craig Hawkins says. "I keep the natural vegetation, I keep bees on the farm and make honey. In the end you're planting a vine to make wine, and the vine has to be number one, but it's crucial to find a balance with everything else. I can't say that the natural vegetation I've preserved results in better wine, but it matters to me. That's enough."

Hawkins is part of the nascent natural wine movement in South Africa, making skin-contact white wines together with his wife, Carla, in the northern mountains of Swartland. He currently farms about ten acres of vines, with plans to expand to twenty-three or so, and purchases fruit from several local old vineyards. "We farm organically," he says. "We always have and we always will." His winemaking follows the general blueprint of the natural wine movement: no additives or corrections, no fining, only native yeast fermentations, minimal to no sulfur.

"I'm not from a winemaking family," he says. "I got into wine—well, through drinking, really!" But after university, he worked as a cellar hand for Eben Sadie at Sadie Family Wines, "then worked at wineries around Europe for a while." Back in South Africa, he started his own winery with Carla in 2008, initially inspired to make skin-contact white wines (or-ange wines, if you'd rather). "I'd fallen in love with the skin-contact wines of Georgia and Friuli, and when I got back to S.A., I looked around and said, 'Well, where are they?'" They weren't anywhere, he discovered; no one in South Africa was mining that particular vein. "So I thought I'd bet-ter make them myself."

His initial efforts were aggressively tannic, "but I've changed my approach somewhat. It's easy to make a very hoppy beer, for instance. You just throw hops at it. And all it tastes like is hops. It's easy to do that with skin-contact whites, too, which is what I was doing initially. But done right, skin contact can give you lift, a kind of complexity and playfulness at the same time."

The **Testalonga El Bandito Skin ($$)** is fourteen-karat gold in hue, with light cheese-rind and dried herb notes, earthy flavors, and zippy acidity. (Hawkins is a fan of acidity: "My father was an insur-ance broker, and I learned a lot about insurance from him. All good acidity is like an insurance policy for your wine.") His **El Bandito Cortez ($$)** is apple-pineapple tangy, full-bodied, and also driven by that sharp, focused tartness. "I got these grapes originally in exchange for doing pruning work in the vineyard," Hawkins recalls.

PRODUCERS PROFILED IN THIS CHAPTER

Hamilton Russell Vineyards   Testalonga
Mullineux Family Wines

OTHER SOUTH AFRICA PRODUCERS TO LOOK FOR

Alheit

Anysbos

A. A. Badenhorst

Boschkloof

City on a Hill

Craven Wines

David & Nadia

Glenelly

Intellego

Joostenberg

Kanonkop

J. H. Meyer

Miles Mossop

Reyneke

Sadie Family Wines

Sijnn

Thistle and Weed

Lelie van Saron

ACKNOWLEDGMENTS

First off, a massive thanks to everyone at Scribner, particularly to my extraordinary editor, Kara Watson, but also to everyone else who has helped see this project through: Jason Chappell, Davina Mock Maniscalco, Lauren Dooley, Brian Belfiglio, Georgia Brainard, and Joie Asuquo. (And a big thanks to Roz Lippel, who had the crazy idea that publishing more than two hundred thousand words about these wines would be a good idea in the first place.)

Without the help of David Black (an amazing agent who also loves wine—how rare is that?) this book would not be a book. It wouldn't even have been a *proposal* for a book. Many thanks, my friend. And to everyone else at the David Black Agency, who navigate so serenely the jagged shores of book deals.

Kristen Green, thank you for your ongoing, insightful help. A book no one knows about doesn't stand much of a chance.

I've had a home at *Food & Wine* for many years now, with far too many great colleagues past and present to call out without making an already weighty book even more so. Still, I'm indebted to editor in chief Hunter Lewis for his constant support, as well as to former editor in chief Dana Cowin, who hired me twice: if that's not also support, what is? A big thanks also to *Travel + Leisure*'s incomparable Jacqui Gifford. Melanie Hansche, how you manage to run a brilliant restaurant and be *F&W*'s deputy editor at the same time, I have no idea; regular administrations of excellent Riesling seem to me the only possible explanation. Karen Shimizu, you are the calm center of an always enjoyable but often frantic editorial storm. The *Food & Wine* drinks team—Oset Babür-Winter and Lucy Simon—definitely needs a shout-out, because they make life there a continual joy. And Steve Dveris, how many years has it been now?

To May Parsey, mapmaker extraordinaire, bravo! And thank you.

Every single winemaker and vigneron who took time out of their days to talk with me has my undying gratitude (I should note also that some of these interviews took place over the course of years, and have been condensed and edited for clarity). But a special thanks for going above and beyond to Youmna and Tony Asseily, Clare Carver, Valter Fissore and Nadia Cogno, Jason Haas, Jasmine and David Hirsch, Martin Foradori Hofstätter, Maria José López de Heredia, Steve and Jill Matthiasson, Alecia Moore, Pepe Raventós, Dan Petroski, and Baron Ziegler. Loïc Lamy, thank you for hours of wonderful companionship in Burgundy, and please make more wine so I can put you in the next edition (God willing, there will be one).

Without the help of many remarkable importers, there's no chance I would have been able to taste all the wines I needed to here, nor speak to everyone I needed to reach. Again, the list is way too long, but a special thanks to Xavier Barlier and Cyprien Roy of MMD USA, Stephen Bitterolf at Vom Boden, Bethany Burke of Taub Family Selections, Molly Choi at Broadbent Selections, John Coyle at T. Edward Wines, Catherine Cutier and Greg Doody of Vineyard Brands, Alyssa Faden at Vintus, Claire Gibbs at Wilson Daniels, Sunil Khanna at Hand Picked Selections, Marilyn Krieger, Suzie Kukaj, Charles Lazzara at Volio Imports, Jenny Lefcourt, Cat Miles at The Sorting Table, Korinne Munson at Winebow Imports, Michael Nelson at Grand Cru Selections, Monica Nogues of Think Global Wines, Neal Rosenthal, Victor Schwartz of VOS Selections, Jane Scott at Santa Margherita USA, Harmon and Michael Skurnik (and with additional thanks for videoing your winemaker presentations, a lifesaver when I could not—as with Jacky Blot—decipher some of my own notes), Eric Solomon, André Tamers of De Maison Selections, Paul Wasserman, Billy Weiss of North Berkeley Imports, and Kirk Wille of Loosen Bros. Thanks as well to the invaluable resources at the Oregon Wine History Archive at Linfield University for additional interview material with Doug Tunnell, and for several winemakers' recollections of Jimi Brooks.

Similarly, without the friendship of many people in the wine (and writing) business over the years, I would have never learned enough to even contemplate writing this damn thing. So, ongoing affection and thanks to Lara Abbott, Charles Antin, Nancy Bean, Stephanie Caraway, Jean-Louis Carbonnier, Alyson Careaga (for help and friendship beyond measure), Melissa Clark, Mikayla Cohen, Brie Conway, Tali

Dalbaha, Vicki Denig, Christine Deussen, Tony DiDio, Alice Feiring (for being a pal but also for inimitable natty wine knowledge), Odila Galer-Noel, Anthony Giglio, Josh Greene, Jack Hecker, Claire Hennessy, Christian Holthausen, Beck Hopkins, Karissa Kruse, Katherine Jarvis, Kelley Jones, Kerrin Laz, Pascaline Lepeltier (MS/MOF/walking encyclopedia of the Loire Valley), Amanda McCrossin, Kyle McLachlan (can we just admit that wine is better than coffee, already?), David Millman, Kristen Reitzell, Jessica Rodriguez, Leslie Sbrocco (my partner in *Today* show crimes), Jay Strell, Tara Thomas, Vanessa Vega, Donna White, Kelli White, Scott "best wine store in Maine" Worcester. Thank you to Jeremy Parzen for translating Luigi Veronelli's inimitable words. And to the Florida Room—you know who you are!

My friends who are not in the wine business have been tolerant enough to listen to me natter on about wine, and at the very least pretend to find it interesting for many years. I owe you all several bottles in recompense: Jim McManus (with many, many thanks for incisive design advice), Akhil Sharma, Gwen Richard, Marisa Ferrarin and Paul Etienne Lincoln, Rob Boynton, Rupa Bhattacharya, and Barbara and Max Riganti (not least for translating the high-speed words of several Italian winemakers in situ).

I was lucky to grow up surrounded by books (though not wine). My father isn't here to see this one, but I sure wish he were. My mother and brother are here, and I hope have the patience to read this damn thing, and perhaps even enjoy it. And my stepmother, Pam Johnson, has been a passionate advocate for local, environmentally responsible farming for many, many years, as well as the reason I have such excellent stepbrothers, and their equally excellent families.

To my ever-growing troupe of remarkable in-laws, look: despite it being a horrible, horrible game, "Oh Hell" is a lot of fun. The key is to enhance it with a glass (or two, or three) of wine. As you know.

Finally, none of this would be meaningful without the people I love most: my wife, Cecily Cook, and my daughter, Marie Isle.

FINDING AND BUYING THE WINES IN THIS BOOK

A t last count, there were more than forty-six thousand wine and liquor stores in the U.S.: no winery in this book, even a relatively large producer such as Allegrini or Guigal, makes enough wine to appear in all those stores. And a small property like Valentin Zusslin in Alsace (i.e., most of the wineries here) might make only a few thousand cases of wine a year, of which only a percentage arrives in the U.S. That translates, for many of these producers, to very little wine spread very thinly around the country, resulting in either a treasure hunt (if you're a positive sort of person) or a big pain in the neck (if you aren't) for anyone trying to find and buy that one must-have bottle.

If wine were hot sauce, or chocolate, or anchovies, none of this would present the slightest problem. But since the U.S. is riddled with wildly outdated state liquor laws that prohibit stores from shipping alcoholic beverages across state borders in much of the country, having someone ship you the bottle of Zusslin Riesling you'd like to drink may be impossible where you live. For commercial, mass-production wines, this isn't an issue—if you're after a bottle of Apothic Red or Yellow Tail Shiraz or Yes Way Rosé, you can walk into the nearest supermarket or beverage chain store and find one. (Yellow Tail imported about 6 million cases of wine into the U.S. in 2022. It's not exactly elusive.) The Zusslins of the world are a different story.

The single best solution to finding the wines in this book is to find a wine shop in your area—or in your state, since it's generally legal to ship *within* state boundaries—that focuses on wines like the ones written about here. Independent stores staffed by people who really care about what they're selling, in other words. Seek them out. If they don't have what you're looking for, tell them what it is and ask if they can get it, or whether they have something similar that's really great (there are also plenty of excellent, independent, ecologically conscious wineries working in the same vein who *aren't* in this book). Also, utilize a wine-locating site like wine-searcher.com, which can pull up stores in your area when you search for a specific wine. Apps such as Vivino can be helpful, too.

For small-production wines from California, Oregon, or Washington, another route is to go direct to the winery. They may be able to ship to your state. If not, email them and ask if the wines are for sale where you live, and if they know who carries them. It's more work than grabbing a bottle off the shelf at Kroger or Safeway when you're doing the weekly shopping, but the rewards are more than worth it. (Also, with truly small wineries, the person on other other end of that email address is likely to be the owner/winemaker/head-barrel-washer/chief guru/etc., because when you only make a couple of thousand cases of wine a year, the staff is you. And maybe your spouse, if they aren't working full-time in some other job to support this crazy wine dream of yours.)

Here's the thing, though: hunting for new wines to try actually is fun. Be flexible. If Thierry Germain's wines simply aren't available where you are, there's probably another Loire Valley producer in this book whose wines are. Also see Appendix Two, on p. 679, which lists many of the importers for the wines in this book. A few of them, such as Weygandt or Old Bridge Cellars, sell directly. Others, such as Kermit Lynch or North Berkeley Imports, have retail stores that can also ship wines. And regardless, importer websites can offer a wealth of information (and usually have contact information listed). It's entirely reasonable to email an importer and ask if there's a place near you that carries a specific wine in their portfolio. After all, the one thing wine importers like to do more than anything else is sell wine.

Lastly, become a wine collector. But let's redefine that term. When people hear the words "wine collector," they usually think of some wealthy man—it's always a man—hoarding thousands of rare bottles in a temperature-controlled vault under a mansion, or, if in Europe, some ancient cobwebbed cellar under a castle. Here's a new definition: consider yourself a wine collector if what you love doing is collecting new tastes and new experiences that just happen to be about wine. No temperature-controlled storage required, because your cellar is portable; it lives in your mind.

GO-TO WINE IMPORTERS

Banville Wine Merchants (Italy)
Bowler Wine (Global)
Brazos Wine (Argentina/Chile)
Broadbent Selections (Global)
Cape Classics (France/South Africa)
Dalla Terra (Italy)
De Maison (France/Spain)
Dreyfus-Ashby (Europe)
T. Edward Wines (Global)
Empson USA (Italy/New Zealand)
Ethica Wines (Italy)
European Cellars / Eric Solomon Selections (France/Spain/Switzerland/Other)
Folio Fine Wine Partners (Europe/Argentina/Australia)
The German Wine Collection (Germany)
Grand Cru Selections (Global)
Hand Picked Selections (France)
IPO Wines (Europe)
Jenny & Francois (Natural Wines)
Kermit Lynch Wine Merchants (France/Italy)
Kobrand (Global)

Kysela Pere et Fils (Global)

Loosen Bros. USA (Germany)

Louis/Dressner (Natural Wines)

Maisons, Marques & Domaines (France/Spain/Portugal)

North Berkeley Imports (France/Italy)

Old Bridge Cellars (Australia/France)

Olé & Obrigado (Spain/Portugal)

The Rare Wine Co. (France/Italy/Spain/Portugal)

Neal Rosenthal Selections (France/Italy/Switzerland)

Zev Rovine (Natural Wines)

Savio Soares (Europe/Natural Wine)

Schatzi Wines (Europe)

Skurnik Wines & Spirits (Global)

The Sorting Table (France/Italy/Germany/Austria)

Taub Family Selections (Global)

Think Global Wines (Spain)

Valkyrie Imports (France/Spain)

Veritas (France/Italy/Switzerland)

Vignaioli Selections (Italy)

Vine Street Imports (Australia/South Africa)

Vineyard Brands (France/Italy/South Africa)

Vintus (France/Italy)

Volio Imports (France/Italy/Spain)

Vom Boden (Germany/Austria)

V.O.S. Selections (Global)

Becky Wasserman & Co. (France)

Weygandt-Metzler (Europe)

Wilson Daniels (Europe/New Zealand)

Winebow Imports (Global)

A SELECTIVE GLOSSARY

Amphora

Amphorae are clay urns used for winemaking, an ancient method dating back to the dawn of winemaking in Georgia eight millennia ago that has come back into vogue in recent years. Because clay is porous and allows some transmission of oxygen, like oak, but does not impart any flavor to wine, like stainless steel, winemakers have found this middle ground intriguing. Amphorae are known by various names around the world—*qvevri* in Georgia, *talhas* in Portugal, *tinajas* in Spain, and so on—and can range in size from twenty-five gallons or so to over one hundred times that size.

Apassimento

The process used in Valpolicella, Italy, to make Amarone or sweet Recioto, for which grapes are dried for weeks or even months before the juice is pressed out of them and fermented. This results in dark, rich, powerful wines, often quite high in alcohol. The method is also used in Valtellina for its Sfursat reds, in Tuscany for sweet Vin Santo, and other places around the world.

Appellation

An appellation is a legally defined place of origin for a wine. Ideally an appellation's geographical boundaries would correspond to the geological and climatic characteristics that make wines from that area distinct. However, politics (and certainly history) usually plays some role as well. Each country has its own system and notation: AVA (American Viticultural Area) in the U.S., AOC (Appellation d'Origine Contrôlée) in France, DOC (Denominazione di Origine Controllata) in Italy, and so on. European appellations also typically have specific rules about what grape varieties can be grown there, how long the wines must be aged, and so on.

Carbonic Maceration

A form of winemaking where, instead of using yeast to start fermentation, whole bunches of grapes are sealed in a tank with carbon dioxide; fermentation begins inside the intact grapes. It produces lighter, brighter, fruitier reds, usually with less color and structure. Beaujolais, particularly Beaujolais Nouveau, is a classic example. With **semi-carbonic fermentation** the vat is not sealed. Instead, the weight of the grapes in the vats crushes those on the bottom, which begin to ferment in the traditional (yeast-driven) way; the carbon dioxide they release then causes carbonic maceration in the grapes above them.

Chaptalization

The process of adding sugar (usually cane or beet) to grape juice before fermentation to increase the potential alcohol in the wine. The name comes from Napoleon's minister of agriculture, Jean-Antoine Chaptal, but the practice goes back centuries if not millennia. It is most common (and more often allowed) in cooler-climate regions, particularly in Europe, where ripeness can be an issue. Its flip side is **acidification**, which is common to warm regions where grapes achieve healthy sugar levels but often lack acidity. Tartaric or malic acid is usually used for acidifying wines.

Clone

Despite the science fiction-y sound, a clone is simply a cutting taken from a specific grape vine and grafted onto rootstock in order to duplicate the first vine's genetic material. The practice originated in Germany in the 1800s, but really took off after World War I. Over the years, grapevine nurseries have isolated specific "clones"—e.g., 115, 667, or Swan, for Pinot Noir—that are known to grow well in certain climates and soils, or are extremely productive, or are distinctively aromatic.

Foundation Plant Services at UC Davis lists more than 120 different Pinot Noir clones, for example.

Cru

A French word meaning a specific vineyard, usually one identified as producing wine of better quality, hence "premier cru" or "grand cru." Sometimes that vineyard may be owned by one estate or person, sometimes by many (for instance, the grand cru of Clos Vougeot in Burgundy is divided among more than eighty different growers, though that's an extreme example). As with almost all wine terminology, there are exceptions to the rule: in Bordeaux, for instance, the term *grand cru classé*, or "great classified growth," applies to the estate overall, whether or not its vineyards are contiguous.

Dosage

A small amount of sugar or sugar plus wine that is added to sparkling wines just before the bottle is sealed, to help balance out the acidity in the wine. The process originated in Champagne, where, because of the region's cold climate, by nature the wines are very tart. Dosage varies: for example, *brut* Champagnes are not allowed more than twelve grams per liter of sugar. There is a current vogue, particularly among grower Champagne producers, for zero dosage (or *brut nature*) wines. They can be excellent, though they can also be aggressively tart and lean—no sugar is not necessarily better.

Grower Champagne

Most Champagnes, and certainly all of the most familiar brands, come from large Champagne houses, who purchase fruit from hundreds (even thousands) of small independent farmers throughout the Champagne region. Grower champagnes, instead, are the product of small producers who farm all of their own land. Both styles can be excellent; which you prefer is often more a philosophical question.

Lees

Lees are sediments left in the bottom of a barrel or tank after fermentation, mostly dead yeast cells. They can be filtered out, but some winemakers prefer leaving them in the wine during the aging process; aging the wine with lees contact, or *sur lie,* can add texture and character, and also protect against oxidation. Lees stirring (or *bâttonage*) is exactly that: regularly stirring up the lees to put them back into suspension in the wine, which allows for more exposure to their effects.

Lieu Dit

A *lieu dit* is typically part of a larger appellation (or larger vineyard) that has its own individual character. The term is most often used in Burgundy for small parcels that express a distinctive terroir character but do not have premier or grand cru status.

Massale Selection

Or *sélection massale,* is the practice of propagating new vines from a selection of older vines chosen from a specific vineyard. It gives genetic variety, and possibly identity, to the new planting. This was a common way of planting vineyards before the advent of varietal planting (e.g., planting your entire vineyard with Cabernet Sauvignon) and single-clone selections.

Négociant

Generally speaking, a *négociant* is a person or company who buys finished wine, or grapes or juice (which they then make into wine), then bottles and sells it under their own name. To make matters somewhat confusing, these days many *négociants* (like Louis Jadot in Burgundy, to take one well-known example) also make domaine wines—i.e., wine from vineyards they own themselves. Recently, particularly in Burgundy, there are a growing number of **micro-*négociants***—a trend tied to skyrocketing prices of vineyard land there—who purchase fruit from high-quality vineyards, often farming the vines themselves, and make excellent wines from it.

Orange Wine

Orange wine, or, as wine world denizens would prefer it were called, skin-contact white wine (this is a losing battle), is essentially white wine made in the same manner as red wine. When making most white wines, the juice is removed from contact with the skins almost immediately. For orange/skin-contact whites, the skins of the grapes are allowed to macerate in the juice for some amount of time, imparting an orangish hue and some structure and tannins (the same way that red wines acquire their color and structure). This method is actually far older than making white wines *without* their skins—it dates back to the dawn of winemaking, some eight thousand years ago.

Pét-nat

Pét-nat is short for *pétillant-naturel*, an old-school method of sparkling winemaking. For *pét-nats*, the wine is bottled before the initial alcoholic fermentation is finished. As fermentation continues, sometimes to dryness and sometimes not, the carbon dioxide it releases is trapped in suspension in the wine inside the sealed bottle. (In the traditional or Champagne method, the wine is first fermented to dryness, then bottled with a small amount of yeast and sugar added to induce a secondary fermentation.)

Phenols

Phenols and polyphenols are naturally occurring compounds, mostly from the skins of grapes but also from seeds and stems, that produce a wine's color and mouth-feel, and help allow it to age over time. Red wines, simply by virtue of being fermented with the grape skins, typically have higher phenolic content than white wines.

Phylloxera

Phylloxera, a microscopic root louse, was responsible for destroying most of Europe's vineyards in the late 1800s. The damage was catastrophic, viticulturally and economically, until the discovery that grafting European *vitis vinifera* vines onto American *vitis aestiva* and similar rootstocks would foil the bug's predations (the sap in American vines literally gums up its jaws). Phylloxera remains a problem, for instance in California in the late 1980s, when it became evident that the supposedly phylloxera-resistant AxR1 rootstock used widely in Napa Valley and other regions was not, in fact, resistant. Again, the economic damage was vast. **Pre-phylloxera** vines are ancient grapevines planted before phylloxera's arrival; they are usually planted on sandy soil (phylloxera doesn't thrive in sand) and, needless to say, are rare.

Spontaneous Fermentation

At a basic level, wine fermentation is simple: yeasts eat the sugar in grape juice, turning it into alcohol and carbon dioxide. There are two ways to go about this. The first is to inoculate the juice with a specific, cultured yeast (typically lab-grown and then freeze-dried). The second is to use the wild yeasts present on the skins of the grapes (often called indigenous or native yeasts). This allows the grapes to ferment spontaneously. Native yeast fermentation is by its nature less controlled and predictable (it can produce off aromas or flavors, or the yeasts can die off before the wine is finished), but proponents feel it produces wines whose character is more expressive of their terroir.

Sulfur/Sulfites

Big topic. Sulfur has been used as an antioxidant and antibacterial agent in wine for hundreds of years. Though there's some evidence that the Romans may have used sulfur (Pliny the Elder seems to suggest as much), widespread use came after the advent of glass bottles in the 1600s.

In recent years there's been somewhat of a backlash against the use of sulfur (most often sulfur dioxide, SO_2) for two reasons. First, the natural wine community, which is broadly against any intervention or additives, tends to feel that sulfur deadens a wine's flavor and taste. Second, many consumers feel they are allergic to sulfites. However, I say "feel" here because the incidence of sulfite allergies is actually extremely low; research suggests that headaches from red wine, particularly, stem from a sensitivity to biogenic amines that are a natural by-product of wine grape fermentation. Sulfites, at much higher levels than in wine, are also found in many prepared foods. Short version: if you can eat frozen French fries or dried apricots with no ill effect, then sulfites aren't your problem.

So. What is also true is that unless you have spotlessly, impeccably clean equipment and winemaking, making wines with no SO_2 is a recipe for prematurely oxidized or bacterially funky wine. Even among natural winemakers there's been a realignment to the idea that a small amount of sulfur at bottling is fine (except among the more rigid "zero-zero" group). At the same time, among conventional winemakers, there's also a broad and increasing sense that as little sulfur as possible is the best course. Regardless, it's an ongoing debate. And, it's worth mentioning, there actually are no truly sulfite-free wines, since some sulfur compounds are simply (and inescapably) a product of fermentation itself.

Whole-Cluster Fermentation

Exactly what it says: putting the entire cluster of grapes, including the stems, into the fermentation vessel. (Not, however, any *mog*—the California shorthand for "material other than grapes"—e.g., leaves, twigs, random bees, your keys, etc.) Most wine grapes are destemmed before fermentation, either by hand (rarely these days) or by a machine called a destemmer. Including the stems can add aromatic and textural notes to a wine and help moderate acidity, though if the stems are underripe (green), the result can be vegetal flavors or astringent compounds instead. Also, some varieties work better with whole-cluster fermentation than others: Pinot Noir, Syrah, and Gamay particularly.

PHOTO CREDITS

p. 43: Stéphane Tissot in his cellar, Jura, France. © Ray Isle.

p. 47: Domaine du Cellier aux Moines, Givry, Burgundy, France. © Ray Isle.

pp. 48, 218, 348, 404, 420, 474, 568, 606, 624, 644, 664: Maps © May Parsey.

p. 217: Amarone grapes, Allegrini, Valpolicella, Italy. © Ray Isle.

p. 347: Comando G, Rumbo al Norte Vineyard, Gredos, Spain. Courtesy of Comando G.

p. 403: The Douro Valley, Portugal. © Ray Isle.

p. 419: Weingut Loimer, Kamptal, Austria. Courtesy of Weingut Loimer, © Andreas Hofer.

p. 453: Sighnaghi, Kakheti Valley, Georgia. © Ray Isle.

p. 473: Hirsch Vineyards, Sonoma Coast, California. Courtesy of Hirsch Vineyards.

p. 567: Sokol Blosser, Willamette Valley, Oregon. Photo by Andrea Johnson, courtesy of Sokol Blosser.

p. 605: Bud Break at Cayuse Vineyards, Walla Walla, Washington. Photo by Tyson Kopfer, courtesy of Bionic Wines.

p. 623: Moonrise over Cullen Vineyards, Margaret River, Australia. Courtesy of Cullen Vineyards.

p. 643: Finca Piedra Infinita Vineyard, Mendoza Valley, Argentina. Courtesy of Zuccardi Valle de Uco.

p. 663: Hamilton Russell Vineyards, Hemel-en-Aarde, South Africa. Courtesy of Hamilton Russell.

INDEX

A

Abruzzo, 274–79, 324

Abuladze, Baia, 459–60

Adegas Guímaro, 355–56

aesthetic judgment, 34–35

agriculture:

large-scale, 12

as mediator between nature and
human community, 12

modern methods of, 5–6

organic, 6–7, 11

pre-industrial, 12

regenerative, 20–22

wine as product of, 1–2, 4–8

see also viticulture

Agriculture Department, U.S.,
organic wine certification and,
17, 18, 27

Alessandria, Fabio, 248–49

Alexander & Maria Koppitsch,
424–25

Allegrini, 264–65

Allegrini, Giovanni, 264–65

Alsace, 52–63

Alto Adige-Trentino, 222–28, 270,
272

Álvarez-Villamil, Vicente, 374–75

Álvaro Palacios, 362–64

Amerighi, Stefano, 287–88

Amoreau, Pascal, 79–80

amphora, amphorae, 8, 23, 681

animal welfare, 22

Ánima Négra, 398–99

Anne-Sophie Dubois, 65–66

Antiquum Farm, 571–73

Antiyal, 654–55

António Maçanita, 407–8

apassimento, 681

appellation, 681–82

Argentina, 645–52

Asseily, Gabriel, 75–76

Asseily, Tony, 75–76

Asseily, Youmna, 75–76

Australia, 625–34

Austria, 421–33
Avignonesi, 289–90

B

Baia's Wine, 459–60
Banke, Barbara, 532–33
Barbier, René, 387–88
Barbier Meyer, René, 388–89
Baron, Christophe, 611–13
Barruol, Louis, 196–98
Basilicata, 9, 327–29, 345
Baudry, Bernard, 160–63
Bea, Giampiero, 319–20
Bea, Paolo, 319
Beaujolais, 64–73
Beckmen, Steve, 537–38
Beckmen Vineyards, 537–38
Bedrock Wine Co., 479–81
Bennett, Ted, 517–18
Bergström, John, 573–75
Bergström, Josh, 573–75
Bergström Vineyards, 573–75
Berlucchi, 265–66
Bernabeleva, 374–75
Bernard Baudry, 160–63
Berry, Wendell, 12
Berthaut, Amélie, 88–90
Bertrand, Gérard, 152–53
Bianchi, Fabrizio, 301–2
Bianchi, Laura, 301–2
Big Table Farm, 575–77
Bilbro, Sam, 505

Billecart-Salmon, 123–25
biodiversity, 21
biodynamic certification, 28
biodynamics, 6–7, 13, 18–20, 21
Bize, Chisa, 91–92
Blot, Jacky, 163–65
Bodega Chacra, 646–49
Bodegas y Viñedos Raúl Pérez,
    378–79
Boffa, Federica, 251–52
Boffa, Pio, 251–52
Bordeaux, 74–85
    sustainable viticulture in, 15
Borgo del Tiglio, 233–35
Borgogno, 244–45
Borgogno, Cesare, 244
Boschis, Chiara, 245–47
Bossard, Guy, 168–69
Bott, Guillaume, 97–98
Bouchon, Julio, 655–57
Brajkovich, Michael, 639–40
Breton, Guy, 23
brettanomyces ("Brett"), 24, 25
Breuer, Theresa, 436–37
Brick House Vineyards, 578–79
Broc Cellars, 481–82
Brockway, Chris, 481–82
Brooks Heuck, Janie, 580–81
Brooks, Jimi, 580–81
Brooks Winery, 580–81
Bucci, 281–82
Bucci, Ampelio, 281–82
Bucklin, Will, 483–84

Bucklin Old Hill Ranch, 482–84
Bueno, Marisol, 357
Burgundy, 8, 86–120
Busch, Clemens, 437–39

C
Ca' dei Zago, 267–68
Cadence, 609–10
Cahn, Deborah, 517–18
Cahn Bennett, Aaron, 517
Cahn Bennett, Sarah, 517–18
Calabria, 327–29, 345
California, 473–565
    Central Coast and beyond,
        536–65
    North Coast, 478–535
    sustainable viticulture in, 14, 15
California Sustainable Wine
        Alliance, 15
Campania, 330–34, 345
Campbell, Adam, 586–88
Campbell, Joe, 586–87
Campbell, Pat, 586–87
Campolmi, Eugenio, 299
Can Sumoi, 389–91
carbon footprint, 14, 15
carbonic maceration, 682
carbon sequestration, 21
Carlisle Winery, 485–87
Cartier, Eve, 186–87
Cartier, Luc, 186–87
Carver, Clare, 575–77

Castello di Monsanto, 301–2
Castiglione, Sebastiano, 308–9
Castilla y León, 371–80
Catalunya, 381–96
Cathiard, Daniel, 81
Cathiard, Florence, 81
Cayuse Vineyards, 611–13
Cecillon, Julien, 192–94
Cerdá, Miquel Ángel, 398
Cerdeira, João António, 414–15
Ceretto, 249–51
Ceretto, Bruno, 249–50
Ceretto, Federico, 249–51
Ceretto, Marcello, 249
certification, of wine, 17, 18, 26–28
Champagne, 8, 121–35
Chandon de Briailles, 96–97
Chanterêves, 97–99
chaptalization, 682
Château Biac, 75–76
Château Bourgneuf, 76–77
Château de Beaucastel, 191–92
Château de Saint Cosme, 196–98
Château du Champ des Treilles,
        77–78
Château le Puy, 79–80
Château Les Trois Croix, 82–83
Château Maris, 153–55
Chateau Musar, 465–67
Château Smith Haut Lafitte, 81–82
Château Thivin, 71–72
Chauvet, Jules, 17, 23
Chêne Bleu, 194–95

Cherry, Cris, 563–64

Chevrot, Pablo, 99–101

Chevrot, Vincent, 99–101

Chiara Boschis, 245–47

Chidaine, François, 165–66

Chile, 653–62

Cilia, Giambatista, 338

Cinzano, Francesco Marone, 290–91

Ciolli, Damiano, 322

Cistercian monks, 8

Clemens Busch, 437–39

climate change, 13, 14

clone, 682–83

Clos Cibonne, 184–86

Clos Mogador, 387–89

Cloudy Bay winery, 3

Cobb, 487–88

Cobb, David, 487–88

Cobb, Ross, 487–88

Cogno, Elvio, 253–55

Col D'Orcia, 290–91

Colette, 1, 71–72

Collobiano, Laura di, 316–17

colorant additives, 10

Comando G, 376–78

Comme, Corinne, 77–78

Comme, Jean-Michel, 77–78

conservation, of natural resources,
       14–15

Constellation Brands, 3

Conterno, Diego, 255–56

copper sulfate, 18, 21

Corison, 489–91

Corison, Cathy, 489–91

Cornelissen, Frank, 336–37

Cornu, Pierre, 101–3

Corsica, 183–88

COS, 338–39

cover crops, 21–22

Crawford, Kim, 2–3

Cristom Vineyards, 582–83

cru, 683

Cruse, Michael, 491–92

Cruse Wine Co., 491–93

Cuilleron, Yves, 198–99

Cullen, Diana, 626

Cullen, Vanya, 626–27

Cullen Wines, 626–27

D

Daldin, Andrea, 297–98

Damiano Ciolli, 322

d'Amico, Noemia, 320–21

d'Amico, Paolo, 320–21

Day, Brianne, 584–86

Day Wines, 584–86

de Benoist, Pierre, 24, 116–18

Defilè, Graziella, 244–45

Dehours et Fils, 125–27

Dehours, Jêrome, 125–27

Deiss, Jean-Michel, 53–55

Delaporte, Matthieu, 167–68

Delecheneau, Coralie, 173–75

Delecheneau, Damien, 20, 24,
       173–75

De Martino, 658–59

de Martino, Sebastián, 658–59

Demeter, 27

de Nicolay, François, 96–97

Derenoncourt, Christine, 83–84

Derenoncourt, Stéphane, 83–84

Deriaux, Nicole, 141–43

Desforges, Claude, 184–86

designer yeasts, 9

Dettori, Alessandro, 339–40

Diego Conterno, 255–56

Do Ferreiro, 353–54

Domaine Agnès Paquet, 112–14

Domaine Alain Graillot, 199–201

Domaine André et Mireille Tissot,
    146–48

Domaine aux Moines, 180–81

Domaine Berthaut, 88–90

Domaine Bruno Lorenzon, 107–9

Domaine Chevrot, 99–101

Domaine Christian Moreau,
    109–10

Domaine de Cassiopée, 92–94

Domaine de l'A, 83–84

Domaine de la Butte, 164–65

Domaine de la Côte, 539–41

Domaine de la Janasse, 205–7

Domaine Delaporte, 167–68

Domaine de la Renardière, 145–46

Domaine de la Taille aux Loups,
    163–64

Domaine de l'Ecu, 168–70

Domaine de Montbourgeau, 141–43

Domaine des Roches Neuves,
    171–73

Domaine des Tourelles, 467–69

Domaine de Villaine, 24, 116–18

Domaine du Cellier aux Moines,
    94–95

Domaine du Pegau, 209–10

Domaine Edmond Cornu, 101–3

Domaine Eleni et Edouard Vocoret,
    118–19

Domaine François Chidaine,
    165–66

Domaine Georges Vernay, 211–12

Domaine Henri Gouges, 103–5

Domaine Huet, 175–77

Domaine La Monardière, 207–8

Domaine Lapierre, 68–69

Domaine Marcel Deiss, 53–55

Domaine Moreau-Naudet,
    110–12

Domaine Ratte, 143–44

Domaine Simon Bize & Fils,
    91–92

Domaine Trimbach, 55–56

Domaine Valentin Zusslin, 61–62

Domaine Weinbach, 57–59

Domaine Zind-Humbrecht, 7, 19,
    59–60

Dominguez, Javier, 352

Dominio de Águila, 373–74

Dominio do Bibei, 352–53

dosage, 683

Dottori, Corrado, 13, 282–83

Draper, Paul, 524–26
Drew, Jason, 493–95
Drew Wines, 493–95
Dr. Loosen, 444–45
Dubois, Anne-Sophie, 65–66
Dubourg, Talloulah, 92–94

E
economic viability, sustainability and,
    14
Eden, Robert, 153–55
E. Guigal, 202–5
Elena Fucci, 328–29
Elk Cove Vineyards, 586–88
Elvio Cogno, 253–55
Emidio Pepe, 275–77
Emilia-Romagna, 229–31, 270, 271,
    325
Erskine, James, 629–30
Espe, Hans-Bert, 446
Espinoza, Alvaro, 654–55
European Union, organic wine
    certification in, 17, 18
Eyrie Vineyards, 588–90

F
Faller, Catherine, 57–59
Faller, Laurence, 57, 58
Familia Torres, 393–95
Familia Zuccardi, 649–51
Farinetti, Oscar, 244–45

farming, see agriculture; viticulture
farmworkers, 22
Fattoria di Petroio, 38, 304–5
Fattoria Poggerino, 306–7
Fattoria Selvapiana, 314–16
Felluga, Livio, 235–37
Felton Road, 26, 636–37
Féraud, Laurence, 209–10
fertilizers, synthetic, 4, 5, 11, 14, 16
Feudo Montoni, 341–42
Figgins, 615–16
Figgins, Chris, 615–16
Figgins, Gary, 615
Figgins, Nancy, 615
Filipa Pato & William Wouters,
    412–13
Fissore, Valter, 253–55
Foillard, Jean, 23
Foléat, Emeric, 140–41
Fonti, Angela, 296–97
Fontodi, 294–96
food:
    genetically modified (GM), 6
    home-cooked vs. store-bought,
        10–11
    production of, 5
Foradori, 223–24
Foradori, Elisabetta, 223–24
Foradori Hofstätter, Martin,
    226–27
Forjas de Salnés, 354–55
Forlorn Hope, 542–44
François Villard, 212–14

Frank Cornelissen, 336–37

Frey, James, 602–3

Fritz Haag, 441–42

Friuli-Venezia Giulia, 232–41, 270, 271

Frog's Leap Vineyards, 495–96

Fucci, Elena, 9, 328–29

Fukuoka, Masanobu, 22

fungicides, 6, 16

G

Gahier, Michel, 137–39

Galicia, 351–60

García, Fernando, 376–78

Garlider, 225

Gates, David, 524–26

Gaudry, Vincent, 170–71

G. B. Burlotto, 247–49

G. D. Vajra, 260–62

genetically modified (GM) crops, 6, 16

Geoffray, Claude-Edouard, 71–72

Georg Breuer, 436–37

Georgia, 458–63

Gérard Bertrand, 152–53

Germain, Thierry, 171–73

Germany, 434–52

Gerrie, Tom, 582–83

Giovanni Rosso, 258–59

Girolamo Russo, 343–44

Giugni, Gina, 545–47

Giugni, Mikey, 545–48

Giuntini, Federico, 314–15

Giuntini Antinori, Francesco, 314–15

glass bottles:
    carbon footprint of, 13
    introduction of, 8

glyphosate, 15

Godard, Mee, 66–67

Goëss-Enzenberg, Michael, 227–28

Götze, Alex, 447–48

Gouges, Grégory, 103–5

Gouges, Henri, 103–5

Graillot, Alain, 199–201

Graillot, Maxime, 200–201

Gramona, 383–84

Gramona, Xavier, 383–84

Granja Nuestra Señora de Remelluri, 365–66

Gravner, 238–40

Gravner, Josko, 23, 238–40

Greening, Nigel, 26, 636–37

Green Revolution, 5

Greywacke, 3–4, 637–38

Grgich, Miljenko "Mike," 497

Grgich Hills Estate, 21, 497–99

grower Champagne, 122, 683

Guibert, Aimé, 156–57

Guigal, Etienne, 202–5

Guigal, Philippe, 202–5

Gurabanidze, Keti, 461–62

Gut Oggau, 4, 422–24

H

Haag, Oliver, 441–42
Haag, Wilhelm, 441–42
Haas, Jason, 14, 21, 554–56
Hagen, Stephen, 571–73
Halcon Estate, 499–500
Hall, Ted, 512–13
Hamilton Russell, Anthony, 666–67
Hamilton Russell, Olive, 666–67
Hamilton Russell Vineyards,
    666–67
Hawkins, Craig, 669–70
Henschke, 628–29
Henschke, Prue, 628–29
Henschke, Stephen, 628–29
herbicides, 4, 5, 11, 14
    chemical, 8, 15
Hill, William McPherson, 453
Hill Smith, Michael, 632–33
Hirsch, David, 500–502
Hirsch, Jasmine, 501, 502–3
Hirsch Vineyards, 500–503
Hiyu Wine Farm, 590–92
Hochar, Serge, 465–67
Honig, Louis, 503
Honig, Michael, 503–4
Honig Winery, 503–4
Horsepower, 611–13
Huët, Gaston, 175–76
Huët, Victor, 175
Humbrecht, Olivier, 7, 19,
    59–60
Hume, David, 25

I

Idlewild, 505–6
Incisa della Rocchetta, Piero,
    646–49
Institut National de l'Origine et de la
    Qualité (INAO), 22
Issa, Faouzi, 467–69
Istine, 296–97
Italy, 217–346
    Central, 273–325
    Northern, 221–72
    organic viticulture in, 16
    Southern, 326–46

J

Jackson, Chris, 532–33
Jackson, Jess, 531–32
Jacky Blot, 163–65
Jauma, 629–31
J. Bouchon, 655–57
Jermaz, Ivo, 21, 497–98
J. Hofstätter, 226–27
Joliveau, Benjamin, 176–77
Joly, Nicolas, 177–80
Judd, Kevin, 3, 637–38
Julien Cecillon, 192–94
Jura, 136–49

K

Kahneman, Daniel, 35
Keplinger, Helen, 506–7

Keplinger Wines, 506–7
Kerschbaumer, Christian, 225
Kerschbaumer, Veronika, 225
Kim Crawford Wines, 2–3
Kings Carey, 544–45
Kingston, Courtney, 657–58
Kingston Family Vineyards, 657–58
Koppitsch, Alexander, 424–25
Koppitsch, Maria, 424–25
Kristancic, Ales, 456–57
Kumeu River, 639–40
Kuntz, Sybille, 443–44
Kurdadze, Nukri, 461–62
Kuriyama, Tomoko, 97–99
Kutch, 507–9
Kutch, Jamie, 507–9

L
La Coulée de Serrant, 177–80
La Distesa, 13, 282–83
Lady of the Sunshine, 545–48
La Grange Tiphaine, 20, 24, 173–75
Lamole di Lamole, 297–98
Landi, Daniel, 376–78
Landon, Erica, 596–98
Languedoc-Roussillon, 150–58
Lanza, Piero, 306–7
Lapierre, Marcel, 17, 23, 68–69
Lardy, Laura, 69–70
Larmandier, Arthur, 127–28
Larmandier, Pierre, 127–28
Larmandier-Bernier, 127–28

Laroche, Tessa, 180–81
Lassa, Andrea, 602–3
La Stoppa, 4, 230–31
Latta, Andrew, 613–14
Latta Wines, 613–14
Laura Lardy, 69–70
Lazio, 318–25
Lebanon, 464–70
Lécaillon, Jean-Baptiste,
    133–34
lees, 683–84
Lefcourt, Jenny, 24
Le Macchiole, 299–300
Le Marche, 280–83, 324, 325
Lemon, Ted, 509–12
Lenzi, Diana, 38, 304–5
Léon, Bertrand, 82–83
Leonetti Cellar, 615–16
Lett, David, 588–89
Lett, Jason, 588–90
Lewis, C. S., 18–19
lieu dit, 684
Liger-Belair, Thibault, 105–7
Littorai, 509–12
Livio Felluga, 235–37
Loimer, Fred, 7, 425–27
Loire Valley, 159–82
Long Meadow Ranch, 512–13
Loosen, Ernst "Erni," 444–45
López de Heredia, María José,
    366–68
Lorenzon, Bruno, 107–9
Louis Roederer, 133–34

Luis Seabra Vinhos, 413–14
Lynch, Kermit, 23, 24

M
Maçanita, António, 407–8
Macron, Emmanuel, 15
Magician's Nephew, The (Lewis),
    18–19
Magnaghi, Jason, 615–16
Maha Estate, 563–64
Mahle, Pam, 521
Mahle, Pax, 499, 521–22
Manelli, Michele, 7, 311–14
Manetti, Dino, 294–95
Manetti, Giovanni, 294–96
Manferrari, Nicola, 233–35
Manincor, 227–28
Marcy, Brian, 576–77
Markus, Brother, 462–63
Marlborough, 2–3
Martin, Evan, 592–94
Martin Woods, 592–94
Mas de Daumas Gassac, 156–57
Mas de Gourgonnier, 186–87
Mas Martinet, 384–87
massale selection, 684
Massican, 513–14
mass production, of wine, 2–9, 11,
    13, 23, 26, 36–37
Mastroberardino, 331–32
Mastroberardino, Antonio, 331–32
Mata, Ton, 392

Mathurin, Hugo, 92–94
Matthiasson, 515–17
Matthiasson, Jill, 515–16
Matthiasson, Steve, 7–8, 515–16
Maximin Grünhaus, 439–41
Mayer, 631–32
Mayer, Timo, 631–32
Maysara Winery, 594–96
McNutt, Gaye, 609–10
Mediterranean Coast, 381–96
Mee Godard, 66–67
Melville, Chad, 548–49
Melville Winery, 548–49
Méndez, Gerardo, 353
Méndez, Juan Jesús, 399–400
Méndez, Rodrigo "Rodri," 354–55
Merli, Cinzia, 299–300
Merret, Christopher, 8
Messana, Silvio, 302–4
Michel Gahier, 137–39
Milliken, Beth Novak, 530–31
Mills, Nick, 640–41
modification, in winemaking, 10
Moët Hennessy-Louis Vuitton
    (LVMH), 3
Moio, Luigi, 333–34
Molise, 330–34, 345
Momtazi, Moe, 594–96
Montesecondo, 302–4
Monzón, Jorge, 373
Moore, Alecia (P!nk), 561–62
Moorman, Sashi, 539–41
Moreau, Christian, 109–10

Moreau, Stepháne, 110–12

Morganti, Giovanna, 292–93

Moser, Kathi, 428–29

Moser, Nikolaus "Niki," 428–29

Mottura, Sergio, 323

Moussé, Cédric, 129–31

Moussé Fils, 129–31

Movia, 456–57

Muller, Melissa, 341–42

Mullineux, Andrea, 668–69

Mullineux, Chris, 668–69

Mullineux Family Wines, 668–69

N

Napa Green, 15

natural wines, 13, 17–18, 22–26

Naudet, Virginie, 113

Navarra, 361–70

Navarro Vineyards, 517–19

Neal, Mark, 6, 519–20

Neal Family Vineyards, 6, 519–20

négociant, 684

New Zealand, 2–3, 635–42

    sustainable viticulture in, 14

Nicolas Joly, 177–80

Niepoort, Dirk, 409–11

Niepoort Vinhos, 409–11

Niger, Claire, 168–69

Niger, Frédérick "Fred," 168–69

Nikolaihof, 37, 429–31

Nik Weis—St. Urbans Hof, 448–49

No Girls, 611–13

Novak, Jack, 530

Novak, Mary, 530–31

O

Obrador, Pere, 398

Occhipinti, Giusti, 338

Oddero, 256–58

Oddero, Mariacristina, 256–58

Officer, Mike, 485–87

Olney, John, 524, 525–26

One-Straw Revolution, The
    (Fukuoka), 22

orange wine, 684–85

Oregon, 567–604

organic certification, 28

organic farming, 6, 7, 11

organic viticulture and winemaking,
    9, 13, 16–18

Osborne, Angela, 559–61

Ossian Vides y Vinos, 375–76

Overnoy, Pierre, 23

P

Pago de Carraovejas, 375–76

Pahlow, Ken, 596–98

Palacios, Álvaro, 362–64

Pantaleoni, Elena, 4, 230–31

Paolo Bea, 319–20

Paolo e Noemia d'Amico, 320–21

Papari Valley Winery, 461–62

Paquet, Agnès, 112–14

Parker, Robert, 31
Parr, Rajat, 539–41
Parra, Pedro, 659–61
Pascal, Philippe, 94–95
Passalacqua, Tegan, 552–53
Pataille, Sylvain, 114–16
Pato, Filipa, 412–13
Pax Wines, 521–22
Pazo Señorans, 357
Peay, Andy, 522–24
Peay, Nick, 522–24
Peay Vineyards, 522–24
Pedro Parra y Familia, 659–61
Pennyroyal Farm, 517–19
Pepe, Emidio, 275–77
Pérez, Raúl, 378–79
Pérez, Sara, 384–87
Perrin, Marc, 191–92
pesticides, 4, 5, 16
Péters, Pierre, 131–32
Péters, Rodolphe, 131–33
Petit, Jean-Michel, 145–46
pét-nat, 685
Petrini, Moreno, 316–17
Petroski, Dan, 513–14
phenols, 685
phylloxera, 685
Piedmont, 242–62, 270, 271
Piedrasassi, 539–41
Pieropan, 268–69
Pieropan, Leonildo, 268–69
Pierre Péters, 131–33
Pinguet, Noël, 175–76

P!nk (Alecia Moore), 561–62
Pio Cesare, 251–52
Pisa, University of, 9
Pisoni, Gary, 550–51
Pisoni Vineyards, 550–51
place, sense of, *see* terroir
Podere le Boncie, 292–93
Pollan, Michael, 11
Pomares, Eulogio, 358–59
Portugal, 403–18
Prisons et Paradis (Colette), 1
Provence, 183–88
Puglia, 327–29, 345

Q
Querciabella, 308–9
Quintodecimo, 333–34

R
Ratte, Françoise, 143–44
Ratte, Michel-Henry, 143–44
Raventós, Manuel, 389–90
Raventós, Pepe, 389–91
Raventós i Blanc, 389–91
Ready, Nate, 590–92
real wine, 4, 10, 24–25, 36–38
Rebholz, Eduard, 23
Recaredo, 392–93
regenerative agriculture, 20–22
Regenerative Organic certification,
    21, 28

regenerative viticulture, 13
"Renewing Husbandry" (Berry), 12
Rhône Valley, 189–215
Ricasoli-Firidolfi, Marco, 310–11
Ricks, Christopher, 29–30
Ridge Vineyards, 524–27
Rioja, 361–70
Rippon, 640–41
R. López de Heredia, 366–69
Rocca di Montegrossi, 310–11
Rodero, Isabel, 373
Rodriguez, Pedro, 355–56
Rodriguez, Telmo, 365–66
Rodriguez Hernandorena, Amaia, 365
Rodríguez Salís, Jaime, 365
Roederer, Louis, 133
Roland-Billecart, Matthieu, 124–25
Rolet, Xavier, 194–95
Rorick, Matthew, 542–44
Rosenthal, Neal, 24
Rosso, Davide, 258–59
Roussillon, see Languedoc-Roussillon
Roux, Andre, 184–86
Ruiz, Pedro, 375–76
Russo, Giuseppe, 343–44

S
Saahs, Nikolaus, 37, 429–30
Sabon, Isabelle, 205–7
Salcheto, 7, 311–14

Sandhi, 539–41
Sandlands, 552–53
Sans Wine Company, 527–28
Sardinia, 335–46
Saverys, Virginie, 289–90
Savoie, 136–49
Scar of the Sea, 545–48
Scherrer, Fred, 528–30
Scherrer Winery, 528–30
Schober, Gina, 527–28
science, winemaking and, 9
Seabra, Luis, 413–14
Sepp Moser, 428–29
Sergio Mottura, 323
Serôdio Borges, Jorge, 415–17
Shavnabada, 462–63
Shaw, Martin, 632–33
Shelter, 446
Sicily, 335–46
Sireci, Fabio, 341–42
Slovenia, 455–57
Small, Rick, 617–18
Smith, Ben, 609–10
Soalheiro, 414–15
social equality, sustainability and, 14, 15
soil health, 7–8, 16, 19, 21
Sokol Blosser, 598–600
Sokol Blosser, Alison, 598–600
Sonoma County Winegrowers association, 14
Soter, Michelle, 600
Soter, Tony, 600–602

Soter Vineyards, 600–602
South Africa, 663–71
Spain, 347–401
   islands of, 397–401
   organic viticulture in, 16
Sparks, James, 544–45
spontaneous fermentation, 686
Spottswoode, 530–31
Stefano Amerighi, 287–88
Steiner, Rudolf, 19
Stonestreet Wines, 531–33
Stover, Jake, 527
Strano, Cirino, 338
sulfur, sulfites, 25, 686–87
   added, 17–18
sustainability, 14–15
   certification of, 27–28
sustainable viticulture, 6–7, 13,
   14–15
Sybille Kuntz, 443–44
Sylvain Pataille, 114–16
synthetic fertilizers, 4, 5, 11, 14

T
Tablas Creek, 14, 21, 554–56
Tavares da Silva, Sandra, 415–17
Tenuta Dettori, 339–40
Tenuta di Valgiano, 316–17
terroir, 4, 6, 7–8, 11, 17, 25
Testalonga, 669–70
tetrahydropyridines, 24–25
Thacher, Sherman, 557–58

Thacher Winery, 557–58
Thévenet, Jean-Paul, 23
Thibault Liger-Belair, 105–7
Thierry Germain, 171–73
Thinking Fast and Slow (Kahneman),
   35
Thomson, Alison, 561
Tiberio, 277–79
Tiberio, Antonio, 277–78
Tiberio, Cristiana, 277–79
Tiberio, Riccardo, 277–78
tillage, 21
Tissot, Stéphane, 146–48
Tolpuddle, 632–33
Torres, Miguel A., 393–95
Trentino, *see* Alto Adige-Trentino
Tresemer, China, 590–92
A Tribute to Grace, 558–61
Trimbach, Jean, 55–56
Trisaetum, 602–3
Tscheppe, Eduard, 4, 422–23
Tscheppe-Eselböck, Stefanie,
   422–23
Tunnell, Doug, 578–79
Turley Wine Cellars, 552–53
Tuscany, 284–317, 324, 325
Twain-Peterson, Morgan,
   479–81
Two Wolves, 561–62

U
Umbria, 318–25

V

Vache, Christian, 207–8

Vache, Damien, 207–8

Vajra, Aldo, 260–61

Vajra, Giuseppe, 260–62

Vayron, Frédérique, 77

Vayron, Marie, 76–77

Veneto, 263–70, 272

Venica, Giampaolo, 240–41

Venica & Venica, 240–41

Venus La Universal, 384–87

Vernay, Christine, 211–12

Vernay, Georges, 211–12

Veronelli, Luigi, 29

Vignerons les Matheny, 140–41

Villa Creek, 563–64

Villard, François, 212–14

Viñátigo, 399–400

Vincent Gaudry, 170–71

Vincor, 3

Vin en Question, Le, (Chauvet), 23

viticulture:

    biodynamic, 7, 13, 18–20, 21

    earth-friendly, 7–8, 9, 10, 13–22

    organic, 9, 11, 13, 16–18

    regenerative, 13

    soil health in, 7–8, 16, 19, 21

    sustainable, 6–7, 13, 14–15

    see also winemaking

Vocoret, Edouard, 118–19

Vocoret, Eleni, 118–19

volatile acidity (VA), 24, 25

Von Schubert, 439–41

von Schubert, Carl, 439

von Schubert, Maximilian, 439–41

W

Walter, Blair, 636–37

Walter Scott Wines, 596–98

Wasenhaus, 447–48

Washington, 605–19

Weingut Loimer, 7, 425–27

Weingut Ökonomierat Rebholz, 23

Weingut Wittmann, 450–51

Weinkauf, Aron, 530

Weis, Nik, 448–49

whole-cluster fermentation, 687

Wieninger, 431–32

Wieninger, Fritz, 431–32

Williams, Chris, 580–81

Williams, John, 495–96

Wine & Soul, 415–17

winemaking:

    carbon footprint of, 14, 15

    early history of, 8

    home cooking compared to,
        10–11

    modification in, 10

    organic, 16–18

    science and, 9

    technology and, 8–9

    see also viticulture

wines:

    aesthetic judgment and, 34–35

    as agriculture product, 1–2, 4–8

wines (*cont.*)
  certification of, 17, 18, 26–28
  contextual experience of, 32–34,
    36–38
  descriptive language for, 29–31
  distinct personalities of, 6, 10, 11
  mass-produced, 2–9, 11, 13, 23,
    26, 36–37
  natural, 13, 17–18, 22–26
  nature of, 1–8
  organic, 6
  point scores for, 31–32, 33, 35
  real, 4, 10, 24–25, 36–38
  three questions to ask about, 11
  unique personalities of, 24–25,
    36–38
Wittmann, Philipp, 6, 450–51
Wolber, Christoph, 447–48
Wolf, Silke, 446

Wong, Vanessa, 522–23
Woodward Canyon Winery,
    617–18
Wouters, William, 412–13

Y
yeasts, designer, 9
Yves Cuilleron, 198–99

Z
Zago, Christian, 267
Zarate, 358–59
Ziegler, Baron, 499
Ziliani, Cristina, 265–66
Ziliani, Franco, 265–66
Zuccardi, Sebastián, 649–51
Zusslin, Marie, 61–62

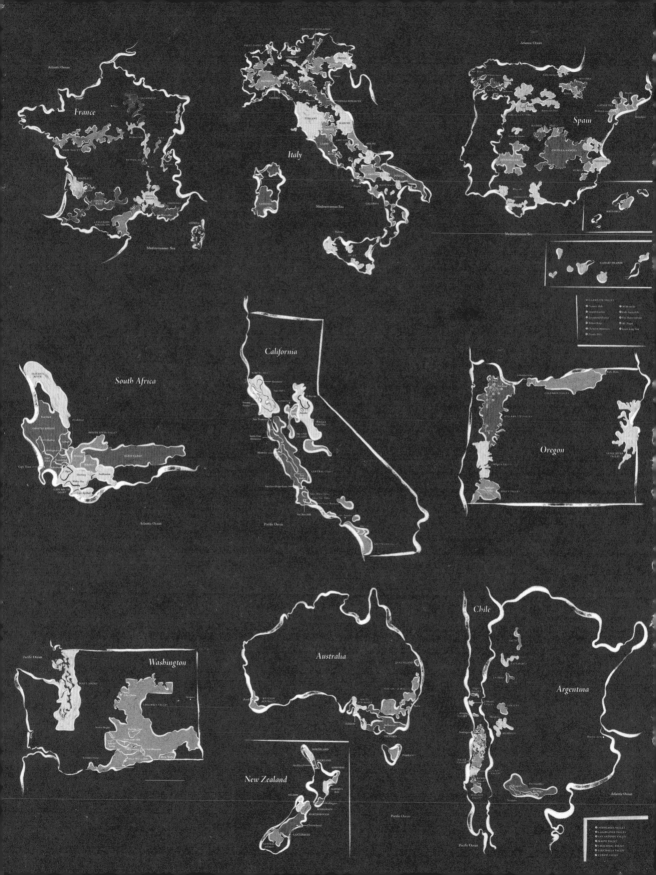